ALL THAT GLITTERS IS OURS
The Theft of Indian Mineral Resources

Other books by Roberta Carol Harvey from Sunstone Press

The Earth is Red: The Imperialism of the Doctrine of Discovery

The Eclipse of the Sun: The Need for American Indian Curriculum in High Schools

The Iron Triangle: Business, Government, and Colonial Settlers' Dispossession of Indian Timberlands and Timber

Social Contributions of Colorado's American Indian Leaders

Warrior Societies. A Manifesto

ALL THAT GLITTERS IS OURS
The Theft of Indian Mineral Resources

ROBERTA CAROL HARVEY
A Citizen of Diné (Navajo Nation)

SUNSTONE
PRESS

SANTA FE

Sunstone books may be purchased for educational, business, or sales promotional use. For information please write: Special Markets Department, Sunstone Press, P.O. Box 2321, Santa Fe, New Mexico 87504-2321.

Printed on acid-free paper

⊗

Library of Congress Cataloging-in-Publication Data

Names: Harvey, Roberta Carol, 1950- author.
Title: All that glitters is ours : the theft of Indian mineral resources / Roberta Carol Harvey, a citizen of Dineʼ¹ (Navajo Nation).
Description: Santa Fe, NM : Sunstone Press, [2023] | Includes bibliographical references and index. | Summary: "This book centers on the wars Indians fought to counter the theft of Indian copper and lead in the Great Lakes region and gold and silver in the Pacific Northwest, the Black Hills, the Great Plains and the Southwest by the invasive flood of white settlers and military forces"-- Provided by publisher.
Identifiers: LCCN 2023041885 | ISBN 9781632936332 (paperback) | ISBN 9781632936295 (hardback) | ISBN 9781611397314 (epub)
Subjects: LCSH: Indians of North America--Government relations. | Indians of North America--Legal status, laws, etc. | Settler colonialism--United States--History--19th century. | Indian Removal, 1813-1903. | Sovereignty.
Classification: LCC E91 .H368 2023 | DDC 323.1197--dc23/eng/20230908
LC record available at https://lccn.loc.gov/2023041885

WWW.SUNSTONEPRESS.COM

SUNSTONE PRESS / POST OFFICE BOX 2321 / SANTA FE, NM 87504-2321 /USA
(505) 988-4418

DEDICATION

FOR HADLIE, CALLAN, SANDER, KENNEDIE AND COOPER—
I AM SO VERY PROUD OF YOU.

ACKNOWLEDGMENTS

My Family

Nobody has been more helpful to me in the pursuit of this project than the members of my family for whom I am so very thankful. I could not have the time for research and writing without their active support. They encouraged me and made sure that whatever resources I needed for this project were available: computer, printer, supplies, etc. Thank you *to my most beloved husband* (who made breakfast, lunch and dinner and took over all daily family responsibilities so I could focus on this project) whose love provides such joy and stability in my life.

CONTENTS

Civil War Debt
Indian Nations Not Parties to Disposal of Their Resources
 Pacific Railway Act
 1885: Arizona State Legislature Recommends Removing Indians on
 San Carlos and White Mountain Reservations to Indian Territory in
 Present-Day Oklahoma
Land Speculation and Atchison, Topeka and Santa Fe Railway
Natural Resource Exploitation and Corruption
Mining Tycoons
Savages Cheated and Robbed Were Starving
Notes: Mineral Economic Development

1891: Leasing Minerals on Tribal Lands
        Unilateral Federal Action
U.S. Control of Indians
Notes: Federal Indian Policy

7: MILITARY POLICY ~ 107

Military Policy Aligned to Political Objective of Indian Relinquishment of
All of Their Country; Keep Indians Ignorant of This Objective; Extinction of
Indians
Fragments of Great Indian Nations
Consolidation of West through U.S.' Military Arm
Military Intelligence
Army Expeditions of the 19th Century
1865: Right after End of Civil War—Finish Indian Subjugation in One War
U.S. Military Command Structure—Great Plains
Methods of War
U.S. Expansionist and Mercantilism Policies Induce Westward Expansion
Priority Given to Protecting Explorers and Surveyors
U.S. Army Forts
Indian Tribes Aversion to Military Settlements
U.S. Military Armaments
Facilitate Civil-Military Cooperation
Railroads' Military Importance
Destruction of Buffalo
Military Commanders' Philosophies
Department of the Interior v. War Department
1872: Indian Reservation Policy
Small War Campaigns
Surprise Attacks
Destruction of War-Making Potential
1879: Limited Indian Resistance
Military's Constabulary Duties
Notes: Military Policy

8: INDIAN POLICY OF TERRITORIAL GOVERNMENTS ~ 127

Arizona
Dakotas
Idaho
Montana
New Mexico

Utah
Wyoming
     Georgia
Colorado
Notes: Indian Policy of Territorial Governments

9: COLORADO ~ 137

Indians in Colorado Pre-Contact
Ute Bands
Contact with Spain
Mexican Land Grants
U.S. Military Expeditions
1849: Treaty of Abiquiú—U.S. Jurisdiction Over Capote and Muache Bands,
Safe Passage for Settlers, Presence of Military Forts and Trading Posts—No
Cession of Lands
U.S. Indian Treaties
1851: Treaty of Fort Laramie—Safe Passage for Settlers, Presence of Military Forts
1853: Commissioner: Cheyenne, Arapaho and Western Sioux Starving
1854–1855: Military Campaign against Utes
U.S. Indian Agencies in Colorado
     Upper Arkansas Indian Agency
     Conejos Indian Agency (Utes)
     Middle Park Indian Agency (Utes)
     Denver Special Indian Agency (Utes)
     Los Piños Indian Agency (Utes)
     White River Ute Agency (Utes)
1857: Denver City Promoters
1858: Discovery of Gold in Colorado
1859: Clear Creek Gold Discovery
1859: Miners' Court
1859: Colorado Mineral Belt, Domain of Arapaho, Cheyenne and Ute
1859: Upper Platte, Agent Twiss, Diminution of Game
1859: Upper Arkansas Agency, Sup. Bent, Encroachments of Whites on Indian Lands
1859: Commissioner Report to Secretary Interior, Critical State
1860: Whites in Colorado Gold Region in Violation of Federal Law
Fort Wise
1861: Treaty of Fort Wise, Confine Cheyenne and Arapaho on Reservation,
1/13 Size of Fort Laramie Treaty Lands
1861: Colorado Established as Territory

1861: Colley Appointed Indian Agent for Upper Arkansas Indian Agency

1861: Commissioner—Difficult to Manage Indian Affairs due to Lack of Treaties

1861: 1ˢᵗ Regiment Colorado Volunteer Infantry Organized

1862: Colorado Territorial Delegate—Miners Overrunning Ute Lands

1862: Middle Park Agency Established for Utes

1862: Commissioner Dole: Colorado and WASH Gold Rushes Infringing on Indian Rights

March 1863: Delegation of Cheyenne, Arapaho, Comanche, Kiowa and Caddo Chiefs Visit Washington, DC—Dissuade Them from Joining Confederacy

1863: Commissioner Dole to Governor/Superintendent Evans—Get Cheyenne and Arapaho that Have Not Signed Treaty of Fort Wise to Do So

August 1863: Governor/Superintendent Evans Council with Cheyenne and Arapaho Leaders, Big Timbers

October 1863: Commissioner Dole Confirms Mineral Wealth of Colorado Territory

October 1863: Treaty of Conejos Only with Tabeguache Utes—Cede Land East of Continental Divide and Middle Park

November 1863: Letter from Governor Evans to Commissioner Dole regarding Indian State of War

April–May 1864: Colorado Volunteer Forces Make Unprovoked Attacks on Cheyenne Villages in Colorado Territory

April 12, 1864: Battle of Fremont's Orchard, Colorado Volunteer Cavalry and Cheyenne, NE/Colorado

May 3, 1864: Without Provocation, Colorado Volunteer Cavalry Attacks Peaceful Cheyenne Leaders at Cedar Bluffs, Kansas

May 31, 1864: Letter to Major Wynkoop from Colonel John Chivington, Whip Cheyennes

June 1, 1864: Mystery of Hungate Family

1864: Four Colorado Forts

June 3, 11, 13, 1864: Governor Evans Demands Federal Troops Be Sent to Denver

June 14, 1864: Governor Evans Wires Secretary of War to Muster Colorado Volunteer Cavalry into U.S. Service

June 15, 1864: Major McKenny Warns General Curtis that Colorado's Volunteer Cavalry May Start Plains Indian War

June 27, 1864: First Proclamation, Governor Evans, Colorado Superintendency Indian Affairs, Denver

August 10, 1864: Governor Evans Requests 10,000 U.S. Troops from Secretary of War; Requests Commissioner Dole to Lobby for His Troops Request

August 11, 1864: Governor Evans Proclamation to Citizens of Colorado Authorizing Them to Kill Hostile Indians

Analysis of Governor Evans' Second Proclamation of August 11, 1864—University of Denver's John Evans Study Committee

August 12, 1864: 3rd Regiment Authorized for 100 Days

August 18, 1864: Governor Evans Sends Letter to Secretary of War that Colorado Is in Danger of Destruction from Indians

August 19, 1864: Secretary of War Informs Governor Evans, due to Civil War, Shortage of U.S. Army Troops

August 29, 1864: Chief Black Kettle and Other Chiefs Have Letters Sent to Agent Colley and Major Wynkoop Seeking Peace Talks

Sep. 4-18, 1864: Chief Black Kettle Letter, Peace Talk Request Delivered to Major Wynkoop; Major Wynkoop Meets with Black Kettle at Smoky Hill River and Confirms Cheyenne and Arapaho Seeking Peace; Wynkoop Agrees to Escort Cheyenne and Arapaho Chiefs to Meet with Governor Evans regarding Peace

Sep. 4, 1864: Governor Evans Informed by Agent Colley that Cheyenne and Arapaho Desire Peace

Sep. 14, 1864: Governor Evans Forwards Agent Colley's Letter that Cheyenne and Arapaho Desire Peace to Colonel Chivington

Sep. 18, 1864: Major Wynkoop Reports Meeting with Cheyenne and Arapaho regarding Peace to Acting Assistant Adjutant-General, District of Upper Arkansas

Sep. 28, 1864: Governor Evans Meets with Cheyenne and Arapaho Peace Party; Rejects Peace Offer Alleging State of War with Military in Control Notwithstanding Commissioner Dole's Directive to Him to Negotiate for Peace

Sep. 29, 1864: Governor Evans Sends False Letter to Major Curtis, U.S. Army, that Sioux Plan to Attack Colorado

Sep. 29, 1864: Governor Evans Sends Letter to Agent Colley regarding Meeting with Cheyenne and Arapaho Peace Party; That He Rejected Peace Offer due to U.S. State of War

Sep. 29, 1864: Governor Evans Forwards Letter from Agent Colley to Colonel Chivington that Cheyenne and Arapaho Peace Offer Denied

October 14, 1864: Colonel Chivington Orders Capt. Nichols, Colorado Third Regiment, to Kill All Indians He Encounters

October 15, 1864: Commissioner Dole Orders Governor Evans to Negotiate for Peace with Indians when They Offer, Regardless of U.S. State of War

November 4, 1864: Major Wynkoop Relieved of Command

November 15, 1864: Majors Anthony and Wynkoop Meet with Cheyenne and Arapaho Who Continue to Press for Peace

November 15, 1864: Commissioner Dole Reports to Secretary of Interior that Cheyenne and Arapaho Urge Peace

November 16, 1864: Major Anthony Reports to Headquarters that Cheyenne and Arapaho Appealing for Peace

November 28, 1864: Major Anthony Reports Arrival of Colorado Third Regiment at Fort Lyon—1000 Soldiers

November 28, 1864: Major General Curtis Reports to Brigadier General Carleton that Cheyenne and Arapaho Are Begging for Peace

November 29, 1864: Sand Creek Massacre—Colonel Chivington Reports Killing 400-500 Indians; Scalped Every Man, Woman and Child, Mutilated Their Bodies; Removed Private Parts as War Trophies

Report on Sand Creek Massacre by Agent Leavenworth

Commissioner Cooley, Sand Creek Massacre

December 7, 1864: Colonel Chivington's Second Report to Governor Evans: Killed 500 Indians, Still in Pursuit of Cheyenne and Arapaho

December 15, 1864: Major Anthony Reports Sand Creek Massacre Was Terrible; Should Be Done to All Hostile Tribes

Governor Evans Culpability in Sand Creek Massacre—University of Denver's John Evans Study Committee

January 16, 1865: Sand Creek Military Investigation

1865: U.S. Condemns Sand Creek Massacre

April 28, 1865: Treaty with Arapaho and Cheyenne for Colorado Land, Offer No Money, No Specific Land for New Reservation

1865: Superintendent Taylor, Upper Platte; Obstruction of Mining Prejudicial to U.S.

October 11-13, 1865: U.S. Treaty Delegation, Arapaho and Cheyenne Still Recovering from Sand Creek, Not Ready to Agree to Relinquish Land in Colorado

October 13, 1865: Treaty Council with Arapaho and Cheyenne— Unfortunately for You, Gold Discovered in Your Country

October 14, 1865: Cheyenne and Arapaho Treaty Signed Removing Them from Colorado

Little Arkansas Treaty—Land Specified for Reservation for Arapaho and Cheyenne in Indian Territory Already Given to Another Tribe

January 1–February 2, 1865: Indian Military Campaign

1865: Battle of Fort Rankin

1866: Governor Evans' Speech on Minerals, Agriculture Promoting Colorado

1866: Gold, Silver and Coal Discovered on Ute Land; Fertile Land, Timber, Water Power, All Requirements for Profitable Occupation

1867: American Express Co., Shoot Indians

1867: Central City Indian Scalp Bounty

1867: Medicine Lodge Treaties—Cheyenne and Arapaho Treaty Establishing Reservation in Indian Territory

1868: Battle of Beecher Island

1868: Ute Treaty of 1868—Utes Cede Central Rockies

1869: Battle at Summit Springs
1871: Indian Appropriations Act Ends Treaty-Making with Indian Nations
1872: Colorado Citizens Want 1868 Treaty Revised for Utes to Cede San Juan Mts. due to Silver Discoveries
1873: San Juan Mountains—Richest Mining District
1874: Brunot Agreement—Utes Cede Mineral Rich San Juan Mountains
1876: Colorado Statehood
1877: Stay Friendly with Utes
1877: Comanche Peace Treaty with Utes
1877: Commissioner Recommends Removing All Indians in Colorado and AZ to Indian Territory to Facilitate Mining and Farming by Whites
Colorado Petitions for Removal of All Utes
1879: Battle of Milk Creek and Meeker Incident—Through No Fault, Utes Forced out of Colorado
Sample News Headlines from Colorado Rocky Mountain News (1878–79)
October 1879: Leadville Chronicle
1879: Governor Pitkin's Order: Bring in, Dead or Alive, All Hostile Indians
1880: Cong. Investigation—Battle of Milk Creek
1880: General Pope—Utes Worthless
Commissioner in Favor of Utes Removal to Utah
1880: After Thornburgh/Meeker Incidents Ute Delegation Forced to DC to Punish Them by Dispossessing Them of Their Reservation
1880: Utes Bribed to Sign Agreement to Cede Colorado Lands
1880–1881: Commission Removes Utes
1881: Forced Military Removal of 200 Miles
1881: Whites Pour onto Land Left by Utes with No Shred of Common Decency
1881: Cattle Enterprises
1881: Legislative Assembly of Colorado Territory: Bill for an Act to provide for the Destruction of Indians and Skunks
1890: Commissioner Morgan—Southern Utes to Stay in Colorado
1895: Hunter Act—Opened Up Ute Strip to Homesteading and Sale
1906: Mesa Verde Carved Out of Southern Ute Lands
Colorado Moguls
Mining and Real Estate
Metal Processing Enterprises
City Developers, Denver, Colorado
City Developers, Durango, Colorado
Investment Banking
Colorado Gold Production History
Colorado's Mining Millionaires
Colorado Counties

Farming

Mesa Verde Land Acknowledgments

Adams County (1902)

Alamosa County (1913)

Arapahoe County (1861)

Archuleta County (1885)

Baca County (1889)

Bent County (1870)

Boulder County (1861)

Broomfield County (2001)

Chaffee County (1879)

1862: Butterfield Overland Despatch, Mail and Freight Service, Great Plains

Cheyenne County (1889)

Clear Creek County (1861)

Conejos County (1861)

Costilla County (1861)

Crowley County (1911)

Custer County (1877)

Delta County (1883)

Denver County (1902)

Dolores County (1881)

Douglas County (1861)

Eagle County (1883)

El Paso County (1861)

Elbert County (1874)

Fremont County (1861)

Garfield County (1883)

Gilpin County (1861)

Grand County (1874)

Gunnison County (1877)

Hinsdale County (1874)

Huerfano County (1861)

Jackson County (1909)

Jefferson County (1861)

Kiowa County (1889)

Kit Carson County (1889)

La Plata County (1874)

Lake County (1861)

Larimer County (1861)

Las Animas County (1866)

Lincoln County (1889)

Logan County (1887)

Mesa County (1883)
Mineral County (1893)
Moffat County (1911)
Montezuma County (1889)
Montrose County (1883)
Morgan County (1889)
Otero County (1889)
Ouray County (1877)
Park County (1861)
Phillips County (1889)
Pitkin County (1881)
Prowers County (1889)
Pueblo County (1861)
Rio Blanco County (1889)
Rio Grande County (1874)
Routt County (1877)
Saguache County (1866)
San Juan County (1876)
San Miguel County (1883)
Sedgwick County (1889)
Summit County (1861)
Teller County (1889)
Washington County (1889)
Weld County (1861)
Yuma County (1889)
Notes: Colorado
U.S. Colorado Indian Treaties

10: NEVADA ~ 305

Great Basin
Goshutes: People of Desert (Newe)
Shoshone: People of High Growing Grasses (Newe)
Paiutes
       Northern Paiutes
       Southern Paiutes
Washoes
Waší·šiw—The People from Here
Changes to Washoe Life
Spanish Contact
Contact with 'White Men'
       Various Treaties with Shoshones in 1863

1859: Comstock Gold Composition
1859: Mining Districts Established on Comstock
Comstock Litigation Fever
Water, Water
Anarchy and Confusion from 1857–1861
1859 Forward: White Farming and Open Range Ranching
Eastern Public Administration Strategies for Establishing Towns
Fear of Indian Attacks Results in Military Presence Wherever Warranted by Revenue
Mormons' Insubordination to U.S. Laws
1859: Captain Simpson's Exploration for Route across Great Basin
1860: Paiutes-Pyramid Lake War
Pony Express and Stage Station Attacks
1861: Hot Springs and Yellow Pine Mining District, Southern Nevada
1861: Opal (Eldorado) Mountains, Gold/Silver Discoveries, Southern Nevada
Indians Face Starvation
1861: James Nye Appointed as Territorial Governor of Nevada
Indians Consider White Miners and Settlers Trespassers
Mormon Incursions; Comstock Lode; Butterfield Overland Mail and Pony Express; Invasion of White Settlers and Miners Engulf Indian Lands
1862–1863: Connor's Thugs and Massacre at Bear Creek
1862: Legislation for Treaties to Be Negotiated with Shoshonees
1863: Treaty Commissioners for Various Shoshonee Treaties
1863: Indian Treaties—Unlimited Mining, Farming, Ranching, Travel and Military Access
Importance of Treaties with Shoshonees to U.S.
Treaties Ratified with an Amendment by Senate
Evolution of U.S. Territories, States, and Indian Agencies from Late 1840s through 1870s in Today's Southern Nevada—(California, New Mexico, Colorado, Arizona, Utah, Idaho and Nevada) Result in Incoherent Indian Policy
1863: Pioche, Southern Nevada—Gold/Silver Discoveries
1864: Gold and Silver Discoveries in Humboldt Mountains
Timber Depletion
Truckee River Channel into Pyramid Lake Blocked by Logging Debris
Changes to Humboldt Region's Ecology
Silver and Gold Production Priority for Funding Civil War
Confederacy Seeks to Win Western Part of U.S. to Exploit Precious Metals
Confederacy Piracy
1865: Extinguish Goshutes' Title
1866: Scalp Bounties

~ 19 ~

11: ARIZONA ~ 429

1852: U.S.-Apache Treaty
1854: Mining Company
1861: Bascom Affair, Fort Bowie
1862: General James Carleton, Kill Apache Men
1863: Mangas Coloradas
1863–1874: Cochise Insurgency Tactics
1863: Territory of Arizona
Exterminating Apaches
Mining Required Mercenary Protection
Deathly Inflammatory Rhetoric
1865–1886: Apache Wars
1866 Forward: Indian Scalp Bounties
1867–1870: Indian Attacks
1862–1871: U.S. Military Campaigns
1868: Department of the Interior—Indians
1871: Reservations Established
1871: Camp Grant Massacre
1871: General Crook—Apache Wars, Use of Indian Scouts
Chiricahua Apache Reservation Proposals
1872: Chiricahua Apache Reservation
1870s: Concentration of Apaches on San Carlos Reservation
1874: Death of Cochise
Pacification of Apaches Permits Mining
1874: Indian Ring
1882–1886: General Crook's Use of Apache Scouts in Second Apache Campaign
1879–1886: Apache Wars
1871: Arizona Copper
1885: Arizona Copper Mining Companies
1861–1868: Army's Constabulary Duties—Apache Wars
Railroads: Territories of New Mexico and Arizona
1883: Indians Had "Little Use for Precious Metals"
1916: Arizona's Mineral Production
Aftermath, Loss of ~5,900,000 Acres
Notes: Arizona

12: CALIFORNIA ~ 457

1848: California Gold Discovered
1852: California—Ratification of 18 Treaties Negotiated Withheld by Senate;

Injunction of Secrecy; Indians Complied with Terms of Removal Only to Be Denied Land
California: Gold Discovered on Indian Lands Forces Genocide of California Indians
Gold Production in California by 1852
Notes: California

13: DAKOTAS ~ 465

1855: Fort Pierre
Routes Connecting Forts Mapped
1856: Fort Randall
1856: Tens of Thousands of Dollars Appropriated for Sioux Go Unexpended
1858: "Treaty of Washington" or Treaty of Yankton Sioux
1860s: Suffering of Sioux—Starvation, Destitution, Exposure
1863: Yankton Sioux Must Be Whipped
Black Hills Should Be Exploited for Whites
1866: U.S. Negligent and Fraudulent in Complying with Indian Treaties
1867: Department of the Interior and Dept. of Treasury Support Miners Who Want to Invade Black Hills
Fort Laramie Treaty of 1868, Establishment of Great Sioux Reservation
1868: Establishing Indian Agencies to Control Sioux—Barely Enough Annuities Doled Out for Survival—Many Died
Lakota Indian Agencies
    1859: Yankton Agency
    1869: Grand River Agency
    1869: Whetstone Agency (Name Changed to Spotted Tail Agency in 1874)
    1869: Cheyenne River Agency
    1871: Red Cloud Agency (1877 Name Changed to Pine Ridge Agency)
    1874: Crow Creek Agency
    1875: Lower Brule Agency
1869: General Sherman Publishes Letter in Press Advocating for Territorial or State Militias to Destroy Marauding Indians
July 1874: Custer's Black Hills Expedition
1875: Whites Taking Over Black Hills; Demand for President Grant to Annex Them
1875: USGS Newton Geological Expedition
April 1875: Military Command
May 1875: Lakota Delegation to DC—President Grant—Cede Black Hills or Lose Rations

July-August 1875: Miners Settling in Black Hills Evicted by General Crook
September 17, 1875: Allison Commission to Buy Black Hills or Lease Mining Rights Fails
October-November 1875: Presidential Scheming to Get Black Hills

November 3, 1875: President Grant Meets with Cabinet—White Settlers May Enter Black Hills

November 9, 1875: Manufacture Complaints against Lakotas—Bureau Inspector Watkins' Report Completed Six Days after White House Secret Meeting
December 3, 1875: Impossible Deadline—Sioux Must Be on Reservation by January 31, 1876, or Be Attacked
December 6, 1875: Commissioner of Indian Affairs Sends Notice of Deadline to Agencies
President Grant's Indian Peace Policy Breached
December 7, 1875: President Grant's Message—Gold in Black Hills; Sioux Unwilling to Cede Them; End Rations
December 20, 1875: Deadline Notice Received by Cheyenne River Agency
December 22, 1875: Deadline Notice Received by Standing Rock Agency, Agent Requests Extension of Time due to Weather Conditions
January 31, 1876: Deadline for Sioux to Be on Their Reservation
Prepare for Winter Military Campaign
January 21, 25, 1876: Department of the Interior to Provide Military Intelligence to War Department
February 1, 1876: Indians Turned Over to War Department
February 7, 1876: War Dept. Assumes Authority
Base of Military Operations

August 1876: Congress: Cede Black Hills or Lose Rations

February 1876: Preparations for U.S. Army's Big Horn Expedition

March 1-26, 1876: U.S. Army's Campaign to Destroy Crazy Horse's Village
Failed Crazy Horse Village Attack Results in Court Martial of Colonel Reynolds and Others
Winter 1876: U.S. Army's Operations a Bust

April 1876: Black Hills Gold Rush

Spring 1876: U.S. Army's Yellowstone Military Expedition: Three Columns Led by General Crook, General Terry and Colonel John Gibbon

June 17, 1876: Battle of Rosebud
July 25, 1876: Little Big Horn Battle
Summer 1876: General Crook's Operations

August 1876: Lieutenant General Sheridan—Disarm and Dismount Lakota, Subjugate on Reservation
Failure of Summer 1876 Campaign

Great Sioux War: 1876–1877

Fall 1876: Slim Buttes: Counterproductive: Lakotas Were Surrendering, Headed to Agencies
Appropriations Act of August 15, 1876, None for Sioux Until They Cede Black Hills
August 1876: Manypenny Commission Sent to Negotiate to Buy Black Hills
November 25, 1876: U.S. Army's Dull Knife Battle in Wyoming
1877: Surrender of Northern Cheyenne and Sioux
Congressional Inquiry
Home for Arapaho
1877: Forced Legislation Confiscates Black Hills
Total Disrespect for Indian Commissioners
1889: Dawes Act
1889–1890: Ghost Dance Movement
Pine Ridge Requests Troops
December 29, 1890: Massacre at Wounded Knee

1898–1904: Lakota Indian Reservations—Not Suitable for Farming, Not Enough Land for Ranching

> Cheyenne River
> Devils Lake
> Pine Ridge
> Rosebud
> Lower Brule Agency
> Crow Creek
> Standing Rock

October 24, 1903: Battle of Lightning Creek
Summary of Military Operations
Notes: Dakotas

14: GEORGIA ~ 513

Secretary of War Threatens Cherokees. They Will Be Left to Whims of Georgia
Georgia Enacts Laws Abolishing Cherokee Indian Sovereignty, Self-Government and Right to Land
Gold Discovered on Cherokee Lands, 1829
Notes: Georgia

History of Idaho Territory 1863–1890
1855: Nez Perce Treaty Establishing Reservation
1860: Idaho, Discovery of Gold, Nez Perce Reservation Overrun; Settlers'
Lawlessness to Be Generously Rewarded at Substantial Cost to Nez Perce
1860: Legislative Assembly of Washington Territory: MEMORIAL ASKING
THE APPOINTMENT OF A COMMISSIONER TO TREAT WITH THE
NEZ PERCE INDIANS FOR A CHANGE IN THEIR RESERVATION
April 1861: Nez Perce Reservation Invaded by 10,000 Whites;
Superintendent Geary Appeals for Military Aid
August 1861: U.S. Army Alerts Its Command to Potential for Hostilities
November 1861: Commissioner Dole Alerts Secretary Smith to Invasion of
Ten Thousand Whites on Nez Perce Land and Need for New Treaty
April 1861 Agreement: Unbelievable Encroachment—Nez Perce Give Right
to Mine on Their Lands without Remuneration
Spring 1862: Most Base Outrages by Whites on Indians; No Military
Response
Idaho Gold Rush: Nez Perce Reservation Completely Overrun by White
Miners and Squatters
Military Command Garrisoned at Lewiston
New Treaty Will Take More than Clothing
No New Reservation Location Available
Volunteer Militia's Opinion: If Nez Perce Reservation Opened, Millions Will
Be Added Annually to Moneyed Wealth of U.S.
Unauthorized Occupation of Gold Mines
Major General Howard, No Spirit Will Hinder Me
1863: Nez Perce "Thief Treaty"
1863: General Land Office Recommends Appropriation for Surveys
1864: "Inquietude and Discontent" of Nez Perce
1865: Kootenai and Coeur d'Alene Indians Retarding Development of
Minerals and Agricultural Land
1866: Governor Ballard: Idaho's Precious Metals, Profitable Investments for
Capitalists
1866: Concentration of Indians on Single Reservation
Bounty for Scalps
1867: Decaying Carcasses
1868: Governor Duplicitous in Pushing for Cession of Mineral and
Agricultural Lands of Shoshone and Bannock Indians
1887: Dawes Act
1893: Nez Perce Agreement
Values of Minerals in Idaho

    Gold
    Silver
Notes: Idaho

16: WYOMING ~ 541

Indians in Powder River Basin
Manifest Destiny
Indian Battles in Wyoming
1863: Bozeman Trail
Frontier Forts
Cantonment Reno
Fort Kearny
1866: Colonel Carrington—Whip Indians
Capt. Fetterman Disobeys Orders Resulting in Destruction of His Command
Battle at Crazy Woman Creek
Battle of Clear Creek
Wyoming Territory
Discovery of Gold at South Pass
Cattle Business
Farming
Wyoming Superintendency, Fort Bridger Treaty, 1868
1872: Reduce Wind River Indian Reservation ("WRIR")
Relinquish Part of WRIR with Mineral Discoveries, 1874 Lander Purchase
Further Reduction of WRIR with Agricultural Land, Coal and Minerals
U.S. Army's Sioux Nation Mission
Retrospective View of Military Policy by General John Pope
Notes: Wyoming

17: MICHIGAN ~ 565

The Iron Triangle, Chapter 6, The Carving Up of Michigan

Indigenous Discoveries of Copper in Keweenaw Peninsula
1805: Michigan Territory, Extinguish Indian Title in State
1820: Mineral Survey
1840: Report on Keweenaw's Copper Deposits
Copper Mining
F.C.L. Koch, German Mining Engineer, 1850
Saginaw Mining Company
Ohio and Isle Royale Company
Pittsburg & Isle Royale Mining Company

1842: Ojibwe Treaty of La Pointe
1843: Department of the Interior's Continued Celebration of U.S. Stripping of Tribes Agriculturally Valuable Land and Mineral Resources
1844: Continued Removal, Re-Locating Tribes Delayed; Chippewas of Mississippi and Lake Superior
1846: President Polk, Removal of Chippewa Indians from Mineral Lands on Lake Superior
1846: Commandeering Valuable Chippewa Land and Resources
Wealth Derived from Ancillary Businesses
1875: Copper Extracted
Notes: Michigan

18: MINNESOTA ~ 565

The Iron Triangle, Chapter 7: Minnesota: Fraudulent Legislation Enabling Acquisition of Indian Land
1866: Gold Mining NE Minn (Bois Forte Impacted)
Value of an Indian Scalp
Minnesota's "Knights of the Forest"
Reign of Terror for Bowels of Earth
Notes: Minnesota

19: WISCONSIN ~ 579

The Iron Triangle, Chapter 8: Wisconsin's Forced Indian Removal
Mining in Northern Wisconsin
1827: Upper Mississippi Valley: Illinois, Wisconsin and Iowa
1829: Lead Mining in Southwestern Wisconsin
1832: City of Galena
Eliminating Indians' Land Base
1842: Confirmation by Army of Vast Quantity of Mineral Land
1855: Copper Mining in Northern Wisconsin
1865: Post Civil War
Resolution of Legislature of Wisconsin for Removing Wisconsin Indians
Notes: Wisconsin

20: MONTANA ~ 585

The Iron Triangle, Chapter 9: Montana: Big Business' Corrupt Political Clout
1862: Gold Discovered
Railroads
1862 Homestead Act; 1877 Desert Land Act

Indian Hostilities
1864: Montana Territory Created
1864: Commissioner of Indian Affairs' Indian Policy
1865: Indian Policy—Protect White Settlers and White Miners Over Indian Interests
Copper Kings
U.S.' Failure to Fulfill Treaty Obligations Causes Indian Depredations
1868: Bitter Root Valley—White Intruders on Flathead Tribal Lands
Montana's Indian Wars (1865–1887)
1869: Use of "Hard" Military Tactics
1870: Piegan Massacre (aka Baker Massacre)
August 18, 1869: Department of the Interior Superintendent General Sully Reports Blackfeet in State of War
Sep. 9, 1869: Military Investigates and Concludes War Mongering
October 21, 1869: Lieutenant General Sheridan Recommends Winter Attack
November 4, 1869: General Sherman Approves Lieutenant General Sheridan's Plan
November 18, 1869: Lieutenant General Sheridan Orders Piegans 'Struck Hard'
January 6, 1870: Colonel Baker's Force of 355 Leaves to 'Chastise' Indians
January 23, 1870: Colonel Baker Attacks Wrong Village
January 29, 1870: Lleutenant General Sheridan Reports "Complete Success" of Attack
February 1, 1870: General Sully Reports Massacre of Women and Children
February 10, 1870: Montana Resolutions Praise Military Victory
February 23, March 9, 10, 1870: New York Times Reports Massacre
March 12, 1870: General Sherman Requests Detailed Report of Indians Killed
March 18, 1870: Lieutenant General Sheridan Justifies Killings
March 24, 1870: Military Investigation—No Guilt
March 27, 1870: Colonel Baker Files Second Report; Reports Vast Majority Killed Were Male Warriors
Indians to Stay Under Control of Department of the Interior
Itomot' ahpi Pikun'i: "Killed Off the Piegans"
1870–1890: Montana's Unswaying Industrial Boom
Starvation of Montana's Reservation Indians
1884: Fort Belknap Reservation—Gold Discovered While Whites Illegally Prospecting
Notes: Montana

1864–1868: Snake War—Indians Hunted like Wolves
1866: Umatilla Indians Threatened with Violent Removal by White Settlers
1871: U.S. Secretary of Treasury Documented Gold Yield in NE Oregon
White Settlers Demand Removal of Modoc Indians
1873: Peace Commission Doomed to Fail
1873: Modocs to Be Punished
1877: Nez Perce 'Thief' War
1878: Bannock War
1878: President Hayes: Lack of Food
1895: Second Bannock War
Stolen Opportunities
Notes: Oregon

23: NEW MEXICO ~ 633

1850: New Mexico Established as Territory
1852: Territorial Governor Calhoun Fears Indian Hostilities
1862: Military's Objective—Subjugation of Mescalero Apaches
1863: Mescalero Apaches Imprisoned at Fort Sumner
1863: Geological Surveys
1866: Volunteer Campaigns against Indians
1866: Concentrating Indians on Reservations
1871: Scalping Apaches
Indian Battles in New Mexico
1877: Carve Up Mescalero Reservation to Exclude Discoveries of Silver
1877: Land and Cattle Companies
1878–1881: Lincoln County War
1879: Discovery of Silver in White Mountains, Northwestern Boundary of
Mescalero Reservation
Relocation of Mescalero Indians
1880: Mescaleros Accused of Supporting Victorio's Outbreak
1880: Gold Discovered on Mescalero Reservation
1881: Nogal Mining District Petitions Military Support in Reducing Size of
Mescalero Reservation
1882: President Arthur's Executive Order to Redefine Mescalero Reservation
Boundaries
1883: Lincoln County Exhibit
1900: Proposal to Open Mescalero Reservation for White Settlement
Notes: New Mexico

Utah's Metals
1858: Gold Discovery
Indian Tribes in Utah
     Utes
     Paiutes
     Gosiutes
Conflicts
Indian Wars
1849: Battle Creek Massacre
1853: The Walker War [Mormons and Utes]
1853: Gunnison Massacre
1856: Tintic War [Mormons and Utes]
1857–1858: Mormon War
1860: SW States' Residents Petition for Extinguishing Indian Title
1860: Indians Surrounded by Mormons (Indian Agent)
1860: President Sets Aside Uinta Valley Reservation
1863: Bear River Massacre
1864: Gold Discovery in Bingham Canyon
Indian Battles in Utah
Mining as Vital Industry
1865: Congress Authorizes President to Enter into Treaties with Indians in Utah Territory to Extinguish Indian Title to Lands Suitable for Agricultural and Mineral Purposes
1865–1867: Black Hawk War—Mormons and Utes (April 9, 1865)
1865: Silver Discovered in SW Utah, May 4, 1865
1865: Spanish Fork Treaty between U.S. and Ute Tribes in Utah, June 8, 1865 (Unratified)
1865: Weber (Cumumbah) Treaty between U.S. and Weber Ute Indians, October 1865 (Unratified)
1866: Circleville Massacre [Mormons and Koosharem Band of Paiute Indian Tribe of Utah]
1867: Most of Uintah Utes Removed to Uintah Valley Reservation
1870: Vernon H. Vaughan, Eighth Governor of Utah Territory, 1870–1871
1871: George Lemuel Woods, Ninth Governor of Utah Territory, 1871–1875
1875: George W. Emery, Eleventh Governor of Utah Territory, 1875–1880; Advocated for Abolishing Tribal Relations
1879: Uintah Utes at Peace
1880: Eli Houston Murray, Twelfth Governor of Utah Territory, 1880–1886
1881: White River & Uncompahgre Utes Removed from Colorado

1886: Fort Duchesne

1886: Uncompahgre Band of Utah Indians Reservation Barren; Vile and Hateful Report on Utes by Agents

1887: Illegal Grazing on Uintah Indian Reservation

1888: Southern Utes Agree to Move to Utah, But Congress Fails to Ratify Agreement

1888: Congress Reduces Uintah Reservation for Mining of Gilsonite by Whites

1889: Unlawful Gilsonite Mining by Whites Continues after Establishment of Uintah Reservation in 1881

1889: Arthur Lloyd Thomas, Fourteenth Governor of Utah Territory, 1889–1893; Requests Early Allotment of Uintah Reservation Lands

1890: Utah Opposed to Southern Utes Removal from Colorado to Utah

1891: Members of Former Pi Ute, Shoshone, Pah Vants, Piedes and Ute Tribes Need Aid

1893: Value of Gold & Silver Extracted $16,276,818

1894: Utah's Legislative Push for Opening Both Uintah and Ouray Reservations

1898: Allotments Made on Ouray (Uncompahgre) Reservation

1904: Congress Approved Allotments for Uintah and White River Utes of Uintah Reservation

1905: Uintah Forest Reserve Established

1906: White River Utes Head to Pine Ridge

1934: Ute Indian Tribe of the Uintah and Ouray Reservation

Bingham Canyon Silver and Gold

1902: MacNeill-Penrose Group ($250,000 Cash Investment)

Copper Enterprise's Financial Backing

Smelters-Bingham Consolidated Mining and Smelting Company, United States Mining Company ("ASARCO"), Utah Consolidated

Railroad Lines

Notes: Utah

25: MAYHEM ~ 683

Doctrine of Settler Colonialism
Fraudulent Doctrine of Discovery
Grants of Right of Way for Railroads and Locations for Settlements
Railroads Recruited Emigrants
Military Posts Built Along Transcontinental Routes
Requiem for Buffalo
Reservation Policy

U.S. Mission to Destroy Tribal Governments, Decimate Sovereignty and
Obliterate Indian Individual Identity
Savage Aristocracy
Policy Conflict between War Department and Interior Department
Failure to Fulfill Trust Relationship
Concealing Peace Treaty Commissions' Purpose
U.S.' Willingness to Break Indian Treaties
Failure to Protect Indian Land
Executive Order Reservations
Encroachments on Indian Lands by White Settlers
Government's Segregation of Minerals from Indian Lands
Deliberate Undervaluation of Indian Mineral Lands by U.S.
Mining Dependent on Timber, Agricultural Land and Water
Theft of Indian Mineral Resources
Theft of Indian Timber
Theft of Indian Water Resources
Mining Magnates
Strategic Military Policy
Cost-Benefit Analysis of Total Destruction of Indians
Shock and Awe Tactics
Railroads: Weapon against Indians
Military Massacres
Consequences of Indian War
Military Used to Enforce Reservation, Assimilation Policies
Private Vigilante Wars Paid for by U.S.
Extermination of Indians by Pioneer Vigilantes
Mayhem to Instill Fear among Indians
Reducing Reservation Size to Acquire More Indian Land
      1872: Reduce Wind River Indian Reservation to Get Mineral Lands
      1874: Further Reduction of WRIR to Get Agricultural Land, Coal
      and Minerals
Consolidation of Different Indian Tribes to Free Up Lands for White Settlers
Loss of Tribal Lands due to Allotment
Opening Surplus Reservation Lands after Allotment to White Settlers
Truth about Quality of Indian Lands
Unfair Advantage due to Indians Unfamiliarity with English Language
Land Descriptions
Deeds for Land Transactions
Type of Document Proffered

Chief Old Dog, 1851–1928
Indian Claims Commission
Notes: Mayhem

PREFACE

Series of Books

This book on the theft of Indian mineral resources is part of a series on the dispossession of Indian natural resources by the iron triangle of the federal government, big business and colonial settlers: *The Earth Is Red: The Imperialism of the Doctrine of Discovery* and *The Iron Triangle: Business, Government, and Colonial Settlers' Dispossession of Indian Timberlands and Timber.*

It would be impossible to treat this subject extensively and without date limitations so the writer has selected arbitrary date limits of about 1850-1900. The areas focused on are the primary western mineral resource states: Oregon, Washington, Idaho, Montana, Wyoming, Colorado, Nevada, Arizona, Utah, New Mexico and the Dakotas.

In-Depth Review

This book is based on an in-depth review of relevant historical documents pertaining to the U.S.' treatment of the mineral resources of Indian Nations over the course of more than one hundred years. This format relies on quotes from the actual entity unfiltered by time or latter-day interpretations and revisions.

Names of Indian Nations, Individuals and Places

Please be aware that variations in spellings as well as cognates exist in regard to names of Indian Nations, individuals and places.

Quotes Reflect Original Text

Quotes used reflect original text, which may have different spellings, punctuation or mis-spellings or mis-punctuation.

Settler Colonialism

If one only reads this section of the book, they would understand the doctrine of settler colonialism. It is presented in a crystal clear manner in this speech by General Pope in 1878. Headings have been provided.

After the Civil War, General Pope was assigned command of the Department of the Missouri. On October 26, 1882, officials promoted Pope to the rank of major general in the regular army. Despite waging war against the Plains Indians during his second stint as commander of the Department of the Missouri, Pope made political enemies in Washington for criticizing the government's harsh treatment of Native Americans and for exposing corruption in the Bureau of Indian Affairs. https://www.americanhistorycentral.com/entries/john-pope/ (accessed online March 9, 2023).

"The Indian Question" by John Pope: Address by General John Pope before the Social Science Association, at Cincinnati, Ohio, May 24, 1878. Delivered by Request of the Association (Cincinnati: n.p., 1878).

General John Pope Verifies Doctrine of Settler Colonialism

> *I presume it will not be disputed that all history shows that when a savage and a civilized people are brought together in the same country, the inevitable result has been the dispossession of the savage and the occupation of the lands by civilized man. ... [I]t is certain that the larger part of the country claimed by him will, in some manner, pass into the possession of the white race.* The abstract wrong or right of this process it seems useless to discuss, as it is quite certain that great district [sic] of country on this continent, capable of maintaining many millions of civilized men, will not be left in the possession of a few thousand nomadic Indians.
>
> In view of this necessity, a policy of dealing with the Indians, based on that of Penn, was adopted; a policy which, with some not very important modifications, to be hereafter referred to, has been pursued by the government to this day.

That policy is briefly as follows:

Whenever the march of emigration began to press upon lands claimed or roved over by wild tribes of Indians, a treaty was made with the Indians which provided for the surrender of that portion of their lands which was immediately in demand, leaving to the Indian what remained. It will be well, before proceeding further, to inquire what such a treaty was and, practically, still is:

Treaties with Indians, unwise under almost any circumstances, are made by the government for one of three objects—first, to buy land; second, to buy peace; and third, and most generally, to buy both. If it be proposed to make a treaty, commissioners are named by the government to conduct and conclude the negotiations up to the point of submitting their work to the U.S. Senate, by which body even Indian treaties must be ratified.

The first demand by the Indians, as the principal condition of the treaty, is that the white man shall not intrude upon his reserved lands, nor destroy his game, nor interfere with his people. This condition is the first and most important to the Indian. In every case of which I know anything, it has been readily agreed to, and the government, through its commissioners, binds itself to this obligation. Is it possible that any white man, official or private citizen, believes that, even if the government intends to enter into this obligation in good faith, it is practicable to fulfill the engagement? *What means has the government to enforce compliance? Consider, for a moment, the vast extent of country which it guarantees against intrusion. Look at the great numbers of adventurous people pressing forward, urged by curiosity, speculation, love of excitement, thirst for gold, or craving for land. From every direction and from all points, the whites throng to these unexplored and unknown regions. Who is to keep them from crossing imaginary lines of Indian country? Is it proposed to employ the army for this purpose? If so, the number of troops required to picket that whole region and the infinite number of routes leading to it would, I fear, appall the stoutest man that ever sat in Congress. ...*

Treaties with Indians, in the process of negotiating them, are carefully gone over, paragraph by paragraph, by the chiefs, and only after the closest examination of each provision is it inserted in the treaty. The Indian, vested with full authority himself, understands, of course, that the white commissioner has equal power, and that the treaty, once signed, is binding on both.

General Pope Confirms Senate's Unlawful, One-Sided Mutation of Treaties

But when the commissioners have completed their work, it is submitted to the United States Senate, which proceeds to modify or change its provisions as it pleases, and then ratifies the amended version, which, in some cases, strikes out what the Indian considers most important and inserts provisions to which he would never have agreed. I will not say that such amended treaties are not resubmitted to the Indian, but as a general rule, I believe they are not, but become binding obligations whether the Indian consents or not. It is also true, within my own experience, that in some cases—I know not how many—the Senate has joined with the House in making appropriations having the direct effect of violating the very treaties which they themselves have ratified. Of course, the Senate did not intend to do such wrong, but acted without remembrance or without knowledge of the obligations to which itself had pledged the United States. [Even in 1865, the commissioners dispatched by Secretary Harlan were instructed that "these treaties might be amended by the Senate and such amendments would not require the concurrence of the Indians."]

I have, for instance, known of more than one case in which a treaty with the Indians contained a solemn provision that their country should not be intruded on by the whites—a treaty duly ratified by the Senate, and yet the Senate joined the House in passing a bill appropriating money to build a wagon road for public use through the very heart of the country thus guaranteed against intrusion. *The very fact that this provision of all treaties with Indians is constantly and systematically violated, and that the Indian wars and outrages have oc-*

curred with increasing frequency on that very account, created the necessity of almost continuous treaty-making, even with the same tribe, until there remained of the tribe no one to treat with, and this I believe to be the natural end of all Indians who engage in this sort of diplomacy. ...

The first treaty made with an Indian tribe only alienated a small portion of his lands, but as the emigrants pressed forward, increasing daily both their numbers and the routes by which they entered the Indian country, it soon became necessary to make another treaty, and then another, until in time, and a very short time, as it appears, one tribe of Indians after another was dispossessed of its lands until the whole of the vast region east of the Mississippi River fell into possession of the whites. In consideration, or rather as payment for the surrender of these lands, large money annuities, as well as annuities of goods, arms, and ammunition, were granted to the Indians, and an Indian agent was appointed for each tribe as custodian and disbursing agent of the money and goods.

The first effect of this process was to establish a class of Indians who, while still maintaining their wild life and their relations with the wilder tribes west of them, were also connected with the white settlers to the east of them through the annuities of money and goods paid annually for the surrender of that portion of their lands bordering the white settlements. *The yearly or semiannual distribution of these annuities required their presence at stated periods on the frontier of the white settlements. The money and goods thus distributed by the Indian agent necessarily attracted all the gamblers, whiskey sellers, Indian traders, and other unprincipled characters who infest the frontier, whilst the purchase and transportation of large quantities of goods brought also into the Indian system an army of contractors and their followers.* The Indian was thus provided with the worst possible associations and surrounded by the most corrupting influences, and these payments became scenes of wild debauch until the Indian had parted with both his money and goods. If this had been the worst, it is possible that some remedy might in time have been applied, but *unfortunately it was only the first step in a long course of demoralization and wrong.*

But a little while and the resistless movement of the white race began again to be felt upon the lands not ceded by the Indians. Of course, the Indian, after more or less resistance, again sold, mainly because he had not power to keep, and the same results followed. This process was repeated at short intervals, the Indians becoming less numerous and more debased by every treaty, until finally they were left with a small fragment of the possessions they once occupied, and being no longer able to subsist themselves and emasculated of their manhood, they became paupers and vagabonds dependent upon the government for support.

General Pope Corroborates Outrages against Indians

Even the small reservation still left them soon became valuable by the growth of settlements around it, and Congress was besieged by land speculators and their friends to make another treaty, involving another removal of the Indians and the distribution of more money and more goods, whilst the lands fell into the possession of the most adroit operator. *The white settlers in contact with these Indians, whether on large or small reservations, inflamed by report or experience of Indian atrocities and unrestrained by law or any sound public opinion, settled all disputes and avenged all injuries in which Indians were concerned, however trifling, with a pistol or rifle, themselves being both judges and executioners. The Indians retaliated* for these acts by horrible outrages common to Indian warfare, and thus provoked renewed attacks. In this manner, a never-ended strife has been kept up from the beginning, which no measures yet taken have sufficed even to check. ...

The Indian country is penetrated everywhere by the seekers for gold or for land; highways are made through it without his consent, and the game driven off or destroyed. No one will say, even if he can, what outrages are committed upon the Indian by irresponsible crowds of white men ... What the white man does to the Indian is never known. It is only what the Indian does to the white man which reaches the public. ...

Every proposition to build railroads (and some are already built) through the Indian Territory, and for the establish-

ment of a territorial government, has but one object and leads to but one result, the dispossession of the Indian and the occupation of his lands by white men. ...

I know no occupation requiring more thorough acquaintance with business methods, greater knowledge of men, and power to influence and control them, than the supply, management, and control of Indian tribes. The man whose life has been devoted to religious duties as a clergyman cannot of necessity have had the training and experience to conduct large business operations carried on with businessmen sharp and unscrupulous, nor to be the best judge of those who can; nor can the duties of religious instructor and business manager, especially for large bodies of wild Indians, be combined without injury to both. ...

General Pope Admits Starvation of Reservation Indians

Whether these opinions be accepted or not, it is certain that the physical condition of the Indian is as bad, if not worse, today than I have ever known it. It is a fact so notorious as to require only the statement of it, that the *reservation Indians are insufficiently fed at all times*, and that for considerable periods during each year, *they are in a condition of want and suffering revolting to humanity*. It is also true that in many cases the articles of food to be daily issued to them are specified in detail in the treaties, but only in part are furnished— and at times not furnished at all. *In short, it is a fact that thousands of Indians placed on reservations by the actual use of superior force are slowly starved.*

There can be little said for the practical sense of people who, in view of this result, insist upon making the Indian support himself by becoming a day laborer on a farm, with the idea of making the whole Indian race an agricultural people. What would be thought of the same attempt upon the white people of this country, or any other? The idea of such people seems to be that all Indians are alike, and that an Indian is the same wherever he is found. ...

Relations of Army to Indian System

In order that the whole subject may be clearly understood, it seems necessary to explain the relation of the army to the Indians and the Indian Bureau, and I will therefore state it as succinctly as possible. Whilst the Indians remain on their reservations and are peaceful, the troops stationed near them have no jurisdiction whatever, and consequently no certain knowledge of their feelings and purposes, and no power to take any action, either of a precautionary or aggressive character. The Indians thus placed are generally furnished with passes, signed by the Indian agent, permitting them to go almost anywhere or for any purpose except war.

The first that is known by the military of Indian hostilities is a sudden report that they have begun a war a hundred miles or more distant from a military post, and have devastated settlements and killed people. By the time such information reaches the military commander, the worst has been accomplished and the Indians have escaped from the scene of outrage, and in most cases have again rejoined their agencies. Nothing is left to the military except pursuit, and generally unavailing pursuit.

Should the Indians succeed in regaining their reservations before they are overtaken, they are safe from punishment, as the military cannot act against them at all unless they are beyond the limits of their reserved lands. In point of fact, the troops are kept near the agencies practically to protect the civil agent and his employees, and are without the slightest authority to interfere in any manner with whatever transactions may be carried on by them.

It is a most painful duty to be forced to witness suffering and privation day after day, and to see whole tribes of Indians so destitute that it makes the heart sick to witness it. The military authorities have not even the right to relieve the hungry and the destitute from the public stores in their charge, but whatever goes on, they must remain silent and on no account interfere with the transactions of the Indian agent, whatever he does or fails to do. It has often happened, and indeed is of frequent occurrence now, that urged by spectacles of suffering, which human nature could not contemplate without horror, the officers have exceeded their authority, and laid themselves liable therefore, by issuing scanty articles of food to the starving Indians from the public stores under their charge, rather than to see people—men, women, and children—die of starvation in their very sight, but even this interference is not lawful, and is only put up with without complaint because it in no manner touches the jurisdiction of the agent. In short, *it appears to be the only function of the army stationed near the Indian agencies to force the Indian to submit to suffering quietly and without disturbance,* whether the necessity results from the deficiency of appropriations, bad management of the agent, or actual fraud. *If the Indian, pressed by want, leaves his reservation, the troops are ordered to attack him, and he is treated as the common enemy of mankind.*

The army is the victim and not the author of wars with Indians.

Suggestions Concerning Improvement of Present Indian System

Accepting as inevitable the proposition that in the nature of things, the lands on this continent must in some manner and in large pass from the possession of the Indian into that of the white man ...

It will not answer for us to say that we have paid the Indians for his lands, and that if he has squandered the money and failed to learn to work, his is the fault, and he and not we are responsible for his sorry condition. It is no more honest to make this excuse in the case of Indians than in the case of children whose property we have filched from them through the agency of toys and trinkets, or even money, which the child knows no better than to squander for such things. *The Indian was and still is as ignorant of values as the child,* and has no more care for the future nor capacity to anticipate or provide for its necessities.

We bought from the Indians: first, because the pressure of emigration demanded it, and second, because the interests of the country were benefited. The Indian sold: first, because he could not keep without continual warfare, if even then, and second, because acquaintance with the whites taught him pleasant and unusual vices which he could not indulge without the white man's money or something he could convert into it.

General Pope Affirms Goal of Relinquishment of All of Indian Country as U.S.' Objective

We bought his lands by driblets, knowing very well that every purchase demanded another purchase in geometrical ratio, and that with every sale the means of livelihood upon which the Indian race had depended for ages, and which was the only mode they knew, were restricted more and more, and that in time every tribe of Indians must, in the nature of the case, be left destitute, except insofar as the government chose to feed and clothe them. The Indian did not know this in the beginning, nor indeed until want was upon him. We knew that he must relinquish in time all of his country. He did not know it, nor in the least comprehended the merciless and resistless progress of white populations. In short, we began the system, knowing perfectly what would be the results; the Indian began and for a long time continued it in ignorance of these ends."

We have the greater part of the Indian's lands; we are bound to see that he does no (sic) undergo physical suffering through his own ignorance or our superior acuteness. I do not suppose that any Christian man will contest this proposition, and relying upon its soundness, I proceed to make one suggestion for improving our treatment of the Indians:

This necessity has created the reservation system, to which many of the Indian tribes have been subjected already, and which is assuredly the future condition of all. ... And yet, if our forefathers could have foreseen the history of this last ninety years—what torrents of blood, what nameless horrors, what lavish and wasteful expenditure of money, what reproach upon themselves and their posterity might have been spared for us. ...

Bearing in mind the obligation, sacred and binding, to protect all Indians whom we have dispossessed of their lands, and whose modes of support we have absolutely destroyed, against actual physical destitution or violence, the question to be considered is, "Where shall we locate the Indian whose restriction to reservations has become necessary, and under what conditions?" ...

It is plain from history and from experience that none of these conditions are fulfilled if the reservation of the tribe be located upon part of the Indian's own lands, where he is subject to precisely the same difficulties already recounted and must go through them to the same end.

I suggest, therefore, that whenever an Indian tribe is in a condition to be placed on a reservation, or is so placed now, it be removed to the rear and not to the front of the advancing emigration ...

The second suggestion I shall make relates to the civilization of the Indian and his conversion to Christianity. ... The Indian, who is but a child in all such matters as Christianity and civilization, has been placed in an environment by the use of mixed persuasion and force, the most unfavorable possible for any improvement whatever. ...

These younger Indians should be taught trades and industries such as they incline to, or can be induced to learn, so that in time, if capable of becoming civilized people like ourselves, they may follow the example of our own youth, leave their reservations and be absorbed among the people, and thus disappear as a distinct race from our midst. I therefore offer for consideration these two propositions:

If the Indian prove capable of becoming a part of our population, pursuing the same avocations and restrained by the same influences, we shall have accomplished a great and beneficent work. If, however, he be unable to profit by the opportunity, and as a necessary consequence disappear from among us, we at least shall not be in fault, but must accept the melancholy result as the unavoidable failure of an honest and earnest effort to do right in the right way. Nothing, then, will be left us except to care for him as he is and, as far as possible, smooth his pathway to inevitable extinction. If God, indeed, will it that the once populous Indian race—our predecessors on this continent—shall shrivel up and disappear before us, let it at least be truly said that we, a Christian people, played our part in its melancholy history and awaited its final obsequies as mourners, and not as executioners.

1: MINERAL ECONOMIC DEVELOPMENT

Natural Resources

Natural resources can be categorized as renewable and non-renewable. Renewable natural resources, when sustainably used, can be regenerated by natural processes of growth. Non-renewable natural resources are exhaustible and can't be regenerated after exploitation, e.g., gold and silver. The other aspect of renewable and non-renewable natural resources includes the environmental functions of ecosystems when not degraded, e.g., water purification and nutrient cycling and the capacity to assimilate wastes.

Indians possessed an abundant natural resource environment which included (1) renewable natural resources such as timber, water and arable land, along with wildlife resources such as fish and game; and (2) non-renewable natural resources, such as gold, silver, copper, iron ore, coal and oil.

The deliberate policy of the U.S., the Indians' trustee, was to expropriate Indian mineral resources.

1855: Nez Perce Treaty Deliberately Excludes Gold Discoveries

A blatant example of this was the Nez Perce 1855 Treaty:[1]

> *Gold* has been found in the country above yours. Our people are very fond of it. When our people hear this they will come here by hundreds. Among them who come there will be some bad people. Those bad people will steal your horses and cattle. There are but few of you. You cannot prevent it. When you are scattered over a great extent of country you cannot prevent it. But if you are living on the Reservation we can protect you and your family. Why then would you refuse to receive our talk and refuse to allow us to protect you? (Emphasis added).[2]

~ 51 ~

1865: Cheyenne and Arapahos - Since Gold Was Discovered in Their Country, They Were Removed

No. 13. Treaty Council held in camp on the Little Arkansas River, October 13, 1865:

> We all fully realize that it is hard for any people to leave their homes and graves of their ancestors; but, **unfortunately for you, gold has been discovered in your country**, and a crowd of white people have gone there to live, and a great many of these people are the worst enemies of the Indians men who do not care for their interests, and who would not stop at any crime to enrich themselves. These men are now in your country—in all parts of it and there is no portion where you can live and maintain yourselves but what you will come in contact with them. The consequences of this state of things are that you are in constant danger of being imposed upon, and you have to resort to arms in self defence. Under the circumstances, there is, in the opinion of the commission, no part of the former country large enough where you can live at peace. The white men who are there do not regard law, and the President desires to punish them, yet it will not come until they have committed actual hostilities against the Indians.

> Before the President can hear of their bad deeds a state of hostilities is created, and you are the sufferers. Under the circumstances the commissioners desire you to carefully consider whether it is not best for you to go to some other country where you will not be disturbed in this manner.

> *We want to give you a country that is full of game and good for agricultural purposes, and where the hills and mountains are not full of gold and silver*. In such a country as this the government can fully provide for your wants ...

> We believe that in the country where we desire you to go you will gradually become rich, and your numbers increase; but we are fully convinced that it is impossible for you to stay, and that if you do stay, you will gradually diminish, until you are finally swept from the earth.

> We are sorry that we have bad people among us, as you are

sorry that you have bad people among you; but this is unfortunately the case with all people, and however severe we make laws; *it is impossible to prevent crime*.

You may accede to our wishes, and be happy and prosperous, or you may refuse to make a treaty, and be ruined in health and happiness. (Emphasis added).[3]

Minerals Were to Be Segregated from Reservations

In concentrating Indians on reservations in New Mexico, the Office of Indian Affairs was adamant that the reservations were not to be located in areas 'abounding' in mineral wealth.

A military force should be posted at or near each reservation. *... The reservations should not be selected near the mountains, which abound in mineral wealth and will attract the whites*. J.K. Graves, Special Agent Relative to Indian Affairs in New Mexico. (Emphasis added).[4]

Wealth Inherent in Natural Resources

The wealth embodied in natural resources was the key component in Indian lands that aggravated the greed of colonial settlers and businesses. The immediacy of revenues that could be derived from natural resources was undeniable. A study by the U.S. Geological Survey in 1923 is very specific as to the value of minerals in Colorado, alone. *The total gross value of Colorado's gold, silver, copper, lead and zinc was calculated to be $1,531,000,000 from 1859-1923*. (Emphasis added).[5]

Entrepreneurs

A gold rush is never really just about the gold. It's about the people it attracts and the businesses they launch.

Farming Enterprises

From 1780 to 1850 the population of the U.S. grew nearly eightfold, from nearly three million to about 23 million. It took about three acres of cropland to feed each person. In Colorado alone, the Commissioner of Indian Affairs recognized the cropland required to feed the miners, characterized as being of 'paramount importance.' The arable land was required for the 'white settlers' and there was no surplus for Indians. Their removal was recommended by their trustee.[6]

Ranching

The development of the railroad made it profitable to raise cattle on the Great Plains. In 1860, some five-million longhorn cattle grazed in the Lone Star state. Cattle that could be bought for $3 to $5 a head in Texas could be sold for $30 to $50 at railroad shipping points in Abilene or Dodge City in Kansas. Cowboys had to drive their cattle a thousand miles northward to reach the Kansas railheads. This was the start to another business endeavor which led to a new breed—the wealthy western cattle baron.

Banking, Shipping and Transportation Enterprises

In the 1830s and 1840s, Henry Wells and William Fargo started shipping and transportation enterprises to the West. They were the leading forces behind the founding of American Express in Buffalo, New York in 1850. In 1850, three competing express companies: *Wells & Company*; *Livingston, Fargo & Company* (Fargo and William A. Livingston); and *Wells, Butterfield & Company*, were consolidated and became the American Express Company, with Wells as President and Fargo as Secretary

1867: American Express Co., Shoot Indians

Thomas Murphy, the Superintendent of Indian Affairs, Upper Arkansas Agency, Fort Larned, Kansas, on May 27, 1867, issued a complaint to his superior Commissioner Taylor. He wrote:

> "I have the honor to transmit herewith a circular issued by the superintendent of the American Express Company to their employes on the Smoky Hill route from Fort Harker to Denver City. I would call your attention particularly to the paragraph marked, viz: "If Indians come within shooting distance, shoot them; show them no mercy, for they will show you none."
> ... According to existing treaty stipulations the Cheyennes, Arapahos, and Apaches have permission to live in and roam over the country lying between these two rivers until the President orders their removal to reservations selected for them.
> ... I respectfully request that you will take such immediate steps as in your judgement will the soonest and most effectually put a stop to these arbitrary and cruel orders."[7]

Valuing Natural Resources

The easiest way to quantify the value of a natural resource, such as fish or timber, is its market price. The option value is the ability to choose between use and non-use. By dispossessing Indians of their natural resources, they lost this total value. Many times in compensating Indians for this loss, either due to legislation or litigation, the only determinable value was the commodity price, which was invariably discounted to an incredible minimal amount.

Nez Perce Awarded $3 Million from $20,000,000 Gold Production

The Indian Claims Commission awarded the Nez Perce Nation

> "a fair and reasonable estimate of the dollar value of the *gold* produced from the Nez Perce Reservation discounted for production costs and producer's working interest. From $20,000,000, it was determined that "70 percent of the dollar value of the *gold* removed from the reservation would represent production cost;" that the net profit that would have been realized on the *gold* would have been 30 percent, or $6,000,000; that "a royalty agreement providing for the Nez Perce Tribe to receive 50 percent of the net profit ... should have been negotiated," and that the Nez Perce Tribe therefore was entitled to recover "50 percent of the net profit ... or $3,000,000, less such offsets, if any, to be later determined by this Commission."

Thus, more than 100 years after the offending conduct, the parties settled for $3,000,000, or 15 percent of the estimated value of the *gold* taken, without interest.[8]

Metals Are Sole Reliance to Liquidate Interest on National Debt

Given the federal government's need for money, especially after the Civil War, Indians were seen as an obstacle whenever their interests collided with the U.S.' favored self-interest support for mining.

> The precious metals, our sole reliance to liquidate the accruing interest upon the national debt, are derived chiefly from the mining districts of Colorado, Oregon, California, Nevada, Idaho, and Montana, and any barrier which obstructs emigra-

tion to these mines, and retards their development, must prove highly prejudicial to the financial prosperity of the country.[9]

Civil War Debt

In 1860, the year before the American Civil War started, the U.S.' debt was $64.8 million. Once the war began, debt grew quickly. The financial cost of the war was significant, totaling an estimated $5.2 billion.

Individual Confederate States owed $67 million. The Confederated States of America owed about $1.4 billion. Following the Civil War, the South was bankrupt. It's industry and farms were ruined and their credit was depleted. To pay down this huge debt, some eastern congressmen regarded western miners as squatters who were robbing the public patrimony, and they proposed seizure of the western mines to pay the huge war debt. In June 1865, Representative George Washington Julian of Indiana introduced a bill for the government to take the western mines from the discoverers and sell them at public auction. Representative Fernando Wood proposed that the government send an army to California, Colorado, and Arizona to expel the miners "by armed force if necessary to protect the rights of the Government in the mineral lands." He advocated that the federal government itself work the mines for the benefit of the treasury.

Western representatives successfully argued that western miners and prospectors were performing valuable services by promoting commerce and settling new territory. The Chaffee Law of 1869 and the Placer Law of 1871 were combined into the General Mining Act of 1872.[10]

In a Congressional debate on taking mining income, this need for mineral revenue was highlighted by Mr. Hendricks:

> I am in favor of that policy that will encourage the miner to produce two dollars now where in past years he has produced but one. Let us add $100,000,000 a year, if we can, to the gold in the country. ... The condition of our country demands an increase in currency, hundreds of millions where but thousands were required before. The commerce and the business of the Army require it.[11]

To pay for the war, Congress authorized the Treasury Department to issue several types of debt instruments, including bonds, interest bearing notes, and compound interest notes. It would require more than 30 years from the end of the war for the Union to pay off its Civil War debt.

Indian Nations Not Parties to Disposal of Their Resources

Indian Nations were not permitted to participate in determining the disposal of their resources. Over and over again, Indians resources were stolen over claims that they weren't using them. The discriminatory stereotypes applied to them made the theft acceptable—here the Indians are characterized as a *"vicious horde of savages, a curse and a plague to civilization and a danger and disgrace to the Territory."*

Pacific Railway Act

The Pacific Railway Act[12] granted two charters—one to the Union Pacific Railroad Company, and one to the Central Pacific Railroad Company. The charters granted 10 miles of land for each mile of track laid, *which included the mineral rights*, plus loans... *Under the Pacific Railway Act, the U.S. would extinguish any Indian title along the route.*

In 1867, General Sherman wrote to General Ulysses S. Grant, "we are not going to let thieving, ragged Indians check and stop the progress of the railroads." (Emphasis added).[13]

In the Report of General G. M. Dodge, Chief Engineer, Union Pacific 1874, 1880, he wrote: "Experience proves the *Railroad* line through Indian Territory a *Fortress* as well as a highway." (Emphasis added).[14]

As the railways expanded, they allowed the rapid transport of troops and supplies to areas where Indian battles were being waged.

> Indeed, the progress of two years more, if not of another summer, on the Northern Pacific Railroad will of itself completely solve the great Sioux problem, and leave the ninety thousand Indians ranging between the two transcontinental lines as incapable of resisting the Government as are the Indians of New York or Massachusetts. *Columns moving north from the Union Pacific, and south from the Northern Pacific, would crush the Sioux* and their confederates as between the upper

and the nether millstone; while the rapid movement of troops along the northern line would prevent the escape of the savages, when hard pressed, into the British Possessions, which have heretofore afforded a convenient refuge on the approach of a military expedition. (Emphasis added).[15]

1885: Arizona State Legislature Recommends Removing Indians on San Carlos and White Mountain Reservations to Indian Territory in Present-Day Oklahoma

The Arizona State Legislature recommended to Congress that the Indians on the San Carlos and White Mountain Reservations be removed to Indian Territory in present-day Oklahoma to open their mineral and agricultural lands for white settlement.

No. 14. MEMORIAL In reference to the San Carlos and White Mountain Reservations. ... *the Indians now occupying these vast reservations, comprising the richest mineral, agricultural and timber lands of the Territory, have made no use of said lands, but simply withhold the same from public use and occupation, and are a perpetual menace to the peaceful settler, retarding progress, paralyzing prosperity, and rendering the richest and grandest portions of the Territory useless and valueless.* That the San Carlos and White Mountain Reservations include *thousands upon thousands of acres of the most productive country within the Territory, magnificently watered, and covering the fountain heads of all our most important streams,* now rendered of no use, but *serving as the abode and lurking places of a discontented, idle and vicious horde of savages, a curse and a plague to civilization and a danger and disgrace to the Territory.* ... *That your Memorialists believe that these Indians ought and should be removed from our midst to some part of the Indian Territory...* Approved March 11, 1885. (Emphasis added).[16]

Land Speculation and Atchison, Topeka and Santa Fe Railway

Cyrus Holliday secured a charter from the Kansas legislature in 1859 to build the Atchison, Topeka & Santa Fe Railway. The railroad needed developable land close to Topeka. The problem was that some of the most fertile and well-watered ground was on the Potawatomi Indian Reservation northwest of town. Led by Senator Pomeroy, the railroad entered into negotiations that resulted in an 1868 treaty (15 Stat. 531) approved by Congress whereby the railroad purchased 338,766 unallotted acres from the Potawatomi at $1 an acre with easy six-year, 6 percent terms.

The Railway Company turned around and put this land on the market to settlers for 20 percent down and the balance in five equal installments. Some tracts were sold for as much as $16 per acre, but others went to insiders like Pomeroy and his brother-in-law at only $1 per acre. The advertisement text for the sale of the land provided brief descriptions of the cities and towns in the area; the railroads available; fuel and lumber that are native to the area; and general descriptions and prices of the land.[17]

On July 7, 1868, Senator Julian submitted the following Resolution regarding the Potawattomie Indian Lands which was adopted by unanimous consent:

> Whereas a contract, has been made which purports to be a treaty between certain commissioners acting in the name of the United States and the Pottawatomie Indians, by which the unallotted lands of said Indians, amounting to 342,000 acres, have been sold to the Atchison, Topeka and Santa Fe Railroad Company, *at the price of one dollar per acre; and where as these lands are known to be valuable, and said price is believed to be in monstrous disproportion thereto*, and said treaty, so called, is declared by prominent and respectable men in the State of Kansas to be similar in character to the late Osage treaty, which has been emphatically condemned by this house: Therefore, Resolved, That the Committee on Indian Affairs be instructed to inquire into the facts and circumstances of said so-called treaty, that they have power to send for persons and papers, and that they report to this house by bill or otherwise. (Emphasis added).[18]

This is another instance of business enterprises being built on the undervalued sale of Indian Land.

Natural Resource Exploitation and Corruption

Natural resource abundance lends itself easily to corruption by governments and businesses impeding growth and development. The concentration of control over resources and resource revenues among a small group of firms and governmental officials sets up a situation in which corruption is probable. The Comstock Lode in Nevada was on Northern Paiute land. The corruption that occurred in regard to this massive silver mine is described by the U.S. National Park Service:

> Two prime characteristics of the Comstock Lode from 1860 to 1880 were wildcat speculation and expensive litigation. In this atmosphere of frantic financial manipulation and unscrupulous rigging of the market, the "Kings of the Comstock" struggled for power, *bought and sold seats in the U.S. Senate*, and brought ruin to the Bank of California. Speculative investment in San Francisco touched a new high, and, as the hectic trading continued without any regulation, a wildly fluctuating market resulted in the rise and fall of many fortunes. But the Comstock Lode was not inexhaustible. In 1880 Nevada's mining stocks, which had been valued at $30,000,000 five years before, were worth less than $7,000,000. Nevada sank quickly into sleepy lethargy ... (Emphasis added).[19]

Mining Tycoons

While Indians were lied to about the value of their lands, mining tycoons became wealthy from producing their minerals. In the mid-1870s in Nevada, the Millionaires Club of the Washoe was formed by the elite gentlemen of the Comstock in the hey-day of the mining activity, termed the "Silver Seventies." The Club's exclusive quarters housed one of the finest libraries east of San Francisco, an elegant billiard room, a parlor adorned with Italian marble and bronze statuettes, and a wine room that boasted an elaborately carved black walnut sideboard. The prominent members and guests included General Sheridan, President U.S. Grant, inventor Thomas Edison, General Sherman, mining tycoons James G. Fair, John Mackay, and many more of the Who's Who of Comstock and Pacific Coast history.[20]

Savages Cheated and Robbed Were Starving

While the federal government failed to act to protect the Indians' natural resources, Indians starved to death, froze to death, died from imported diseases and were wantonly exterminated.

> At one hour a famishing, begging, and half naked crowd would surround my office on a freezing cold morning and implore me to go to their lodges and see their old people and children, who from starvation or want of clothing were unable to come out. To these I doled out provisions in quantities barely suf-

~ 60 ~

ficient to keep them· alive. … At another time, men wearing nothing but a stroud and robe or blanket, with a belt and knife in it, and carrying their tomahawks or other weapons, would come, and with loud, and, from starvation, hollow sounding voices, accompanied by exciting and threatening gestures, demand the cattle or other food. J. B. Hoffman, United States Indian Agent, Ponca Agency.[21]

Notes: Mineral Economic Development

1. Nez Perce 1855 Treaty, 12 Stat. 957.
2. Record of Official Proceedings of 1855 Treaty Negotiations at 68 (on file with the U.S. National Archives).
3. Report of the Commissioner of Indian Affairs to the Secretary of the Interior, United States. Office of Indian Affairs. U.S. Government Printing Office, 1865, p. 523.
4. Report of the Commissioner of Indian Affairs to the Secretary of the Interior, United States. Office of Indian Affairs. U.S. Government Printing Office, 1866, p. 136.
5. MINING IN COLORADO A HISTORY OF DISCOVERY, DEVELOPMENT AND PRODUCTION BY CHARLES W. HENDERSON, DEPARTMENT OF THE INTERIOR, Hubert Work, Secretary, U.S. GEOLOGICAL SURVEY, George Otis Smith, Director, Professional Paper 138, Washington Government Printing Office, 1926, p. 249.
6. Report of the Commissioner of Indian Affairs to the Secretary of the Interior, United States. Office of Indian Affairs. U.S. Government Printing Office, 1877, p. 6.
7. Report of the Commissioner of Indian Affairs to the Secretary of the Interior, Accompanying Papers. REPORT TO THE PRESIDENT BY THE INDIAN PEACE COMMISSION, JANUARY 7, 1868. United States. Office of Indian Affairs. U.S. Government Printing Office, 1868, p. 38.
8. Opinion of the Commission, *Williams v. United States*, No. 180-A (Indian Cl. Comm'n December 31, 1959). Final Judgment, *Williams v. United States*, No. 180-A (Indian Cl. Comm'n July 5, 1960).
9. Report of the Commissioner of Indian Affairs to the Secretary of the Interior, United States. Office of Indian Affairs. U.S. Government Printing Office, 1865, p. 400.
10. The Government's Grab for Gold - A History of Mining Claim Law, Arthur Leger. https://www.linkedin.com/pulse/governments-grab-gold-history-mining-claim-law-arthur-leger (accessed online October 4, 2022).

11. CONG. GLOBE, 38th Cong., 1st Sess. 2558-60 (1864).

12. Pacific Railway Act (12 Stat. 489).

13. The Papers of Ulysses S. Grant: January 1-September 30, 1867, Volume 17 of Papers of Ulysses S. Grant, Ulysses Simpson Grant, Editor John Y. Simon, SIU Press, 1991, p. 162. https://digitalcommons.law.ou.edu/cgi/viewcontent.cgi?article=2714&context=indianserialset (accessed online September 2, 2022).

14. Born Modern: An Overview of the West. https://ap.gilderlehrman.org/essays/born-modern-overview-west#:~:text=%E2%80%9CExperience%20proves%2C%E2%80%9D%20 (accessed online March 7, 2023).

15. Report of the Commissioner of Indian Affairs to the Secretary of the Interior, United States. Office of Indian Affairs. U.S. Government Printing Office, 1872, p. 9.

16. Arizona Acts, Resolutions, and Memorials, 1885, p. 374.

17. A New Home in an Old Settlement: Come and see the "New Land in an Old Country." Date: May 1, 1876. https://www.kansasmemory.org/item/213108/page/1 (accessed online December 15, 2022).

18. Journal of the House of Representatives of the United States, Volume 40, Issue 2, United States, Congress. House, U.S. Government Printing Office, 1868, p. 994.

19. UNITED STATES DEPARTMENT OF THE INTERIOR NATIONAL PARK SERVICE THE NATIONAL SURVEY OF HISTORIC SITES AND BUILDINGS Theme XV, Westward Expansion and the Extension of the National Boundaries to the Pacific 1830-1898 THE MINING FRONTIER. Edited by William C. Everhart Region Four, San Francisco 1959, p. 33. http://npshistory.com/publications/nhl/theme-studies/mining-frontier.pdf (accessed online December 18, 2021).

20. The Washoe Club. https://www.thewashoeclubmuseum.com/history/ (accessed online January 17, 2023).

21. Report of the Commissioner of Indian Affairs to the Secretary of the Interior, United States. Office of Indian Affairs, Cheyenne and Arapaho Agency, Captain J.M. Lee, 9th Infantry, Acting Agent. U.S. Government Printing Office, 1886, p. 118.

Report of the Commissioner of Indian Affairs to the Secretary of the Interior, United States. Office of Indian Affairs, Dakota Superintendency. U.S. Government Printing Office, 1865, p. 267.

2: MINERAL PRODUCTION IN U.S.

Value of Nonfuel Minerals Production in U.S.

The Western Mining History website regarding "Where To Find Gold: The Top Ten US Counties" has very valuable statistics regarding the **Value of Non-fuel Minerals Production by state and their percentage ranking.** https://westernmininghistory.com/2195/where-to-find-gold-the-top-ten-us-counties/ (accessed online August 16, 2022).[1]

U.S. Bullion Product: 1860-1870

U.S. Bullion Product (US$) States and Territories 1860–1870	Estimates[2]
Year	Amount (US$)
1866	17,617,076
1867	19,265,376
1868	17,367,000
1869	15,502,457
1870	20,492,055

The Statistics Of Mines And Mining In The States And Territories West Of The Rocky Mountains: Annual Report Of U.S. Commissioner Of Mining Statistics to Secretary of Treasury, 1872, p. 516, sets out tables of production from various states in 1869, 1870, 1871, 1872, 1873, 1874 and 1875.

Top Ten Gold Producing States as of 1965

From 1799 through 1965, the U.S. produced over 300,000,000 ounces of gold, which at the current price of around $1,500 per ounce (as of August 2019) would be valued at over $450 billion dollars.

The period of production from 1848 to the 1930s is considered the golden era of mining. During this period the bulk of all the rich gold districts of the West were discovered. These discoveries drove exploration and settlement of the vast American West, a geographic area that was mostly wilderness before this time.

These are the top ten historical gold producing states in America as of 1965.[4] The information is derived from the following article: Koschmann, A. H., and M. H. Bergendahl. "Principal Gold-Producing Districts." United States Geological Survey Professional Paper 610, U.S. Government Printing Office, 1968.

1. California

The well-known discovery in El Dorado County in 1848 sparked a series of gold rushes that indirectly led to colonization of the entire mountain West. The rich gold placers of California yielded phenomenal wealth in the early years, and as the placers were depleted, prospectors searched for and found the source of the placer gold—the high-grade gold-quartz veins of the Mother Lode and Grass Valley.

Others explored the forbidding mountain ranges of southern California and found productive lodes in the Cove, Rand, and Stedman districts. Placer mining was rejuvenated in the early 1900s with the introduction of large bucket dredges. From the late 1930s onward, dredging operations were responsible for a major part of California's gold output.

California has produced more gold than any other State—more than 106 million ounces from 1848 through 1965.

2. Colorado

Colorado ranks second among the gold-producing States; its gold output through 1965 was about 40,776,000 ounces. The first publicized discovery of gold in Colorado was in 1858.

3. South Dakota

The first documented discovery was made in 1874, during General George A. Custer's expedition to reconnoiter the Black Hills. The actual discovery is credited to two miners named Ross and McKay, who were attached to the expedition and found gold in gravel bars along French Creek. News of this discovery attracted many prospectors to the area, even though the country then belonged to the Sioux Indians.

In 1876 the Black Hills were expropriated by the U.S., and prospectors flooded into the area and found gold in Deadwood Gulch and Rockerville. By 1880, from $6 to $8 million worth of placer gold had been mined, about half of which came from Deadwood Gulch.

South Dakota produced over 31 million ounces of gold at the time this USGS report was made, however the Homestake mine continued to operate until 2002, and this one mine produced over 40 million ounces, so South Dakota's total production is significantly higher than what was reported in 1965. The Homestake mine, located in Lead, was the longest operating and deepest mine in America.

4. Alaska N/A

5. Nevada

Mining began in Nevada in the early 1850s, and 1859-79 was the boom era of the Comstock Lode and the Reese River districts. Mining, except in the Comstock Lode, declined steadily after 1880 until the discoveries of the silver ore deposits of Tonopah in 1900 and the bonanza gold deposits of Goldfield in 1902. Nevada is known as the "Silver State" due to the enormous silver production that came out of the early bonanza mining centers.

Nevada produced over 27 million ounces of gold between 1859 and 1965. However, production in recent decades has significantly increased Nevada's total. If the statistics for this article were compiled today, Nevada would be the number one gold producer in America.

6. Utah

Most of the ore deposits in Utah are found in its western part—in the mountain ranges in and flanking the Great Basin. The most productive districts, principally the Bingham, Tintic, Camp Floyd, and Park City, are south and east of Salt Lake City.

While gold districts are scattered throughout the state, the bulk of historical production can be credited to the Bingham district where gold was first mined in placer operations, and later was a byproduct of Bingham's spectacular copper mines.

Through 1960 Utah produced about 17,765,000 ounces of gold and ranked sixth among the States in total gold production. However, the Bingham open-pit mine has continued to produce significant gold as a byproduct of copper production, and Utah has likely moved up at least a few spots on this list.

7. Montana

In 1852, gold was first discovered in Montana in gravels along Gold Creek in Powell County. The influx of prospectors, however, started with the discovery in 1862 of placers along Grasshopper Creek, near Bannack, in Beaverhead County. Other discoveries, both placer and lode, came in rapid succession.

In Montana, 54 mining districts distributed in 17 counties (most of which are in the southwest part of the state), have each produced more than 10,000 ounces of gold. Four districts—Butte, Helena, Marysville, and Virginia City—have produced more than 1 million ounces, and 27 other districts produced between 100,000 and 1 million ounces.

Montana produced almost 18 million ounces of gold from 1862 through 1965. Almost half of the state's production was from placer mines, most of which occurred before 1870. The great copper mines of Butte produced much of the state's gold after 1900.

8. Arizona

Deposits of silver and copper in Arizona were known to the Indians and Spaniards long before the Territory was acquired by the U.S. Because of the inaccessibility of the area, lack of water, and Indian raids, only a small amount of prospecting was done by Americans in the 1850s, mostly near the old Mexican settlements of Tucson and Tubac, and in the Dome (Gila City) district where rich placers were discovered in 1858. Little or no lode gold was mined in these early years.

During the Civil War, prospectors among the California troops in Arizona organized parties to hunt for gold. In 1862, rich placer deposits were found near the Colorado River at La Paz in western Yuma County, and from 1862 to 1870 other placer deposits were found in Yavapai County. Soon lode deposits were discovered in most districts.

Arizona produced over 13 million ounces of gold between 1860 and 1965. While gold mining occurred in many districts during the second half of the 1800s, it was gold as a byproduct of the great copper mines developed after 1900 that contributed significantly to Arizona's production numbers.

9. Idaho

Gold placers were discovered in Idaho in 1852 along the Pend O'reille River; however, the placer discovery at Pierce City in 1860 is considered the earliest discovery of consequence in the State. Other placers were discovered in Elk City, Orofino, and along the Salmon River in 1860 and 1861, and a year later discoveries were made at Florence, Warren, and Boise Basin.

Placers were the major source of gold in Idaho before 1900; however, most of them were exhausted after the period of feverish exploitation from 1860 to 1870. Lode deposits, which had been known and worked on a small scale since 1861, became more important, though placering was rejuvenated in 1897 by cheaper dredging operations and it continued to furnish most of the gold.[5]

10. Oregon

Gold placers were discovered at Rich Gulch in Jackson County and Josephine Creek in Josephine County in 1852. The more widely publicized discoveries of placer gold at Griffin Gulch in Baker County in 1861 and at John Day and Canyon Creek in Grant County triggered an avalanche of prospectors and miners of sufficient magnitude to eventually establish the gold mining industry in the state.

After the initial period of high production during which the richer placers were exhausted, discoveries of lode mines helped stabilize the mining economy. The earliest lode mining began as early as 1859 on the Gold Hill vein in Jackson County, although the most important lode mining region was later established in the opposite side of the state in Baker and Grant counties.

Oregon produced just under 6 million ounces of gold between 1852 and 1965. The primary gold producing regions are in the northeast and southwest corners of the state.

Mineral Production Environmental Costs

Western mining wrought havoc on the local environment. Rock dust from drilling was often dumped into river-beds, forming silt deposits downstream that flooded towns and farmlands. Miners and farmers were often at loggerheads over the effects of one enterprise on the other. Poisonous underground gases, mostly containing sulfur, were released into the atmosphere. Removing gold from quartz required mercury, the excess of which polluted local streams and rivers. Strip mining caused erosion and further desertification.

Hardrock mining has devastated tribal communities. Many mines, such as the Zortman-Landusky mine, south of the Fort Belknap Indian Reservation in north central Montana, and the silver, lead, and zinc mines of Idaho's Silver Valley, adjacent to the Coeur d'Alene Reservation, polluted public water systems, poisoned fish and wildlife populations, and contaminated sacred sites before becoming federal Superfund sites. Other mines, such as the Midnite uranium mine in eastern Washington, created serious health risks.

On May 20, 2021, John Dilles' Testimony to the Oregon House Committee on Agriculture & Natural Resources briefly discussed the major environmental costs associated with mineral production:

(1) Modification of land surface
- Cultural and historical features are removed
- Reclamation can partly restore the surface (but is difficult with large open pit mines)

(2) Disturbance of and local pollution of groundwater and surface waters
- Turbidity or sediment discharge
- Acid mine drainage (with dissolved metals)

(3) Heavy metal pollution (5 most toxic metals: lead, cadmium, arsenic, mercury, and chromium)
- Present in impounded tailing ponds
- Present in "stripped" waste rock or pit walls
- Dispersed via sediment transport in water/air or dissolved in water

Notes: Mineral Production in U.S.

1. https://westernmininghistory.com/2195/where-to-find-gold-the-top-ten-us-counties/ (accessed online August 16, 2022).
2. Statistics Of Mines And Mining In The States And Territories West Of The Rocky Mountains: Annual Report Of U.S. Commissioner Of Mining Statistics to Secretary of Treasury, 1872, p. 516.
3. Ibid., p. 511.
4. Koschmann, A. H., and M. H. Bergendahl. "Principal Gold-Producing Districts." United States Geological Survey Professional Paper 610, U.S. Government Printing Office, 1968.
5. https://www.fs.usda.gov/Internet/FSE_DOCUMENTS/stelprdb5356586 (accessed online October 8, 2022).

3: NATION'S NATURAL RESOURCES SURVEYS

Land Ordinance of 1785

The Land Ordinance of 1785, enacted by the U.S. Congress under the Articles of Confederation, reserved "one-third part of all gold, silver, lead, and copper mines to be sold or otherwise disposed of, as Congress shall thereafter direct."[1]

Not only did the Land Ordinance require surveying the public domain lands, but it also imposed the duty to determine and record mineral and non-mineral lands. The decision not to hold public lands as a capital asset, but to dispose of them for revenue, was to encourage settlement.

The Confederation was deeply in debt to France and other creditors from borrowing to fund the Revolutionary War. As the Confederacy Congress had no power to levy taxes on the land or states, the "Northwest Territory loomed as the only asset the new country had which might be turned into hard money. If the vast public domain could be sold to settlers, it could return millions of dollars to the treasury and solve the pressing immediate need for money."[2]

Jared Mansfield, Surveyor General, sent instructions to district surveyors, with a copy to the Hon. Albert Gallatin, Secretary of the Treasury. Their field notebooks were to contain survey markers (e.g., tree was 'blazed' or marked at the section corners), as well as detailed notes, in particular of "all rivers, creeks, springs and smaller streams of water, with their width, and the course they run in crossing the lines of survey, and whether navigable, rapid or mountainous; the kinds of timber and undergrowth with which the land may be covered, all swamps, ponds, stone quarries, coal beds, peat or turf grounds, uncommon, natural, or artificial productions, such as mounds, precipices, caves, etc., all rapids, cascades or falls of water; minerals, ores, fossils, etc.; the quality of the soil and the true situation of all mines, salt licks, salt springs and mill seats." Once a township was finished, the surveyors made a map of the area.[3]

Surveying, with registration of purchases in an official land office, was planned so as to reduce litigation over boundaries, etc. "Thousands of boundary disputes already in the courts made the rectangular system and prior survey sound attractive even to many of the conservative group."[4]

"Only the land that had been purchased from the Indians was to be surveyed. This provision would appease the Indians, follow the practice of purchase traditional in the colonies, and since only Congress could buy land from the Indians, would prevent private claims based on private purchases." (Emphasis added).[5]

As to Indian lands, the Northwest Ordinance provided:

> the utmost good faith shall always be observed towards the Indians; their lands and property shall never be taken from them without their consent; and in their property, rights, and liberty, they shall never be invaded or disturbed, unless in just and lawful wars authorized by Congress; but laws founded in justice and humanity shall, from time to time, be made, for preventing wrongs being done to them and for preserving peace and friendship with them. [6]

Thomas Jefferson wrote to William Carmichael on August 18, 1785, that Congress had purchased the Indian rights to fifty million acres under the Land Ordinance of 1785 and that the sale of the land will pay all the foreign debt.

> "They have purchased the Indian right of soil to about fifty millions of acres of land, between the Ohio and lakes, and expected to make another purchase of an equal quantity. They have, in consequence, passed an ordinance for disposing of their lands, and I think a very judicious one. They propose to sell them at auction for not less than a dollar an acre, receiving their own certificates of debt as money. I am of opinion all the certificates of our domestic debt will immediately be exchanged for land. *Our foreign debt, in that case, will soon be discharged*." (Emphasis added).[7]

The 1785 Land Ordinance effectively divided the nation into a grid of square miles. The grid had no connection to the ecological landscape that underlay it, which led to a total rearrangement of that landscape, with serious ecological consequences for the future. It made settlement of the land west of the Mississippi orderly and made it possible to buy land without seeing it. They had only to describe the Township, Range, and Section or part thereof.

Norhwest Ordinance of 1787 (Political Organization)

The Ohio Company of Associates, a land-speculating company led by Manasseh Cutler, Samuel Parsons, and Rufus Putnam, pressed Congress for a land grant in Ohio and succeeded in getting Congress to pass the Northwest Ordinance of 1787 which provided for establishing governments in the territories and later statehood. An appointed Governor and three judges would rule a Territory until the population reached 5,000. At that time, the citizens could elect a legislature, and, when the population numbered 60,000, the Territory could apply for admission to the Union as a State on a basis of full equality with the original thirteen states. The Ordinance would govern settlement of millions of square miles of the American continent, until superseded by the 1862 Homestead Act.[8]

As territorial and statehood status were determined by population numbers, marketing was rampant to motivate westward expansion. The Northwest Ordinance promulgated a pattern of westward expansion that would result in laying out state after state from coast to coast. The settlement and creation of permanent non-Indian family-sized farms would go unchecked. Land subsidies and preemptive rights for squatters were used as tools for compact settlement of lands. Compact settlements made defense against Indians easier which reduced the cost to the government of having to provide military services. It increased the ability to clear lands and reduce game habitat for Indian hunting, making their willingness to move more likely. It made the migration of a group of settlers possible, rather than having them migrate singly. This facilitated the development of settler communities, which in turn encouraged the migration of additional settlers. The resources from these lands would help the federal government reduce its national debt and accumulate capital for its own use and as collateral for credit.

Geological Surveys: State and Federal

It became necessary to take stock of these lands. Gold-bearing rock was discovered in North Carolina in 1824. In 1825, Denison Olmsted, Professor of Chemistry, Mineralogy, and Geology at the University of North Carolina, reported on the gold mines of North Carolina.[9]

Discoveries thereafter were made in Virginia, South Carolina, and Georgia. Prospectors and miners flooded into these areas. Geologists seized upon these gold discoveries in the southeastern states to promote state-funded geological surveys. In the 1830s, several of the eastern and central States recognized the need for information on the geological structure, mineral resources, and products within their states and ordered state surveys. The bureaucracy of the federal government would limit federal mineral surveys for another thirty years.

In 1834, Congress authorized the first federal examination of the geological structure, mineral resources, and products of the public lands by permitting the Topographical Bureau of the U.S. Army to use $5,000 of its appropriation for geological investigations and the construction of a geological map of the U.S. The head of the Bureau, Colonel J.J. Abert, had based his request for funds on the importance of mineral resources. The Army engineers' surveys were used instead to prepare estimates for roads and canals for national military, commercial, or postal purposes.[10]

Four Major Surveys of West

The proper evaluation of the geology and resources of the country became a matter of the highest concern in 1866. Joseph S. Wilson, the Commissioner of the General Land Office, in his Annual Report written in the fall of 1866, remarked that "Eighteen sixty-seven marks, in the history of national geological work, a turning point, when the science ceased to be dragged in the dust of rapid exploration and took a commanding position in the professional work of the country."[11]

On March 2, 1867, Congress for the first time authorized western explorations in which *geology would be the principal objective*: a study of the geology and natural resources along the fortieth parallel route of the transcontinental. Clarence King was appointed to lead the Exploration.

Starting in the 1850s, Ferdinand V. Hayden, M.D., conducted surveys in the Nebraska and Western Territories. In 1867 he was appointed geologist-in-charge of the U.S. Geological and Geographical Survey of the Territories. He explored the Yellowstone area in 1871.

In 1869, John Wesley Powell led a geographic expedition down a three-month river trip of the Green and Colorado rivers, including the first official U.S.

government-sponsored passage through the Grand Canyon. He served as the second director of the U.S. Geological Survey (1881–1894).[12]

The mining geology program began in earnest in 1879 with studies of the geology and technology of three great mining districts--Leadville in Colorado and the Comstock and Eureka in Nevada. Mineral data was to be collected and analyzed in all of the western States so that the probability of development could be assessed. A trend analysis was to be made of the copper-bearing rocks of Michigan and Wisconsin through northeast Minnesota to the Canadian boundary. The investigations in general geology were to include the Colorado Plateau region, Utah, and the Rocky Mountain region north of New Mexico and west of the 94th Meridian.[13]

The drought of 1886 led Congress in 1888 to authorize a survey to investigate the extent to which the arid region of the U.S. could be reclaimed by irrigation, to segregate the irrigable lands, and to select sites for reservoirs and other hydraulic works for the dual purpose of storage and utilization of water for irrigation and prevention of floods and overflows. To prevent speculation, Congress then stipulated that all lands that might be irrigated by the reservoirs and canals located by the surveys be withdrawn from entry.[14]

President Polk further requested that Congress require a geological and mineralogical examination of New Mexico and California given the presence of mines of gold, silver, copper, and quicksilver corroborated by two investigations by federal and military officials. Polk's plan was to adopt measures to preserve the mineral lands for the use of the U.S., or "if brought into market, dispose of them in such manner as to *secure a large return of money to the Treasury* and at the same time to lead to the development of their wealth by individual proprietors and purchasers." (Emphasis added).[15]

Generalized Geographical Distributions of Minerals

Hailed as an event of considerable importance to mining engineers and metallurgists was the 1878 publication of the Volume on Mining Industry of the Report of the United States Geological Exploration of the Fortieth Parallel. It reviewed the mining and metallurgical processes of the principal mining districts, with an analysis of their geological features and vein-phenomena.[16]

It is extremely important to be aware of the significant amount of data avail-

able to the Department of the Interior regarding mining in states with Indian populations. Congress appropriated funds in 1866 to enable the Secretary of Treasury to collect "reliable statistics of the mineral resources of the United States" and to assure the proper payment of taxes. The 1872 Statistical Report identified the three mineral trends in the western states.

> Through Mexico, Arizona, Middle Nevada, and Central Idaho is another line of silver mines.... Through New Mexico, Utah, and Western Montana lies another zone of argentiferous galena lodes. To the east, again, the New Mexico, Colorado, Wyoming, and Montana gold belt is an extremely well-defined and continuous chain of deposits.[17]

Notes: Nation's Natural Resources Surveys

1. Rabbitt, Mary C. The United States Geological Survey: 1879–989, U.S. Geological Survey Circular 1050, p. 1.
2. A History of the Rectangular Survey System, U.S. Department of the Interior. Bureau of Land Management, p. 11. https://www.blm.gov/sites/blm.gov/files/histrect.pdf (accessed online August 27, 2022).
3. Ibid., p. 237.
4. Ibid., p. 11.
5. Ibid., p. 14.
6. Northwest Ordinance, 1 Stat. 51, art. 3 (1787).
7. "From Thomas Jefferson to William Carmichael, 18 August 1785," Founders Online, National Archives, https://founders.archives.gov/documents/Jefferson/01-08-02-0316. [Original source: The Papers of Thomas Jefferson, vol. 8, 25 February–31 October 1785, ed. Julian P. Boyd. Princeton: Princeton University Press, 1953, pp. 401–402.] (accessed online August 14, 2022).
8. Northwest Ordinance, Act of August 7, 1789, ch. 8, 1 Stat. 50, 52.
9. Denison Olmsted, "On the Gold Mines of North Carolina," American Journal of Science 9 (1825): 5-15.
10. Rabbitt, Mary C. The United States Geological Survey: 1879–1989, U.S. Geological Survey Circular 1050, p. 2.
11. Ibid., p. 4. Clarence King, U.S. Geological Survey, 1st Annual Report, 1880, p. 6.
12. Rabbitt, Mary C. The United States Geological Survey: 1879–1989, U.S. Geological Survey Circular 1050, p. 7.
13. Ibid., p. 11.

14. Id.

15. James K. Polk, Fourth Annual Message Online by Gerhard Peters and John T. Woolley, The American Presidency Project. https://www.presidency. ucsb.edu/node/200618 (accessed online March 7, 2023).

16. Professional Papers of the Engineer Department, U.S. Army, No. 18. Report of the Geological Exploration of the Fortieth Parallel made by order of the Secretary of War according to acts of Congress of March 2, 1867, and March 3, 1869, under direction of Brigadier and Brevet Major General A. A. Humphreys, Chief of Engineers.

17. Statistics Of Mines And Mining In The States And Territories West Of The Rocky Mountains: Annual Report Of U.S. Commissioner Of Mining Statistics to Secretary of Treasury, 1872, p. 503. Browne, John Ross, and James Wickes Taylor. Reports upon the mineral resources of the United States. U.S. Government Printing Office, 1867. Report of James W. Taylor, special commissioner for the collection of statistics upon gold and silver mining east of the Rocky mountains. February 15, 1867. 39th Congress, 2d Session. House of Representatives. Ex. Doc. No. 92.

4: CHASING THE GOLD

Placer Mining

Manual labor placer deposits were quickly exhausted leaving mining and its wealth to big business. Technological advances for further gold placer production included river sluicing and hydraulic mining. Hydraulic mining used pressurized water cannons to propel hundreds of gallons of water per second to wash away hillsides into sluices where the heavy gold could be separated from lighter particles and debris. It took capital and required large-scale mining corporations for financing. While it was damaging to the region's ecosystem, clogging and flooding rivers and burying farmland under silt and debris, the government demanded the revenue derived from mining, even at the expense of its ecological consequences.

Surface and Deep Mining

Without the engineering complexity, Mark Twain, in his book, *Roughing It*, simplified the arduous process of refining the ore as follows:

> Workers, wielding sledgehammers, broke up the ore, which was then pulverized by machines. The dust was mixed with water, mercury, and salt in heated tubs. The mercury attracted particles of silver and gold. When heated, the mercury evaporated, leaving pure gold and silver.[1]

From (1) mucking (hammering at quartz rock, picking at rock cleavages, then shoveling the ore into bins pulled on narrow gauge underground railways by mules); to (2) drilling patterned holes for the blasting of explosives (nitroglycerine and/or dynamite); to (3) milling; and to (4) smelting, the work is arduous and dangerous. Unexploded dynamite, falling rock, timber cave-ins, and the silent killer, silicosis, took their toll.

The discovery of the Comstock Lode in Nevada in 1859 initiated a pattern of lode mining that "ended the poor man's day in mining and ushered in the era of the financier and the engineer."[2] While placer deposits could be exploited with simple equipment, lode deposits required extensive -- and expensive -- tunnels, stamp mills, and refining processes. The Comstock lode mines set the pattern for technology, cooperative activity, and capital markets that shaped the mining industry and national mining legislation.[3]

The Comstock Lode was on Northern Paiute land.

The initial developments on the Comstock were "coyote holes," small surface excavations using placer mining techniques. By the time Congress passed the Lode Mining Act of 1866, however, engineers had developed a mine-timbering system that permitted tunnels to depths of 3,000 feet; 46 corporations had constructed 57 1/2 miles of tunnels, shafts, and inclines.[4] Precious minerals were extracted from the ores in stamp mills. By 1866, mills operating on the Comstock refined 57,112 tons of ore each month.[5]

Individuals and partnerships could not raise the capital needed to engage in such sophisticated mining operations; so, beginning in April of 1860, mining corporations formed to pool resources, including claims, and to attract investments and loans from eastern and foreign financiers. Soon, stock companies owned nearly every important claim on the Comstock Lode. Stocks in many of the corporations were traded on the San Francisco Stock Exchange after its formation in 1862.[6] With the establishment of the San Francisco Stock Exchange Board in 1862, needed capital was infused into numerous mining ventures, including those in California and Nevada. The San Francisco Stock Exchange Board was followed in January 1872 by the California Stock and Exchange Board, and on June 7, 1875, by the Pacific Stock Exchange. By 1875 the shares of thirty Comstock corporations listed on the San Francisco Stock Exchange were valued at $262,669,940.[7]

The corporate mining pattern begun on the Comstock Lode was replicated at major mineral strikes throughout the West.

Example of Milling Operations in Colorado

So as not to oversimplify what was needed to extract the gold discovered, this excerpt gives us an insight into the engineering complexity of milling operations:

> An important addition to the mechanical and metallurgical appliance of the county is the new mill of the Stewart Sil-

~ 78 ~

ver Reducing Company just below Georgetown, which commenced operations about the 1st of September. The works are said to cover 142,000 square feet, and to have required 175,000 feet of lumber, 145,000 brick, and over 6,000 cubic yards of excavation for foundations in their construction. The plans were made by Mr. J. O. Stewart, an experienced mill-man; and the work is an excellent specimen of the silver-mills of the Reese River type. The machinery, weighing 98 tons, was made at the Eagle Works, in Chicago. Power is furnished by a 100 horse-power steam engine, with two large tubular boilers. The ore is first passed through a Dodge crusher, of which the mill has two, then dried upon a floor, heated by the escaping gases of the furnaces, then weighed and conveyed to the stamps. There are four batteries, of five stamps each, with high mortars and double discharge, and geared to run separately. The weight of each stamp is about 700 pounds; speed, 80 drops per minute; fineness of screens, fifty holes per linear inch; estimated crushing capacity, 24 tons daily, or about 0.85 ton daily per horse-power developed. Roasting is performed with the addition of salt in six reverberatory furnaces, of the well-known small Nevada pattern. Each furnace requires the attendance of two men. The length of the roasting depends upon the character of the ore. The Terrible ore, which forms a chief source of supply, is roasted ten hours, in charges of 1,200 pounds. In working this material, therefore, the capacity of the furnaces is inadequate to that of the stamps. There is room left in the mill for the erection of four additional reverberatories. After the chloridizing roasting, the ore is cooled, and amalgamated in Varney pans. The amalgamating room is furnished with ten pans and five settlers, and supplied with water-power from a dam on the creek by a race 650 feet in length. The economical defect in this is the employment of the old-fashioned reverberatories, which are more wasteful of fuel and labor than either the Bruckner cylinder or the Stetefeldt furnace. The daily consumption of wood at this mill must be four cords for the engine, and from one to one and a half for each of the furnaces. ... here the Stewart Company has the great advantage of capital, by which it is enabled to buy ores upon assay, and pay for them in cash before treatment. This system is more convenient to the miners and more profitable for the works.[8]

Private Business Method of Mineral Acquisition

Businessmen in the mineral industry establish, cultivate, and maintain relationships with regulatory agencies and industry competitors. They are familiar with the exploration for, production of, and marketing of their products. The Indian Agent lacked the personnel, acumen or time to engage in the mineral analysis that mineral companies routinely performed.

A review of conveyances by Fairfield Gold Mining Company, organized in Colorado in January 1865, confirmed the legal and financial sophistication already in play. The same is true of the Montana Gold Mining Co. which had access to the Union Pacific Railroad from Middle Park.[9]

It is fair to say that mining enterprises, in conjunction with railway building and the timber industry, played a great, and probably decisive, role in the grant of federal lands to private enterprise. In the U.S. this included the famous 1872 mining law-still in force today-which allowed free access to individuals and to corporations to explore for minerals on public lands, and upon their detecting ore, to make a claim on the ore deposit. Once development work had begun, the claim holder could apply for a patent of title to both surface and underground rights. If the patent was approved, the mining company had to pay a mere $5.00 fee for a lode deposit, or $2.50 for a placer deposit. Many critics, then and now, saw this as a "giveaway" of the nation's resources without sufficient recompense.

Generous as this law was, many claimants nevertheless found ways to abuse it by staking claims for non-mineral purposes or without having discovered valuable mineral deposits.[10]

Stages of Management in Mining Industry

The development of the mining industries is normally categorized according to three stages.

The first period is that of the "rushes" where prospectors, including some veterans and many more inexperienced migrants, move into hitherto untapped wilderness areas where surface mineral deposits can be opened up by placer techniques. Their extraction technology-rockers, cradles, and chutes-usually fabricated by hand out of wood, was simple and inexpensive. A set of modern writers, focusing on the California, Colorado, and Nevada gold and silver rushes have termed this "petty commodity production."

In the next phase, identified as the "entrepreneurial capitalist stage," the common features are the integration of a number of mines into larger holdings, recruitment of a "low wage" labor force, heavy infusions of capital-first through personal funds raised by the founders and then through the sale of shares to the public and by debentures, and finally, of course, by applications of heavy machinery to ore crushing and mineral separation.

The third stage involves the transition to modern "systematic and scientific management." Greater departmental specialization and the increased use of trained professionals is required, especially experienced mining engineers, to head these departments and to run mining operations in the field. These managers were skilled in the formulation of long-term, as well as short-term, investment and mining strategics through better accounting practices, the careful staking out of new ore areas for development work based on increasingly scientific investigation, plus greater vigilance in replacing outworn machinery and competence in the application of new and more efficient machine power.

With the twentieth-century behemoths of the Guggenheims and the massive Consolidated Selection Trust (or CAST), run by Chester Beatty, we can catch glimpses of the transition to a fourth or "contemporary phase" in mining history—that of multinational conglomerates controlling a vast range of different classes of companies in order to achieve balance and maintain profits in fluctuating markets through diversified operations in many regions and continents of the world.[11]

Strikes

As far as the western U.S. was concerned, nearly all of the American tycoons covered here (1) adhered to low workers' wages policies, (2) were opposed to mineworkers' unions in principle, and (3) pursued strongly anti-union tactics, including strike-breaking. When the mine workers at Horace Tabor's Chrysolite mine at Leadville, led by eastern organizers for the Knights of Labor, struck for higher wages and less stringent working rules in 1883. Tabor, through his political connections got the governor to call out the National Guard to break up the strike and force workers to return to the job, without concessions. Some of the worst labor conflicts in U.S. history were associated with mining in the western states, including that of the Arizona copper miners.

In 1907, Governor Oakes Murphy was criticized for forming a private police force called the "Arizona Rangers," supposedly for the purpose of protection, but whose prime aim was to control labor and prevent strikes and walkouts. There were major strikes against the Guggenheim-owned copper mines of

Utah and Nevada in 1912. But for the greater part of the nineteenth century, most groups of western mine workers were unsuccessful in gaining even recognition of their unions because the power of mining capital, backed by territorial and state governments, was so great.

Essentials for Mineral Development

Low wages, populous settlements, agriculture, and a favorable attitude of the authorities toward mining all made for a successful mining environment. Obstacles included a lack of transportation, Indian conflicts and in the arid west, the scarcity of water.

These elements are evidenced in Commissioner of Indian Affairs E. A. Hayt's report to the Secretary of the Interior in 1877 that all Indians in Colorado and Arizona should be removed to the Indian Territory in what is now Oklahoma. Then, miners, in search of gold and silver, could claim lands without regard to Indian reservations established by the federal government by treaty or legislative authority. He further stated that all of the arable land was required by white settlers and feeding them was of paramount importance. Certainly, this evidences, without a doubt, the government's favorable attitude toward mining and the need for agriculture to feed the influx of miners and their suppliers of goods.[12]

James W. Taylor, a renowned mineral statistician, alerted Congress in 1867 to his prerequisites for successful mining: "There are two indispensable requisites to the development of the western mines: *security from Indian hostilities*, and the establishment of railway communication to the Pacific coast." (Emphasis added).[13]

"Gobble gobble" economics and unbridled self-interest prevailed.

Notes: Chasing the Gold

1. http://www.digitalhistory.uh.edu/disp_textbook.cfm?smtID=2&psid=3149 (accessed online August 14, 2022).
2. Barger, Harold, and Sam H. Schurr. "Mining in the Nation's Economy." The Mining Industries, 1899-1939: A Study of Output, Employment, and Productivity. NBER, 1944. 249-265 at 101.
3. COMMENT: The 1872 Mining Law: Historical Origins of the Discovery Rule., 53 U. Chi. L. Rev. 624, Spring 1986.
4. Lord, Eliot. Comstock mining and miners, United States Geological

Service, No. 4. Govt. Printing Office, 1883, p. 227.

5. Id.

6. Ibid., p. 131.

7. Mayer, Carl J. "The 1872 Mining Law: Historical Origins of the Discovery Rule." The University of Chicago Law Review, vol. 53, no. 2, 1986, pp. 640.

8. http://npshistory.com/publications/nhl/theme-studies/mining-frontier.pdf (accessed online August 1, 2022).

9. Denver Public Library, Special Collections.

10. GEORGE CAMERON COGGINS & ROBERT L. GLICKSMAN, PUBLIC NATURAL RESOURCES LAW § 2.02[3][b] (1990).

11. Dumett, Raymond E., ed. *Mining tycoons in the age of empire, 1870-1945: Entrepreneurship, high finance, politics and territorial expansion.* Ashgate Publishing, Ltd., 2009.

12. Report of the Commissioner of Indian Affairs to the Secretary of the Interior, United States. Office of Indian Affairs, U.S. Government Printing Office, 1877, p. 6.

13. Report of James W. Taylor, special commissioner for the collection of statistics upon gold and silver mining east of the Rocky mountains. February 15, 1867. 39th Congress, 2d Session. House of Representatives. Ex. Doc. No. 92, p. 28.

5: WESTWARD EXPANSION

Louisiana Purchase, Annexation of Texas (1845); Oregon Country (1846); Mexican-American War (1848) and Gadsden Purchase

In the 1840s and 1850s, the nation expanded quickly and in the span of just five years, the U.S. increased its size by a third. It annexed Texas; negotiated with Britain for half of the Oregon country; and acquired much of the West and Southwest including what would become the states of California, Nevada, Utah, parts of Arizona, Colorado, New Mexico, and Wyoming as a result of the Mexican-American War. In 1853, the Gadsden Purchase solidified the border of Mexico along New Mexico and Arizona. General Santa Ana accepted $10 million for a strip of territory south of the Gila River, which is now southwestern New Mexico and southern Arizona (about the size of Pennsylvania).

People began to move in record numbers into Texas, California, and Oregon. The California Gold Rush, the Mormons' pilgrimage to Utah, the existence of westward routes, such as the California Oregon and Santa Fe Trails, all contributed to the expansion of the west.

President Fillmore in his First Annual Message on December 4, 1849, took it a step forward pointing out the importance of establishing cross-country communication and transportation with the Pacific coast region. He recommended reconnaissance commence on a transcontinental railroad route.[1]

Location of Minerals

The initial pattern of settlement of the west was largely determined by the location of its mineral wealth. The process begun in California was repeated time and again—in Nevada and Arizona, in Colorado and Idaho, in Montana, Wyoming, and South Dakota. Gold was the magnet which attracted the first settlers, advertised the wealth of the territory, and provided it with a permanent population.

> The discovery of gold accelerated the need to establish regular territorial governments and extend the revenue laws over these territories. Without an extension of the laws and appointment of collectors, no revenue could be received into the U.S.' coffers. With this done, President Polk anticipated the rapid enlargement of our commerce and navigation. He forecast that with *"the addition to the national wealth that the present generation may live to witness the controlling commercial and monetary power of the world transferred from London and other European emporiums to the city of New York."* (Emphasis added).[2]

In his First Annual Message in 1857, President James Buchanan announced that "four hundred millions of gold from California" had "flowed in upon us within the last eight years."[3]

In 1857, Congress approved the construction of a number of wagon roads across the territories to aid emigrant travel and speed mail delivery to the West Coast.[4]

In President Lincoln's Third Annual Message in 1863 he submitted to Congress a request for more expedient western immigration due to "a great deficiency of laborers in every field of industry, especially in agriculture and in our mines, as well of iron and coal as of the precious metals." (Emphasis added).[5]

Eastern Public Administration Strategies for Establishing Towns

Settlers poured into the territories, seeking work in their mining, timber and agriculture industries. The territory leaders and land speculators had a special interest in seeing the development of particular towns and regions.

From the methods of the East, business men started to bring organization into the chaos. They could not allow the chaos to thwart their plans. They applied the public administration strategies known to them for establishing towns: planning, organizing, developing procedures, budgeting, staffing, securing resources, managing and critiquing the process.

Boundaries were established. Counties were created. Appointments and elections were planned. The offices of officials included Senators, Councilman, and Representatives under Territorial law. At the county level, the following offices were promptly established: County Commissioners, Probate Judges, District Attorneys, County Sheriffs, County Clerks, County Treasurers, County Assessors, County Recorders, County Superintendents of Schools, County Surveyors, Public Administrators, Collectors, and other positions as needed.

Financial and political matters were addressed, including capital acquisition. This was obtained through leveraging their natural resources as collateral to secure credit. Bonds bearing a high rate of interest were issued to pay for public works. Property values were determined and taxed. Mining, farming and ranching provided sources of revenue. Schools and churches were opened.

The elected officials meticulously analyzed, tabulated, planned and, most importantly, imposed and collected taxes on land, livestock and income. Statistics were maintained for the population, mineral production, the amount of land under cultivation and the various products of the same, cattle ranching, the business enterprises and the stores, hotels, homes and other useful buildings.

Interested in having their lands surveyed and opened to public sale, rival promoters pushed to improve their village sites to attract buyers. They advertised heavily in the east, willing to lay out the money to attract settlers and merchants. They hoped their land would host a major railroad hub, giving it an economic edge.

Land speculation was one of the most significant business opportunities on the frontier. Land offices attracted settlers, lawyers, merchants, money lenders, and speculators. Although these people brought business to the towns in the early formative years, extractive resources and accessible transportation routes were far more reliable indicators of a town's potential to become a major city. Most of the wealth generated through trade and land sales was directed toward construction and land investment. Building construction centered primarily on homes, stores and hotels, needed to supply the local trade and to accommodate the immigrants pouring in.

Consequences for Indians

Westward expansion had serious consequences for Indians since continental expansion implicitly meant the occupation and annexation of their lands. The U.S. continued the European practice of recognizing only limited land rights of indigenous peoples and sought to expand into the west through the nominally legal purchase of Indian land in treaties. In many cases, these treaties were negotiated and signed by tribal members who didn't have the authority to do so, and in some cases, by signers who lacked knowledge of what they were signing. Despite the legality of a treaty, once one was signed, the government often used force to move the Indians from their homelands.

In 1860, President Buchanan transmitted eight memorials to Congress from residents of New Mexico, Utah, Kansas, and Nebraska seeking "the early extinguishment of the Indian title, a consequent survey and sale of the public land, and the establishment of an assay office in the immediate and daily reach of the citizens of that region, along with granting territorial status."[6]

Railroads Spur Western Settlement with Pioneer Vigilantes

In his 1871 Report to the Hon. George S. Boutwell, Secretary of the Treasury, R. W. Raymond, U.S. Commissioner of Mining Statistics, captured the role of the settlers: They would have carte blanche to deal with the Indians as they saw fit.[7]

Notes: Westward Expansion

1. https://millercenter.org/the-presidency/presidential-speeches/december-4-1849-first-annual-message (accessed online October 4, 2022).
2. https://www.presidency.ucsb.edu/documents/fourth-annual-message-6 (accessed online October 4, 2022).
3. https://millercenter.org/the-presidency/presidential-speeches/march-4-1857-inaugural-address (accessed online October 4, 2022).
4. Historic Trails Management Plan United States. Bureau of Land Management, Publisher: The Bureau, 1986, p. 47.
5. https://www.presidency.ucsb.edu/documents/third-annual-message-9 (accessed online October 4, 2022).
6. https://www.presidency.ucsb.edu/documents/special-message-2969 (accessed online October 4, 2022).
7. Statistics Of Mines And Mining In The States And Territories West Of The Rocky Mountains: Being The 6th Annual Report Of U.S. Commissioner Of Mining Statistics to Secretary of Treasury, 1871, p. 280.

6: FEDERAL INDIAN POLICY

The Presidents from Washington to Jackson recognized that Western settlement was intimately related to the country's future wealth and power. In 1783, 2 percent of colonists lived west of the Alleghenies; by 1830 the figure was 28 percent. Soon it became obvious that removal of the eastern tribes alone was not enough—the vast migration of over three and a half million settlers from 1860 through 1880 required land for settlement.

1817: President James Monroe: Extinguishment of Indian Title Inevitable; Removal of Indians Paramount; Assimilation Policy Defunct; Severalty; Agrarian Policy

Our fifth President, James Monroe, in his First Annual Message on December 2, 1817, to Congress proclaimed his success in *extinguishing Indian title* in seven states: Ohio, Michigan, Indiana, Georgia, North Carolina, Tennessee and Alabama and pursuing his goal also of individual allotted Indian ownership of land. Monroe *encompassed in 1817* what would become the strategy of future executives: cessions of land, establishment of reservations, land ownership in severalty, and assimilation to an agrarian lifestyle.

> From several of the Indian tribes inhabiting the country bordering on Lake Erie *purchases* have been made of lands on conditions very favorable to the United States, and, as it is presumed, not less so to the tribes themselves. It is gratifying to know that the *reservations* of land made by the *treaties* with the tribes on Lake Erie were *made with a view to individual ownership among them* and to the *cultivation of the soil* by all, and that an annual stipend has been pledged to supply their other wants. (Emphasis added).[1]

U.S. policy toward Indians from the end of the Revolutionary War through the 1830s focused mainly on keeping Indian and white societies separate. The first major U.S. law dealing with Indians, the Nonintercourse Act (aka Indian Trade and Intercourse Act), mainly limited the ways in which American citizens could interact with Indians, for instance by requiring a federal license to engage in trade; this law, which was reauthorized and revised several times before being made permanent in 1834, was the primary legislation in effect during this period.[2]

Indian Civilization Act in 1819

Monroe had come to believe that "independent savage communities" could no longer exist within the "civilized population" of the United States. That is he believed that if the United States did not take complete control of the Indian tribes and "civilize them", they would become extinct.

In Monroe's 1818 State of the Union address, he wrote these words:

> "Experience has clearly demonstrated that independent savage communities can not long exist within the limits of a civilized population. The progress of the latter has almost invariably terminated in the extinction of the former, especially of the tribes belonging to our portion of this hemisphere, among whom loftiness of sentiment and gallantry in action have been conspicuous. To civilize them, and even to prevent their extinction, it seems to be indispensable that their independence as communities should cease, and that the control of the United States over them should be complete and undisputed. The hunter state will then be more easily abandoned, and recourse will be had to the acquisition and culture of land and to other pursuits tending to dissolve the ties which connect them together as a savage community and to give a new character to every individual. I present this subject to the consideration of Congress on the presumption that it may be found expedient and practicable to adopt some benevolent provisions, having these objects in view, relative to the tribes within our settlements."[3]

Congress responded in 1819 by approving $10,000 annually for Indian education under the Indian Civilization Act, also known as the Civilization Fund Act. The act was passed on March 3, 1819 to encourage benevolent societies to provide education for the Indian tribes and provided the authorization to encourage the civilization programs.

SEC. 1 ...For the purpose of providing against the further decline and final extinction of the Indian tribes, adjoining the frontier settlements of the United States, and for introducing among them the habits and arts of civilization, the President of the United States shall be, and he is hereby authorized, in every case where he shall judge improvement in the habits and condition of such Indians practicable, and that the means of instruction can be introduced with their own consent, to employ capable persons of good moral character, to instruct them in the mode of agriculture suited to their situation; and for teaching their children in reading, writing and arithmetic.... SEC. 2. And be it further enacted, That the annual sum of ten thousand dollars be, and the same is hereby appropriated, for the purpose of carrying into effect the provisions of this act ; and an account of the expenditure of the money, and proceedings in execution of the foregoing provisions, shall be laid annually before Congress. APPROVED, March 3, 1819.[4]

Indian Removal Act

The geographical boundary between white and Indian   drawn first down the Appalachian mountain range in a royal proclamation in 1763— was moved progressively further west until finally, in 1830, the Indian Removal Act set it at the Mississippi River.

The Indian Removal Act of 1830 was followed by numerous removal treaties, by which eastern tribes ceded their current lands in exchange for new lands in the west, along with monetary payments and other inducements. It was widely believed that it would be decades before white settlement in the west would be substantial enough to seriously encroach on Indians.

Westward Expansion

However, in the 1840s and 1850s, the nation expanded quickly and in the span of just five years, the U.S. increased its size by a third. It annexed Texas; negotiated with Britain for half of the Oregon country; and acquired much of the West and Southwest including what would become the states of California, Nevada, Utah, parts of Arizona, Colorado, New Mexico, and Wyoming as a result of the Mexican-American War. In 1853, the Gadsden Purchase solidified the border of Mexico along New Mexico and Arizona. General Santa Ana accepted $10 million for a strip of territory south of the Gila River, which is now southwestern New Mexico and southern Arizona (about the size of Pennsylvania).

The discovery of gold in California was the capstone — the pace of white migration to the west accelerated far beyond the expectations of the previous decade. It became clear as the pace of westward migration accelerated that Indians would have years, not decades, to transform themselves into "civilized" Americans, or be wiped out by the rising tide of emigration.

The Indian country," Francis Paul Prucha observed, "was invaded, crossed and crisscrossed, and it was no longer possible to solve the question of the Indians' destiny by the convenient scheme of repeated removal."[5]

The U.S. actively supported this emigration through supporting westward routes, such as the California, Oregon and Santa Fe Trails. A military policy was established to protect the emigrants.

Vast Reservation Areas v. Concentrated Holdings

From 1840 onwards, the idea that the U.S. should afford the Indians the huge expanse of land that was the Trans-Mississippi west became difficult for the government to support. Not only did emigrants increasingly use the area for transit to the west coast, but economic interests emerged in the form of producing the minerals, but also the construction of a transcontinental railroad. Only two options appeared open to the government: submit to the will and desires of the electorate by permitting unhindered American access to the region or protect the Indians and their right to hold the land from white intrusion. The U.S. was caught between public pressure and its own treaty guarantees.

In 1848, Commissioner of Indian Affairs, William Medill, proclaimed the continuation of President Monroe's reservation policy, except with the designation of smaller, well-defined tracts of land for Indians and civilization through Christianization. White people would be free to occupy and utilize the country around them, and the government would prevent Indian interference. The U.S. would protect the Indians, turn them into farmers, and slowly civilize them through Christianity. His recommendation was supported by succeeding Commissioners Orlando Brown, Luke Lea and Manypenny.[6] Even though Congress did not immediately enact legislation to accomplish this, within the Indian Bureau this policy would be advocated and implemented for the next three decades.

1850 Forward: Extinguish Indian Title to West

In the 1850s, a movement started to extinguish Indian title to their lands in the west.

The Act of June 5, 1850, 9 Stat. 437, authorized the President to negotiate with Indian tribes of the Oregon Territory to extinguish title to lands west of the Cascade Mountains, and to remove Indians to east of the Cascades.

In February of 1851, Congress passed the Indian Appropriations Act, 9 Stat. 574, mandating the new reservation policy and providing monies to negotiate treaties.

The Appropriations Act of March 3, 1853, 10 Stat. 226, authorized the President to enter into negotiations with Indians to secure Indian lands west of Iowa and Missouri for settlement and to extinguish Indian title to the lands.

Indians were coerced into selling their vast tribal lands making more land available for homesteading by white Americans. The smaller land base would compel Indians, as the game decreased, to resort to agriculture and other kinds of labor to obtain a subsistence, in which aid may be afforded and facilities furnished them out of the revenue obtained by the sale of their former possessions. These sales would be made at land-grab prices under the prevailing Land Sales Acts.

The government fixation on making Indians into farmers was part of Thomas Jefferson's legacy—his famous vision of the U.S. as a nation of self-sufficient "yeoman farmers" and small tradesmen, all owning property of their own and making their living from the products of their labor.

For those tribes who chose an "obstinate adherence to aboriginal modes and habits," Commissioner Lea, in 1852 had the solution:

> Deep seated maladies can be remedied by no superficial curatives; and it has been the work of hunger, disease, and death to arouse in the survivors a perception of the only conditions upon which human life and comfort can be sustained on earth.[7]

Making Indians into farmers wasn't just to encourage economic self-sufficiency. Behind it was the complete elimination of the Indian race. It would tie them to specific pieces of land; encourage them to invest in and improve those lands, and require them to purchase seed, stock, and other goods, thus bringing them into the market. Their individual interests would collide with tribal communal interests, thereby weakening the individuals' connection and loyalty to his/her tribe. Tribal relationships would be destroyed; tribal sovereignty over a people and a communal land base would be disrupted. Indians would be assimilated into the U.S. polity, the "melting pot." Languages and cultures would be expunged.

> In all, more than fifty concentration treaties were negotiated by 1856, bringing more than 4000 square miles of new territory under the responsibility of the Indian Bureau, and designating reservations for many of the western tribes. Indian title to over 174 million acres of land was extinguished by these treaties. Treaties in new territories such as Utah and New Mexico would be negotiated through the end of the 1860s.[8]

Post Civil War: Remove Indians Out of Major Immigration Routes and Mineral Areas

Following the Civil War, the reservation system evolved into a hybrid policy: Indians would be "concentrated" on a few large reservations, removing them from the western emigration and railroad routes, and areas with valuable mineral discoveries (e.g., gold in Colorado and the Black Hills).

In 1865, Acting Commissioner Charles E. Mix authorized Governor Stevens to conduct treaty negotiations with the Pacific Northwest Indians. He provided him with policy guidelines and with several recently concluded treaties to use as models but left much to his discretion and experience.

It is the expectation of the Department that the sum appropriated, will prove sufficient to defray all expenses incurred in and incidental to making conventional arrangements *designed to be permanent*, with all the Tribes and fragments of Tribes within your Superintendency, by which the United States will extinguish their claim of title to all the lands within the Territory … you will endeavor to *unite the numerous bands and fragments of tribes into tribes and provide for the concentration of one or more of such tribes upon the reservations which may be set apart for their future homes*. (Emphasis added).[9]

The idea behind this was not only to minimize the amount of land occupied by Indians; it was also to dissolve tribal relations and identity. These officials hoped to advance Indian assimilation into American society by making tribal distinctions or divisions irrelevant, and they tried to achieve this in part by treating them as if they already were.

1871: End Treaty Making

Given the difficulty of selling this new policy to Indians who did not want to move from their homelands, the U.S. came up with a solution: end treaty-making. In this vein, in 1869, Commissioner of Indian Affairs Ely S. Parker urged an end to treaty-making and described the Indians as "helpless and ignorant wards:"

> "...because treaties have been made with them, generally for the extinguishment of their *supposed absolute title to land inhabited by them* or over which they roam, they have been falsely impressed with the notion of national independence. It is time that this idea should be dispelled and the government *cease the cruel farce* of thus dealing with its helpless and ignorant wards." (Emphasis added).[10]

In 1871 Congress banned any further use of the treaty power in dealing with the Indians, retaining legislative plenary power over Indian lives and lands. Act of March 3, 1871, 16 Stat. 566.

The motivation for the executive branch to determine where Indians would be located was to free Indian lands for white settlement.

> In 1871, Secretary Columbus Delano pointed out that concentrating the entirety of the American Indian population within the Indian Territory "would release from Indian occupancy 93,692,731 acres of land, and throw it open to white settlement and cultivation."[11]

1872: Indian Reservation Policy

In 1872, Commissioner Walker endorsed harsher policies for reservations. Indians were to be placed under strict reformatory control:

> The reservation system affords the place for thus dealing with tribes and bands, without the access of influences inimical to peace and virtue. It is only necessary that Federal laws, judiciously framed to meet all the facts of the case, and enacted

in season, before the Indians begin to scatter, shall *place all the members of this race under a strict reformatory control by the agents of the Government*. (Emphasis added).[12]

Indians were to be harassed and scourged if they resisted the reservation procedures, especially those requiring Indians to remain within reservation boundaries.

In the first announcement made of the reservation system, it was expressly declared that the Indians should be made as comfortable on, and as uncomfortable off, their reservations as it was in the power of the Government to make them; that such of them as went right should be protected and fed, and *such as went wrong should be harassed and scourged* without intermission. (Emphasis added).[13]

Commissioner Walker further elucidated his opinion on what should become of Indians:

No one certainly will rejoice more heartily than the present Commissioner when the Indians of this country cease to be in a position to dictate, in any form or degree, to the Government; when, in fact, the last hostile tribe becomes reduced to the condition of *suppliants for charity*. This is, indeed, the only hope of salvation for the aborigines of the continent. (Emphasis added).[14]

He proclaimed the need to "relentlessly crush" them and with the sentiment of Manifest Destiny he saw it as an aspect of God that they were being defeated or killed.

If they stand up against the progress of civilization and industry, *they must be relentlessly crushed*. The westward course of population is neither to be denied nor delayed for the sake of all the Indians that ever called this country their home. The Indian must yield or perish; and there is something that savors of *providential mercy* in the rapidity with which their fate advances upon them, leaving them scarcely the chance to resist before they shall be surrounded and disarmed. (Emphasis added).[15]

1873: President Grant's Peace Policy

In his inaugural address on March 4, 1873, President Grant stated: "The proper treatment of the original inhabitants of this land—the Indians—is one deserving of careful study. I will favor any course towards them which tends to their civilization and ultimate citizenship."[16]

To implement a Peace Policy, Grant reversed President Johnson's policy of using military personnel as Indian superintendents and agents. Under Grant, civilians associated with various Christian denominations, would manage Indian reservations, including Catholics, Methodists, Baptists, and Quakers. They would replace the military officers. Common practice, however, continued to allow the temporary appointment of military officers as Indian agents in hostile areas.[17]

A major impetus behind Grant's Peace Policy lay in the need to defuse the public's cries of corruption and mismanagement in the Indian Bureau. In addition to appointing members of religious orders as Indian Agents, Congress authorized a commission of philanthropic citizens, outside of the government, who would advise the government in matters concerning Indian policy. More important, Secretary J.D. Cox stated: these civilian advisors were authorized by executive order to "...inspect all the accounts and records of the Bureau, to be present at the purchases of Indian goods and advise them to the conduct of the same, and to visit and inspect the tribes in their reservations and examine the business of all the agencies."[18]

> Grant also discovered that not every Indian nation was ready to embrace the changes his administration proposed. Some Indians had no interest in moving to reservations, farming, Christianity, or becoming U.S. citizens. For tribes who refused to abide by the "Peace Policy," a different plan that might be described as "Peace by Force" was developed. As violence between Indians and settlers increased, Grant described this plan in an 1872 letter to General John Schofield: "Indians who will not put themselves under the restraints required will have to be forced, even to the extent of making war upon them, to submit to measures that will insure [sic] security to the white settlers of the Territories," he argued.[19]

Despite the auspicious plans embodied in the Peace Policy, affairs did not improve noticeably for the Indians.

While President Grant espoused peace, he was willing to invite war if the public treasury would be benefitted. Under extreme political pressure, he had to decide what to do about the Black Hills given the vast discoveries of gold. Given the Treaty of 1868, Grant had no legal basis for seizing the Black Hills, so he invented one ... *no fixed resistance by the military should be made to the miners going in. ...* (Emphasis added).[20]

The invasion of thousands of miners led to the Great Sioux War of 1876 and the continuing warfare from 1877.

Commissioner Smith, in 1876, put the burden on Indians to adapt to agricultural lifestyles and become self-supporting, notwithstanding that "the adventurous, grasping Anglo-Saxon race is dominant and in possession of the fairest and richest portions of the land. He pronounced that "The next twenty-five years are to determine the fate of a race. If they cannot be taught, and taught very soon to accept the necessity of the situation and begin in earnest to provide for their own wants by labor in civilized pursuits they are destined to speedy extinction. ..." He recommended: First. Concentration of all Indians on a few reservations. Second. Allotment to them of lands in severalty. Third. Extension over them of United States law and the jurisdiction of United States courts.[21]

1877: President Hayes - Large Reservations No Longer Desirable, Assimilation Necessary

In 1877, the Indians highest trust official secretary of Interior Schulz would bulldoze their interests. He declared the "system of large reservations" as "utterly untenable." The manner in which he justified his position completely denigrated Indians.

"... it is not unnatural that the withholding of large tracts from settlement and development so as to maintain a *savage aristocracy* in the enjoyment of their chivalrous pastimes, should be looked upon by many as a system incompatible with the progress of civilization and injurious to the material interests of the country. ... It is most desirable for the interests of the Indians themselves, therefore, that *we should substitute for the system of large reservations a "new system" of assimilation and merger in the body of citizens*. (Emphasis added).[22]

~ 98 ~

It was as if justifying this shift of policy could only be made by immorally attacking Indians.

> The shift away from the reservation policy did not occur immediately. Meanwhile, the reservation system continued to be modified, as it had been during the Grant years, away from the concentration of the Indians in large centralized locations. Instead, the reservations were smaller entities incorporating the Indians along loose tribal lines, and this "small reservation approach" was the cornerstone of the Hayes strategy. As a result, after President Hayes took office in 1877, "over sixty tribes resettled in the Indian Territory, while many more were shifted from their homeland to new locales."[23]

Commissioner Smith, in 1876, listed the deficiencies in many of the reservations and the need to reduce the number of reservations:

> Many of the present reserves are almost worthless for agricultural purposes; others are rich in soil, mineral wealth, and timber. Nearly all are too small to subsist the Indians by hunting, and too large for them to occupy in agricultural and civilized pursuits. Many are so remote and difficult of access, that needed supplies can be furnished only at great expense. Nearly all are surrounded by white settlers, more or less numerous. Wherever an Indian reservation has on it good land, or timber, or minerals, the cupidity of the white man is excited, and a constant struggle is inaugurated to dispossess the Indian, in which the avarice and determination of the white man usually prevails.[24]

Reduce Number of Indian Reservations

Consolidation. In 1878, at the verbal request of the House Committee on Indian Affairs, a bill was drawn in the Secretary of Interior's office and sent to the committee, providing for the removal and consolidation of certain Indians in the States of Oregon, Colorado, Iowa, Kansas, Nebraska, Wisconsin, and Minnesota, and the Territories of Washington and Dakota.[25]

The objects sought to be attained by the bill were as follows:

> First. The reduction of the number of agencies, and consequently a large annual reduction of the expense attending

the civilization of the Indians and the management of their affairs.

Second. The consolidation of the Indians upon reservations where they might be best protected in their personal and property rights.

Third. The sale of the lands vacated by the consolidation, and the use of a portion of the funds arising therefrom in the removal and settlement of the Indians, now residing on the reservations to be vacated, on the reservations where the consolidation is to be effected, the balance of the money to be funded for their use, the interest thereon to be expended in lieu of direct appropriations for the benefit of all the Indians on the reservation as created by the bill.

Without attempting to particularize, it may be said that the various tribes and bands of Indians embraced in the bill now occupy thirty-six reservations, containing 21,922,507 acres of land, under charge of twenty agents and the necessary attendant corps of teachers and other employes. Upon the reduction proposed in the bill they will occupy nine reservations, containing 4,239,052 acres, under the charge of nine agents, all of whom are now provided for by law. A reduction of twenty-five reservations and eleven agencies will thus be effected. There will be restored to the public domain 17,642,455 acres of land, and an annual saving in agency expenses to the amount of $120,000 will be effected ...

He went on to recommend further consolidations of the Indians of New Mexico, Colorado, and Arizona.

The Klamath Indians of Oregon can, with material advantage to themselves and the government, be removed to Yakama Reservation, in Washington Territory, to which reservation the Bannocks and Malheur Indians will also be immediately sent. This policy should also be pursued with the Indians of Western Dakota, Montana, Idaho, and other sections; the paramount object being to locate them on good agricultural lands to which permanent title can be given, and to sustain and aid them thereon until they become self-supporting.[26]
...

His justification was that the Indians were only using a small portion of the lands previously reserved to them.

Washington: In 1884, Governor Squire of Washington Territory fully endorsed this approach:

> *There are fifteen Indian reservations in the Territory…. The land occupied by these reservations consists largely of the best agricultural, grazing, timber, and mineral lands in the Territory … if they could be induced to concentrate, and altogether abandon certain reservations, it would conduce much to the development of the Territory by the settlement and cultivation of large tracts of valuable land that are now unproductive.* (Emphasis added).[27]

> Between 1877 and 1900, federal appropriations for Indian schools rose from $20,000 to $2,936,000; in the same period, the number of Native children enrolled in school went from 3,598 to 21,568. The main point for my purposes here is that concentration of Native groups on well-defined reservations was widely seen as a prerequisite for making the education programs work.[28]

Destroy Tribal Relations

The continuing federal policy continued in its belligerent posture. Commissioner Atkins in 1885 did not seem at all concerned over the procedures used to control Indians:

> The policy of the Government for many years past has been to destroy the tribal relations as fast as possible, and to use every endeavor to bring the Indians under the influence of law. To do this the agents have been accustomed to *punish for minor offenses, by imprisonment in the guard-house and by with holding rations* … (Emphasis added).[29]

"Indians Must Conform to "The White Man's Ways," Peaceably if They Will, Forcibly if They Must"

In 1889, Commissioner T.J. Morgan continued advocacy for the policy of assimilation and allotment:

First.-The anomalous position heretofore occupied by the Indians in this country can not much longer be maintained. The reservation system belongs to a "vanishing state of things" and must soon cease to exist.

Second.-The logic of events demands the absorption of the Indians into our national life, not as Indians, but as American citizens.

Third.-As soon as a wise conservatism will warrant it, the relations of the Indians to the Government must, rest solely upon the full recognition of their individuality. Each Indian must be treated as a man, be allowed a man's rights …

Fourth.- The Indians must conform to "the white man's ways," peaceably if they will, forcibly if they must. They must adjust themselves to their environment, and conform their mode of living substantially to our civilization. This civilization may not be the best possible, but it is the best the Indians can get. They can not escape it, and must either conform to it or be crushed by it.

Sixth.-The tribal relations should be broken up, socialism destroyed and the family and the autonomy of the individual substituted. The allotment of lands in severalty, the establishment of local courts and police, the development of a personal sense of independence, and the universal adoption of the English language are means to this end.[30]

Of the land actually acquired 17,400,000 acres, or about one seventh of all the Indian lands in the United States, might seem like a somewhat rapid reduction of the landed estate of the Indians, but when it is considered that for the most part the land relinquished was not being used for any purpose whatever, that scarcely any of it was in cultivation, that the Indians did not need it and would not be likely to need it at any future time, and that they were, as is believed, reasonably well paid for it, the matter assumes quite a different aspect. The sooner the tribal relations are broken up and the reservation system done away with the better it will be for all concerned.[31]

1890: Forego Indian Consent for Land Acquisition through Legislative Taking

Commissioner T.J. Morgan described the reservation system in bleak terms in 1890:

The entire system of dealing with them is vicious, involving, as it does, the ***installing of agents, with semi-despotic power over ignorant, superstitious, and helpless subjects***; the keeping of thousands of them on reservations practically as prisoners, isolated from civilized life and dominated by fear and force; the issue of rations and annuities, which inevitably tends to breed pauperism; the disbursement of millions of dollars worth of supplies by contract, which invites fraud; the maintenance of a system of licensed trade, which stimulates cupidity and extortion, etc. (Emphasis added).[32]

1890: No More Frontier

The Superintendent of the U.S. Census reported in 1890 "there can no longer be said to be a frontier line and hence the country's westward movement can no longer have a place in the census reports."[33]

1891: Leasing Minerals on Tribal Lands

In 1891, Congress enacted the first legislation for leasing minerals on tribal lands, authorizing ten-year mineral leases of land not needed for agriculture or allotments. The leases required the approval of the Secretary of the Interior and the consent of the tribe. Unfortunately, the stipulation for tribal consent meant very little because tribes frequently did not have the knowledge and experience to make informed decisions about leasing, while economic hardship and external forces put significant pressure on tribes to develop. 25 U.S.C. § 397 (1988).

Unilateral Federal Action

After *Lone Wolf v. Hitchcock*, 187 U.S. 553 (1903), Congress immediately began to change the way that it dealt with Indian property.

> Commissioner of Indian Affairs William Jones in testimony before the House Indian Affairs Committee stated: "The decision in the Lone Wolf case will enable you to dispose of [Indian] land without the consent of the Indians. If you wait for their consent in these matters, it will be fifty years before you can do away with the reservations." ... "Supposing you were the guardian or ward of a child 8 or 10 years of age," he told, "would you ask the consent of a child as to the investment of its funds? No; you would not."[34]

Congress followed Jones' suggestion and, without even initiating negotiations, proceeded to adopt allotment statutes for many Indian reservations.

U.S. Control of Indians

Concentration, then could be seen as the central organizing factor:

(1) It would limit the mobility of Native groups, making them easier to locate and control.

(2) It would reduce alternative possibilities for subsistence, thereby encouraging them to take up farming.

(3) It would make them more dependent on government support if they did not take up farming, *giving federal officials additional leverage*.

(4) It would facilitate the allotment of land, by restricting the area to be divided.

(5) It would simplify the reliable identification of individuals, clarifying their family relationships.

(6) Finally, it made possible a much clearer picture of the number of Native children who would need to be enrolled in schools, as well as keeping track of their progress.[35]

Notes: Federal Indian Policy

1. James Monroe, First Annual Message Online by Gerhard Peters and John T. Woolley, The American Presidency Project. https://www.presidency.ucsb.edu/node/205560 (accessed online November 4, 2020).
2. U.S. Statutes at Large, 1:119 (1802); "From Thomas Jefferson to the Senate and the House of Representatives, 27 January 1802," *Founders Online,* National Archives, https://founders.archives.gov/documents/Jefferson/01-36-02-0289. [Original source: *The Papers of Thomas Jefferson*, vol. 36, *1 December 1801–3 March 1802*, ed. Barbara B. Oberg. Princeton: Princeton University Press, 2009, pp. 440–443.] (accessed online November 4, 2020).
3. https://www.presidency.ucsb.edu/documents/second-annual-message-1 (accessed online March 27, 2023).
4. *U.S. Statutes at Large,* 3:516-17.
5. Prucha, Francis Paul. The Great Father: The United States Government

and the American Indians. Lincoln; University of Nebraska Press, 1984: 1:316.

6. Banner, Stuart. *How the Indians lost their land: Law and power on the frontier*. Harvard University Press, 2005:231.

7. Report of the Commissioner of Indian Affairs to the Secretary of the Interior, United States. Office of Indian Affairs. U.S. Government Printing Office, 1852, p. 4.

8. "Pensioners upon Our Humanity": Governmentality and the Reservation System in the 19th Century. John Mark French, DePaul University, Paper presented at the Annual Meeting of the Western Political Science Association, San Diego, CA, April 18-21, 2019, p. 13.

9. Text of Proceedings of Chehalis Council. https://www.washingtonhistory. org/wp-content/uploads/2020/04/chehalisCouncil-1.pdf (accessed online May 21, 2022).

10. Report of the Commissioner of Indian Affairs to the Secretary of the Interior, United States. Office of Indian Affairs. U.S. Government Printing Office, 1869, p. 36.

11. Report of the Secretary of the Interior, United States. Office of Indian Affairs. U.S. Government Printing Office, 1871, p. 6.

12. Report of the Commissioner of Indian Affairs to the Secretary of the Interior, United States. Office of Indian Affairs, U.S. Government Printing Office, 1872, p. 11.

13. Ibid., p. 6.

14. Ibid., p. 9.

15. Id.

16. President Ulysses S. Grant Inaugural Address. https://www.presidency. ucsb.edu/documents/inaugural-address-37 (accessed online April 14, 2022).

17. President Ulysses S. Grant and Federal Indian Policy. https://www.nps. gov/articles/000/president-ulysses-s-grant-and-federal-indian-policy.htm (accessed online March 20, 2023).

18. The Abridgment ... Containing the Annual Message of the President of the United States to the Two Houses of Congress ... with Reports of Departments and Selections from Accompanying Papers, United States. President, 1870, p. 614.

19. President Ulysses S. Grant and Federal Indian Policy. https://www.nps. gov/articles/000/president-ulysses-s-grant-and-federal-indian-policy.htm (accessed online March 20, 2023).

20. Library of Congress. Cozzens, Peter. "Ulysses S. Grant Launched an Illegal War Against the Plains Indians, Then Lied About It." *Smithsonian Magazine,* November 2016. https://www.smithsonianmag.com/history/ ulysses-grant-launched-illegal-war-plains-indians-180960787/?utm_ medium=email&utm_source=govdelivery (accessed online September 11, 2022).

21. Report of the Commissioner of Indian Affairs to the Secretary of the Interior, United States. Office of Indian Affairs. U.S. Government Printing Office, 1876, pp. VI, VII.

22. H.R. Rep. No. 1401, 46th Cong., 2nd Sess. (1880) Agreement with Ute Indians of Colorado, pp. 2-3.

23. Major Russel D .Santala, The Ute Campaign of 1879: A Study in the Use of the Military Instrument. U.S. Army Command and General Staff College, Fort Leavenworth, Kansas, p. 17.

24. Report of the Commissioner of Indian Affairs to the Secretary of the Interior, United States. Office of Indian Affairs. U.S. Government Printing Office, 1876, p. 386.

25. Annual Report of the Secretary of the Interior, Report of the Commissioner of Indian Affairs to the Secretary of the Interior, United States. Office of Indian Affairs. U.S. Government Printing Office, 1878, pp. iv-v.

26. Annual Report of the Secretary of the Interior, Report of the Commissioner of Indian Affairs to the Secretary of the Interior, United States. Office of Indian Affairs. U.S. Government Printing Office, 1878, pp. iv-v.

27. Report of Governor of Washington (Squire) to Secretary of Interior (Teller). H.R. Exec. Doc No. 1, 48th Cong., 2nd Sess. (1884), p. 613.

28. "Pensioners upon Our Humanity": Governmentality and the Reservation System in the 19th Century. John Mark French, DePaul University, Paper presented at the Annual Meeting of the Western Political Science Association, San Diego, CA, April 18-21, 2019, p. 28.

29. Report of the Commissioner of Indian Affairs to the Secretary of the Interior, United States. Office of Indian Affairs. U.S. Government Printing Office, 1885, p. XXI.

30. The Abridgment ... Containing the Annual Message of the President of the United States to the Two Houses of Congress ... with Reports of Departments and Selections from Accompanying Papers, United States. President, 1889, p. 620.

31. Report of the Commissioner of Indian Affairs to the Secretary of the Interior. United States. Office of Indian Affairs. U.S. Government Printing Office, 1890, pp. XXXVIII-XXXIX

32. Report of the Commissioner of Indian Affairs to the Secretary of the Interior. United States. Office of Indian Affairs. U.S. Government Printing Office, 1890, p. V.

33. "Frederick Jackson Turner." Wisconsin Authors and Their Works. Madison: The Parker Educational Company, 1918. 302-307.

34. House Report No. 443, 58-2, Serial 4578, p. 4.

35. "Pensioners upon Our Humanity": Governmentality and the Reservation System in the 19th Century. John Mark French, DePaul University, Paper presented at the Annual Meeting of the Western Political Science Association, San Diego, CA, April 18-21, 2019, p. 32.

7: MILITARY POLICY

Military Policy Aligned to Political Objective of Indian Relinquishment of All of Their Country; Keep Indians Ignorant of This Objective; Extinction of Indians

In an 1878 Speech, General Pope set forth the political and economic objectives of the U.S. in regard to Indians. As the goal of the military is to provide support to fulfill these objectives, the U.S.' military policy must begin here.

> *We bought his lands by driblets, knowing very well that every purchase demanded another purchase in geometrical ratio, and that with every sale the means of livelihood upon which the Indian race had depended for ages, and which was the only mode they knew, were restricted more and more, and that in time every tribe of Indians must, in the nature of the case, be left destitute, except insofar as the government chose to feed and clothe them. The Indian did not know this in the beginning, nor indeed until want was upon him. We knew that he must relinquish in time all of his country. He did not know it, nor in the least comprehended the merciless and resistless progress of white populations. In short, we began the system, knowing perfectly what would be the results; the Indian began and for a long time continued it in ignorance of these ends."* (Emphasis added).[1]

Fragments of Great Indian Nations

Continuing in his speech, General Pope provides the best evidence of the U.S.' partial fulfillment of its objectives.

What has become of the great tribes once famous in our history? The Delaware, the Miami, the Shawnee, the Sac and Fox, the Pottawattomie, the Kickapoo, and many others—where are they, those beneficiaries of a wise and humane policy? Only a few feeble, helpless, and hopeless fragments of these great Indian nations yet remain. Transferred, through scenes of violence and bloodshed, from one reservation to another, they have at last been established on small reservations in the Indian Territory and on the Upper Missouri—poor, forlorn dependents upon the insufficient charity of the government and the forbearance of the imperious white settlers. There, let us hope, they may be left to die in peace, and their race and name to pass out of the history of the country and be comfortably forgotten by those who have suffered this wrong to be inflicted upon them.[2]

Consolidation of West through U.S.' Military Arm

The military campaigns in the western U.S. were not as haphazard as articulated at different times. In order to secure the freedom of movement for the expansion of settlers along the major trails and rail lines, the Army was able to define its critical area of operations.

Military Intelligence

From the time of President Jefferson's secret message to Congress on January 18, 1803, the U.S. was fully cognizant of the unwillingness of Indian Nations to sell any more of their lands and the need of more land for a burgeoning population.[3]

The military expeditions ordered by President Jefferson and his successors included covert action to gather detailed intelligence on the number, strength, allies and military capacity of Indians should the U.S. continue its westward expansion. Lewis & Clark, in their Military Expedition, were ordered to (1) have Indian Nations acknowledge the authority of the U.S.; and (2) in regard to the Louisiana Territory, after its purchase from France, of the U.S.' sovereignty.[4]

Army Expeditions of the 19th Century[5]

An excellent chart of the various Army Expeditions is located online with information on 21 Expeditions from 1804-1867, ordered chronologically with Explorer, Time, Place, and Major Accomplishments. It is an excellent teaching tool.

https://history.army.mil/museums/TRADOC/frontier-army-museum/docs/
Army-Earth-Day_Topographic-Explorations_Lesson_Plan.docx (accessed
online November 16, 2022).

Gathering military information was a priority given the number of tribes and
the territory they controlled. The Army relied on the data from its numerous
expeditions, along with the support of the Department of the Interior, and the
use of armed Indian scouts and secret observers among the reservation Indians.

1865: Right after End of Civil War - Finish Indian Subjugation in One War

Right after the end of the Civil War, Secretary of War Edwin M. Stanton
proposed to use the standing Regular Army, that had not yet been dispersed, to
attack the Indians in the west in one sweep. There were 50,000 soldiers, triple
the 1860 strength. The military commanders concurred, with General Pope
advising General Grant: "I think the government will find it true economy to
finish this Indian war this season, so it will stay finished. We have the troops
enough now on the plains to do it now better than hereafter." An offensive
was planned to begin in April 1865 but was delayed until the summer. By
that time, popular opposition to a standing army in peacetime, resulted in its
disbandment, with a smaller force retained.[6]

With troop strength and quality dissipated, the U.S. military campaign against
the Indians would have to rely on a piecemeal offensive posture against
individual tribes. Less than 5,000 troops were employed, and the majority of
forces were territorial and state militias rather than Regular formations.

In the first months after Appomattox, General Grant was preoccupied with the
occupation of the South and Army reorganization. Admitting his ignorance of
Indian affairs, he gave broad discretionary powers to his western commanders:
Generals William T. Sherman, Pope, Sheridan, Schofield, Miles, Howard
and Crook. He appointed General Sherman as the Commanding General of
the Army, to superintend the U.S.' engagement in the Indian Wars. General
Sherman favored a harsh policy from his Civil War battle experience.[7]

U.S. Military Command Structure - Great Plains

A military command structure was put in place, with designated zones of
operations, the establishment of garrisoned forts to assure the control of
territory and the ability to procure, transport and distribute armaments and
supplies. The telegraph allowed the military command to monitor operations

by communication between forces. Railroads served as fortresses and the strategic movement of forces.

The Departments of the Platte in Omaha and Missouri at Fort Leavenworth would lead the military response. Responsibility was delegated as follows:

COMMANDING GENERAL OF THE U.S. ARMY, GEN. WILLIAM TECUMSEH SHERMAN

THE DEPARTMENT OF THE COLUMBIA: 1874 - Department Commander, General Otis A. Howard

THE DEPARTMENT OF THE MISSOURI: Missouri, Arkansas, Kansas, the Indian Territory, Colorado and Nebraska. Department Commanders included:

> Winfield Scott Hancock (1866–1867)
> Philip Sheridan (1867–1869)
> John Schofield (1869–70)
> John Pope (1870–1883)
> Christopher Columbus Augur (1883–1885)
> Nelson Appleton Miles (1885–1886)
> Thomas Howard Ruger (1886)
> Orlando Bolivar Willcox (1886–1887)

THE DISTRICT OF NEBRASKA: Commanding Officer, Brigadier General Robert B. Mitchell
> SubDistrict of Western Nebraska: Commanding Officer, Lieutenant Colonel William O. Collins
> SubDistrict of Eastern Nebraska: Commanding Officer, Colonel Samuel W. Summers

THE DEPARTMENT OF THE PLATTE: [Part of Department of the Missouri]
Responsible to protect the Overland Route (or Oregon Trail) to Salt Lake City, the Montana Road (or Bozeman Trail) and the construction route of the Union Pacific Railroad.

Commanding Officer(s)

> Brigadier General Philip St. George Cooke, March 5, 1866
> Major General Christopher C. Augur, January 23, 1867

Brigadier General Edward Ord, November 18, 1871
Brigadier General George Crook, April 27, 1875
Brigadier General Oliver O. Howard, September 5, 1882
Colonel John Gibbon, March 6, 1884 (temporary)
Brigadier General Oliver O. Howard, October 25, 1884
Brigadier General George Crook, April 28, 1886
Brigadier General John R. Brooke, 1888
Brigadier General John J. Coppinger, March 17, 1895
District of Colorado: Commanding Officer, Colonel Thomas Moonlight

THE DEPARTMENT OF KANSAS: 1864, Kansas, Nebraska Territory, Colorado Territory (except Fort Garland), Indian Territory, and Fort Smith, Arkansas—Merged into The Department Of The Missouri, Department Commander, Major General Samuel R. Curtis.

Methods of War

Prussian General and military theorist Carl von Clausewitz wrote in his seminal treatise on military strategy still studied today that "War is thus an act of force to compel our enemy to do our will."[8] The U.S. Army used the methods outlined by Clausewitz: The *first* of these is invasion, that is the seizure of enemy territory; not with the object of retaining it but in order to exact financial contributions, or even to lay it waste. The immediate object here is neither to conquer the enemy country nor to destroy its army, but simply to cause general damage. The *second* method is to give priority to operations that will increase the enemy's suffering. The *third*, and far the most important method, judging from the frequency of its use, is to wear down the enemy. ... Wearing down the enemy in a conflict means using the duration of the war to bring about a gradual exhaustion of his physical and moral resistance.[9]

U.S. Expansionist and Mercantilism Policies Induce Westward Expansion

The expansionist and mercantilism policies of the U.S. induced westward expansion. The military, by Presidential Proclamation, protected the white explorers, considered part of the intelligencia, creating new routes, along with the white settlers, miners and surveyors who traversed them.

James K. Polk, in his First Annual Message to Congress on December 2, 1845, recognized the importance of the link between settlers and the military. He ordered the military to erect stockades and forts along the frontier trails for their protection.

For the protection of emigrants whilst on their way to Oregon against the attacks of the Indian tribes occupying the country through which they pass, I recommend that a suitable number of stockades and blockhouse forts be erected along the usual route between our frontier settlements on the Missouri and the Rocky Mountains, and that an adequate force of mounted riflemen be raised to guard and protect them on their journey. (Emphasis added).[10]

Senators David R. Atchison and Benton, with the aid of others, put through a bill in 1846 which provided for the establishment of a regiment of mounted riflemen and a line of military posts along the route to Oregon.

In January 1867, General Grant wrote to Secretary of War Stanton that, "The protection of the Pacific railroad, so that not only the portion already completed shall be entirely safe, but that the portion yet to be constructed shall in no way be delayed either by actual or apprehended danger is indispensible (sic)."[11]

In his Third Annual Message on December 3, 1867, President Andrew Johnson extended protection from hostile Indians to railroad construction workers:

It is of vital importance that our distant Territories should be exempt from Indian outbreaks, and that the construction of the Pacific Railroad, an object of national importance, should not be interrupted by hostile tribes.[12]

Priority Given to Protecting Explorers and Surveyors

On April 30, 1874, President Grant, in a Special Message, ordered that the 'educated, scientific gentlemen' of the Engineer Corps of the Army conduct explorations of the country, with the protection of military escorts. This is important as many of these surveys were mineralogical.

"As the country to be explored is occupied in great part by uncivilized Indians, all parties engaged in the work at hand must be supplied with escorts from the Army..."[13]

U.S. Army Forts

Army frontier forts were strategically located to protect emigrants and settlers. Numerous forts were built along the emigrant passage corridors: the California Trail, the Oregon Trail, the Smoky Hill Route, the Platte River Route and the Santa Fe Trail, to name a few. They were used as depots to stockpile supplies and to enable military-escorted wagon trains to rest, regroup and resupply.

COLORADO: Fort Wise, Fort Collins, Fort Lyon, Camp Weld, Camp Rankin

WYOMING: Platte River Route, Fort Laramie

KANSAS: Smoky Hill Trail, Fort Riley, Fort Ellsworth, Fort Hays, Fort Wallace, Santa Fe Trail Fort Zarah, Fort Larned, Fort Dodge

NEBRASKA: Platte River Route, Fort Kearny, Camp Cottonwood

Indian Tribes Aversion to Military Settlements

As early as 1853, tribes expressed their 'aversion' to military settlements in their midst.

> There is a decided aversion among all the wild tribes of Indians to the establishment of military settlements in their midst. They consider that they destroy timber, drive off the game, interrupt their ranges, excite hostile feelings, and but too frequently afford a rendezvous for worthless and trifling characters. Their efficacy, too, for insuring the security of the country, is perhaps overrated, as at present existing, although under the command of excellent and efficient officers, who are always zealous in the performance of their duties; yet, so small is the force usually at their disposal, that they maintain their own position in the country more by the courtesy of the Indians than from any ability to cope with the numbers that surround them. Instead of serving to intimidate the red man, they rather create a belief in the feebleness of the white man. In fact, it must be at once apparent that a skeleton company of infantry or dragoons can add but little to the security of five hundred miles square of territory; nor can the great highways to Utah and New Mexico be properly protected by a wandering squadron that parades them once a year. Thomas Fitzpatrick, Indian Agent, Upper Platte and Arkansas.[14]

U.S. Military Armaments

The U.S. Military, since 1795 with the Harpers Ferry rifle, standardized the weapons and ammunition used by soldiers. Every cartridge and weapon adopted by the U.S. military was recorded and used consistently across the branches in a specific date range.

1795: Harpers Ferry Rifle
1853: Emfield Pattern
1860: Spencer Carbine Henry Lever Action Colt Army Mode
1861: Colt Navy Model Gallager Carbine
1866: Springfield Model 1866
1873: Winchester Lever Action, Springfield Model
1875: Sharps Rifle 187

Large numbers of improved arms were issued to the regular army in 1869, and it was reported:

> The cavalry have all been supplied with Spencer carbines or with Sharp's carbines altered to take the musket metallic cartridges calibre .50. About 30,000 of these later arms have been altered. The Spencer carbine at the end of the war was generally regarded with favor, and as being the best arm in the service, and it continues to be regarded as a superior arm by the cavalry. The altered Sharp's carbine gives great satisfaction, and in some respects—particularly in the ammunition—which is the same as the breech-loading musket ammunition—it is decidedly superior to the Spencer carbine.[15]

The Chief of Ordnance reported increased interest in the Gatling gun in his report for 1873.

> He said that fifty .45 caliber Gatlings had been "contracted for and it is expected will be placed in service in the early spring [of 1874] for the use of troops on the frontier. These are of such dimensions and weights as to be easily transported on pack-animals. It is thought that they will be far more effective in Indian warfare than the mountain howitzers heretofore in use."[16]

Facilitate Civil-Military Cooperation

To facilitate civil-military cooperation, department boundaries were drawn to equate roughly with the boundaries of territories and states. In addition, the east-west orientation of the Departments corresponded with the routes of the major lines of communication to the west. State militias of volunteer citizens augmented the regular Army.

A letter from Joel Palmer, Superintendent, to Commissioner Manypenny, dated April 11, 1856, elucidated the strategy to keep the settlers up in arms, at the cost of Indian lives. Importantly, it highlights the dissension between the governing entities in the War.

> It is a well-known fact that the easiest way to prevent success in war is the inability to express and act upon a unified plan. No decisive victory was possible due to the splintered approach for war. The political infighting led to the Indians out maneuvering, outflanking, and soundly beating the disunited forces fighting them. ... The dissensions between the different functionaries of the government, civil and military, tends greatly to destroy the efficiency of the service: crimination & recrimination but adds to the flame, and whilst a considerable portion of the energies of the respective parties are exhausted in striving to gain the ascendancy and convince others of the correctness of their policy, the enemy goes unwhipped, their forces continually augmenting, our citizens slaughtered, and our settlers cut off and destroyed. (Emphasis added).[17]

Railroads' Military Importance

General Sherman believed military protection for *the construction of the railroads* was a task for the Army.

> These roads, although in the hands of private corporations have more than the usual claim on us for military protection, because the general government is largely interested pecuniary. They aid us materially in our military operations by transporting troops and stores rapidly across a belt of land hitherto only passed in the summer by slow trains drawn by oxen, dependent on the grass for food.[18]

Many of the railroad's builders and its military protectorate viewed the Indians as obstacles to be removed. Grenville Dodge (UP's Chief Engineer) was unsentimental: "We've got to clean the damn Indians out or give up building the Union Pacific Railroad. The government may take its choice."[19]

As the railways expanded, they allowed the rapid transport of troops and supplies to areas where Indian battles were being waged.

In his 1871 Report to the Hon. George S. Boutwell, Secretary of the Treasury, R. W. Raymond, U.S. Commissioner of Mining Statistics, captured the role of the settlers in its triangle with the military and railroad owners. They would have carte blanche to deal with the Indians as they saw fit.

> But what the Government has not been able to do in the past the South Pacific or Texas Pacific Railroad will certainly do. As in the case of the Union and Central Pacific roads, it will attract population, and *the citizens, less hampered in regard to Indians than the military powers, will soon dispose of the question in their own way.* (Emphasis added).[20]

The telegraph, alongside the railway routes, allowed the military command to monitor operations by, and protect, communication between forces.

Destruction of Buffalo

The destruction of the bison was a primary objective. Lieutenant General Philip Sheridan, Commander of the Division of the Missouri, had witnessed first-hand the weakening of Indian opposition in his area of command largely due to the work of professional hunters, who, in the course of two years, removed the great southern buffalo herds upon which the Indians based their subsistence.[21]

He supported this effort wholeheartedly congratulating the hunters stating:

> By 1870, the Army witnessed the destruction of major Indian opposition, other than the Lakota, through the work of professional buffalo hunters using the railroads. In the course of two years, they removed the great buffalo herds upon which the Indians based their subsistence.[22]

Lieutenant Colonel Dodge, a high-ranking military officer, once said in a conversation with Frank H. Mayer: "Mayer, there's no two ways about it, either the buffalo or the Indian must go. Only when the Indian becomes absolutely dependent on us for his every need, will we be able to handle him. He's too independent with the buffalo. But if we kill the buffalo we conquer the Indian. It seems a more humane thing to kill the buffalo than the Indian, so the buffalo must go."[23]

Massive hunting parties arrived in the west by train on excursions for "hunting by rail." Hundreds of men aboard the trains climbed to the roofs and took aim, or fired from their windows, leaving countless 1,500-pound animals where they died.

Harper's Weekly described these hunting excursions:

> Nearly every railroad train which leaves or arrives at Fort Hays on the Kansas Pacific Railroad has its race with these herds of buffalo; and a most interesting and exciting scene is the result. *The train is "slowed" to a rate of speed about equal to that of the herd; the passengers get out fire-arms which are provided for the defense of the train against the Indians, and open from the windows and platforms of the cars a fire that resembles a brisk skirmish.* Frequently a young bull will turn at bay for a moment. His exhibition of courage is generally his death-warrant, for the whole fire of the train is turned upon him, either killing him or some member of the herd in his immediate vicinity. (Emphasis added).[24]

> Herds of buffaloes were seen on the eastern plains of Colorado up to 1871, but all have since disappeared, as the commercial spoil of huntsmen and hide gatherers. The wholesale decimation began in great force and for a distinct purpose—that of collecting hides—in 1869-70. The railways afforded transportation for the hides ($1-2 apiece), heads, and the edible parts of the carcasses. Then came a cloud of bone gatherers, who collected the whitened remnants of skeletons and sold them at five dollars a ton, to be converted into buttons, knife handles, combs and fertilizers. At nearly all the railway stations vast heaps of these bones were stacked up, awaiting shipment to markets east of the Missouri. The Kansas Pacific and Atchison, Topeka & Santa Fe took away hundreds of carloads. "In a little more than three months," says one writer, "in the fall of 1874, over 50,000 hides were shipped from the stations on the Santa Fe road, and it was estimated that the shipments for the year over that and the Kansas Pacific

aggregated 125,000. During the winter season of five months about 2,000,000 pounds of buffalo meat were shipped to all parts of the country. At Kansas City large quantities were cured and packed for eastern consumption."[25]

Leavenworth became a trading center for buffalo hides, and tanneries found even more, [sic] uses for the material, such as making drive belts for industrial machines and grinding buffalo bones into fertilizer. In some places, buffalo tongues became a delicacy in fine restaurants. Soon, the demand for buffalo had increased to such a degree that year-round work was available for buffalo hunters.... Armed with powerful, long-range rifles, individual hunters could kill as many as 250 buffalo a day. Tanneries paid as much as $3.00 per hide and 25¢ for each tongue, which made a nice living for hundreds of men, including Wyatt Earp, Bat Masterson, Pat Garrett, Wild Bill Hickok, and William F. Cody, just to name a few. Unfortunately, once these hides and tongues were taken from the carcasses, the edible buffalo meat was often left to rot on the Plains. By the 1880s, over 5,000 hunters and skinners were involved in the trade.[26]

General Sheridan stated:

These men have done more in the last two years, and will do more in the next year, to settle the vexed Indian question, than the entire regular army has done in the last forty years. They are destroying the Indians' commissary. And it is a well known fact that an army losing its base of supplies is placed at a great disadvantage. Send them powder and lead, if you will; but for a lasting peace, let them kill, skin and sell until the buffaloes are exterminated. Then your prairies can be covered with speckled cattle.[27]

Military Commanders' Philosophies

The western generals brought with them the legacy of "hard war" tactics they had used in the Civil War. General William Tecumseh Sherman wrote in 1867:

We must act with vindictive earnestness against the Sioux, even to their extermination, men, women, and children. Nothing else will reach the root in this case. *The more we can*

~ 118 ~

kill this year, the less will have to be killed in the next war, for the more I see of these Indians the more convinced I am that they all have to be killed or be maintained as a species of paupers. Their attempts at civilization are simply ridiculous. (Emphasis added).[28]

Lieutenant General John M. Schofield, commander of the Department of Missouri from 1869 to 1870, stated his career goal as follows: "With my cavalry and combined artillery encamped in front, I wanted no other occupation in life than to ward off the savage and kill off his food until there should no longer be an Indian Frontier in our beautiful country."[29]

Sheridan's two principal subordinates were Generals Crook and Pope, experienced Indian fighters and astute soldier-politicians who cultivated political favors and supporters. The currying of political favor was a continuation of a tradition that reached its peak during the Civil War.

General Pope preferred to remain at his department headquarters or at a location that afforded him the use of the railroad and telegraph. His command method put him in the position of monitoring operations from afar while maintaining contact with superiors and Eastern political allies.

Soldiers tended to view General Crook as a publicity-hungry leader more concerned with his image than fighting Indians. This was not the case with President Hayes who served under Crook in the Civil War.

> A soldiers' ditty that was popular in Crook's command went:
> I'd like to be a packer.
> And pack with George F. Crook
> And dressed up in my canvas suit
> To be for him mistook.
> I'd braid my beard in two long tails,
> And idle all the day
> In whittling sticks and wondering
> What the New York papers say.[30]

In the estimation of William T. Sherman, Crook was the most effective Indian-fighting general the army ever produced. But he was also the tireless champion of Indian rights. He worked incessantly to promote acculturation on the Apache reservations of Arizona and to protect the bands he defeated in battle from corrupt Indian agents, governmental indifference, and abusive white settlers. As Hayes remarked to the chief justice of the Supreme Court upon Crook's promotion in 1888 to major general in the Regular Army, "his appointment will be especially gratifying to all who take an interest in just and humane treatment of the Indian."[31]

Department of the Interior v. War Department

Dealing with the Indians by diplomatic rather than military means was debated in political and military circles. Senior members of the military establishment actively campaigned for the control of Indian affairs to be transferred to the War Department. The Army saw itself removed from the corruption and inconsistent administration that plagued the Bureau of Indian Affairs as administered by the Department of the Interior. In 1867, a bill to return the Department of Interior's Indian Bureau to the War Department. It was a given to fail since President Grant led the element opposed to the military's passed the House but failed in the Senate.[32]

1872: Indian Reservation Policy

In 1872, *Commissioner Walker endorsed harsher policies for reservations which the military would enforce*. Indians were to be placed under "strict reformatory control. Indians were to be harassed and scourged if they resisted the reservation procedures, especially those requiring Indians to remain within reservation boundaries. ... Force was permitted to accomplish assimilation, along with the destruction of tribal relations.[33]

Small War Campaigns

Randolph B. Marcy, in his book Thirty Years of Army Life on the Border, described the difficulties of Indian fighting:

"To act against an enemy who is here to-day and there to-morrow; who at one time stampedes a herd of mules upon the head waters of the Arkansas, and when next heard from is in the very heart of the populated districts of Mexico, laying waste haciendas, and carrying devastation, rapine, and murder in his steps; who is everywhere without being any where; who assembles at the moment of combat, and vanishes whenever fortune turns against him; who leaves his women and children far distant from the theater of hostilities, and has neither towns or magazines to defend, nor lines of retreat to cover; who derives his commissariat from the country he operates in, and is not encumbered with baggage wagons or pack-trains; who comes into action only when it suits his purposes, and never without the advantage of numbers or position-with such an enemy the strategic science of civilized nations loses much of its importance, and finds but rarely, and only in peculiar localities, an opportunity to be put in practice."[34]

To deal with the Indians' guerrilla military tactics, the Army focused its efforts on a series of small war campaigns against Indian combatants. They took on tribes, piecemeal, tribe by tribe, to suppress insurrection activities.

Surprise Attacks

Over time, the military came to realize the success of surprise attacks. The only way the soldiers could make a decisive attack at all was through surprise attacks on Indian camps. By relying on Indian scouts, this tactic was widely used. If this meant killing women and children, this was part of the punitive, hard war tactics of the higher echelons of the military learned from the Civil War.

Destruction of War-Making Potential

The Army used its power to suppress subversive and insurrection activities. Recognizing Indians on reservations were feeding hostiles and providing supplies, along with warriors using the reservations as a base, the Army required disarming and taking ponies of Indians on reservations and preventing them leaving at will. All of the enemy's war-making potential would be crushed.

1879: Limited Indian Resistance

Lieutenant General Sheridan stated in 1879, "Indian troubles that will hereafter occur will be those which arise upon the different Indian reservations or from attempts made to reduce the number and size of these reservations by the concentration of the Indian tribes."[35]

Military's Constabulary Duties

A Letter from Lieutenant General Sheridan to General Sherman, dated March 18, 1870, following the Piegan Massacre, listed the duties of the military beyond combat operations. His frustration was evident, given the split in public perception about their responsibilities. His resentment about the public reproach of a thankless task is clear:

> We cannot avoid being abused by one side or the other. If we allow the defenseless people on the frontier to be scalped and ravished, we are burnt in effigy and execrated as soulless monsters, insensible to the sufferings of humanity. If the Indian is punished to give security to these people, we are the same soulless monsters from the other side. This is a bad predicament to be in...[36]

He notes that tribes do not willingly move to reservations—*they must be forcibly compelled and it is the military that must do the compulsion*. He cites the example of "the Cheyennes, Arapahoes, Comanches, Kiowas, and Apaches" who "have just been forced on by the troops."

> "The reservation is the last ditch to the wild Indian, but to get him there he must be forced on by the troops. Those who think he can be induced to go there by other means are mistaken."[37]

He further confirms that Indians do not willingly stay on reservations—again they must be forcibly compelled to remain and it is the military that must do the coercion. The Department of the Interior expected "*severe treatment by the military*" against those who left the reservation to serve as a deterrent. When on the reservation Indians would be kept there by the presence of the troops.

Without Indians remaining on reservations they couldn't be 'civilized,' forced to become farmers on land unsuited for farming, without the necessary equipment and supplies. Thus, the military was involuntarily conscripted to engage in the assimilation process.

Worse, was the emigrants' invasion of reservation lands, in huge numbers:

> he [Indian] can only be protected in his rights while there by the troops keeping off the emigrants who encroach on his land.[38]

Protecting the Indians' land was impossible at times when the invasion was in the tens of thousands:

> During the last year, as soon as I withdrew the troops from the Sac and Fox reservation, the emigrants took possession. A flood of immigration, almost ten thousand strong, moved in solid mass and occupied the Osage reservation, because there were no troops to keep them off. All the other reservations on which the Indians may yet be placed will be lost in the same manner, unless guarded by the military.[39]

In another letter, Sheridan stated:

> So far as the wild Indians are concerned, the problem which the good people of the country must decide upon is, who shall be killed, the whites or the Indians; they can take their choice.[40]

Jeremy Siegrist in analyzing these "constabulary" duties noted that the military is untrained, understaffed, unsupported and able to be reactive only, thus resulting in failure and further castigation by the Department of the Interior and settlers. *Without the enemy "feeling the sting of defeat," success is impossible.*[41]

Notes: Military Policy

1. General John Pope, Social Science Association speech, May 24, 1878, on 'The Indian Question.'
2. Id.
3. From Thomas Jefferson to the Senate and the House of Representatives, 18 January 1803," *Founders Online,* National Archives, https://founders. archives.gov/documents/Jefferson/01-39-02-0303. [Original source: *The Papers of Thomas Jefferson,* vol. 39, *13 November 1802–3 March 1803,* ed. Barbara B. Oberg. Princeton: Princeton University Press, 2012, pp. 350–354.] (accessed online November 16, 2020).
4. From Thomas Jefferson to Meriwether Lewis, 22 January 1804," *Founders Online,* National Archives, https://founders.archives.gov/documents/Jefferson/01-42-02-0285. [Original source: *The Papers of Thomas Jefferson,* vol. 42, *16 November 1803–10 March 1804,* ed. James P. McClure. Princeton: Princeton University Press, 2016, pp. 325–326.] (accessed online November 16, 2020).
5. https://history.army.mil/museums/TRADOC/frontier-army-museum/docs/

Army-Earth-Day_Topographic-Explorations_Lesson_Plan.docx (accessed online November 16, 2022).

6. Wooster, The Military and United States Indian Policy, 1865-1903, 112-13.

7. Annual Report of the Secretary of War, 1865, pp. 528-529. Waltmann, Henry George, "The Interior Department, War Department and Indian Policy, 1865-1887" (1962). Dissertations, Theses, & Student Research, Department of History, p. 27.

8. Von Clausewitz, Carl. On war. Vol. 1. Jazzybee Verlag, 1950.

9. Id.

10. https://millercenter.org/the-presidency/presidential-speeches/december-2-1845-first-annual-message (accessed online October 9, 2022).

11. H.R. Exec. Doc. No. 71, 39th Cong., 2nd Sess. (1867), p. 12. 3-8-1867 Letter of the Secretary of War, communicating, in compliance with a resolution of the Senate of February 5, 1867, information in relation to an order issued by Lieutenant General Sherman in regard to the protection of trains on the overland route.

S. Exec. Doc. No. 2, 40th Cong., 1st Sess. (1867).

12. https://www.presidency.ucsb.edu/documents/third-annual-message-10 (accessed online October 4, 2022).

13. https://www.presidency.ucsb.edu/documents/special-message-1918 (accessed online March 18, 2023).

14. Report of the Commissioner of Indian Affairs to the Secretary of the Interior, United States. Office of Indian Affairs. Robert Armstrong, Printer, 1853, p. 122.

15. House Executive Document No. I, Part 2, 41 Cong., 2 Sess., Report of the Secretary of War, 1869 (Washington: Government Printing Office,1869). 442. Rickey Jr, Don. *Firearms in the Indian Wars 1862 to 1891*. Diss. 195, p. 43

16. Ibid, p. 60. Report .of the Secretary of War [1873], III, 10.

17. NARA Series M234, Letters Received by the Office of Indian Affairs, Reel 609 Oregon Superintendency 1856, frames 647-662. To James Clugage Esq. Grand Ronde NARA Series M2, Microcopy of Records of the Oregon Superintendency of Indian Affairs 1848-1873, Reel 6; Letter Books E:10, pages 184-185.

18. Report of the Secretary of the War, 1867, p. 36.

19. Ambrose, Stephen E. Nothing Like It In the World: The Men Who Built the Transcontinental Railroad 1863-1869, Simon and Schuster, 2001, p. 223.

20. Statistics Of Mines And Mining In The States And Territories West Of The Rocky Mountains: Being The 6th Annual Report Of U.S. Commissioner Of Mining Statistics to Secretary of Treasury, 1871, p. 280.

21. Hutton, Phil Sheridan and His Army, 120.

22. Id.

23. The Buffalo Harvest by Frank H. Mayer with Charles B. Roth. https://www.pbs.org/kenburns/the-west/the-buffalo-harvest (accessed online November 4, 2022).

24. "Buffalo Hunting: Shooting Buffalo From the Trains of the Kansas Pacific Railroad," Harper's Weekly, December 14, 1867.

25. Hall, Frank. History of the State of Colorado, Embracing Accounts of the Pre-historic Races and Their Remains: The Earliest Spanish, French and American Explorations... the First American Settlements Founded; the Original Discoveries of Gold in the Rocky Mountains; the Development of Cities and Towns, with the Various Phases of Industrial and Political Transition, from 1858 to 1890... Vol. 4. Blakely Printing Company, 1895, p. 355.

26. Buffalo Hunters. https://www.legendsofamerica.com/we-buffalo-hunters/ (accessed online February 18, 2023).

27. "Buffalo Hunting: Shooting Buffalo From the Trains of the Kansas Pacific Railroad," Harper's Weekly, December 14, 1867.

28. Ambrose, Stephen E. Nothing Like It In the World: The Men Who Built the Transcontinental Railroad 1863-1869, Simon and Schuster, 2001, p. 223.

29. John M. Schofield, Forty-six years in the Army, 1869, p. 428. https://www.perseus.tufts.edu/hopper/text?doc=Perseus%3Atext%3A2001.05.0131%3Achapter%3D23%3Apage%3D428 (accessed online March 25, 2023).

30. James T. King, "Needed: A Re-evaluation of General George Crook," Nebraska History Magazine 65 (September 1964): 229.

31. "George Crook and Rutherford B. Hayes: A Friendship Forged in War", Peter Cozzens, Presented by Cozzens on the occasion of the 11th Hayes Lecture on the Presidency, February 20, 2000, in the Hayes Museum auditorium. https://www.rbhayes.org/hayes/george-crook-and-r.b.h.-a-friendship-forged-in-war/ (accessed online March 20, 2023).

32. THE TRANSFER OF THE INDIAN BUREAU TO THE WAR DEPARTMENT. H.R. Rep. No. 241, 45th Cong., 2nd Sess. (1878).

33. Report of the Commissioner of Indian Affairs to the Secretary of the Interior, United States. Office of Indian Affairs. U.S. Government Printing Office, 1872, pp. 6, 9, 10, 11.

34. http://www.npshistory.com/publications/waba/special-report.pdf (accessed online February 18, 2023).

35. Paul Andrew Hutton, ed., "Philip H. Sheridan," in Soldiers West: Biographies from the Military Frontier (Lincoln: University of Nebraska Press, 1987), 93.

36. Piegan Indians. Letter from the Secretary of War in answer to a resolution of the House, of March 3, 1870, in relation to the late expedition against the Piegan Indians, in the Territory of Montana. H.R. Exec. Doc. No. 269, 41st Congress, 2nd Sess. (1870), p. 71.

37. Id.

38. Id.

39. Id.

40. Tovias, Blanca. (2012). A blueprint for Massacre: The United States army and the 1870 blackfeet Massacre. 10.1515/9780857453006-013.

41. Siegrist, Jeremy T. Apache Wars: A Constabulary Perspective. ARMY COMMAND AND GENERAL STAFF COLL FORT LEAVENWORTH KS SCHOOL OF ADVANCED MILITARY STUDIES, 2005, p. 63.

8: INDIAN POLICY
OF TERRITORIAL GOVERNMENTS

The territorial governments of the U.S. unanimously opposed the presence of Indians and petitioned for their removal and/or opening of their reservations to settlement, given the presence of valuable minerals, agricultural, grazing and water resources. Also, many times the territories would argue about alleged Indian depredations against white settlers or erroneous surveys which included valuable mineral deposits within a reservation. These territorial demands had a strong impact on the Department of the Interior and a segregation of minerals would later follow through a cession occasioned by misrepresentation of the value of the ceded lands or unilateral Congressional action.

Arizona

Report of Governor of Arizona (Tritle), to Secretary of Interior (Teller), 1883

Up to the year 1874 they [Apaches] terrorized the entire Territory, kept out immigration and capital, and had life and property virtually at their mercy. In that year they were placed on a reservation, where those of them who are not absent in Mexico yet remain. When this was accomplished the people of Arizona congratulated themselves on the end of the Indian difficulties, and it was thought that savage warfare was forever at an end... But the raids of the past two years have rudely awakened them from their dream of security, and taught them that there can be no lasting peace while a single Apache remains in the Territory. The country has been set back at least five years in the path of progress and prosperity. *The people of*

Arizona demand that the Apaches be removed to the Indian Territory. ... Some of the richest mineral and finest farming lands in the Territory are embraced within their reservation and closed against the industrious white settler. Remove them to where they properly belong... (Emphasis added).[1]

Report of Governor of Arizona (Murphy) to Secretary of Interior (Noble), 1892

It is very important for the progress and prosperity of the Territory that the mineral and coal lands of the San Carlos Reservation be segregated and opened for settlement and development. As this property is not now being utilized by the Indians, nor any revenue from it derived by them, it would seem just that the segregation be made, and sale and occupation authorized in the same manner as other public lands are settled, and the Government price of the land placed in a trust fund for the use of the Indians. At any rate, it is earnestly requested that a resurvey of the western boundary of this reservation be ordered, as the line as now marked is disputed, and it is believed that a new survey will prove that the present boundary is improperly placed and that much mineral land now included in the reservation properly belongs to the public domain.[2]

Dakotas

Report of Governor of Dakotas (Church) to Secretary of Interior (Lamar), 1887

The Black Hills produce all the gold and silver mined in Dakota, and nearly the entire output is credited to just four mines. The Hills are full of the precious minerals, and other mines, which are quite as rich in gold and silver as the four now paying heavy dividends to stockholders, are simply awaiting capital for their development. *The opening of the Great Sioux Indian reservation, the settlement of this expanse of unsettled territory, and the building of railways through to the Black Hills will bring this about.* (Emphasis added).[3]

Idaho

Report of Governor of Idaho (Stevenson) to Secretary of Interior (Lamar), 1886

The Coeur d'Alene Lake, which lies midway in the reservation, is a deep navigable body of water, and three large rivers, whose head waters are among the mining camps, supply it. For miles around it are *magnificent pastural meadows, and beyond them are the forests of splendid timber, while the precious metals are abundant along the streams and throughout the mountains, and yet 600 Indians hold and own 600,000 acres of this land of inexhaustible resources*, without ambition to develop them for their own benefit, and refusing to permit others to do so.

South of the Coeur d'Alene is the Nez Perce Reservation, consisting of grazing and timber lands, abounding with streams and rivers, capable of phenominal (sic) production, nearly three quarters of a million of acres inhabited by 1,500 Indians. Better for themselves and assuredly better for the growth of our Territory would be the carrying out of the "lands in severalty" plan. The same arguments will apply to all Indians and reservations in Idaho. (Emphasis added).[4]

Report of Governor of Idaho (Stevenson) to Secretary of Interior (Lamar), 1887

The Lemhi Indian reservation is situated on the Lemhi river and embraces 140,000 acres of the best land in the county. Practically it is of no use to the Indians.

Fort Hall or Shoshone and Bannock Reservation: This reservation is situated in Bingham county, on the Snake, Blackfoot, Port Neuf, and Ross Fork rivers, and comprises 1,202,330 acres of land, most of which is of very superior quality. There are at the present time only about 1,500 of all sexes occupying this vast tract, embracing some of the choicest agricultural lands in this Territory.[5]

Montana

Report of Governor of Montana (Crosby) to Secretary of Interior (Teller), 1884

Opening the Reservations.

These vast reservations no longer afford any means of support to the Indian in his traditional mode of life. The large game is gone. The Indians are in many cases driven to kill the white man's cattle or starve. The situation of the Piegans and Blackfeet has been most deplorable as reported by me in detail at different times; *hundreds died from starvation*.

Notwithstanding the temporary relief afforded the Northern Indians by an increase of supplies to the amount of half a ration daily to last until March 1, *their condition from exposure, destitution, and starvation experienced during the past two years is utterly astounding and deplorable, and I have great fears that many will die during the coming winter.*

The recent report of the discovery of gold mines in the Little Rockies ... lying in the very heart of the great northern reservation, is already attracting hundreds from all parts of the Territory and beyond. If it were possible to prevent this intrusion it would not be good policy to do so. It is for the interest of the whole country that the mines should be worked, and the surrounding country be opened to permanent settlement. (Emphasis added).[6]

New Mexico

Report of Governor of New Mexico (Ross) to Secretary of Interior (Lamar), 1885

In May and June last very destructive raids into this Territory were made by renegade bands of Apache Indians, located on the White Mountain or San Carlos Indian reservation in Arizona ... San Carlos reservation is but some 30 miles from the west line of this Territory, inside of which lies a region 150 by 200 miles in extent, *constituting the richest mineral and grazing district in the southwest. ...*[7]

Report of Governor of Utah (Thomas) to Secretary of Interior (Noble), 1891

I have nothing new to add to my former statements respecting the 1,500 or more Indians who have renounced their tribal relations and are scattered throughout the Territory. At the last session of Congress an appropriation of $10,000 was made for the relief of the Shebit Indians. Similar action should be taken for the relief of the Indians in Tooele County, who are anxious to own their land, and those in Garfield, San Juan, Sevier, Kane, and Iron counties.

The people of the Territory through their legislative assembly have protested against the unloading of the Indians upon them. After a full investigation of the matter by the Senate Committee on Indian Affairs it was decided not to recommend the passage of the bill authorizing the removal. In justice to the Territory the matter should no longer be agitated.

Much land within these [Indian] reservations is useless for either cultivation or grazing, while some of it is of *immeasurable value for mining. ... The early adoption of an Indian policy which will abolish the tribal organization of the Indians, and give them in severalty whatever land they can use, will be worth millions of dollars to the people of the Territory.* (Emphasis added).[8]

Wyoming

Report of Governor of Wyoming (Hoyt) to Secretary of Interior (Schurz), 1878

Owing to the occupation of the greater portion of Wyoming by hostile Indians until very recently, the mineral resources of the Territory have been but little developed, or even ascertained with much definiteness. ... Enough has been determined, however, to settle the matter beyond all question that they are vast and varied.[10]

Report of Governor of Wyoming (Warren) to Secretary of Interior (Noble), 1889

The mining industries of Wyoming present perhaps the greatest possibilities of any of its resources. They comprise not only the precious metals, gold and silver, but inexhaustible quantities of coal, petroleum, iron, and soda. Copper, lead, tin, asbestos, mica, magnesium, sulphur, graphite, kaolin, fire-clay, glass, sand, and other valuable deposits exist, and many of them in large deposits. ...

While the development of the Territory is retarded by having this large Indian reservation within its borders, it can hardly be expected that it be given up without a proper regard for the rights of the Indians. In my report for 1886 I recommended the opening up for settlement of all abandoned military reservations and of the Shoshone Reservation, except so much as might be necessary for the support of the Indians, or a *division in severalty among them*. (Emphasis added).[11]

Georgia

State Legislature, 1832

When gold was discovered on Cherokee land, the State of Georgia passed another act, entitled An act to authorize the Governor to take possession of the gold, silver, and other mines lying and being in that section of the chartered limits of Georgia commonly called the Cherokee country, and those upon all other unappropriated lands of the State, and for punishing any person or persons who may hereafter be found trespassing upon the mines.[12]

Colorado

June 27, 1864: First Proclamation, Governor Evans, Colorado Superintendency Indian Affairs, Denver

TO THE FRIENDLY INDIANS OF THE PLAINS:
Agents, interpreters, and traders will inform the friendly Indians of the plains that some members of their tribes have gone to war with the white people. They steal stock and run

it off, hoping to escape detection and punishment. In some instances they have attacked and killed soldiers and murdered peaceable citizens. For this the Great Father is angry, and will certainly hunt them out and punish them, but he does not want to injure those who remain friendly to the whites. He desires to protect and take care of them. For this purpose I direct that all friendly Indians keep away from those who are at war, and go to places of safety. Friendly Arapahoes and Cheyennes belonging on the Arkansas River will go to Major Colley, U.S. Indian agent at Fort Lyon, who will give them provisions, and show them a place of safety. Friendly Kiowas and Comanches will go to Fort Larned, where they will be cared for in the same way. Friendly Sioux will go to their agent at Fort Laramie for directions. Friendly Arapahoes and Cheyennes of the Upper Platte will go to Camp Collins on the Cache la Poudre, where they will be assigned a place of safety and provisions will be given them.

The object of this is to prevent friendly Indians from being killed through mistake. None but those who intend to be friendly with the whites must come to these places. The families of those who have gone to war with the whites must be kept away from among the friendly Indians. The war on hostile Indians will be continued until they are all effectually subdued.[13]

Governor Evans, August 11, 1864: Proclamation to Citizens of Colorado Authorizing Them to Kill Hostile Indians

PROCLAMATION.
Having sent special messengers to the Indians of the plains, directing the friendly to rendezvous at Fort Lyon, Fort Larned, Fort Laramie, and Camp Collins for safety and protection, warning them that all hostile Indians would be pursued and destroyed, and the last of said messengers having now returned, and the evidence being conclusive that most of the Indian tribes of the plains are at war and hostile to the whites, and having to the utmost of my ability endeavored to induce all of the Indians of the plains to come to said places of rendezvous, promising them subsistence and protection, which, with a few exceptions, they have refused to do:

Now, therefore, I, John Evans, governor of Colorado Territory, do issue this my proclamation, authorizing all citizens of Colorado, either individually or in such parties as they may organize, to go in pursuit of all hostile Indians on the plains, scrupulously avoiding those who have responded to my said call to rendezvous at the points indicated; also, to kill and destroy, as enemies of the country, wherever they may be found, all such hostile Indians. And further, as the only reward I am authorized to offer for such services, I hereby empower such citizens, or parties of citizens, to take captive, and hold to their own private use and benefit, all the property of said hostile Indians that they may capture, and to receive for all stolen property recovered from said Indians such reward as may be deemed proper and just therefor.

I further offer to all such parties as will organize under the militia law of the Territory for the purpose to furnish them arms and ammunition, and to present their accounts for pay as regular soldiers for themselves, their horses, their subsistence, and transportation, to Congress, under the assurance of the department commander that they will be paid.

The conflict is upon us, and all good citizens are called upon to do their duty for the defence of their homes and families.

In testimony whereof, I have hereunto set my hand and caused the great seal of the Territory of Colorado to be affixed this 11th day of August, A. D. 1864.
John Evans.[14]

Governor Pitkin's Order: Bring in, Dead or Alive, All Hostile Indians

It was not until October 13, 1879, that the newspapers reported on the Neeker Agency incident. The headlines blazed, "A SCENE OF SLAUGHTER." Governor Pitkin denounced the attack in no uncertain terms, and incidentally pointed out that 12,000,000 acres could be opened with the removal of the Utes. [Frederick Pitkin, quoted in the Denver Daily News, October 13, 1879.] Herein lay the perfect opportunity to be rid of the Indians for good.[15]

The Governor mustered two companies of the Colorado militia: His War Order No. 1 was to "bring in, dead or alive, all hostile Indians found off the reservation ... consider all Indians off the reservation hostile, and bring them in, dead or alive, and we will determine their docility afterward."[16]

In the view of Colorado citizens, the Utes were both dangerous and an impediment to progress. ... Pitkin commented to the press: "It will be impossible for the Indians and whites to live in peace hereafter ... This attack had no provocation and the whites now understand that they are liable to be attacked in any part of the state ... *My idea is that, unless removed by the government they must necessarily be exterminated.*" (Emphasis added).[17]

Notes: Indian Policy of Territorial Governments

1. Report of Governor of Arizona to Secretary of Interior (Teller), H.R. Exec. Doc. No. 1, 48th Congress, 1st Sess. (1883), p. 9.
2. Report of Governor of Arizona (Murphy) to Secretary of Interior (Noble), 1892. Report of the Secretary of the Interior; Being Part of the Message and Documents Communicated to the Two Houses of Congress at the Beginning of the Second Session of the Fifty-second Congress: In Five Volumes. Volume III, U.S. Government Printing Office, 1893, p. 28.
3. Report of Governor of Dakotas (Church) to Secretary of Interior (Lamar), 1887. H.R. Exec. Doc. No. 1, 50th Cong., 1st Sess. (1887), p. 780.
4. Report of Governor of Idaho (Stevenson) to Secretary of Interior (Lamar), 1886.
5. Report of Governor of Idaho (Stevenson) to Secretary of Interior, 1887. H.R. Exec. Doc. No. 1, 50th Cong., 1st Sess. (1887), pp. 823-824, 828, 843.
6. Report of Governor of Montana to Secretary of Interior. H.R. Exec. Doc No. 1, 48th Cong., 2nd Sess. (1884), pp. 559-560.
7. Report of Governor of New Mexico (Ross) to Secretary of Interior (Lamar). H.R. Exec. Doc. No. 1, 49th Cong., 1st Sess. (1885), p. 1011.
8. Report of Governor of Utah (Thomas) to Secretary of Interior (Noble), 1891. H.R. Exec. Doc. No. 1, 52nd Cong., 1st Sess. (1891), pp. 367-368, 375.
9. Report of Governor of Washington (Squire) to Secretary of Interior (Teller). H.R. Exec. Doc No. 1, 48th Cong., 2nd Sess. (1884), p. 613.
10. Report of Governor of Wyoming to Secretary of Interior. H.R. Exec. Doc.

No. 1, 45th Cong., 3rd Sess. (1878), 1139.

11. Report of Governor of Wyoming (Warren) to Secretary of Interior (Noble). H.R. Exec. Doc. No. 1, 51st Cong., 1st Sess. (1889), pp. 586, 593.

12. Laws of the Colonial and State Governments, Relating to Indians and Indian Affairs, from 1633 to 1831, Inclusive: With an Appendix Containing the Proceedings of the Congress of the Confederation ; and the Laws of Congress, from 1800 to 1830, on the Same Subject. United States. Continental Congress, United States. Thompson and Homans, 1832, p. 223.

13. Report of the Commissioner of Indian Affairs to the Secretary of the Interior, United States. Office of Indian Affairs. Colorado Superintendency. U.S. Government Printing Office, 1864, pp. 218-219.

14. Report of the Commissioner of Indian Affairs to the Secretary of the Interior, United States. Office of Indian Affairs. Colorado Superintendency. U.S. Government Printing Office, 1864, pp. 230-231.

15. Athearn, Frederic J. An Isolated Empire: A History of Northwestern Colorado. 3rd ed. Colorado Bureau of Land Management, Cultural Resource Series No. 2, 1982, p. 53.

16. U.S. Congress, House, Extinguishment of Indian Title, 46th Cong., 1st sess., Congressional Record, vol. 9, pt. l, 21 April 1870, 615.

17. Report of the Commissioner of Indian Affairs to the Secretary of the Interior, United States. Office of Indian Affairs. U.S. Government Printing Office, 1879, p. 69.

9: COLORADO

Indians in Colorado Pre-Contact

Prior to the Europeans, Colorado was historically populated by three tribes of Indians. Of these groups, the Ute were centered in the mountains and canyonlands, and the Arapaho and Cheyenne on the Great Plains. The hunting or wintering sites overlapped along the Front Range of the Rocky Mountains. Comanche and Kiowa also lived and hunted within the present boundaries of the state.

Within the Ute tribe there were subdivisions including Uncompahgre, Weeminuche, Muache, Capote, and others. These subdivisions related primarily to geographic locations and not major cultural differences. The Ute expanded to the point that by the time Europeans came into their land, they ranged from Pike's Peak on the east to the Great Salt Lake on the west, and from Taos in the south, to Wyoming's Green River country on the north.[1]

In 1840, the Kiowa, Comanche, and Lakota joined the Cheyenne and Arapaho in an unprecedented alliance to resolve territorial disputes and counter the growing number of emigrants headed west.

Ute Bands

The largest of the Ute Bands lived in west-central Colorado along the Gunnison and Uncompahgre river valleys. These were the Tabeguache (Taviwatch) or Uncompahgre Utes. North of them the Parianuche (Parusanuch), or Grand Valley Utes, lived along the Colorado River. The Yampa River Valley was home to the Yampa band, which also occupied North and Middle Parks. When the White River Agency was established in Meeker, the Grand Valley and Yampa bands came to be known as the White River Utes. In the Uintah Basin near today's

Dinosaur National Monument in northeastern Utah and northwestern Colorado, were the Uintah Utes. The Tabeguache, White River, and Uintah bands together are now known as the Northern Utes. For the next 20 years there was the constant pressure on the Utes to relinquish their land by the U.S., the State of Colorado, and mining and railroad interests. This was done by a series of negotiations and treaties entered into by the U.S.

Contact with Spain

In 1595, the viceroy of New Mexico selected Juan de Onate y Salazar to lead an expedition of northern New Spain in search of gold. Onate began the expedition in January 1598 with 400 settlers, soldiers, and livestock. The expedition crossed the Rio Grande at present-day El Paso, Texas, and on April 30, 1598, he claimed all of New Mexico for King Phillip II of Spain, including what is today southern Colorado. That summer, his party established the colony of New Mexico for Spain and became New Mexico's first governor. Hearing about plentiful game to the north in the San Luis Valley, Oñate sent an expedition there to hunt bison. The party came across a village of about fifty Ute lodges; the Utes greeted them warmly, and some of the Ute men volunteered to help the inexperienced Spaniards hunt bison. Their relations with the Utes remained friendly until the 1630s, when Spaniards attacked a band and took about eighty Utes as slaves. Thereafter, Utes began raiding Spanish parties and communities for livestock and goods.

During the seventeenth and eighteenth centuries, the San Luis Valley remained largely indigenous, barely even a remote outpost of the Spanish Empire. Comanche raids on New Mexican communities increased during the eighteenth century.

In 1776, the Dominguez and Escalante Expedition, explored and mapped the region from Santa Fe, New Mexico to as far north as today's Dinosaur National Monument in Colorado to the Uintah Valley and Salt Lake in Utah and across northeastern Arizona. The Franciscan Friars Atanasio Domínguez and Silvestre Vélez de Escalante were searching for a route to the missions in Monterrey, CA. They encountered the Utes (Yutahs) who provided two guides who they named "Silvestre," and "Joaquin," a 12 year old boy who helped guide the party through its entire journey. They traveled and headed west to the Uintah Valley where they reached Salt Lake. Another 12 year old guide from the Timpanagos who they named Jose Maria helped them out from near Provo to Cedar City. With winter approaching, they drew lots to decide whether to continue on or return to Santa Fe. They chose to return to Santa Fe, but without a guide they lost a significant amount of time finding a site to ford the Colorado River.

Their prolific and renowned cartographer, Don Bernardo Miera y Pacheco, was a retired military engineer who lived in Santa Fe. He had earlier mapped "Nuevo Mexico" which described the entire province, its twenty-two pueblos, population statistics, livestock numbers, and men and military equipment available for defense. His map is crucial in understanding the extent of the land inhabited by various Ute Bands ("Yutahs") and the Arapaho ("Rapahu") in western Colorado. Traveling into Utah, he mapped the Timpanogos who lived in the Utah and Salt Lake Valleys and "indios barbones"—bearded Indians in central Utah. Traveling south into Arizona, he mapped the region inhabited by the Havasupai ("Cosninas") and the Hopis ("Moquinos"). Coming back into New Mexico, he mapped the Pueblos of Zuni and Acoma. His legendary map opened up the region to future exploration and trade.

In 1779, the Spanish war party of Juan Bautista de Anza picked up Ute and Jicarilla Apache warriors on its way to fight the Comanche leader Cuerno Verde who had been raiding villages in northern New Mexico. With 800 men and 2,500 horses, de Anza led an expedition from New Mexico through Colorado and across the Arkansas River to engage the Comanches. Cornering the chief near Rye, Colorado, the campaign killed him and several other headmen, which eventually precipitated the longest-lasting peace treaty ever signed by the Comanche with any of the governments of Spain, Mexico, or the U.S.

Colorado's first permanent settlers were citizens of Spain who made homes along the southern edges of Colorado settling in the San Luis Valley.

Mexican Land Grants

After winning independence from Spain in 1821, Mexico issued land grants in present-day New Mexico and Colorado to encourage settlement as a bulwark against rising American influence in the Southwest. In 1833, the Mexican government awarded the Conejos Grant, roughly spanning land between the Rio Grande and Conejos Creek near present-day Alamosa, to fifty families. In 1841, Mexico gave the Canadian trader Charles Beaubien and Mexican official Guadalupe Miranda the contested Maxwell Grant. In 1843-44, the Luis Maria Baca Grant No. 4 and the Sangre de Cristo Grant were granted in south-central Colorado (present-day Costilla County).

U.S. Military Expeditions

The U.S. Military Expeditions were part of the contested struggle for possession of the west. A large part of this vast domain was claimed by Spain and, thereafter, Mexico. Part of the expeditions included gathering intelligence on Spain's control of the southwest, which the U.S. might challenge. The U.S. knew Spain was too weak to go to war to defend its 'discovery' claim in the southwest.

When France sold Louisiana to the U.S. in 1803 it conveyed: "for ever and in full Sovereignty the said territory [Louisiana] with all its rights and appurtenances as fully and in the Same manner as they have been acquired by the French Republic in virtue of the above mentioned Treaty concluded with his Catholic Majesty."[1] (Treaty of San Ildefonso, 1800). France's Foreign Minister Talleyrand was deliberately vague and unhelpful about the boundaries: "You must take it as we received it."[2] Congress approved the purchase on October 31, 1803, and the U.S. took possession on December 20, 1803.

After the Purchase, President Jefferson wanted to claim as much territory as possible given the vague description of the boundaries. There was limited geographical knowledge of North America, as well as confusion resulting from the competing territorial claims of the European powers. In an 1803 Letter, Jefferson claimed land on the west to the Rio Norte or Bravo.

From Thomas Jefferson to Thomas Paine, Monticello, August 10, 1803

> The unquestioned extent of Louisania [sic] on the sea is from the Iberville to the Mexicana river, *or perhaps the high lands dividing that from the Missisipi [sic]*. it's original boundary however as determined by occupation of the French was Eastwardly to the river Perdido (between Mobile & Pensacola) & Westward to the Rio Norte or Bravo. (Emphasis added).[6]

In 1805, U.S. Army General James Wilkinson ordered Lieutenant Zebulon Pike to lead 20 soldiers on a reconnaissance of the upper Mississippi River. On a second expedition in 1806-1807, Pike ultimately explored the west and southwest, including today's Kansas, Colorado, New Mexico, Texas and Louisiana. Most importantly, Pike was to ascertain what the Spanish were doing along the uncertain southwestern border of the Louisiana Territory. A letter between Pike and Wilkinson, written on July 22, 1806, directed Pike to scout as close as possible to Santa Fe, allowing for the possibility that he might be captured by Spanish authorities. If discovered, he would use the cover story that he had become lost while en route to Natchitoches, Louisiana. On February 26, 1807, a troop of Spanish soldiers rode up to Pike's stockade and informed him that he was in Spanish territory. The Spanish patrol rounded up the frostbitten stragglers, escorting the entire party to Santa Fe. Pike's papers were confiscated, and he was sent south to Chihuahua. Neither Pike nor his men were mistreated; the majority were returned to the U.S. at Natchitoches on June 30, 1807. The Spanish Governor was reprimanded by his King for releasing Pike before receiving an apology from the U.S. for trespassing.

Major Stephen Long's 1819-1820 expedition mapped the central Plains to the Rocky Mountains. Long was the first Army explorer to include professional scientists on his survey team. He also was the first to use a steamboat for exploration purposes. Setting out from Council Bluffs, he crossed the plains to Colorado, explored the Front Range of Colorado, and then followed the Rocky Mountain Front down into New Mexico.

The orders regarding these military expeditions included gathering detailed intelligence, not only on Spain, and thereafter, Mexico, but on the number, strength, allies and military capacity of Indians should the U.S. continue its westward expansion.

Zebulon Pike: 1805-06; 1806-07; Upper reaches of the Mississippi; the southwest. Pike's Peak; explored much of the Mississippi's upper regions.

Stephen A. Long: 1819-20; Plains along the Platte River to the Colorado Rockies. Explored and named Long's Peak; measured the height of Pike's Peak; collected plant, rock, and animal specimens for public viewing; more accurate maps.

John C. Fremont: 1842; Plains up the Platte River to Fort Laramie to the South Pass gateway to Oregon to the Wind River Range. Removed the label of "Great American Desert" from the plains which provided for farming and supplies for emigrants.

James W. Abert & Thomas Fitzpatrick: 1845-46; New Mexico, Oklahoma, Texas. Mapped locations of water, wood, and grass; information on Comanche and Kiowa; described Rio Grande Valley, its uses, and possibilities for region.

William H. Emory: 1846; New Mexico, California. Provided intelligence that NM would require irrigation, scarce fertile lands that would make slavery unprofitable; Mexican government not responsive to citizens, therefore there would be little local resistance to American roads or railroads; first accurate maps of Southwest.

1849: Treaty of Abiquiú - U.S. Jurisdiction Over Capote and Muache Ute Bands, Safe Passage for Settlers, Presence of Military Forts and Trading Posts - No Cession of Lands

The Utes initially benefited from the fact that the large immigrant trails and the transcontinental railroad skirted their mountain home but it didn't last long. The one point of friction between the white and Ute cultures originated with the movement of settlers from New Mexico into the fertile San Luis Valley in south-central Colorado.

In late December 1849, in his capacity as Indian Agent, James Calhoun brought together Ute leaders—mostly from the Capote and Muache bands—and American officials at Abiquiú, a village along the Chama River in northern New Mexico.

The U.S. sought to *pacify the Territory of New Mexico and the San Luis Valley which had been acquired as a result of the Mexican-American War.* The U.S. sought *free passage" of American citizens through Ute territory, as well as for the construction of "military posts," Indian agencies, and "trading houses" on Ute lands.* In return, it promised to protect Utes against depredations by American citizens, as well as provide "such donations, presents, and implements" deemed necessary for the Utes to "support themselves by their own industry." These "donations" would come in the form of annuities—annual deliveries of food and supplies. The Treaty involved no cession of lands and did not set apart any reservation to the Indians, though it clearly recognized the rights of the Utes in the territory covered by the Treaty.

The resulting Treaty of Abiquiú (9 Stats., 984) was signed by twenty-eight leaders of the "Utah tribe of Indians," placing the Utes *"lawfully and exclusively under the jurisdiction of the [U.S.] government"* in *"perpetual peace and amity."* (Emphasis added).

The agency designated to provide the "donations" was in Taos which made securing the promised annuities difficult. The Treaty failed to give the Utes the reliable food supply they had sought through diplomacy. More importantly, it failed to protect the Indian lands from being overrun by whites and two more treaties would be demanded of the Utes to secure mineral resources.

This is an instance recognized by General John Pope regarding Indian treaties in his 1878 speech:

> *The first demand by the Indians, as the principal condition of the treaty, is that the white man shall not intrude upon his reserved lands, nor destroy his game, nor interfere with his people.* This condition is the first and most important to the Indian. In every case of which I know anything, it has been readily agreed to, and the government, through its commissioners, binds itself to this obligation. Is it possible that any white man, official or private citizen, believes that, even if the government intends to enter into this obligation in good faith, it is practicable to fulfill the engagement? *What means has the government to enforce compliance?* (Emphasis added).[4]

U.S. Indian Treaties

The high cost of military campaigns impressed upon the U.S. the need for negotiations with Indians. The Treaties entered into weren't for the benefit of the Indians—they were to satisfy the U.S.' Manifest Destiny political goal. From the time of George Washington the goal of a continental empire from sea to sea was the overriding plan. The Indians were an impediment and would be dealt with initially by a three prong strategy—(1) use settlers to achieve military objectives of seizing territory and exterminating or otherwise controlling Indians; (2) implement an administrative policy of forced removal with the aid of the military and private contractors; and (3) when more land was needed for emigrants enter into treaties of peace or treaties of cession of land.

1851: Treaty of Fort Laramie - Safe Passage for Settlers, Presence of Military Forts

In 1834, during the height of the fur trade in the American West, American traders William Sublette and Robert Campbell established what became Fort Laramie in present-day Wyoming, at the confluence of the Laramie and North Platte Rivers. The Cheyenne, Arapaho, and Sioux often gathered there to trade bison robes for weapons, iron cookware, coffee, and other American goods. In the 1840s, increasing numbers of white migrants began traveling west to settle in the newly acquired territories of Oregon and California. Fort Laramie, then known as Fort John, became a popular waystation for migrants traveling the Great Platte River Road. Their wagon trains drove away game, trampled grazing grasses for bison, and the emigrants consumed timber and other important resources on the Great Plains. This put the migrants in competition with the Cheyenne, Arapaho, and other local Indians.

In 1851, the U.S. invited all the Indian Nations of the northern Great Plains to gather for a treaty council at the mouth of Horse Creek, near Fort Laramie, where Nebraska and Wyoming now meet. The U.S.' purpose was to *ensure a protected right-of-way for the emigrants crossing Indian lands and the establishment of military posts*.

In attendance were: Oglala Sioux, Assiniboine, Arapaho, Shoshone (attended though not invited), Brule Sioux, Mandan, Crow, Arikara, Rees, Cheyenne, Gros Ventre, Hidatsa and Snake. The Comanche, Kiowa and Apache refused to attend.

It was the largest gathering of Plains Indian Nations in American history— more than ten thousand people (men, women and children) attended. The Fort Laramie Treaty is also referred to as the Horse Creek Treaty since the treaty location had to be moved from the Fort due to insufficient forage for the thousands of horses.

The 1851 Treaty of Fort Laramie recognized the sovereignty and territories of the different signatory tribes who pledged an end to warfare and to live in peace with one another. To compensate for their diminishing subsistence base, the Nations were promised annuities, so long as white travelers were allowed free and unmolested travel across Colorado and the Army could build and man forts. Many of the emigrants were headed for California and Oregon.

Whereas the government promised to distribute $50,000 in annuities among all nine nations for fifty years, the U.S. Senate ratified the treaty, adding Article 5, which *adjusted the compensation from fifty to ten years*, if the tribes accepted the changes. All tribes accepted the change with the exception of the Crow.

Each nation then selected delegates to tour the eastern U.S.; these trips were designed to showcase the wealth and power of the U.S. so that Indian nations would abide by the treaty.[5]

The government's failure to deliver the promised annuities undercut the Treaty's two fundamental goals: to preserve peace between Indian nations and between Indians and whites. As their food sources diminished and government annuities failed to supplement the loss, the Indian Nations fought each other for the best hunting grounds and attacked settlers intruding upon their lands.

1853: Commissioner: Cheyenne, Arapaho and Western Sioux Starving

In 1853, Thomas Fitzpatrick, Indian Agent, Upper Platte and Arkansas, reported that the Cheyenne, Arapaho, and western Sioux were "in a starving state ... Their women are pinched with want, and their children constantly crying out with hunger."[6]

1854–1855: Military Campaign against Utes

On December 25, 1854, a small band of Mouache Utes, under the leadership of Tierra Blanca, killed four trappers. The Army gathered a force of twelve companies of Regulars and militia at Fort Garland to pursue the Utes but quickly came to the conclusion that winter was not the best season for active campaigning in the Rockies. The size of the Army force, however, impressed the Utes, who had avoided contact with the troops by melting away into the mountains. A peace was negotiated in the fall of 1855.

U.S. Indian Agencies in Colorado

The federal regulation of Indian affairs in the U.S. first included development of the position of Indian agent in 1793 under the Second Trade and Intercourse Act. The legislation also authorized the President to "appoint such persons, from time to time, as temporary agents to reside among the Indians," and guide them into acculturation of American society by changing their agricultural practices and domestic activities. Eventually, the U.S. ceased using the word "temporary" in the Indian agent's job title.

The two principal types of field jurisdictions of the Office of Indian Affairs in the 19th century were superintendencies and agencies, which would come into play in Colorado. Superintendents of Indian Affairs for a specific locality existed from approximately 1803 until 1878, when the last Superintendency was abolished. A Superintendent of Indian Affairs was an administrator whose duties included the supervision of relations between the tribes and non-Indians, the supervision of the conduct and accounts of agents responsible to them, the communication of instructions from the Commissioner to agents, and the granting of leaves of absence to subordinates. It was also common practice for them to receive contract bids, enter into contracts, and issue annuities to the Indians. Under each superintendent were agents, subagents, or special agents immediately responsible for one or more tribes. The records of the Superintendencies evidence the broad areas of responsibility including documents relating to negotiation and enforcement of treaties; land surveys and allotments; Indian removal; annuity and other payments; Indian delegations; intrusions on Indian lands; traders and licenses; enforcement of federal laws and regulations; hostilities and military operations; depredation claims; location of agencies; school attendance and curricula; medical treatment; production at blacksmith, gunsmith, and wheelwright shops; construction and repair of buildings; and purchase and transportation of goods and supplies.

The St. Louis Superintendency was established in 1822 and was responsible for the agencies located in the Midwest, including Colorado. It operated until 1851, when it was succeeded by the Central Superintendency. The Central Superintendency was originally responsible for most of the Indians in what is now Kansas and Nebraska, and in the upper regions of the Missouri, Platte, and Arkansas Rivers in the Dakotas, Wyoming, and Colorado. The agencies assigned to the Central Superintendency include the Upper Platte, Upper Missouri, Upper Arkansas, Ponca, and Yankton agencies. The Colorado Superintendency of Indian Affairs was not established until 1861 when Colorado received Territorial status. The Territorial Governor served as the *ex officio* Superintendent of Indian Affairs. John Evans assumed that position on May 16, 1862.

The Tabeguache and Muache Utes were attached to the Taos Agency in northern New Mexico under the jurisdiction of Kit Carson by 1856. Despite being administered by the Taos Agency, the Tabeguache Utes resided in western and south-central Colorado, including the Uncompahgre and San Luis Valleys. The Muache band roamed farther south and was more closely attached to the Taos Agency. Annuity goods—annual payments made to Indians as stipulated by treaties—for the Tabeguache and Muache Utes were distributed at Conejos in the San Luis Valley beginning in 1858. For convenience, the goods were stored and distributed at Lafayette Head's ranch at Conejos in 1859. In order to more effectively administer the Tabeguache Utes, the Conejos Agency was established in 1860 at Head's ranch, and Head was appointed Indian agent.

The Indian agencies in Colorado were as follows:

Upper Arkansas Indian Agency

The Upper Arkansas Indian Agency was established in 1855 at Bent's New

Fort to superintend Nations along the upper part of the Arkansas River in eastern Colorado and western Kansas. The original agency was assigned to the Central Superintendency and was under its supervision until the establishment of the Colorado Superintendency in 1861. In 1866 the agency was moved to Kansas.[7]

Conejos Indian Agency (Utes)

Annuity goods—annual payments made to Indians as stipulated by treaties—for the Tabeguache and Muache Utes were distributed at Conejos in the San Luis Valley beginning in 1858. For convenience, the goods were stored and distributed at Lafayette Head's ranch at Conejos in 1859. In order to more effectively administer the Tabeguache Utes, the Conejos Agency was established in 1860 at Head's Ranch, and Head was appointed Indian agent. After the Treaty of 1868 established a reservation for the Utes west of the Rocky Mountains, a new agency was established in 1869 on the reservation and the Conejos Agency was abandoned.

Middle Park Indian Agency (Utes)

The Middle Park Agency was established in 1862 for the Grand River, Uinta, and Yampa Utes. After the Treaty of 1868 established a reservation for the Utes west of the Rocky Mountains in Colorado, the agency was moved to a location on the White River in 1869 and became known as the White River Agency.

Denver Special Indian Agency (Utes)

To deal with the large number of Utes off the reservation, the Board of Indian Commissioners appointed Robert Campbell and Felix R. Brunot to a committee to meet with Colorado Governor Edward M. McCook in 1870. They concluded that the best solution was to establish a special agency in Denver rather than create a conflict by forcing the Utes onto the reservation. These off-reservation Utes received their annuity goods—items promised to them by treaty in return for their land—at the Denver Agency. McCook's brother-in-law, James B. Thompson, began serving the Utes in Denver in 1869, when he arrived in Colorado as McCook's private secretary. On January 17, 1871, Thompson was officially appointed the special agent for the Denver Agency; he also took over the administration of Indian affairs in Colorado from the Governor The Agency served Utes who were accustomed to collecting supplies from Denver's Middle Park Agency during the 1860s, even though reassigned to a reservation west of the Rocky Mountains. It was decommissioned in November 1874 but this did not prevent Utes from spending the winter in the Denver area. They still came to Denver expecting provisions so the agency was reestablished and operational through 1875.

Los Piños Indian Agency (Utes)

Under provisions of the 1868 treaty, an agency was to be established by the Office of Indian Affairs on the Los Piños River in extreme southern Colorado to serve some of the Ute bands. For various reasons the agency could not be constructed on the river. Instead, it was established in the high mountains near Cochetopa Pass south of Gunnison, which was close to the eastern boundary of the new reservation. It could not be easily supplied and the surrounding land was unsuitable for growing crops. It was relocated in 1875 to the Uncompahgre Valley. It was abandoned in 1881 after the Utes were forcibly removed by the military to Utah in the fall of 1881.

White River Ute Agency (Utes)

The White River Ute Agency at Meeker, Colorado was established at the same time as the first Los Piños Agency under provisions of the Treaty of 1868. The agency was intended to serve the White River Ute band as well as some of the other bands from northwestern Colorado. As the site of the Meeker Incident and the Battle of Milk Creek, the White River Agency was the focal point of important episodes of violence between Indians and whites that led to the removal of many Utes from the state. It was abandoned after the White River Utes were forced into Utah.

1857: Denver City Promoters

Denver already had promoters in 1857. The Denver City Town Company was formed in 1858 with the following members: E. I. Stout, president; General William Larimer, E. E. Whitsitt, James Reed, J. H. Dudley, Charles Blake, Norman Welton, A. J. Williams, General John Clancy, Samuel Curtis, Ned Wyncoop, McGaa and Charles Nichols. Most of their names have been perpetuated in the names of Denver's prominent streets.[8]

1858: Discovery of Gold in Colorado

The first publicized discovery of gold in Colorado was in 1858. Prospectors traveling west to California's Gold Rush panned small amounts of gold at Cherry Creek, the South Platte River, and Ralston Creek. William Green Russell and a team of prospectors traveled to the South Platte River the next year and discovered gold at the Little Dry Creek which is credited with launching the Pike's Peak Gold Rush in 1859. The immediate rush to the Denver area resulted in important placer finds near Idaho Springs and Central City. Panning gold from stream and terrace gravels is called placer mining, derived from the Spanish word placer or "pleasure"—the gold is available at one's pleasure.

Gold and other ore deposits were mostly in a northeast-trending belt, known as the Colorado mineral belt. From near Boulder on the northeast this belt extended southwest to the San Juan Mountains and beyond. The Cripple Creek District, the largest gold producer in Colorado, and several minor districts lay southeast of the mineral belt.

1859: Clear Creek Gold Discovery

In January of 1859, the prospector George A. Jackson found the first substantial amount of gold in Colorado where Chicago Creek empties into Clear Creek in present day Idaho Springs.

1859: Miners' Court

The first miners' court was created in the Gregory District of Gilpin County, in 1859. Subsequent courts followed the Gregory model. The Gold Hill District was organized by a mass convention on July 23, 1859. Boulder's town company was organized on February 10, 1859.

1859: Colorado Mineral Belt, Domain of Arapaho, Cheyenne and Ute

The gold discoveries in the Colorado mineral belt were made on Indian land. Without regard to their rights, prospectors, miners and mercantilists flooded onto their land. The year 1859 was a critical one for Colorado's Indians. Commissioner Greenwood informed Secretary Thompson that the U.S. had essentially deprived the Indians living in or hunting and gathering or visiting spiritual sites in the Colorado area of any means of traditional subsistence.

> A crisis has now, however, arrived in our relations with them. Since the discovery of gold in the vicinity of "Pike's Peak," the emigration has immensely increased; the Indians have been driven from their local haunts and hunting grounds, and the game so far killed off or dispersed, that it is now impossible for the Indians to obtain the necessary subsistence from that source. In fact, we have substantially taken possession of the country and deprived them of their accustomed means of support. ... They have also been brought to realize that

a stern necessity is impending over them; that they cannot pursue their former mode of life, but must entirely change their habits, and, in fixed localities, look to the cultivation of the soil and the raising of stock for their future support. There is no alternative to providing for them in this manner but to exterminate them, which the dictates of justice and humanity alike forbid. *They cannot remain as they are; for, if nothing is done for them, they must be subjected to starvation, or compelled to commence robbing and plundering for a subsistence.* (Emphasis added).[9]

1859: Upper Platte, Agent Twiss, Diminution of Game

On August 16, 1859, Thomas S. Twiss, the U.S. Indian Agent for the Upper Platte, submitted his grave concerns of possible Indian hostilities due to the incursion of whites on their lands to the Superintendent of Indian Affairs. His report, regarding the Arapaho and Cheyenne, was *"animated solely with a desire to prevent their utter extinction."* (Emphasis added). His Report was brought to the attention of the Senate in response to a resolution they passed for an "estimate of the amounts that will be required to hold councils with certain Indians of the plains and in the State of Minnesota." It was referred to the Committee on Indian Affairs.[10]

Agent Twiss expressed the fears of the Indians regarding the diminution of game due to penetration of their hunting grounds by whites:

> The state of the Indian mind among the wild tribes is one of extreme suspicion in all matters relating to the preservation of game, their only means of subsistence; and when it disappears the Indian must perish. Hence it has happened that, in some parts of the prairie country, the Indians have stopped white people, and even United States topographical parties, when they have endeavored to penetrate to their hunting grounds, and have turned them back, pretty roughly too, for fear that the buffalo would be destroyed or scared away, and never return again. According to Agent Twiss, the buffalo "no longer covers the valleys of the North Platte and its tributaries, and makes the prairie appear black, as formerly, as far as the eye could scan the horizon..."[11] A Sioux chief in council expressed his fear regarding the discovery of gold: "On the south fork of the Platte the white people are finding gold, and the Arapahoes and Cheyennes have no longer any hunting grounds. Our

~ 150 ~

country has become very small, and, before our children are grown up, we shall have no more game." [12]

This emigration, according to Agent Twiss, had resulted in "a tendency to irritate, excite, and exasperate the Indian mind, and fill it with alarm and jealousy to such a degree that an interruption to our friendly relations with the wild tribes may occur at any moment." [13]

1859: Upper Arkansas Agency, Sup. Bent, Encroachments of Whites on Indian Lands

Agent Twiss' fears were confirmed by the renowned Agent Bent. He announced that the Cheyenne and Arapaho were willing to treat with the U.S., due to the influx of gold miners taking over choice Indian lands and emigration through their hunting grounds reducing their subsistence on game.

> They ask for pay for the large district known to contain gold, and which is already occupied by the whites, who have established the county of Arapahoe and many towns. They further ask annuities in the future for such lands as they may cede and relinquish to the government. ... [14]

The Cheyenne and Arapaho demand for pay for the gold in the region was fully warranted based on Agent Bent's substantiation and confirmation:

> *The explorations of this season have established the existence of the precious metals in absolutely infinite abundance and convenience of position.* The concourse of whites is therefore constantly swelling, and incapable of control or restraint by the government. This suggests the policy of promptly rescuing the Indians, and withdrawing them from contact with the whites ... (Emphasis added). [15]

In accord with Agent Twiss' report, Agent Bent *warned* of possible predatory attacks on whites by the Comanches:

> A smothered passion for revenge agitates these Indians, perpetually fomented by the failure of food, the encircling encroachments of the white population, and the exasperating sense of decay and impending extinction with which they are surrounded. ... A desperate war of starvation and extinction is therefore imminent and inevitable, unless prompt measures shall prevent it. [16]

~ 151 ~

1859: Commissioner Report to Secretary Interior, Critical State

In November 1859, Commissioner Greenwood, in his Report to the Secretary of the Interior Jacob Thompson, compelled "*special attention* to the reports of Messrs. Twiss and Bent, the agents for the Indians within the upper Platte and Arkansas agencies, embracing Sioux, Cheyenne, Arapahoe, Comanche, Kioway, and a portion of the Apache Indians. There is evidently a very critical state of affairs existing within those agencies, and serious difficulties must soon occur, unless timely measures are adopted to avert them." (Emphasis added).[17]

1860: Whites in Colorado Gold Region in Violation of Federal Law

Stephen A. Douglas pointed out on the Senate floor on May 16, 1860, that "every man in Pike's Peak is there in violation of law; every man of them has incurred the penalty of $1,000 fine and six months' imprisonment for going in violation of the Indian intercourse law, and claiming land which was under Indian title."[18]

Four memorials of residents at and near the eastern slope of the Rocky Mountains, praying for the extinguishment of the Indian title, a survey and sale of the public lands, the establishment of an assay office, and the erection of a new territory from contiguous portions of New Mexico, Utah, Kansas, and Nebraska, were communicated to President Lincoln. In an address by General O.O. Howard, he recounted Lincoln's support for the miners: "Tell the miners for me I shall promote their interests to the best of my ability because their prosperity is the prosperity of the nation, and we shall prove in a very few years that we are indeed the treasury of the world."[19]

Fort Wise

Fort Wise, established just west of Bent's New Fort in Colorado, was built in 1860 and named for Henry Wise, Governor of Virginia. That same year, the U.S. Army leased William Bent's New Trading Post, which consisted of 12 rooms surrounding a central courtyard. Bent's New Fort buildings were used as a commissary for the Fort and housed the Upper Arkansas Indian Agency. It served as an important military link on the Santa Fe Trail between Fort Leavenworth, Kansas, and Fort Union, New Mexico. In 1861, the U.S. changed the name of the Post to Fort Lyon in honor of General Nathaniel Lyon, killed at the Battle of Wilson's Creek, Missouri, on August 10, 1861. Cooperating with detachments from Fort Larned, Kansas, and Fort Union, New Mexico, its troops escorted traffic along the upper reaches of the Mountain Branch of the Santa Fe Trail from the Arkansas River to Raton Pass.

1861: Treaty of Fort Wise, Confine Cheyenne and Arapaho on Reservation, 1/13 Size of Fort Laramie Treaty Lands

Under the 1851 Treaty of Fort Laramie, there was no authority for settlers to settle or mine for gold on any of the Indians lands. The fifty thousand miners and traders who came to Colorado in 1859 alone, *squatted* on the legal homelands of the Cheyenne and Arapaho. The influential lobby of the miners and mercantilists that settled in Denver pressured the U.S. to renegotiate the 1851 Treaty and redefine Cheyenne and Arapaho lands to allow for continued settlement of the gold-rich Rocky Mountains, without fear of violence.

To this end, the U.S. sent Commissioner Greenwood to Bent's New Fort in the fall of 1860 to negotiate a treaty. It was planned to cordon the Cheyenne and Arapaho onto a subdivided, roughly triangular reservation of 4 million acres in the area near Sand Creek (bounded by the Arkansas River near the northern border of New Mexico and the Big Sandy Creek). However, only ten chiefs signed the treaty: six Cheyennes, including Black Kettle (Motevato), and four Arapahos. Cheyenne chief Black Kettle protested since under Cheyenne political doctrine all tribal and military leaders (most of whom were not in attendance) had to be consulted before the treaty could be consummated. Many would later say they did not understand the terms, and had not intended to cede the lands granted them under the 1851 Fort Laramie Treaty, which *encompassed over 44 million acres*. The majority of the Cheyenne and Arapaho did not move to the Reservation which was *one-thirteenth the size of their former territory*. The Indian Office considered the Treaty of Fort Wise to be applicable only to those bands whose leaders had agreed to it. Historian Frank Hall in his 1895 History of Colorado concurred with the Indians that it was secured by "presents and mystification."

> A treaty made with the Cheyenne and Arapaho at Bent's Fort in 1860, procured the cession of their lands east of the mountains to the government. It was no sooner signed than regretted. *They had been persuaded to the point of affixing their names to the instrument which dispossessed them of their ancient heritage by the usual means, presents and mystification.* The more the act was contemplated the more resolute they became to expel the settlers and regain what they had foolishly surrendered. (Emphasis added).[20]

The Treaty was signed by President Lincoln on February 15, 1861.

Younger Cheyenne and Arapaho, especially those in the Cheyenne Dog

Soldiers and other warrior societies, refused to abide by the terms of the Treaty. For more than a decade after the Treaty, the Dog Soldiers and similar groups staged raids throughout eastern Colorado, plundering small stagecoach and later railroad station towns.

It was on that reservation, along Sand Creek in present-day Kiowa County, that Colonel John Chivington and the Third Colorado Volunteers slaughtered peaceful Cheyenne and Arapaho—mostly women, children, and the elderly—in 1864.

1861: Colorado Established as Territory

On February 28, 1861, Colorado was established as a Territory. John Evans was appointed as Governor and *ex oficio* Superintendent of Indian Affairs. The Territory was opened to white settlement, even though Indian title had not been fully extinguished. Many tribes continued to view the land as theirs. Territorial officials lost no time in establishing seventeen counties, all of which were on Indian land. On November 1, 1861, the State of Colorado was divided into 17 counties. From northwest to southeast they were: Summit, Larimer, Weld, Boulder, Gilpin, Clear Creek, Arapahoe, Jefferson, Douglas, Lake, Park, El Paso, Fremont, Pueblo, Guadalupe (Conejos), Costilla, and Huerfano. There also was the Cheyenne and Arapaho reservation, abutting the eastern boundaries of El Paso and Pueblo Counties. Present-day Colorado is divided into 64 counties.

1861: Colley Appointed Indian Agent for Upper Arkansas Indian Agency

On July 26, 1861, Samuel G. Colley was appointed as the Indian Agent for the Upper Arkansas Indian Agency from 1861 to 1865. Around that same time Colley's cousin, William P. Dole, was appointed the Commissioner, which provided an avenue for communication of Indian issues.

1861: Commissioner - Difficult to Manage Indian Affairs due to Lack of Treaties

In late 1861, Commissioner William A. Dole reported the difficulties faced in the newly established Colorado Territory due to the *lack of treaties* with the tribes:

> The recent discovery of gold within this Territory has drawn thither a rapid tide of emigration, which being precipitated amongst the tribes occupying the gold bearing regions of the

Territory, thus mingling the white and red races, ***without any*** ***treaties*** contemplating so radical a change in their relations, has greatly increased the difficulties in the way of a successful administration of its Indian affairs. (Emphasis added).[21]

1861: 1ˢᵗ Regiment Colorado Volunteer Infantry Organized

On August 26, 1861, Territorial Governor Evans organized the 1st Regiment of Volunteer Infantry. John Chivington was commissioned as a Major.

1862: Colorado Territory Delegate - Miners Overrunning Ute Lands

In 1862, the *Colorado* Territorial delegate to Congress (Hiram Pitt Bennet) noted that the miners were "entirely overrunning the hunting grounds of Ute *Indians* ... taking out large quantities of *gold*, killing and driving out game," and that despite treaties conferring ostensible protection, the "demand for Ute land continued unabated." (Emphasis added).[22]

1862: Middle Park Agency Established for Utes

The Middle Park Agency was established in 1862 for the Grand River, Uinta, and Yampa Utes. The Utes spent their summers hunting elk, mule deer, and other game in Middle Park before returning to their winter camp in present-day Glenwood Springs. In addition to hunting, they were proficient gatherers and took from the landscape a wide assortment of wild berries, roots, and plants, such as the versatile yucca plant. By the mid-seventeenth century the Utes had obtained horses via the Spanish. The animals greatly improved Ute mobility and changed Ute culture.

Historian Frank Hall in his 1895 History of Colorado vividly described Middle Park and the Utes attachment to it.

> The Middle Park was the favorite home and hunting ground of the northern Ute Indians. Prior to the invasion of the Park by white settlers, quadruped and other game abounded elk, deer, mountain sheep, antelope, buffalo and all varieties of bear, including grizzlies; grouse, sage hens, ducks, geese, turkeys, etc. ... It was, in reality, the best hunting range in all the mountain region. It is watered by Grand river, a large and noble stream, fed by many strong tributaries; a beautiful and picturesque basin well grassed, and the mountains which

surround it on all sides are heavily timbered. It is a lovely place in summer, and the winters are not rigorous except upon the ranges; there the snows fall to great depths. But one of the principal attractions to the Indians was the large hot sulphur spring, to which they resorted for the cure of various ailments; a broad circular pool of hot steaming water, strongly impregnated with sulphur, soda and other minerals. It is fed by a constant flow from smaller springs in the neighboring hillside .... Trout swarmed in all the streams, and Grand lake, in which Grand river takes its rise, contains thousands of these beautiful fish. In the melting seasons Grand river runs full to the height of its banks. The Park being a sheltered retreat, well nigh inaccessible to their enemies, the plains Indians, and possessing all the advantages which an Indian desires, it is not surprising that the Utes should have made vigorous efforts to retain it.

1862: Commissioner Dole: Colorado and WASH Gold Rushes Infringing on Indian Rights

Commissioner William P. Dole, in 1862, confirmed that the Indians claimed the land:

> Considerable difficulty has been created in Colorado and Washington with the tribes in those Territories by the great increase of immigration, attracted by newly discovered gold mines. The Indians claim that the land belongs to them, while the miners, in search of new veins, are disposed to pay but little respect to their claims. A sufficient extent of country should be assigned to the Indians, and they should be protected in its enjoyment.[23]

March 1863: Delegation of Cheyenne, Arapaho, Comanche, Kiowa and Caddo Chiefs Visit Washington, DC - Dissuade Them from Joining Confederacy

According to newspaper accounts,

> "The savages were dressed in full feather—buffalo robes, Indian tanned, and bead worked leggings, with a profusion of paints upon their faces and hair, etc. ... They squatted themselves down upon the floor in a semicircle—fourteen chiefs and two squaws—and were instantly surrounded by the

curious crowd." One of the delegates, a Kiowa chief named Yellow Wolf, drew special attention for the large silver peace medal he wore, given to the Kiowas by President Thomas Jefferson. The medal had been handed down for generations and was held in the highest esteem by the tribe.

Two Cheyenne chiefs, Lean Bear and Spotted Wolf, each addressed the President, amazed at what they had seen. They pledged their tribal friendship but expressed dire concern about the encroachment of white settlers on their lands. President Lincoln responded by telling the Indians that "It is the object of this Government to be on terms of peace with you and all our red brethren. We constantly endeavor to be so. We make treaties with you, and will try to observe them" Lincoln continued, "The palefaced people are numerous and prosperous because they cultivate the earth, produce bread, and depend upon the products of the earth rather than wild game for a subsistence. This is the chief reason of the difference; but there is another. Although we are now engaged in a great war between one another, we are not, as a race, so much disposed to fight and kill one another as our red brethren."[24]

The President was speaking truthfully when he said the U.S. would *try* to observe the treaties made with the Indians. If fact, it was rarely done. As the President was seeking to secure peaceful relations with the Indians and to dissuade them from joining forces with the Confederacy, it was untoward to speak of the comparison of the two races in regard to warfare. In July of the same year, the Battle of Gettysburg would be fought with more than 50,000 estimated casualties alone, the bloodiest single battle of the Civil War. Also, many times reservations set aside were barren, arid and without irrigation.

1863: Commissioner Dole to Governor/Superintendent Evans - Get Cheyenne and Arapaho that Have Not Signed Treaty of Fort Wise to Do So

Still trying to get all of the Cheyenne and Arapaho that had not signed the Treaty of Fort Wise, on July 16, 1863, Commissioner Dole wrote to Evans: "I hope you will find it possible to arrange with the Cheyennes and Arapahos that have not signed the Treaty to do so and put them together, or make some other arrangement that will be just to them, and satisfactory to the whites."[26] In short, Superintendent Evans's top priority from the Indian Office was to secure the rest of the Indian signatories.

August 1863: Governor/Superintendent Evans Council with Cheyenne and Arapaho Leaders, Big Timbers

Governor Evans scheduled an August 27, 1863, council with Cheyenne and Arapaho leaders at Big Timbers to get them to sign the Fort Wise Treaty. After traveling there, he received news that the Cheyenne were unable to meet due to widespread sickness that was circulating among them. Even though the Cheyenne's encampment on Beaver Creek was only located approximately twenty-five miles from the Republican River Council site, Governor Evans did not elect to travel to the diphtheria and whooping cough infested camp. In numerous instances, epidemics of diphtheria and whooping cough were fatal diseases in Indian communities, with high mortality rates among children and the elderly.[27]

October 1863: Commissioner Dole Confirms Mineral Wealth of Colorado Territory

On October 31, 1863, Commissioner William P. Dole, confirmed the mineral wealth of the Colorado Territory in his Annual Report to the Secretary of the Interior, without referring to the destitution and desperation of the Cheyenne and Arapaho which might lead to war:

> *Colorado Territory, resting upon the headwaters of the Platte and Arkansas rivers and the western slope of the Rocky mountains, is rich in mineral wealth, containing gold, silver, copper, iron, coal and salt, alabaster, limestone, and gypsum.* None but gold mines have been worked to any extent; these are proving remunerative ... (Emphasis added).[28]

He stressed the importance of the Treaty negotiated with the Tabequache band of Utahs extinguishing their title to white settlements in Colorado, and more importantly to valuable mining districts:

> It will be seen that by the treaty negotiated with the Tabequache band of Utahs, as above stated, *the Indian title is extinguished to one among [sic] the largest and most valuable tracts of land ever ceded to the United States. It includes nearly all the important settlements thus far made in Colorado, and all the valuable mining districts discovered up to this time.* (Emphasis added).

October 1863: Treaty of Conejos Only with Tabeguache Utes - Cede Land East of Continental Divide and Middle Park

White immigrants occupying Ute lands during the Colorado Gold Rush of 1858-59 and after the passage of the Homestead Act in 1862, increased Ute hostilities against the trespassers.

Anticipating more treaty negotiations with the Utes, Lafayette Head, Agent at the Conejos Indian Agency in the San Luis Valley, brought a Ute delegation to Washington, DC, in February 1863. Leaders from each of Colorado's Ute bands, including the Tabeguache leaders Shavano and Ouray, rode a train to DC and visited New York City. It was clear that the trip was intended to favorably influence the U.S. position in negotiations, demonstrating that the Utes didn't stand a chance against a U.S. war given the strength in numbers and technology that would be brought to bear by the U.S.

On October 7, 1863, at the Tabeguache Agency in Conejos, Governor John Evans, ex-officio Superintendent of Indian Affairs for Colorado, Michael Steck, Simeon Whitely and Lafayette Head negotiated a treaty with the Tabeguache Band of Utes. The U.S. had hoped that more of Colorado's Ute bands would sign the treaty, but only the Tabeguache were willing to attend the negotiations in any significant number.

The Tabeguache Utes relinquished claims to all land in Colorado's Rocky Mountains east of the Continental Divide, along with Middle Park. In exchange, the Tabeguache Utes were confined to a region that stretched from the Uncompahgre Valley in the west to the Sawatch Range in the east, and from the Colorado River valley in the north to the Gunnison River valley in the south. The Utes would receive $10,000 worth of annuities—food and provisions—each year for ten years.

Since the other Ute Bands didn't agree to allow miners, soldiers, and homesteaders to trespass or build on their land, the Conejos Treaty's objective to prevent violence failed. In addition, as with most other Indian treaties, the U.S. failed to provide the promised annuities; in 1865, just one year after the Treaty was ratified, Governor Evans was already complaining about a delay in annuity shipments.[30]

November 1863: Letter from Governor Evans to Commissioner Dole regarding Indian State of War

Governor Evans wrote to Commissioner Dole in November 1863, *based on a rumor of a white settler*, that the Comanches, Apaches, Kiowas, the northern band of Arapahoes, and all of the Cheyennes, with the Sioux, were forming an alliance to go to war in the spring. Mexicans, along with the Comanche and Apache Indians, promised to help.

[Inclosure No. 2.] EXECUTIVE DEPARTMENT, Denver, November 10, 1863.

Honorable W. P. Dole, Commissioner Indian Affairs: STATEMENT.

> Having recovered an Arapaho prisoner, a squaw, from the Utes, I obtained the confidence of the Indians completely. I have lived with them (Utes) from a boy, and my wife is an Arapaho. In honor of my exploit in recovering the prisoner the Indians recently gave me a "big medicine dance" about 55 miles below Fort Lyon, on the Arkansas River, at which the leading chiefs and warriors of several of the tribes of the plains met. *The Comanches, Apaches, Kiowas, the northern band of Arapahoes, and all of the Cheyennes, with the Sioux, have pledged one another to go to war with the whites as soon as they can procure ammunition in the spring.* ... There are a great many Mexicans with the Comanche and Apache Indians, all of whom urge on the war, promising to help the Indians themselves, and that a great many more Mexicans would come up from New Mexico for the purpose in the spring. John Evans, Governor Colorado Ter. and ex officio Supt. Indian Affairs. (Emphasis added).

> MEMORANDA.
> I received letters from Major S. G. Colley, U.S. Indian agent for the Upper Arkansas, and from Major Loree, U.S. Indian agent for the Upper Platte Agency, as well as other corroboration of these statements, which were also sent forward with them. John Evans, Governor of Colorado Territory.[31]

April-May 1864: Colorado Volunteer Forces Make Unprovoked Attacks on Cheyenne Villages in Colorado Territory

Tensions between Colorado's burgeoning white population and the Cheyenne Indians reached a feverish pitch in the Spring of 1864. Colorado Volunteer forces made unprovoked attacks on Cheyenne villages in Colorado Territory. The Cheyenne retaliated by raiding mail and freight wagon trains, stage stations and outlying farms. Thus begin a period of conflict known as the Indian War of 1864.[32]

In skirmishes the 1st Regiment Colorado Volunteer Calvary announced that *this one was the beginning of the war, creating a frenzy of excitement*. The Rocky Mountain News printed a front-page editorial advocating the "extermination of the red devils" and urging its readers to "take a few months off and dedicate that time to wiping out the Indians."[33]

April 12, 1864: Battle of Fremont's Orchard, Colorado Volunteer Cavalry and Cheyenne, NE/Colorado

The U.S. War Records document the Battle of Fremont's Orchard in April 1864.

Lieutenant Dunn of the 1st Regiment Colorado Volunteer Calvary encountered a group of Cheyenne, who had reportedly stolen livestock and downed telegraph lines in northeast Colorado. Although the initial contact with the Cheyenne was friendly, hostilities broke out when Lieutenant Dunn and his men attempted to disarm the group. The resulting fight became known as the Battle of Fremont's Orchard.

Geo. L. Sanborn, Captain, First Colorado Cavalry, Commanding, requested 8,000 more cartridges for the carbines for his command.[34]

May 3, 1864: Without Provocation, Colorado Volunteer Cavalry Attacks Peaceful Cheyenne Leaders at Cedar Bluffs, KS

Under the command of Lieutenant George S. Eayre, the 1st Regiment Colorado Volunteer Cavalry, part of Chivington's command, scouting for presumed "hostiles", carried out an attack on a camp of "friendly" Cheyennes under the leadership of Black Kettle and Lean Bear. When the soldiers were seen advancing in formation as if to attack, Lean Bear went out to meet them peacefully, with a number of Indians following him. He wore the medallion presented to him in Washington and carried official papers underlining his friendliness to the United States. As the small group neared the soldiers, Lieutenant Eayre gave the order to fire. Lean Bear and another leader, Star, fell to the ground. The soldiers then rode over to them and shot them again to make sure that they were dead. The attack at Cedar Bluffs was one of three fights that Chivington's troops had with Cheyennes in a little over a month's time and inaugurated a pattern of U.S. Army murders of Indian peace leaders.[35]

Major Downing's (First Colorado Cavalry) report did not mention Lean Bear. He stated:

> I then directed the men to confine their efforts to killing as many Indians as possible, which, after a fight of about three hours, they succeeded in killing about 25 Indians and wounding about 30 or 40 more, when the carbine ammunition getting rather scarce, and the Indians so concealed that after 50 shots I could scarcely get a men [sic] ... *I believe now it is but the commencement of war with this treble [sic], which must result in exterminating them.* (Emphasis added).[36]

May 31, 1864: Letter to Major Wynkoop from Colonel Chivington, Whip Cheyennes

Colonel Chivington directed Major E.W. Wynkoop as follows:

> "[T]he Cheyennes will have to be roundly whipped — or completely wiped out — before they will be quiet. I say that if any of them are caught in your vicinity, the only thing to do is kill them." He copied Captain William H. Backus on this order.[37]

Colonel Chivington's public speeches advocated killing all of the Indians in Colorado. A month later, while addressing a gathering of church deacons, he dismissed the possibility of making a treaty with the Cheyenne: "It simply is not possible for Indians to obey or even understand any treaty. I am fully satisfied, gentlemen, that to kill them is the only way we will ever have peace and quiet in Colorado."[38]

June 1, 1864: Mystery of Hungate Family

On June 1, 1864, the Hungate Family was found murdered 25 miles southeast of Denver. Their mutilated bodies were brought to Denver and displayed, causing wide-spread panic. The coroner's inquest indicated the family "came to their death by being feloniously killed by some person or persons... supposed to be Indians(.)"[39] The Hungate Massacre of 1864 crystalized public sentiment against the Indians, even though it was not confirmed that they were responsible for the killings.

1864: Four Colorado Forts

In the summer of 1864, General Robert B. Mitchell received 1,000 troops to both patrol the Platte River Road and to establish outposts. At the same time, four sites were located and forts built throughout northeastern Colorado.[40]

Camp Rankin, renamed Fort Sedgwick, along the South Platte River near Julesburg and the stage route to Denver was assigned the responsibility of protecting wagon trains, pioneers, and the Overland Stage from Plains Indians in the area. The Iowa Volunteer Cavalry patrolled the Trail east and the Colorado Militia patrolled the area west of Julesburg. It is important to emphasize the use of volunteer militia in Colorado.

Further upstream, the South Platte Valley Station, near present day Sterling, was taken over for military use. This Station was built in 1859 and served from the beginning of the South Platte Trail to the end under four stage companies: The L&PP, the COC&PP, the Overland Stage Company, and Wells Fargo and Company.

Near the mouth of Bijou Creek, Camp Tyler was established. The construction of the post began by Colorado Volunteers under the leadership of General Sam Brown. It was soon renamed Camp Wardell as construction continued by "Galvanized Yankees" under the command of Captain Williams. These troops were Confederate soldiers released from prison because they joined the union army and moved west to fight the Indians. When the fort buildings were complete, a detachment of federal soldiers from the Missouri Cavalry under Lieutenant Colonel Willard Smith were garrisoned at the post, which was finally christened "Fort Morgan" in honor of Colonel Christopher A. Morgan. The post was about the size of one square city block.

In early 1864, Lieutenant Colonel William L. Collins, the commander of the Military Department of the Platte River, headquartered at Fort Laramie, Wyoming, came to the Cache la Poudre Valley in search of a location for a military post. To protect the Overland mail route that had recently been located through the region, Camp Collins was established on the Cache la Poudre River, near the settlement of Laporte. However, the post was short-lived, as a flood destroyed the camp in June 1864. Soon, the post was moved several miles further down the Cache la Poudre River to present-day Fort Collins. Two 11th Ohio Volunteer Cavalry companies initially manned the post. The six square mile military reservation was renamed Fort Collins the following year. Soon, the town of Fort Collins grew up around the post.[41] Instead of using typical wooden stockades, these "citadels" were constructed of sod and adobe. By 1865, the Army had its forts established.[42]

June 3, 11, 13, 1864: Governor Evans Demands Federal Troops Be Sent to Denver

Governor Evans contacted Colonel Chivington, Major-General Curtis, General Carleton (NM) and General Mitchell to dispatch troops to Denver. Due to the ongoing Civil War and their commitment to other locales, they could not commit their troops. This meant that Colorado would have to use undertrained and undisciplined volunteer soldiers to "whip these red-skin rebels into submission at once" as directed by Governor Evans.

Letter from Governor Evans to Major-General Curtis, Commanding Department of Kansas, June 3, 1864:

> It will be destruction and death to Colorado if our lines of communication are cut off, or if they are not kept so securely guarded as that freighters will not be afraid to cross the plains, especially by the Platte River, by which our subsistence comes. We are now short of provisions and but few trains are on the way. I would respectfully ask that our troops may be allowed to defend us and whip these red-skin rebels into submission at once. John Evans.[43]

> Having received a letter reporting that the Indians had driven off stock from Mr. Van Wormer's ranch, burned his house, and murdered a man who was in Mr. Van Wormer's employ, his wife, and two children, and burned his house, Governor Evans, without confirming the veracity, ordered Colonel J. M. Chivington to "send a detachment of soldiers after [them] to recover the stock and chastise the Indians. *As the Indians are probably a war party in considerable force, I suggest that the detachment be as strong as you can make it.*" (Emphasis added).[44]

In a letter from J. S. Maynard, Acting Assitant Adjutant-General, June 13, 1864, to Major C. S. Charlot, Assitant Adjutant General, Department of Kansas, Maynard expressed his concerns with the 1st Regiment Colorado Volunteer Calvary as never drilled and inefficient:

Afternoon of 11th, Indians stole 100 horses and mules from parties on Box Elder, Kiowa, and Coal Creeks, about 20 miles from Denver; burned houses on two ranches; murdered ranchman, his wife, two children; ravished woman before killing. I sent orders to Captain Davidson, commanding Company C (detained on Cherry Creek by flood), to send out detachment 50 men in pursuit, with orders to rejoin command en route to Lyon within two days; also ordered Lieutenant Chase, with detachment from Fremont's Orchard, in pursuit. *Governor Evans has called upon militia, who are unmounted, never drilled, scattered, and consequently inefficient.* Settlements so scattered they cannot be guarded. J. S. Maynard, Acting Assistant Adjutant-General. (Emphasis added).[45]

June 14, 1864: Governor Evans Wires Secretary of War to Muster Colorado Volunteer Cavalry into U.S. Service

When Governor Evans' demands for federal troops to be dispatched to Denver failed, he appealed directly to Secretary of War Edwin M. Stanton by wire on June 14, 1864, stating that Indians of the Colorado plains had committed "extensive murders" within a day's ride of Denver. He stated he could "furnish 100-days' men, if authorized to do so to fight Indians. Militia cannot be made useful, unless in the U S service, to co-operate with troops. Shall I call regiment of 100-days' men or muster into U.S. service the militia?"[46]

June 15, 1864: Major McKenny Warns General Curtis that Colorado's Volunteer Cavalry May Start Plains Indian War

Major T.I. McKenny, sent to Fort Larned by General Curtis to assess the growing Indian hostilities in western Kansas, reported:

"In regard to these Indian difficulties, I think if great caution is not exercised on our part there will be a bloody war. It should be our policy to try and conciliate them, guard our mails and trains well to prevent theft, and *stop these (military) scouting parties that are roaming over the country who do not know one tribe from the other, and who will kill anything in the shape of an Indian*. It will require but few murders on the part of our troops to unite all these warlike tribes of the plains who have been at peace for years and intermarried amongst one another." (Emphasis added).[47]

A day later, Governor Evans wrote to Major-General Curtis to *whip the "infernal barbarians":*

> The Indian alliance is so strong that I am sure our settlement or our lines of communication cannot be protected without more force. I have applied for authority to raise a regiment of 100-days' men. I have also asked General Carleton to aid on the Arkansas and below. It is very important that Colonel Chivington operate with his command on these infernal Indians, and the troops under General Mitchell at Laramie, Cottonwood, and Kearny ought to be brought into service.
>
> I have ordered camps for friendly Indians at Fort Lyon, Fort Larned, and on the Cache la Poudre, and hope all the friendly bands of the Sioux may come to Fort Laramie; then, as we whip and destroy, others will join them, and we will bring it to a close. This requires vigorous war, and it can be effected soon. As we are at home powerless but to defend, and almost so even for that purpose, we rely upon you to pour down this hostile alliance of the infernal barbarians. I appeal to you to consider our situation, and to protect our lines of communication and our settlements by whipping these Indians. John Evans. (June 16, 1864).[48]

June 27, 1864: First Proclamation, Governor Evans, Colorado Superintendency Indian Affairs, Denver

Without any direction from the President or anyone else, *Governor Evans issued a Proclamation to the Indians that the "Great Father is angry and will hunt them out and punish them."* He ordered them to go to camps for friendly Indians at Fort Lyon, Fort Larned, and on the Cache la Poudre, and for the Sioux: Fort Laramie.

> TO THE FRIENDLY INDIANS OF THE PLAINS:
> Agents, interpreters, and traders will inform the friendly Indians of the plains that some members of their tribes have gone to war with the white people. They steal stock and run it off, hoping to escape detection and punishment. In some instances they have attacked and killed soldiers and murdered peaceable citizens. For this the Great Father is angry, and will certainly hunt them out and punish them, but he does not want to injure those who remain friendly to the whites. He desires

to protect and take care of them. For this purpose I direct that all friendly Indians keep away from those who are at war, and go to places of safety. Friendly Arapahoes and Cheyennes belonging on the Arkansas River will go to Major Colley, U.S. Indian agent at Fort Lyon, who will give them provisions, and show them a place of safety. Friendly Kiowas and Comanches will go to Fort Larned, where they will be cared for in the same way. Friendly Sioux will go to their agent at Fort Laramie for directions. Friendly Arapahoes and Cheyennes of the Upper Platte will go to Camp Collins on the Cache la Poudre, where they will be assigned a place of safety and provisions will be given them.

The object of this is to prevent friendly Indians from being killed through mistake. None but those who intend to be friendly with the whites must come to these places. The families of those who have gone to war with the whites must be kept away from among the friendly Indians. The war on hostile Indians will be continued until they are all effectually subdued.[49]

Given his belligerent language about the President's "anger" and how the President intends to hunt them down and punish them, it is unlikely that any Indian would go to a military fort. Governor Evans continued to exhort war on "hostile Indians," without any authority.

August 10, 1864: Governor Evans Requests 10,000 U.S. Troops from Secretary of War; Requests Commissioner Dole to Lobby for His Troops Request

Governor Evans vituperative language accelerated on a daily basis. On August 10, 1864, he wrote to Secretary of War Stanton that Denver was on the verge of destruction from the "largest Indian war" of all the Plains Indians.

Denver, Colorado, August 10, 1864, Honorable E. M. Stanton:

The alliance of Indians on the plains reported last winter in my communication is now undoubted. A large force, say 10,000 troops, will be necessary to defend the lines and put down hostilities. Unless they can be sent at once we will be cut off and destroyed. John Evans, Governor of Colorado Territory.[50]

Denver City, Colorado, August 10, 1864. Honorable W. P. Dole, Commissioner of Indian Affairs:

> I am now satisfied that the tribes of the plains are nearly all combined in this terrible war, as apprehended last winter. *It will be the largest Indian war this country ever had, extending from Texas to the British lines, involving nearly all the wild tribes of the plains.* Please bring all the force of your department to bear in favor of speedy re-enforcements of our troops, and get me authority to raise a regiment of 100-days' mounted men. Our militia law is inoperative, and unless this authority is given we will be destroyed. John Evans, Governor of Colorado Territory and Superintendent of Indians. (Emphasis added).[51]

August 11, 1864: Governor Evans Proclamation to Citizens of Colorado Authorizing Them to Kill Hostile Indians

The next day, Governor Evans issued a Proclamation to the citizenry of Colorado that the Indians had refused to come into the forts he designated for their safety. He explicitly authorized settlers to organize killing parties targeting Indians perceived as a threat; to take captives; and to hold "for their private use and benefit" any property they capture. Evans further offered to furnish arms and ammunition and to pay any parties that will organize under the militia law of the territory to seek out and kill Indians, recruiting citizens to join the hundred-day volunteers for which Evans had been lobbying Secretary of War Stanton. He had no authority at this time to basically declare war.

> PROCLAMATION.
>
> Having sent special messengers to the Indians of the plains, directing the friendly to rendezvous at Fort Lyon, Fort Larned, Fort Laramie, and Camp Collins for safety and protection, warning them that all hostile Indians would be pursued and destroyed, and the last of said messengers having now returned, and the evidence being conclusive that most of the Indian tribes of the plains are at war and hostile to the whites, and having to the utmost of my ability endeavored to induce all of the Indians of the plains to come to said places of rendezvous, promising them subsistence and protection, which, with a few exceptions, they have refused to do:

Now, therefore, I, John Evans, governor of Colorado Territory, do issue this my proclamation, authorizing all citizens of Colorado, either individually or in such parties as they may organize, to go in pursuit of all hostile Indians on the plains, scrupulously avoiding those who have responded to my said call to rendezvous at the points indicated; also, to kill and destroy, as enemies of the country, wherever they may be found, all such hostile Indians. And further, as the only reward I am authorized to offer for such services, I hereby empower such citizens, or parties of citizens, to take captive, and hold to their own private use and benefit, all the property of said hostile Indians that they may capture, and to receive for all stolen property recovered from said Indians such reward as may be deemed proper and just therefor.

I further offer to all such parties as will organize under the militia law of the Territory for the purpose to furnish them arms and ammunition, and to present their accounts for pay as regular soldiers for themselves, their horses, their subsistence, and transportation, to Congress, under the assurance of the department commander that they will be paid.

The conflict is upon us, and all good citizens are called upon to do their duty for the defence of their homes and families.

In testimony whereof, I have hereunto set my hand and caused the great seal of the Territory of Colorado to be affixed this 11th day of August, A. D. 1864. John Evans.[52]

Analysis of Governor Evans' Second Proclamation of August 11, 1864 - University of Denver's John Evans Study Committee

The Report of the University of Denver's John Evans Study Committee, of November 2014, castigated Governor Evans.

Evans's Proclamation of August 11 essentially created an unregulated vigilante force. ... No criteria are offered for violence-hungry settlers, who have been bombarded with anti-Indian sentiment from the state, the military, and local newspapers, and who would be outfitted and paid by the state, to differentiate hostile from friendly Indians. *The proclamation does not merely carry a "vigilante tone,"... it is a blanket endorsement of citizen violence against Native people in partnership with territorial civil leadership.* (Emphasis added).

The policy laid out in this fateful document was tantamount to a declaration of war, and it was one which Evans had no legal authority to make.

As for issuing such a proclamation as Superintendent of Indian Affairs, not in any stretch of the imagination could the laws that were in place at the time be interpreted as permitting a superintendent to send cadres of armed citizens to exterminate and loot unidentified Indian people.

In the direct aftermath of these events Colonel John Chivington declared martial law on August 23, 1864, at the request of Denver businessmen who "hoped to promote enlistments of 100-day men to rid our territory of all hostile Indians."

According to Gary Roberts, Evans chillingly "told Wynkoop matters were out of his hand, and that the Indians needed to be punished more to insure peace. More than once Evans asked, 'What will I do with the 3rd Regiment if I make peace?' He told Wynkoop, 'The 3rd Regiment was raised to kill Indians, and kill Indians it must.'" Evans asserted that his credibility in Washington would be lost if, having agitated so stridently for war, he now made peace.[53]

August 12, 1864: 3rd Regiment Authorized for 100 Days

On August 12, 1864, Evans finally received his authorization for the 3rd Regiment, but the term of enlistment was only for 100 days, prompting the Rocky Mountain News to hail the 3rd as the "Hundredazers."

On August 13, 1864, Major-General Curtis: C. S. Charlot, Assistant Adjutant-General, authorized the regiment. Colonel John M. Chivington, Denver Your Governor has been authorized to raise a mounted 100-days' regiment. The ordnance, quartermaster, and commissary officers in your district will furnish the necessary supplies upon proper requisitions.[54]

August 18, 1864: Governor Evans Sends Letter to Secretary of War that Colorado Is in Danger of Destruction from Indians

On August 18, 1864, Governor Evans raised the stakes in a letter to Secretary of War Stanton:

> Extensive Indian depredations, with murder of families, occurred yesterday thirty miles south of Denver. Our lines of communication are cut, and our crops, our sole dependence, are all in exposed localities, and cannot be gathered by our scattered population. Large bodies of Indians are undoubtedly near to Denver, and we are in danger of destruction both from attacks of Indians and starvation. I earnestly request that Colonel Ford's regiment, Second Colorado Volunteers, be immediately sent to our relief. It is impossible to exaggerate our danger. We are doing all we can for our defense. Jno. Evans, Governor.[55]

August 19, 1864: Secretary of War Informs Governor Evans, due to Civil War, Shortage of U.S. Army Troops

On August 19, 1864, Secretary Stanton ordered troops to Colorado.

> Orders have been sent General Rosecrans to send the Colorado regiment of cavalry to your Territory if he can possibly spare it. EDWIN M. STANTON, Secretary of War.[56]

August 29, 1864: Chief Black Kettle and Other Chiefs Have Letters Sent to Agent Colley and Major Wynkoop Seeking Peace Talks

George Bent, son of trader William Bent and his Cheyenne wife Owl Woman, and Edmund Guerrier, another mixed blood, wrote letters to Indian Agent S.G. Colley and the commander of Fort Lyon, Major Wynkoop, on behalf of Chief Black Kettle and other chiefs, seeking peace talks in response to Governor Evans Proclamation. *As noted below, repeated efforts for peace were sought by the Cheyenne and Arapaho for naught. Governor Evans was hell-bent on war.*

Sep. 4-18, 1864: Chief Black Kettle Letter, Peace Talk Request Delivered to Major Wynkoop; Major Wynkoop Meets with Black Kettle at Smoky Hill River and Confirms Cheyenne and Arapaho Seeking Peace; Wynkoop Agrees to Escort Cheyenne and Arapaho Chiefs to Meet with Governor Evans regarding Peace

Sep. 4: Cheyenne Chief One Eye, his wife, and a Cheyenne named Min-im-mic deliver the Bent/Guerrier letter to Fort Lyon. Major Wynkoop sees this as an opportunity to restore peace and free several white hostages, who the chiefs have offered in exchange for Cheyenne prisoners.

Sep. 6-18: Major Wynkoop rides out from Fort Lyon with 127 men to meet with Chief Black Kettle and other leaders on the Smoky Hill River. During the meeting, the Cheyenne and Arapaho Chiefs agree to turn over 4 white children taken as captives. Wynkoop agrees to escort Chief Black Kettle and other Cheyenne and Arapaho chiefs to meet with Governor John Evans.[57]

Sep. 4, 1864: Governor Evans Informed by Agent Colley that Cheyenne and Arapaho Desire Peace

On Sep. 4, 1864, Governor Evans, Superintendent of Indian Affairs was informed in writing of the Cheyenne and Arapaho's plea for peace:

> Two Cheyenne Indians and one squaw have just arrived at this post. They report that nearly al (sic) of the Arapahoes, most of the Cheyennes, and two large bands of Ogallala and Brule Sioux are encamped near the "Bunch of Timbers" some 80 to 100 miles northeast of this place; that they have sent runners to the Comanches, Apaches, Kiowas, and Sioux requesting them to make peace with the whites. They brought a letter purporting to be signed by Black Kettle and other chiefs, a copy * [Not Found] of which is here inclosed. They say that the letter was written by George Bent, a half-breed son of W. W. Bent, late U.S. Indian agent for this agency. They also state that the Indians have seven prisoners. One says four women and three children, the other states three women and four children. Major Wynkoop has put these Indians in the guard-house, and requested that they be well treated in order that he may be able to rescue the white prisoners from the Indians. S. G. Colley, U.S. Indian Agent, Upper Arkansas.[58]

Sep. 14, 1864: Governor Evans Forwards Agent Colley's Letter that Cheyenne and Arapaho Desire Peace to Colonel Chivington

Sep. 14, 1864, Colonel J. M. CHIVINGTON, Commanding District of Colorado:

> SIR: I herewith inclose for your information a copy of a

letter received from Major Colley, U.S. Indian agent, Upper Arkansas Agency, dated September 4, 1864, Fort Lyon, stating the location of the Arapahoes and portions of other tribes of Indians, and inclosing a proposition for peace from Black Kettle and other chiefs. JNO. EVANS, Governor of Colorado Territory.[59]

Sep. 18, 1864: Major Wynkoop Reports Meeting with Cheyenne and Arapaho regarding Peace to Acting Assitant Adjutant-General, District of Upper Arkansas

Fort Lyon, Colorado Ter., September 18, 1864.
Lieutenant J. E. Tappan, Acting Assistant Adjutant-General, District of Upper Arkansas:

They came, as they stated, bearing with them a proposition for peace from Black Kettle and other chiefs of the Cheyenne and Arapahoe Nations. Their propositions were to the effect that they, the Cheyennes and Arapahoes, had in their possession seven white prisoners whom they offered to deliver up in case that we should come to terms of peace with them. They told me that the Cheyennes, Arapahoes, and Sioux were congregated for mutual protection, at what is called "Bunch of Timber," on headwaters of the Smoky Hill, at a distance of 140 miles northeast of this post numbering altogether about 3,000 warriors, and desirous to make peace with the whites. I told them I was not authorized to conclude terms of peace with them, but if they acceded to my proposition I would take what chiefs they might choose to select to the Governor of Colorado Territory and state the circumstances to him, and that I believed it would result in what it was their desire to accomplish, viz, *peace with their white brethren*. I had reference particularly to the Cheyenne and Arapahoe tribes ... they brought and turned over into my possession four white prisoners, all that was possible at the time being for them to turn over, the balance of the seven being, as they stated, with another band far to the northward ... I have the principal chiefs of the two tribes with me, and propose starting immediately to Denver City, Colorado Ter., to put into effect the proposition made aforementioned by me to them. E. W. Wynkoop, Major First Cavalry of Colorado, Commanding Post. (Emphasis added).[60]

Sep. 28, 1864: Governor Evans Meets with Cheyenne and Arapaho Peace Party; Rejects Peace Offer Alleging State of War with Military in Control Notwithstanding Commissioner Dole's Directive to Him to Negotiate for Peace

Sep. 1864 The Cheyenne and Arapaho seeking peace, traveled to Denver for a meeting with Governor and Superintendent of Indian Affairs Evans seeking peace. Governor Evans and Colonel Chivington met with the Cheyenne and Arapaho Chiefs at Camp Weld, near Denver.

Sep. 28, 1864 Meeting at Camp Weld

> We have come with our eyes shut, following [Major Wynkoop's] handful of men like coming through the fire. All we ask is that we have peace with the whites. We want to hold you by the hand. You are our father. We have been traveling thro' a cloud. The sky has been dark ever since the war began. These braves who are with me are all willing to do what I say. We want to take good tidings home to our people, that they may sleep in peace. *I want you to give all the chiefs of these soldiers to understand that we are for peace, and that we have made peace, that we may not be mistaken by them for enemies.* I have not come here with a little wolf bark, but have come to talk plain with you. We must live near the buffalo or starve. When we came here we came free, without any apprehension to see you, and when I go home and tell my people that I have taken your hand, and the hand of all the chiefs here in Denver, they will feel well, and so will all the different tribes of Indians on the Plains, after we have eaten and drank with them. (Emphasis added).[61]

Evans accused the leaders—men who had already signed the Fort Wise Treaty and who had now come to him at great personal risk—of being allied with the Lakota and having committed depredations …

Several of the Indians in attendance responded, asserting, "This is a mistake. We have made no alliance with the Sioux, or any one else."

As the meeting report shows, the Cheyenne and Arapaho also pointed out that they did not know the reasons for the fighting launched by Chivington's forces in the three battles of the spring, with White Antelope raising this question to Evans, who simply ignored it.

Toward the end of the meeting, Evans claimed that he was obligated to turn the Cheyenne and Arapaho over to the Army, given his claim that the settlers and Indian peoples were at war: "Another reason that I am not in a condition to make a treaty, is that war is begun, and the *power to make a treaty of peace has passed from me to the Great War Chief,*" he asserted. (Emphasis added).[62]

When faced with a last desperate attempt by leaders from those nations to make a peace that might have changed the trajectory of events, Evans blamed and rebuffed them, and arbitrarily, without sufficient cause, passed off his authority to the military. This pattern of irresponsible leadership amounted to dereliction of his duties as superintendent. (Emphasis added).[63]

This statement is particularly startling as it clearly indicates an abdication of his responsibility under Commissioner Dole's instruction, as well as in his role of Indian Superintendent, to negotiate for peace at every opportunity.

Sep. 29, 1864: Governor Evans Sends False Letter to Major Curtis, U.S. Army, that Sioux Plan to Attack Colorado

Denver, September 29, 1864. Major-General Curtis:

A party of the most reliable chiefs of Cheyennes and Arapahoe tribes, brought in by Major Wynkoop, say a very large party of Minneconjou and other Sioux Indians from the north are now on the Republican, nearly opposite the Cottonwood; that they soon will strike the Platte and make for the settlements of Colorado. General Sully has doubtless driven them down upon us. We must have a strong force after them at once or we will be destroyed by their cutting off our communication. JNO. EVANS, Governor. COLORADO SUPERINTENDENCY OF INDIAN AFFAIRS[64]

Sep. 29, 1864: Governor Evans Sends Letter to Agent Colley regarding Meeting with Cheyenne and Arapaho Peace Party; That He Rejected Peace Offer due to U.S. State of War

Denver, September 29, 1864. S. G. Colley, U.S. Indian Agent:

> SIR: The chiefs brought in by Major Wynkoop have been heard. *I have declined to make any treaty with them, lest it might embarrass the military operations against the hostile Indians of the plains.* The Arapahoe and Cheyenne Indians being now at war with the United States Government must make peace with the military authorities. Of course this arrangement relieves the Indian Bureau of their care until peace is declared with them, and as their tribes are yet scattered, and all except Friday's band are at war, it is not probable that it will be done immediately. You will be particular to impress upon these chiefs the fact that my talk with them was for the purpose of ascertaining their views and not to offer them anything whatever. They must deal with the military authorities until peace, in which case alone they will be in proper position to treat with the Government in relation to the future. JNO. EVANS, Governor Colorado Ter. and ex-officio Supt. of Indian Affairs. (Emphasis added).[65]

Sep. 29, 1864: Governor Evans Forwards Letter from Agent Colley to Colonel Chivington that Cheyenne and Arapaho Peace Offer Denied

[Inclosure to Letter to Colonel Chivington] FORT LEAVENWORTH, September 29, 1864. JOHN EVANS:

> General Mitchell is hunting Indians up the Platte, and General Blunt south of Arkansas also searching for them. Try and give them any information you think reliable. The chiefs you named are not reliable, and desire to save their friends, who are near the Arkansas, by extravagant reports of forces elsewhere. They ought to be made to go and show our enemies. Their chiefs are all implicated in the attacks where they have depredated. All they fear is winter approaching and therefore they desire peace, which they cannot have at present. I was far up the Republican and Mitchell was farther. I will try to have new scouts sent out from Cottonwood to ascertain the truth of this report. If such a force is there it must be attacked

as soon as possible. The idea of Sioux being driven down by Sully is not reasonable; that was the report before my visit to the Platte, and **I found nothing to justify it**. S. R. CURTIS, Major-General. (Emphasis added).[66]

October 14, 1864: Colonel Chivington Orders Capt. Nichols, Colorado Third Regiment, to Kill All Indians He Encounters

HEADQUARTERS DISTRICT OF COLORADO, Denver, October 14, 1864. Captain D. H. NICHOLS, Third Regiment Colorado Cav., Valley Station, Colorado Ter.:

CAPTAIN: Be vigilant. *Kill all the Indians you come across.* Strengthen your squads at stations below you to Julesburg. Ammunition leaves by to-morrow's coach.

J. M. CHIVINGTON, Colonel, Commanding District. (Emphasis added).[67]

October 15, 1864: Commissioner Dole Orders Governor Evans to Negotiate for Peace with Indians when They Offer, Regardless of U.S. State of War

Sir: I have the honor to acknowledge the receipt of your letter of the 29th ultimo, stating that at a council held with certain Arapahoes and Cheyenne Indians, you informed them, in answer to their expressed desire for peace, that you had no treaty to make with them, that they must make terms with the military authority. In reply, I have to say that while I approve of your course as a matter of necessity, while these Indians and the military authorities are at war, and the civil authority is in abeyance, yet, *as superintendent of Indian affairs, it is your duty to hold yourself in readiness to encourage and receive the first intimations of a desire on the part of the Indians for a permanent peace, and to cooperate with the military in securing a treaty of peace and amity.*
I cannot help believing that very much of the difficulty on the plains might have been avoided, if a spirit of conciliation had been exercised by the military and others. (Emphasis added).[68]

November 4, 1864: Major Wynkoop Relieved of Command

Orders relieving Major Wynkoop of command and directing him to report to district headquarters at Fort Riley in Kansas are issued.

I. Major E. W. Wynkoop, First Cavalry of Colorado, is hereby relieved from the command of Fort Lyon, Colorado Terr., and is ordered to report without delay to headquarters District of the Upper Arkansas, for orders. II. Major Scott J. Anthony, First Cavalry of Colorado, will proceed to Fort Lyon, Colorado Terr., and assume command of that post, and report in regard to matters as stated in Special Orders, No. 4, paragraph VII, from these headquarters, dated Fort Riley, October 17, 1864. By order of Major Henning: A. HELLIWELL, Lieutenant and Acting Assistant Adjutant-General.[69]

November 15, 1864: Majors Anthony and Wynkoop Meet with Cheyenne and Arapaho Who Continue to Press for Peace

Major Anthony (New Commander at Fort Lyon) and Major Wynkoop (Relieved of Fort Lyon Command) meet with about 60 Cheyenne and Arapaho chiefs and headmen at Fort Lyon.

> *Major Anthony advises the Cheyenne to return to their camps at Sand Creek and allows the Arapaho under Little Raven to move down the Arkansas about 60 miles and there wait until he receives further instructions from his superior officers.* (Emphasis added).[70]

November 15, 1864: Commissioner Dole Reports to Secretary of Interior that Cheyenne and Arapaho Urge Peace-Military Says Further Punishment Needed

> ... on the 4th of September Agent Colley forwarded to the superintendent a letter signed by several of the Cheyenne chiefs, proposing terms of peace. On the 28th an interview took place between Governor Evans and these chiefs, at which, it appears, from the annual report of that officer, they seemed earnest for peace; but the governor deemed it his duty, under the existing circumstances, to decline acceding to their terms, or indeed to make any terms with them, and the interview ended with leaving the chiefs referred to, or any others who might be disposed towards peace, to communicate with the military authorities. *This course seems, from the paper accompanying Governor Evans's report, to have commended itself to Major General Curtis as the proper one to be pursued, that officer deeming it necessary, in order*

to a permanent peace and the future good behavior of the Indians, that they should receive further punishment; ... Governor Evans advocates the policy of a winter expedition against the offending tribes. (Emphasis added).[71]

November 16, 1864: Major Anthony Reports to Headquarters that Cheyenne and Arapaho Appealing for Peace

HEADQUARTERS, Fort Lyon, Colorado Ter., November 16, 1864.

SIR: I have the honor to report that since my last report on the 7th [6th] instant the Cheyenne Indians, numbering about 200, under their head chief, Black Kettle, have sent into the post a request to meet me for a council. I met them and had a talk. They profess friendship for the whites, and say they never desired war, and do not now. They were very desirous of visiting the post and coming in with their whole band. I would not permit this, but told them they might camp on Sound [sic] [Sand] Creek, twenty-five miles northeast of the post, until the pleasure of the commanding officer of the district could be learned. They appear to want peace, and want some one authorized to make a permanent settlement of all troubles with them to meet them and agree upon terms. I told them that I was not authorized as yet to say that any permanent peace could be established, but that *no war would be waged against them* until your pleasure was heard. *I am satisfied that all of the Arapahoes and Cheyennes who have visited this post desire peace ... Neither of these tribes are satisfied with me for not permitting them to visit the post, and cannot understand why I will not make peace with them.* My intention, however, is to let matters remain dormant until troops can be sent out to take the field against all the tribes. SCOTT J. ANTHONY, Major First Cavalry of Colorado, Commanding Post. (Emphasis added).[72]

November 28, 1864: Major Anthony Reports Arrival of Colorado Third Regiment at Fort Lyon: 1000 Soldiers

Fort Lyon, Colorado Terr., November 28, 1864. Lieutenant A. HELLIWELL, Acting Assistant Adjutant-General, Fort Riley, Kans.:

SIR: I have the honor to report that Colonel John M. Chivington, First Cavalry of Colorado, arrived at this post this day with *1,000 men of the Third Regiment* Colorado Cavalry

(100-day's men) and two howitzers, on expedition against Indians. This number of men has been required for some time, and is appreciated by me now, as *I believe the Indians will be properly punished— what they have for some time deserved. I go out with 125 men and two howitzers* to join his command. SCOTT J. ANTHONY, Major First Cavalry of Colorado, Commanding Post. [KNEW AND PREVIOUSLY WROTE INDIANS WANTED PEACE]. (Emphasis added).[73]

November 28, 1864: Major General Curtis Reports to Brigadier General Carleton that Cheyenne and Arapaho Are Begging for Peace

HEADQUARTERS DEPARTMENT OF KANSAS, Fort Leavenworth, November 28, 1864. Brigadier General J. H. CARLETON, Commanding Department of New Mexico:

> GENERAL: ... *The Arapahoes and Cheyennes have come into Lyon begging for peace, turning over prisoners, horses, &c., for that purpose.* The hardest kind of terms are demanded by me and conceded by some of these Indians. They insist on peace or absolute sacrifice, as I choose. Of course, they will have to be received, but there still remains some of these tribes and all the Kiowas to attend to, and *I have proposed a winter campaign for their benefit. This, if successful, must be secret and well arranged beforehand.* I have written the War Department, and Governor Evans, of Colorado, has gone to Washington to urge my plans. S. R. CURTIS, Major-General. (Emphasis added).[74]

November 29, 1864: Sand Creek Massacre - Colonel Chivington Reports Killing 400-500 Indians; Scalped Every Man, Woman and Child, Mutilated Their Bodies; Removed Private Parts as War Trophies

On November 29, 1864, from in the field at the South Bend of the Big Sandy, John M. Chivington, First Colorado Cavalry, reported:

> In the last ten days my command has marched 300 miles, 100 of which the snow was two feet deep. After a march of forty miles last night *I, at daylight this morning, attacked Cheyenne village of 130 lodges, from 900 to 1,000 warriors strong; killed Chiefs Black Kettle, White Antelope, Knock Knee, and Little Robe [Little Raven], and between 400 and*

500 other Indians, and captured as many ponies and mules. Our loss, 9 killed, 38 wounded. All died nobly. Think I will catch some more of them eighty miles, on Smoky Hill. Found white man's scalp, not more than three days' old, in one of lodges. (Emphasis added).[75]

Report on Sand Creek Massacre by Agent Levenworth

I have the honor to enclose herewith papers relating to the late massacre of friendly Indians by Colonel J.M. Chivington,* near Fort Lyon. It is impossible for me to express to you the horror with which I view this transaction; it has destroyed the last vestige of confidence between the red and white man. Nearly every one of the chiefs and headmen of the Arapahoe and Cheyenne tribes who had remained true to the whites, and were determined not to fight the whites, were ***cruelly murdered when resting in all the confidence of assurances from Major Wyncoop, and I also believe from Major Anthony, that they should not be disturbed.*** Major Wyncoop, of the Colorado cavalry, was doing all that it was possible for an officer to do to pacify the Indians, and had restored comparative peace to this frontier, when all his work was destroyed, and an Indian war inaugurated that must cost the government millions of money and thousands of lives. These are the bitter fruits of Governor Evans's proclamation that I sent you last summer: "to the victor belongs the spoils." I then stated that those men could not stop to inquire if the Indians they should come in contact with were friendly or hostile. When Major Wyncoop went to Denver with the chiefs of tribes under his charge, why did Governor Evans refuse to act in any way, for or against them ... they were determined not to fight the whites... Little Bear escaped with his band; and it is due to him and to humanity that no effort be spared, in my opinion, to save him and his from certain destruction. I'm making every effort possible to find the Comanches and Kiowas; but I have little hope of succeeding. J. H. Leavenworth, U.S. Indian Agent (Emphasis added).

*The papers referred to above were not received.[76]

Commissioner Cooley, Sand Creek Massacre

The 'disastrous and shameful occurrence': the Sand Creek Massacre was reported:

> *Most disastrous and shameful occurrence of all, the massacre of a large number of men, women and children of the Indians of this agency by the troops under command of Colonel Chivington, of the United States volunteer cavalry of Colorado. ... Several hundred of them had come in to a place designated by Governor Evans as a rendezvous for those who would separate themselves from the hostile parties, these Indians were set upon and butchered in cold blood by troops in the service of the United States.* (Emphasis added).[77]

The Sand Creek Indian Fight.—This memorable struggle for the permanent immunity of southern Colorado from strife with hostile Indians began on September 9th and ended on December 29, 1864, thus lasting one hundred and twelve days. Mr. Stubbs was an active participant in it from the beginning to the end, as a member of Company G, Third Colorado Cavalry. His company was formed at Denver and went into camp four miles below Pueblo, and a few days later marched down the Arkansas river to Fort Lyon, being three days on the march and suffering many hardships therein. The soldiers were obliged to sleep on the snow, and as the emergency was great, all men whom they met on the road were impressed into the service despite its hardships. At nine o'clock one night the force was ordered out to march north and surprise the enemy. After spending the whole night on the march, and being led by their scouts and half-breed Indian guides through a pond, in which the horses floundered and the men suffered intensely from the cold, the Cheyenne Indian village was discovered at a distance of three miles from the camp at sunrise on the morning of November 29th. The men then became wild with excitement and could not be restrained, but rushed upon the Indians, who were still sleeping and unprepared for the attack. The noise awakened them and numbers succeeded in escaping, but *five hundred of the nine hundred in the band were killed*, with the loss of only one man of Company G, whose fate was due to his own carelessness. The battle lasted until five o'clock in the evening and during its progress *two cannon were used by the whites to great advantage*. Company G found a high enjoyment in burning the tepees of the Indians after the latter were routed. On the morning of November 30th they marched to the junction of Sand creek with the Arkansas and went into camp ... Nearby they found Indians in force and drove them far into the plains. On December 3d the company was ordered home. ... This war freed southern Colorado from the danger of savage attacks and established lasting security for the settlers. Mr. Stubbs escaped without injury. (Emphasis added).[78]

December 7, 1864: Colonel Chivington's Second Report to Governor Evans: Killed 500 Indians, Still in Pursuit of Cheyenne and Arapaho

December 7, 1864. Governor JOHN EVANS: (Care of National Hotel, Washington, D. C.)

Had fight with Cheyennes forty miles north of Lyon. I lost 9 killed and 38 wounded. *Killed 500 Indians*; destroyed 130 lodges; took 500 mules and ponies. Marched 300 miles in ten days; snow two feet deep for 100 miles. Am still after them. J. M. CHIVINGTON, Colonel, Commanding District of Colorado and First Indian Expedition. (Emphasis added).[79]

December 15, 1864: Major Anthony Reports Sand Creek Massacre Was Terrible; Should Be Done to All Hostile Tribes

HEADQUARTERS FORT LYON, COLORADO Territory, December 15, 1864.

... *The massacre was a terrible one and such a one as each of the hostile tribes on the plains richly deserve. I think one such visitation to each hostile tribe would forever put an end to Indian war on the plains*, and I regret exceedingly that this punishment could not have fallen upon some other band. Major Anthony, Major First Cavalry of Colorado, Commanding Post (Emphasis added).[80]

Governor Evans Culpability in Sand Creek Massacre - University of Denver's John Evans Study Committee

Evans abrogated his duties as superintendent, fanned the flames of war when he could have dampened them, cultivated an unusually interdependent relationship with the military, and rejected clear opportunities to engage in peaceful negotiations with the Indian peoples under his jurisdiction. Furthermore, he successfully lobbied the War Department for the deployment of a federalized regiment who executed the worst of the atrocities during the massacre.[81]

January 16, 1865: Sand Creek Military Investigation

Major General S. R. CURTIS, Fort Leavenworth, Department of Kansas. [Inclosure Numbers 5.] FORT LYON, COLORADO Territory, January 16, 1865.

Personally appeared before me Lieutenant James D. Cannon, First New Mexico Volunteer Infantry, who, after being duly sworn, says: That on the 28th day of November, 1864, I was ordered by Major Scott J. Anthony to accompany him on an Indian expedition as his battalion adjutant. The object of that expedition was to be a thorough campaign against hostile Indians, as I was led to understand. I referred to the fact of there being a friendly camp of Indians in the immediate neighborhood, and remonstrated against simply attacking that camp, *as I was aware that they were resting there in fancied security under promises held out to them of safety from Major E. W. Wynkoop, former commander of the post at Fort Lyon, as well as by Major S. J. Anthony, then in command.* Our battalion was attached to the command of Colonel J. M. Chivington, and left Fort Lyon on the night of the 28th of November, 1864. About daybreak on the morning of the 29th of November *we came in sight of the camp of the friendly Indians aforementioned, and was ordered by Colonel Chivington to attack the same*, which was accordingly done. The command of Colonel Chivington was composed of about 1,000 men. The village of the Indians consisted of from 100 to 130 lodges, and, as far as I am able to judge, of from 500 to 600 souls, the majority of which were women and children. In going over the battle-ground next day I did not see a body of man, woman, or child but was scalped, and in many instances their bodies were mutilated in the most horrible manner-- men, women, and children's privates cut out, &c. I heard one man say that he had cut a woman's private parts out, and had them for exhibition on a stick. I heard another man say that he had cut the fingers off of an Indian to get the rings on the hand. According to the best of my knowledge and belief, these atrocities that were committed were with the knowledge of J. M. Chivington, and I do not know of him taking any measures to prevent them. I heard of one instance of a child a few months' old being thrown in the feed-box of a wagon, and after being carried some distance left on the ground to perish. I also heard of numberless instances in which men had cut out the private parts of females and stretched them over the saddle bows, and wore them over their hats while riding in the ranks. All these matters were a subject of general conversation, and could not help being known by Colonel J. M. Chivington. JAMES D. CANNON, First Lieutenant, First Infantry, New Mexico Volunteers. Sworn and subscribed to before me this 27th day of January, 1865, at Fort Lyon, Colorado Ter. W. P. MINTON, Second Lieutenant, First New Mexico Volunteers, Post Adjutant. (Emphasis added).[82]

1865: U.S. Condemns Sand Creek Massacre

After a lengthy investigation of the Sand Creek Massacre, the U.S. condemned it and decided to offer reparations to the afflicted parties in exchange for peace. In addition, the removal of the Cheyenne and Arapaho from Colorado was part of the U.S.'s renewed focus on pacifying the indigenous population of the American West to make way for homesteads, railroads, mines, and cities.

April 28, 1865: Treaty with Arapaho and Cheyenne for Colorado Land, Offer No Money, No Specific Land for New Reservation

By the Spring of 1865, President Abraham Lincoln appointed Vital Jarrot as the Indian Agent to the Upper Platte Agency. He had served in the leading role of Adjutant General during the Black Hawk War in 1832 in which Lincoln served as a volunteer.[83]

On April 28, 1865, Jarrot was notified by Charles Mix, Acting Commissioner, that President Lincoln had selected him to head the Upper Platte Agency based on his "influence ... arising from your long residence among and intimate acquaintance." He was to negotiate with the Arapaho, Cheyenne and Sioux affiliated with them and Cheyenne for a cession of their lands. His instructions were as follows:

> Agreements to pay money will not be approved. If a treaty is made, it will be one of occupancy only: no title to lands will be acknowledged in the Indians of the country they abandon, nor will any be conferred upon them in the country they are to inhabit; Just an article may be inserted providing that the whites will be excluded from settlement in the country assigned to them.[84]

1865: Superintendent Taylor, Upper Platte; Obstruction of Mining Prejudicial to U.S.

Edward B. Taylor, Superintendent, Upper Platte, advised that obstruction to the development of the mines in this region should be avoided:

> The precious metals, our sole reliance to liquidate the accruing interest upon the national debt, are derived chiefly from the mining districts of Colorado, Oregon, California, Nevada, Idaho, and Montana, and any barrier which obstructs emigration to these mines, and retards their development, must prove highly prejudicial to the financial prosperity of the country.[85]

October 11-13, 1865: U.S. Treaty Delegation, Arapaho and Cheyenne Still Recovering from Sand Creek, Not Ready to Agree to Relinquish Land in Colorado

To accomplish the joint goals of reparations and removal, the U.S. sent a treaty delegation—led by Colonel Henry Leavenworth and including Colorado notables Kit Carson and William Bent—to the banks of the Little Arkansas River, where they arrived on October 4, 1865. There the party waited until several Cheyenne and Arapaho bands arrived on October 11, with their numbers eventually totaling more than 4,000. Among them were Black Kettle's Cheyenne and Little Raven's Arapaho—both of whom had been at Sand Creek—as well as five other Cheyenne bands and six other Arapaho bands.

On October 13, 1865, the surviving Arapaho and Cheyenne chiefs met with government commissioners. The Arapaho didn't want to agree on land at the time—few were present, the rest were up north. They were still reeling from the Sand Creek Massacre:

> *Little Raven There is something very strong for us-that fool band of soldiers that cleared out our lodges, and killed our women and children. This is strong (hard) on us. There, at Sand creek, is one chief, Left Hand; White Antelope and many other chiefs lie there; our women and children lie there. Our lodges were destroyed there, and our horses were taken from us there, and I do not feel disposed to go right off in a new country and leave them.* (Emphasis added).[86]

October 13, 1865: Treaty Council with Arapaho and Cheyenne - Unfortunately for You, Gold Discovered in Your Country

No. 13. Treaty Council held in camp on the Little Arkansas River, October 13, 1865

> We believe that in the country where we desire you to go you will gradually become rich, and your numbers increase; but we are fully convinced that it is impossible for you to stay, and that if you do stay, you will gradually diminish, until you are finally swept from the earth.
> Wise and good men have for many years, at Washington, been studying what is best for Indians to do. They have arrived at the conclusion that it is best for the two races to be separated. From the earliest history of our country, where the white man has come in contact with the Indians, you have gradually wasted away from the earth; and for this reason they have concluded it best for the two races to be separated.[87]

October 14, 1865: Cheyenne and Arapaho Treaty Signed Removing Them from Colorado

The treaty which had been prepared was now read, article by article, by President Sanborn, and interpreted by John Smith to the Indians present. An article was submitted authorizing the Senate to make amendments without reference back to the Indians, but was objected to by the Indians, and withdrawn.

The treaty was then signed by the commissioners and the chiefs and headmen of the Cheyenne and Arapaho tribes, and witnessed by the secretaries and other persons present, when the council adjourned. John R. Sanborn. President of the Commission. (Emphasis added).[88]

Article 6 of the Treaty of the Little Arkansas, 14 Stat. 703, negotiated on October 14, 1865, ratified May 22, 1866, and proclaimed February 2, 1867, provided for land and money reparations to survivors:

> The United States being desirous to express its condemnation of, and, as far as may be, repudiate the gross and wanton outrages perpetrated against certain bands of Cheyenne and Arapahoe Indians, on the twenty-ninth day of November, A.D. 1864, at Sand Creek, in Colorado Territory, while the said Indians were at peace with the United States, and under its flag, whose protection they had by lawful authority been promised and induced to seek, and the Government being desirous to make some suitable reparation for the injuries then done, will grant three hundred and twenty acres of land by patent, as well as individual payments for property lost.

This promise has not yet been kept.

Descendants of those killed in the Sand Creek Massacre have been fighting for these lost reparations throughout the twentieth century and into the twenty-first.[89]

Little Arkansas Treaty - Land Specified for Reservation for Arapaho and Cheyenne in Indian Territory Already Given to Another Tribe

The Little Arkansas Treaty refers to a pair of treaties signed between the U.S. and Indian Nations in Kansas: one with the Southern Arapaho and Southern Cheyenne Nations and one with the Comanche and Kiowa. Of the two, the Treaty signed on October 14, 1865, with the Cheyenne and Arapaho, was the most significant within Colorado because it removed the two Indian Nations to a new reservation in Indian Territory (present-day Oklahoma) and offered them reparations for the Sand Creek Massacre of the previous year. However, the U.S. had already removed other Indians to the same area and would have to move them to make space for the newcomers. Instead of issuing money to the individuals listed in the treaty for reparations, the Interior Department gave some of the money to the Nations and, in a common move, "returned the rest" to the Treasury as "surplus." Once money is returned to the Treasury it is final. The only method for securing money returned to the Treasury is by

Congressional action—new legislation to appropriate monies is required.

January 1–February 2, 1865: Indian Military Campaign

After the Sand Creek Massacre of the Cheyenne and Arapaho on November 29, 1864, a number of Colorado and Kansas tribes allied to conduct hostilities against the U.S. Army and white settlers. Many of the Cheyenne survivors had fled north to the Republican River, where a large contingent of "Dog Soldiers" were camped.

Among the Cheyenne Indians one of the most important military societies was the Dog Soldiers, of which Tall Bull was chief. It was considered a great honor to belong to this band of warriors. In battle, a Cheyenne Dog Soldier would stake his dog rope in the ground. Dog ropes were made out of rawhide leather and decorated with porcupine quills and feathers. One end was tied to a red wooden stake. During combat, a Cheyenne Dog Soldier would plant the stake in the ground as a sign of perseverance and standing one's ground. The area over which the Dog Soldier could fight was limited to the length of the rope. Dog Soldiers would not remove the stake until their people had safely retreated or a comrade removed it, so it was used as a last resort.

On January 1, 1865, the Indians met at present-day St. Francis, Kansas, to plan a concerted strategy against the invasive settlement and trespass of white settlers on their land. In the meeting were the Cheyenne Dog Soldiers, the Northern Arapaho, and two Bands of Lakota Sioux, including the Brule, under Chief Spotted Tail, and the Oglala, under War Leader Pawnee Killer. The U.S. had failed to provide any protection of Indian lands and lives, affording military protection by Presidential Proclamation to the settlers, resulting in these Indians having to fight against insurmountable odds.

As many as 2,000 Cheyenne, Sioux, and Arapaho warriors shifted their camps closer to the South Platte River, where it cut through the northeast corner of Colorado. In the midst of this area was Fort Rankin (later Fort Sedgwick), an Overland Trail stagecoach station and the station town of Julesburg.

These warriors would lead a campaign between the 1st Battle of Julesburg on January 7, 1865 and the 2nd Battle of Julesburg on February 2, 1865, over a 150 mile stretch of the Overland Trail near the South Platte River in Northern Colorado.[90]

1865: Battle of Fort Rankin

On January 6, 1865, a small party of Indians hit a wagon train and killed 12 men. In the early morning hours of January 7th, the Indians attacked Fort Rankin. While the majority of the Indians concealed themselves in some sandhills a short distance from the Fort, Cheyenne Chief Big Crow and about ten of his warriors charged the Fort and then quickly retreated as a decoy. In response, Capt. Nicholas O'Brien led a 60-man cavalry troop out of the Fort to chase the would-be attackers.

About three miles from the Fort, up to 1000 warriors were hidden in the nearby bluffs. Some Indian warriors fired prematurely, alerting Capt. O'Brien. His troops fled back to the Fort with the Indians in pursuit, cutting off some of the soldiers before they reached safety. Of those who didn't reach the Fort, they dismounted to defend themselves. In the battle, 14 soldiers and four civilians were killed. Capt. O'Brien and the rest of his men made it back to the Fort.

As the remaining troops prepared to defend the Fort against further attack, the Indians looted the stage station, store, and warehouse at Julesburg. Julesburg was only 200 miles east of Denver. It was an important waystation for immigrants and settlers traveling along the Platte River on the Oregon Trail, which built up around the home station for the Overland Trail Stagecoach Lines.

In response to the attack on Fort Rankin, General Robert Byington Mitchell gathered 640 cavalry, a battery of howitzers, and some 200 supply wagons at Cottonwood Springs, which was located near present-day North Platte, Nebraska. He then marched southwest to find and punish the Indians who had attacked Fort Rankin and Julesburg. On January 19th, he found their deserted camp and returned to his base.

In the meantime, the Indians raided ranches and stagecoach stations up and down the South Platte River Valley. The Sioux struck east of Julesburg, the Cheyenne west of Julesburg, and the Arapaho in between. George Bent, the mixed-race son of William Bent, the founder of Bent's Fort, and his Cheyenne wife, was with this group of Indians. He would later say that at night "the whole valley was lighted up with the flames of burning ranches and stage stations, but the places were soon all destroyed, and darkness fell on the valley."

Just weeks after the first attack at Julesburg, the warriors returned in force on February 2, 1865, where they once again looted the town and, this time, burned it to the ground. They also looted some wagon trains. The 15 soldiers and 50 civilians sheltered at nearby Fort Rankin did not venture outside the Fort's walls. As the fire and smoke poured from the settlement, Capt. O'Brien and 14 of his men, who had been away from the Fort, returned to Julesburg. O'Brien scattered the Indians with a round from his field howitzer, and the Indians fled.

1866: Governor Evans' Speech on Minerals, Agriculture Promoting Colorado

Colorado Governor Evans, in November 1866, remarked at a public meeting in Chicago:

> "I have just returned from visiting a district about one hundred miles by ten or fifteen in extent, lying across the main mountain range west of Denver City, which is pervaded throughout by extensive and rich veins of silver; some are of pure silver ores, but the majority of them are argentiferous galena ores, varying in richness, many of them yielding in the smelting furnace as high as six hundred dollars of silver to the ton of ore. Salinas, or extensive deposits of salt, are accessible, as in New Mexico; and even petroleum is found near the eastern base of the mountains. The forests supply timber even for exportation to Kansas, and the mountain streams are generally available for the uses of machinery and irrigation. The area of Colorado is 67,723,520 acres, and the most sanguine view of its future agriculture is comprised in a statement by Surveyor General Pierce, in 1866, that *"there are about 4,000,000 acres of agricultural land susceptible of irrigation, which will make productive farms."* (Emphasis added).

> "The whole of the plains," according to the testimony of Governor Evans, "and the parks in the mountains of Colorado, are the finest of pastoral lands. Stock fattens and thrives on them the year round, large herds and flocks being kept there in the finest possible condition. In some parts, it is true, the snow covers the grass for a part of the winter, but in other places cattle and sheep are wintered without feeding, with entire success. The celebrated parks, North, Middle, South and San Luis, are fine agricultural valleys for grass and small grains."[91]

1866: Gold, Silver and Coal Discovered on Ute Land; Fertile Land, Timber, Water Power, All Requirements for Profitable Occupation

The Central Superintendency reported the following:

> Colorado Territory. Last summer gold, silver, and coal were discovered in this section, which is reported to have many fertile valleys, abundance of timber and water powers, a fine climate, and all the requirements for profitable occupation. Many parties are preparing to invade this new land early in the spring … It is important that a treaty be made with the Grand River and Uintah bands at as early a day as possible. *I need scarcely allude to the necessity of limiting, as far as possible, the amount which the government will be called upon to pay for a cession of the right of occupancy of the land by the Indians*, but deem it of importance that, so far as possible, no promises of money annuities shall be made, but that all payments shall be made in stock animals, implements, goods adapted to their wants, and for other beneficial objects. (Emphasis added).[92]

1867: American Express Co., Shoot Indians

Upper Arkansas Agency, Fort Larned, Kansas, May 27, 1867

Thomas Murphy, the Superintendent of Indian Affairs, on May 27 issued a complaint to his superior Commissioner Taylor. He wrote:

> "I have the honor to transmit herewith a circular issued by the superintendent of the American Express Company to their employes on the Smoky Hill route from Fort Harker to Denver City. I would call your attention particularly to the paragraph marked, viz: "If Indians come within shooting distance, shoot them; show them no mercy, for they will show you none."
> … According to existing treaty stipulations the Cheyennes, Arapahos, and Apaches have permission to live in and roam over the country lying between these two rivers until the President orders their removal to reservations selected for them. If the government countenances these arbitrary acts of military commanders and superintendents of express

companies in violating treaties, it is unreasonable to expect that the Indians will keep their part of these treaties. If this condition of affairs is permitted to exist much longer, every effort that has been made during the past two years by the civil officers of the government to promote peace and friendship among those Indians, and to prevent depredations, will have been utterly in vain, and it is but reasonable to expect that an Indian war of gigantic proportions will ensue, which will astonish the American people and cost millions of treasure. In view of these facts, I respectfully request that you will take such immediate steps as in your judgement will the soonest and most effectually put a stop to these arbitrary and cruel orders."[93]

1867: Central City Indian Scalp Bounty

The citizens of Central City have raised $5,000 to pay for Indian scalps, and offer $25 each for "scalps with the ears on."[94]

1867: Medicine Lodge Treaties - Cheyenne and Arapaho Treaty Establishing Reservation in Indian Territory

The Medicine Lodge Treaties in 1867 were a series of three treaties between the U.S. and the Comanche, Kiowa, Plains Apache, Southern Cheyenne, and Southern Arapaho nations. By treating with multiple tribes at once, the appointed Peace Commission's goal was to "establish security for person and property along the lines of railroad now being constructed to the Pacific." Leading the negotiations would be Acting Indian Affairs Commissioner Nathaniel G. Taylor, Senator John B. Henderson of Missouri, General William T. Sherman, and Christian reformer Samuel F. Tappan, among others. President Grant was pursuing a "Peace Policy," preferring cultural warfare over military campaigns.

The U.S. had the upper hand as the military had already established forts in the region, the tribes were fractured along lines of peace and warfare, and the tribes needed annuities to survive, given the depletion of their subsistence base.

On October 28, the Cheyenne and Arapaho chiefs signed a treaty creating a reservation in western Indian Territory. Capt. Barnitz of the 7th U.S. Cavalry, who recorded the speeches during the negotiations, expressed his misgivings.

"They have no idea that they are giving up, or that they have ever given up the country which they claim as their own...*The treaty amounts to nothing, and we will certainly have another war* sooner or later with the Cheyennes, at least, and probably with the other Indians..." (Emphasis added).

The eastern plains of Colorado were cleared of Indians by 1870, primarily because superior military power and the physical removal to Indian Territory eliminated the presence of these peoples. Unlike the northern plains, there was no continual warfare between new-comers and Indians, nor was there inter-tribal squabbling. Colorado's Indians were simply overwhelmed by the 100,000 immigrants that poured across the plains in 1859, and small bands like the Arapaho were inundated.[95]

1868: Battle of Beecher Island

The Battle of Beecher Island was fought on Sep. 17, 1868, on the Arikaree River, near present-day Wray, Colorado. Fifty-one scouts and frontiersmen under the command of Colonel George A. Forsyth engaged the combined forces of the Northern Cheyenne, Arapaho, and Oglala after hunting them for several days due to their attacks on settlers. The advantage of the frontiersmen was a new firearm, the Spencer Seven repeating rifle; it shot seven times without re-loading. Unaware of this new rifle, the Indians tried making a direct charge on the frontiersmen, but were cut down. The frontiersman took cover on a sandbar island. The battle changed to a siege; starvation was the Indian plan. The frontiersmen lay in their sand pits for a whole week, drank river water, and ate horse meat. Two of their scouts were able to escape and go for help. Three military rescue parties departed following different routes due to the uncertainty of Forsyth's location. The Battle had the makings of a disaster until the Tenth Cavalry and other units arrived and routed the Indians.

1868: Ute Treaty of 1868 - Utes Cede Central Rockies

The Ute Treaty of 1868, also known as the "Kit Carson Treaty," was negotiated between agents of the U.S., including Kit Carson, and leaders of seven bands of Nuche living in Colorado and Utah. The treaty created for the Utes a massive reservation on Colorado's Western Slope in exchange for ceding the Central Rockies to the U.S. For the miners, it opened a huge portion of the mineral-rich Rocky Mountains to development. A reservation was created in northeast Utah for the Uintah Utes.

In 1870 Governor Edward M. McCook wrote a letter declaring:

> "I have never been able to comprehend the reasons which induced the Colorado officials and the General Government to enter into a treaty setting apart one-third of the whole area of Colorado for the exclusive use and occupation of the Ute nation." He claimed: "***The greater part of this country is the best agricultural, pastoral, and mining land on the continent*** ... The Ute reservation includes mines which will pay $100 per day to the man, grasses are luxuriant and inexhaustible, and a soil richer and more fruitful than any other in the Territory." McCook closed his letter with an appeal to the ideals of Manifest Destiny: "I believe that God gave to us the earth, and the fullness thereof, in order that we might utilize and enjoy His gifts. I do not believe in donating to these indolent savages the best portion of my Territory." (Emphasis added).[96]

1869: Battle at Summit Springs

In response to a series of Cheyenne Indian raids in north-central Kansas in 1868 and 1869, after the Washita Massacre, Colonel Eugene Carr, with 244 men of the 5th U.S. Regiment of Cavalry and 50 Pawnee Scouts led by Major Frank North, were given orders to *clear the Republican River country of all Indians*. On July 11, 1869, Carr's force came upon an unsuspecting Cheyenne camp and attacked at 3 p.m., from three sides at once.

Southern Cheyenne Chief Tall Bull along with Heavy Furred Wolf, Pile of Bones, Lone Bear, Black Sun, White Rock, Big Gip, Powder Face and 45 Cheyenne and Sioux men, women and children were killed at Summit Springs, near Sterling, Colorado, by the U.S. Cavalry. The Indian camp contained 84 lodges housing approximately 450 people. Even though the battle took place in the middle of the afternoon it came as a complete surprise to the Indians.[98]

The battle lasted nearly three hours. When the shooting finally stopped, around 6 p.m., a powerful prairie thunderstorm rolled in from the southwest and pummeled the battleground with rain and hail and everyone was forced to take cover wherever they could.

The diary of Major Frank North reads:

> "Sunday, July 11, 1869. Marched this morn at 6 A.M. with

fifty of my men and two hundred whites, with three days' rations. Follow trail until three P.M. and came up to the village. Made a grand charge and it was a complete victory. Took the whole village of about 85 lodges. Killed about sixty Indians. Took seventeen prisoners and about three hundred ponies and robes, etc., innumerable. Rained pretty hard tonight."

By capturing the Dog Soldiers' village, many of the ponies, and practically all of their supplies and equipment, Carr's offensive effectively ended Cheyenne resistance on the Southern Plains.

One story told from the Battle is worth repeating:

As the mounted horsemen galloped toward the hide-covered lodges a young boy, later identified as 12-year-old Little Hawk, was caught between the advancing Cavalry and the horses that he had been herding. The horses he was guarding were spooked by the advancing troops and began to scatter. Although the boy could have made his escape he mounted his own pony, gathered up the horses that had broken away and drove them into the camp ahead of the charging troops.... at the edge of the village he turned and joined a band of warriors that were trying to hold us back, while the women and children were getting away, and there he died like a warrior. No braver man ever existed than that 15 year old boy." His actions so impressed Capt. Luther North that he recorded the events in his book "Man of the Plains."[99]

Mr. Clarence Reckmeyer visited the site of the battle with Capt. Luther H. North, who took part in the Battle. The Battle of Summit Springs was the last important battle fought by Plains Indians on Colorado soil.

The lodges and all the contents of the village, except such articles as the soldiers desired to keep were burned. A footnote in Mr. Reckmeyer's article notes in part:

On a plate opposite page 128 of Our Wild Indians, by R. I. Dodge, is shown a tobacco pipe the description of which reads: "Tall Bull's tobacco pipe, ornamented with feathers and scalp locks." Tall Bull was chief of a band of

the area which included the principal mines. Even after this concession there still remained to them 15,577,120 acres.[101]

1873: San Juan Mountains - Richest Mining District

> *The country ceded by the Utes, including, as it does, probably the most extensive and richest mining district in the United States, embraces about four million acres of land, of very little value to Indians, being unfit for agricultural purposes and devoid of game, but of almost incalculable value to Colorado and the nation.* (Emphasis added).[102]

1874: Brunot Agreement - Utes Cede Mineral Rich San Juan Mountains

In 1872 by authority of Congress, a commission consisting of Hon. John D. Tong, Gen. John McDonald and Governor E. M. McCook was appointed, with instructions to negotiate a treaty with the Southern Colorado Utes for a reduction of their reservation, which then covered a tract nearly 300 miles long by 200 miles wide.

Prospectors had entered the San Juan mountains and there discovered valuable mines of silver and gold, but as it was a part of the Indian reservation, they were in danger of conflicts with the savages. Hence, they appealed to delegate Jerome B. Chaffee, who introduced the resolution providing for the commission. This negotiation failed. (Emphasis added).[103]

As a result of the discovery of gold and silver, the treaty between the U.S. and the Utes of Colorado would be revised three times, accounting for each new mineral discovery.

The Brunot Agreement of 1873 was ratified by the U.S. in 1874, and is most often remembered by Utes as the agreement when their land was fraudulently taken away. The Utes were led to believe that they would be signing an agreement that would allow mining to occur on the lands located only in the San Juan Mountain area, the site of valuable gold and silver ore. About four million acres of land not subject to mining would remain Ute territory under ownership of the tribe. However, they ended up forcibly relinquishing the lands to the U.S.

With completion of the agreement, the San Juan Mountains saw a mining rush that resulted in many towns being established in 1874 and 1875, including Silverton. When the boundaries of the ceded lands were surveyed, the surveyor

~ 199 ~

failed to exclude Uncompahgre Park, and it was quickly settled, much to the dissatisfaction of the Utes. Seeing the abundant farm and grazing land that surrounded the ceded territory, the Colorado citizenry became even more covetous of the Utes' land, making it only a matter of time before most of the Utes were forced from their Colorado homeland.

1876: Colorado Statehood

Colorado became a state in 1876.

1877: Stay Friendly with Utes

> Every day it becomes of higher importance that friendly relations should be maintained with the Utes, for it is in their power to stop, for a time at least, the development of the great San Juan mining district, which borders on the reservation. Los Pinos, Co., Agent W. D. Wheeler.[104]

Mining in southwestern Colorado was not of the placer-type that characterized early activity in the central Rockies. In order to effectively extract the mineral wealth in the mountains, lode mining techniques were essential. Lode deposits could only be recovered by skilled labor and technology. In milling, ore was crushed into sand and then washed over copper plates embedded with mercury, or simply into sluice boxes to recover the gold. It was relatively inefficient, with as little as 25 percent of the gold content recovered. The inefficiency came because milling is only a physical separation process and does not break the chemical bonds between the rock and gold. The result was a need for large machinery, a substantial labor force, smelters and transportation.

1877: Comanche Peace Treaty with Utes

In the 1700s the Ute and Comanche tribes began peace negotiations to ensure peace between two powerful tribal allies that reigned over the southwestern plains, however, peace talks were interrupted and a fifty-year war followed. Peace talks began again and in 1877 the Ute Comanche Peace Treaty was finalized. Representatives of the Comanche Tribe traveled to Ignacio, Colorado, to finalize the Ute Comanche Peace Treaty.

1877: Commissioner Recommends Removing All Indians in Colorado and AZ to Indian Territory to Facilitate Mining and Farming by Whites

Commissioner E. A. Hayt reported to the Secretary in 1877 that all Indians in

Colorado and Arizona should be removed to the Indian Territory in what is now Oklahoma. Miners, in search of gold and silver, could claim lands without regard to Indian reservations established by the U.S. by treaty or legislative authority. He further stated that all of the arable land was required by white settlers and feeding them was of paramount importance. [105]

The Military And The Colorado Frontier, Marshall Sprague

These "ignorant savages" were blocking all progress in Colorado mining progress, railroad progress, homestead progress, city-making progress, stage road progress-west of the Ute reservation line. That line ran along the 107th parallel from the New Mexico border for 240 miles north through the present site of Pagosa Springs, Gunnison, Aspen, Gypsum, Glenwood Springs and up to 20-Mile Park in the Yampa River area. All those future townsites and all the country west of them to the Utah border were in the Ute reservation. [106]

Colorado Petitions for Removal of All Utes

At this time, articles headlining "The Utes Must Go" were being prepared by members of the staff of Governor Frederick W. Pitkin. Pitkin was a former miner who used his wealth (acquired from a gold mine in the San Juan Mountains of Colorado) to influence the revision of the Ute treaty in 1873 and to become the first governor of Colorado on its statehood in 1876. His view of the Utes was an expression of the statewide view among whites that they were an impediment to the development of the richest part of the state and should be removed to the Indian Territory or elsewhere.

William Vickers, an adviser to the Governor, wrote in the Denver Tribune:

Honorable N. C. Meeker, the well-known Superintendent of the White River Agency, was formerly a fast friend and ardent admirer of the Indians. He went to the Agency in the firm belief that he could manage the Indians successfully by kind treatment, patient precept and good example. But utter failure marked his efforts and at last he reluctantly accepted the truth of the broader truism that the only truly good Indians are dead ones. [107]

On February 4, 1878, the Colorado delegation introduced the first of three bills designed to remove the Utes from Colorado. House Resolution 351 was typical of the three. It empowered the Secretary of the Interior to negotiate with the Utes and "establish by law the extinguishment of title to their lands, removal from their present locations and consolidation on certain reservations."[108]

Early in 1879, an editorial in the Denver Times stated what had become obvious to most white Colorado residents. Since the 1873 Brunot Agreement, pressure had continued to mount for the removal of the Utes from Colorado.

> "Either they [the Utes] or we go, and we are not going. Humanitarianism is an idea. Western empire is an inexorable fact. He who gets in the way of it will be crushed."[109]

1879: Battle of Milk Creek and Meeker Incident - Through No Fault, Utes Forced out of Colorado

Nathan C. Meeker, White River Ute Reservation Indian Agent, was the wrong person to appoint as the White River Indian Agent. He had no experience working with Indians and the White River Utes resented his paternalistic attitudes. He expressed his unfavorable opinions about the Utes in the press and to Nevada's popular Senator Teller:

In an article in the Greeley Tribune on January 29, 1879, Meeker had written: "The habits of this sui generis [unique] American aristocracy seem almost identical with those of the European. Neither will work, neither attach any value to learning, both have the lower classes do work for them, both find occupation and happiness in gambling and horseracing, and the women in both are of no account."[110]

Captain Jack and thirteen other Utes went to see Governor Pitkin in Denver where they asked him to remove Meeker.[111]

Meeker believed the Indians must be brought down to the level of basic survival in order to guide them to civilized and agrarian lifestyles. He reported to Colorado's influential Senator Teller, "I propose to cut every Indian down to the bare starvation point if he will not work."[112]

Nathan Meeker wrote the following in an article published in the American Antiquarian Newsletter, 1878:

> "They are savages, having no written language, no traditional

history, no poetry, no literature... a race without ambition, and also a race deficient in the inherent elements of progress. Vermin abound on their persons..."

The Utes suspected him of direct involvement with the anti-Ute movement in the State.[113]

On Sep. 10, 1879, Meeker requested a telegram be sent to Commissioner Hayt requesting troops to repress a threatened uprising by the White River Utes after a Ute pushed him during an argument. The message reached Commissioner Hayt on Sep. 13, 1879. It was forwarded by Secretary of the Interior Carl Schurz to Secretary of War George W. McCrary, and ultimately received by General of the Army William T. Sherman. The location of the White River Agency was at the end of the Army's operational reach. General Sherman approved the request for troops and instructed the Commander of the Division of the Missouri, Major General Phillip H. Sheridan, to order "the *nearest* military commander" to send troops to White River.

The Commander of the Department of the Platte, Brigadier General George Crook, gave the following order to the forces at Fort Steele: You will move with a sufficient number of troops to White River Agency under special instructions. The special instructions that General Crook spoke of were to contact the agent on the scene and "develop" the situation. Major Thomas T. Thornburg began his march to the White River Agency on Sep. 22, 1879, with a total of 153 soldiers and 25 civilians.

On Sep. 25, 1879, Major Thornburgh wrote to Agent Meeker seeking instructions. Thornburgh continued his march toward the Agency. En route, a delegation of eleven Utes met with Thornburgh, voicing their concern over the arrival of troops and denouncing Agent Meeker.

On Sep. 27, 1879, Meeker sent a letter to Major Thornburgh:

> "the Indians are greatly excited, and wish you to *stop at some convenient camping place, and then that you and five soldiers of your command come into the Agency, when a talk and a better understanding can be had.* ... The *Indians seem to consider the advance of the troops as a declaration of real war.* ... *The first object is to allay apprehension.* (Emphasis added).[114]

Major Thornburgh unilaterally decided that instead of sending a small group to meet with Meeker as Meeker and the Indians personally requested of him, he would enter the Reservation with all of his soldiers, fearing trouble. He sent Agent Meeker the following message:

> *I have, after due deliberation, decided to modify my plans*: ... I shall move with my entire command to some convenient camp near, and within striking distance of your agency, reaching such point during the 29th. ... *I have carefully considered whether or not it would be advisable to have my command at a point as distant as that desired by the Indians who were in camp last night*, and have reached the conclusion that under my orders, which require me to march this command to the agency, *I am not at liberty to leave it at a point where it would not be available in case of trouble*. (Emphasis added).[115]

When Thornburgh's command reached Milk Creek, twenty-five miles from the agency, and within the Reservation, a large body of Indians confronted it ... For seven days, Thornburgh was besieged by the Utes. Major Thornburgh and thirteen of his men were killed.[116]

On the same day, other Utes attacked the Indian Agency, killing Agent Meeker, his 10 male employees and taking five women and children captive.

Troops proceeded to Colorado from all directions.

Sample News Headlines from Colorado Rocky Mountain News (1878-79)

1878

2 January "Indian Hostilities"
3 March "Utes on Rampage, Whites Fear Uprising"
5 March "Utes Kill Cattle on Snake River"
18 April "Ute Massacre in Pagosa Springs"
23 April "Rumors of Ute War"
28 April "Utes' Gold Locations Secret from Whites"
24 May "Utes Rebellious Through Neglect of Indian Bureau"
21 July "Movements of Ute Indians"
3 August "Utes Kill Joe McLane, Stockmen Seek Revenge"
1 September "Ute Uprising Feared in Grand County"
12 September "Utes in Trouble over Murder of Settlers"

1879

1 January "Utes Make Trouble in Middle Park"
27 June "Utes Threaten Miners in North Park"
9 July "Ute Hostile Attitude Excites State Officials"
16 July "Shall We Kill or Starve the Indians? [editorial]"
6 August "The Indians Must Go"
14 August "Utes Arrested and Charged with Arson"
10 September Letter to the editor from Meeker complaining of his treatment by the Utes

October 1879: Leadville Chronicle

> [T]he savages are sweeping through the outlying settlements of the State, murdering miners and ranchmen ... Some man is needed who will out Chivington—some man who will duplicate Sand Creek... Murder is the Indian game. Give them enough of it.

1879: Governor Pitkin's Order: Bring in, Dead or Alive, All Hostile Indians

It was not until October 13, 1879, that the newspapers reported on the Meckor Agency incident. The headlines blazed, "A SCENE OF SLAUGHTER." Governor Pitkin denounced the attack in no uncertain terms, and incidentally pointed out that 12,000,000 acres could be opened with the removal of the Utes. [Frederick Pitkin, quoted in the Denver Daily News, October 13, 1879.] Herein lay the perfect opportunity to be rid of the Indians for good.[117]

The Governor mustered two companies of the Colorado militia: His War Order No. 1 was to "bring in, dead or alive, all hostile Indians found off the reservation ... consider all Indians off the reservation hostile, and bring them in, dead or alive, and we will determine their docility afterward."[118]

In the view of Colorado citizens, the Utes were both dangerous and an impediment to progress. ... Pitkin commented to the press:

> "It will be impossible for the Indians and whites to live in peace hereafter ... This attack had no provocation and the whites now understand that they are liable to be attacked in any part of the state .... *My idea is that, unless removed by the government they must necessarily be exterminated.*" (Emphasis added).[119]

~ 205 ~

William Vickers, an adviser to the Governor, wrote in the Denver Tribune:

> The Utes are actual, practical Communists and the Government should be ashamed to foster and encourage them in their idleness and wanton waste of property. Living off the bounty of a paternal but idiotic Indian Bureau, they actually become too lazy to draw their rations in the regular way but insist on taking what they want wherever they find it. Removed to Indian Territory, the Utes could be fed and clothed for about one half what it now costs the government.

> Honorable N. C. Meeker, the well-known Superintendent of the White River Agency, was formerly a fast friend and ardent admirer of the Indians. He went to the Agency in the firm belief that he could manage the Indians successfully by kind treatment, patient precept and good example.

1880: Cong. Investigation - Battle of Milk Creek

One contemporary historian postulates that the *Utes attack was "directly ascribable to the neglect and indifference of the Indian Bureau at Washington. The time for the distribution of the annuities to the White River Utes had passed*, and the Bureau at Washington *calmly ignored the whole business*." Flour, blankets, and other supplies sat in depots at Rawlins, Wyoming, and rotted. (Emphasis added).[120] *Meanwhile, the Indians went hungry and naked.* Then they began to wander off the reservation and make reprisals upon the settlers. (Emphasis added).[121]

In a Congressional investigation, the ambiguity in whether the Army intended to attack the Utes was sharply questioned. The soldiers did not have a flag of truce with them, officer Cherry waved a hat to arrange a parley with the Indians. The Utes thought it was a signal to attack. The investigation found it was contentious since it was not a typical signal, such as using a white flag:

> By Mr. POUND:
> Q. Would the Indians have respected a flag of truce?
> A. I, of course, cannot say as to that. .... *They did not respect what was intended as a flag of truce, this waving of my hat.*
> *Q. Would not the waving of a hat be as much a sign of war as of Peace? Might it not be so considered by them?*
> A. I know nothing of their customs in that respect, but the manner of my men stopping and sitting there quietly on their

horses, and my own attitude, looking right towards the Indians, and not towards my men, and waving my hat in a friendly manner-all these things considered, it seems to me that there was no possibility of such a mistake. (Emphasis added).

By Mr. Errett:
Q. If you were going out to hold a parley, wouldn't it have been more prudent for you to have taken a flag of truce along. A. Well, it might have been better, but still I don't think that it would have made any difference. Indeed, I don't know that I had such a thing as a white handkerchief about me. I think the only handkerchief I had was a silk one around my neck, and that was of a different color.

By Mr. Poeiiler:
Q. Was Mr. Meeker asked to come out with the command?
A. Yes ....

Jack, a chief of the Utes, was recalled and further examined (through Ouray and another interpreter), as follows:

The soldiers when they got down to Milk River instead of stopping there as I thought they would, crossed the river they took the trail which led up to where the Indians were, and came up very fast until they got to a little creek there, and stopped on the north side of the creek ... About this signal that it was said the soldiers made I did not see any, but I understood that some Utes who were off quite a distance from me on the lower side saw some signal-saw a soldier take off his hat and wave it, but I did not see that, nor did anybody near me.[122]

1880: General Pope - Utes Worthless

The White River band of Utes is in no sense different from the other bands of that nation. They are worthless, idle vagabonds, who are no more likely to earn a living where they are by manual labor than by teaching metaphysics.[123]

Commissioner in Favor of Utes Removal to Utah

Thus, the Indian Bureau presented its desire to relocate the tribe as a matter of military and practical expediency. Commissioner Ezra A. Hayt stated:

The reason I favored it [transfer of the Utes to Indian Territory] is this: The Indian Territory has enough fertile land to enable those Indians to settle down comfortably. It has a superabundance of fertile land. Again, the country is not broken, ridged, and labyrinthine like this region in Colorado; *it is a country where the Army could use artillery*; and wherever our troops can use artillery the Indians know very well that it is useless for them to go upon the warpath, so that, as a defensive measure, I think it would be wise to take them out of their fortresses and put them where they will be less formidable ... I think, then, if we wish to avoid expensive war and to save the lives of our soldiers, it is very desirable to put these Indians out of their fortresses in Colorado. (Emphasis added).[124]

A settlement was entered into that would lead to the forcible removal of the majority of the Utes from Colorado to Utah.

1880: After Thornburgh/Meeker Incidents Ute Delegation Forced to DC to Punish Them by Dispossessing Them of Their Reservation

Otto Mears accompanied Chief Ouray and an Indian delegation *ordered* to Washington, where an agreement was forced upon them. *In order to punish the Indians for a massacre, dispossess them of their reservation, and remove them from Colorado, Congress passed the Act of June 15, 1880*, 21 Stat. 199, which ratified and embodied an agreement by their leaders to cede to the U.S. all territory of "the present Ute Reservation," which would be restored to the public domain for sale. An Executive Order of 1882 restored the lands to the public domain.

The Southern Utes agreed to remove to and settle upon the unoccupied agricultural lands on the La Plata River, in Colorado ... The Uncompahgre Utes agreed to remove to and settle upon agricultural lands on Grand River, near the mouth of the Gunnison River, in Colorado, if a sufficient quantity of agricultural land shall be found there, if not then upon such other unoccupied agricultural lands as may be found in that vicinity and in the Territory of Utah. The White River Utes agreed to remove to and settle upon agricultural lands on the Uintah Reservation in Utah.

It was proposed to settle the Uncompahgre Indians at the junction of the

~ 208 ~

Uncompahgre and Grand River, in Colorado. The Ute commission found that land at this point was unsuitable for the Indians, being neither adapted to agricultural nor pastoral pursuits; and *removed said Uncompahgre Indians to the Territory of Utah*.

1880: Utes Bribed to Sign Agreement to Cede Colorado Lands

The Utes at home refused at first to accept the legislation which would force their removal but were paid two dollars a piece by a commissioner, Otto Mears, to sign the Agreement. Commissioner Manypenny pressed bribery charges against Mears. Mears' hearing resulted in Interior Secretary Kirkwood agreeing to reimburse him for his personal expenses of $2,800 paid to the Indians. [Official documentation on allegations uncertain.]

> As part of the Commission to select a site for the Uncompahgres Indians' new reservation, Mears gave the stipulations of the Ute Treaty a very **"elastic"** interpretation, and accordingly the Umcompahgre Utes were removed from Colorado to a reservation in eastern Utah. They thought they were going to be removed to Grand Junction. They had to be forcibly removed by the U.S. Army to Utah.

1880-1881: Commission Removes Utes

A commission was appointed to superintend the physical removal and settlement of the Utes: former Commissioner George W. Manypenny; Alfred B. Meacham of Washington, DC; John J. Russell of the Department of the Interior; John B. Bowman, a mining man from Kentucky; and Colorado's Otto Mears, mining and transportation promoter.[125]

1881: Forced Military Removal of 200 Miles

In late August 1881 the commissioners said it was time for the move to begin.

> Finally, with his troops surrounding the Ute camp, Brevet Brigadier General Mackenzie threatened that he would use force if necessary, and the sad cavalcade started down the Gunnison River at dawn on September 1. … they arrived at their destination on September 13, having accomplished the two hundred-mile journey in less than two weeks.

1881: Whites Pour onto Land Left by Utes with No Shred of Common Decency

General Pope wrote of the occasion:

> "... the whites who had collected, in view of [the Utes] removal were so eager and unrestrained by common decency that it was absolutely necessary to use military force to keep them off the reservation until the Indians were fairly gone ..."[126]

The legislation cleared the way for the settlement of the valleys of the Gunnison, the Grand and the White Rivers. Throughout the state there was rejoicing. The Ouray Times said:

> Sunday morning the Utes bid adieu to their old hunting grounds and folded their tents, rounded up their dogs, sheep, goats, ponies and traps, and took up the line of march for their new reservation, followed by General McKenzie and his troops. This is an event that has been long and devoutly prayed for by our people. How joyful it sounds, and with what satisfaction one can say, "The Utes have gone". The great menace to the advancement and development of this grand southwestern country is no more. Eastern people can now come to this section in the most perfect security. Besides it throws open to the dominion of white men one of the most fertile and beautiful valleys in all Colorado; a valley that will be to those who are so fortunate as to become owners of its broad acres, a happy land of Canaan.[127]

1881: Cattle Enterprises

Once the Utes were moved to Utah in 1881, the open range cattle industry expanded. As the U.S. forced the Cheyenne and Arapaho off their Colorado land, cattle could graze for free on thousands of acres. For a scant $10,000 investment, John Wesley Iliff soon became the largest landowner in northeast Colorado, with approximately 15,500 acres. Feeding his herds on the open range created an opportunity for large profits. While grazing on the range was free, buying land and appropriating water rights secured Iliff water along the South Platte River. He sold cattle to Indian reservations, army posts like Fort Laramie, the city of Cheyenne, and Union Pacific railroad construction crews in Nebraska, Wyoming and Utah. With refrigerated cattle cars, he could ship cattle and dressed beef to Chicago's Union Stockyards.[128]

1881: Legislative Assembly of Colorado Territory: Bill for an Act to provide for the Destruction of Indians and Skunks

John Coulter, a lawyer, justice of the peace, Territorial Legislator in 1881, and Mayor of Georgetown in 1891 and 1892, introduced on January 29, 1881, in the Colorado House of Representatives, H.B. No. 178, a bill for an act to provide for the destruction of Indians and skunks. Section 1 provided as follows:

> Section 1: That any person who shall produce the scalp of any Indian or skunk found in this State, shall receive a reward or premium of twenty-five (25) dollars for each and every Indian or skunk scalp produced, to be paid out of the State treasury... p. 321

> On February 2, 1881, the bill was referred to a special committee: H. Bill. No. 178, a bill for an act for the destruction of Indians and skunks, Was read a second time. Mr. Brush moved that the bill be referred to a special committee of five, with Mr. Coulter as chairman, Which motion prevailed.

> On February 2, 1881, the special committee recommended that it be passed· The special committee to whom was referred H. B. No. 178, presented the following report: Mr. Speaker: Your special committee to whom was referred H.B. No. 178, a bill for an act for the destruction of Indians and skunks, have had the same under consideration, and instruct me to report said bill back to the House with the recommendation that it be passed. Jno. A. Coulter, Chairman.

> On February 4, 1881, it was scheduled for a special order: H.B. No. 178, a bill for an act to provide for the destruction of Indians and skunks, and instruct me to report the same back to the House with the recommendation that it be made a special order for 7:30 P.M., February 11, 1881.

> On February 11, 1881, it was moved that it be considered for final passage. The special order for this day and hour, being H.B. No. 178, a bill for an act in relation to Indians and skunks, Was taken up. Mr. Coulter moved that the bill be ordered engrossed and placed on its third reading and final passage. Mr. Lee moved that it be "chucked under the table," Which motion prevailed.[129]

1890: Commissioner Morgan - Southern Utes to Stay in Colorado

Colorado continued to advocate for removal to Utah of the one remaining Indian tribe in Colorado, the Southern Utes.

> The legislative assembly of [Utah] Territory at its last session adopted a memorial to Congress protesting against the proposed removal [of the Southern Colorado Utes] ... the presence of these Indians would be a menace and a hindrance to the settlement of the country... Utah has now her share of Indians, and should not be made to receive more at the selfish behest of a neighboring State.

They did not succeed and the Commissioner noted Colorado should not be too overly concerned:

> ... the Southern Utes are the only Indians now remaining in Colorado, and they number less than two thousand. Minnesota, Michigan, and Wisconsin each have over three times as many, Montana five, and California six times as many, North Dakota and South Dakota four and ten times as many, respectively, and the State of Washington five times as many; so that *in the distribution of our Indian population, to those who regard their presence as a detriment, Colorado seems to have been much more fortunate than many of her sister States*. (Emphasis added).[130]

1895: Hunter Act - Opened Up Ute Strip to Homesteading and Sale

In 1895, the Hunter Act enabled lands within the Ute Strip to be allotted to tribal members, and the surplus lands homesteaded and sold to non-Indians. The Utes were divided. The Weenuchiu under the leadership of Chief Ignacio opposed allotment. They moved westward and settled near what is today Towaoc. The Southern Utes (Mouache and Caputa bands) agreed to allotment.[131]

1906: Mesa Verde Carved Out of Southern Ute Lands

The prehistoric relics of Mesa Verde were first brought to public attention in 1876 with the publication of the Hayden Surveys of 1874 and 1875-76.[132] Establishing a National Park was advocated.

One of the main obstacles to the park was the fact that some of the most important cliff dwellings, including Cliff Palace, were not on public land, but within the Southern Ute Indian Reservation. In the spring of 1906 a survey was made by the Bureau of American Ethnology, with the help of Edgar Lee Hewett, to fix the park boundaries. Hewett accompanied the surveyors and identified the ruins to be included.[128] As thus described, the proposed Mesa Verde park comprised a strip of land along the Mancos River fourteen and a half miles long and several miles wide, embracing a total area exceeding sixty-five square miles. Concerned over important omissions from the park proposal, Hewett wrote Commissioner Francis E. Leupp of the Office of Indian Affairs and suggested an amendment to Hogg's bill providing that all prehistoric ruins situated on Indian lands within five miles of the boundaries of Mesa Verde National Park also be included within the jurisdiction of its officers for administrative purposes. This strip contained an additional 274 square miles. The amendment was promptly accepted by the House Public Lands Committee. As Hewett wrote, "This secures what has been so much desired by all namely the inclusion of all the great Mesa Verde and Mancos Canyon ruins within the National Park." [133]

On June 15 the House Committee on Public Lands reported the Mesa Verde National Park bill favorably, and eight days later it had passed both the House and Senate. It was signed by President Roosevelt on June 30, only twenty-two days after he approved the Antiquities Act.[134]

> An Act Creating the Mesa Verde National Park SEC. 3. That the Secretary of the Interior be, and he is hereby, authorized to permit examinations, excavations, and other gathering of objects of interest within said park ... undertaken only for the benefit of some reputable museum, university, college, or other recognized scientific or educational institution, with a view to increasing the knowledge of such objects and aiding the general advancement of archaeological science. Approved, June 29, 1906.[135]

According to the agreement with the Wiminuche, the government would obtain 12,760 acres on the Southern Ute Indian Reservation and agree to give the Indians a tract lying west and within the park boundary containing about 6,000 acres and a second tract.[136]

Colorado Moguls

Mining and Real Estate

Spencer Penrose came from a very accomplished eastern family; his brothers were a U.S. senator and Republican Party leader, a noted geologist, and a successful medical doctor. Penrose came west and as a businessman, miner, mill owner, and investor who worked primarily in the Pike's Peak region, he built up the city of Colorado Springs. He had assets in Colorado, Utah, Arizona, and Kansas, including mines and real estate properties. He is most notable for owning the Cash On Delivery mine in Cripple Creek and for building the Broadmoor Hotel.

In 1902, with the Cripple Creek gold rush slowing down, Spencer Penrose and Charles L. Tutt, Sr., along with the Guggenheims, invested in the speculative technology for extracting copper from low-grade ore proposed by Daniel Jackling, a mineralogist. The Bingham Canyon Mine in Utah started with underground mining and switched to open-pit mining, using steam shovels, with railway access to transport the ore for processing. It produced about 30 percent of all the copper used by the Allied Forces for weapons, equipment, tools, and communication wires. One of the largest man-made excavations on earth, it is visible from outer space. In 2013, it reached a width of 2.5 miles and a depth of 3,900 feet. Still in operation, it has produced more copper than any other mine in the world.

With his immense fortune, Penrose contributed to virtually every prominent landmark in Colorado Springs. Penrose built the world-famous Broadmoor Hotel, the Pike's Peak Highway, the Cheyenne Mountain Zoo, and the Will Rogers Shrine. He also started the Pike's Peak Hill Climb and along with his wife, Julie, was central in the founding of the Colorado Springs Fine Arts Center, the rejuvenation of Central City Opera, and the expansion of Colorado College. His philanthropy is continued through the El Pomar Foundation.

Metal Processing Enterprises[137]

Nathaniel Peter Hill (1832-1900) was a mining entrepreneur and U.S. senator from Colorado. In the 1860s, Hill, an accomplished chemist and metallurgist, bought mining interests in Black Hawk and developed the first successful smelter in Colorado, revolutionizing the mining industry in the fledgling territory and beyond. Hill recognized that Colorado's gold miners needed a new extraction method. In 1867, he founded the Boston and Colorado Smelting Company, opened Colorado's first successful smelter in January 1868. In the decade before Hill's smelter opened, miners in Gilpin County had extracted a total of $9.4 million in gold. In the decade after Hill's smelter opened, Gilpin County miners more than doubled their gold production to $20.2 million. Hill's company ruled Colorado's smelting industry in those years, and Hill also acquired mining interests in Central City. He was a friend of President Hayes and served as a U.S. Senator.

After his move to Denver, Hill expanded his business interests. He acquired real estate and helped develop property around the growing city. In 1887 he helped form the Denargo Land Company and served as its president. He also served as president of the United Oil Company and purchased a local newspaper, the Denver Republican. In his later years, he sat on the board of trustees of the Colorado School of Mines, where he also taught classes.

With the usual social congregation of the wealthy, his neighbors included the Evanses, Iliffs and the Byers. Byers owned the Rocky Mountain News and fifteen years after the Sand Creek Massacre still believed that Sand Creek had "saved Colorado and taught the Indians the most salutary lesson they ever learned."[138] This led to financial and political leverage, along with the consolidation and integration of common industrial interests.

Meyer Guggenheim made his fortune (one of the largest of the 19th century) through business ventures in mining and smelting, mostly in the U.S. After investing in silver mines in the Leadville mining district of Colorado, he expanded into ore smelting in Colorado. He built a number of smelters across the U.S. and in northern Mexico. Later, he expanded into copper (Utah's Bingham Canyon, Canada and Chile) and lead—needed in telephone and electrical systems. Internationally, he engaged in rubber and diamond production in the Belgian Congo.

City Developers, Denver, Colorado

Early arrivals such as Walter Cheesman, David Moffat, and James Archer led efforts to bring reliable and safe water service to Denver. They provided the financing for constructing and maintaining extensive ditch systems.

In 1868 Cheesman, John Evans and David H. Moffat began work to build the Denver Pacific Railroad to Cheyenne, Wyoming. Cheesman was president of the railroad for several years. He planned for the construction of the Union Station, and he was active in the building of the Denver Boulder Valley Railroad and South Park Road. The railroad helped Denver become a major city. He also was a director of the Denver, Northern, and Pacific Railway Company.

Cheesman was an organizer of the International Trust Company and served as a member of its executive committee for more than 15 years, and he was a member of the Denver Real Estate Exchange. He bought real estate throughout the years, established financial institutions, and helped develop mines.

In 1870, he became a principal in a company to provide water to Denver. With David Moffat and Thomas Hayden, they consolidated two water plants into the monopolistic Denver Union Water Company in 1894, which grew to a $25 million organization. Cheesman built dams, reservoirs, and filtration and distribution systems.

City Developers, Durango, Colorado

General William J. Palmer, president of the Denver & Rio Grande Railway railroad, along with William A. Bell and John A. Porter formed the Durango Trust to establish the townsite and buy and sell property. As investors in the New York and San Juan Mining and Smelting Company, they built a smelter in Durango, purchased a limestone quarry and several nearby coal mines. On July 8, 1882, the Denver & Rio Grande Railroad made its way into Silverton. In that year, the "Silvery San Juan" produced $20,000,000 worth of ore.

Investment Banking

Jay Cooke was an American financier who helped finance the Union war effort during the Civil War and the postwar development of railroads in the northwestern U.S. He is generally acknowledged as the first major investment banker in the U.S. and creator of the first wire house firm. On January 1, 1861, just months before the start of the American Civil War, Cooke opened the private banking house of Jay Cooke & Company in Philadelphia. Soon after the war began, the state of Pennsylvania borrowed $3,000,000 to fund its war efforts.

> In the early months of the war, Cooke worked with Treasury Secretary Salmon P. Chase to secure loans from the leading bankers in the Northern cities. Cooke's own firm was so successful in distributing Treasury notes that Chase engaged him as special agent to sell the $500 million in "five-twenty" bonds—callable in five years and matured in 20 years— authorized by Congress on February 25, 1862. The Treasury had previously tried and failed to sell these bonds. Promised a sales commission of 0.5 percent of the revenue from the first $10 million, and 0.375 percent of subsequent bonds, Cooke

financed a nationwide sales campaign, appointing about 2,500 sub-agents who traveled through every northern and western state and territory, as well as the Southern states as they came under control of the Union Army. Meanwhile, Cooke secured the support of most Northern newspapers, purchasing ads through advertising agencies, and often working directly with editors on lengthy articles about the virtues of buying government bonds. His editorials, articles, handbills, circulars, and signs most often appealed to Americans' desire to turn a profit, while simultaneously aiding the war effort. Cooke quickly sold the $500 million in bonds, and $11 million more. Congress immediately sanctioned the excess.

Cooke influenced the establishment of national banks, and organized a national bank at Washington and another at Philadelphia almost as quickly as Congress could authorize the institutions.

In the early months of 1865, the government faced pressing financial needs. After the national banks saw disappointing sales of "seven-thirty" notes, the government again turned to Cooke. He sent agents into remote villages and hamlets, and even into isolated mining camps in the west, and persuaded rural newspapers to praise the loan. Between February and July 1865, he disposed of three series of the notes, reaching a total of $830,000,000. This allowed the Union soldiers to be supplied and paid during the final months of the war. In 1870 his firm financed the construction of the Northern Pacific Railway.

Colorado Gold Production History

The total Colorado production of the precious and allied metals from 1859 to 1870, inclusive, was: Gold $27,213,081; silver $330,000; copper $40,000; total, $27,583,081.

The annual gold output of the state increased from $4,150,000 in 1890 to $28,702,036 in 1900.

A study by the U.S. Geological Survey in 1923 is very specific as to the value of minerals in Colorado. Even though it was written in 1923, an extrapolation of current monetary values can be made from this past data.

This history of mining in Colorado will be useless unless the facts set forth for the period 1859-1923 can point in some way to the future. That Colorado has been a large producer of metals is definitely known. That it has been chiefly a producer of gold and silver is shown by the fact that of the calculated gross value of recovered gold, silver, copper, lead, and zinc, amounting to $1,531,000,000, $673,000,000 in gold, or 44 per cent of the total, and 628,850,000 ounces of silver, with a commercial value of $501,734,000, or 33 per cent, represent the gold and silver added to the world's supply. Thus 77 per cent of the total gross value of Colorado's production of these five metals is represented by gold and silver. Most of the gold is still in existence. A great part of the silver was coined and in this form represents a value of $1.29 an ounce. The copper produced, chiefly as a by-product of gold and silver mining, amounting to 263,000,000 pounds, with a gross calculated value of $40,328,000, has not all been dissipated. The enormous quantity of lead recovered, 4,200,000,000 pounds, with a gross value of $189,662,000, and the large quantity of zinc recovered, 1,740,000,000 pounds, with a gross calculated value of $126,216,000.

It seems hardly a mere coincidence that the total gross value of these five metals-$1,531,000,000 to the end of 1923, is very close to the assessed valuation of the State of Colorado for 1923, $1,550,000,000. The fact that the curve of the assessed value from the early days of Colorado-when mining or labors dependent on mining had developed the only assessable wealth-to the present time not only parallels but actually coincides with the curve of the gross production of the five metals can not be a mere accident. Denver in particular owes its growth to mining. Colorado Springs owes a great part of its development to mining. Pueblo owes its industrial existence to mining and metallurgy.[139]

Colorado's gold output through 1965 was about 40,776,000 ounces.[140]

Other minerals and commodities currently mined in the state include oil, natural gas, coal, carbon dioxide, helium, molybdenum, sand, gravel, quarry aggregate, clay, limestone, gypsum, nahcolite (sodium bicarbonate), and dimension and decorative stone (e.g., marble, sandstone).[141]

Colorado's Mining Millionaires

By 1892, there were thirty-nine millionaires in Colorado. This article is set forth in its entirety. Many of these men had made their fortunes through mining or by supporting the development of mining in the state.

> Official statistics show that Colorado produced from 1859 to December 31, 1904 at the current market prices for the metals: Gold $355,014,347; silver $386,457,857; lead $121,118,146; copper $17,835,820; zinc (a recent product) $10,740,207; total, $891,259,375.
>
> The total Colorado production of the precious and allied metals from 1859 to 1870, inclusive, was: Gold $27,213,081; silver $330,000; copper $40,000; total, $27,583,081.
>
> The annual gold output of the state increased from $4,150,000 in 1890 to $28,702,036 in 1900.
>
> Note that this list does not include those millionaires who later benefited from the Cripple Creek gold boom of the 1890s. The average mine worker earned $3.00 per day in 1892.
>
> There are few who have any idea of the number of millionaires in Denver and in Colorado. One would hardly believe that there are thirty-three ... in this city. .... Besides there are six millionaires in the state outside of Denver.
> [Horace] Tabor heads the list with several millions, all made in mining.
> Then comes [Nathaniel] Hill, whose money was made in the mining [and smelter] business...
> David Moffatt accumulated his money in the banking and railroad business...
> E. Eildy is another mining and smelting man.
> Charles Kountze...is in mining.
> William James accumulated his wealth in the same business.
> John Reithmann is also in the mining business.
> Samuel Morgan was a miner.
> Jerome Chaffee was in the mining business.
> H.M. Griffin of Georgetown was also a miner."

John W. Mackey, Comstock, from 1880 to 1888 owned and

operated the Freeland mine, Clear Creek County, Colorado, which during his ownership produced $3,350,000 worth of mineral, mostly gold, within 600 feet from the surface.

The late L. Z. Leiter, of Chicago, and the late William H. Stevens, of Detroit, were the principal owners in the famous Iron Silver mine at Leadville. This mine since 1879 ... has produced upwards of $15,000,000 and is still paying dividends.

The late M. Guggenheim, of New York, ... and Charles Graham, of Philadelphia, made large fortunes out of their joint ownership and operation of the phenomenal A.Y. & Minnie mine at Leadville, which since 1870 has produced upwards of $8,000,000 from a comparatively small area and is still producing. ...

N.K. Fairbank, of Chicago, the late Charles D. Arms, of Youngstown Ohio; Robert McCurdy, also of Youngstown, Ohio, and D.M. Hyman, of Cincinnati, Ohio, made large sums out of the bonanza silver mines of Aspen in the '80s.

The late Joseph Reynolds (often known as "Diamond Joe"), of Chicago and St. Louis, made a large portion of his fortune from various mines in Clear Creek County.

The late Edmund C. Bassick ...made a handsome fortune out of the Bassick mine, Custer county, Colorado, and died a few years ago in his native state, Connecticut.

R. G. Shannon, of New York, is a large stockholder in the Portland mine, Cripple Creek, which produced from 1894 to December 31, 1904, produced $20,679,363 worth of gold and paid $5,377,080 in dividends.

Among the millionaire Colorado mining men now deceased were the following:

Ex-Senator H.A.W. Tabor made a large fortune from various mines in Leadville...

W.S. Stratton made his fortune in the 90s in the famous

Independence mine, Cripple Creek ... In 1894 Winfield Scott Stratton became the first millionaire to come out of the District.

William Church made a large fortune in the 90s in copper mines in Graham county, Ariz. ...

Among the Colorado men who made fortunes by mining in Colorado and are not now residents of the state are the following:

Eben Smith, now resident in Los Angeles, Calif., during a period of over 30 years mined successively in Gilpin and Boulder counties and at Leadville, Aspen and Cripple Creek.

Thomas F. Walsh, now resident in Washington, DC, made his fortune in the 90s and since out of the famous Camp Bird mine, near Ouray.

D.R.C. Brown, Jerome B. Wheeler and W.B. Devereux, all now residents in New York city, made handsome fortunes out of mining at Aspen in the 80s.

J.J. Hagerman, now resident in the Pecos valley, New Mexico, derived a considerable part of his fortune from mining in Aspen.

Henry R. Wolcott, still a resident of Denver, but mostly resident in New York city, profitably mined at Leadville, Creede and Cripple Creek, Colorado, also in Montana and is now mining in New Mexico.

Edward G. Stolber, now traveling around, made a fortune out of the Silver Lake mine, near Silverton, Colorado

William Bailey and O.P. Posey, both resident at Los Angeles, Calif., each made very considerable sums out of the famous Boy mine near Telluride.

Partial list of present residents of **Denver alone** ... who have individually made anywhere from $50,000 up to millions of dollars from mining operations ... does not include any "professional promoter" or "company-monger" ... [Similar lists could be made of residents in Colorado Springs, Pueblo, or elsewhere.]

Frank Adams, (Telluride); Charles Armstrong, (Ouray); A. Ashbaugh, M.D., (Gilpin county).

William Barth, (Cripple Creek); T. Walter Beam, (Telluride); J.W. Benson, (Ouray); John Best (Gilpin county); Max Boehmer, M.E., (Leadville); Charles Boettcher, (Leadville); Henry Boltholf, (Leadville); S.G. Bonney, M.D., (Cripple Creek); James J. Brown, (Leadville); L.B. Brown, (Leadville); W. G. Brown, Banker, (Leadville); D.W. Brunton, (Aspen); Charles Burns, (Aspen, Creede); Hugh Butler, attorney, (Gilpin county, Aspen, Leadville); W.H. Bryant, attorney (Creede).

F.J. Campbell, (Cripple Creek, Colorado, Goldfield, Nev.); L.E. Campbell (Leadville, Creede, Cripple Creek); John F. Campion, (Leadville, Breckenridge); Rodney Cavanaugh, (Creede); Charles Cavender, attorney, (Leadville); Walter S. Cheeseman, (Leadville, Creede, Cripple Creek, Red Cliff); A.J. Clark, (Telluride); Judge E.A. Colburn, (Cripple Creek); Edward Collingwood, (Breckenridge); T.T. Cornforth, merchant, (Black Hills, S.D.); E.B. Costigan (Telluride).

Thomas F. Daly, insurance, (Leadville); W.H. Davis, (Cripple Creek); Royal J. Donnen, (Leadville); D.H. Dougan, banker, (Leadville); James Doyle, (Cripple Creek and La Plata county); John Dumont, (Clear Creek county).

James H. Emerson, (Cripple Creek); Augustus L. Engelbach, (Leadville); Robert Esty, (Leadville).

John B. Farish, M.E., (Old Mexico); Charles Finding, (Breckenridge); Michael Finnerty, (Leadville, Cripple Creek); John Fortune, (Park county); E. Le Neve Foster, M.E., (Georgetown and Summit county); Peter J. Fredericks, (Cripple Creek); W.A. Fullerton (Gilpin county).

J. Gavin, (Leadville); Judge L.M. Goddard, (Leadville); Timothy Goodwin, (Leadville); J.W. Graham, M.D., (Cripple

Creek, Colorado, Goldfield, Nev.); Horace Granfield, (Cripple Creek); ex-Governor James B. Grant, (Leadville).

Percy Ham, (Leadville); Charles Harker, (Gilpin county); E.H. Hendrie, merchant, (Leadville); Charles. L. Hill, (Leadville); George Hook, (Leadville); B.A. Hopkins, (Georgetown and Summit county); Charles J. Hughes, attorney, (Aspen, Cripple Creek); Albert E. Humphreys, (Creede).

Harry C. James, (Leadville).

Silas S. Kennedy, (Boulder county); E.A. Kent, manufacturer, (Hinsdale county); Benjamin Kimber, (Gilpin county); Charles B. Kounizo, banker, (various districts).
Judge Owen Le Fevre, (Creede); Lewis E. Lemen, M.D., (Clear Creek County); W.R. Leonard, (Coeur d'Alene, Idaho); Henry P. Lowe, (Gilpin county).

A. P. Mackoy, (Aspen, Cripple Creek); Alfred Mann, M.D., (Arizona); James McClurg, (Cripple Creek); Governor Jesse F. McDonald, (Leadville); Robert L. Martin, (Clear Creek and Gilpin counties); D.G. Miller, (Ouray, Creede, Aspen); David H, Moffat, Jr., banker, (Leadville, Creede, Aspen); John. G. Morgan, (Leadville, Creede).

Samuel D. Nicholson, (Leadville, Lake City).

T.J. O'Donnell, attorney, (Hinsdale county); Harper M. Orahood, (Gilpin county); Judge Frank W. Owens, (Leadville).

W. Bryd Page, M.E, (Leadville); A.D. Parker, general auditor, Colorado and Southern railroad system, (Tonopah and Goldfield, Nev.); Charles C. Parsons, attorney, (Leadville, Colorado, Utah); Henry M. Porter, (New Mexico, Arizona); John A. Porter, (Telluride); Thomas H. Potter, banker, (Gilpin county).

Albert H. Reynolds. (Aspen, Ouray, etc.); Link Reynolds (Leadville); W.O. Reynolds, (Leadville); August Riche, (Leadville); J.H. Robeson, (Georgetown); Julius Rodman, (Creede, Lake City, Leadville); R.T. Root, (Arizona, New Mexico, etc.); ex-Governor John L. Routt, (Leadville).

Jacob F. Sanders, (Creede); Otto Sauer, (Gilpin County); D.J. Sayer, (Telluride, Colorado, Arizona); Hal Sayre, (Gilpin county); T.S. Schlesinger, (Leadville); Dennis Sheedy, banker, (Leadville); Fred L. Sigel, (Cripple Creek, Colorado, Goldfield, Nev.); Michael E. Smith, (Leadville); Link Spangler, (Cripple Creek); J. Standley, (Gilpin county); H.C. Stuchfield, manufacturer, (Hinsdale county); Dennis Sullivan, (Gilpin county, Leadville and Cripple Creek, Colorado, Arizona and Old Mexico); S.J. Sullivan, (Leadville, Colorado, Old Mexico); William Sullivan, (Silverton, Ouray); David Swickhelmer (Rico, Telluride).

Willard Teller, attorney and his brother, U.S. Senator Henry M. Teller, (Gilpin and Boulder counties); Joseph A. Thatcher, banker, (Gilpin county); ex-Governor Charles S. Thomas, (Leadville, Aspen, Creede); Judge C.I. Thomson, (Leadville, Aspen, etc.).

W.S. Ward, (Leadville); Joseph Watson, (Georgetown); Frank G. White, (Leadville); Edward W. Williams, (Gilpin and Clear Creek counties); R.R. Williams, (Gunnison county); G.S. Wood, (Cripple Creek, Colorado, Goldfield, Nev.); Lee Wood, (Rico, Cripple Creek).

W.H. Yankee, (Aspen, etc., etc.).

Adolph J. Zang, brewer, (Cripple Creek, Ouray).

All present indications are that during 1905 Colorado will equal, if not exceed, her greatest past annual record production of the precious and allied metals, viz, that of 1900, which was $50,314,010; also that Colorado will continue to produce annually from $40,000,000 to $50,000,000 worth of the precious and allied metals for many years yet to come.[142]

Colorado Counties

All of today's 64 Colorado counties have a history of Indian inhabitation. On November 1, 1861, the new Colorado Territory created 17 original counties: Arapahoe, Boulder, Clear Creek, Costilla, Douglas, El Paso, Fremont, Gilpin, Guadalupe, Huerfano, Jefferson, Lake, Larimer, Park, Pueblo, Summit, and Weld. It is important to understand that these counties initially covered immense areas and were later reduced in size. *For example, seven counties now occupy the area originally assigned to Weld County.*

One of the more dominant tribes were the Utes. The Tabeguache or Uncompahgre Bands lived in west-central Colorado along the Gunnison and Uncompahgre River Valleys. They considered Pike's Peak the heart of their lands. The Yampa Band of Utes lived in the Yampa River Valley and North and Middle Parks. The Parianuche or Grand Valley Band lived along the Colorado River. The Uintah Utes lived in the Uintah Basin in northeastern Utah and northwestern Colorado. The Weeminuche, Muache and Capote Bands lived in southwest Colorado. The 1776 Dominguez and Escalante Expedition's Map clearly demarcated the different areas of the various Ute Bands ("Yutahs") and the Arapaho ("Rapahu").

The Cheyenne and Arapaho formed an alliance in 1811. In 1840, the Kiowa, Comanche, and Lakota joined the Cheyenne and Arapaho in an unprecedented alliance to resolve territorial disputes and counter the growing number of emigrants headed west. After the Sand Creek Massacre, the Cheyenne, Arapaho and Lakota formed an alliance to engage in the 1865 Indian War. The Cheyenne, Arapaho and Lakota fought together in the 1st and 2nd Battles of Julesburg in 1865; the Battle of Beecher Island in 1868; and the Battle of Summit Springs in 1869.

The Comanche were Bent Fort's major trading partner.

The Navajo Nation has two of their Four Sacred Mountains within the State of Colorado. Blanca Peak, marking the eastern boundary of its traditional homeland, is in present-day Alamosa County. Mt. Hesperus, marking the northern boundary of its traditional homeland, is in present-day Montezuma County.

Various tribes engaged in battle with one another for control of different areas. For example, the Utes fought the Jicarilla Apache and the Comanche for control of southern Colorado. The Pawnee also had a presence in Colorado. Other tribes have a history in the area as 48 contemporary tribes are historically tied to the lands that make up the State of Colorado.

So while a tribe or tribes may be associated with a particular area, it is important to understand the widespread areas in which tribes shared summer or wintering grounds, in areas with game or along rivers with cottonwood trees for shelter or visited Hot Springs such as those at Pagosa.

Denver City Council's Land Acknowledgment is as follows:

> The land on which we reside is the traditional territory of the Ute, Cheyenne, and Arapaho Peoples, and the 48 contemporary tribal nations that are historically tied future, and those who have stewarded this land throughout generations. We also recognize that government, academic and cultural institutions were founded upon and continue to enact exclusions and erasures of Indigenous Peoples. May this acknowledgment demonstrate a commitment to working to dismantle ongoing legacies of oppression and inequities and recognize the current and future contributions of Indigenous communities in Denver.[143]

A very cursory analysis of what happened in the counties of Colorado from Frank Hall's 1895 History of Colorado is set forth below. It is important to know about the mining, farming, ranching, railroads and urban development that occurred on Indian lands that were forcibly ceded to the U.S. As public domain lands they were opened for homesteading usually at $1.25/acre. Squatters were given preference to purchase the land they had illegally settled, including land on Indian reservations.

After the Ute removal in 1880, townsite companies organized within northwestern Colorado.[144]

The comprehensive research done by History Colorado and Colorado Encyclopedia has been invaluable in understanding the many counties of Colorado, and is reflected herein. See Chart of Counties in the last Chapter.

Farming

Colorado's Gold Rush changed farming in northeastern Colorado almost overnight. Miners needed supplies and at first, depended upon foodstuffs imported from the Midwest. Flour cost as much as $50 a barrel here but hungry miners were more than willing to pay these inflated prices. Further, because many of Colorado's Fifty-niners had farming backgrounds they turned to agriculture after they were unable to survive in the mines. These people found the mountain meadows and lands along the foothills fertile and they took up farms in those places. Farmers did not plant crops for survival but rather to sell. Agriculture in northeastern Colorado rapidly changed from subsistence to commercial farming. As fast as Indian title was extinguished by treaties, farmers filed claims.[145]

In the 1870s, railroads in the mining districts and discoveries of gold and silver in the San Juan Mountains, the Gunnison Valley, and Leadville re-ignited the minerals industry. The forced removal of much of Colorado's Ute population in 1881 made industrial mining possible in places such as Aspen (silver) and the San Juan Mountain towns of Ouray, Silverton, and Telluride (gold and silver).

When gold deposits seemed to be depleted again in the late nineteenth century, miners applied modern industrial technology to the ancient concept of gold panning, creating monstrous machines called dredges. A dredge was a floating platform equipped with a mechanical chain of buckets attached to a boom on a huge flat-bottom barge. The dredge buckets scooped large volumes of riverbed gravel into rotating steel cylinders. Small materials, including gold, filtered down into a sluice while jettisoning larger pieces of waste rock off the back of the dredge via a conveyer belt. The "waste" gravel was then stacked by a conveyor belt in piles still visible in such places as along the Blue River near present-day Breckenridge.

Mesa Verde Land Acknowledgments

Visit USA Parks Land Acknowledgment:

Today, there are 24 tribes that have a special relationship with this landscape and its long history; the 19 Pueblo Tribes of New Mexico: Taos, Picuris, Sandia, Isleta, Ohkay Owingeh, Santa Clara, San Ildefonso, Nambe, Tesuque, Jemez, Cochiti, Pojoaque, Santo Domingo, San Felipe, Santa Ana, Zia, Laguna, Acoma, and Zuni, the Hopi Tribe in Arizona, the Ysleta del Sur Pueblo in Texas, the Ute Mountain Ute Tribe in Colorado, the Southern Ute in Colorado and Navajo Nation in Colorado, Arizona, and New Mexico.[147]

Land Acknowledgement:

Today, we acknowledge that the ground beneath our feet is historically the home of Indigenous Peoples. It is the ancestral lands of the Puebloan, Ute tribes and Dine, who have occupied this land before colonization. The Weenuchiu band are now recognized as Ute Mountain Utes who are located in Towaoc just outside of Cortez, Colorado. The Mouache and Caputa bands make up the Southern Ute Indian Tribe of Ignacio, Colorado. Hesperus Peak, located just west of Durango, is the tallest peak in the La Plata mountain range, and is identified as one of the four sacred mountains by the Dine people, aka Navajo.

The history of these lands have been told from a western perspective, without fully acknowledging the indigenous people who occupied this land before it was La Plata County and Montezuma County. It is imperative to know that we are living and working on stolen lands.

We are here to create a peaceful environment for all and to be inclusive of history, culture, and humanity. Thank you for acknowledging the history of lands with me today.

Ahe'hee.[148]

Southwest Conservation Corps - Four Corners Land Acknowledgement: Today we want to recognize the original stewards of the land we are occupying and working on. The land we stand on is the traditional land of the Puebloan and Ute tribes, who have taken care of this land for generations. Members of the Weenuchiu band are now recognized as the Ute Mountain Utes, headquartered in Towaoc, and the Mouache and Caputa bands make up the Southern Ute Indian Tribe headquartered in Ignacio. Additionally, Hesperus Peak, the tallest peak in the La Plata Mountain range, is one of the four sacred mountains of the Navajo, or Diné, People. It is important to acknowledge that we are working on stolen land. The main narrative of this area has been that of the dominant voice, without the recognition of the people who lived here before colonization and their descendants, many of whom still live here today. It is important to know that this statement is not made to ask for apologies or guilt. We are seeking to create accomplices to help to dismantle the false narratives and oppression of the original habitants of this space. Thank you for acknowledging this history with us as we begin and continue our work with Southwest Conservation Corps.[149]

Adams County (1902)

Historically, the Cheyenne, Arapaho, Ute and Lakota lived in what is today Adams County. Most of its population is concentrated in the Denver metro area, in the cities of Arvada, Aurora, Commerce City, and Thornton. It was named in honor of Governor Alva Adams, who served two terms and sixty days as governor of the state.

The Arvada Center's Land Acknowledgment is as follows:

> Our facilities stand atop ancestral lands that include the Tsétséhéstaestse (Cheyenne), the Hinono'eiteen (Arapaho), Nuche (Ute), and Oceti Sakowin (Lakota) nations.

> We further acknowledge that the lands that make up the current state of Colorado are historically linked to 48 contemporary tribal nations.

> We offer respect to people of these nations—past, present and future. As we strengthen our resolve to honor their legacies we ask that you do so as well by giving pause to acknowledge the history of deceit, wrongdoing and Western settlement on their lands as well as the beauty of their languages, knowledge and strengths that informs our human experience today.[150]

Alamosa County (1913)

Historically, the Utes, primarily the Capote and Mouache Bands, lived in what is today Alamosa County. Blanca Peak is one of the Four Sacred Mountains of the Navajo Nation marking the eastern boundaries of its traditional homelands. The first Spanish explorer to enter the San Luis Valley was Juan de Zalvídar in 1596. Through irrigation from the Rio Grande the farmers produce potatoes, barley, alfalfa, wheat, and other crops. Ranching and tourism are current industries. The Great Sand Dunes National Park encompasses 30 square miles and the tallest dune towers 750 feet high.

Alamosa is a Spanish word meaning "cottonwood grove". Spanish pioneers gave the name to a creek within the existing county. The name was next given to the town and finally to the county.

The Adams State University's Land Acknowledgment is as follows:

> We, the Adams State University community, gratefully acknowledge the Indigenous peoples on whose ancestral lands we gather. This beautiful San Luis Valley is sacred to many Indigenous nations, including the Nuchu (Utes), Abáachi (Jicarilla Apaches), Numunu (Comanches), Ka'igwu (Kiowas), InunaIna (Arapahoe), Tsistsistas (Cheyenne), Diné (Navajo Nation), Pueblos, and all other First peoples who once made this valley their home. We honor the diverse communities that historically dwelled here and those who currently reside in the San Luis Valley. We know that honoring these lands is a reflective process that demands continued engagement and action.[151]

Arapahoe County (1861)

Historically, the Arapaho, Cheyenne, Ute, and Očhéthi Šakówiŋ lived in what is today Arapahoe County.

Arapahoe has the distinction of being Colorado's first county, as it was created as part of the western limits of the Kansas Territory in 1855. It was named for the Arapaho who inhabited the area. The Cheyenne and Arapaho struck an alliance in 1811.

In 1848 a group of prospectors on the way to California stopped to pan a few streams just west of present-day Denver. They found gold near present-day Englewood, where Dry Creek ran into the South Platte River. This was the first important discovery of gold in Colorado.

In 1851 and 1853, the U.S. signed treaties with the Cheyenne and Arapaho, along with several other Plains groups, in which Indians agreed not to attack whites traveling along the overland routes. Many Cheyenne and Arapaho began to realize that the ceaseless flow of whites into their lands meant the complete destruction of their resource base; thus, the earlier treaties were broken and raiding resumed.

On July 6, 1858, Russell found gold along Dry Creek, just downstream from where traces had been panned out ten years earlier. Several months later, on the east side of Cherry Creek, William Larimer, Jr., founded Denver City, the first seat of Arapahoe County.

In 1867, the Medicine Lodge Treaty established the Cheyenne-Arapaho Reservation in central Oklahoma, then known as "Indian Territory."

Meanwhile, G. A. Snow, a cattle rancher from New York, owned some 12,000 acres—almost half his ranch—in the eastern part of the county. The Snow family maintained the ranch from 1871 until 1957. Other large ranches included Parrett Ranch, Owens Ranch, and Price Ranch.

Arapahoe Community College's Land Acknowledgment is as follows:

> "As a means of expressing our gratitude, and in recognition of whose territory we reside in, we want to start our meetings by acknowledging the indigenous history of the land our institution is occupying, and specifically the peoples of the Arapaho, Cheyenne, Ute, and Očhéthi Šakówiŋ tribes. We are obligated to reflect on, and actively address, the history of this area, including the Sand Creek Massacre, as we continue in our work to move this institution towards a more inclusive and welcoming place for all people."[152]

Archuleta County (1885)

Historically, the Utes inhabited what is today Archuleta County. Other Indian Nations traveled to the "Healing Waters" to soak in Pagosa Springs and other springs, some too hot to touch. Pagosah is the Ute word meaning "healing waters" so the area became known as Pagosa Springs, the deepest hot spring aquifer in the world, 75-feet across, with a temperature of 155 degrees.

The first official report of the springs is from the "exploring expedition from Santa Fe, New Mexico, to the junction of the Grand and Green Rivers of the great Colorado of the West, in 1859, under the command of Capt. J.N. Macomb, U.S. Army Topographical Engineer."[153] Captain John N. Macomb led the 1859 San Juan Exploring Expedition whose purpose was to find a military supply route from Santa Fe, New Mexico to Utah and to map previously unexplored areas along the route.

The botanist with the expedition, John S. Newberry, reported in July, 1859:

> 'In the upperpart of this valley is the Pagosa, one of the most remarkable hot springs on the continent, well known, even famous, among the Indian tribes, but up to the time of our visit, never having been seen by the whites. It can hardly be

doubted that in future years it will become a celebrated place of resort, both for those who shall reside in the surrounding country, and for wonder-hunting health seeking travelers from other lands. There is scarcely a more beautiful place on the face of the earth. The valley is three miles long by one broad; a verdant meadow of the finest grass, thickly strewed with flowers, through which winds the bright and rapid river, margined by clumps of willows, and most graceful groups of cotton-wood. On every side are hills covered with gigantic pines or the slender Oregon spruces, and on the north, far above these, rise the forest-clad slopes and craggy crests of two great Sierras. The Pagosa is at the edge of this prairie.

Here is a great basin, oval in form, 40 by 50 feet in diameter, its walls of white rock, of unfathomable depth, in which the deep-blue water seethes and surges as in a boiling caldron, giving off a column of vapor which in damp weather is visible for miles. The water, though hot, is not at the boiling-point, and the ebullition is produced by the escape of gases, which are generated in enormous quantities.[154]

Some nonnatives began to visit the springs for health reasons in the 1870s. No public bathhouses existed, so people often bathed in seeps near the main spring, which was too hot for humans. Traffic increased after the Brunot Agreement of 1873 opened the San Juan Mountains to mining and white settlement. People began to settle around the springs, which lay along an important route to the San Juan mining camps.

President Hayes (in accordance with acts of Congress passed March 3, 1863, and July 1, 1864) issued an order, during the year 1880, designating a one mile square surrounding the principal spring as a U.S. town site. In 1883, it was platted by the government into streets, avenues, blocks, building lots, large parks and boulevards. It is located in Archuleta County, of which one-quarter of the county is covered by the Southern Ute Indian Reservation.

It was named in honor of Antonio D. Archuleta, who was the Senator from Conejos County when it was divided to form Archuleta County.

By 1900, the prevalence of logging and ranching brought the railroad to Pagosa Springs. When the railroad connected to towns further west, such as Durango, it made the logging and ranching industries the backbone of the regional economy.

Whites clamored for the U.S. to establish a military post nearby which they did in October 1878. The post was initially called Pagosa Springs before being renamed Camp Lewis, in honor of the recently deceased Lieutenant Colonel William Lewis. Garrisoned on October 17, 1878, with about one hundred men in order to safeguard the terms of the Brunot Agreement, it was positioned where the Indian and military trails crossed the San Juan River.

In January 1879 the camp was upgraded to Fort Lewis, signaling an installation that was intended to be permanent. After the 1879 Meeker Incident, about 500 troops were stationed at Fort Lewis. By January 1880, however, the army had decided that Fort Lewis was too isolated to be useful. Most of the troops headed west in May to reestablish the fort near Durango. The Fort was officially abandoned in November 1882.[155]

Baca County (1889)

The Comanche lived in the area of Baca County. It was named, at the suggestion of Senator Barela, for the Baca family of Trinidad. A member of this family was the first white settler on Two Buttes Creek. In the mid-1870s, ranching and agriculture were the primary industries.

Bent County (1870)

The Comanche and Cheyenne lived in the area of Bent County. William Bent (1809-69) and Ceran St. Vrain built an adobe trading post on the Arkansas River, situated along the Santa Fé Trail that connected Missouri and Mexico and quickly became the center of trade on the Great Plains. The Cheyenne were the Bents' primary trading partners, and through trade at the fort they obtained weapons to fight the Comanches. The Comanches raided and fought with Spanish New Mexicans to the south and occasionally clashed with the Arapaho.

In 1840, the Arapahos, Cheyennes, Comanches, Kiowas, and Naishans formed an unprecedented alliance of Plains groups. Importantly, all groups retained the right to winter in the Big Timbers. The peace also allowed the Comanches to begin trading directly with Bent's Fort.

Bent County was in the heart of an expanding Comanche territory that ran north and south between the Arkansas and Cimarron Rivers and stretched from the Sangre de Cristo Mountains in the west to what is today south-central Kansas in the east. Of particular value to the Comanches was a section of the Arkansas River Valley they called "Big Timbers," a veritable plains oasis.

This grove of cottonwood trees stretched east of the Purgatoire River for about sixty miles and provided the Comanches and their horses with food and shelter during the harsh plains winters.

It is uncertain why after a cholera epidemic in the area, Bent blew up the Post. He built another trading post further downriver in 1853, but the escalating tensions between whites and Indians ensured that his trade business would never recover. He leased the new post to the U.S. Army, which renamed it Fort Lyon in 1862.

During the construction of the Kansas Pacific railway across the plains in 1868-69, the Indians were extremely active and troublesome, harassing all routes of travel, killing the freighters, and grading parties, attacking ranches, stealing stock, and murdering and burning wherever the opportunity offered. Troops were sent against them from the east and from Fort Lyon, but it was not until 1870 that their depredations finally ceased.[156]

By the mid-1870s, a combination of resource woes and immense pressure from the American military brought an end to Comanche dominance of the Bent County area.

In 1884, construction began on the Fort Lyon Canal, one of the largest irrigation projects in Colorado history. When completed, the canal supplied water to nearly 100,000 acres of farmland in Bent and Otero Counties.

Ranching and agriculture are the primary industries.

Boulder County (1861)

The University of Colorado – Boulder's Land Acknowledgment is as follows:

> We acknowledge that the land where we work today in Boulder County is within the territory of the Hinóno'éí (Arapaho) people. We honor Chief Left Hand (Nawath), leader of the last Hinóno'éí band to spend their winters in the Boulder Valley. Many Hinóno'éí people were massacred by the U.S. Cavalry at Sand Creek, Colorado, in 1864. The survivors were forced out of Colorado to reservations in Wyoming and Oklahoma, where most Hinóno'éí live today.

~ 234 ~

We recognize that the university sits upon land within the territories of the Ute and Arapaho peoples. Further, we acknowledge that 48 contemporary tribal nations are historically tied to the lands that make up the state of Colorado. In our daily lives, let us honor and respect that the Boulder Valley is home to the Hinóno'éí people and to many other tribes that also camped, hunted, and traded here for centuries. Native people of many Indigenous nations live here today.[157]

Boulder County is named after Boulder City and Boulder Creek, which were given their names from the abundance of boulders in the area. The county straddles three unique geographic zones: mountains in the west, plains in the east, and a natural trough that runs between the plains and foothills.

The county was created in 1861, two years after prospectors discovered gold in Boulder Canyon.

Several distinct Ute bands roamed the Front Range in what would become Boulder County: the Parianuche, or "Elk People," the Tabeguache, or "People of Sun Mountain (Pike's Peak)," and Muaches, or "Cedar Bark People."

Unlike the Ute, who rarely left their mountain homeland, the Arapaho ranged across all three ecological zones in present-day Boulder County.

Arapaho leader, Niwot, attended the signing of the Treaty of Fort Laramie in 1851, which preserved Arapaho rights to the Boulder Creek area. After gold was found along the South Platte, few whites felt obligated to obey the treaty.

In 1861, Arapaho leaders, Niwot and Little Raven, were forced to negotiate another treaty, the Fort Wise Treaty, which surrendered the Front Range to the whites and carved out a small reservation for the Arapaho and Cheyenne in southeast Colorado. Niwot's and Little Raven's people spent two more lean and violent years in the Boulder Creek area before they moved to the Sand Creek Camp, near Fort Lyon in present-day Kiowa County.

The southern Arapaho under Little Raven were removed to Indian Territory (present-day Oklahoma) after the Medicine Lodge Treaty of 1867.

In the mountains west of Boulder City, Nederland was founded in 1871, as Middle Boulder, serving as a mill and supply town for the nearby mining community of Caribou.

Broomfield County (2001)

Historically, the Arapaho, Cheyenne and Ute lived in what is today Broomfield County.

Broomfield's Open Space Foundation Land Acknowledgment is as follows:

> We acknowledge that the land upon which we reside is the ancestral home of the Arapaho, Cheyenne, and Ute peoples. We further recognize that their connection to this place, both today and for countless generations, stewards the natural and cultural resources that we value so deeply. By acknowledging this connection, we strive to learn from, honor and respect these native ties in our open space landscapes.[158]

When the Colorado Gold Rush began in 1858-59, farms sprang up at the feet of the Front Range to feed the mining camps in the mountains. Present-day Broomfield began as one of these agrarian communities, due to its proximity to some of the early mines in Boulder, Clear Creek, and Gilpin Counties. In 1884, the U.S. Post Office opened a station in the town and named it Broomfield, after broomcorn, a crop that grew well in the area.

Chaffee County (1879)

Southwest Conservation Corps' Land Acknowledgment is as follows:

> Southwest Conservation Corps—Salida Land Acknowledgement: Salida, Colorado—home of Southwest Conservation Corps, Los Valles Region and we are on stolen land. Our entire service area, from the San Luis Valley, up the Upper Arkansas River Valley along the Collegiate Peaks, and into South Park is within the traditional land of the Ute People. The Mouache band lived in the eastern Rockies from Denver to New Mexico—along the Front Range and the West Mountain Valley, and the Caputa band lived east of the Continental Divide and south through the San Luis Valley. Both bands are known today as the Southern Ute and they are headquartered in Ignacio, Colorado. The southernmost tip of Los Valle's range runs into the traditional land of the Jicarilla Apache and to the north, the Cheyenne. The Spanish settlement of the San Luis Valley is also a vital part of the story of this area. It is important to us that we continue the Ute tradition

of stewardship of this land and as you travel around and work these trails, you'll see their names, Tabeuache, Weminuche, and hear their words, Saguache. Please take a moment to acknowledge the people who came before us, appreciate how resilient they were in this challenging environment. They did not migrate to this place. In their own words—they have always been here and will always be here.[159]

Chaffee County was named in honor of Senator Jerome B. Chaffee who retired from the U.S. Senate the year the county was formed.

Historian Frank Hall in his 1895 History of Colorado had some interesting stories of early miners, including Mr. Tabor, and fighting over water for irrigation:

> The Cache creek placers were discovered and opened in the spring of 1860. It was here that H. A. W. Tabor took his initiatory lessons in the labors and uncertainties of mining... Cache creek has for more than thirty years been regarded as one of the best placers in the mountains, and though worked almost continuously from 1860 to the present is not wholly exhausted. ... Gold in considerable quantities was scattered all through this part of the valley.[160]

> The following tragic incident related by Emerson, was one of the most exciting events that occurred in the upper Arkansas, between 1860 and the rise of Leadville in 1879: "The numerous streams coming into the Arkansas from the west afforded abundant water for irrigation, but early in the spring of 1874, a *difficulty arose in regard to water* and certain ditches from Brown creek, that resulted in the killing of George Harrington, a ranchman, and a neighbor, Elijah Gibbs, with whom he had had a dispute the day before, was arrested and tried for the murder, but acquitted, there being no evidence against him, the trial taking place in Denver. After he had returned to his ranch in the fall of 1874, an attempt was made to arrest and lynch him, which resulted in his killing three of the party making the attempt. (Emphasis added).

Insight into justice in the west also came into play in this saga:

> Judge E. F. Dyer, then county and probate judge, but acting as

a justice of the peace, upon complaint being made before him, issued warrants for the arrest of certain of this committee. In obedience to the summons, they, with associates, appeared at Granite for trial. They were heavily armed, the sheriff claiming his inability to disarm them, and after the dismissal of the case on the morning of July 3rd, 1875, Judge Dyer was brutally assassinated, shot dead in the court room. The assassins escaped, and but little effort was made to discover or arrest them."

Historian Frank Hall in his 1895 History of Colorado noted:

[L]arge bodies of Indians made a hunting ground and favorite retreat of this region. ... There were buffalo, elk, mountain sheep, deer, game birds and other sources of food supply. When the white hordes came to dig for gold, both Indians and game fled to the parks and valleys to the westward.

For centuries, the mountain Indians made the Poncha Hot Springs one of their chief resorts. There are ninety-nine of these springs.

Throughout the late nineteenth century, numerous mines operated throughout Chaffee County, producing gold, silver, iron ore, copper, and zinc. The Mary Murphy Mine in the Chalk Creek District, operated by the Mary Murphy Gold and Silver Mining Company of St. Louis, was the most famous.

Numerous hay, grain and vegetable ranches were located and cultivated along the alluvial bottom lands, deltas of the affluents of the Arkansas River, and some of them yielded large crops, under irrigation.[161]

1862: Butterfield Overland Despatch, Mail and Freight Service, Great Plains

In 1862, Atchison, Kansas resident, and entrepreneur David A. Butterfield moved his family west to the newly established mining town of Denver in western Kansas Territory. He returned to Atchison in 1864 with dreams of establishing a more direct overland route than the Arkansas and Platte River routes. That year, he commissioned a re-survey for a direct route between Atchison and Denver in advance of launching a fast freight and stagecoach line through Kansas. The survey expedition was commanded by Major James B. Pond with four companies of the 3rd Wisconsin Cavalry and two companies of the 13th Missouri Cavalry, Colonel Isaac Eaton, surveyor Lieutenant Julian

Fitch, and others which reported favorably that the Smoky Hill River road provided access to water and grass for animals and was safe. The route passed directly across Cheyenne and Arapaho lands.

David A. Butterfield organized a joint-stock express and passenger-carrying service between the Missouri River and Denver, Colorado, along the Smoky Hill River route. The first stage left Atchison, Kansas, on June 4, 1865, arriving in Denver, Colorado, on Sep. 23. Along the 592-mile-long route, relay stations were built about every 12 miles for passengers' rest, food, and changing of horses. Cheyenne Wells was a home station for the Overland Mail and Freight Service which had 17 stops in Colorado with 6 home stations. The line was an initial success, providing tri-weekly express service between Atchison, Kansas, and Denver, Colorado, in only 8-12 days.

Soldiers were also posted along the Trail to protect the stations and travelers from Indian attacks. However, the soldiers could not keep up with the Indian attacks against the invaders. Stations and ranches were burnt. At length a company of cavalry under Colonel Alexander was sent to keep the Indians in 'check.'

During this time, the Kansas Pacific Railroad was also pushing towards Denver, and by 1870, the stage line was no longer needed. When the Kansas-Pacific Railroad reached the Cheyenne Wells station in 1870, railroad agent Louis McLane bought land and laid out a town. The first lot was sold in 1887, and Cheyenne Wells was incorporated in 1890.[162]

Cheyenne County (1889)

Historically, the Kiowa, Cheyenne and Arapaho lived in what is today Cheyenne County. They claimed most of the plains east of the mountains and west of Kansas.[163]

By 1790 the Kiowa had moved onto the plains from the mountains of Montana. That year an agreement with the Comanche, the dominant group on the southern plains, gave the Kiowa a large territory that included the Cheyenne County area and other parts of eastern Colorado, as well as parts of present-day Kansas, Oklahoma, and the Texas Panhandle.

Finding themselves in the same territory and fighting common enemies such as the Lakota and Ute, the Cheyenne and Arapaho formed an alliance in the early 1800s. In 1840 the Kiowa, Comanche, and Lakota joined them in an unprecedented alliance with a similar goal—to resolve territorial disputes and better deal with the growing number of whites, who were by then migrating west along the Oregon and Overland Trails and competing with Indians for resources on the plains.

Indian hostilities against whites invading their territory are part of the history of this County:

> The entire length of the county from east to west is traversed by the Kansas Pacific railway ... The famous Smoky Hills, rendered historic by the fact of their having been the main headquarters of hostile Indians, lie in the northeastern portion, extending into Kansas. It was there that many parties of gold hunters in 1859 and subsequent years were attacked and roughly handled by savages. The first Pike's Peak stage and freight lines came to Denver by that route, starting from Leavenworth, and some years later it was occupied by the "Butterfield Overland Dispatch." From these bluffs or hills, the Indians sent out war parties that desolated the border, intercepted and destroyed stages and freight trains, burnt ranches and stations, and killed all companies of white men that were not too strong for them. In the summer of 1878 a band of Ute Indians under Chief Shawano, while hunting in this region, killed Mr. Joseph McLane (July 30th), a brother of Mr. L. N. McLane, now, and for many years, a resident of Cheyenne Wells. There were 500 Indians and 250 warriors in the band. Why they killed him, if for any special reason, is not known.[164]

On July 11, 1869, the U.S. military and its Pawnee allies delivered a fatal blow to Cheyenne resistance in the Battle of Summit Springs near present-day Sterling, where the Dog Soldiers' supplies were destroyed and their leader Tall Bull was killed.

Cheyenne County was established on April 11, 1889. Farming was and still is productive. Ranchers came, too; by 1890, about 10,000 head of cattle and just as many sheep roamed the plains of Cheyenne, Kiowa, Kit Carson, and Yuma Counties.

Clear Creek County (1861)

Historically, the Cheyenne, Arapaho and Ute lived in what is today Clear

Creek. One of Colorado's seventeen original counties, it covers 396 square miles, including Mt. Evans, and spans Clear Creek Canyon, from which it takes its name.

The Front Range Community College's Land Acknowledgment is as follows:

Front Range Community College acknowledges that, with respect, the lands that our campuses occupy are the ancestral and traditional homelands of the Arapaho, Cheyenne and Ute nations. We honor the land, the water, all peoples both living and past, and we are grateful to be here—recognizing that the original stewards of this land were those ancestors who have lived here for thousands of years, prior to written histories, as well as the many diverse and vibrant Native communities who are still connected to this land on which we gather today.

Through oral histories we know that these areas were also the sites of day-to-day life, gathering, trade, community and healing for many other Native Nations—the Apache, Comanche, Hopi, Kiowa, Lakota, Shoshone and the Zuni being among at least 48 contemporary Native Nations that have been part of the recent history of the lands that make up the state of Colorado.

However, we must also acknowledge the impacts of manifest destiny, including the painful histories of genocide, broken treaties, forced removal from these lands, silencing and exploitation, as well as the continued racism and the magnitude of inequities that Indians continue to experience to this day. In recent times, the United States government legally recognized the Cheyenne and Arapaho Nations as the owners of these lands through the Fort Laramie Treaty of 1851—although, presently, many tribes including the Arapaho have been fully displaced and have no legally recognized land in Colorado.

As we speak these words of acknowledgement, our intention is to recognize the ties that those Native Nations have to their traditional homelands, while also recognizing our responsibilities as an institution that is the beneficiary of unceded land. While we cannot expect the descendants living today to forgive or forget what has happened, we can offer a promise to remember the past and pledge to forge a new path forward to treat our tenure in these lands with respect. Consistent with the college's commitment to equity, inclusion and diversity, Front Range Community College commits itself to action towards positive outcomes for Indigenous peoples by: funding to support Native American students with scholarship opportunities; supporting our staff, faculty and our communities through continuous learning and education; community service, outreach and enrollment efforts; historical recognitions; and community partnerships.[165]

In January 1859, George Jackson discovered placer gold in the gravel along the north fork of Clear Creek, south of modern Idaho Springs. More mining districts were located in areas that would become the cities of Dumont, Empire, and Georgetown. Empire sprang up after Henry DeWitt, Clinton Cowles and Edgar F. Freeman found gold in the area in 1860. Georgetown began when the Griffith brothers discovered gold at the base of a nearby mountain, creating the Griffith Mining District.

A rich silver ore deposit was discovered near Georgetown but wasn't extensively mined until smelters were built in the late 1860s. At that time, entrepreneurial chemistry professor Nathaniel P. Hill applied a process he learned in Wales to build the state's first successful smelter in Black Hawk. Smelters use heat to melt milled ore and chemically separate the precious metals.

Other silver strikes in the early 1870s led to the creation of the Burleigh, Marshall and Lebanon mines, as well as the town of Silver Plume. Prosperity brought by silver mining only lasted until the Panic of 1893. Although Clear Creek County mines continued to produce silver, the steady drop in the metal's value from nearly $1 per ounce in 1891 to about $0.58 by 1898 caused a major economic decline.

Conejos County (1861)

Historically, the Capote Utes lived in what is today Conejos County. It was originally named Guadalupe, from the patron Saint of Mexico, but was quickly changed. Conejos County covers 1,287 square miles of the southern San Luis Valley and eastern San Juan Mountains in south central Colorado. The San Luis Valley covers Conejos, Costilla, Rio Grande, and Saguache Counties. Classified as a high alpine desert, the San Luis Valley generally receives fewer than eight inches of precipitation per year, forcing local farmers and ranchers to rely on underground aquifers and mountain reservoirs for water.

Frank Hall documents the taking of seisin by the Mexican land grant owners:

> I led them over the tract and granted to them the land: and they plucked up grass, cast stones and exclaimed in voices of gladness, saying: "Long live the Sovereignty of our Mexican Nation!" taking possession of said tract quietly and peaceably without any opposition the boundaries designated to them.[166]

Indians harassed the settlers who moved out:

> While Martinez, Gallegos and Valdez took possession as stated, the Indians, resenting the intrusion upon their cherished hunting and camping grounds, harassed the settlers continually and finally drove them out.[167]

On another day, the Utes and Apaches did not fare as well:

> On the 13th of March, 1854, the Utes and Apaches surrounded the town and a lively fight ensued, lasting from just before sunrise until noon, when the savages were driven away. Several of Mr. Head's party were wounded but none killed. The Indians carried off their dead and wounded.[168]

Although Congress had confirmed the legitimacy of the neighboring Sangre de Cristo Grant in 1860, the confirmation of the Conejos/Guadalupe Grant was rejected at the end of the century due to lost documents. As a result, many early Hispano settlers of the Conejos Grant lost their claims over the following decades, and much of the area was partitioned into 160-acre farmsteads in accordance with the Homestead Act of 1862.

Farming

Farming.—There are several immense farms in this region, the largest, under the management of Mr. T. C. Henry of Denver. These are the Empire (17,000 acres), the San Luis, Excelsior (5,000 acres) and Mosca farm (5,000 acres) companies; the Empire Land and Canal Co., and the San Luis Land and Water Co. From 1882-1884, Henry, of the Colorado Loan and Trust company of Denver, built the Empire, Del Norte and Citizens' canals. In the spring of 1884 he opened up the North Side farm of 7,000 acres, irrigated by water from the Del Norte canal.[169]

In 1888, Henry and his associates purchased the San Luis Canal system, widened and extended it, which irrigates 80,000 acres. These farming enterprises built upon former Indian land created intergenerational wealth for the colonial settlers.[170]

Like other counties in the arid San Luis Valley, Conejos County relies on aquifers and sparse rivers to sustain its agricultural economy.

Costilla County (1861)

Historically, the Capote Utes lived in what is today Costilla County. In 1851 New Mexicans founded San Luis, the first permanent settlement in what would become Colorado, on the Sangre de Cristo Grant. To protect the new settlements in the San Luis Valley, the U.S. built Fort Massachusetts in 1852, and then replaced it in 1858 with Fort Garland. The Costilla County area, along with most of the San Luis Valley, came under the jurisdiction of the Colorado Territory upon its establishment in 1861.

Crowley County (1911)

Historically, the Kiowa, Cheyenne, Arapaho and Comanches lived in what is today Crowley County. The Comanches area known as the Comancheria reached from the foot hills of the Rockies to New Mexico, eastward to the cross timbers of Texas and Oklahoma and from the Arkansas River to Kansas, south to the Texas Pecos River, Rio Grande area. The Nation was 600 miles from north and south, 400 miles from east to west. Among the first Plains Indians to acquire horses from Spanish settlers, Comanches soon became legendary horsemen.

After their removal, white ranchers and farmers arrived, towns were laid out and railroads followed. Ranchers such as John Cowden and George Dennis grazed herds near the station, driving them north to market in Denver. In 1889 irrigation investor Theodore Henry began construction on the Colorado Canal. Henry quickly sold the canal to the Colorado Land and Water Company, which set up its headquarters in Ordway. The town of Ordway, named after local homesteader and Denver businessman George N. Ordway, was established in 1890. By 1892, former ranchers and new homesteaders were setting up farms on newly irrigated land.

It was named for John H. Crowley, who was the Senator from Otero County at the time that county was divided to form Crowley.

~ 244 ~

Agricultural development in Crowley County outpaced the local water supply. In 1935 the Twin Lakes Reservoir and Canal Company completed a $2 million trans-mountain diversion system that carried water from the west side of the Continental Divide to the Arkansas River. In the 1970s, Crowley County farmers sold their Twin Lakes Reservoir water rights to the Crowley County Land and Development Company, which then sold the rights to Pueblo, Colorado Springs, Pueblo West, and Aurora—all growing cities along the Front Range. The water sale devastated the County.

Custer County (1877)

Historically, the Utes lived in what is today Custer County. It was "one of their favorite resorts for camping and hunting, the climate being equable, the surroundings picturesque, and game abundant."[171]

In 1874, prospectors found copper and silver ores south of present-day Rosita in what would be called the Humboldt-Pocahontas Vein. The find produced over $900,000.

Mr. Bassick discovered another vein and "It remained for Mr. Bassick to unlock here a treasure vault that has few equals anywhere. It is impossible to give the total value of the product, as the former owner kept no books and did not preserve all his smelter receipts. It is thought to have produced nearly $2 million in gold and silver by 1885, when the mine closed."[172]

In another tale by Frank Hall of claim jumping, we have an abbreviated account:

> Colonel Boyd and Walter A. Stuart engaged Major Graham, an ex-convict, to lead a party of desperadoes to take forcible possession of Mr. Herr's mining claim. They succeeded, and held it for a week. While Graham and his confederates were in town drinking, carousing and shooting, a citizen, was severely wounded. Next morning, all the saloons were closed and the main roads leading from the town guarded. A company of well-armed citizens, while marching to capture the jumpers, met Graham coming down from the mine and killed him, whereupon the remainder of the gang fled, were pursued and taken, but released upon their pledge to leave the camp at once.[173]

Speculation ran riot, mines were staked, bonded and sold without development, and upon the flimsiest of surface indications; prospecting took wide range, and it really seemed as if the newest settlement was destined to become a large and permanent city.[174]

At its 1880 peak, Silver Cliff hosted fourteen stamp mills and smelters and a population of 5,000; residents even campaigned to make it the capitol of Colorado. They did not secure that title, but the region was populous enough to warrant its own county. Custer County, named after General George Armstrong Custer, was officially carved out of the southern portion of Fremont County in 1877.

Mr. Frank's prognosis for the County was as follows:

The mines of precious metals which have been developed and worked for years, the still larger and richer fields of gold and silver to be discovered in the future, the almost exhaustless fecundity of the soil, and the vast area of nutritious grazing lands, constitute advantages that will speedily stimulate the building of another railroad and attract numbers of speculators and capitalists.[175]

Delta County (1883)

Historically, the Ute Bands the Parianuche, or "elk people," and the Tabeguache, or "the people of Sun Mountain" lived in what is today Delta County. It is situated upon the broad and fertile delta at the junction of the Gunnison and Uncompahgre rivers. Agriculture and ranching are the chief industries. Historian Frank Hall wrote in 1895:

The slopes of the mountains are covered with yellow pine, much of it suitable for fine lumber. There is a belt of timber beginning near Ouray and running parallel with and on the west side of the Uncompahgre and Gunnison to Utah, which is fifty to sixty miles long, by five to twenty in width, that furnishes lumber equal to the best Chicago or Milwaukee products.[176] The better lands lie in the valleys of the Gunnison, Uncompahgre and North Fork rivers, and the cultivated portions are irrigated by canals taken from these streams. Bordering the valleys are elevated mesas, known as California, Rogers, Gomet and Cushman, all well adapted to wheat, oats, rye, barley and alfalfa. Some remarkable crops are produced upon these rich table-lands, and they are also useful for pasturing horses, cattle and sheep.

After the removal of the Ute Indians from this region in Sep. 1881, stock growers, realizing the great advantage of the valleys and mesas for their purposes, came in considerable numbers and occupied the land, not alone with Texas stock, but with fine breeding cattle of imported blood. The broad, well grassed and abundantly watered ranges afforded exceptional facilities for the advancement of this pursuit. The south side of Grand Mesa, the elevated slopes of the North Fork valley, Smith's Fork and Muddy district were almost immediately taken up. The growth of the business has been large and profitable. ...

Denver County (1902)

Historically, the Cheyenne and Arapaho lived in what is today Denver County. There are 48 contemporary tribal nations that are historically tied to the lands that make up the State of Colorado.

Gold and silver ores mined in the mountains rode the rails into Denver's smelters. Smelters became Denver's biggest employers by the 1890s. Acrid, black smelter smoke hung over the city, signaling its emergence as an industrial center. The city drew not only Colorado's gold and silver, but also attracted the state's mining magnates.

It was named after General James W. Denver, who was Governor of Kansas in 1858. When Denver was founded it was located in Kansas Territory.

Dolores County (1881)

Historically, the Utes lived in what is today Dolores County. It derived its name from the Dolores River. The full Spanish name, which was reported by Father Escalante in 1776, was Rio de Nuestro Senora de los Dolores (River of our Lady of Sorrows). It is sparsely populated. Miners had to be fed, and the rich grass of the Dolores River valley provided excellent fodder for cattle-raising. Whites murdered a group of Utes at a campsite along Beaver Creek in 1885.[177]

The County experienced exaggerated reports of the new Eldorado.

The hills were soon honey-combed with prospect holes, and, in a short time, the country for a radius of several miles from the common center, where Rico has since been built, was covered in many places three or four deep by overlapping mining claims. The boom was of short duration. It was followed by a relapse, when a majority of those who came expecting to soon reap a rich silver harvest went away in disgust, cursing the camp …

The start of the cemetery is recorded by Hall:

The last day of August, 1879, George McGoldrick, alias the Kid, shot and killed a man called "Frenchy," who was buried next day. This was the first start of the cemetery.

From Dolores County, we also have the story of the burro casualty:

The night of October 5th, 1879, the inhabitants of Rico experienced a first class Indian scare, barricaded themselves upstairs against the expected onslaught. The only casualty was one burro killed by an excited guard, who mistook it for a bloodthirsty Ute.[178]

Mr. Hall couldn't end his story without a jab at the demonetization of silver:

It is said that large beds of good anthracite coal have been discovered and partially opened there. The mountains about Rico seem to be literally ribbed with veins of precious metal bearing minerals, and at no distant day, when our national monetary problems shall have been readjusted on a bimetallic basis, this portion of Dolores county will be one of the most productive mining fields in the West.[179]

Douglas County (1861)

Historically, the Cheyenne, Arapaho and Utes lived in what is today Douglas County. It was named after Stephen A. Douglas, a popular politician in the 1850s. It was one of Colorado's original seventeen counties.

Eagle County (1883)

Historically, the Yampa and the Parianuche Utes lived in what is today Eagle County. Formed in 1883, it covers 1,692 square miles of mountainous terrain in northwest Colorado. It is named for the Eagle River and home to Vail.[180]

Mining

Eagle County's first major strike came in 1874, when silver ore was found in limestone deposits on the west side of Battle Mountain. Miners set up a permanent mining camp there, which became the town of Red Cliff in 1879. Some 100 claims were filed. The Gilman Mining District, north of Red Cliff, developed in the 1880s and included the Belden silver mine and the Ground Hog mine, the most productive in the area. Mining in Eagle County continued throughout the twentieth century, moving from gold and silver to other metals, including copper, lead, molybdenum, and zinc. By 1970 the mines in the Gilman District had produced more than 393,000 ounces of gold, 66 million ounces of silver, 105,000 tons of copper, 148,000 tons of lead, and 858,000 tons of zinc.

Ranching

Not all early communities in Eagle County were related to mining. Many homesteaders came seeking free land. Edwards, for instance, was first settled by two ranchers in 1882. It was known as "Berry's Ranch" until 1887, when the Denver & Rio Grande Railroad established a station there. Two other ranching communities, Eagle and Gypsum, were first settled in 1882. By 1884 there were thirty-one ranches in Gypsum.

El Paso County (1861)

Historically, the Tabeguache Utes, the people of Sun Mountain, lived in what is today El Paso County. By 1881, the Tabeguache were removed onto a reservation in eastern Utah. Manitou Springs and the Garden of the Gods are popular tourist spots. El Paso is the Spanish word for "the Pass". Ute pass, west of Colorado Springs, was the famous pass the name references.

The earliest documented peoples also include the Apache, Arapaho, Comanche, and Cheyenne.

The Cultural Office of the Pike's Peak Region Land Acknowledgment is as follows:

> The Pike's Peak region is situated on the ancestral homeland of the Ute Peoples, who are the Southern Ute, Ute Mountain Ute, and Northern Ute. Other tribes who lived and hunted on this land include the Cheyenne, Arapaho, Comanche, and Apache. Even through forced relocation and land dispossession, we recognize that the land still holds Ute traditions, language, stories, and history. Today, Indigenous people from many Native nations reside here and continue to make significant contributions to our community.[181]

Elbert County (1874)

Historically, the Kiowa, Cheyenne and Arapaho lived in what is today Elbert County. It was named for former Colorado Territorial Governor Samuel H. Elbert.[182]

Historian Frank Hall wrote: It has large pine forests in the western part, from which much of the lumber was taken in 1859 that was used in building early Denver. During the early settlement of the county, portions of it were frequently raided by the Indians, and many of the inhabitants were murdered.

Coal was found in abundance.

Today agriculture remains the main economic driver in Elbert County. The county raises more than 30,000 head of cattle and is also one of the state's top producers of horses and other draught animals, with more than 1,400. Elbert County also ranks in the top third of Colorado counties in wheat production.

Fremont County (1861)

It was named for General John C. Fremont, who explored the region before 1850.

Historically, the Utes lived in what is today Fremont County. Coal Creek and Coaldale, reflect the role of the coal industry in the county's development. Colorado Coal Company, the predecessor of the Colorado Fuel and Iron Company (CF&I), owned nearly seventy coal mines in Fremont. The first commercial production of oil in Colorado was the Florence Oil Field.

D&RG in Cañon City and the Atchison, Topeka & Santa Fe Railway in Pueblo began an aggressive competition to extend a rail line to Leadville through the narrow Royal Gorge in Fremont County, which had space for only one rail line. The gorge is 1,000 feet deep and 10 miles long. In 1879, after gunfights between the two railroad crews and a legal battle that ended at the U.S. Supreme Court, the D&RG was granted the primary right to build a line through the gorge. D&RG won.

The Ku Klux Klan held political power in the region from 1924 to 1928, not only controlling the Cañon City government but also influencing Fremont County and the state government in Denver.

Garfield County (1883)

Historically, the Utes lived in what is today Garfield County. It was named for President James A. Garfield. Coal mines were first discovered in 1882. The coal belt runs diagonally across the county from southeast to northwest, and is readily traceable.[183]

Gilpin County (1861)

Historically, the Cheyenne and Arapaho lived in what is today Gilpin County. It was established in 1861 as one of the original seventeen counties, named for William Gilpin, Colorado's first Territorial Governor. It is the home of Central City and Blackhawk, respectively known for gold and smelters.

Grand County (1874)

Historically, the Arapaho, Cheyenne and Utes lived in what is today Grand County. The Utes fought the Cheyenne and Arapaho for control of the hunting grounds. Grand County, named for the Grand River (now the Colorado River), was established in 1874. It is home to Winter Park.[184]

Winter Park Resort's Land Acknowledgment is as follows:

> Winter Park Resort acknowledges and honors that the land on which we operate today is the traditional and ancestral homelands of the Nookhose'iinenno (Northern Arapaho), Tsis tsis'tas (Cheyenne), and Nuuchu (Ute). We recognize and honor these Native Nations, their people, and their continued connection as the original stewards of these lands and waters where we recreate today. We reaffirm and recognize that

connection both through our words here and through our actions.[185]

Historian Frank Hall vividly describes this area and the reluctance of the Utes to part with it. [186]

Gold and silver mines situated in the Rabbit Ear range were not profitable due to the lack of a railway.

The town of Grand Lake was laid out in 1879, and in 1881 the county seat was moved there due to a brief mining boom. This led to a feud between two political factions, one supporting Grand Lake and the other supporting Hot Sulphur Springs. The feud culminated in a deadly shooting in Grand Lake in 1883, which left three county commissioners and the county clerk dead; the county sheriff, a backer of Hot Sulphur Springs, shot and killed a pro-Grand Lake official during the incident and later killed himself. The county seat was returned to Hot Sulphur Springs in 1888, ending much of the bitterness.

Gunnison County (1877)

Historically, the Utes lived in what is today Gunnison County. It was named for the western explorer John W. Gunnison. It is the home of Crested Butte Ski Resort.

The country belonged to, or was claimed by, the Ute Indians. Nevertheless, a number of bold prospectors had ventured in, made discoveries, and in due course … camps opened for gold, silver, coal and iron mines.[187]

The gold and silver was not a large find, though the coal mining was significant.

Hall describes how the Los Pinos creek was named due to the obstinacy of the Utes:

> In 1868, when Governor Hunt's treaty with the Utes for their location upon reservations at White river and the Los Pinos was made, the Uncompahgres, Mouaches, Capotes, and Weeminuches were encamped in the vicinity of Fort Garland, in the eastern part of the San Luis valley. In attempting to remove them to the Los Pinos they could only be gotten as far as Cochetopa creek... The Los Pinos where it was designed that they should be settled is some 60 miles southwesterly. But here they were determined to remain, and, consequently,

~ 252 ~

the agency was established at Cochetopa in 1869. But in order to conform in some degree to the terms of the treaty, a small creek running into the Cochetopa at that point was named Los Pinos. Here they remained until removed to the Uncompahgre reservation under the treaty of 1873.[188]

In describing how Gunnison was set up in the late 1800s, it was fairly simple: The town company was organized in 1879 ... survey made April 1st, 1880 ... plat filed May 9th, 1880 ... and Gunnison laid off by the Gunnison Town and Land company.

The granite from which the state capitol was built came from quarries at Aberdeen.[189]

In typical fashion for many mining communities, Hall describes the rise and fall of Gunnison:

> The great burst of excitement passed away in 1883 ... distance from markets, high transportation charges, the collapse of local reduction works, disappointment in not finding vast beds of carbonate ores worth millions, the severity of the winters in the higher altitudes and the lack of capital for investment, together with the general decline of interest after the blow which struck Leadville in 1881-82, all combined to bring about depression in Gunnison.[190]

The Crested Butte Film Festival's Land Acknowledgment is as follows:

> The Crested Butte Film Festival is located on the ancient homeland and traditional territory of the Ute (Núu-agha-tʉvʉ-pʉ) people. As a public and cultural institution, it is our responsibility to acknowledge the sovereignty and the traditional territories of these tribal nations, the treaties that were used to remove these tribal nations, and the histories of dispossession that have allowed for us to be present here today. We pay respect to Ute peoples past, present, and future and their continuing presence in the homeland and throughout the Ute diaspora.[191]

Hinsdale County (1874)

It was named in honor of George A. Hinsdale, a prominent pioneer and leader in southern Colorado, former Lieutenant Governor of Colorado, who died during the month preceding the creation of Hinsdale County.

Historically, the Weenuche and Capote Utes lived in what is today Hinsdale County. On August 27, 1871, the prospectors Harry Henson, Joel Mullen, Albert Meade, and Charles Godwin found gold and silver while trespassing on Ute land. The Ute Ulay Mine eventually became a rich source of gold, silver, lead, and copper, and was among the largest producers of silver and lead in the state.

Among the records of Hinsdale county is the following entry among the expense bills:

"To W. T. Ring, on account of fees in the matter of inquest and burial of five men found dead, $37." These were the mutilated remains of [cannibalist] Alfred Packer's victims, given final rest on Gold Hill Bar about a mile above Lake City, in what is known as Dead Man's Gulch ...[192]

Armory Hall was the headquarters of a military organization, known as the "Pitkin Guard," then a strong, well drilled and efficient company which rendered good service in the many Indian disturbances that threatened that part of the country.[193]

In typical fashion for many mining communities, Hall once more describes the decline in Hinsdale County in the 1880s:

> After a few years of marked prosperity, continuing until about the close of 1879, the lack of markets for ores, inexperience of the miners, the great cost of supplies, its distance from the great centers and general inaccessibility began to undermine the courage and endurance of the people. ... To crown the disasters, on the 8th of November, 1879, a destructive fire occurred which swept away the better part of the business center of Lake City. From that time the decadence became general, until only a small remnant of force remained to preserve its existence. ... The paralysis continued, therefore, with scarcely a ray of hope until midsummer of 1889 when, Mr. D. H. Moffat, president of the Denver & Rio Grande company, built a branch to Lake City.[194]

In closing, here is another Frank Hall report on a lynching and return of the remains to their jail cells. Billy Le Roy and his brother were tracked down by a posse after robbing a stagecoach and shooting the driver in the leg. After threats, the Sheriff was able to secret the arrestees into jail cells.

> Jumping out of bed to ascertain the cause, he [the Sheriff] found the house surrounded by armed men, most of whom were masked. On opening the door he was immediately seized, and in spite of his struggles and remonstrances the keys of the jail were taken from him. Putting him under guard, the leaders assembled their forces, marched to the prison, and taking the Le Roys from their cells proceeded to a cluster of tall cottonwoods on the bank of the Rio Grande river just below the town and there hanged them. *Half an hour later the lifeless bodies were cut down, taken back to the prison and replaced in the cells, when all who had been engaged in the execution passed noiselessly to their homes.* (Emphasis added).[195]

Huerfano County (1861)

Huerfano is the Spanish word for "orphan". The county was named after the Huerfano River which flows through the area. It was so named from Huerfano Butte which is an isolated, cone-shaped butte located in the river bottom area.

Historically, the Utes, Apache and Comanche Indians vied for control of Huerfano County. In south-central Colorado, its capital, Walsenburg is known as "The City Built on Coal". The late nineteenth century saw the rise of railroad, steel, and oil tycoons who amassed huge amounts of money at the expense of their workers. Tensions escalated until 1914, when National Guard soldiers killed nearly twenty men, women, and children in the nearby Ludlow Massacre, the climax of the Colorado Coalfield War.

Jackson County (1909)

Historically, the Yampa Utes lived in what is today Jackson County. In August 1865, for instance, Utes drove a party of prospectors out of North Park. The county is named for Andrew Jackson. In 1925 the Continental Oil Company struck oil northeast of Walden, and in 1926 a well was completed on what became the North McCallum Oil Field.

Jefferson County (1861)

Historically, the Cheyenne and Arapaho lived in what is today Jefferson County. "Jeffco" is the home to Golden, Morrison, Evergreen and Red Rocks, Dinosaur Ridge.

COUNTY OF JEFFERSON STATE OF COLORADO RESOLUTION NO. CC22-047 RE: Parks and Conservation - Open Space - Indigenous Peoples Land Acknowledgement

> The original caretakers of the lands we now call Jefferson County Open Space Parks include the Tabeguache and Moghwachi bands of the Ute Nation, the Arapaho and Cheyenne Tribes, and other Indigenous Peoples. Their knowledge, resilience, and cultural and spiritual ties to these lands inspire us to continue their legacy by practicing informed stewardship, providing equitable access, teaching sound outdoor ethics, and treating nature and humanity with respect.[196]

Kiowa County (1889)

Historically, the Cheyenne and Arapaho lived in what is today Kiowa County. The Comanche, Kiowa, Cheyenne, and Arapaho forged an agreement in which the Cheyenne and Arapaho would live north of the Arkansas River, making those two groups the dominant presence in the Kiowa County area.

The County derived its name from the Kiowa Indians who hunted and lived in eastern Colorado before European's arrived. Beyond agriculture, Kiowa County also remains active in oil and gas production, with some seventy-three active oil wells and fifty-five active natural gas wells.

Kit Carson County (1889)

Historically, the Kiowa, Cheyenne and Arapaho lived in what is today Kit Carson County. The county, named after Kit Carson, was frequented by land disputes between ranchers and homesteaders that sometimes resulted in violence. The Ogallala Aquifer sits below the eastern two-thirds of the county. Today, the county ranks second in corn production and is the top wheat producer in the state, with nearly 225,000 acres of winter wheat. As of 2012 Kit Carson County is also one of the state's top cattle producers, with more than 350,000 head.

La Plata County (1874)

Durango's Land Acknowledgment is as follows:

Durango recognizes, publicly and intentionally, that we live, work, and organize on stolen and occupied traditional land that is just one piece of a larger, boundless terrain for Indigenous Peoples; Ute Tribe, Jicarilla Apache, Arapaho, Comanche, and the Diné Nations, and others. We acknowledge that 48 contemporary tribal nations are historically tied to the lands that make up the state of Colorado. Visit Durango would like to pay our respects to their elders, past and present, and choose to honor and acknowledge the original stewards of this land in hopes of building mutual respect and understanding across all cultures—those that reside here and those that pass through here today and in the future."[197]

Fort Lewis College's Land Acknowledgment is as follows:

We acknowledge the land that Fort Lewis College is situated upon is the ancestral land and territory of the Nuuchiu (Ute) people who were forcibly removed by the United States Government. We also acknowledge that this land is connected to the communal and ceremonial spaces of the Jicarilla Abache (Apache), Pueblos of New Mexico, Hopi Sinom (Hopi), and Diné (Navajo) Nations. It is important to acknowledge this setting because the narratives of the lands in this region have long been told from dominant perspectives, without full recognition of the original land stewards who continue to inhabit and connect with this land.[198]

Hall documents the Utes campaign against white settlers trying to settle in the area which discouraged them. Benjamin H. Eaton (in 1884 elected governor of Colorado) led a group into southwest Colorado:

> ... the Indians were becoming hostile and were burning the bridges and massacreing [sic] all the white people found in small unprotected squads. ... Incomers were being massacred by the Indians, and the party was nearly out of provisions. [They ended up retracing their steps to Denver.][199]

Of interest, historian Frank Hall reported the following:

[T]he Aspen, Prospector, Susquehanna and other mineral lodes were discovered, some of which afterward became noted producers of precious metal. ... This was the primary impulse which led to the treaty [accord] with the Ute Indians whereby, under the act of Congress approved September 3, 1873, that part of their reservation was ceded to the United States and opened to settlement.[200]

Even before the cession of Ute lands, Capt. John Moss' party negotiated its own agreement with the Utes for the right to mine:

In the summer of 1873 a band of prospectors [arrived] from California, led by Capt. John Moss, with whom were Richard Giles, John Merritt, Thomas McElmel, John McIntire, John Thompson, John Madden, Henry Lee and John Robinson. ... *Capt. Moss conceived and executed a private treaty with Ignacio, then, as now, chief of the Southern Utes, for the right to mine and farm 36 square miles of that country,* with the center at a point where Parrott City now stands, for which privilege 100 ponies and a quantity of blankets were given the Indians. From the fact that the treaty with the United States then pending had not been fully consummated, and all the country was still held by these Indians, the movement exhibited much tact and wisdom. The contract was made by Moss for Parrott & Co. of San Francisco on the side, and Ignacio for the Utes on the other, and secured to these prospectors peaceful occupation of what they termed "California district." Armed with a copy of this treaty and also with many samples of gold quartz and free gold, as indications of immense wealth awaiting development in the La Plata mountains, the party proceeded to San Francisco. The new enterprise was presented to Parrott & Co., with a glowing account of the country, and soon an expedition was completed under Moss's direction, who was granted carte blanche to draw on Parrott & Co. for all requisite funds to revisit and explore the country. (Emphasis added).[201]

Under the Brunot Agreement, the Utes ceded 3.5 million acres of the San Juan Mountains to the U.S. in exchange for annual payments of $25,000. The cession left a narrow strip of land at the southern end of the state for the Weenuche, Capote, and Muache Utes. This land became the Southern Ute Indian Reservation.

Therefore, within 30 days after the ratification of the treaty with the Indians of September 3rd, 1873, which opened to settlers the whole San Juan country, save a 15-mile strip along the southern boundary of the territory (that now occupied), every acre of available land in the valley had been located and staked off in ranch claims. No surveys having been made, squatters' rights prevailed. (Emphasis added).[202]

The town of Silverton was laid out and incorporated. The first lode discovery was made by Almerian Root and named the Comstock. W. H. Jackson, the photographer for Hayden's U.S. Geological Survey, discovered and reported upon what is today Mesa Verde.[203]

To demonstrate the importance of these mineral discoveries, the following episodes are recounted by Hall:

During the summer a report was sent to Silverton that an Indian war had broken out, and that all settlers were in danger. *In less than an hour nearly 100 miners, well armed, were on the way to the Animas valley.* They traveled nearly all night, but on their arrival found that the cause of alarm had been removed. (Emphasis added) [204]

General Hatch, department commander of New Mexico, sent in a company of cavalry and *stationed them at or near the mills of Scott, Earl & Cooper.* The final result was the location of a military post at Pagosa Springs and an agency for the Southern Utes on Pine river, with Rev. Mr. Weaver as agent. (Emphasis added).[205]

Otto Mears and his associates built their two railways for the express purpose of controlling the ore traffic from Ouray and San Juan counties.[206]

In his report for 1886, State Inspector John McNeil, in reviewing the coals of La Plata county, says: "Extensive coal beds are found to underlie the greater part of the county. It is principally bituminous and well adapted for coking."[207]

Hall conclusively describes the value of La Plata County after its cession:

Leaving its gold and silver mines out of the question, the great extent and excellence of its coals, the production of its farms, its quarries of lime, granite and sandstone, deposits of iron ores, its splendid watercourses, its great forests of timber, and, above and beyond all, its advantages for the location of large reduction works, are sufficient to attract and must inevitably acquire millions of new capital and thousands of industrious people in the next few years.
(Emphasis added).[208]

Lake County (1861)

Historically, the Parianuche Utes lived in what is today Lake County. One of Colorado's original seventeen counties, Lake County is a mountainous, 384-square mile county in the west-central part of the state.

In 1860 the prospector Abe Lee found gold in California Gulch, just south of present-day Leadville. As many as 8,000 people arrived shortly thereafter, and in five years they panned or sluiced out nearly all of the surface gold—worth some $4 million. By 1875 several miners had purchased claims, but they had to wait until a smelter was built to start making any profit. They sent samples to a refining company in St. Louis, and a smelter was built in 1877. Mines sprung up on Iron and Carbonate Hills, and the town of Leadville was established in 1877.

In May 1878, two miners discovered another silver lode near Leadville on Fryer Hill. By 1880 the area was the continental center of silver and lead mining, with fifteen smelters and thirty-seven blast furnaces processing millions of dollars' worth of ore.

Horace Tabor's investments in mines and in Denver real estate made him one of the richest men in the nation. He served as mayor of Leadville and even briefly as a stand-in U.S. senator. His wealth dissipated when the mines began to play out and the price of silver crashed in 1893.

In 1896 the Twin Lakes Reservoir and Canal Company dammed Lake Creek at Twin Lakes to bolster the water supply for farmers in Colorado's eastern Arkansas River valley. The dam dropped the water level in the lakes and made it stagnant.

The crash in silver prices during the Panic of 1893 wiped out about 90 percent of the jobs in Leadville. But silver was only one of Lake County's geologic riches. Before the silver crash was a year old, James Joseph Brown, a mine superintendent and the husband of Margaret "Molly" Brown, found gold in the Little Johnny Mine. Other mines continued to produce zinc, lead, copper, bismuth, iron, manganese, and even silver, although it had lost considerable value.

In the early twentieth century, molybdenum, a metal used in the production of structural steel and other alloys, was discovered north of Leadville and led to the opening of the Climax Molybdenum Mine in 1918.

The Bureau of Reclamation's Fryingpan-Arkansas Project involved diverting water from dams built at Turquoise and Twin Lakes to deliver water to approximately 280,600 acres of irrigated farmland in the Arkansas River valley east of Pueblo; water diverted by the project also helps meet the municipal needs of cities such as Colorado Springs and Aurora.

Larimer County (1861)

Fort Collins is home to Colorado State University, a land-grant university founded in 1870 with funds from the federal Morrill Act of 1862.

Colorado State University's Land Acknowledgment is as follows:

> Colorado State University acknowledges, with respect, that the land we are on today is the traditional and ancestral homelands of the Arapaho, Cheyenne, and Ute Nations and peoples. This was also a site of trade, gathering, and healing for numerous other Native tribes. We recognize the Indigenous peoples as original stewards of this land and all the relatives within it. As these words of acknowledgment are spoken and heard, the ties Nations have to their traditional homelands are renewed and reaffirmed.
>
> CSU is founded as a land-grant institution, and we accept that our mission must encompass access to education and inclusion. And, significantly, that our founding came at a dire cost to Native Nations and peoples whose land this University was built upon. This acknowledgment is the education and inclusion we must practice in recognizing our institutional history, responsibility, and commitment.[209]

Larimer County was named in honor of General William Larimer, who was one of the founders of Denver and a "prominent pioneer of Colorado".

Frank Hall describes another mysterious claim regarding Larimer county:

> The principal settlements of Larimer county, one of the most fertile and productive agricultural sections of northern Colorado, are situated on a beautiful stream called the Cache-la-Poudre The gold fever broke out in 1858 ... Soon after locating my [Antoine Janise] claim, I moved over from Laramie and settled upon it. The place is just above Laporte. One hundred and fifty lodges of Arapahoes moved there with me at the time. They asked me if I wanted to settle there. I told them I did. Bald Wolf, the chief, then called a council of his braves, and they finally gave us permission to locate there, and donated to us all the land from the foot of the mountains to the mouth of Box Elder creek (which is about eight miles from the mountains). My associates in the donation were Elbridge Gerry and Nicholas Janise. In the winter of 1858-59 settlers and prospectors came flocking in.[210]

In 1862, the U.S. Army established Camp Collins to protect settlers on the Overland Trail from Indian raids. In Sep. 1864, it was moved and renamed Fort Collins.

According to the census report of 1870, the population of Larimer county was 838. Ten years later it had increased to 4,892. The assessed valuation of property in 1880 was $388,000, and in 1889 it had increased to $1,000,000.

The Big Thompson Irrigating and Manufacturing Ditch Company used the Big Thompson and Little Thompson Creeks for irrigation. In 1867, Loveland was organized and named after the Hon. W. A. H. Loveland, under whose supervision the Colorado Central railway was extended from Longmont to Wyoming Territory, enabling it to serve as a trade center. Berthoud, named for the chief engineer of the Union Pacific system in Colorado, at one time was an Indian trading post owned by Joe Knight. Arapahoes, Utes and Cheyennes obtained their supplies of sugar, flour, coffee and tobacco; trading furs and skins therefor.

> Most of the productive farms are in the valleys of the Cache-la-Poudre, and on Big and Little Thompson creeks and their adjacent table-lands. The county is widely renowned as the

agricultural garden of the state, unsurpassed in fertility of soil and the abundance of its harvests.[211]

Las Animas County (1866)

Animas River Watershed Land Acknowledgment

We would like to start this study by acknowledging that the land surrounding the Animas River Watershed is the ancestral lands and territories of the Nuchu (Ute), Apache, Pueblos, Hopi, Zuni, and the Diné (Navajo) Nation. These tribal nations are the traditional stewards of the land and water, and we would like to honor these tribes by providing this acknowledgment. We believe it is important to provide this recognition because the narratives of this land and region have long been told from one dominant perspective, without full acknowledgment of the Indigenous peoples who lived on this land since time immemorial and long before it was Silverton, Durango, Aztec, Farmington, and the Animas River as they are known today.[212]

Las Animas took its name from the main river which flows through the area. The complete name of this river, discovered and christened by the early Spanish explorers, is El Rio de los Animas Perdidas en Purgatorio (River of the Souls Lost in Purgatory).

In an effort to affirm ownership of that area, the Mexican government began issuing land grants in what is now New Mexico and Colorado in 1832. In 1841 Mexico gave the Canadian trader Charles Beaubien and Mexican official Guadalupe Miranda the Maxwell grant, which included land in present New Mexico as well as what is now the southwest corner of Las Animas County. Two years later, Mexico awarded a land grant to Cornelio Vigil and Ceran St. Vrain, a naturalized Mexican citizen and partner of William Bent. This massive grant covered the western half of present-day Las Animas County, stretching between the Purgatoire and Arkansas Rivers and into the San Luis Valley. Conflict with white Texans and Comanches, however, delayed Mexican settlement of the land grants.

Again, Frank Hall provides an interesting story about the Utes in the area:

"In the fall of 1846 [John] Hatcher [a wagon master for St. Vrain and Vigil, claimants of the Las Animas Land Grant]

~ 263 ~

brought his teams, tools and peons (Mexican slaves) from Taos, N. M., built his cabin on the north side of the Purgatoire, 18 miles east of Trinidad, and began taking out a ditch on the south side. It was surveyed only by the eyes of unskilled men. In May, 1847, Hatcher planted such land as he had cleared and plowed—some 40 acres—to corn. In July his crop was a novel, interesting sight in the valley of tall cottonwoods, smaller box elders, dense willows, plum, locust and hop vines. About roasting ear time the Indians waited upon Mr. Hatcher, told him the land was theirs and farming would not be permitted. On his refusing to give up the crop, the Indians killed his oxen, took his mules and destroyed his crop, telling him they would kill him also unless he moved away at once.[213]

Despite the U.S.' earlier attempts to remove the Utes by treaty, in 1865 there was still a significant population of Muaches near the Spanish Peaks who refused to abide the Anglo/Hispano encroachment on their homelands. Amid growing distrust and discord between federal Indian officials and the Utes in 1866, Muaches led by Kaniache began attacking white and Hispano ranches and other settlements in the Purgatoire Valley. The U.S. cavalry arrived, and with the help of local volunteers, defeated the Utes in battle.

Many Utes continued to travel to their traditional hunting grounds, including the Purgatoire Valley. As late as 1873 the Denver News reported that "Kanneache [sic] and his band, which have never yet obeyed the treaty of 1868 ... have been in the habit of annoying the settlers of the valleys of the Cucharas and the Huerfano." The paper opined that this activity "should be stopped -peacefully, if possible, forcibly, if necessary."

Small farming was evidenced by the 89 main ditches. The vast cattle enterprises were undone by overusing the feeding grounds. The Mexican population, which for many years predominated, was overwhelmed by the influx of whites.

What really hurt the development of Trinidad, though, was the rivalry of the Colorado Coal and Iron Company in Pueblo promoting its city, El Moro. Instead of extending the Denver & Rio Grande five miles to Trinidad, it stopped at El Moro in 1876 and did not add the extra five miles until 1888.

By the early twentieth century, Trinidad's coal mines were among the most productive in the nation with three rail lines into the city. Due to poor working conditions though, the coal miners struck in 1914. The state's largest private employer, the Colorado Fuel and Iron Company (CF&I), employed most of the striking miners. Colorado Governor Elias M. Ammons deployed the National Guard to keep the miners under control.

The Guard was supposed to maintain the peace, but since the mine owners worked out a deal with the state to pay for the cost of the deployment of the Guard there was no eagerness on their part to end the conflict.

The powder keg finally exploded on April 20, 1914, when gunfire erupted between the National Guard and strikers near the union's Ludlow tent colony north of Trinidad. Many of the miners' families fled the tent colony once the fighting began, so the National Guard believed the camp to be empty when they set it on fire. Hidden in a pit underneath one of the tents, however, were thirteen women and children, who died of smoke inhalation.

After hearing about the events at Ludlow, other miners went on a rampage across the southern coalfields, killing mine operators and guards. It is still not known how exactly how many people died during the entire conflict, but at least nineteen died at Ludlow, making the event the deadliest labor conflict in American history.

The primary object of union and public hostility after the Ludlow Massacre was John D. Rockefeller, Jr., the oil baron's son and primary stockholder of CF&I. Coal mining continued in Las Animas County until the 1920s, when demand tapered off due to the availability of other fuels.

Trinidad and Raton Pass are part of the I-25 corridor between Colorado and NM. Raton Peak derives its name from a peculiar species of rodents that inhabit it. The Indians called it Chuquirique (Rat), in the Spanish "Raton."

Lincoln County (1889)

Historically, the Kiowa, Cheyenne and Arapaho lived in what is today Lincoln County. It was named after President Abraham Lincoln, covers 2,586 square miles of Colorado's Great Plains southeast of Denver. The western portion of the Smoky Hill route, including parts of today's Lincoln County, became known as the "Starvation Trail" on account of the many immigrants who became lost and starved to death.

Though the soil is favorable for farming, the residents initially chose to engage in cattle ranching and sheep herding. Disputes between cattle ranchers and sheep herders led to the formation of the Lincoln County Cattle Growers' Association and the Lincoln and Elbert Counties Wool Growers' Association.

Later, agriculture became the main driver of the economy with irrigation from the Ogallala Aquifer.

Logan County (1887)

Historically, the Kiowa, Cheyenne and Arapaho lived in what is today Logan County.

Logan County, named for Civil War General John A. Logan, covers 1,845 miles of the Great Plains in northeast Colorado. The Overland Trail passed along the South Platte through present-day Logan County on its way to Denver. By the mid-1870s rancher John Wesley Iliff was grazing thousands of his cattle in the area. Agriculture was one of the main industries with sugar beets, the leading crop.

Sterling is the largest and most important town in the county. Soon after founding the settlement they were threatened by Indians, but escaped serious damage. A fort was built that was large enough to shelter all the families. S. S. Kempton was elected captain of a temporary military company. Arms and ammunition were supplied by the state.

Mesa County (1883)

Historically, the Uncompahgre Utes lived in what is today Mesa County. It is situated on 3,341 square miles of the eastern Colorado Plateau in western Colorado. The county is named for the wide, flat-topped mountains within its borders. The Spanish called such mountains *mesas*—meaning "tables." The county's largest mesa, Grand Mesa, rises more than 11,000 feet and sprawls 500 square miles over the county's eastern reaches.

Up to the year 1881 all the region comprised the Uncompahgre Reservation of the band of Ute Indians. The Thornburgh/Meeker incidents led to their forcible military removal in August 1881.

> In 1883 some of the philanthropic spirits conceived the idea of establishing a school for the moral and mental training of young children from the Ute Indian tribes stationed in Utah. ... It is unnecessary to dwell upon the benefits derivable from schools of this nature, for we all comprehend that, if the remnants of the savage races are ever to be humanized and adapted to civilization, it must be done by taking the young out of the camps and away from the wild roving life, and fashion them for citizenship by education.[214]

Frank Hall gives us his opinion of the region and the Indians:

> In his [Hon. George A. Crawford] expeditions to the western part of our state he traveled on horseback, and at length discovered at the junction of the Uncompahgre and the Gunnison, and also at the confluence of the Gunnison and Grand rivers, two of the most admirable sites within our jurisdiction, and there, *as soon as permitted by the expatriation of the Indians, planted the colonies of Delta and Grand Junction.* (Emphasis added).[215]
>
> Less than a month after the Utes had been removed to Utah, *George A. Crawford, "the father of Grand Junction", purchased squatter rights* from W. O. Stephens located at the juncture of the Uncompahgre and Gunnison Rivers. Crawford's interest in the area led to the organization of the Uncompahgre Town Company. Associated with Crawford in this venture were M. C. Vandeventer and three officials of the Denver and Rio Grande Railroad, whose participation foretold the importance of the expanding railroad for the proposed townsite. (Emphasis added).[216]

The Grand Valley had an estimated area of 150,000 acres of good tillable land. Four canals, projected in 1882-83, were all completed and in running order in 1885. Due to the favorable agriculture and horticulture other immense canals were projected for the reclamation of 75,000 to 100,000 acres of land. North of Grand Junction large deposits of coal were discovered, much of it along the standard gauge of the Denver & Rio Grande and the Colorado Midland railways. In 1890, some copper was mined.

Fruit Industry

In the early 1880s—at the same time the Utes were being removed from the Gunnison, Colorado, and Uncompahgre River valleys—Anglo-American horticulturalists and prospective farmers noticed that with sufficient irrigation from the rivers, the area was ideal for growing fruit. Denver & Rio Grande Railroad in 1883 set the stage for an agricultural boom in the Grand Valley.

> Mr. C. W. Steele, statistical reporter for the bureau of statistics in Washington, in his report for 1891, says: "Long seasons and warm summers, with immunity from insect pests, tend to make this one of the best localities in the United States for the growth of the finer fruits, as well as the more hardy.

Apples and pears grow to a phenomenal size and of surpassing flavor." Of the other advantages he notes, "an abundance of water for irrigation; a low altitude in the Rocky Mountain system; freedom from hailstorms and tornadoes; and, owing to the dryness of the atmosphere, no late destructive frosts in the spring, no insects such as are common to the Mississippi valley."[217]

By 1910 more than a million trees stood on 20,000 acres of fruit orchards in the valley, watered by massive irrigation projects such as the Grand Valley Project and Orchard Mesa Canals. The Highline Project was another ambitious canal project involving a series of dams and ditches designed to irrigate some 50,000 acres at the base of the Book Cliffs north of Grand Junction; it was completed in 1918.

Ranching

Large-scale herders—including the Kimball Brothers, the YT outfit, and the Smith brothers -introduced the first cattle herds to the county in 1882. They quickly realized that Grand Mesa offered some of the best grazing land in the country. After the railroad arrived, livestock raising became big business in Mesa County; stockyards developed in Appleton, De Beque, Grand Junction, and Whitewater, and by 1920, more than 50,000 cattle grazed on upward of 44,000 acres of alfalfa and hay.[218]

This is the region the Uncompahgre Utes thought they were being removed to, not Utah. They blamed Otto Mears for his sleight of hand in moving them over the state line into Utah based on the argument there was no sufficient land base for a reservation in northwestern Colorado when that was far from the truth.

Mineral County (1893)

Historically, the Weeminuche and Capote Utes lived in what is today Mineral County. Located in the heart of the San Juan Mountains west of the San Luis Valley, the county takes its name from the rich mineral deposits found there in the nineteenth century. N. C. Creede made the first discoveries. He sought financial backing from David H. Moffat. Moffat sent his famed mining manager, Eben Smith to investigate. He bought out Creede. It was not long before a settlement arose in the narrow winding cañon of Willow Creek, which was called Creede.

To provide an idea of how grub-staking worked, Hall gives us his "Creede" description:

> Ralph Granger and Erl von Buddenbock had opened a meat market and were making money. One day a prospector named Theodore Renniger happened in, and said if they would "grub stake" him he would prospect for them on shares. They accepted the proposition ... In August they found on what is now Bachelor mountain a well-established outcrop, and began to work upon it. Soon afterward Mr. N. C. Creede came that way and stopped to examine it. His well-trained eye told him that a great find had been made though the discoverers were unconscious of it. He asked Renniger to define and stake his claim, which he did, naming it "The Last Chance." Creede immediately staked off a claim adjoining on the outcrop for Moffat, Campbell and himself, and named it "The Amethyst." In course of their development these two properties became the largest producers of rich ore in that district...[219]

Then, a newspaper correspondent writing of Creede in January, 1892, epitomizes the situation there as cited by Hall:

> "The train when it comes is a sight to behold, the smoking car being an especial marvel. It is jammed. Men sit on one another, and on the arms of the seats, stand in the aisles and hang on to the platforms. Pipes, blankets, satchels form the major part of their equipment. At night there are no policemen to interfere with the vested right of each citizen to raise as much Cain as he sees fit, and it is a reasonable estimate to say that fully three-fourths of the population are of that kind which does see fit. ...The saloons and dance houses are in full blast, and such dance houses as they are, and such discarded remnants as the old fairies who flaunt around in them never were seen before. Along in the morning, when the wheezy accordeon [sic] lets up, the time is occupied by a riot. Nobody bothers. Drunken men come out occasionally and empty their revolvers into the air or somebody's legs. The latter process indicates a cultivated softening of the old brutal habits. There are a few bad men in Creede, and many who are reckless."[220]

Moffat County (1911)

Historically, the Yampa, Uintah and Parianuche Utes lived in what is today Moffat County. The Utes' expulsion led to the establishment of many towns in northwest Colorado, including Craig, the future seat of Moffat County, in 1889. In 1902, David Moffat, a Denver entrepreneur worth some $25 million, financed a rail line that would run through the Yampa valley and link Denver with Salt Lake City. Moffat's plan hinged on getting the line, nicknamed the "Moffat Road," to the Yampa valley so he could tap the coal reserves that would fund the line's completion.

The county economy is mostly supported by energy development, including coal mining and natural gas drilling, although ranching and agriculture also contribute.

Montezuma County (1889)

Montezuma County acquired its name from the famous chief of the Aztec Indians of Mexico. The prehistoric building ruins of Mesa Verde National Park, which are located in the county, were originally thought to have been built by the Aztecs.[221]

Historically, the Muache, Capote and Weenuche Utes lived in what is today Montezuma County. Navajo and Southern Paiute people also frequented the Four Corners area. It is known as the Four Corners region, where the boundaries of four states intersect.

Under the Brunot Agreement, the Ute leader Ouray agreed to cede the San Juan Mountains, including the eastern part of present-day Montezuma County, to the U.S. The agreement also established the Southern Ute Indian Reservation, south of the ceded territory for the Weenuche, Capote, and Muache Utes.

Tension between whites and Utes in Montezuma sometimes resulted in violence, such as when Utes killed at least a dozen ranchers in the spring of 1881, or when whites murdered a group of Utes at a campsite along Beaver Creek in 1885. That same year Weenuches burned the Genthner home on Totten Lake, near Cortez, and killed the family patriarch, though his wife and six children survived. Sporadic violence continued until the last major conflict in 1915, which left several Utes and members of a joint Anglo-American-Mexican posse dead.

Later, the Dawes Act of 1887 directed that reservation land be allotted to individual tribal members, but many Weenuches rejected the idea of allotment and preferred one large reservation. To that end, in 1895 the government established the Ute Mountain Ute Reservation out of the western edge of the Southern Ute Reservation. Weenuche Utes began settling the reservation in 1897, and they gained federal recognition as the Ute Mountain Ute Tribe in 1915.

At the turn of the century, the county's economy began a transition from ranching to farming after the construction of great canals in the Montezuma, in 1885-86. In 1885 the Montezuma Valley Water Supply company was organized to take water from the Dolores River from the North and South Forks. In May 1889, the irrigation corporations combined, forming the Colorado Consolidated Land and Water company. It has about 100 miles of constructed canals, including mains and laterals, and covers some 80,000 acres of fine agricultural land. The chief market for produce is the Navajo Indian Reservation, thirty miles south, in New Mexico, where about 20,000 Indians are located. The produce is sold under government contracts to be delivered to the Navajos. A great amount of corruption is known to exist in this market which led to the Santa Fe Ring's willingness to fight for the contracts in Lincoln County, New Mexico. The tract known as the Mesa Verde is reported to be extensively underlaid with coal. Some gold-bearing placers have been found on the upper Mancos, and some silver lodes in the La Plata mountains.

Montrose County (1883)

Historically, the Parianuche, Tabeguache, and Weeminuche Utes lived in what is today Montrose County. Also, Paiutes frequented the area. *This is the region the Uncompahgre Utes thought they were being removed to, not Utah.*

Montrose County received its name from the City of Montrose which is surmised to have been named after Sir Walter Scott's The Legend of Montrose, published in 1819.

Montrose County was opened to settlers in 1881, when, General McKenzie effected the forcible removal of the Uncompahgre Utes to their new reservation in Utah. Large numbers of whites, knowing the value of the lands for agricultural purposes, came. Some of the more impatient crossed the line in advance of the withdrawal of the Indians but were expelled by the troops. In 1882 the price of town lots ranged from $50 to $150 each.[222]

The Black Cañon

Thousands of tourists take the Denver & Rio Grande railroad through the Black Cañon. Here are many miles of deep and very narrow chasms environed by towering cliffs bearing the marks of glacial action, the rocks worn smooth by the plunging stream. The Gunnison, which is considered the most beautiful of Colorado rivers, finds its tortuous way through these wondrous depths, winding and twisting and turning like a serpent, followed along its margins, by the railway, which, when shut out on one side, crosses to the other and back again as the varying changes occur, in obedience to the caprices of the torrent. The dark overhanging walls shut out the sunlight most of the day, and impart to it its name, "The Black Cañon."

At Cimarron, resides Capt. M. W. Cline, one of the oldest white settlers on the Indian reservation, also one of the founders of Ouray, and who achieved much distinction as a member of the General Charles Adams party that recaptured the white women carried into captivity by the Utes after the awful massacre at the White River agency in 1879. ...[223]

Natural Resources

The county is well timbered along the valleys and streams; beds of lignite coals have been located to the southeast of Montrose, but they are comparatively undeveloped. Large deposits of gypsum, limestone, fine building stone, and fine brick clays lie in the near vicinity. The timber of the mountain sides is chiefly yellow pine, cedar and pinon. There are vast areas of fine grazing lands, watered by small lakes and springs, where herds of cattle and flocks of sheep find pasturage the year round, owing to the mildness of the winters, the purity of the climate, and the luxuriance of the native grasses. According to the assessment roll for 1890 there were 34,846 head of cattle, and 10,784 sheep. Here, as elsewhere in the well-watered agricultural sections, the rich alluvial bottomlands were first taken up and improved, for the reason that little or no irrigation is required; next, the uplands, where a different but equally valuable soil is found, but requiring artificial canals to render them tillable. It is estimated that there are fully 200,000 acres of irrigable land in the county.[224]

Irrigation

The Uncompahgre river and other streams afford an abundant and never-failing supply of water for irrigation. The largest canal is the Uncompahgre, taken out seven miles above Montrose, which irrigates about 65,000 acres. *Eighteen flumes* or aqueducts are required, most of them long and high, aggregating more than one mile in length. Nearly *850,000 feet of lumber* was used in these flumes and the entire *cost of the canal was $210,000*. ... (Emphasis added).[225]

Still other natural resources, that must ultimately contribute much to the wealth of the country, are the extensive placer mines, located on the Dolores river.[226]

Hydraulic Mining Flume Required at Cost of $100,000

> The Montrose Placer Mining company, formed of *St. Louis capitalists* owns six and a half miles of mining ground on the Dolores river. To successfully work them by hydraulic process a flume was required. *For more than six miles this flume is supported on brackets from an overhanging cliff, ranging from 100 to 150 feet above the river and from 250 to 500 feet below the summit of the gorge*. ... A wagon road was constructed along the cliff at the apex, from which workmen were let down by ropes for the purpose of drilling into the face of the cliff, inserting the iron brackets and setting the flume thereon, using 1,800,000 feet of lumber in its construction. *It carries 80,000,000 gallons of water each twenty-four hours. ... Its cost was something over $100,000*. ... To the south are the mighty ranges of the San Juan, Mount Sneffels and the Uncompahgre Peaks... producing nothing but treasure. (Emphasis added).[227]

Fort Crawford to Keep Indians in Check

> Eight miles above Montrose, near the Uncompahgre river, is the abandoned military post known as Fort Crawford, built in 1880 and garrisoned by Federal troops commanded by General McKenzie, to keep the Indians "in check." In the neighborhood was the historic site of the Uncompahgre Indian Reservation, opened to settlement in 1881, and now mainly occupied by farmers.[228]

Otto Mears, Pathfinder of San Juan Mts.

In Montrose, Otto Mears continued his toll road building and operated freighting outfits over the roads and pack mule trains on the trails. Then he began railroad construction, building the Rio Grande Southern and the Silverton Railroad. He also acquired an interest in certain mining and smelter properties in the District. His portrait, Otto Mears, the Pathfinder of the San Juan, is in the dome of the State Capitol building.[229]

Assessed Valuation of $1,885,187

> The assessed valuation of taxable property in the county in 1884, the first year after its organization, was $757,878. The next year it amounted to $1,112,710. There has been a steady increase of value to 1890, when the total was $1,885,187.50. The county at this writing is only seven years old. When organized in 1883, it was simply a wilderness, sort of a primitive desolation, an Indian "hunting ground!" (Emphasis added).[230]

Other Minerals

While agriculture has been the backbone of the Montrose County economy since its creation, the area also has a rich history of copper and uranium mining.

Morgan County (1889)

Historically, the Cheyenne and Arapaho lived in what is today Morgan County. It covers 1,294 square miles of the South Platte valley and the Great Plains northeast of Denver. Its name is derived from Fort Morgan, a military post established along the South Platte River in 1865 built to protect white travelers on the Overland Trail from Indians.

By 1882, irrigation enterprises made Fort Morgan the center of a productive agricultural region. Water from the Platte was Fort Morgan's lifeblood for its crop of sugar beets.

Otero County (1889)

With their resource base seriously threatened, the Cheyenne and Arapaho decided to invade Comanche territory along the Arkansas River. There they vied with the Comanche for access to stands of cottonwood trees along the river, which offered essential shelter, fuel, and forage during the plains' harsh winters.[231]

This area became Otero County, named for Miguel Otero, the nineteenth-century New Mexican politician who helped found the county seat of La Junta. The La Junta and Rocky Ford areas are known for producing high-quality cantaloupe and watermelons.

Trade Development and Bent's Fort

During the eighteenth century, French, Spanish, and Indian traders frequented what became known as the Santa Fé Trail in southeastern Colorado. The trail, which connected Missouri and New Mexico, followed the Arkansas and Purgatoire Rivers in present-day Otero County. In the early nineteenth century, the trail cut across the Comanche heartland. Jealously patrolled by the Spanish, it was opened to American traders after Mexican Independence in 1821.

In 1830, the traders Ceran St. Vrain and William and Charles Bent relocated their trading post on the Arkansas River to a large adobe fort further downstream, which was completed in 1833, just east of present-day La Junta.

American cattle and sheep raisers established ranches in the Otero County area in the 1860s. In 1876, the Santa Fe Railroad made La Junta a stop on its Chicago-Los Angeles line, saving the region. La Junta was incorporated in 1881. Rocky Ford's famous melons, along with beans and alfalfa were farmed and, of course, cattle and sheep were a mainstay.

Ouray County (1877)

Historically, the Tabeguache Utes lived in what is today Ouray County. It was named for Chief Ouray, a leader of the Tabeguache Utes in the nineteenth century. It lies in southwest Colorado and has a prominent mining history from gold and silver mines in the late nineteenth century.

By the summer of 1872, gold and silver ore worth more than $30,000 per ton were being carved out of the region. The San Juan Cession of 1873, also known as the Brunot Agreement, cleared the way for present-day Ouray County by removing the people who had called it home for centuries. The agreement gave the U.S. a 4-million-acre chunk of the mineral-rich San Juan Mountains. The government paid the Utes seven and a half cents per acre for their land, even as it simultaneously charged homesteaders $1.25 per acre for inferior land elsewhere. For his role in negotiating the agreement, Ouray got 160 acres and a $1,000 pension for the rest of his life that would help support Chipeta until her death in 1924.

Otto Mears spent $2,800 of his own money bribing individual Utes to sign the cession Agreement. The Department of the Interior reimbursed the money he spent. It was completed on Sep. 11, 1880, and took all of the Utes' land in western Colorado.

Otto Mears helped relieve transportation in 1883 with the construction of a toll road between Ouray and the now-defunct town of Ironton to the south. The road formed the base of today's U.S. 550 and greatly eased the transport of supplies and ore between the county's mining towns. Mears' timing could not have been better, as an enormous amount of silver had been discovered in the Red Mountains south of Ironton in 1882. The silver deposit was so large that the Red Mountain mining district was second only to Leadville silver production at the time and was served by two towns, Ouray and Silverton. The Yankee Girl was the district's most profitable mine, producing $8 million in ore over the next decade.

In 1887 the Denver & Rio Grande Railroad arrived in Ouray, and Mears' Silverton Railroad reached the Red Mountain mines in 1888. In 1890 another Mears railroad, the Rio Grande Southern, was under construction in the Uncompahgre Valley to the north and was the basis for the town of Ridgway, founded the same year. The cost of ore transportation decreased even further with the arrival of the railroads.

A few miles below Ouray is a semi-tropical region—the fertile Uncompahgre Park—where there are no mines, but well-cultivated farms instead, bearing grand crops of grain, vegetables, fruits, alfalfa, etc. *Only a few years ago this valley was an Indian hunting ground, nothing more.* (Emphasis added).[232]

Hall has the last word here:

> *Some millions of English and American capital have been invested* there, the most improved appliances for hoisting, mining, milling and concentrating ores supplied, and the facilities afforded by railway switches leading from all the greater mines to the Rainbow railway for transportation to the ore buyers at Durango, Pueblo and Denver are unequaled by any other mining quarter. (Emphasis added).[233]

Park County (1861)

Tabeguache Utes, Kiowa, Cheyenne and Arapaho and Comanche hunted in South Park. In 1859, Tabeguaches killed a handful of prospectors near Tarryall, and several other white men were killed in South Park. In the 1860s the area was also the site of clashes between the Utes and the Arapaho.

The discovery of gold along Tarryall Creek northwest of Como in 1859, along with subsequent discoveries in the area, enticed some 10,000 people to present-day Park County, including prospectors, merchants, laborers, and a host of other people hoping to cash in on mining and related activities. Miners and mining companies established camps throughout South Park, including the Mosquito Mining District Park. It was in the summer of 1864 that Mr. Hall met H.A.W. Tabor, who, then the proprietor of a small grocery store, would in fifteen years became one of the "celebrities of the nation."

Phillips County (1889)

Historically, the Arapaho, Cheyenne, Comanche, Kiowa, Pawnee, and Lakota were present in what is today Phillips County. It was named for the secretary of the Lincoln Land Company, R.O. Phillips, who organized several towns in eastern Colorado. It covers 688 square miles on the Great Plains of northeastern Colorado. It was hard hit by drought and after 1900 the county became home to thriving communities of Anglo-American farmers, which were hit hard by the Dust Bowl of the 1930s but bounced back in future decades. Today the county is one of the state's top producers of corn, sheep, pigs, and cattle, thanks to water pumped from the vast Ogallala Aquifer.

Pitkin County (1881)

Historically, the Parianuche Utes lived in what is today Pitkin County. It is named after former Colorado Governor Frederick Pitkin. Located in west-central Colorado, it spans 973 square miles of mountains and the Roaring Fork River valley. In the summer of 1879, H.B. Gillespie and twenty-three other prospectors entered the Roaring Fork Valley and began staking silver claims. Aspen, the county seat, was founded during a silver boom during the 1870s paying millions in dividends. Much litigation arose over claim boundaries. From the best data procurable it is estimated that from 1880 to the close of 1892, Pitkin county contributed about $44,000,000 to the wealth of the state in silver and lead.[234]

The County is home to six of Colorado's Fourteeners, mountains standing 14,000 feet or higher: Pyramid Peak (14,025), Snowmass Peak (14,099), Capitol Peak (14,137), Castle Peak (14,279), and the Maroon Bells—Maroon Peak (14,163) and North Maroon Peak (14,019). The White River National Forest occupies most of the southern portion of Pitkin County.

Aspen Historical Society's Land Acknowledgment is as follows:

> Aspen Historical Society: We gratefully acknowledge we gather on the land of the Uncompahgre band of the Ute Nation,

or Nuche, past and present. We honor this land and the people who lived in harmony with the natural world for generations before their forced removal. We are committed to sharing the complete history of the land, recognizing and partnering with Native Peoples, and supporting the advancement of Native places and heritage. This calls us all to be better stewards of the land we inhabit and the natural resources we benefit from today.[235]

Prowers County (1889)

Historically, the Comanche, Kiowa, Cheyenne and Arapaho lived in what is today Prowers County. The Comanche occasionally clashed with the Arapaho, and other nomadic plains people who arrived north of the Arkansas in the late eighteenth and early nineteenth centuries. In 1803, while still under Comanche control, the area was claimed by the U.S. as part of the Louisiana Purchase. It was named for one of Colorado's prominent early ranchers, John W. Prowers.

Hiram S. Holly, who owned several quartz mills in the Rocky Mountains, bought 1,300 cattle and set up his ranch in what is now eastern Prowers County in 1871. To get around the Homestead Act's 160-acre limit, Holly made deals with cowboys to file for claims on the surrounding land and turn them over to him. By 1881 Holly had thirty miles of waterfront land on the Arkansas and 15,000 head of cattle.

The U.S. land office, whose district embraces Bent, Kiowa, Baca and Prowers counties, is located there, and during the brief period of its existence has disposed of immense quantities of government land to immigrants.

Thousands of acres have been irrigated and planted, more than 300 miles of canals and ditches built, nearly half a million acres rendered irrigable. These are now in use and there is in the course of construction four storage reservoirs having capacity for supplying water to 120,000 acres. Ranching and agricultural are present industries.

Pueblo County (1861)

Historically, the Arapaho lived in what is today Pueblo County. Pueblo is the Spanish word for "town" or "village". The group of adobe houses built at the site of the present City of Pueblo in 1841-1842 came to be known as "the pueblo". The name was then adopted by the city and then suggested as the name for the county.

Rio Blanco County (1889)

Rio Blanco is the Spanish name for White River. The county adopted the name Rio Blanco from the river which runs through the area. It is said that the Spanish explorer, Father Escalante, originally named the stream Rio San Clemente.

Historically, the Parianuche, or "Elk People," and the Yampa, or "Root Eaters," and the Uintah Utes lived in Rio Blanco County. The Yampa wintered in the White River valley and ranged into the Flat Tops and southern Wyoming; the Parianuche wintered near present-day Glenwood Springs and ranged into eastern Utah and the Flat Tops.

On March 2, 1868, the Senate of the U.S. ratified a treaty whereby two agencies were to be established, one for the Grand River, Yampa and Uintah bands on White River, and the other for the southern Utes on the Rio de las Pinos. Nathan Meeker was appointed as the agent for White River. Hall discusses the lack of "harmony and good fellowship almost from the beginning:"

> [Meeker] put too much nervous force and methodical, exacting energy into his proceedings. In attempting to establish the same order and enforce the same discipline which had governed the organization of Union Colony [in Greeley], he soon discovered that the Indians would not have it so. They were sullen, suspicious and wholly unwilling to change their old habits and customs for the new. While it is true that he did induce some of them to plow and seed certain patches of ground, after the crops began to appear they expected him to care for and bring them to harvest for their benefit, while they went off to hunt and fish among the mountains according to immemorial custom. They believed the country belonged to them; that the agent and his followers were hired by the government and paid to work for them, and when in his sharp, brusque and uncompromising manner he notified them that they must plant and cultivate and reap for themselves or starve, they broke out in a tempest of opposition. There was a total lack of harmony and good fellowship almost from the beginning. They did not understand his ways, nor he their natures. After the spring of 1879 Mr. Meeker realized that his mission would fail. During the summer he came back to Greeley, and in a visit to Denver had a conference

with General John Pope, then commanding this department, but with headquarters in Leavenworth, Kansas, to whom he related his trials, saying it would be impossible to enforce his project for the reclamation of the Utes without the presence of Federal troops, and if these could not be furnished he was ready to resign. Pope encouraged him to retain his position. When Mr. Meeker returned to his post he found the Indians ready for revolt. They had come to hate him and all his plans for their redemption.[236]

The Thornburgh and Meeker incidents which occurred thereafter in what is today Rio Blanco County have been previously presented.

Rio Grande County (1874)

In 1820, Mexico began issuing land grants to attract settlers to the former Spanish "far north." One such grant, the 1833 Conejos Guadalupe Land Grant, included parts of present-day Saguache, Rio Grande, and Conejos Counties. An attempt to settle the grant in 1843 was thwarted by Utes and Navajos, but later attempts were more successful.

The county derived its name from the river of the same name which flows through it. The original name given to the river by the Spanish was Rio Grande del Norte (Great River of the North). In its prime a considerable wholesale trade was carried on there, but most of this disappeared when the D. & R. G. railway penetrated the San Juan by a different route. Agriculture and stock raising are features of the region.

Routt County (1877)
Steamboat Springs' Land Acknowledgment is as follows:

WHEREAS, The First Peoples known to live in the Yampa Valley trace their origins through their Numic speaking descendants. Today, they are known to be part of the Ute Nation. Their oral history traditions are without a migration story because they claim the Rocky Mountains as their origin and understand themselves to have been here for at least 10,000 years; and WHEREAS, regionally the Ute tribe that inhabited the Yampa Valley are known as the Yamparika or Yampatika people who were later forcibly removed from their ancestral home and relocated to reservations in Utah and Southern Colorado after the Battle of Milk Creek in 1879; and WHEREAS, we further recognize all other Native American

~ 280 ~

tribes who passed through or made the Yampa Valley their home throughout time; and their stewardship cared for a Yampa Valley teeming with herds of American Bison, Colorado Elk, and Gray Wolf Packs, which subsequently became extinct in the 20th century.[237]

The County is named after John L. Routt, the first Governor of the State of Colorado. It is by far the largest grazing section of the state. It is quite thoroughly watered. The county seat was located at the town of Hahn's Peak, where gold was discovered, with mining starting in 1866.

Saguache County (1866)

Saguache County acquired its name from a Ute Indian word meaning "blue earth" or "water at blue earth". The name was initially applied to a stream in the area, then the town and eventually to the county.

The Tabeguache, Muache, and Capote Utes lived in Saguache County but Navajo, Comanche, Cheyenne, Arapaho, and Kiowa are historically tied to the area, also. Saguache County is known as the northern gateway to the San Luis Valley.

Large cattle-ranching operations developed in the 1880s, which caused land-use conflicts between Anglo-American cattle ranchers and Hispano shepherds.

One of the ambitious men who homesteaded the Saguache area in the mid-1860s that would help shape the region for decades was Otto Mears. He arrived in the area in 1865 and began farming wheat and milling flour for the fledgling mining communities. Sensing a future for trade through the San Luis Valley and surrounding communities, Mears built toll roads over Poncha Pass in 1867, Cochetopa Pass in 1871, and Marshall Pass in 1878. He sold the latter road to the Denver & Rio Grande Railroad (D&RG), which used the path to extend its narrow gauge line to Gunnison ahead of its rivals. Mears founded a local newspaper—the Saguache Chronicle—in 1874, and even started his own railway in the San Juans. Mears single-handedly improved road infrastructure and encouraged travel and trade amongst the early mountain communities of southern Colorado, earning himself the title "pathfinder of the San Juans."

The County's history is closely tied to mining. The first gold rush to the area—modest in scale compared to those along the Front Range of the Rocky Mountains—began in 1879, when silver-lead-manganese veins were discovered along Kerber Creek. The mining camp of Bonanza to the west of

Villa Grove was founded as a central hub for other small mining operations in the area; the smelter there was completed by 1879 and continued operation for three years. Mines soon opened up in Orient in the northeastern San Luis Valley to exploit local iron ores. Gold discoveries near Cochetopa and at the base of the San Juans contributed to the mining boom, and local populations ballooned as thousands of miners came to the valley seeking fortunes. Prominent local mines included the Rawley, Antoro, Michigan, Paragon, Cocomongo, and Eagle.

Between 1880 and the closing of local mines in 1923, Saguache County produced over $2.7 million in minerals, $1.6 million of which was in silver.

San Juan County (1876)

San Juan County was originally part of La Plata County. Its name is Spanish for Saint John. Early explorers to the region applied the name to the river and mountain ranges. Eventually, the name was given to the region and the county.

Historically, the Utes lived in what is today San Juan County. Silverton, at an elevation of 9,318 feet along the Animas River, is the county seat. San Juan County covers 388 square miles of the San Juan Mountains. U.S. 550, the "Million Dollar Highway," is the main thoroughfare.

In 1872 gold and silver ore worth some $30,000 per ton was being produced from the San Juans. The riches flowing out of the mountains prompted Colorado territorial Governor Edward McCook to openly lament the 1868 treaty that barred nonnatives from the mountains. For its part, the U.S. responded by ordering miners to leave Ute lands, and even sent in troops to enforce the treaty. The miners, however, banded together before any conflict took shape and convinced the government to negotiate a new treaty that would take more land from the Utes.

The Brunot Agreement, also known as the San Juan Cession, cleared the way for present-day San Juan County by removing the people who had lived there for more than four centuries. The government coveted a rectangular chunk of the San Juan Mountains that measured 4 million acres and that included most of what is today southwest Colorado. In 1873 Felix R. Brunot, then-president of the U.S. Board of Indian Commissioners, hatched a plot to find Ouray's lost son, Pahlone, believed to be in Arapaho possession, and trade him to the chief for the land.

Although Brunot's men could not find Ouray's son, at negotiations in September Ouray still wanted to provide for his wife and was impressed enough by Brunot's effort that he agreed to sell the San Juans to the U.S. The river valleys suitable for farming were supposed to remain in Ute possession, but the final agreement was struck along lines of latitude and longitude—a concept the Utes were not familiar with—so the U.S. got all 4 million acres. The government paid the Utes seven and a half cents per acre, a poor deal considering that it simultaneously charged white homesteaders $1.25 per acre for other, grossly inferior land.

Otto Mears

Otto Mears constructed, between 1867 and 1886, no less than nine wagon roads in the southwestern mountains. For San Juan County, he was the principal engaged in the construction of a narrow or three-foot gauge railway, seventeen miles in length, including several switchbacks, from Silverton across the intervening range to Red Mountain and Ironton on the western slope, over a five per cent, grade, or an elevation of 262 feet per mile average. Its cost was $725,000. From the terminus of the main line he installed eight miles of switches or branches, leading to all the great mines of the Red Mountain district which also included Telluride and Rico for convenience in delivering supplies and in transferring ores for shipment to the sampling mills at Silverton, or direct to the D. & R. G. railway for conveyance to Durango, Pueblo and Denver. All the switching at the mines was without charge. Mr. Mears derives his revenue from his monopoly of the traffic between the points of reception and delivery. The building of a railway connection between Red Mountain and Silverton was a must, resulting in an increase in the number of mines and an increase of receipts at the smelters, and a hefty revenue accruing to the County.

San Miguel County (1883)

Historically, the Utes lived in what is today San Miguel County. Formed in 1883, it includes the historic mining-turned-ski town of Telluride. San Miguel is the Spanish word for Saint Michael. The name was used by the Spanish to reference the main river of the area. It was later chosen as the name for the county.

Among the early prospectors was a group led by Linnard Remine that reached the San Miguel Valley in 1872. They were likely the first white Americans to explore the area near present-day Telluride. Remine built a cabin—illegally, as he was on Ute lands—and his group panned gold worth about $15 per day from the San Miguel River. Richer strikes were made to the southeast, in present-day San Juan County. Otto Mears' narrow gauge railway from Silverton included a branch for Telluride and enhanced the silver mining in the area.

During an era marked by nationwide disputes between capital and labor, violent strikes rocked San Miguel County in 1901 and 1903-4. During the 1903-4 strike, the Colorado National Guard was brought to Telluride on behalf of mine owners and citizens. As the town grew increasingly polarized, vigilante groups such as the pro-company Citizens' Alliance confronted union members and sympathizers. Anti-union Governor James Peabody appointed Bulkeley Wells, manager of the Smuggler-Union Mine, as a National Guard captain. Wells declared martial law and illegally deported miners to neighboring Ouray County. To keep the deportees out, Wells built a machine gun nest atop Imogene Pass, the only way into San Miguel County from the east.

San Miguel River Smuggler-Union Hydroelectric Plant was built in 1907 to power the Smuggler-Union Mining Company's mines and mills. San Miguel and Montrose Counties became worldwide centers of radium mining. Between 1910 and 1922, demand for vanadium rose because it was used as an alloy for steel, and mining occurred near Placerville.

In the 1940s, the federal Manhattan Project—the covert mission to develop atomic weaponry—used uranium from mines in San Miguel and Montrose Counties.

Sedgwick County (1889)

Historically, the Kiowa, Cheyenne and Arapaho lived in what is today Sedgwick County. It was named for Fort Sedgwick, a military post along the Platte Trail, which existed from approximately 1864-1871.

The town of Julesburg was founded at an important crossing of the South Platte River. Camp Rankin was established near Julesburg in the early 1860s to protect the stage lines and white travelers from Indians. Tensions between Indians and whites erupted into all-out war after U.S. troops under Colonel John Chivington slaughtered more than 150 peaceful Cheyenne and Arapaho Indians—mostly women, children, and the elderly—at Sand Creek in November 1864. The Indians were camped on the agreed-upon reservation in present-day Kiowa County. In January 1865 a retaliatory force of some 1,000 Lakota, Cheyenne, and Northern Arapaho raided Julesburg, destroyed surrounding ranches, and drove away cattle and horses. In this first assault, Julesburg's buildings were left intact. But in a second attack, on February 2, the warriors burned Julesburg to the ground.

Three years later, under the terms of the Medicine Lodge Treaty the Cheyenne and Arapaho were to relocate to present-day Oklahoma. But many, especially the younger members of both tribes, decided to keep fighting. In 1869 the U.S. Army defeated the Cheyenne leader Tall Bull's Dog Soldiers at the Battle of Summit Springs in present-day Washington County marking the end of Indian resistance on the Colorado plains.

> The third Julesburg ... became the terminus of the U. P. railway for a time, a town of tents and shanties, whither drifted and lodged the most notorious and reckless gang of outlaws, thieves, thugs and assassins ever congregated at any one point on the western frontier. Gambling, drinking, rioting, murders, robberies ... marked both night and day, until the crowd was dispersed and scattered by the advance of the railroad to Cheyenne, where, in due course, similar scenes were enacted, but upon a limited scale.[238]

As far as natural resources, the County is situated upon an open plain which is solely adapted to agriculture and grazing. The principal stream is the South Platte River and it is located within the Ogallala Aquifer.

Summit County (1861)

The county derived its name from the many mountain summits located within the county.

> Historically, the Kiowa, Cheyenne and Arapaho lived in what is today Summit County. The Arapaho also followed a seasonal migration route, tracking game up to the high country in the Summit County area during the summer and returning to the edge of the foothills for the winter. The Utes, meanwhile, had been ranging out of their mountain homeland for summer buffalo hunts since the late seventeenth century; the overlapping territory was often a source of tension and conflict between the Ute and Arapaho peoples.[239]

The first gold seekers arrived in the Summit County area in 1859. In August, a prospecting party led by Ruben J. Spaulding, a miner who participated in the 1849 California Gold Rush, found gold in Georgia Gulch a few miles northeast of present-day Breckenridge.

Between 1859 and 1879, several different mining processes helped Summit County produce nearly $7 million in gold. As early as 1863, the surface gold in Summit County mines began to be depleted. To reach deeper deposits, miners turned to a process called hydraulic mining, which uses high-pressure hoses to blast away rock and free gold tumbling down through sluices. The gold would then sink to the bottom of the sluices, where it was recovered the same way it was in the panning process. Hard-rock mining, or the manual extraction of gold and silver in mine tunnels, was also employed to get at deeper deposits.

In addition, a number of silver lodes were discovered in the area during the 1870s, and Summit County soon found itself in the midst of a second mining boom. The center of mining production shifted from the Breckenridge area to the Tenmile Mining District near Frisco, which produced an estimated $2 million in silver in 1881.

Benjamin S. Revett, a mining mogul known as the "Father of Gold Dredging in the United States," began operating Colorado's first dredge in Summit County in 1898.

Teller County (1889)

Historically, the Arapaho and Utes lived in what is today Teller County. They fought for control of the area.

Teller County, named for U.S. Senator Henry M. Teller, was formed in 1889 to alleviate tension between wealthy mine owners in Colorado Springs (El Paso County) and working-class miners in Victor and Cripple Creek. It encompasses 559 square miles of the western flank of Pike's Peak and the southern Front Range. *Its county seat is Cripple Creek, the site of the last great gold rush in Colorado history*.

> **Cripple Creek** A new gold-extraction process gained traction
> in Colorado during the Cripple Creek gold boom of the 1890s.
> Using cyanide to separate gold was, as mining historian Jay
> Fell writes, "far more efficient than stamp milling and far
> less expensive than smelting." Like earlier stamp milling,
> the process involved crushing the gold ore into sand, but

instead of running it over copper plates or through sluices, the cyanide mills sent the sand into vats of a cyanide solution which dissolved gold for extraction. Despite the success of cyanide in gold processing, silver-lead-zinc ores still had to be smelted.[240]

Winfield Scott Stratton discovered gold on Battle Mountain and the Independence Lode, one of the richest gold deposits in American history, above present-day Victor. The Cripple Creek-Victor areas were producing almost $20 million worth of gold per year. Cripple Creek had grown to a population of 10,000 and Victor claimed to have 18,000 residents.

Five lumber mills converted the area's dense timber stands into boards for houses in Colorado Springs and mining structures in Cripple Creek as well as ties for railroads across the state. By 1892, timber was being extracted at such a frantic pace that the U.S. established the Pike Forest Reserve to control the damage caused by uncontrolled and wasteful timber cutting.

In January 1894, in the midst of skyrocketing production, mine owners in Cripple Creek and Victor announced a wage reduction. The local chapter of the Western Federation of Miners (WFM), a national hard-rock miners' union formed the previous year, initiated a strike, and in March Colorado Governor Davis Waite sent in the state militia to keep the peace. The troops left without incident at the end of the month, but El Paso County sheriff M. F. Bowers was apparently determined to break the strike himself. He illegally deputized more than 1,000 men and in May led them to a clash with armed strikers at Bull Hill, east of Cripple Creek. The skirmish prompted Governor Waite to visit the miners and seek a resolution. In a rare move, Waite sided with the miners, which cost him his seat in the next election.

This time, the state government, led by anti-union Governor James Peabody, was firmly on the side of big business. Peabody sent in the state militia and National Guard to arrest union leaders and break the strike, but it went on throughout 1903, crippling the Teller County economy.

On June 6, 1904, a local railroad depot in Independence, near Victor, was mysteriously bombed, killing fourteen men and releasing months of mounting tension between the strikers and groups aligned with the owners. With accusations flying on both sides, Governor Peabody declared martial law, and several skirmishes between militia and strikers resulted in deaths, injuries, deportations, and mass arrests. Eventually, the WFM was forced out of the district and the mine owners secured victory over the strikers.

The depot bombing remains unexplained to this day. Nonetheless, the station bombing was a catalyst for one of organized labor's biggest defeats in Colorado history.

Mining Accidents

Frequent mining accidents helped illustrate why workers fought so hard for better pay and safer conditions. In 1896 accidents killed twenty-six miners in the Cripple Creek Mining District alone. But perhaps the most tragic accident occurred at the Independence Mine during the strike of 1903-4, when faulty machinery and a snapped cable sent fourteen non-union miners plummeting 1,500 feet to their deaths.

In 2013 CC&V donated several ounces of gold used to refurbish the state capitol dome in Denver.

Washington County (1889)

Historically, the Kiowa, Cheyenne and Arapaho lived in what is today Washington County. It is named for the U.S.' first president. The county generally lacks the major water sources of its neighbors, such as the South Platte River in Morgan County or the Ogallala Aquifer underneath Yuma County. Ranching and agricultural are the only present industries.

Weld County (1861)

It was named for Lewis Ledyard Weld, who was appointed by President Abraham Lincoln as the first Secretary of the Colorado Territory. Historically, the Cheyenne and Arapaho lived in what is today Weld County. The Arapaho and Lakota are also included. One of Colorado's original seventeen counties, Weld County covers 4,017 square miles in northeastern Colorado and is home to more than 250,000 people. A major agricultural county, Weld has a population of 252,825. More than a third of the population resides in Greeley. Seven counties now occupy the area originally assigned to Weld.

Records exist for the area from 1859. In December 1869, Meeker, Greeley, and Robert A. Cameron organized the Union Colony Association.

By the early 1900s, the Great Western Sugar Company built thirteen communities in Weld County.

In 1960 Monfort's company partnered with Capital Packing, Inc. to build a meat-packing plant in Greeley.

The Niobrara Shale formation, a subterranean rock formation containing oil and natural gas at depths between 3,000 and 14,000 feet, is being produced. The county currently hosts approximately 20,000 oil and gas wells, more than any other county in the state. The energy industry is a huge contributor to the local economy.

The University of Northern Colorado's Land Acknowledgment is as follows:

> The University of Northern Colorado sits upon the territories of the Ute, Cheyenne, Arapaho, and Lakota peoples. The University also acknowledges the 48 tribes that are historically tied to the state of Colorado. UNC appreciates this connection and has great respect for this land. Additionally, the University community pays its respect to Elders past, present, and future, and to those who have stewarded this land throughout the generations.[241]

Yuma County (1889)

> Yuma County was used as a hunting range by Cheyenne, Arapaho, Kiowa and Pawnee. The Cheyennes, Arapahoes and Sioux frequently raided settlements in the area, but committed no depredations after 1881. Yuma County covers 2,369 square miles in northeast Colorado. It was named after the ancient Yuma Indians who inhabited the area.[242]

It is one of the state's most productive agricultural counties, drawing water from the Ogallala Aquifer to support more than 800 farms and more than 260,000 head of cattle.

County Development

After the American Indians left, the only people living in the Yuma County area before 1880 were ranchers. Joseph W. Bowles had a ranch near the North Fork of the Republican River, about twenty-three miles from present-day Yuma, while William L. Campbell had a ranch near the Nebraska state line and Frank and Charles Reeks grazed their cattle in the area of Beecher Island.

Abundant rainfall during the 1880s led many people to believe that eastern Colorado was situated in a rainbelt, which it turned out was false. Yuma, like Sedgwick, Phillips and other counties were hard hit by the droughts in the 1880s and 1890s, leaving many farmers destitute. Irrigation and semi-arid farming techniques had to be developed. Agriculture is the leading industry in Yuma, with irrigation from the Ogallala Aquifer.

> Joseph Yule, considered generally the *leading and most substantial ranchman in the county of Garfield*, and living on a fine ranch of five hundred and twenty acres on the creek of the same name not far from Newcastle, is essentially a self-made man and a good product of his own energy and capacity. ... *Mr. Yule has been ranching and raising cattle for himself, having located a squatter's claim on what was then an Indian reservation. When the land was surveyed he pre-empted his claim of one hundred and sixty acres, and he has since added to it by purchase until he now owns five hundred and twenty acres* ... (Emphasis added).[243]

Notes: Colorado

1. Warren L. d'Azevedo, et al. (eds.), (The Current Status of Anthropological Research in the Great Basin; 1964. (Reno: Desert Research Institute, 1966, p. 178. See also: James Grady, Environmental Factors in Archaeological Site Location, Piceance Basin, Colorado. (Denver: Bureau of Land Management, 1980). Athearn, Frederic J. An Isolated Empire: A History of Northwestern Colorado. 3rd ed. Colorado Bureau of Land Management, Cultural Resource Series No. 2, 1982, p. 3. https://upload.wikimedia.org/wikipedia/commons/8/86/The_new_empire_of_the_Rockies_-_a_history_of_northeast_Colorado_%28IA_newempireofrocki00mehl%29.pdf (accessed online December 7, 2022).
2. American Blood on American Soil, U.S. History. https://www.ushistory.org/us/29c.asp (accessed online November 11, 2020).
3. Around the world with General Grant: a narrative of the visit of General U.S. Grant, ex-President of the United States, to various countries in Europe, Asia, and Africa, in 1877, 1878, 1879 to which are added certain conversations with General Grant on questions connected with American politics and history, John Russell Young, 1879: 448.
4. Address by General John Pope before the Social Science Association, at Cincinnati, Ohio, May 24, 1878. Delivered by Request of the Association

(Cincinnati: n.p., 1878).

5. 1904 - Indian Affairs - Laws and Treaties, Treaties Vol. II, Charles J. Kappler (2019). U.S. and Indian Relations. 594.

6. Report of the Commissioner of Indian Affairs to the Secretary of the Interior, United States. Office of Indian Affairs. U.S. Government Printing Office, 1853, p. 128.

7. King, Judy. "Upper Arkansas Indian Agency." Colorado Encyclopedia. https://coloradoencyclopedia.org/article/upper-arkansas-indian-agency (accessed online December 23, 2021).

8. ALICE POLK HILL, COLORADO PIONEERS IN PICTURE AND STORY, 1915. https://archive.org/details/coloradopioneers00hill_0 (accessed online December 23, 2021).

9. Report of the Commissioner of Indian Affairs to the Secretary of the Interior, United States. Office of Indian Affairs. U.S. Government Printing Office, 1859, p. 21.

10. Ibid., p. 129.

11. Id.

12. Id.

13. Ibid., pp. 130-131.

14. Ibid., p. 137.

15. Ibid., p. 138.

16. Report of the Commissioner of Indian Affairs to the Secretary of the Interior, United States. Office of Indian Affairs. U.S. Government Printing Office, 1859, pp. 138-139.

17. Report of the Commissioner of Indian Affairs to the Secretary of the Interior, United States. Office of Indian Affairs. U.S. Government Printing Office, 1859, p. 20.

18. Stephen Arnold Douglas, Speeches of Senator S. A. Douglas: On the Occasion of His Public Receptions by the Citizens of New Orleans, Philadelphia, and Baltimore, L. Towers, 1859, Harvard University.

19. Reminiscences of Lincoln, Address by General O.O. Howard to Young Men's Republican Club, Montpelier, Vt., February 12, 1896. https://library.bowdoin.edu/arch/mss/ooh-pdf/M91b40f039.pdf (accessed online March 12, 2023). S. Exec. Doc. No. 15, 36th Cong., 1st Sess. (1860).

20. Hall, Frank. History of the State of Colorado, Embracing Accounts of the Pre-historic Races and Their Remains: The Earliest Spanish, French and American Explorations... the First American Settlements Founded; the Original Discoveries of Gold in the Rocky Mountains; the Development of Cities and Towns, with the Various Phases of Industrial and Political Transition, from 1858 to 1890..., Vol. 4, Blakely Printing Company, 1895.

21. Report of the Commissioner of Indian Affairs to the Secretary of the Interior, United States. Office of Indian Affairs. U.S. Government Printing

Office, 1861, p. 17.

22. *Cuthair v. Montezuma-Cortez Colorado Sch. District No. Re-1*, 7 F. Supp. 2d 1152, 1156 (D. Colorado 1998).

23. Report of the Commissioner of Indian Affairs to the Secretary of the Interior, United States. Office of Indian Affairs. U.S. Government Printing Office, 1862, p. 13.

24. Washington National Republican, March 27, 1868.

25. Annual Report of the Department of the Interior, Vol. II, Report of the Commissioner of Indian Affairs, Office of Indian Affairs, United States. U.S. Government Printing Office, 1916, p. 58.

26. Letter of William P. Dole to John Evans, 07-16-1863, Governor's Papers, Transcript of original Letter Press Book Record. Governor John Evans. Colorado State Archives, History Colorado. MSS Evans 226.

27. Report of the John Evans Study Committee, University of Denver, November 2014, Denver, p. 45.

28. Report of the Commissioner of Indian Affairs to the Secretary of the Interior, United States. Office of Indian Affairs. U.S. Government Printing Office, 1863, p. 28.

29. Ibid., p. 139.

30. Encyclopedia Staff. "Conejos Treaty." Colorado Encyclopedia. https://coloradoencyclopedia.org/article/conejos-treaty (accessed online February 3, 2023).

31. The War of the Rebellion: A Compilation of the Official Records of the Union and Confederate Armies, United States War Department, U.S. Government Printing Office, 1891. Series I, Vol. XLI, Part IV, Chapter XLVI, CORRESPONDENCE, ETC. - UNION, p. 101.

32. A Timeline of events relating to the Sand Creek Massacre. National Park Service. https://www.nps.gov/sand/learn/timeline.htm (accessed online February 19, 2023).

33. Draper, Kenneth E. The Pike's Peakers and the Rocky Mountain Rangers: A History of Colorado in the Civil War. Xlibris Corporation, 2012, p. 320.

34. The War of the Rebellion: A Compilation of the Official Records of the Union and Confederate Armies, United States War Department, U.S. Government Printing Office, 1891. LOUISIANA AND THE TRANS-MISSISSIPPI. Chapter XLVI, SKIRMISH NEAR FREMONT'S ORCHARD, COLORADO, p. 883.

35. Report of the University of Denver John Evans Study Committee, p. 55.

36. The War of the Rebellion: A Compilation of the Official Records of the Union and Confederate Armies, United States War Department, U.S. Government Printing Office, 1891. Series I, Vol. XXXIV, Part I, Chapter XLVI, LOUISIANA AND THE TRANS-MISSISSIPPI, SKIRMISH AT CEDAR BLUFFS, Colorado., pp. 909-910.

37. The War of the Rebellion: A Compilation of the Official Records of the Union and Confederate Armies, United States War Department, U.S. Government Printing Office, 1891. Series I, Vol. XXXIV, Part IV, CORRESPONDENCE, ETC. - UNION, p. 151.

38. John M. Chivington. http://www.shoppbs.pbs.org/weta/thewest/people/a_c/chivington.htm (accessed online February 19, 2023).

39. https://www.nps.gov/sand/learn/news/hungate-family-murdered.htm (accessed online December 27, 2021).

40. Mehls, Steven F. The new empire of the Rockies: A history of northeast Colorado. No. 16. Bureau of Land Management, 1984, p. 43. https://upload.wikimedia.org/wikipedia/commons/8/86/The_new_empire_of_the_Rockies_-_a_history_of_northeast_Colorado_%28IA_newempireofrocki00mehl%29.pdf (accessed online December 7, 2022).

41. Kathy Alexander. https://www.legendsofamerica.com/fort-collins/ (accessed online October 5, 2022).

42. Mehls, Steven F. The new empire of the Rockies: A history of northeast Colorado. No. 16. Bureau of Land Management, 1984, p. 43.

43. The War of the Rebellion: A Compilation of the Official Records of the Union and Confederate Armies, United States War Department, U.S. Government Printing Office, 1891. Series I, Vol. XXXIV, Part IV, CORRESPONDENCE, ETC. - UNION, p. 206.

44. The War of the Rebellion: A Compilation of the Official Records of the Union and Confederate Armies, United States War Department, U.S. Government Printing Office, 1891. Series I, Vol. XXXIV, Part IV, CORRESPONDENCE, ETC. - UNION, p. 320.

45. Ibid., p. 353.

46. Ibid., p. 381.

47. Ibid., pp. 402-404.

48. Ibid., pp. 421-422.

49. Report of the Commissioner of Indian Affairs to the Secretary of the Interior, United States. Office of Indian Affairs. Colorado Superintendency. U.S. Government Printing Office, 1864, pp. 218-219.

50. The War of the Rebellion: A Compilation of the Official Records of the Union and Confederate Armies, United States War Department, U.S. Government Printing Office, 1891. Series I, Vol. XXXIV, Part IV, CORRESPONDENCE, ETC. - UNION, p. 658.

51. Id.

52. Report of the Commissioner of Indian Affairs to the Secretary of the Interior, United States. Office of Indian Affairs. Colorado Superintendency. U.S. Government Printing Office, 1864, pp. 230-231.

53. Report of the John Evans Study Committee, University of Denver, November 2014, Denver, pp. 63, 64, 65, 66, 69.

54. The War of the Rebellion: A Compilation of the Official Records of the Union and Confederate Armies, United States War Department, U.S. Government Printing Office, 1891. Series I, Vol. XXXIV, Part IV, Chapter LIII, CORRESPONDENCE, ETC. - UNION, p. 695.

55. Ibid., p. 765.

56. Ibid., p. 775.

57. A Timeline of events relating to the Sand Creek Massacre. https://www.nps.gov/sand/learn/timeline.htm (accessed online Sep. 25, 2021).

58. The War of the Rebellion: A Compilation of the Official Records of the Union and Confederate Armies, United States War Department, U.S. Government Printing Office, 1891. Series I, Vol. XLI, Part III, Chapter LIII, CORRESPONDENCE, ETC. - UNION, pp. 195-196.

59. Ibid., p. 195.

60. Ibid., p. 242.

61. Condition of the Indian Tribes: Report of the Joint Special Committee, Appointed Under Joint Resolution of March 3, 1865, United States, Congress. Joint Special Committee to Inquire into Condition of the Indian Tribes, Kraus Reprint Company, p. 87.

62. The Sand Creek Massacre Weld Council Transcript. https://www.kclonewolf.com/History/SandCreek/sc-documents/sc-weld-council.html (accessed online October 2, 2021).

63. Report of the John Evans Study Committee, University of Denver, November 2014, Denver, p. 13.

64. The War of the Rebellion: A Compilation of the Official Records of the Union and Confederate Armies, United States War Department, U.S. Government Printing Office, 1891. Series I, Vol. XLI, Part III, Chapter LIII, CORRESPONDENCE, ETC. - UNION, pp. 494-495.

65. The War of the Rebellion: A Compilation of the Official Records of the Union and Confederate Armies, United States War Department, U.S. Government Printing Office, 1891. Series I, Vol. XLI, Part III, Chapter LIII, CORRESPONDENCE, ETC. - UNION, p. 495.

66. Ibid., p. 525.

67. Ibid., p. 876.

68. Report of the Commissioner of Indian Affairs to the Secretary of the Interior, United States. Office of Indian Affairs. U.S. Government Printing Office, 1864, p. 256.

69. The War of the Rebellion: A Compilation of the Official Records of the Union and Confederate Armies, United States War Department, U.S. Government Printing Office, 1891. Series I, Vol. XLI, Part IV, Chapter LIII, CORRESPONDENCE, ETC. - UNION, p. 433.

70. Ibid., p. 876.

71. Report of the Commissioner of Indian Affairs to the Secretary of the

Interior, United States. Office of Indian Affairs. U.S. Government Printing Office, 1864, p. 23.

72. The War of the Rebellion: A Compilation of the Official Records of the Union and Confederate Armies, United States War Department, U.S. Government Printing Office, 1891. Series I, Vol. XLI, Part III, Chapter LIII, CORRESPONDENCE, ETC. - UNION, p. 914.

73. Ibid., p. 708.

74. Ibid., p. 709.

75. The War of the Rebellion: A Compilation of the Official Records of the Union and Confederate Armies, United States War Department, U.S. Government Printing Office, 1891. Series I, Vol. XLI, Part I, LOUISIANA AND THE TRANS-MISSISSIPPI, Chapter LIII0, p. 948.

76. Report of the Commissioner of Indian Affairs to the Secretary of the Interior, United States. Office of Indian Affairs. Central Superintendency. U.S. Government Printing Office, 1865, p. 387.

77. Report of the Commissioner of Indian Affairs to the Secretary of the Interior, United States. Office of Indian Affairs. U.S. Government Printing Office, 1865, p. 24.

78. AW Bowen & Co. Progressive Men of Western Colorado... AW Bowen & Company, 1905, pp. 627-628. https://babel.hathitrust.org/cgi/pt?id=uc2.ark:/13960/t9n29vf9s&view=1up&seq=668&q1=Sand%20creek (accessed online December 7, 2022).

79. The War of the Rebellion: A Compilation of the Official Records of the Union and Confederate Armies, United States War Department, U.S. Government Printing Office, 1891. Series I, Vol. XLI, Part IV, LOUISIANA AND THE TRANS-MISSISSIPPI, Chapter LIII, CORRESPONDENCE, ETC.- UNION, p. 797.

80. Ibid., pp. 953-954.

81. Report of the John Evans Study Committee, University of Denver, November 2014, Denver, p. iii.

82. The War of the Rebellion: A Compilation of the Official Records of the Union and Confederate Armies, Chapter LIII. ENGAGEMENT ON SAND CREEK, COLORADO Territory., United States War Department, U.S. Government Printing Office, 1891. Series I, Vol. XLI, Part IV, CORRESPONDENCE, ETC. - UNION, pp. 970-971.

83. Patrick J. Jung, The Black Hawk War of 1832 (Norman: University of Oklahoma Press, 2007), 33-210.

84. Report of the Commissioner of Indian Affairs to the Secretary of the Interior, United States. Office of Indian Affairs. U.S. Government Printing Office, 1865, p. 431.

85. Ibid., p. 400.

86. Ibid., p. 525.

87. Ibid., p. 523.

88. Ibid., p. 527.

89. Encyclopedia Staff. "Little Arkansas Treaty." *Colorado Encyclopedia.* https://coloradoencyclopedia.org/article/little-arkansas-treaty (accessed online February 3, 2023).

90. https://thejulesburgproject.org/ (accessed online February 4, 2023).

91. Browne, John Ross, and James Wickes Taylor. Reports upon the mineral resources of the United States. U.S. Government Printing Office, 1867. Report of James W. Taylor, special commissioner for the collection of statistics upon gold and silver mining east of the Rocky mountains. February 15, 1867. 39th Congress, 2d Session. House of Representatives. Ex. Doc. No. 92.

92. Report of the Commissioner of Indian Affairs to the Secretary of the Interior, United States. Office of Indian Affairs, Central Superintendency. U.S. Government Printing Office, 1866, pp. 158-160.

93. Report of the Commissioner of Indian Affairs to the Secretary of the Interior, Accompanying Papers. REPORT TO THE PRESIDENT BY THE INDIAN PEACE COMMISSION, JANUARY 7, 1868. United States. Office of Indian Affairs. U.S. Government Printing Office, 1868, p. 38.

94. The Burlington Weekly Sentinel, June 28, 1867; The Chicago Evening Post, June 26, 1867.

95. Athearn, Frederic J. Land of Contrast: A History of Southeast Colorado. Colorado Bureau of Land Management, Cultural Resource Series No. 17, 1985, p. 79.

96. Report of the Commissioner of Indian Affairs to the Secretary of the Interior, United States. Office of Indian Affairs. U.S. Government Printing Office, 1870, p. 163.

97. Report of the Commissioner of Indian Affairs to the Secretary of the Interior, United States. Office of Indian Affairs. U.S. Government Printing Office, 1872, p. 89.

98. https://www.ghosttowns.com/states/co/summitspringsbattlefield.html (accessed online February 4, 2023).

99. The Battle of Summit Springs, Clarence Reckmeyer, The Colorado Magazine, The State Historical Society of Colorado, Vol. VI, No. 6, November 1929.

100. Thomas, J. Noel, "Summit Springs Battlefield Site", [Otis, Colorado], SAH Archipedia, eds. Gabrielle Esperdy and Karen Kingsley, Charlottesville: UVaP, 2012. http://sah-archipedia.org/buildings/Colorado-01-WS09 (accessed online February 4, 2023).

101. Hall, Frank, pp. 191-192.

102. Report of the Commissioner of Indian Affairs to the Secretary of the Interior, United States. Office of Indian Affairs. U.S. Government Printing

Office, 1873, p. 258.

103. Hall, Frank, pp. 60-61.

104. Report of the Commissioner of Indian Affairs to the Secretary of the Interior, United States. Office of Indian Affairs. U.S. Government Printing Office, 1877, p. 45.

105. Report of the Commissioner of Indian Affairs to the Secretary of the Interior, United States. Office of Indian Affairs. U.S. Government Printing Office, 1877, p. 6.

106. The American Military on the Frontier: The Proceedings of the 7th Military History Symposium, United States Air Force Academy, 30 September-1 October 1976, Ed. James P. Tate, Office of Air Force History, Headquarters USAF, 1978.

107. Dee Brown, Bury My Heart at Wounded Knee (New York: Henry Holt and Co., 1970), 367.

108. U.S. Congress, House, Extinguishment of Indian Title, 46th Cong., 1st sess., Congressional Record, vol. 9, pt. l, 21 April 1870, 615.

109. Carl, Ubbelohde, Maxine Benson, and Duane A. Smith, A Colorado History (Boulder, Colorado: Pruett Publishing, 1988), 190.

110. https://upload.wikimedia.org/wikipedia/commons/8/86/The_new_ empire_of_the_Rockies_-_a_history_of_northeast_Colorado_%28IA_ newempireofrocki00mehl%29.pdf (accessed online December 7, 2022).

111. U.S. Congress, House, The Committee on Indian Affairs, Testimony in Relation to the Ute Indian Outbreak, p. 10.

112. Parkhill, Forbes. The Wildest of the West. "The Meeker Massacre." Denver: Sage, 1957, p. 235.

113. Brown, Dee. Bury My Heart at Wounded Knee.

114. Elmer R. Burkey, "The Thornburgh Battle With the Utes on Milk River," The Colorado Magazine 13 (May 1936): 93.

115. War Department, General of the Army, Annual Report of the Secretary of War (1880).

116. Hall, Frank, p. 500.

117. Athearn, Frederic J. An Isolated Empire: A History of Northwestern Colorado. 3rd ed. Colorado Bureau of Land Management, Cultural Resource Series No. 2, 1982, p. 53.

118. U.S. Congress, House, Extinguishment of Indian Title, 46th Cong., 1st sess., Congressional Record, vol. 9, pt. l, 21 April 1880, 615.

119. Report of the Commissioner of Indian Affairs to the Secretary of the Interior, United States. Office of Indian Affairs. U.S. Government Printing Office, 1879, pp. xxi-xxii.

120. Athearn, Frederic J. An Isolated Empire: A History of Northwestern Colorado. 3rd ed. Colorado Bureau of Land Management, Cultural Resource Series No. 2, 1982, p. 49.

121. Hall, Frank, pp. 494-495.

122. United States Congress. House. The Committee on Indian Affairs. Testimony in Relation to the Ute Indian Outbreak. Hearings 46th Cong., 2d Session. House Misc. Doc. 33, March 1880.

123. Testimony in Relation to Ute Outbreak, 46th Congress, 2nd Session, House Miscellaneous Documents no. 38, 1880, p. 101.

124. Ibid., p. 2.

125. LeRoy R. Hafen, "Otto Mears, 'Pathfinder of the San Juan'," The Colorado Magazine, 9 (March 1932):73.

126. The Ute Campaign of 1879: A Study in the Use of the Military Instrument, Russel Dale Santala, U.S. Army Command and General Staff College, 1994, University of Georgia Libraries, p. 70. Citing Thomas C. Leonard, Above the Battle: War-Making in America from Appomattox to Versailles (New York: Oxford University Press, 1978), p. 46.

127. Denver Daily Times, Sep. 12, 1881.

128. Athearn, Frederic J. An Isolated Empire: A History of Northwestern Colorado. 3rd ed. Colorado Bureau of Land Management, Cultural Resource Series No. 2, 1982, p. 4.

129. House Journal of the Legislative Assembly of the Territory of Colorado, Colorado. Legislative Assembly. House of Representatives, 1881, pp. 321, 388, 409, 455, 756.

130. Report of the Commissioner of Indian Affairs to the Secretary of the Interior, United States. Office of Indian Affairs. U.S. Government Printing Office, 1890, p. XLIV. Letter from the Secretary of the Interior, transmitting a communication from Attorney-General and report of Commissioner of General Land Office, also report of Commissioner of Indian Affairs, in response to Senate resolution of January 10, 1882, calling for information touching the opening for settlement under the pre-emption laws of the United States of part of the Ute Reservation in Colorado. 130 S. Exec. Doc. No. 108, 47th Cong., 1st Sess. (1882).

131. Letter from the Secretary of the Interior, transmitting, in response to Senate resolutions of January 27, 1881, copy of report of Ute Commission, and copies of all correspondence between this department and the Ute Commission, and also the Governor of Colorado, concerning the same since June 15, 1880. S. Exec. Doc. No. 31, 46th Cong., 3rd Sess. (1881).

132. Edmund B. Rogers, "Notes on the Establishment of Mesa Verde National Park, The Colorado Magazine. XXIX, 1 (January 1952).

133. https://www.nps.gov/articles/lee-story-creating.htm (accessed online October 1, 2022).

134. Mesa Verde National Park, House Rep. No. 4944, 59th Cong., 1st Sess. (1906), pp. 1-2.

135. Congressional Record. 59th Congress, 1st Session, 1906, XL, Part 9, p. 8818.

136. Secretary of the Interior to Commissioner of the General Land Office, May 25, 1911, NA-RG 79. Assistant Secretary to Acting Superintendent Wright, Mesa Verde, July 25, 1911, NA-RG 79. 7. Superintendent, Annual Report, 1910; Acting Superintendent Wright to the Secretary, June 29, 1911, NA-RG 79.

137. Philip F. Anschutz with William J. Convery and Thomas J. Noel, *Out Where the West Begins: Profiles, Visions and Strategies of Early Western Business Leaders* (Denver: Cloud Camp Press, 2015), p. 236.

138. Flowers, Kaylyn Mercuri. "William N. Byers." Colorado Encyclopedia. https://coloradoencyclopedia.org/article/william-n-byers (accessed online December 15, 2022).

139. MINING IN COLORADO A HISTORY OF DISCOVERY, DEVELOPMENT AND PRODUCTION BY CHARLES W. HENDERSON, DEPARTMENT OF THE INTERIOR, Hubert Work, Secretary U.S. GEOLOGICAL SURVEY, George Otis Smith, Director, Professional Paper 138, Washington Government Printing Office, 1926, p. 249.

140. Koschmann, A. H., and M. H. Bergendahl. "Principal Gold-Producing Districts." United States Geological Survey, Professional Paper 610, U.S. Government Printing Office, 1968.

141. https://coloradogeologicalsurvey.org/minerals/ (accessed online December 28, 2021); Western Mining History. https://westernmininghistory. com/2099/the-top-ten-gold-producing-states/ (accessed online January 31, 2023); Annual Report of the Department of the Interior, Volume 3, U.S. Government Printing Office, 1890, p. 645.

142. Mining and Engineering World, Volume 22, 1905, pp. 604-605; Aspen Evening Chronicle (October 5, 1892).

143. https://buffalobill.org/about-us/denver-city-council-land-acknowledgement/ (accessed online February 24, 2023).

144. Athearn, Frederic J. An Isolated Empire: A History of Northwestern Colorado. 3rd ed. Colorado Bureau of Land Management, Cultural Resource Series No. 2, 1982, p. 100.

145. Athearn, Robert G. The Coloradans, (Albuquerque: University of New Mexico Press, 1976), pp. 107-109; Propst, Forgotten, p. 38, and W.L. Hays interview, CWA, CSHS, vol. 341; Mehls, Steven F. The new empire of the Rockies: A history of northeast Colorado. No. 16. Bureau of Land Management, 1984. https://upload.wikimedia.org/wikipedia/commons/8/86/The_new_empire_of_the_Rockies_-_a_history_of_northeast_

Colorado_%28IA_newempireofrocki00mehl%29.pdf (accessed online December 7, 2022).

146. Hall, Frank.

147. https://visitusaparks.com/indigenous-heritage-in-the-american-southwest/ (accessed online February 23, 2023).

148. https://swcahec.org/?mailpoet_router&endpoint=view_in_browser&action=view&data=WzIxMCwiNzcxNDM0NmUxNDEyIiwwLCIiL-DI1MCwxXQ (accessed online February 23, 2023).

149. https://conservationlegacy.org/land (accessed online February 23, 2023).

150. https://arvadacenter.org/land-acknowledgement (accessed online February 23, 2023).

151. https://www.adams.edu/about/land-acknowledgement-statement/ (accessed online February 23, 2023).

152. https://www.arapahoe.edu/about-acc/locations/accs-land-acknowledgement (accessed online February 23, 2023).

153. Newberry, John S. Report of the exploring expedition from Santa Fe, New Mexico, to the junction of the Grand and Green Rivers of the great Colorado of the West, in 1859: under the command of Capt. J.N. Macomb, Corps of topographical engineers. Washington, DC: Government Printing Office, 1876, pp. 74-75.

154. Report of the exploring expedition from Santa Fé, New Mexico, to the junction of the Grand and Green Rivers of the great Colorado of the West, in 1859 under the command of Capt. J.N. Macomb. With geological report by J.S. Newberry. United States Army, Macomb, J.N. (John N.), 1810 or 11-1889, pp. 74-75. https://quod.lib.umich.edu/cgi/t/text/text-idx?c=moa&cc=-moa&sid=95e3f6e828e116b80d4cccd93c806bc1&view=text&rgn=main&id-no=AET7181.0001.001 (accessed online February 23, 2023); hhttps://quod.lib.umich.edu/cgi/t/text/text-idx?c=moa&cc=moa&sid=95e3f6e828e116b-80d4cccd93c806bc1&view=text&rgn=main&idno=AET7181.0001.001 (accessed online February 4, 2023).

155. https://westernmininghistory.com/2195/where-to-find-gold-the-top-ten-us-counties/ (accessed online August 16, 2022).

156. Hall, pp. 75-76.

157. https://www.colorado.edu/ics/land-acknowledgement-statement (accessed online February 23, 2023).

158. https://broomfieldopenspacefoundation.org/contact-us/ (accessed online February 23, 2023).

159. https://conservationlegacy.org/land (accessed online February 23, 2023).

160. Hall, pp. 78-79.

161. Hall, p. 85.

162. Butterfield Overland Despatch. https://www.legendsofamerica.com/butterfield-overland-despatch/ (accessed online February 23, 2023). https://

www.kshs.org/resource/national_register/nominationsNRDB/Dickinson_
SmokyHillTrail&BODSegmentNR.pdf (accessed online February 23, 2023).
163. Hall, p. 87.
164. Hall, pp. 88-89.
165. https://www.frontrange.edu/about-frcc/equity-inclusion-diversity/
land-acknowledgement (accessed online February 23, 2023). (Boulder, Larimer, Westminster).
166. Hall, p. 92.
167. Id.
168. Id.
169. Hall, p. 96.
170. Hall, p. 97.
171. Hall, p. 107.
172. Hall, p. 110.
173. Hall, p. 109.
174. Hall, p. 111.
175. Hall, p. 113.
176. Hall, pp. 113-114.
177. Hall, p. 117.
178. Hall, p. 120.
179. Hall, p. 122.
180. Hall, p. 123.
181. https://www.culturaloffice.org/land-acknowledgement-for-the-arts com-
munity/ (accessed online February 23, 2023).
182. Hall, p. 127.
183. Hall, p. 129.
184. Hall, p. 145.
185. https://www.winterparkresort.com/the-mountain/land-acknowledgement
(accessed online February 23, 2023).
186. Hall, p. 136.
187. Hall, p. 147.
188. Hall, p. 145.
189. Hall, p. 153.
190. Hall, p. 149.
191. https://cbfilmfest.org/landacknowledgment (accessed online February
23, 2023).
192. Hall, p. 152.
193. Hall, p. 158.
194. Hall, p. 158.
195. Hall, p. 161.
196. https://www.jeffco.us/DocumentCenter/View/31920/22-047-Indige-
nous-Peoples-Land-Acknowledgement (accessed online February 24, 2023).

197. https://www.durango.org/responsible/land-acknowledgement/ (accessed online February 23, 2023).

198. https://www.fortlewis.edu/about-flc/leadership/presidents-office/land-acknowledgment (accessed online February 23, 2023).

199. Hall, p. 167.

200. Hall, p. 168.

201. Hall, pp. 167-168.

202. Hall, p. 169.

203. Hall, p. 170.

204. Hall, pp. 173-174.

205. Hall, p. 174.

206. Hall, p. 177.

207. Hall, p. 177.

208. Hall, pp. 179-180.

209. https://oeo.colostate.edu/land-acknowledgment/ (accessed online February 23, 2023).

210. Hall, pp. 180-181.

211. Hall, p. 184.

212. Perceptions of The Animas River. Jasmine Williams, Michael Clements, Andrew Teck, Ellis McNichol, Ninalani Grimes, Josh Andrews. https://storage.googleapis.com/wzukusers/user-17111544/documents/74ab31d-6f4b24b988367d2883bc7280f/Perceptions%20of%20the%20Animas%20River%20FLC%20Report.pdf (accessed online February 23, 2023).

213. Hall, p. 193.

214. Hall, p. 215.

215. Hall, p. 212.

216. The Permanent Settlement of Southwest Colorado, Frontier in Transition: A History of Southwestern Colorado, BLM Cultural Resources Series (Colorado: No. 10), p. 83. https://www.nps.gov/parkhistory/online_books/blm/co/10/chap7.htm#:~:text=%5B8%5D%20Crawford's%20interest%20in%20the,railroad%20for%20the%20proposed%20townsite (accessed online December 18, 2022).

217. Hall, p. 219.

218. O'Rourke, Paul M., Frontier in Transition: A History of Southwestern Colorado, BLM Cultural Resources Series (Colorado: No. 10), 1980.

219. Hall, p. 225.

220. Hall, p. 225.

221. Hall, p. 226.

222. Hall, pp. 232-233.

223. Hall, pp. 233-234.

224. Hall, p. 234.

225. Hall, p. 234.

226. Report of the American Society Civil Engineers, 1886.

227. Hall, p. 235.

228. Hall, p. 237.

229. http://hometownchronicles.com/co/ourayco/bio-mears,otto%5b2%5d. html (accessed online February 1, 2023). Otto Mears, "Pathfinder of the San Juan," Leroy R. Hazen. The Colorado Magazine, The State Historical Society of Colorado, VOL. IX, Denver, Colorado, March, 1932, No. 2, p. 73.

230. Hall, p. 237.

231. Hall, p. 242.

232. Hall, p. 258.

233. Hall, p. 257.

234. Hall, p. 272.

235. https://aspenhistory.org/about-us/land-statement/ (accessed online February 23, 2023).

236. Hall, p. 285.

237. http://docs.steamboatsprings.net:10100/OnBaseAgendaOnline/ Documents/ViewDocument/PROCLAMATION.DOCX.pdf?meetingId=1189&documentType=Agenda&itemId=15423&publishId=15264&isSection=false (accessed online February 23, 2023).

238. Hall, p. 321.

239. Hall, p. 326.

240. Hall, p. 102.

241. https://www.unco.edu/hss/sociology/#:~:text=The%20University%20 of%20Northern%20Colorado,great%20respect%20for%20this%20land (accessed online February 23, 2023).

242. Hall, p. 354.

243. AW Bowen & Co. Progressive Men of Western Colorado... AW Bowen & Company, 1905, pp. 251-252.

Colorado Indian Treaties [See Chart in the last Chapter]

1849: Abiquiu - Pacify the Territory of NM and San Luis Valley acquired as result of Mexican-American War (1846-48). Capote and Muache Ute bands agree to U.S. jurisdiction over them, safe passage for settlers, presence of military forts and trading posts. 9 Stat. 984, December 30, 1849, Ratified September 9, 1850, Proclaimed September 9, 1850.

1851: Treaty of Fort Laramie protects Cheyenne and Arapaho sovereignty along westward wagon roads in northern Colorado in exchange for allowing U.S. citizens and government to travel and build forts on Indigenous land.

1861: Colorado Territory established; **Treaty of Fort Wise** ends government-recognized sovereignty of Cheyenne and Arapaho, creating a reservation for them in eastern Colorado.

1863: Conejos Treaty sees the Tabeguache band of Utes relinquish claims to the Front Range of the Rockies and Middle Park. Government designates Ouray as de facto leader of all Utes. October 7, 1863 | 13 Stat., 673 | Ratified March 25, 1864 | Proclaimed December 14, 1864

1865: Little Arkansas Treaty offers reparations for the Sand Creek Massacre of 1864 and reserves the right of the Cheyenne and Arapaho to hunt in the Arkansas River valley in western Kansas and southeast Colorado.

1867: Medicine Lodge Treaties remove the Cheyenne, Arapaho, and other Plains Nations to so-called Indian Territory (present-day Oklahoma).

1868: Ute Treaty of 1868 creates a consolidated reservation for all of Colorado's Ute bands on the Western Slope.

1871: Indian Appropriations Act ends treaty making with Indigenous nations.

10: NEVADA

Great Basin

At the time of European contact, the indigenous people inhabiting the Great Basin each had their own unique form of governance, traditions and identities spanning millennia. The Great Basin is a 220,000 square-mile natural bowl nesting between the Sierra Nevada to the west and the Wasatch Mountains to the east.

Once the bottom of an ancient sea, the waves, at some distant period, rolled hundreds of feet above the present plains. Far up on the sides of the mountains can be seen the chalky white outlines of the previous water levels. The white sands and colored clays are the relics of by-gone ages, when the whale and other sea creatures roamed over what are now vast sage covered plains, extending as far as the eye can see.[1]

Hundreds of mountain ranges rise in north-south parallel rows, separated by broad sagebrush valleys. One writer colorfully described it:

> "Salt desert and sagebrush steppe. Sun-tempered mountains
> the color of steel. Heat and eye-scalding dust, turbid streams
> and briny waterholes ... miles and miles with no water at all."[2]

Mark Twain in Roughing It, an account of his 1861 stagecoach trip west, gave us his memorable description:

> Imagine a vast, waveless ocean stricken dead and turned to
> ashes; imagine this solemn waste tufted with ash-dusted sage-
> bushes; imagine the lifeless silence and solitude that belong
> to such a place .... The sun beats down with dead, blistering,
> relentless malignity; ... there is not the faintest breath of

air stirring; there is not a merciful shred of cloud in all the brilliant firmament; there is not a living creature visible in any direction ....[3]

The Forty-Mile Desert, the terror of the early emigrants, lay ahead where hundreds, or rather thousands, of wagons, harnesses and yokes were left behind. A survey made in 1850 produced these appalling statistics: 1,061 dead mules, almost 5,000 dead horses, 3,750 dead cattle, and 953 graves.

Yet, all of this was home to the Indians living in the Great Basin:

> Washoes, who lived primarily around Lake Tahoe;
> Goshutes;
> Western Shoshones; and
> Northern and Southern Paiutes.

They lived in independent groups of from three to five families, so as not to deplete the natural resources in their homeland, maintaining a sustainable balance in their ecosystem.

They traversed in unison with the seasonal plant growth and animal availability. No portion of the area's fauna–from ants to deer–was overlooked as a food source. Sage, willows, flowers, and rabbit brush were medicinal plants, and were also processed into dyes. Sagebrush, willows and junipers were used for housing and clothing. Red willow was gathered, made into fibrous material, and transformed into baskets. Pine nuts were harvested in the higher elevations. Seeds, roots and greens were gathered. Rabbits, squirrels, marmots, deer and antelope were harvested to provide the meat the people needed.

> The fact that Native Americans have occupied every cranny of the continent for at least 10,000 years, and have maintained the rich diversity and high productivity of American landscapes throughout the millennia, must be understood as a consequence of the sophisticated systems of Traditional Environmental Knowledge developed and passed down the generations by all Native American tribes. ... Thus we recognize in the knowledge systems of Native American people an alert intelligence and an aesthetic sense for connection that we admire in the scientists and poets of all cultures.[4]

Goshutes - People of Desert (Newe)

The Goshutes exemplify the historic Great Basin desert way of life because of the climatic condition of their territory. They lived in small camps in a crescent area around the southern half of the Great Salt Lake Desert. The aridity is the result of the rain shadow caused by the Sierra Nevada, the distance of the Basin from the ocean, and latitudes inimical to recurrent storm patterns.

Yet, the Goshutes knew and used at least eighty-one species, digging for roots, tubers, bulbs, also, gathering wild vegetable foods, nuts and insects and hunting for small land animals. Their knowledge of their environment permitted them to live in what appeared to be an inauspicious eco-system.

Shoshonu - People of High Growing Grasses (Newe)

At the time of the incursion of the Great Basin and the Snake River areas in the 1840s by white settlers, there were numerous distinct Shoshoni bands:

(1) The Eastern Shoshoni, numbering about 2,000, occupied the region from the Wind River Mountains to Fort Bridger;

(2) the Goshute Shoshoni, about 900 in number, lived west and southwest of the Great Salt Lake;

(3) the Western Shoshonu, with as many as eleven major bands, about 8,000 strong, inhabited what is today a wide swath of central Nevada and south central California, established at the center of a vast trade network, supported by their use of horses and well-trod trails;

(4) the Northwestern Shoshoni, about 1,500 people, resided in the valleys of northern Utah, especially Weber Valley and Cache Valley, and along the eastern and northern shores of the Great Salt Lake; and

(5) the Northern Shoshoni were composed of three groups: (a) the Fort Hall Shoshoni, of about 1,000 people, lived with a band of about 800 Northern Paiutes; (b) the Lemhi, numbering some 1,800 people, lived in southwestern Montana westward to the Salmon River area; and (c) in western Idaho, along the Boise and Bruneau rivers, a third alliance of about 600 Shoshoni practiced a lifestyle centered around fishing for salmon, their basic food.

By the 1840s, certain Shoshonus had acquired the horse, permitting mobility and the hunting of game.

Paiutes

Prior to their contact with Euro-Americans, the Paiutes' aboriginal land covered an area of more than 30 million acres, from southern California to southern Nevada, south-central Utah, and northern Arizona. They moved across their lands in accord with the seasonal ripening of natural plants and animal migration patterns. Living in independent groups of three to five families, they stewarded the fragile environment, without overtaxing its resources.

Northern Paiutes

The Northern Paiutes lived in the very diverse ecological zones afforded by Pyramid Lake and the Walker River, utilizing hunting, plant-gathering, and fishing for subsistence strategies.

Southern Paiutes

The entire Western division of the Southern Paiute Tribe was known as the Paranayi (Southern Paiute). That term is translated into English as "people with their feet in the water." The water referred to is that flowing down the Moapa River and the Virgin River into the Colorado River, including the Meadow Valley Wash upstream.[5]

Local lineages did not live autonomously. A specialized corps of runners carried messages from theocratic leaders to local social units interconnecting Southern Paiutes as a society.[6]

Paiutes cultivated crops by using flood plain, oasis, and riverine irrigation and dryland techniques. They provided subsistence and trading bases. Their foot trails still manifest the routes used in their exchange economy.

> An early Spanish explorer, Escalante, in 1776 described the Southern Paiutes as cultivating the irrigable lands within their territory. The Mormon explorer, John D. Lee, in 1852 observed Paiutes in the Santa Clara River Valley cultivating 100 acres of corn and squashes. A few days later, in the narrow but fertile stream bottoms of the Virgin River at the edge or possibly in Kaibab Paiute territory, Lee again observed that: "Their corn was waist high; squashes, bean, potatoes, etc. look well. They had in cultivation four or five acres; their wheat had got ripe and was out". When Euroamericans first traveled down the Colorado River, past Southern Paiute territory, they

found small fields of maize planted along the river. Powell stated that all of the Southern Paiutes cultivated the soil prior to settlement of the area by Euroamericans.[7]

Euroamerican colonization concentrated in the Virgin River watershed dispossessed the Southern Paiute of their core territory and terminated forever their pre-contact food economy. Just as agricultural settlements spread rapidly among the core water resource areas of the Southern Paiute lands, mining districts would follow just as fast, including.

> Hiko (1865–1871);
> Crystal Spring (1865);
> Logan City (1865);
> Grand Gulch (1868: copper);
> Ivanpah, part of the Clarke District spanning lands in California and Nevada (1860s);
> New York District, including lands in California and Nevada;
> Timber Mountain District (1869);
> Yellow Pine District (1870s);
> Southeastern District (1870); and
> Ferguson Mining District (1892—with silica dust problem).

Major epidemic and endemic mortality from 1851 reduced Southern Paiute population by well over 75 percent within a decade.

The Spanish, the Navajos and Utes raided Indian villages and captured women and children to trade as slaves in the Rio Grande Valley and in California. For many, their desert environment didn't have enough feed for horses, so they were not able to incorporate the horse into their lifestyles. This restricted their mobility and ability to counter the brazen assaults by those on horseback.

Washoes

Prior to the arrival of white settlers, the Washoes lived in the Lake Tahoe area and at least one and a half million acres spanning California and Nevada. As presented by the Washoe Tribe in their account of their history:

> "The center of the Wá·šiw world is dá?aw (Lake Tahoe) both geographically and spiritually." Like most native peoples our lifestyles revolved around the environment; the people were part of the environment, and everything was provided by the environment.

Cave Rock is a pivotal part of the Washoe religion and spiritual existence. Seen as an impediment to transportation, white settlers created overlapping travel routes that went over, around and through. A toll road for freight teams was made immediately adjacent to the towering, sacrosanct rock.

Wašíšiw—The People from Here

The family unit was the core of the Tribe. Groups of families comprised local groups and local groups made up a band. The Wá·šiw were recognized by what part of the territory they came from—[north, west, south or east.]

Changes to Washoe Life

> During the California gold rush followed by the subsequent silver rush in Nevada a few years later, thousands of miners and immigrants flooded Wá·šiw lands in a relatively short time period and they stayed here, disrupting the balance; changing the Wá·šiw world forever in only a few short years. The demand on the natural resources by the immigrant population depleted much of it. The logging industry denuded the forests and scarred the Pine Nut Mountains to support the mining industry and towns that sprang up everywhere. The fisheries of Lake Tahoe once bountiful with the native cutthroat trout had been reduced to nothing and livestock replaced the native herbivores.[8]

Washoe resistance to incursions on their lands proved futile, and the last armed conflict with the Washoes and non-Indians was the Potato War of 1857, when starving Washoes were killed for gathering potatoes from a European-American farm near Honey Lake in California. The locals received re-enforcements from the California state arsenal, volunteer fighters from Sierra Valley, and a band of Piutes. During the skirmish several Washo were killed and many wounded. In the aftermath, the Washo withdrew from the lower end of Honey Lake Valley and never ventured north of Long Valley.

> By 1851, Indian Agent Jacob Holeman recommended that the government sign a treaty with the Washoe and wrote, "…the Indians having been driven from their lands, and their hunting ground destroyed without compensation, therefore—they are in many instances reduced to a state of suffering bordering on starvation."[9]

By December 1862, the Washoe Tribe had lost all of its lands. After contact with non-Indian cultures (or the "encroachment" as the Washoe and Federal Government describe it), the Washoe endured as a people, with many continuing ties to the Lake, after being forced to upland resource areas.

In his first Annual Report, Agent H.G. Parker, stated scant information was available to him, due to the "confused state of the agency" as Governor Nye had ceased to be ex officio Superintendent more than a year before, and Agent Lockhart had six months previously left his post. *No papers or records of importance had been transmitted to [Agent Parker]. Nonetheless*, he proceeded to state his evaluation of the Washoes and whether they should be granted a reservation.

> This is a small tribe of about five hundred Indians, living in the extreme western part of the State. They are usually a harmless people, with much less physical and mental development than the Pi-Utes, and more *degraded morally. They are indolent, improvident, and much addicted to the vices and evil practices common in savage life. They manifest an almost uncontrollable appetite for intoxicating drinks. They are sensual and filthy, and are annually diminishing in numbers from the diseases contracted through their indulgences*. A few have learned the English language, and will do light work for a reasonable compensation. They spend the winter months about the villages and habitations of white men, from whom they obtain tolerable supplies of food and clothing. The spring, summer, and autumn months are spent in fishing about Washoe and Tahoe lakes and the streams which flow through their country. They also gather grass-seed and pine-nuts, hunt rabbits, hares, and ducks. *There is no suitable place for a reservation in the bounds of their territory, and, in view of their rapidly diminishing numbers and the diseases to which they are subjected, none is required*." (Emphasis added).[10]

This *uninformed perspective* by a newly appointed Indian Agent resulted in a denial of the request for a reservation made by Agent Holeman in 1851. Between 1871 and 1877 several more requests for a reservation for the Washoe were made by agents, but again they were ignored. The U.S. made no attempt to secure rights for the Washoe or to stop the destruction of their lands by the white settlers.

Loss of their subsistence base drove most Washoe to dependency on menial jobs for servile wages on white ranches and farms, on lands once owned by them, and in cities. The areas where they settled became known as Indian colonies.

Today, some 1500 enrolled members of the Washoe Tribe of Nevada and California live in "Colonies," tribal lands scattered in the Reno, Carson Valley, and Gardnerville areas of Nevada and in Woodfords, California. An active tribal government continues to lobby for a land base in the Lake Tahoe basin and works with federal and state agencies and private land owners to protect locations important to the Washoe.

Spanish Contact

The first Europeans to come to the area were the Spanish in 1776. The Shoshones' land formed part of the alleged Viceroyalty of New Spain and was called Nevada, due to the snow which covered the mountains in winter. It became part of Mexico when it gained independence in 1821 from Spain.

Contact with 'White Men'

For me, the term 'white' didn't sit well; it was foreign to me. As a child, I was taught by my family the reference, 'Anglo.' I never questioned it; it was simply a part of my *vernacular*. I felt uncomfortable with the word 'white'; it was uncouth, chilling.

In writing this Book, I became fully aware of the federal government's use of the term—'white,' denominating a powerful, influential and privileged racial group. It was used in Treaties and in common communication as evidenced below. I will use it in my writing and speaking, as a legal and political matter. It doesn't or probably won't ever flow easily off the tip of my tongue. Regardless, 'white men' wield significant power in Indian relations.

Various Treaties with Shoshones in 1863

It was used in the various Treaties with the Shoshones in 1863.

> Eastern Shoshone Treaty, (18 Stat. 685), July 2, 1863:
> Article II. The several routes of travel through the Shoshonee country, now or hereafter used by *white men*, shall be and remain forever free and safe for the use of the government of the United States, and of all emigrants and travellers under its

authority and protection, without molestation or injury from any of the people of said nation. (Emphasis added).

Western Shoshone Treaty, Ruby Valley (Vigorously Contested by Shoshones Up to Present Day), (18 Stat. 689), October 1, 1863: Article II. The several routes of travel through the Shoshonee country, now or hereafter used by *white men*, shall be forever free, and unobstructed by the said bands, for the use of the government of the United States, and of all emigrants and travelers under its authority and protection, without molestation or injury from them. (Emphasis added).

Shoshonee-Goship Treaty, (13 Stat. 681), October 12, 1863: Article II. It is further stipulated by said bands that the several routes of travel through their country now or hereafter used by *white men* shall be forever free and unobstructed by them, for the use of the Government of the United States, and of all emigrants and travellers within it (sic) under its authority and protection, without molestation or injury from them. (Emphasis added).

Mixed Bands Treaty, (5 Kapp. 693), October 14, 1863: Article III. The said bands, in addition, agree that the roads now used by *white men* between Soda Springs and the Beaver Head mines, and between Salt Lake and the Boise River mines, as also such other roads as it may be necessary or convenient for the *white men* to make and use between said places, or between other points within their country, shall at all times be free and safe for travel; and no depredations shall be committed upon *white men* in any part of their country. (Emphasis added).

Here are statements in the Annual Reports of the Commissioner of Indian Affairs to the Secretary of the Interior using the term 'white' to identify a specific racial group. The list could go on and on.

Indians Compensated for Lands Stolen by 'White Men' by Working for 'Whites' as Menial Laborers

Starting as early as 1866, there were *repeated warnings* to the Secretary of the Interior regarding the elimination of the Nevada Indians' subsistence base. Platitudes of the availability of menial employment by whites were proffered.

~ 313 ~

[Indians] begin to regard these reservations as their homes and only sure hope for a support. Their country is rapidly passing from them. Every garden spot and tillable acre of land is now being sought out and occupied by *white men*. Their groves of pinon are disappearing before the strokes of his axe, their grass-seed is consumed by his herds, the antelope and mountain sheep are killed or driven away, and, although there is *some compensation in the employment given in the harvest field and elsewhere*, still the Indian must look for a reliable and permanent supply of his wants to the products of these *lands sacredly set apart for him*. (Emphasis added).[11]

The Indians, in whose territory mines have been found of sufficient richness to warrant the erection of quartz mills and the settlement of the country, have been in a great measure *compensated for the destruction of their resources in the pay received from the whites for labor performed*, and, in accommodating themselves to the new order of things, have shown great aptitude. (Emphasis added).[12]

The most encouraging characteristic of these people is their *willingness to work whenever they see an opportunity to earn fair wages*. They are in demand as sheepshearers, hay hands, ranch hands, vaqueros, and do all the freighting and irregular labor on the reservation. Calvin Asbury, Superintendent and Special Disbursing Agent. (Emphasis added).[13]

Federal Government Aware that 'White Men' Disregard Indian Rights

White men are too apt to act upon the hypothesis that an Indian has no rights ... (Emphasis added).[14]

Carson City: *I will here remark, that until the metes and bounds of the reserve are authoritatively established, it will not be free from the encroachments of a bad class of white men, who seldom believe in according any rights to Indians.* (Emphasis added).[15]

Department of the Interior Recommends Abandoning Nevada's Indian Reservations

Due largely to the efforts of Indian Agent James Dodge, two sizable reservations—Pyramid Lake, including over 400,000 acres and Walker River, consisting of approximately 320,000 acres were formally withdrawn in 1859 and designated as reserves in 1874. Notwithstanding this withdrawal, the Department of the Interior and white settlers continued repeatedly to seek the elimination or reduction of these reservations, enlisting the aid of the powerful "Silver Senator" Stewart.

> There are from twelve to fifteen thousand Indians, and three reservations in the State for Indian occupancy, known as Walker River and Pyramid Lake, and one on Truckee River, of timber for the use of the Indians at Pyramid Lake. The Pah-Utes, numbering about eight thousand, for whose use and benefit they were set apart, do not all reside upon them, many being scattered through the towns and settlements. *The superintendent suggests that the reservations be abandoned, as the Indians will be more benefited by being settled with the whites, for whom they could work*, though they will not farm for themselves. They will labor for farmers, and *none need suffer for want of employment, as it can be given by the Pacific railroad contractors and by miners*. (Emphasis added).[16]

Under Watch of Department of the Interior, 'White Men' Seek to Appropriate Indian Fisheries

> There are two reservations in this superintendency [Pyramid Lake Paiutes' and Walker River] ...The fisheries at the mouths of the rivers are excellent and of immense value as sources of subsistence; quite a large income is derived from the sale of fish caught at these fisheries, so much so that the *cupidity of white men* has been *excited*, and *they have endeavored to appropriate the fisheries and realize the profits, which of right belong to the Indians*. (Emphasis added).[17]

Death Warrants for Indians by "Bad White Men"

> *A suspicion against an Indian is tantamount to his death-warrant, to be executed by bad white men, without fear of prosecution or molestation at the hands of civil authorities*. (Emphasis added).[18]

Indians Swindled by 'Evil-Disposed White Men' Due to Apathy of Civil Authorities

The anomalous position which the Indians sustain toward the Government, being neither aliens nor citizens, the *apathy and inertness of civil authorities in protecting them in their lives and property*, and the ease with which they can be swindled and outraged by *evil-disposed white men*, demand that something commensurate with the designs of the Government be done for the protection and improvement of its dependent and destitute wards. *The Indians in Nevada desire good reservations set apart for their exclusive use; they desire assistance from the Government in developing their agricultural resources; and, above all, protection in their rights.* (Emphasis added).[19]

Indians Misled to Get Them to Cede Land

In council with the Indians *great care was taken not to implant in their minds the idea that the Government was willing to pay them for yielding lands which white men needed*, and that as a recompense for such lands they would be furnished with clothing and food, and thus *enabled to live in idleness*. (Emphasis added).[20]

'White Men' Fomenting War at Duck Valley Indian Reservation

Rumors of war by the Shoshones at Duck Valley Indian Reservation were being circulated. The Department of the Interior sent Levi Gheen to Duck Valley to investigate and report back. He found that the reports were untrue and without foundation.

I believe that some of the white men were more anxious for an Indian war than the Indians themselves. (Emphasis added).[21]

Warfare was sought due to the desire of the white settlers to get rid of the Indians, and not the actual threat imposed by them. As a result, Indian lives would be needlessly lost—while federal dollars would be expended on a private war. The frightening motives of the white settlers included generating federal money for their enclaves.

Law Is All for 'White Man' and None for Indian

The Pah-Utes and Pi-Utes, on the Walker River and Pyramid Lake Paiutes Reservations, told their Agent, Joseph M. McMaster, of their fear of the one-sidedness of the law:

> One thing that they do not just understand is why the trespassers are not removed from the reservation. The agent has informed them that the whole matter has been referred to Washington, and that soldiers have been promised to remove them. But the soldiers fail to come, and they think the law is all for the *white man* and none for the Indian. (Emphasis added).[22]

Stockmen, Mining Men and Railroad Company Conspire to Expropriate Indian Lands

White stockmen and miners, along with the Carson and Colorado Railroad Company, conspired to expropriate Indian lands, using the political clout of Nevada Senator Stewart. He introduced Senate Bill No. 99 as discussed below:

> The Bill proposed to reduce the Pyramid Lake Paiutes' Reservation, selling the southern part of the Reservation, which included the town of Wadsworth and surrounding lands. It also proposed to move the Paiutes on the Walker River Reservation to the Pyramid Lake Paiutes' Reservation and sell their land, consisting of 318,815 acres of land, to homestead settlers at $1.25 per acre.
>
> *It was approved by the Senate Committee on Indian Affairs*, chaired by the Hon. James K. Jones, a Confederate Army veteran, plantation owner, lawyer, U.S. Congressional Representative, U.S. Senator and chairman of the Democratic National Committee from Arkansas. (Emphasis added).[23]

The Gold Rush brought Senator Stewart west where he *amassed a fortune as a mining litigator*. He represented the people of Nevada for more than 20 years in the Senate, serving as Chairman of the Committee on Pacific Railroads and the Committee on Indian Affairs. (Emphasis added).[24]

Indian Agent I.J. Wooten expressed his opinion on the clout of the wealthy supporting this legislation:

The Indians of both of the reserves are unanimous in their opposition to the propositions contained in the bill, and it would require the strongarm of the Government to force them to change their opinions. Moreover, even if the Indians were willing to give their voluntary approval to the provisions of the bill, I would deem it my bounden duty to enter a protest against its enactment, for the reason that it would be an *unfair, unjust, unwarranted, and uncalled-for piece of legislation, enacted solely in the interest of a few wealthy stockmen and mining men and the Carson and Colorado Railroad Company as against the best interests of the Pah-Ute Indians.* ... (Emphasis added).[25]

In an address on July 2, 1873, by General Garfield on The Future of the Republic Its Dangers and Hopes, he deplored the political control railroad companies exerted over state government:

It is painfully evident from the experience of the last few years that the efforts of the States to regulate their railroads have amounted to but little more than feeble annoyance. ... In these contests the corporations [railroad companies] have become conscious of their strength and have entered upon the work of controlling the States. ... the corporations have grasped the sources and fountains of power.

"Waste of Money" to Irrigate Pyramid Lake Paiutes' and Walker River Indian Reservations

Most likely, the Indians on the Pyramid Lake Paiutes' and Walker River Indian Reservations were never told irrigation needed on both reservations would be too costly and a waste on the Walker River Indian Reservation due to the exploitative use of water by white farmers.

Agriculture on these reservations can only be prosecuted by irrigation, which involves considerable expense to obtain water for that purpose. *It would be a waste of money for the Government to undertake the irrigation work for both reservations.* There is an abundance of land on either reservation for the Indians, if furnished with water. Pyramid Lake Reservation is the better for all purposes. The supply of water from the Truckee River is sufficient and reliable. *There is more difficulty on the Walker River on account of the*

~ 318 ~

use of the water above by farmers, which would deprive the
Indians of water at every dry season, even if irrigation works
were constructed. (Emphasis added).[26]

Water for Indian Reservations Appropriated by 'White Water Users'

The Walker River Reservation's water supply was inadequate due to whites appropriating water upstream before it could reach the Reservation. The Agent thought the only way Indians could get relief was through the DOJ suing the white users.

> Due to a shortage of supply, the *white water users* along the stream above the Indian reservation are utilizing practically all of the available water, so that very little other than seeped and return flow reaches Indian lands. The situation became so serious last spring that aid from the Department of Justice was sought. It is apparent from existing conditions that court action will be necessary in this case before the Indians will be granted their full rights, owing to the location of their lands with relation to lands of the *whites* subject to irrigation. (Emphasis added).[27]

Not until 1908, did the U.S. Supreme Court hold that when Congress reserves land (i.e., for an Indian reservation), Congress also reserves water sufficient to fulfill the purpose of the reservation for future uses, not just present uses. Since these water rights date to the establishment of the reservation, Indians reserved water rights customarily pre-date other water users' claims. The doctrine conflicts with many state laws, including Nevada's, in establishing priorities and the rights of existing users. The Nevada State law is based on the doctrine of appropriation, rights being acquired by diverting water from a natural course for "beneficial," continued use, with the first in time, first in right rule.

'White Men' Are Judge, Jury and Executioner of Indians

Repeatedly, without a legal system in place to protect Indians, whites took the law in their own hands and served as the judge, jury and executioner of Indians.

> August 1, 1864. During the present season a report reached me that the Indians had driven off from a ranch ... a number of

cattle. [The rancher] [s]ending for the principal or head men of the band in the vicinity, they came. They were told that, unless the cattle were immediately brought back, together with the thieves. ... *white men would punish the Indians* severely, whenever and wherever found. They left, promising that the cattle should be returned and the thieves caught and delivered up. In two days the cattle, all but one which had been killed, were brought back and delivered to their owners, but the Indian who is said to have stolen them made his escape to the Shoshonees. *They have been told that the whole band will hereafter be held accountable for any misdemeanor of any one of their people...* (Emphasis added).[28]

Broken Promises - All Way from Atlantic to Pacific

General Nelson A. Miles expressed the dichotomy in the federal relations between the federal government and Indians, creating a conflict of interest, where the U.S. had to protect its interest versus protecting the rights of Indians as their trustee.

Our relations with the Indians have been governed chiefly by treaties and trade, or war and subjugation. By the first we have invariably overreached the natives, and we find the record of broken promises all the way from the Atlantic to the Pacific, while many of the fortunes of New York, Chicago, St. Louis, and San Francisco can be traced directly to Indian tradership. By war the natives have been steadily driven toward the setting sun—a subjugated, a doomed race.[29]

Fur Trappers Decimate Beaver Population

In 1826, Jedidiah Smith, David Jackson and William Sublette of the Rocky Mountain Fur Company engaged in fur trapping and trading in the Rocky Mountains, traversed what would become Nevada. Desperate for supplies, Smith crossed over into California, which was then under the control of Spain. General Echandia, Military Commandant of Spain's Presidio in California, permitted him to purchase supplies in California, after reviewing his documents, including "*passports* produced by him from the Superintendent of Indian Affairs for the Government of the United States of America."

In the same year, Peter Skene Ogden of the British Hudson's Bay Company came to Nevada in a prelude to his later exploration of the Humboldt River in 1828. The Hudson Bay Company claimed the region west of the Rocky Mountains to the Pacific for trapping and trading. They had six establishments on the coast, sixteen in the interior and nine substantial manned forts. Their coastal businesses were protected by six armed vessels. Settlements for farming produced wool, tallow and agricultural produce for export in trade, with their trappers producing hides. With the U.S. as a rival, tensions existed for control and supremacy in trade.[30]

By 1829, the commercial demand for beaver hides ended up decimating the beaver population.[31]

> When beavers formed part of the fauna of the riverine oases, their dams and their ponds also constituted part of the oasis environment. Beaver ponds were desirable environments for at least some of the fish species present in the river system. Ponds attracted migratory waterfowl, and probably supported local oasis populations of resident birds such as herons. Thus, beaver ponds increased the animal protein productivity of the riverine oases, and facilitated both hunting and fishing success. In addition, beaver ponds must have contributed to alluvial soil building over periods of time. The streams forming the Virgin River watershed in many instances have steep gradients, especially upstream. Beaver ponds would have slowed the rate of stream flow, and impounded flood waters during storms, minimizing erosion. Whatever soil the streams carried would have built up in the ponds, forming fertile alluvial deposits Paiutes could cultivate once a pond dried up and its beavers moved elsewhere. Euroamerican beaver trappers set in motion an inexorable process of environmental deterioration of the riverine oases, significantly detrimental to the Southern Paiute food economy.[32]

In July 1832, an expedition led by Milton Sublette for trapping encountered severe difficulties.

> [They] were forced to eat the flesh of the beavers they caught … The season was one of famine for these little animals, which were forced in their hunger to subsist upon wild parsnips, which poisoned their flesh and made them unwholesome food for the trappers, many of whom were made ill from eating them. Because of this it became necessary to at once abandon the river, and strike across the country towards the

north, where after being four days with almost no food, and several weeks in a state of famine ... They were forced, as they passed over the country, to subsist upon ants, crickets, parched moccasins, and puddings made from blood, taking a pint at a time from their almost famished animals. (Emphasis added).[33]

1831: Walker-Bonneville Expedition

In 1831, Captain Benjamin Louis De Bonneville led an expedition to collect geographical data and conduct military surveillance of the Indians from the Great Salt Lake to the Pacific Ocean, authorized by Alexander Macomb, Major-General, Commanding the Army. Captain Bonneville chose an experienced scout, Joseph Reddford Walker.

Bonneville's August 3, 1831, instructions were to ascertain "the nature and character of the several tribes of Indians inhabiting those regions, the trade which might be profitably carried on with them, the quality of the soil, the productions, the minerals, the natural history, the climate, the geography and topography, as well as geology." In particular, the Army wanted more information on Indian warfare capability, asking Captain Bonneville to observe:

> ... *the* **number of warriors that may be in each tribe or nation** *that you may meet with their alliances with other tribes, and their relative position as to a state of peace or war, and whether their friendly or warlike dispositions towards each other are recent or of a long standing.*

He was further requested to note the Indians:

> ... *manner of making war; of the mode of subsisting themselves during a state of war, and a state of peace; their arms, and the effect of them; whether they act on foot or on horseback; detailing the* **discipline and maneuvers of the war parties;** *the power of their horses, size, and general description...* (Emphasis added).[34]

The Walker-Bonneville Expedition was met by Northern Paiutes in the Humboldt Sink area. Irving stated that the men of the Walker-Bonneville attacked the Northern Paiutes without provocation, killing 30 or 40 of them. On his return through the Humboldt Sink area in 1834, his men once again attacked Northern Paiutes living in the vicinity. *By the end of the Walker-Bonneville Expedition in 1834, Walker and his men had killed more than 50 Indians* and their livestock had caused even more destruction of critical food resources, such as grasses that provided seeds. (Emphasis added).[35]

"In his journal of 1844-1845, Edward Kern, who was traveling with Joseph Walker at the time, mentioned that he found near Carson Lake the 'skulls of the natives killed here by Walker's party some ten years since.'"[36]

1840s: Frémont's Massacres

Influential U.S. Senator Thomas H. Benton of Missouri made arrangements for his son-in-law, John Charles Frémont, to lead exploration expeditions into the little-known region beyond the Rocky Mountains. In the 1840s, Frémont led five expeditions into the western U.S. When he explored the Wind River Range, he climbed a 13,745-foot mountain which he named Frémont's Peak, planting an American flag and claiming the Rocky Mountains and the West for the U.S.

Frémont's journals provide incredible, vivid details of his expeditions. His account of April 6, 1846, is as follows:

> The temperature at sunrise the next day (April 6th) was 42°, with a northeasterly wind. We continued up the Sacramento, which we crossed in canoes at a farm on the right bank of the river. The Sacramento was here about one hundred and forty yards wide, and with the actual stage of water, which I was informed continued several months, navigable for a steamboat. We encamped a few miles above, on a creek wooded principally with large oaks. Grass was good and abundant, with wild oats and pea vine in the bottoms. The day was fine, with a cool northwesterly breeze, which had in it the air of the high mountains. The wild oats here were not yet headed. The snowy peak of Shastl [Shasta] bore directly north, showing out high above the other mountains. Temperature at sunset 57°, with a west wind and sky partly clouded.

He completely fails to mention the Sacramento Lake Massacre of the Wintu Indians led by him, given by Kit Carson of the same day in his Journal:

Kit Carson notes that during their stay at Lassen's (he fails to note that there were two visits) "some Americans that were settled in the neighborhood came in stating that there were about 1000 Indians in the vicinity making preparations to attack the settlements; requested assistance of Frémont to drive them back. He and [his] party and some few Americans that lived near started for the Indian encampment. Found them to be in great force, as was stated. *They were attacked. The number killed I cannot say. It was a perfect butchery*. Those not killed fled in all directions, and we returned to Lawson's (sic)." Another of JCF's men affirms that an attack was made on the Indians in April and Henry L. Ford said that he organized one of the companies. (Emphasis added).[37]

Eyewitness William Isaac Tustin testified that men of Frémont's band mounted on horses chased down the running Indians and tomahawked them to death, while riflemen stood on the shores of the river and took potshots at the Indians trying to swim to safety. He described the scene as "a slaughter." According to his testimony, at least 600-700 Indians were killed on land, with another 200 or more dying in the water. There are no records of any expedition members being killed or even wounded in the massacre.[38]

Frémont and his band continued up the Sacramento River, killing Indians on sight as they went. The Indians had heard about the Sacramento River Slaughter, and on May 9, 1846, killed three members of Frémont's party in retaliation. This led to the Klamath Lake Massacre three days later where 14 Klamath Indians lost their lives.[39]

Frémont's response to the Klamath Lake Massacre by him and his expeditionary force was as follows:

When the Tlamaths tell the story of the night attack where they were killed, there will be no boasting. They will have to tell also of the death of their chief and of our swift retaliation and how the people at the fishery had to mourn for the loss of their men and the destruction of their village. It will be a story for them to hand down while there are any Tlamaths on their lake.[40]

Both in the memoirs, and in his description of his California expedition, JCF takes responsibility for chastising the Indians *after the return from Oregon* but notes extreme provocation—in fact, he alleges protection of the settlers against impending attack. "I then descended into the Sacramento valley where I found the American settlers in excitement & alarm. I learned that General Castro (Military Commandant of Mexico) had caused a general rising of the Indians, with the avowed object of destroying the crops & farms of the Americans & extirpating them from the country. The settlers came to me & requested my protection & assistance which I undertook to give them. Being joined by about 20 of them I proceeded to the head of the lower Sacramento valley, where four or five hundred Indians had gathered together and anticipating them in the very act of their descent on the settlements, *I* attacked & defeated & entirely dispersed them." (Emphasis added).[41]

Neither Frémont nor any of his expedition members were charged or punished in any way for the killings.

Western-Bound Emigrants

The central corridor of the western trails had been used for thousands of years by Indians in a vast trading network. It became the interstate of successive waves of European trappers, missionaries, soldiers, teamsters, stagecoach drivers, Pony Express riders, and overland emigrants bound for opportunity in the California goldfields, the Oregon territory and the silver mines of the Great Basin.

The expansionist and mercantilism policies of the U.S. induced westward expansion. The military, by Presidential Proclamation, protected the white explorers, considered part of the intelligencia, creating new routes, along with the white settlers, miners and surveyors who traversed them.

All of this traffic trespassing across Indian land damaged the fragile ecosystem. The wagon wheels created ruts in the ground and the cattle traveling with the emigrants for food consumed the grass in the area and compacted the soil. The ecological damage was difficult to recover from in a desert environment.

1844: Humboldt River Emigrant Route

The Humboldt River route in northern Nevada across the Great Basin offered water over most of its length. The Bidwell-Bartleson Party in 1841 of 34 wagons was the first to traverse its length.

Franklin Langsworthy, an emigrant in 1850, provided an excellent description:

> The Humboldt is a singular stream; I think the longest river in the world, of so diminutive a size. Its length is three or four hundred miles, and general width about fifty feet. From here, back to where we first saw it, the quantity of water seems about the same. It rather diminishes in size as it proceeds.

As noted somewhat derisively in this year in the diary of Elisha D. Perkins:

> The stream itself does not deserve the name of river being only a good sized creek...For the first days travel in its valley the grass is splendid, then the valley begins to narrow and feed to get poorer and less of it all the rest of its course, till for the last 80 miles, except in special spots we could hardly get enough for our mules to eat and water barely drinkable from saline and sulphurous impregnation and having a milky color. I think Baron [Alexander von] Humboldt would feel but little honored by his name being affixed to a stream of so little pretension.[42]

Thousand Springs Valley was on the route from Fort Hall to the headwaters of the Humboldt River. In 1849, E. D. Perkins wrote:

> The valley where we are Encamped is a remarkable fine one abounding in rich grass, and presents quite a live appearance just now, *there being wagons and camps up and down as far as we can see*... About noon we came to a hot spring. ... Certainly there is something very mysterious in the appearance of nearly boiling water at the surface of the ground. ... What is a little singular is that a spring of clear cold water issues from the ground not 1/4 of a mile from the other. (Emphasis added).[43]

Edwin Bryant described his days' travel across Independence Valley to Mound

Springs on August 7, 1846:

> Crossing this valley, *the sun pouring its scorching rays down upon us with such fervor as nearly to parch our bridle reins into a crisp,* we found on the slope of the western side, near the foot of the mountains [Spruce Mountains], another small oasis, of an acre or two of green vegetation, near the center of which were one or two small springs or wells of cool fresh water. The waters of these springs rise to the surface and sink immediately, moistening only the small patch of fertile ground. (Emphasis added).[44]

The emigrants then had to cross the Wasatch Mountains on the eastern edge of the Great Basin, with its peaks towering up to 12,000 feet, and deep, narrow canyons below. There was no trail. Using axes, shovels, and picks, the men bladed a track.

James E. Reed in his report in 1847 wrote:

> After traveling eighteen days they accomplished the distance of thirty miles, with great labor and exertion, being obliged to cut the whole road through the forest of pine and aspen.[45]

In Sep. 1854, a member of Colonel E.J. Steptoe's detachment searching for a feasible military route across central Nevada found "rubies" (actually garnets) in his gold pan while prospecting one of the streams above Ruby Valley (east side of the Ruby Mountain range) near Hastings Pass (later renamed Overland Pass). The range was then named the Ruby Mountains by Colonel Steptoe, replacing the name Humboldt Mountains assigned by John C. Frémont in 1845 during his Great Basin expedition.[46]

The Ruby Mountains are only ten miles wide but they were impassable to wagons. Emigrants had no choice but to travel over one hundred miles around this rugged range.

Sulphur Hot Springs at the foot of the Ruby Mountains were a curiosity to the early emigrants. Madison Berryman Moorman described the springs in 1850:

> We came to a group of boiling springs. I did not count them, but there can not be less than twenty. ... One of the springs I supposed to be twenty feet in diameter, of unfathomable depth and boiling like a pot. From the appearance of the ground

around which is perfectly bare of vegetation, they sometimes overflow. They attract the attention of every passer-by, and this strange phenomenon of nature is only beheld with wonder and surprise.[47]

While traveling across Pilot Creek Valley named after Pilot Peak, John Wood lamented:

> This morning we traveled over one of the most uninhabitable parts of God's creation; not a thing but the bare earth to be seen, but I suppose if it was not for these there would be no pretty places.[48]

James E. Reed described the Valley similarly to John Wood.

> We started to cross the desert traveling day and night only stopping to feed and water our teams as long as water and grass lasted. We must have made at least two-thirds of the way across when a great portion of the cattle showed signs of giving out...[49]

> James A Payne, 1850, decried the alkaline grass: "In many places the alkali lies so thick upon the ground that it lifts up from the earth with the grass ... the stock refuses to touch it."

Heinrich Lienhard told of his journey through the South Fork of the Humboldt River in 1846:

> We entered the deep gorge through which the river cut its way, and through which our road led. The mass of rock rose in several places nearly perpendicular, around which the stream twisted in several great bends, now to the right, now to the left, the gorge becoming more contracted. ... Each moment we had to recross the stream, the water often coming nearly as high as the wagon bed.[50]

At the end of the Humboldt River, it disappeared into a sink, a low-lying wetland area.

One traveler wrote:

> This is the end of the most miserable river on the face of the

earth. The water of the lake, as well as the last one hundred miles above, is strong with salt and alkali, and has the color and taste of dirty soap-suds.

But the water of the Humboldt Sink was the only water available.[51]

In 1849, Rueben Cole Shaw also described the sink in his Journal:

> On arriving at the sink of the Humboldt... there was found a mud lake ten miles long and four or five miles wide, a veritable sea of slime, a slough of despond, an ocean of ooze, a bottomless bed of alkaline poison...[52]

G.W. Thissell further described the area:

> We arrived at the sink of the river. It empties out on the desert, forming a great marsh or meadow of coarse grass, that covers more than a thousand acres. In many places the grass was higher than a man's head.[53]

Applegate Trail, NW Corner of Nevada

Just below the big bend of the Humboldt River, the Applegate Trail crossed the northwestern corner of Nevada, traversing imposing areas such as Black Rock Desert and High Rock Canyon. The emigrants then crossed 40 miles of desert before they reached the Sierra Nevada.

Starting out, they could choose from two routes, one leading to the Truckee River and the other to the Carson River. It didn't really matter which route they took: either way, the sun beat down on them, and they and their livestock never had enough water to drink. The wind blew sand into their sunburned faces, and the stench of dead oxen, lying by the wayside, filled their nostrils.

The emigrant journals described their journeys:

> At Double Hot Springs, two azure "large round sinks" marked the end of a series of springs that extended over five miles from Black Rock. Alonzo Delano stopped here on August 18, 1849:

> On looking around us we saw a beautiful plat of green grass, covering about an hundred acres, which was irrigated by the

water of several hot springs. Two of these were very large, and from them ran a rivulet of sufficient capacity to turn a mill; but fifty rods below the brook was too hot to bear the hand in. The water in the springs was clear and deep, and hot enough to boil bacon. We boiled our coffee by setting the coffee-pot in the water.[54]

The exhausted, starved, and dehydrated oxen could hardly continue pulling the wagons. On September 22, 1849, Joseph Middleton described their plight: "People are driving their poor exhausted cattle behind or sometimes before their wagons—and when they lie down from exhaustion, they will sometimes wait a while for them to rest, at others they will beat them. ... This is all an appalling desert of desolation ... vestiges of the intensity of its power and heat being equalled only by its incomprehensible extent and magnitude."[55]

J. G. Bruff thought he had reached "the jumping-off place" when he came to this rocky, 45-degree descent of about 200 feet into Fly Creek near High Rock Lake. Emigrants lowered their wagons with ropes, locked the wheels with chains or poles, or added an extra team of oxen to keep from pitching down this "very precipitous rocky descent." Although most efforts were successful, occasionally they lost control and wagons crashed to the bottom of the canyon. "It was truly frightful," wrote A. E. Garrison.[56]

In 1849, J. G. Bruff noted the Applegate Trail crossed "a more dreary and wider waste, without either grass or water, and with a harder road before us." There "was scarcely space for wagons to reach the holes, for the ox-carcasses."[57]

Volcanic Black Rock "looked like a mass of black cinders" and resembled "a blacksmith's forge." This "oasis in the desert" with its complex of impressive boiling springs was the first adequate source of water and grass on the 50 mile trek from the Humboldt River and the first water after the Black Rock Desert. The water irrigated about 20 acres of meadow and was "too hot for the hand," but Joseph Middleton noted in 1849 that "the water when cold is good for drinking" and "tasted good to the thirsty traveller."[58]

1852-1869: Nobles Trail

Long before the first white explorers and settlers made it to California, American Indians lived in the areas from Black Rock Hot Springs, Nevada to Shasta City, California. Thousands of emigrants and their cattle, horses and sheep, traveling west of the Mississippi River, trespassed into and across Indian traditional homelands from 1840 to 1880. One Nevada route avoided long stretches of the dreaded Forty-Mile Desert. They named it the 'Nobles Trail' and used it from 1852-1869, until the completion of the Transcontinental Railroad.

J.B. Brown, an emigrant, described a miserable nights camp at Trego Springs on the Nobles Trail in 1859:

> "Such a scene I never wish to see again as being enacted here. ... Some of the loose cattle which have had no grass for two days nor water for 20 miles travel ... and of course are nearly crazed are running about in all directions lowing and bellowing in search of water and grass." The trail continued west across the playa for another 12 miles before good water.[59]

With the loss of critical food resources for the Northern Paiutes and Western Shoshones due to the increased emigration, came an increase in conflicts between the Northern Paiutes and Western Shoshones and the emigrants. These hostilities continued throughout the late 1840s and 1850s and resulted in periodic raids against the emigrant wagon trains by Northern Paiutes and Western Shoshones.

From 1840 to 1860, over 500,000 emigrants trespassed across and into the traditional homelands of the Indians threatening their survival.

Forts Bridger, Kearny and Ruby

Forts would be built along the California Trail and its branches and cutoffs through Nevada to protect the emigrants. The Trail itself was never a straightforward, singular route. Numerous paths, cutoffs, and detours made up the California Trail during its decades of service. It traversed northern Nevada, following the Humboldt River to the deserts near the base of the northern and central Sierra Nevada. The Hastings Cutoff of the California Trail moved south of the Great Salt Lake to join the main trail on the Humboldt. The Pony Express route swung far south of the Great Salt Lake and the Humboldt River Valley to cross central Nevada covering a minimal distance across the Territory.

The California Trail carried over 250,000 gold-seekers and farmers to the goldfields and rich farmlands of the Golden State during the 1840s and 1850s, the greatest mass migration in American history. The Trail passed through Missouri, Kansas, Nebraska, Colorado, Wyoming, Idaho, Utah, Nevada, Oregon and California. At the time, the entire journey took five to six months to complete. The forts served as welcome stopping points and supply stations, along with providing a military deterrent to Indian hostilities. President Polk recognized the importance of the bond between white settlers and the military in ordering the construction of manned military forts and mounted riflemen to guard the wagon trains.

Jim Bridger established Fort Bridger in 1843 in Wyoming as a fur trading post. It served as a vital resupply point for wagon trains on the Oregon, California and Mormon Trails. The Pony Express and Overland Stage used the Fort which was garrisoned by the U.S. Army between 1857 and 1890. A transcontinental telegraph station provided communication.

Fort Kearny, Nebraska, was established by the U.S. Army in 1848 to protect the growing traffic along the Oregon Trail from the threat of Indian attacks. It took on additional roles as a Pony Express station, an Overland Stage station and a telegraph station.

Fort Ruby, in territory dominated by bands of the Western Shoshone, was built in 1862 by the 3rd Infantry, California Volunteers. It protected the overland mail coaches and Pony Express in order to maintain transcontinental transit and communication. William Rogers, an assistant Indian agent, lived at the Fort. Troops from Fort Ruby were involved in the Goshute War of 1863.

1848: Treaty of Guadalupe Hidalgo, Southwest Annexed by U.S.

The Mexican-American War, fought from 1846-1848, was the climax of America's quest for new territory. Mexico had allowed American settlers to claim land in order to augment its population. Settle they did. Enough so, they declared themselves independent from Mexico in 1836, although Mexico never officially recognized their new republic. When the U.S. annexed Texas as a state in 1845, Mexico considered it an act of aggression. President Polk sent John Slidell to Mexico, offering $20 million in exchange for California and the New Mexico territories. Mexico refused to sell.

The U.S. Army sent troops commanded by General Zachary Taylor to the Nueces River to defend against a specious threat of a Mexican invasion. It was clear that Polk's plan to use shock and awe military tactics was intended to favorably influence the U.S. position in negotiations for its proffered purchase of Mexico's southwest territory. The dominant military display was to demonstrate to Mexico that it didn't stand a chance against a U.S. war which would result in its complete physical destruction.

The Nueces River was the accepted U.S. boundary under the Louisiana Purchase. Generating no Mexican military response from its baiting, General Taylor moved his troops to the Rio Grande River, inside Mexico. Mexican soldiers crossed the River and fired on American troops. President James Polk proclaimed, "American blood had been shed on American soil." He asked Congress to declare war, which it did on May 13, 1846. Just 25 years young, Mexico was ill prepared to fight a large-scale conflict with the U.S. Her government was still unsettled; she lacked the financial capital to engage in war; and her military did not have the technological resources the U.S. did. Many felt she had been duped into starting an unwinnable war.

The U.S. took New Mexico without a shot and faced small skirmishes in California which they put down. Still, the Mexican government refused to surrender.

General Winfield Scott, commander of all American forces, felt that the only way to force a surrender would be to occupy Mexico City. To do so he proposed an amphibious assault on Veracruz, then an overland march of less than 200 miles from there to Mexico City. The campaign for Mexico City proved to be costly, for this time Mexicans were defending the heart of their homeland. But Winfield Scott's Army captured the Mexican capital on September 13, 1847.

The Treaty of Peace, Friendship, Limits, and Settlement, better known as the Treaty of Guadalupe Hidalgo, was signed in 1848, and ended the Mexican-American War. The U.S. annexed lands from Mexico without regard for Indian habitation, occupancy and use rights. It increased the land mass of the U.S. by 50 percent and offered citizenship to the 100,000 Mexican nationals within the territory. The mineral resources from the territory conquered created an economic boom for the U.S.

General U.S. Grant, who had served as a young Lieutenant in the War, later commented on it as follows:

> I do not think there was ever a more wicked war than that waged by the United States on Mexico. ... I had a horror of the Mexican War, and I have always believed that it was on

our part most unjust. The wickedness was not in the way our soldiers conducted it, but in the conduct of our government in declaring war. ... We had no claim on Mexico. Texas had no claim beyond the Nueces River, and yet we pushed on to the Rio Grande and crossed it. I am always ashamed of my country when I think of that invasion.[60]

The territory ceded to the U.S. by Mexico on February 2, 1848, added the area of what is now California, Nevada, Utah, Arizona, New Mexico, and a part of Colorado.

Nevada Indian Lands Freely Appropriated by Whites

The Indian title question had not been addressed prior to the invasion of whites into Nevada. It created a legitimized free-for-all stage for the execution of 'might makes right' in taking Indian land, as confirmed by Commissioner Francis Walker.

Commissioner Walker, in his work entitled "The Indian Question" holds that "it is not to be denied that wrong was often done to tribes in the negotiation of treaties of cession; that the Indians were not infrequently overborne or deceived; that more powerful tribes were permitted to cede lands to which weaker tribes had as good if not a better claim; but the United States endeavored to obtain the cession successively of all lands within its limits to which Indians could show color of title, *except in California and Nevada* ... (Emphasis added).[61]

1849: Exploration of Western Shoshone and Northern Paiute Lands

In 1849, under the authority of the U.S., Howard Stansbury began exploration of the areas inhabited by the Western Shoshone and Northern Paiute Indians. In spite of stories about Indian attacks, he and his party did not experience any violent encounters. In the 1850s, the U.S. sponsored surveys for possible railroad and wagon routes through lands inhabited by the Goshutes.

1849: Mormon Invasions

Regardless of the Indian inhabitants, the Mormons proclaimed their broad intentions of creating a vast empire of their own, the "State of Deseret." This would be a Mormon Empire within the western Empire of the U.S.

On the eighteenth of March, 1849, the Mormons assembled in convention at Salt Lake organized a Territorial Government which they designated as the "State of Deseret." The boundaries named for this new Territory included what is now Utah, Nevada, Arizona, a portion of Colorado, a slice from Oregon, and that portion of Wyoming lying south of the Wind River Mountains. It also included part of what is now California—San Diego and Los Angeles Counties, then as far up the coast as Santa Monica, and from there a line running directly north to the ridge of the Sierra Nevada, taking half of Kern County, a part of Tulare, all of Inyo and Mono, part of Alpine and Shasta and Siskiyou Counties, and all of Lassen.[62]

On July 17, 1849, Brigham Young and a company of Mormons entered the Tooele region, the Goshute homeland. The Mormons hoped to find an area suitable for the establishment of a Mormon community, the State of Deseret. To enable the colonization process, on January 28, 1850, their General Assembly ordered the construction of a road from Salt Lake City to Tooele Valley. They established permanent settlements and began building sawmills and gristmills.[63] By the end of the 1850s, the non-Indian population in the Goshute homeland had reached approximately 1,000 people, exceeding that of the Indians. This large non-Indian population placed the Goshutes in a desperate situation.

Mormon leaders sought to appoint headmen to the various Indian communities when no apparent or sympathetic leader was present, seeking to formalize leadership in predictable patterns and to empower leaders who were seen as being amenable to Mormon objectives.

Invading and monopolizing Cache Valley, the traditional homeland of the Northwest Shoshoni, led to conflict. Their land and livelihood threatened, Shoshoni leader Bear Hunter's warriors raided Mormon cattle herds and attacked mining parties traveling to and from Montana.

Within a decade, by the end of 1858, Mormons had established eleven invasive settlements in Indian country, confiscating prime lands and water sources. In southern Nevada, in 1855, Brigham Young assigned 30 Mormon missionaries to the Las Vegas area to convert the Paiute Indians. They soon built a fort that constituted the first non-Indian settlement in the region. The Paiute rejected their teachings, occasionally raiding the fort until it was abandoned in 1857.

The last major Mormon settlement in the region was at Ibapah, or Deep Creek, in 1860. With the establishment of this community, the last of the favored regions in the Goshute homeland had been invaded.[64]

In an ironic turn, Paiutes were hired to provide much of the labor needed to create the new settlements. They helped prepare the fields for planting and performed various domestic chores. Once enough Mormons had moved into the area, they no longer needed or desired Paiute labor. By the 1870s, the Paiutes who lived near the region's Mormon settlements were destitute.[65]

1850: Compromise of 1850 (Utah Territory)

The U.S. Compromise of 1850 defused the confrontation between the slave states and the free states, in part, by creating the State of California as a free state and creating the Territories of Utah and New Mexico. *Most significantly, it emphatically rejected the Mormon petition for recognition of the State of Deseret*.

The Territory of Utah established on September 9, 1850, included what is now Nevada. A decade later, on March 2, 1861, the Territory of Nevada was formed, carved out of the Utah Territory. In just three years, on October 31, 1864, it was admitted to the Union as the State of Nevada, even though it didn't possess the statutorily required number of 60,000 inhabitants. The special privilege of recognition as a state, notwithstanding its deficient population, was due to its silver, the revenue therefrom desperately needed to fund the Union side of the Civil War.

Silver determined the economy and development of the State of Nevada, nicknamed the "Silver State," until exhaustion of the mines and the U.S.' demonetization of silver started a decline in the 1870s.

Squatters' Associations

As explained by Senator Malone of Nevada in 1953,

> ... squatters' right referred to unsurveyed land for mineral claims. A squatter was known as a man who would go out into an area that was unsurveyed and take up what he would call a homestead. You could not take up a homestead on unsurveyed ground, but if he stayed right there he could hold what is known as squatter's right. ... You could not hold any unsurveyed land if you did not stay right on it. If you did stay

right there on the land then when it was surveyed you could
file on it.

Senator Barrett of Wyoming confirmed that "The Federal Government
recognized squatters' rights."[66]

> Squatters would form associations to tide the settlers over
> until Congress should enact a law which would give them
> proper legal protection, or until they were able to pay for their
> claims.[67]

> While these associations were formed to protect squatters
> from the law, the associations were almost universally
> accepted by public opinion. As one newspaper observed, "It
> is useless to say anything in justification or explanation of
> combinations of this character, as they have become a part of
> the established common law of the West, and are based upon
> that fundamental element of democracy—popular will, and
> the first law of nature—self-defence [sic]."[68]

Within this setting the first universal preemption laws were enacted in 1830
and extended thereafter. The Preemption Act in 1841 recognized the rights of
settlers on unsurveyed public domain land who did not hold official title (i.e.,
"squatters"). The purpose of the Act was to encourage settlers to move onto the
public lands west of the Mississippi River.

> The citizens of western Utah assembled on the twelfth
> of November, 1851, at Mormon Station for the purpose of
> organizing a Squatter Government. [Their] [o]bject was to
> adopt a system by which the settlers could subdivide "the
> valley so as to secure each individual in their rights to land
> taken up and improved by them."[69]

Their regulations included:

> No. 1 provided for the survey of land claims and the
> employment of a competent Surveyor for that purpose.
> No. 2 created the offices of Recorder and Treasurer, both
> to be held by the same party, who was to record and issue
> certificates of claims.
> No. 3 limited claims to quarter-sections.
> No. 10 permitted a company to take claims for each individual

of the company and improve only one location to cover the expenses of all of the company claims.

On the first of December 1852, John Reese recorded a one-fourth section claim.

1851: Hostilities on Humboldt River Passage

By the end of 1851, stories of violence between the Indians and the emigrants passing along the Humboldt River were rampant. Tales told of frequent "Indian" attacks with entire wagon trains being wiped out, cattle shot with poison arrows, and horses run off. By this time, the Western Shoshones had formed into larger bands to more effectively carry out raids against the emigrants trespassing across their land. The best known of the newly formed band organizations in northern Nevada in the 1850s was the White Knife (Tosa wihi). They relied upon newly acquired guns and horses, from traders, Mexicans and emigrant battles, to fight the invading whites.

This hostility was the result of the behavior documented in The History of Nevada in 1881:

> The passage of emigrants through the country, among whom were many that were reckless, and some who thought that the *reputation of having killed an Indian would transform them into heroes, resulted in the slaughter of some straggling Shoshones, along the Humboldt in 1849*. Several instances of the kind occurred, where they [Indians] were shot in retaliation for real or fancied aggressions. (Emphasis added).[70]

> In the spring of 1851, Walter Cosser now living in Douglas County, in this State, left Salt Lake for the purpose of going to California. There were five men accompanying Cosser's party, among whom was the since notorious Bill Hickman, the Danite, or destroying angel of Brigham Young. The five were under the leadership of Hickman; and while they were camped at Stony Point, on the Humboldt River, some Shoshones were standing around, when one of the Danite gang shot and killed a couple of them. *Their only reason given for doing it was the pleasure that killing of redskins afforded the murderers.* (Emphasis added).[71]

> On the fifteenth of April [1865?], four parties succeeded in surprising a camp of Indians near Kane Springs. *They*

~ 338 ~

charged in among the redskins, dealing death right and left, and brought away with them eighteen scalps as trophies of their work. (Emphasis added).[72]

1854: Overland Mail Stations Attacked by Indians, American Express' Kill Order

In the summer of 1854, a private mail route was opened that went through Deep Creek and then on to California. This route preceded the Overland Stage route. The U.S. contracted with the Butterfield Overland Mail Company which soon led to the building of stations at some of the most important watering springs in the Goshute homeland. These stations eventually deprived the Goshutes of water, herbs, seeds, fish and waterfowl.[73]

The Goshutes caused the Butterfield Overland Mail Company, its stagecoaches and stage wagons problems by raiding, stealing stock and attacking drivers as they passed through Goshute country. The stage line constructed twenty-two stations on Goshute land, and the loss of resources to the Indians was alarming.

Mark Twain observed the stage company hierarchy in the early 1860s, while traveling across the continent on the Central Overland California Route with his brother, Orion Clemens. He later wrote about the organization in his book, Roughing It.[74]

> The stage company had everything under strict discipline and good system. Over each two hundred and fifty miles of road they placed an agent or superintendent, and invested him with great authority. His beat or jurisdiction of two hundred and fifty miles was called a "division." He purchased horses, mules, harness, and food for men and beasts, and distributed these things among his stage stations, from time to time, according to his judgment of what each station needed. He erected station buildings and dug wells. He attended to the paying of the stationkeepers, hostlers, drivers and blacksmiths, and discharged them whenever he chose. He was a very, very great man in his "division"—kind of Grand Mogul, a Sultan of the Indies, in whose presence common men were modest of speech and manner, and in the glare of whose greatness even the dazzling stage-driver dwindled to a penny dip. There were about eight of these kings, all told, on the overland route.[75]

The American Express Company, successor to Wells Fargo, instructed their employees on the Kansas to Denver route, "*If Indians come within shooting distance, shoot them; show them no mercy, for they will show you none.*" (Emphasis added).[76] Most probably, this directive influenced the attitudes of the Company personnel where they operated.

The Overland Mail service existed until the transcontinental railroad was completed in 1869.

1855: Western Shoshone Treaty of Ruby Valley, Not Ratified

In an attempt to diminish hostilities between the Nevada tribes and the white settlers, Garland Hurt, the Indian Agent assigned to the Nevada area negotiated the Treaty of Ruby Valley in 1855 with some of the Western Shoshone bands. This purported Treaty was, however, not ratified by the U.S. and is still contested by the Western Shoshones today.

1855: Commissioner of Indian Affairs Celebrates White Men's Western Settlement

Rather than taking action to prevent the ingress of white settlers into Indian territory, the Department of the Interior lauded their western arrival. Along with this complicity in the piercing of Indian land for the benefit of 'white men' came the recommendation to "designate suitable tracts or reservations of land in proper localities, for permanent homes for, and provide the *means to colonize*, them [the Indians] thereon." (Emphasis added).

> The *wonderful emigration to our newly acquired States and Territories*, and its effect upon the wild tribes inhabiting them and the plains and prairies, is well calculated at the present period to attract special attention. Not only are our settlements rapidly advancing westward from the Mississippi river towards the Pacific ocean, from the shores of the Pacific eastward towards the Mississippi river but large settlements have been made in Utah and New Mexico between the two. Already the settlements of Texas are extending up to El Paso and spreading into the Gadsden purchase, and those of California have reached into the great valley of the Colorado, whilst the settlers of Minnesota are building cities at the very head of Lake Superior and villages in the remote valley of the Red River of the north, on their way to Puget Sound. Railroads built and building, from the Atlantic and Gulf cities, not only reach the Mississippi river at about twenty different

~ 340 ~

The majority of the profits from mineral extraction would go to California's *Bank Crowd, a* group of wealthy bank representatives who provided the financing and managed the assets of the Union Mill and Mining Company. Their Company held the monopoly over the Comstock for the entirety of the time between the 1860s and 1880s. The *Bank Crowd's* political and economic power ensured its grip on the Lode for the entirety of its profitability.

1859: Comstock Gold Composition

The composition of the gold on the Comstock Lode was problematic, a black substance encased the gold. It was sent to California to be assayed. The "black stuff" proved to be almost pure silver. The original discovery hole became the Ophir mine which eventually yielded more than $17,000,000.[82]

In a Mining Frontier study, the area was vividly described:

> This country is fabulously rich in gold, silver, copper, lead, coal, iron, quicksilver, marble, granite, chalk, plaster of Paris (Gypsum), thieves, murderers, desperados, ladies, children, lawyers, Christians, Indians, Chinamen, Spaniards, gamblers, sharpies, coyotes (pronounced ci-yo-ties), poets, preachers, and jackass rabbits. I overheard a gentleman say the other day that it was 'the d-dest country under the sun'--and that comprehensive conception I fully subscribe to.[83]

Nevada mining was industrial mining; it required capital, organization, and equipment. The surface croppings were soon extracted, forcing the miners to tunnel underground. The ore was so soft, that the tunnels were often subject to deadly cave-ins. Also, hampering the mining activities were heavy flows of water, required for pumping machinery. Quick advances in mining technology would solve these problems.

Based on Philipp Deidesheimer's invention of the square set method of timbering mines, which allowed voluminous subterranean caverns of ore to be readily extracted and replaced with a rigid timber structure, the Comstock's appetite for the region's richly-timbered forests became ravenous.

Extensive logging and saw mill operations throughout the Sierra Nevada Mountains started up. These operations quickly and severely degraded the quality of the Carson River's waters and in the Truckee River, sawdust choked the river's banks and bed, even creating sawdust bars at the river's terminus at

Pyramid Lake, barriers which proved impassable to native fish attempting to spawn upstream. In 1873, the Carson & Tahoe Lumber & Fluming Company became the largest Comstock wood and lumber combine. During its time, it controlled over 50,000 acres of timberland, operated four sawmills, two lake steam tugs, two logging railroads, a planing mill and box factory in Carson City, and employed some 500 men in its logging camps. During its existence, it had taken 750 million board feet of lumber and 500,000 cords of wood from the Lake Tahoe Basin.[84] Timber depletion and reduced Comstock mining closed the company in 1898.

Adolph Sutro developed a solution to the excess water in mines. *A four-mile-long tunnel was blasted from solid rock to drain over 10 million gallons of boiling, rancid water per day from the lower levels of the mines. The water temperature at deeper levels would rise to more than 100 degrees, and often when miners penetrated through rock, steam and scalding water would pour into the tunnel.* (Emphasis added).[85]

> Tapping scalding pockets of geothermal waters, began a process of water diversions and mine dewatering. Water supplies were initially diverted from the Sierra Nevada Mountains (in the Truckee River Basin) to Virginia City (located in the Carson River Basin). Water was also diverted from Lake Tahoe for flumes to float logs over to sawmills in Washoe Valley.[86]

1859: Mining Districts Established on Comstock

Notwithstanding that the Comstock Lode was on Northern Paiute land, the miners established Mining Districts by holding informal meetings which adopted rules for staking claims and appointed recorders. Such meetings on the Comstock were held as early as 1858. Claims were staked, recorded and fiercely protected.[87]

Comstock Litigation Fever

The first few years were filled with litigation as miners and corporations fought over mining claim boundaries.

> The ore deposits discovered in the fall of 1857 by brothers, Ethan Allen and Hosea Ballou Grosh, fell into the hands of Comstock. Before the Grosh brothers could work or file the claim, both would die tragically. Hosea Grosh ran a

pick through his foot, which eventually resulted in lockjaw (septicemia) and he died on September 2, 1857. His brother, Allen, while traveling to Last Chance, California in November 1857, got caught in a snowstorm and suffered severely from exposure. Though he was found before his death and taken to Last Chance, his legs were completely frostbitten, and refusing to have them amputated, he died on December 19, 1857.[88]

Some years after the Comstock Lode had become a heavy bullion producer, the heirs of the Grosh brothers tried to secure their rights on the Comstock by litigation. They employed Benjamin F. Butler, then the most noted lawyer in the United States, to prosecute the case.[89]

He made a comprehensive examination of the matter. He stated to the litigants that there was no legal question about the absolute rights of the heirs to some of the most valuable ground on the Comstock. Still, he gave them the advice that the defendants were men so thoroughly entrenched in possession, and *having unlimited money at their command, they would be able to buy up any jury* that could be selected to try the case, and that, under the circumstances, the winning of such a case would be an impossibility. The heirs of the Groshes abandoned their effort to wrest the big mines from the hands of William Sharon and the Bank of California. (Emphasis added).[90]

The individual miner was forced out, having served his purpose of discovery. Mining claims were purchased by the *Bank Crowd*, quashing mining in Nevada as an entrepreneurial enterprise. They controlled Virginia City, even building the Virginia and Truckee Railroad, which dramatically reduced ore transportation costs. They also built and controlled the Virginia City and Gold Hill Water Company, the first non-mining incorporation on the Comstock Lode.

Water, Water

The real battle in mining was over the water, always scarce in the desert and made even more valuable by the high stakes of gold mining. When water was scarce, mercury could be used to separate the gold, but this method was considerably more expensive. It cost more than most miners could afford, placing a premium on water. As *in western agriculture and ranching, whoever controlled the water supply controlled production, in this case, of gold*. From these circumstances, the doctrine of prior appropriation—the concept of "first in time, first in right"—became enshrined in western water law, setting the stage for much of the conflict that seemed endemic in western life. Mark Twain's adage, 'Whiskey's for drinking, water's for fighting over,' would be played out in the arid west.

In 1876, Levi Gheen, reported on the lack of water for farming for Indians in eastern Nevada:

> The Indians who are farming throughout the eastern part of the State have been greatly annoyed during the past year by the want of land and water. *The country is being fast settled up by white people; and the patches of land heretofore cultivated by the Indians, in many cases, have been taken from them, and in other cases the water used for irrigating purposes has been taken from them, and their crops have dried up and become worthless*. (Emphasis added).[91]

Anarchy and Confusion from 1857-1861

The years 1857 to 1861 were marked by anarchy and confusion without an effective government.

A San Francisco newspaper of the time reported that:

> There is no government. Nominally the Mormon government bears sway over that portion of the territory as well as over Salt Lake City. But practically Mormon laws are a nullity, they are not enforced, nor could they be. Should a Mormon judge or justice of the peace attempt to hold his court at Carson City or Virginia City, he would not only find that he possessed no power to execute the mandates of his court, but also that all attempts to do so would endanger his personal safety. ... Politically, the people are in a chaotic state, without law and without a Constitutional [sic] government. ... The present position of the people is deplorable. The evils to which they are exposed are terrible to contemplate and the coming season it is to be feared, will witness scenes of anarchy and bloodshed, fearful to behold, as the rich silver mines will attract thither a large crowd of desperate and abandoned men,

who, in the absence of law and a well-established government will give full scope to their vicious inclinations.[92]

1859 Forward: White Farming and Open Range Ranching

The discovery of the Comstock Mines and others induced farming and ranching on an extended scale. Men pushed out on the Humboldt and up its various branches.

Granville W. Huffaker drove a herd of 500 cattle from Salt Lake City to the Truckee Meadows. By 1859, he had established an extensive ranching operation near the hills that now bear his name.[93]

In 1859, Nathan Hockett Allen ("Hoc") Mason formed the Walker River Ranch covering over 30 square miles and some 20,000 acres, financed in part by California cattle baron Henry Miller.

In 1862, Lewis R. Bradley, Nevada's second Governor from 1870-1878, moved to the upper Reese River Valley from California with 500 head of Texas longhorn cattle which grew to thousands of longhorn cattle.[94]

Around 1870, the firm of Sparks & Tinnen began cattle operations within the Mary's River sub-basin. It owned about 200,000 acres and through strategic land purchases along streams and around springs controlled many times that amount by using the open range on public domain lands. John Sparks introduced the Shorthorn and Hereford cattle breeds, which soon replaced the Texas longhorns on Nevada's open ranges.[95]

Among the cattle buckaroos and barons in Nevada were: Dr. Glenn & Co. with 30,000; Tod Hunter, with 25,000; Lux & Miller, with 10,000; and N. H. A. Mason, number unknown.

The total number of cattle in Nevada was estimated at 210,900.[96]

Eastern Public Administration Strategies for Establishing Towns

From the methods of the East, business-men started to bring organization into the chaos. They could not allow the chaos to thwart their plans. They applied the public administration strategies known to them for establishing towns: planning, organizing, developing procedures, budgeting, staffing, securing resources, managing and critiquing the process.

Boundaries were established. Counties were created. Appointments and elections were planned. The offices of officials included Senators, Councilman, and Representatives under Territorial law. At the county level, the following offices were promptly established: County Commissioners, Probate Judges, District Attorneys, County Sheriffs, County Clerks, County Treasurers, County Assessors, County Recorders, County Superintendents of Schools, County Surveyors, Public Administrators, Collectors, and other positions as needed.

Financial and political matters were addressed, including capital acquisition. This was obtained through leveraging their natural resources as collateral to secure credit. Bonds bearing a high rate of interest were issued to pay for public works. Property values were determined and taxed. Mining, farming and ranching provided sources of revenue. Lumber for building was brought from the Sierra Nevada. Schools and churches were opened.

The elected officials meticulously analyzed, tabulated, planned and, most importantly, imposed and collected taxes on land, livestock and income. According to the reports of the various Assessors in Humboldt County there were 20,000 acres under cultivation, with 150,000 acres in the county available for agriculture, with the possibility of increasing the amount to 300,000 with proper irrigation. Statistics were maintained for the population, the bullion product, the amount of land under cultivation and the various products of the same, cattle ranching, the business enterprises and the stores, hotels, homes and other useful buildings.

In addition to mining, smelters were needed; copper beds of salt, soda, gypsum and saltpetre would bring revenue as avenues of distribution were developed. Completion of the Transcontinental Railroad provided transport for heavy ores, freight and passengers.

One example of such an early town was Dun Glen, dating back to 1862. A company of U.S. soldiers were stationed there in 1863, "to keep the Indians in check"—to provide protection for the extensive and lucrative stock raising and farming.

> Six thousand head of cattle are pastured in the valley and adjoining mountains. Among the prominent stock-raisers are: Marzen, who owns 2,000 head; Marker Brothers, 2,000, and Carpenter & Lowery, 1,000.

Of grain 1,500 tons are usually grown in the valley, Joseph Marzen, the largest stock-raiser, owns 1,200 acres of highly improved land, the Marker Brothers, about 1,000.[97]

Fear of Indian Attacks Results in Military Presence Wherever Warranted by Revenue

The fear of Indian attacks resulted in a military presence posted wherever justified by revenue. One example was the *extensive and fertile Paradise Valley.*

> April 4, 1865 Major C. McDermit, There can be no doubt that the settlers in that locality [*Paradise Valley*] are in very great danger, and unless speedily relieved and permanently protected from the depredations of the Indians by whom they are surrounded they will undoubtedly be under the necessity of abandoning that valley, which is *one of the most extensive and fertile in this State, and it is settled by an industrious, enterprising, and worthy people, who, if protected, will soon make it the garden of Nevada...* (Emphasis added).[98]

On April 9, 1865, Captain Wells, with 103 men, well armed and equipped were sent to Paradise Valley. His Commanding Officer, Major C. McDermit, Second Cavalry *California Volunteers, declared that "Captain Wells will be able to whip all the Indians that may oppose him."* (Emphasis added).[99]

Mormons' Insubordination to U.S. Laws

In mid-1857, President James Buchanan became alarmed about events that were reported to be occurring in the Mormon-dominated Territory of Utah. The Mormons had "for several years past manifested a spirit of insubordination to the Constitution and laws of the United States, including [opposing] the authority of the Government by military force." The official beginning of the Utah War came in July 1857 when President James Buchanan removed Brigham Young as Territorial Governor and appointed a new, non-Mormon government headed by Alfred Cumming.

President Buchanan issued orders that would send several Army regiments westward to address this 'Mormon Rebellion.' Under the command of Brevet Brigadier General Albert Sidney Johnston, the Army reached Salt Lake City on June 26, 1858, with the city deserted except for newly appointed Territorial

Governor Alfred Cumming, his staff, and a few leaders of the Mormon church.[100]

General Albert S. Johnston selected Cedar Valley to establish a military post for some twenty-four hundred officers and men of the U.S. Army's Utah Expedition to avoid further rebellious activity by the Mormons. He knew he had to open a supply line avoiding the Mormon Trail and Echo Canyon, natural fortresses for the Mormon militia. In 1857, they built a defensive network in the Canyon, using uncut stones stacked on random courses from 1 to 2 feet above ground, 4 to 12 feet in length and spanning 12 miles. They also planned to flood the Canyon if needed.[101]

1859: Captain Simpson's Exploration for Route across Great Basin

Captain J.H. Simpson of the U.S. Army Corps of Topographical Engineers was selected to lead the exploration for a direct wagon route from Camp Floyd to Genoa in western Nevada, avoiding Echo Canyon. The importance of this expedition came from its approval by the Secretary of War, John B. Floyd. The sixty-four members of Simpson's expedition included an artist, geologist, wheelwright, blacksmith, teamsters, twenty soldiers, twelve six-mule wagons, scientific apparatus, and one of Nevada's first citizens, John Reese.

> "The country between Camp Floyd and Genoa is a striking
> example of what geologists and geographers call "basin and
> range." Throughout this extremely arid region, numerous
> mountain ranges run in a north-south direction, appearing at
> almost regularly spaced intervals. Between the mountains are
> flat-bottomed valleys covered with thick growths of sagebrush
> and greasewood. In many of the valleys, there are expanses of
> alkali flats, which support no vegetation whatsoever."[102]

The expedition also carried a number of scientific instruments that were to be used to determine latitude, longitude, and altitude. ... During the expedition, it was the normal practice to take daily observations. At one point in his narrative, Simpson gave a detailed account of a part of this process.

> This afternoon the astronomical transit was set up for
> observations of the transit of the moon and moon-culminating
> stars.... Also observed as usual for time (or longitude) and
> latitude. Also took four sets of lunar observations for longitude
> with sextants and artificial horizons, two sets being on each
> side of the moon.[103]

In Simpson's Journal entry of May 3, 1859, he wrote:

> The California mail-stage passed us on its way to Camp Floyd.
> Cho-kup, chief of the Ruby Valley band of Sho-sho-nees, was
> a passenger, on his way to see the Indian agent.[104]

Captain Simpson's Indian policy, which he instructed his men to follow was:

> I have made it a point to treat the Indians I meet kindly, making
> them small presents, which I trust will not be without their
> use in securing their friendly feelings and conduct. A great
> many of the difficulties our country has had with the Indians,
> according to my observations and experience, have grown
> out of the bad treatment they have received at the hands of
> insolent and cowardly men, who, not gifted with the bravery
> which is perfectly consistent with a kind and generous heart,
> have, when they thought they could do it with impunity,
> maltreated them; the consequence resulting that the very next
> body of whites they have met have not unfrequently been
> made to suffer the penalties which in this way they are almost
> always sure to inflict indiscriminately on parties, whether they
> deserve it or not.[105]

Simpson recorded his reliance on pre-existing Indian trails:

> .... There is an old beaten trail down this cañon, about the
> largest we have seen on the trip. The Indians say it is the trail
> of the To-sa-witch band of the Sho-shonees, living about the
> Humboldt River, who *yearly take this route*, to trade horses
> with the Pahvant Indians about Fillmore. (Emphasis added).[106]

The springs, at times, provided a modicum of water. The animals were watered
by the bucketful and that at intervals of several minutes. Simpson noted: "At
this rate it was evident that the animals would die before we could satisfy
them."[107]

Within a year following Simpson's expedition, emigrant traffic on the outbound
trail had increased to the point that the Army was ordered to begin providing
these travelers some protection. Pack trains, commercial and emigrant wagons,
hand-cart processions, the Pony Express, and the Overland Stage traversed the
route. In May of 1860, an Army patrol, under the command of Lieutenant
Stephen H. Weed, began escorting parties of California-bound emigrants along
the central part of the new trail.[108]

1860: Paiutes - Pyramid Lake War

Two trading Posts, the Buckland and Williams Stations, were built to supply miners and emigrants, as they traveled across the Carson Branch of the California Trail. The Posts provided a welcome rest to emigrants after surviving an inhospitable stretch of desert. Overland Mail and Pony Express stations were posted there so mail from the East may have caught up with the travellers. They were in the heart of Paiute country.

> By 1860 the Paiutes' precarious balance with nature had long tipped toward starvation. Their most important food, fuel, and water resources were taken up by emigrant campgrounds, the military, and a string of stage and mail stations that squatted on every key waterhole.[109]

Only a spark was needed to start a war of survival. On May 7, 1860, an incident at the Williams Station in Carson Valley set off the Pyramid Lake War. Two Paiutes had gone to a white settlers' home, J.O. Williams. Four whites tied up the Paiute man and attacked the woman with him. The Paiutes were later set free, but the Paiute man returned later with friends who forced the four white men into the house. The house was burned with the men in it. In retaliation, the white settlers hastily formed volunteer companies from Virginia City, Silver City, Carson City, and Genoa with 105 men under the command of Major William Ormsby. They planned to attack the Northern Paiutes and Western Shoshones camped at Pyramid Lake.[110]

On May 12, a few miles from Pyramid Lake, the Indians led the armed companies into a well-prepared ambush. Of the 105 volunteers who participated, 76 were killed, including Major Ormsby, and many of the remaining 29 were wounded. The battle brought a short-lived victory for the Northern Paiutes.[111]

Thereafter, a volunteer force and U.S. Army regulars comprising 800 men, commanded by the legendary former Texas Ranger Colonel John Coffee "Jack" Hays, galvanized to fight the Indians. The "Washoe Regiment," named after Washoe County, was composed of 13 companies of volunteers from the areas surrounding Carson City and Virginia City, Nevada; as well as Sacramento, California. U.S. Army regulars were sent from Fort Alcatraz, California, under the command of Captain Joseph Stewart.

Without waiting for Captain Stewart's troops, Colonel Hays led his men towards the site of Williams Station where he and his volunteer thugs encountered the Paiute on June 3, 1860. In a three-hour battle, six of the Indians died and the survivors fled into the hills. Two of the volunteers were also killed.

In the Second Battle of Pyramid Lake, Hays and Stewart's combined force of 800 men defeated the Paiute, killing some 160 Paiute warriors, and suffering four casualties. The outnumbered and outgunned Paiute force then scattered across the Great Basin.

Pony Express and Stage Station Attacks

The end of the Pyramid Lake War of 1860 was the signal for a series of Indian raids throughout the Great Basin, aimed mainly at the Pony Express and Overland stage stations. These routes had gained importance because of the need to transport gold from California and silver from Nevada to the east to fund the Civil War. Soldiers were assigned to each coach to provide protection, while others were located at stations along the route.

During the next decade many stations were overrun, their stock driven off, and some station agents killed. To meet the threat, the U.S. built Fort Churchill along the Carson River, led by Captain Joseph Stewart. Union Nevada Volunteers, 1st Battalion, Nevada Infantry, were assigned to the Fort. It was to serve as a base of operations from which to watch and patrol the Northern Paiutes of Walker River, Fallon, and Pyramid Lake and protect the Buckland Station which was a Pony Express stop. In addition, *more than two dozen military posts* throughout Nevada were established to protect the main travel routes and the important settlements, yet difficulties with the Indians continued into the 1860s.

The Pony Express riders were glorified:

> In mid-century America, communication between St. Joseph, on the fringe of western settlement, and gold mining communities of California challenged the bold and made skeptical the timid. Into this picture rode the Pony Express. In rain and in snow, in sleet and in hail over moonlit prairie, down tortuous mountain path ... pounding pony feet knitted together the ragged edges of a rising nation.[112]

Each courier normally rode three segments, an average of thirty-three miles, before handing off the mail to another, though circumstances frequently required the expressmen to endure considerably longer distances between rider relays. Messages were written on tissue paper to reduce weight, the postage for each half-ounce letter costing $5.00. The riders carried a maximum of ten pounds of mail, secured in locked leather pockets of a mochila, a special removable saddle cover that was transferred from one horse to another during the journey.

When en route to California, author Mark Twain vividly recounts his experience as a Pony Express rider galloped past his stagecoach:

> "We had a consuming desire from the beginning to see a pony-rider ... Away across the endless dead level of the prairie a black speck appears against the sky, and it is plain that it moves. In a second or two it becomes a horse and rider, rising and falling, rising and falling—sweeping toward us nearer and nearer—growing more and more distinct, more and more sharply defined—nearer and still nearer, and the flutter of the hoofs comes faintly to the ear... another instant a whoop and a hurrah from our upper deck, a wave of the rider's hand, but no reply, and man and horse burst past our excited faces, and go winging away like a belated fragment of a storm!"[113]

Indian resistance wasn't the death knell of the glorified Pony Express; it was Congress. Two months after the first rider streaked across the horizon, Congress authorized funding for a transcontinental telegraph. In 1861, Western Union linked the west and east bound segments and coast-to-coast telegraphic communication was a reality.

1861: Hot Springs and Yellow Pine Mining District, Southern Nevada

The natural springs and the area that surrounds what is now Goodsprings, Nevada, in southern Nevada were used by the Paiute Indians. However, across the west, the control of springs by white settlers was highly coveted. They provided that necessary element for survival—water—and also served as luxury resorts, another source of revenue.

Mining also occurred around the area in 1856 when Mormons established a lead mine at nearby Potosi, the oldest lode mine in Nevada. Though a small oasis in the desert, no settlement would be founded until after Joseph Good discovered silver near the springs in 1861. The area was incorporated into the New England Mining District, later renamed the Yellow Pine Mining District.

During its heydays, the Yellow Pine Mining District earned over $30 million from lead, gold, copper, and zinc, providing for 1/3 of the total metal production for Clark County, making it one of the most lucrative mining districts in Southern Nevada.[114]

1861: Opal (Eldorado) Mountains, Gold/Silver Discoveries, Southern Nevada

When a trapper found gold ore in the Opal (Eldorado) Mountains during the spring of 1861, a rush of prospectors from the gold districts of California was attracted to Eldorado Canyon, located 39 miles southeast of Las Vegas. Within a year, the Southwest Mining Company and El Dorado Mining Company had established working mines in the Valley. Eldorado Canyon's principal mine, the Techatticup, opened in 1863 and by this time, four separate town sites had been platted in the area. Millions of dollars in gold were generated, initially transported by steamboat on the Colorado River. As to be expected, a military post was founded in Eldorado Canyon in 1867. The Wall Street and Queen City mines, in 1872 alone, produced $25.2 million of gold and silver.

Indians Face Starvation

While millions of dollars were being made from the gold and silver discoveries on what was Indian land, Indian Agents would report instances of extreme hardship faced by the Indians under their charge to their superiors. Most of the time, there was not enough time or appropriated money for the Department of the Interior to muster a response. Indians died from exposure and hunger.

> The approaching winter will be one of trying and peculiar hardship to all the Indians of this division, if not to those of the other portions of the territory caused by the great scarcity, or rather the utter failure, this year of all the principal productions of their subsistence, such as pine-nuts, seeds, roots, &c., Fish, which, with them, is a large item in the sustainment of life, and which they caught in copious quantities in the lakes and rivers of the country, will also almost entirely fail them this season, owing to the extremely low stage of water in all rivers and lakes, caused by the unusually small amount of snow that fell the past winter. The watercourses and lakes being thus reduced in volume, and the alkali properties greatly predominating in the water, great quantities of the fish have died and drifted on the margin of the streams ... therefore rendering it imperatively necessary on the part of

the government to administer promptly and liberally to their relief and support, *to prevent starvation and disturbance*. (Emphasis added).[115]

1861: James Nye Appointed as Territorial Governor of Nevada

James W. Nye was serving as President of the New York Metropolitan Board of Police when President Lincoln commissioned him as Governor of Nevada Territory on March 22, 1861. It was a patronage appointment. Most western political appointees had no knowledge of the west or of Indians. Nye was a good friend of Lincoln's Secretary of State, William H. Seward, and the two had campaigned in the west for Lincoln during the 1860 election.

Nye, Governor and Acting Superintendent of Indian Affairs for the Territory of Nevada, jumped right into his role as trustee for the Indians. He wrote to the Secretary of Interior in 1861: "Lake Bigler [Tahoe], lying in the county of the Washoes, and from which they formerly obtained large quantities of the best kind of fish, is now taken possession of by the whites, and has become a watering place, to which large numbers from this Territory and California resort, and from which this poor Tribe are virtually excluded."[116]

In his annual report of October 1, 1861, Superintendent Henry Martin wrote of the dire lack of necessity of subsistence for the Nevada Indians and the need to negotiate Treaties with them which would provide protection. Any supplication purporting to be for the benefit of Indians usually has a suspect alternative reason. In this case, Superintendent Martin discloses it: protection, not for the Indians, but for the overland mail and telegraph communication.

> Too little attention, I am fearful, has heretofore been paid to the fact that there is very little game in this Territory, of any description, which the Indians can kill to keep them in food. There is no buffalo whatever that range in this Territory, and very few antelope, elk, deer, mountain sheep, or bear, and these only in certain localities.
>
> Civilization seems to have had the same effect here as has been noticed elsewhere in this country since the first settlement by our forefathers, in driving before it the game natural to a wilderness, and the Indians complain bitterly that since the white man has come among them their game has almost entirely disappeared from their former hunting grounds, and they are now obliged either to beg food from the white settlers

or starve. .... They frequently come to me and *fairly beg for some beef, to keep their squaws and papooses from starving*. (Emphasis added).

The establishment of the overland daily mail and telegraph lines, and their recent completion through this Territory -- consummations of such vital importance to the people throughout the Union -- renders it necessary that steps should be immediately taken by the government to prevent the possibility of their being interrupted by the Indians.

In recent consultations or "talks" with the Wash-a-kee and Sho-kub, the head chiefs of the Shoshones or Snake Indians, Navacoots and Pe-tut-neet, chiefs of the Ute nation, and many of the sub-chiefs of both nations, I find that they are unanimously in favor of a treaty with the United States ...[117]

On February 26, 1862, the Secretary of the Interior wrote the chairman of the House Committee of Indian Affairs in part as follows, further *disclosing the basic aim of control over the Indians*:

The lands owned by the Indians are, most of them, unfit for cultivation, and it is not probable that any considerable portion of them will be required for settlement for many years. *The principal inducement to make treaties with those tribes is the control which the Government would thereby be enabled to exercise over them*, by which additional security would be given to settlers in the Territory, and to the Overland Mail and Telegraph Lines. (Emphasis added).[118]

By the end of 1862, Colonel Patrick E. Connor and his California volunteer thugs were assigned to Ruby Valley to control the Indians. Remember that the vast amount of the Northern Paiutes' confiscated mineral wealth was going to California businessmen who would assure its protection.

Indians Consider White Miners and Settlers Trespassers

Since much of Nevada was unsurveyed, the homestead laws did not immediately apply and, in many areas, white settlers could fence large areas and live on the land for years as squatters, without holding title or any other form of legal consent by Congress.[119]

Charles E. Mix, Acting Commissioner, recommended that a treaty be made with all the tribes embraced within the Territory for the extinguishment of their "real or pretended titles to the land." The 2d Cavalry California Volunteers and local citizens were intent on "exterminating" the Indians.

> **February 3, 1862:** *One great source of difficulty between the whites and the Indians is a continued series of encroachments on the part of the whites upon the reservations of the Indians*. I refer to the reservations of the Pah Utes. These reservations cover a large portion of the *best grazing lands* in the western and middle portions of the Territory. The increasing population bring in their train a large increase of stock, and the great scarcity of forage in the Territory makes it almost a necessity for them to occupy a portion of the reservation. The Indians are exceedingly sensitive to any infractions upon their supposed rights. (Emphasis added).[120]
>
> In the vicinity of the Big Meadows, and where a large band of the Pah Utes reside, is an *extensive gold and silver mining* region, rapidly settling with whites. The *Indians regard them as trespassers*, and subject them to considerable annoyance. (Emphasis added).[121]

Mormon Incursions; Comstock Lode; Butterfield Overland Mail and Pony Express; Invasion of White Settlers and Miners Engulf Indian Lands

The Mormon incursions starting in 1847; the California Gold Rush in 1849; the mail transport running through Deep Creek starting in 1854; the Overland stage coach runs starting in 1858; the Comstock Lode Rush in 1859; the Oregon Gold Rush in 1860; the Pony Express in 1860; the Montana Gold Strikes in 1862; and the overbearing presence of the military all added to the tension between the Indians and the whites. The mail companies and the government responded by distributing provisions to the Indians hoping it would reduce the Indian problems on the route between Salt Lake City and Carson City. Indian attacks continued though with the stage company losing a total of seventeen stations, 150 horses, and sixteen men.[122]

Most of Nevada's Indians were facing the same condition of the Goshutes as described by Territorial Governor Amos Reed in a December 1862 letter to the Commissioner of Indian Affairs, resulting in the raids:

> [T]he largest portion of tillable land in the Goshute country

had been occupied by whites and that the game had been killed or driven off. In response to this loss of resources the Indians had turned to raiding the Overland Mail and stage stations. Reed was convinced that unless the Goshutes received assistance *they would either steal what they needed or starve*. (Emphasis added).[123]

1862-1863: Connor's Thugs and Massacre at Bear Creek

In May 1862, after learning that soldiers would again be stationed in Utah, a New York Times reporter suggested that it was

> "... *much more likely that these Gentile soldiers from California will create difficulties in Utah than that they will ever settle them*. If the troops are designed to operate against the fragments of dying savages west of the Rocky Mountains, we are likely to have an Indian war on our hands this Summer, which, though barren enough of value, will be fertile enough of expenses." (Emphasis added).[124]

This reporter's opinion was played out in the heinous instructions of Colonel Patrick E. Connor to his subordinate officer, Major Edward McGarry, in a September 29, 1862, dispatch.

> If hostile Indians resisted capture "you will destroy them." *If any Indians were known to have committed murder, "immediately hang them, and leave their bodies thus exposed as an example of what evil-doers may expect while I command in this district.* ... This course may seem harsh and severe, but I desire that the order may be rigidly enforced, as I am satisfied that in the end it will prove the most merciful." Connor also ordered McGarry, though, that "in no instance will you molest women or children." Connor's views reflected those of General George Wright, commander of the Department of the Pacific and Connor's immediate supervisor, who wrote that Indian difficulties "have been growing worse and worse for years, and I am determined to settle them now for the last time. *Every Indian you may capture, and who has been engaged in hostilities present or past, shall be hung on the spot*. Spare the women and children." (Emphasis added).[125]

On January 29, 1863, Colonel Patrick Edward Connor and about 200 California volunteer thugs attacked the winter camp of Bear Hunter's Northwestern Shoshoni group of 450 men, women, and children on Beaver Creek at its confluence with the Bear River. As a result of the four-hour carnage that ensued, twenty-three soldiers lost their lives and at least *250 Shoshoni were slaughtered* by the troops, including ninety women and children in what is now called the Bear Creek Massacre. Chief Bear Hunter was killed, and the remnants of his tribe under Sagwitch and the chiefs of nine other Northwestern bands signed the Treaty of Box Elder at Brigham City, Utah, on July 30, 1863. It was most probably under duress due to their resounding loss of lives in the Massacre.

On October 21, 1863, Commissioner Doty commended Colonel Connor:

> He has rendered great service to the government in punishing and subduing them [Indians]. By the rapid and skilful (sic) movement of his troops, and their repeated successful attacks, he has been mainly *instrumental in bringing the Indians to acknowledge, for the first time, that the "Americans" are the masters of the country*. (Emphasis added).[126]

Commended also by General Henry W. Halleck, U.S. Army general-in-chief, for his "heroic conduct and brilliant victory on Bear River," Connor was promoted to brigadier general on March 29, 1863.[127]

1862: Legislation for Treaties to Be Negotiated with Shoshonees

By the Act of July 5, 1862, 12 Stat. 512, 529, Congress appropriated $20,000 "for defraying the expenses of negotiating a treaty with the Shoshonees or Snake Indians…"

On July 22, 1862, the Commissioner of Indian Affairs gave Peace Commissioners James Duane Doty (Superintendent of Indian Affairs for the Territory of Utah, later Governor of that Territory), Luther Mann (Indian Agent, Territory of Utah), and Henry Martin (former Superintendent of Indian Affairs for Utah Territory), a letter of instructions as follows:

> Congress at its recent Session having appropriated Twenty Thousand Dollars for the purpose of making a treaty with the Shoshonees or Snake Indians, you have been designated by the President to carry into effect the object of the said appropriation. No sufficient reports of explorations are in

the custody of this office to enable me to state definitely the boundaries of the country inhabited and claimed by these Indians, but it is understood that they inhabit the country in the northern part of Utah and eastern portion of Washington Territories, through which lies the route of the overland mail, and the emigrant route through Utah and into Washington Territory and *it is mainly to secure the safety of the travel along these routes that a treaty is desirable.* (Emphasis added).[128]

1863: Treaty Commissioners for Various Shoshonee Treaties

News of the January 1863 massacre at Bear River spread quickly among both Indian and white populations, and it generally had the effect General Connor desired.

General Connor was a **Treaty Commissioner** at several of the Shoshonee treaties (Northwestern Shoshonees, Goships, and mixed bands of the Bannacks and Shoshonees); J.B. Moore, lieutenant-colonel Third Infantry California Volunteers, was a Witness for Treaty of the Western Bands of Shoshonees, at Ruby Valley, October 1, 1863 (Vigorously Contested by Shoshones Up to Present Day); and Territorial Governor Doty was a negotiator, as well.

Surely, General Connor's presence as Treaty Commissioner must have had an intimidating influence. The presence of the murderer of *250 Shoshoni men, women and children in cold-blood* could only have resulted in duress, the force of psychological pressure, for the Indians. Surely, if the U.S. wanted to apply coercion, there was no better person than one rewarded and promoted for "punishing and subduing" [Indians] and for "repeated successful attacks."[129]

The Treaties were signed in rapid succession by various bands of Shoshonees: Treaty at Fort Bridger with the Eastern Shoshone Indians (July 2, 1863); Treaty of Box Elder (July 30, 1863) with the Northwestern Shoshonees; Treaty of the Western Bands of Shoshonees, at Ruby Valley, October 1, 1863 (Vigorously Contested by Shoshones Up to Present Day); Treaty at Tuilla (Tooele) Valley with the Goships (October 12, 1863); and Treaty at Soda Springs with the mixed bands of the Bannacks and Shoshonees (October 14, 1863).

1863: Indian Treaties - Unlimited Mining, Farming, Ranching, Travel and Military Access

The Treaties were prepared by the U.S. and were a complete give-away, granting carte blanche authority for whites to overrun the Shoshonees' lands. They required an end to all hostile actions against the whites and permitted unassailed mining, farming, ranching and logging in their country by whites and free, undisturbed travel. They also agreed to the construction of military posts and military presence wherever necessary and that stage lines, telegraph lines, and railways could be built throughout their domain. No adequate compensation was provided for this huge loss of nonrenewable resources. The U.S. agreed to pay minimal compensation.

When the Treaty with the Eastern Shoshonees (which was the format for all of the Shoshonee Treaties,) was transmitted to the Commissioner of Indian Affairs by the Treaty Commissioners with a letter of July 3, 1863, they stated: *"The terms were more advantageous than we had expected to obtain."* (Emphasis added).

In regard to the Treaty of the Western Bands of Shoshonees, at Ruby Valley, October 1, 1863 (Vigorously Contested by Shoshones Up to Present Day), (18 Stat. 689), Former Chief of Western Shoshones Timoke in 1878 regarding Ruby Valley stated:

> He [Former Chief of Western Shoshones Timoke) states that years ago the Shoshones were promised a reservation in Ruby Valley, *but subsequently the same land was sold to the whites and nothing more was said about the reservation; and since that time all the valuable land, water, and timber in his country has been disposed of to the whites*; that the game, heretofore in abundance, has disappeared; that some of the Indians have gone to farming and have greatly improved in civilized habits, notwithstanding the great disadvantages they have labored under, that is, the scarcity of water and the poor quality of land forced to be taken. He states that his Indians are scattered over a large tract of country; that, while many of them, through being employed by the whites, have learned to farm and do almost all kinds of work yet others have become demoralized and are now roving vagabonds, living about mining camps and railroad towns, subsisting upon refuse food thrown away by restaurants and boarding-houses; that they got drunk and committed crimes among themselves; that their

squaws are prostitutes; that loathsome diseases were spreading among them; that in consequence they were degenerating and would soon die off if something was not done to improve their condition. (Emphasis added).[130]

Importance of Treaties with Shoshonees to U.S.

Treaty Commissioner Doty expressed the importance of the treaties he negotiated with the Shoshones to the protection of the white emigrant wagon trains and the white miners, and for overland communication. None of these were made for the benefit of the various Shoshone tribes.

> November 10, 1863 The importance of these treaties to the government and to its citizens can only be appreciated by those who know the value of the continental telegraph and overland stage to the commercial and mercantile world, and the safety and security which peace alone can give to emigrant trains, and to the *travel to the gold discoveries* in the north, which exceed in richness -- at least in the quality of the gold -- any discoveries on this continent. (Emphasis added).[131]

Treaties Ratified with an Amendment by Senate

Each of the five treaties was ratified by the Senate, with an incomprehensible amendment:

> Nothing herein contained shall be construed or taken to admit any other or greater title or interest in the lands embraced within the territories described in said treaty in said tribes or bands of Indians than existed in them upon the acquisition of said territories from Mexico by the laws thereof.

Peace Commissioner Doty met with the Tribes and received their approval to the Treaties, as amended.[132]

The mixed bands of Bannocks and Shoshones were never assembled for the purpose of obtaining their formal assent, apparently for the reason that they became so scattered as to render it impossible to assemble them. Fortunately for them, their treaty was never proclaimed by the President.[133]

The Treaties promised payments of annuities annually for a term certain to the Shoshones, in the form of goods and livestock, but it is uncertain if the U.S. complied.

Evolution of U.S. Territories, States, and Indian Agencies from Late 1840s through 1870s in Today's Southern Nevada - (CA, NM, Colorado, AZ, UT, ID and NEV) Result in Incoherent Indian Policy

In less than twenty years, beginning with the Treaty of Guadalupe Hidalgo in 1848, jurisdiction for the region shifted among five U.S. territories: New Mexico, California, Arizona, Utah and Nevada. It also shifted among different Indian agencies, making it difficult to develop and implement a consistent Indian policy. A Bureau of Land Management Report in 2012 characterized it as "*incoherent.*"

For Nevada the following applied at various times, providing a brief insight (not comprehensive), to change in administrations, locations, etc. [See Chart in the last Chapter.]

Note 1: EXAMPLE OF CHANGE OF PERSONNEL. AGENTS California: Special Agents and Commissioners and Appointment Dates: John Ross Browne **1857**; George Bailey **1858**; Robert J. Stevens **1866**; John G. Ames May 6, **1873**; Charles Q. Wetmore (Special Commissioner) August 10, **1874**; D.A. Dryden March 31, **1875**; Justin Colburn July 12, **1877**; Samuel S. Lawson July 1, **1878**; Adam Johnson (Sub-agent, San Joaquin) April 13, **1849**; John A. Sutter (Sub-agent, Sacramento) November 29, **1849**; George Barbour September 30, **1850**; J. M. Wozencraft September 28, **1850**; Colonel Redick McKee September 30, **1850**; Samuel Sheldon September 1, **1852**; Benjamin Wilson September 1, **1852**.

Superintendents, 1852-60: Edward F. Beale March 5, **1852**; Thomas J. Henley May 31, **1854**; James Y. McDuffie March 9, **1859**.
Northern District: John A. Driehbelbis June 21, **1860**; George M. Hanson April 9, **1861**; Elijah Steele August 10, **1863**.
Southern District: James Y. McDuffie June 21, **1860**; Augustus D. Rightmire December 20, **1860**; John P. H. Wentworth April 16, **1861**.
Superintendents: 1864-73: Austin Wiley, Charles Maltby, Billington C. Whiting, Brevet Major General John B. McIntosh, Billington C. Whiting.
Source: Letter from Commissioner L. Lea to Secretary Alex H.H. Stuart, January 15, 1851.

Note 2: EXAMPLE OF DESPOTIC CONTROL OF SUPERINTENDENT.
Brigham Young (Mormon), Utah Territorial Governor and ex oficio Superintendent of Indian Affairs for Utah Territory from 1850 to 1858. Mormon settlers encroaching on Paiute settlements, excluded them from traditional resource areas by force, even as Young sought to win favor with Tribes.

Major Jacob Holeman, Indian agent to Utah Territory, recommended Treaty negotiation with Paiutes before Mormon encroachment had permanent and damaging effects; call for Paiute treaty ignored. Indian affairs administration under Young's influence tended to default to Mormon strategic, economic, and religious agendas. Deur, Douglas and Confer, Deborah, "People of Snowy Mountain, People of the River: A Multi-Agency Ethnographic Overview and Compendium Relating to Tribes Associated with Clark County, Nevada." Pacific West Region: Social Science Series, National Park Service, Publication Number 2012-01,U.S. Department of the Interior, p. 109.

Note 3: EXAMPLE OF CHAOS. Southern Nevada Indian Agent, 1869, R.H. Fenton: I reported at Saint Thomas, Nevada, October, 1869; there I found no one in charge of the agency, and, from the best information that can be obtained, there never has been an agent in this tribe of Indians (the Pah-Utes) previous to my being assigned to this duty. The range of this tribe extends over portions of Utah and Arizona Territories, also the States of Nevada and California. Report of the Commissioner of Indian Affairs to the Secretary of the Interior, United States. Office of Indian Affairs. U.S. Government Printing Office, 1870, p. 113.

Southern Nevada Indian Agent, 1870, Charles Powell: By the following year, the agency was turned over to Charles Powell, who complained that his predecessor had taken a salary but carried out almost none of his duties. Powell reported to his superiors the precarious condition of the *Southern Paiutes he encountered at the new post, "who have been neglected at this agency, and most shamefully neglected by their former agent."* (Emphasis added). Report of the Commissioner of Indian Affairs to the Secretary of the Interior, United States. Office of Indian Affairs. U.S. Government Printing Office, 1871, p. 561.

Note 4: EXAMPLE OF MISAPPROPRIATION OF FUNDS. Office of Indian Affairs had allocated funds to area Indian agencies through late 1860s and early 1870s to support tribes of Moapa region. In practice, little of funding made its way to the Indians. Misappropriation so egregious and destabilizing that local governments threatened legal action. Deur, Douglas and Confer, Deborah, "People of Snowy Mountain, People of the River: A Multi-Agency Ethnographic Overview and Compendium Relating to Tribes Associated with Clark County, Nevada." Pacific West Region: Social Science Series, National Park Service, Publication Number 2012-01,U.S. Department of the Interior, p. 109.

1863: Pioche, Southern Nevada - Gold/Silver Discoveries

With a significant discovery in southern Nevada at Pioche in 1863, the formation of a town was quick. San Francisco capitalist F.L.A. Pioche purchased several claims in 1868 and had a smelter built.

> In 1872, the city boasted a daily line of six-horse Concord stagecoaches carrying the U.S. Mail and a Wells Fargo express stagecoach that made its way to the Central City Railroad at Palisade, Nevada. The Gilmer & Salisbury stagecoach company also had three daily lines, with two of them running six-horse Concord coaches to Bullionville.

> The first independent narrow-gauge railroad in Nevada was built in 1873 with the Pioche & Bullionville Railroad that was formed to haul ore from the rich Pioche-area mines 20 miles to the milling facilities at Bullionville. Three railroads were also organized to build lines to and from Pioche. These included The Salt Lake, Sevier Valley & Pioche Railroad, the Palisade, Eureka & Pioche from the north, and another from the south. It had two telegraph offices — the Western Union to San Francisco and the Desert Telegraph (Brigham's) through Salt Lake City.[134]

1864: Gold and Silver Discoveries in Humboldt Mountains

The Humboldt Mountains were home to large bands of Indians. The Mountains provided the subsistence base to support their hunting and gathering culture before the massive incursion of white settlers and miners, who made up their own quasi-legal rules to claim land and water. Once destroyed, the Indians were "Faced with a steal or starve situation, many were attracted to the Overland Mail route and the Emigrant Trail as places to carry out their attacks... The segment of the trail between Fort Hall and Wells was one of the more perilous segments of the journey."[135]

Repeatedly, the reports of the Commissioner of Indian Affairs highlighted the conflict between the whites and Indians, yet it would be the whites the U.S. would protect.

> *The Territory in gold and silver bearing quartz is fabulous*
> *in its extent and richness. Gold and silver are discovered*
> *in many portions of the Territory among large bands of*

~ 366 ~

Indians who have recently had undisturbed possession of the country. These discoveries being known, miners move in and settle up the country in a very short time. *These miners drive away the game and cut down the pine-nut trees, upon which the Indians subsist.* In this hurried manner of settling the country, of course *many little difficulties arise. The mining interests have been of so much importance to the general government and the Territory, that every possible precaution has been taken to prevent an outbreak among the Indians,* such as there was in 1860, which set the Territory back. (Emphasis added).[136]

August 10, 1864 Owing to the Ophir-like *mineral richness* of the Humboldt mountains, as well as the *productive qualities of the soil* of the valleys, and the almost irresistible inducements held out to the hardy and industrious miner and agriculturist, the country is fast filling up by settlement. *The mountains, which all contain the precious metals,* are now being thoroughly prospected and worked by the skilful (sic) miner, and are beginning to yield a generous reward to the persistent toiler from their redundant wealth.

The river bottoms and the cañons of the mountains are all taken up as ranches and garden spots, and have been put in a state of cultivation. The game of the mountains and valleys is being frightened away by the appearance of the white man in this wild region, and the continual crack of his unerring rifle. The pine-nut trees are rapidly being cut down and used for building purposes or fuel. The bunch-grasses, the seed of which formerly supplied the Indians with one of their chief articles of food, and which abounds in the Humboldt country, now fails to yield even the most scanty harvest, owing to its being eaten off as fast as it sprouts by the vast amount of stock which has been brought to the country by the settlers and drovers; large herds of cattle from distant California, for the last two years, and more especially during the last fall and winter, having been driven to this region to graze. *Thus you will see that the means of subsistence for the Indians of this section for the past year, and for the whole future, have been greatly impaired if not completely destroyed.* In consideration of these facts, I would respectfully urge upon your excellency to bring to the notice of the department the destitute condition of these Indians, in the hope that some means may be provided for their subsistence and support. The discovery of the rich and precious minerals in southwestern Idaho has induced, for the past two years, a heavy emigration thither from California and our own territory. *The highway to the Jordon creek, Boise, and other mining districts of Idaho, lies through Nevada*, and for over two hundred miles through Humboldt county, and through two different tribes or bands of Indians—the Pah-Utahs and the Pannakes (Bannocks). The destruction of the grass along the route by the stock of the emigrants was a source of great dissatisfaction and discontent among these Indians, as the supply of provender for their own stock, large numbers of which they possess, being thus cut off, they were compelled to seek other more distant and less eligible localities for pasturage. (Emphasis added).[137]

August 1, 1864: Apprehending that trouble or disturbance might arise between some of the bands of Indians and the emigration to Idaho from the cause of *their country being made a highway*, I called together in council, in the month of May, 1863, the principal men of Pah-Ute nation. Among them, and the most important of all, was old Waw-ne-mucka, the head chief of the tribe ... I stated to them that there would be a *large number of white people passing through their country* ... and that I wished them to remain perfectly quiet and friendly to all whites going over the route either way, as also to the coming immigration from the States. ... *I then made him* [Waw-ne-mucka] *a present of a Spanish sombrero, a red silk sash, a pair of heavy red blankets, and sundry other articles*, with which he seemed highly pleased. (Emphasis added).[138]

Allusion is elsewhere made to the fact that the Pai-Utes ... [live in] Meadow valley ... the centre of a rich mining district ... where *fabulous amounts of gold and silver* are to be found. ... (Emphasis added).[139]

In a Letter from Governor Nye to Brigadier General Wright, Commanding Dept. of the Pacific, April 5, 1864, he unambiguously records the priority of protecting miners in Nevada against Indians in the State by providing a concentrated military presence:

The policy of the Government seems to be to encourage the development of our mineral resources as speedily as possible, and believing [sic] that the best way to do it is to protect the miners in their explorations.[140]

Timber Depletion

At Lake Tahoe, a 4,000 foot-long tramway was built by the Sierra Nevada Wood and Lumber Company up a steep grade near present-day Incline Village, Nevada. A unique steam-powered cable railway carried cordwood and lumber a vertical height of 1,800 feet to the summit, at which point the logs were dumped into a V-flume and sluiced to lumber mills in Washoe Valley. From there they were carried by wagons up to the Comstock. *This began a period of extensive deforestation of the Lake Tahoe Basin*. By 1896 most suitable trees within the basin (estimated at up to 60 percent of all mature trees) were cut down and the tramway and flume operation was shut down.[141]

Concern over clear-cutting Tahoe's forest led a local newspaper to cry out in opposition to the lumber barons who were destroying the "gem of the Sierras."

> *But Tahoe is a picture rarer than ever glittered on cathedral walls; older, fresher and fuller than any work by the old masters, and yet they are cutting away her frame and bearing it away. Have we no state pride to stop the work? (Truckee Tribune 9/7/1878)*[142]

> By the 1880s, writers, professionals and scientific groups began to threaten that the country would face a "timber famine" if steps were not taken to stop the plunder and destruction of the country's forests. ... Denouncing timber frauds in Northern California, the General Land Office launched investigations that found lumber companies openly using farmers, sailors, and laborers to file under the Timber and Stone Act of 1878, which allowed acquisition of 160 acres of timbered and stony land at a nominal price. The land conspirators would purchase a claim and then immediately re-sell it to the company at a modest profit and go about their other business. General Land Office agents investigating the cases claimed that perhaps three-fourths of the claims filed were fraudulent. (USDI, Annual Report 1886: 95, 200-213).[143]

Truckee River Channel into Pyramid Lake Blocked by Logging Debris

In a November 1874 letter from the Pyramid Lake Paiutes' Agent to the Commissioner of Indian Affairs, it was reported that the entire Truckee River channel into Pyramid Lake was blocked by logging debris and sawdust, consequently diverting the river's entire flow into Mud [Winnemucca] Lake.[144]

In the Governor's message to the Nevada Legislature, as reprinted in the Nevada State Journal (Reno), he noted:

> "A subject of importance to many citizens of the State...is the preservation of the fisheries of the Truckee River...unless preventive measures are soon adopted and rigidly enforced, their certain destruction is imminent...The mouth of the Truckee [at Pyramid Lake]...is closed by a bar of sawdust at least a mile in length, three hundred yards in breadth and three feet in depth...I saw hundreds of fine trout dead and rotten upon the shores...The air was poisoned with the stench of their decay..."[145]

Changes to Humboldt Region's Ecology

The degradation of Indian natural resources was a direct result of mismanagement by the federal government. The environmental functions of ecosystems, e.g., water purification and nutrient cycling and the capacity to assimilate wastes, were damaged, impaired or destroyed. A Report by The Nevada Department of Conservation and Natural Resources and The United States Department of Agriculture documents this destruction:

> Early mining activities within the Humboldt River Basin prompted rapid population growth and intensified the need to produce agricultural food products for both livestock and people. In response to these requirements, much of the basin's upland wooded hillsides were denuded of usable timber for the mines, railroads, building construction and as a source of fuel. As early as 1862 the increased mining activity throughout much of the basin had caused many of the steep, thin-soiled slopes of upper basin watersheds to become exposed to sheet and gully erosion. ... The deforestation of

the hillsides fostered the establishment of well-developed gully systems in these upper watersheds which reduced their ability to hold moisture and mitigate the flows downstream onto the meadowlands below.[146]

Adding to the effects of erosion on changing the Humboldt River Basin's native landscape, early agricultural activities diverted natural flows out of established stream channels for irrigation purposes and to support large cattle operations. By the late 1800' s, the effects on natural vegetation from the region's extensive open-range cattle grazing operations were exacerbated by extensive and far-ranging sheep herding. The resultant overuse of timber, shrub and natural perennial grasses, both in the basin's lowland meadows and upland watersheds, began an irreversible process of soil and channel erosion, elimination of natural meadows and native grasses, and the influx of invasive plant species (e.g., cheatgrass) which was to accelerate changes to the region's ecology.[147]

Silver and Gold Production Priority for Funding Civil War

Precious metals from the West helped keep Northern banks solvent during the protracted, bloody—and expensive—Civil War and reassured an anxious public that the U.S. would be able to pay its debts. Transporting the gold and silver to banks in the East was difficult. By stagecoach it went as far as San Francisco, where it was loaded onto Pacific steamers bound for Panama, carried by railroad across the isthmus, and loaded onto Atlantic steamers for the final leg of the journey.

When the U.S. began issuing paper money in 1861 to pay for the Civil War, the notes were not trusted by Americans and were derided as "greenbacks" or "shinplasters." Only when the new federal income tax was instituted, and it became clear that greenbacks could be used to pay taxes, did their reputation and value improve. Gold and silver discovered in the West and shipped to the East, especially the output of Nevada's Comstock Lode, made a crucial difference in the Civil War.

Confederacy Seeks to Win Western Part of U.S. to Exploit Precious Metals

The Confederate plan for the West during the Civil War was to raise a force in

Texas, march up the Rio Grande, take Santa Fe, turn northeast on the Santa Fe Trail, capture the stores at Fort Union, head up to Colorado to capture the gold fields and then turn west to take California.

In February 1862, a Confederate army invaded New Mexico Territory. The advance into New Mexico Territory (today's New Mexico and Arizona) under Brigadier General Henry Sibley had several ambitious goals, among them claiming the New Mexico Territory and California for the Confederacy, annexing parts of Mexico, and establishing a presence on the Pacific coast to mitigate the Union blockade of Southern ports. Of particular importance was access to the gold and silver mines in the Western states, especially those of California, Colorado, and Nevada.

The New Mexico Campaign was a dismal failure, effectively thwarting Southern ambitions in the West. With the rich gold and silver mines out of reach, the only course left was to try to pirate Union treasure in transit.[148]

Confederacy Piracy

Stephen Mallory, Confederate Secretary of the Navy, had authorized Acting Master Thomas E. Hogg to lead an expedition to board a Union steamer in Panama as passengers, smuggle arms on board, and commandeer the ship in the name of the Confederate States of America with the intent of fitting it with arms and using it to attack Union shipping in the Pacific. Mallory instructed him:

> *Having secured the steamer, organized your crew, and hoisted the flag of the Confederate States, you will adopt prompt measures to arm your vessel and proceed to cruise against the enemy of the Pacific.*

He went on to make it clear that one of the goals was the acquisition of Union gold:

> *You will endeavor to strike a blow at the California trade and whalemen in the Pacific, and should you capture bullion, it is suggested that, if no better means for shipping it to Europe*

~ 372 ~

offers, you place it in the hands of a British merchant of established character at Valparaiso. A French man-of-war might receive it on board in freight for France.

There wasn't only attempted piracy on the high seas, but on the western plains as well. In one stage coach robbery, the records of the Confederacy record the following:

> Shortly after the first coach had departed, [Captain] Ingram addressed those on the second coach as follows: "Gentlemen, I will tell you who we are. We are not robbers, but a company of Confederate soldiers. Don't act foolish. We don't want anything of the passengers. All we want is Wells, Fargo and Co.'s treasure, to assist us to recruit for the Confederate Army." Ingram presented the driver with the following receipt:

> *June 1864 This is to certify that I have received from Wells, Fargo, & Co, the sum of $____, cash, for the purpose of outfitting recruits enlisted in California for the Confederate States Army. R. HENRY INGRAM, Capt. Com'g Co., C. S. A* (Emphasis added).[149]

1865: Extinguish Goshutes' Title

The government moved quickly to extinguish the Goshutes' aboriginal title to settle them on a reservation of the U.S.' unilateral selection.

> In the treaty with the Shoshonee Goship band, of October 12, 1863, there is a special provision by which those Indians agree to give up their roving life and *settle upon a reservation whenever the President of the United States shall deem it expedient for them. That time has now come,* and advantage may be taken of the existence of that clause, or similar provisions, in treaties with the other bands.

> I have further to suggest, that inasmuch as it has not been the policy of government to acknowledge the full title of these Indians to the lands claimed by them, that *treaties should be so framed that the Indians shall relinquish the right of occupancy of the lands included within defined boundaries,*

and agree to remove to and occupy the lands reserved for their use. (Emphasis added).[150]

1866: Scalp Bounties

Scalp bounties were common in several western jurisdictions. One of these was Nevada. What is amazing is that this subject was just part of the agenda of a War Meeting of Ruby and Silver Cities. No legal impediment appeared to exist.

> In the February 15, 1866, Ruby and Silver City War Meeting, the following Resolution was adopted:
>
> RESOLVED, That three men be appointed to select *twenty-five men to go Indian hunting* ... 2. That *for every buck scalp be paid one hundred dollars, and every squaw scalp fifty dollars, and twenty-five dollars for everything in the shape of an Indian under ten years of age*. 4. That each scalp shall have the curl of the head, and each man shall make oath that the said scalp was taken by the company. G. C. Whitcomb, Sec'y. (Emphasis added).[151]

Destitution and Extermination of Nevada's Indians

Repeatedly, Indian Agents informed the Commissioner of the destitution faced by the Western Shoshonees and pleaded for assistance, only to be ignored, again and again. They faced homelessness, poverty, starvation, and murder. Beyond comprehension, the Western Shoshone endured the ignominy of continuing, unabated cruelty and injustices.

In 1830, in the debates in Congress on the Indian Removal Act, Representative Evans eloquently pleaded what needed to be done:

> If I could stand up between the weak, the friendless, the deserted, and the strong arm of oppression, and successfully vindicate their rights, and shield them in their hour of adversity, I should have achieved honor enough to satisfy even an exorbitant ambition; and I should leave it as a legacy to my children, more valuable than uncounted gold — more honorable than imperial power.[152]

Yet in the case of the Western Shoshonees, there was no one in a position of power to stand up for them. They were pushed to the brink of dehumanization, where all they could do was steal to live, which put them in the crosshairs of the riflemen eager for the "extermination of all Indians."

In 1865, Utah's Superintendent of Indian Affairs, Orsemus H. Irish, notified Commissioner Cooley of the genocide facing the Shoshonees:

> Witnessing the constant stream of emigration, and hearing, as they do, from the emigrants, citizens, and too often the soldiers and officers of the government, the threats of extermination of their race, made against all Indians, and being threatened by the hostile Indians that they will ever regard them as enemies if they do not make common cause with them now against the whites, it is not strange that they are excited and uncertain as to the course that they should pursue. … cruelties practiced by hostile savages have prejudiced our people against the whole race. The emigrants … and *the officers and soldiers who are here for their protection, are almost entirely in favor of the extermination of all Indians*. … I know of only one case of Indian outrage and depredation that has not commenced in the misconduct of the whites. (Emphasis added).[153]

A year later, the threat of extermination of the Indians by the miners was again conveyed to Commissioner Cooley by Utah's Superintendent of Indian Affairs H.G. Parker:

> South of Ruby valley many white settlements are being formed, and the fertile lands of this degraded people [Shoshonees] are being taken from them, their grasses consumed, their groves of pine trees (pinon) destroyed, and the scanty supply of game is being killed or driven away by the invaders, whom the Indian has learned to regard as his natural enemies. The country increases in sterility towards the south until it becomes probably the most barren district on the American continent. The families and bands which dwell in this region are destitute of horses and other domestic animals. They live in the depths of poverty, and are emaciated from hunger. When they steal horses, mules, and cattle, it is to appease the cravings of appetite; to keep themselves and their families from starvation. But these acts, with their utter want of moral perception, and their degraded and wretched condition, have given rife to such a strong and general aversion to them that

the *miners almost universally demand their extermination*. Acts of injustice, wrong, and cruelty are not unfrequent. The civil law cannot protect them at so great a distance. An existence maintained under such natural disadvantages must, of necessity, fade away before the encroachments of a superior race. I beg leave respectfully to recommend that all necessary measures be at once adopted by the department to select and establish a suitable reservation for the Shoshones somewhere in the vicinity of Pahranagat. Lands, with proper facilities for irrigation, adapted to agricultural and grazing purposes, might now be obtained. (Emphasis added).[154]

Again in 1868, Superintendent Parker, graphically portrayed the death facing the Indians in the Nevada Superintendency to Commissioner Taylor. The primary source documents of the federal government contain with them evidence of the abject failure of the federal government to act for the benefit of the Nevada Indians. There is no other way to present it. The only reason that the Nevada Indians were subjected to this depravity and corruption was so the U.S. and its businesses could rape the Indian lands of the gold and silver in them and steal their present and future survival, leaving desolation for them behind.

There are now over 10,000 Indians in this superintendency, all of whom are quietly and peaceably disposed, but whose means of subsistence have been greatly restricted from the increasing *influx of our white population, who are, step by step, encroaching on the favorite haunts of the Indian tribes in this State*.

The streams which formerly afforded them a plentiful supply of fish are now invaded by the miner for milling purposes; the pineries, which formerly afforded them an annual crop of nuts, have been squatted on and are fast giving way before the woodman's axe.

In fact the *means of subsistence for this people, which were always scanty, are now almost completely shut off*. Indeed, they must either be taught the arts of husbandry to sustain themselves, or the alternative will be forced on them to *starve or steal*. (Emphasis added).[155]

In the Carson City Nevada Agency 1867 Report, Agent Franklin Campbell noted that he did not have a single dollar for traveling expenses to investigate or respond to the killing of several Pi-Utes by a desperado named Grayson. He further stated:

> *White men are too apt to act upon the hypothesis that an Indian has no rights ...* (Emphasis added).[156]

Shoshone Sharecroppers

Many Shoshones depended on farming or ranching from white lands for survival. This sharecropping, though, was unstable as the white owners could end it at any time.

> Twenty one of these ranches have been cultivated ... Nearly all of the land so cultivated by Indians [Western Shoshonees] belongs to white people ... I find that something must be done soon for these Indians for the reason *that the white people who own the land cultivated by them are likely to take it at anytime*. They state that they cannot see what is to become of them unless a suitable reservation is established. (Emphasis added).[159]

1867: Proposal to Reduce Pyramid Lake Paiutes' and Walker River Indian Reservations to Exclude Mineral Lands

To gain control of minerals on reservations, the Department of the Interior would discount the value of minerals to Indians, along with the necessity and desirability of large reservations which could be reduced to conveniently carve out mineral lands. The Department of the Interior and those confiscating the profit of the monetized minerals knew what they were doing—it was private profit at the expense and extermination of the indigenous peoples of Nevada—it was genocide.

> *1867: At present they [Pyramid Lake Paiutes' and Walker River Indian Reservations] contain a large area of mineral land which is of no value to the Indians. Miners will not be debarred from working thereon. ... I would propose that the reserves be resurveyed in such a manner as to exclude all mineral lands and the greater portion of both Pyramid and Walker lakes...* (Emphasis added).[160]

> The present size of the Walker river Indian reserve, containing, as it does, about 600 square miles, is both unnecessary and

undesirable. I would recommend that it be reduced to 40 square miles, 10 miles long by four wide … *The abandoned portion would comprise the mineral lands…* (Emphasis added).[161]

Use of Territorial Establishment to Challenge Indian Reservations

In an effort to undermine the validity of Indian reservations in Nevada after the discovery of gold and silver, Walker River Indian Reservation Indian Agent Franklin Campbell reported to Superintendent H.G. Parker that the Indians had never completed a formality of their establishment in the Territory of Nevada—expressing their willingness to the President. This meant their reservations weren't valid. This common effort to undermine the validity of Indian title is conceptualized by Peter d'Errico as " a semantic world created by one group to rule another."[162]

> *Last spring a mining district was formed to the west of the lake and within the limits of this reserve [Walker River Indian Reservation]. The lodes are numerous and contain gold, silver, copper, and lead.* Several companies are now engaged prospecting them for the purpose of testing their permanency and wealth. *The act organizing the Territory of Nevada provides that established Indian reservations shall form no part of the Territory until the Indians express a willingness to the President of the United States that they should. This the Indians have never done.* (Emphasis added).[163]

1868: Commissioner - Agricultural and Mining Lands of Western Tribes Should Be Opened for White Settlers

Commissioner Brown in a further effort to *prescribe* the location of Indian lands in *'rich agricultural districts or mining regions,'* advised Secretary Browning that lands which were 'wastes of country' in the control of Indians could be used by whites. This epidemic of lies repeated over and over in this Chapter must come out of the dark libraries of the Department of the Interior.

> I can but express … the propriety and necessity of there being some treaty arrangements entered into with tribes in New Mexico, Arizona, Nevada, and Washington Territories, having no treaty relations with the government, *especially with those tribes inhabiting or claiming rich agricultural districts or mining regions, in order that their rights may be determined*

~ 378 ~

and secured … the rights of settlers protected, and desirable wastes of country opened for occupancy and improvement by citizens. N.G. Taylor, Commissioner to Hon. O. H. Browning, Secretary of the Interior. (Emphasis added).[164]

1869-1887: Mining in Ruby Mountains

The Ruby Mountains sub-basin, once home to the Shoshones, became a Mining District in 1869. The *Camp of Bullion* stood on the site of mining claims for silver, lead and copper. It is difficult to ascertain the specific amount of wealth generated from any mining site due to theft, underreporting or not reporting at all. Nonetheless, over two decades mining resources of $3.2 million were reported.

> Mining became one of the principal economic activities in the Ruby Mountains ... Between 1869 and 1887, some $3.2 million in silver, lead, copper and some gold was mined in the district.[165]

1869: Menial Labor for Shoshones

As more and more land was homesteaded or squatted on or otherwise acquired, Indian lands were diminished and the Indians were forced to turn to menial labor to survive. Having to leave their homelands, traditional political organization under chiefs or other leaders and traditional culture and religion withered away. It was yet another way to break up reservations and crush tribal relations and individual Indians. Repeatedly, this is noted in the historical record.

> As the mining and ranching interests expanded, the Indian peoples around the state responded in large part by forming settlements on the outskirts of mining camps, railroad towns and farming communities or by attaching themselves to particular ranches.[166]

> Long established subsistence activities were abandoned in favor of menial wage labor. Men hauled and chopped firewood, sold pine nuts and fish, hauled water, dug irrigation ditches, worked as loggers, plowed fields, bounty hunted for rabbits, or commercially hunted large game, while women worked as laundresses, maids, and kitchen helpers. The production and use of most traditional technological items had essentially ceased by 1880.[167]

Canned Justifications for Eradicating Indian Reservations

Since Indians had to leave their reservations, sometimes for extended periods, to work to survive, they were then chastised by the Commissioner with the threat of eradicating their reservations since they didn't live on them. The terminated reservations could then be opened to white settlement, and the Indians would not be harmed by their land stolen as they would have further menial labor opportunities to work for the white settlers.

If mineral discoveries were made on reservations, the canned justifications— language that would result in opening the Indian land for white settlement, without regard to whether the justification was true—included that it was for the benefit of the Indians, the miners weren't disturbing the Indians, the Indians weren't using the land, they had no concept of the value of the minerals, etc.

> In the country of the latter (Shoshones) *great discoveries of mineral wealth have been made, and miners are rapidly coming in who, so far, have not disturbed the Indians, but have been of benefit to them, it is said, by bringing into the country many comforts the Indians were before unable to procure* ... (Emphasis added).[168]

> The Indians are well fixed this fall as regards food and clothing. Their labor is in good demand, and at good wages. It is almost impossible for them to suffer much in any portion of this superintendency now, since the building of the Central Pacific railroad, and the discovery of silver mines in almost every portion of the country. The more this barren desert country is settled by the whites the better it is for the Indians. Every white man who makes himself a farm on any of the strips of cultivable lands adds to the comforts of the Indians more than they could get on fifty miles square in its natural state. *From this time on the yearly appropriation of twenty thousand dollars will not be needed. It is money thrown away to give the Indians* of this superintendency clothing of any amount. If it is given them once, they expect the same amount each year, and will not work for what they think the government owes them. With the exception of giving to families who have been sick or otherwise distressed, it is a detriment to give the Indians of this State anything. *The reservations they have in this superintendency are at the present time of no use or value to them whatever. It would benefit them vastly more if*

they were abandoned and allowed to be settled by the whites for there would be so many more farms for them to work on. I have demonstrated the fact that these Indians will not farm for themselves; at the same time, *they are good hands to work for white men*. (Emphasis added).[169]

A year later, Major Douglas emphatically **contradicted** Agent Parker that the appropriation set aside for the Indians was anywhere near being "adequate."

> *Estimated Enumeration of Indians—it will be seen that the number exceeds 12,000. The annual sum of $20,000, in any form of distribution, is wholly inadequate*. (Emphasis added).[170]

1870: Whites Appropriating Indian Fisheries at Pyramid Lake Paiutes' and Walker River Indian Reservations on Pretext They Were of No Value to Indians

If valuable fisheries existed on reservations, the same canned justifications were used to steal them—"the pretext that they were valueless" was one example. These "canned justifications" were designed to achieve a result, without regard to whether the 'justification' was true or had any merit. One Indian Agent considered they were "*not conceived in an honest spirit.*"

> In this connection it may be proper to speak of the importance of these reserves as means to an end. *It has been the design of some citizens of this country to break them up, on the pretext that they were valueless to Indians*. As it would be a matter of small importance to such persons whether such was or was not the case, unless the reserves in case of withdrawal, might be made valuable to themselves, *I am inclined to believe such designs were not conceived in an honest spirit.*

> The reserves are not valueless, for without man's assistance, nature has endowed them with fisheries, which furnish the Indians with a bountiful supply of food. *That they have not been valuable in other respects is owing to official neglect and maladministration and not to any lack of inherent value.* The reservations, properly developed, must necessarily be of great importance as means for the advancement of Indians in civilization; and were they abandoned, every scheme for the improvement of the condition of the Indian would thereby

be rendered abortive, or at least very difficult of execution. (Emphasis added).[171]

1870: Whites Encroaching on Indian Lands Arguing Indians Had No Surveys to Prove Up Their Land Claims

Another 'canned justification' for whites encroaching on Indian lands was the argument the Indians had no survey to prove it was their land. It was the U.S.' responsibility to survey their lands and adequately mark the boundaries, which they conveniently put-off year after year.

> In previous communications I have called attention to the fact that the limits of reservations have not been designated by any maps or plats indicating a legitimate survey. *I would here respectfully reiterate what I have hitherto said. I deem it of the highest importance that a resurvey be made of the limits of these reserves*, and the limits indicated so as to preclude the possibility of future litigation and dispute. The increase of immigration, and the *disposition of the whites to encroach on the reserves*, renders such a course imperatively necessary. (Emphasis added).[172]

> Carson City: *I will here remark, that until the metes and bounds of the reserve are authoritatively established, it will not be free from the encroachments of a bad class of white men, who seldom believe in according any rights to Indians.* (Emphasis added).[173]

1870: Power of Indian Agents to Lie, Rely on "Canned Justifications"

Only one year after Agent H. G. Parker falsely asserted the fisheries were valueless, the truth was revealed by H. Douglas, Major U.S. Army, Superintendent of Indian Affairs, in his report to the Commissioner. The Indians, *in fact*, relied on the fish for subsistence and the large income derived from selling them to whites. It was the greed of the whites, their cupidity, that was the foundation for wanting to steal the fisheries.

> In connection with this inclosed letter I would respectfully invite attention to what I have written hitherto on the subject of reservations, particularly to my review of Mr. Parker's report for 1869, of yesterday's date, and reiterate my petition

that *the Indian reserves in this State be not touched, and that their limits be minutely and forever defined, so that white people cannot encroach upon them. It is not only politic but just that some portion of the land in this State be set apart to be considered by Indians as exclusively their own.* The abandonment of the present reservations would, in my opinion, be an outrage on the Indians, and, if effected, will, I fear, prove a dangerous experiment. Give the Indians a home, with assistance and encouragement, and, as Sarah [Winnemucca] says, "I warrant that the savage (as he is called to-day) will be a thrifty and law-abiding member of the community fifteen or twenty years hence." (Emphasis added).[174]

1870: Encroachment of Whites on Indian Reservation Land Countenanced by Lack of Legal Protection for Indians

J. M. Lee, First Lieutenant, U.S. Army, Special Indian Agent for Nevada, reported in 1870, that Pyramid Lake had been the *headquarters for whites for grazing stock, fishing, and prospecting for gold and silver mines.* It would appear that this use agreed to by Treaty, in the Agent's determination, could be used as a subterfuge by the whites to expropriate the Indian land.

> *From all information, and appearances as well, the reservation [on Truckee River and Pyramid Lake] had for years been the headquarters of white men, engaged in grazing stock, fishing, and prospecting for gold and silver mines.* (Emphasis added).[175]

1871: All Shoshones in Utah and Nevada Should Be Removed to Indian Territory in Oklahoma

In the latter part of 1871, George W. Dodge, with the status of Special Agent, was sent to Utah to once more investigate the condition of the Indians. He recommended that the Goshutes be sent to the Shoshone Reservation at Fort Hall, Idaho; but later he amended this request and recommended instead that *all the Shoshone Indians in Utah and Nevada be sent to the Indian Territory—present-day Oklahoma.* Dodge justified this recommendation by stating that the Shoshone-speaking Indians in Utah and Nevada were related to the Shoshone-speaking Comanches in Oklahoma. (Emphasis added).[176]

Stock Manipulation

While Nevada Indian's faced destitution, the white mine owners were engaged in devising deceptive means for accumulating yet more wealth. The Comstock mine owners were criticized for stock manipulation in San Francisco, skimming of profits, and poor accounting, all resulting in losses to the common shareholders. This fit with Mark Twain's opinion: "a mine is a hole in the ground with a liar on top."

The original Comstock stock issue was 10,700 shares, selling for between $4 and $5 a share. After "the big bonanza" was struck, the price of the stock went skyward. By the middle of 1875 the speculative value of the two mines was close to $1,000,000,000. Shares went as high as $710.[177]

According to a study by the National Park Service in 1959:

> Two prime characteristics of the Comstock Lode from 1860 to 1880 were wildcat speculation and expensive litigation. *In this atmosphere of frantic financial manipulation and unscrupulous rigging of the market, the "Kings of the Comstock" struggled for power, bought and sold seats in the U.S. Senate, and brought ruin to the Bank of California.* ... (Emphasis added).[178]

Bank of California - Controlling Influence in Virginia City

The Bank of California, under the leadership of William Ralston, acquired the vast majority of the Comstock claims. Eventually, it became the controlling influence in Virginia City, even building the Virginia and Truckee Railroad which dramatically reduced transportation costs. They also built and controlled the Virginia City and Gold Hill Water Company, the first non-mining incorporation on the Comstock Lode. The Bank made money from the predatory practice of buying out mines that defaulted on loans issued at 2% per month.

Frauds to Fleece Shareholders

By selling stock in mines before they open, investors are dependent on ore assays made by the owner's selected engineer. Owners would provide the highest quality of ore to the assayer, leading to a better review of the mine.

Another form of fraud committed with the assays was salting of the ore. Salting of ore is when the ore selected for the assay is artificially mixed with more metal, which makes the ore appear to be richer than it actually is, leading to a good report if the assayer did not catch that the ore had been salted.

Not all mining assayers were true professionals, however, and simply produced a report that the mine owners desired just to get paid. There were no regulations calling for evidence or double checks on assays, making the act of committing fraud very easy.

Often times the vein of ore runs out and a search for another vein is undertaken. Mine owners levy assessments against their shareholders in order to continue the search. However, many times mine owners would levy assessments when there was no need, and instead pocket the money from the stockholders without the stockholders being aware of it.

It was not uncommon for a mine to initiate a shut-in when a bonanza was found so that the mine owners could purchase high volumes of their own stock, relying on inside information, then release the news of the bonanza, and then sell their now highly valued stocks for large, quick profits. Sometimes the bonanzas would be overhyped, and the actual value of ore in the bonanza turned out to be much less than expected, but would still produce a spike in stock values for the mine owners to make profits.

1873: Powell and Ingalls Recommend Removal of Western Shoshonees to Fort Hall, Idaho; Goshutes to Uintah Basin, Utah

Special commissioners J. W. Powell and G. W. Ingalls were appointed to investigate and report on the conditions of the Nevada Indian tribes. They included recommendations in their report as to the disposition that should be made of various tribes.

> The Western Shoshones number 1,945 and are divided into thirty-one tribes. They inhabit Southeastern Oregon, Southwestern Idaho, and Central Nevada. *Of these tribes not more than one-fourth took part in the treaty of October 1, 1863, made at Ruby Valley in Nevada.* The tribes living to the south and west were not present or represented in any manner. Under that treaty it was stipulated that the Western Shoshones could be called to a reservation at the will of the President, and that these tribes should receive annuities to the amount of $5,000 for a term of twenty years. Only the northern tribes,

who took part in the treaty, have received the benefit of this stipulation. ...

> *The southern and western tribes, having taken no part in the treaty, have received no part of the annuities, and consider that they are under no obligations to the General Government, and exhibit some reluctance to their proposed removal to a reservation.* (Emphasis added).[179]

They recommended that all of the Western Shoshones be moved to the Fort Hall Reservation in southern Idaho, but they refused to be relocated.

Powell and Ingalls in a similar familiar refrain recommended that the Nevada Goshute Indians be removed to the Uintah Basin in Utah. Due to a lack of firm government purpose, direction, and organization, the Goshute people remained in their homeland and did not move to any reservation.[180]

Powell and Ingalls Misrepresent Purpose for Removing Indians

Powell and Ingalls' documented cunning and hidden negotiation with Indians is on full display in their Report. Their negotiations were simply to rid whites of the presence of Indians as cheaply and quickly as possible. The need to buy peace was gone. Petty depredations and their demoralizing savage presence were to be done away with, not by justly compensating the Indians for the land the whites needed, but by hypocritically swindling them, all along faking a pretended interest in their well-being.

> All of the Indians who have been visited by the commission finally appreciate the hopelessness of contending against the Government of the United States and the tide of civilization. They are broken into many small tribes, and their homes so interspersed among the settlements of white men, that *their power is entirely broken* and no fear should be entertained of a general war with them. *The time has passed when it was necessary to buy peace. It only remains to decide what should be done with them for the relief of the white people from their petty depredations*, and from the demoralizing influences accompanying the presence of savages in civilized communities, and also for the best interests of the Indians themselves.
>
> In council with the Indians *great care was taken not to implant*

in their minds the idea that the Government was willing to pay them for yielding lands which white men needed, and that as a recompense for such lands they would be furnished with clothing and food, and thus enabled to live in idleness. The question was presented to the Indian something in this light: The white men take these lands and use them, and from the earth secure to themselves food, clothing, and many other desirable things. Why should not the Indian do the same? The Government of the United States is anxious for you to try. If you will unite and agree to become farmers, it will secure to you permanent titles to such lands as you need, and will give you the necessary assistance to begin such a life, expecting that you will soon be able to take care of yourselves, as do white men and civilized Indians. (Emphasis added).[181]

Powell and Ingalls Report - Indians Indict Soldiers as Offensive and Evil

Powell and Ingalls conveyed the Indians' indictment of the presence of soldiers in their midst as offensive and evil. They recommended if their presence was not absolutely required, they be removed.

THE RELATION OF THE ARMY TO THESE INDIANS
Your commission cannot refrain from expressing its opinion concerning the effect of the presence of soldiers among these Indians where they are no longer needed to keep them under subjection. They regard the presence of a soldier as a standing menace, and to them the very *name of soldier is synonymous with all that is offensive and evil*. To the soldier they attribute their social demoralization and the unmentionable diseases with which they are infested. Everywhere, as we traveled among these Indians, the question would be asked us, "If we go to a reservation will the Government place soldiers there?" And to such a removal two objections were invariably urged; the first was, "We do not wish to desert the graves of our fathers," and the second, "We do not wish to give our women to the embrace of the soldiers." If the troops are not absolutely necessary in the country for the purpose of overawing these Indians, or protecting them in their rights against the encroachments of white men, it will be conceded that they should be removed. (Emphasis added).[182]

Powell's' Presumption that Removal of Indians from Homelands Necessary for Their Civilization

Powell's February 1880 letter to Senator Henry Teller acknowledged his clear understanding of the importance of Indian lands to them, yet he *forcefully* concluded their removal and severalty of their land were paramount to eliminating these 'savage societies' and the threat they represented to the U.S.

> All of our Indian troubles have arisen primarily and chiefly from two conditions inherent in savage society. The first is that the land belonging to an Indian clan or tribe is dear to it not only as a region from which it obtains subsistence but chiefly because it is the locus of its religion. The Indian religion is localized. Every spring, creek and river, every valley, hill and mountain as well as the trees that grow upon the soil are made sacred by the inherited traditions of their religion. These are all homes of their gods. When an Indian clan or tribe gives up its land it not only surrenders its home as understood by civilized people but its gods are abandoned and all its religion connected therewith, and connected with the worship of ancestors buried in the soil; that is, everything most sacred to Indian society is yielded up. Powell then concluded: "Such a removal of the Indians is the first step to be taken in their civilization ... The second great step in the civilization of the Indians consists in inducing them to take lands and property in severalty..."[183]

For Powell, assimilation was the only answer as written in the San Jose Weekly Mercury, Volume XXIII, Number 28, October 28, 1875:

> Social problems are so complex that few are willing or able to comprehend all the factors, and so the people are divided into two great parties, one crying for blood, and demanding the destruction of the Indians, the other begging that he may be left in his aboriginal condition, and that the progress may be stayed. Vain is the clamor of either party; the march of humanity cannot be stayed; fields must be made and gardens planted in the little valleys among the mountains of that Western land, as they have been in the broader valleys and plains of the East, and the mountains must yield their treasure of ore to the miner, and, whether we desire it or not, the ancient inhabitants of the country must be lost; and we may comfort

ourselves with the reflection that they are not destroyed, but are gradually absorbed, and become a part of more civilized communities.[184]

1873: Big Bonanza - Gold/Silver Discovery at Comstock

The California Bank was unable to buy out one man named John William Mackay, who had arrived in the area in 1859 from the California goldfields. He formed a business partnership with fellow Irishmen, James Graham Fair, James C. Flood, and William S. O'Brien, whose business dealt in mining stocks and operating silver mines on the Comstock Lode. In 1873, they discovered the richest ore body in the Comstock Lode, which was known as the "Big Bonanza" of the Consolidated Virginia and California Mine.

Boring straight through the flinty mountain rock, the *Consolidated Virginia in 1873 struck the Big Bonanza--the lode at this point was 54 feet wide and filled with gold and silver. It was probably the richest find in mining history.* Between 1873 and 1882 the Comstock Lode and its "Big Bonanza" yielded more than $100,000,000 and during the same time, two adjacent mines of the Bonanza Group produced the same amount. In all, the group produced nearly 400 million dollars in ore by 1882 — half of the silver in the U.S. during the period.

John Mackay was a miner's miner:

> Though millions have come at his call, he [John Mackay] still is studying among the levels. He dons the mining suit, takes his hammer and candle and goes prodding around 2,000 feet under ground, observing the dip of the wall rocks, the stratification and character of the ores, and is just as keen in searching out the secrets of the mine as when he was pleading with Flood and O'Brien to test the ground. He knows from the shade of ore whether it is good or bad; whether to order it mined out for milling, or whether to let it remain where the great convulsion left it. With him it is a science. He searches out the secrets of the Comstock as the astronomer studies the stars, or the movements of a planet or a comet; as the botanist the structure of a plant, or a politician the secrets of political economy. Though money is a factor in the problem the strong motive is the love of knowledge, in his case the knowledge of mines.[185]

Mark Twain, a reporter for the *Territorial Enterprise*, gave a pithy description of life in Virginia City in a letter to his mother: I have just heard five pistol shots down the street.... The pistol did its work well...two of my friends [were shot]. Both died within three minutes.[186]

1873: Crime of '73

In 1873 Congress passed the Mint Act, known in the western U.S. as the Crime of '73. The Mint Act put the U.S. on the gold standard and eliminated the minting of silver coins. With government demand for silver down and demand for gold rising, the price paid and the demand for Nevada's chief industrial product perilously fell. Attempts by the western states to convince Congress to return to bimetallism were defeated with the exception of a few minor, short-lived victories such as the Sherman Silver Purchase Act in 1890, which required the federal government to purchase 4½ million ounces of silver per month. It was repealed in 1893.

The ores of the "Big Bonanza" began to decline after 1878. In 1880 Nevada's mining stocks, which had been valued at $30,000,000 five years before, were worth less than $7,000,000. Nevada sank quickly into sleepy lethargy ... (Emphasis added).[187]

Nevada Indian Reservations Established in Decade of 1870

The Walker River, Pyramid Lake, Duck Valley and Moapa Reservations were established by Executive Order in the decade of 1870. I have included the text to provide an understanding of the brevity used in creating them. They basically consisted of a land description. It did not end white encroachment. Later, they were subject to allotment, with surplus lands opened for white settlement. The Department of the Interior continued its concentration effort.

1874: Walker River Indian Reservation

> Executive Mansion, March 19, 1874.
> It is hereby ordered that the reservation situated on Walker River, Nevada, as surveyed by Eugene Monroe, December, 1864 ... be withdrawn from public sale or other disposition and set apart for the use of the Pah-Ute Indians residing thereon. U. S. GRANT.

Indian agent Calvin Bateman reported on August 31, 1874, that the reservation "is the home of at least six hundred Pah-utes, who if absent at all, are only so temporarily. ... Here the government has promised them an abiding-place, and justice and honor demand that the compact remain inviolate. I am glad that the executive order ... reaffirms the obligation and sets at rest the question of its perpetuity."[188]

In 1902, Congress acted to enable part of the reservation to be opened to settlement. By a series of statutes and an agreement, allotments of irrigable lands and cash payments were made to individual Indians, tribal grazing and timber lands were set aside and the Indians "cede(d) ... and relinquish(ed) to the United States all right, title and interest" to the remaining lands in the reservation. In 1906 the relinquished lands were opened by presidential proclamation to white settlement.

1874: Pyramid Lake Paiutes' Reservation

EXECUTIVE MANSION, MARCH 23, 1874. It is hereby ordered that the tract of country known and occupied as the Pyramid Lake Indian Reservation in Nevada, as surveyed by Eugene Monroe in January, 1865 ... be withdrawn from sale or other disposition and set apart for the Pah-Ute and other Indians residing thereon. U. S. Grant[189]

1874: Reduction of Pyramid Lake Paiutes' Reservation Materially Diminished Agricultural Base

The *Pyramid Lake Paiutes' Reservation* was diminished in 1874. Though the Department of the Interior would admit it was an impermissible error, nothing was done to correct it. If they weren't able to become self-supporting, their aid would be cut-off.

> *By this reduction* [some ten miles from the south] *the tillable land of the reservation [Pyramid Lake Paiutes' Reservation] was materially diminished; an error that, in our opinion, should not have been permitted, for it left the area of farming lands quite small.* (Emphasis added).

The plan adopted by me ever since coming to Nevada has been to impress upon the minds of the Indians the fact that the Government extended aid for the express purpose of benefiting them in the way of their becoming self-supporting at the earliest possible time; and that a reasonable time only would be given to the trial, and, if not improved by then, they would be left to their indolence as unworthy of further aid.[190]

1875: Shoshone Indian Reservation Needed

Consistently, many Department of the Interior representatives reported the need for a reservation for the Shoshonees given the depletion of their subsistence base. For an unknown reason resulting in incomprehensible cruelty, this plea was ignored decade after decade. This is equally incredulous given the huge aboriginal domain of the Western Shoshones. Levi Gheen repeated this request in 1875.

I would respectfully suggest that a suitable reservation be set apart for the Shoshones of Nevada as soon as practicable. The whites are rapidly settling up the country, and in many cases the Indians are compelled to give up their little farms. The game is being driven out, and in a short time there will be no place suitable for a reservation, and the Indians will have nothing to subsist upon. They express an anxiety to be taken to a reservation suitable for them, that they might be assisted in case of necessity, and be able to support themselves without fear of being molested.[191]

Resource poverty was having profound effects upon Shoshones:

Captain Sam, another chief from the north side of the Central Pacific Railroad... stated that he could not see what was to become of the Shoshones in his country; that the game was all gone; the trees that bore pine-nuts were cut down and burned in the quartz-mills and other places; the grass-seed, heretofore used by them for food, was no more; the grass-land was all claimed by the whites, and the grass cut for hay before the seed was ripe; that the good land was or soon would be all claimed and cultivated by the white people; and that *his Indians would soon be compelled to work for the ranchers for two bits (twenty-five cents) per day, or starve.* (Emphasis added).

~ 392 ~

Tsa-wie … states that himself and many others of his tribe are in favor of a tract of land being reserved for the Shoshones. Levi A. Green, Farmer in Charge of Western Shoshonees.[192]

1877: Reservation for Western Shoshone at Duck Valley

DUCK VALLEY RESERVATION. [Partly In Idaho.)
EXECUTIVE MANSION, April 16, 1877.
It is hereby ordered that the following-described tract of country, situated partly in the Territory of Idaho and partly in the State of Nevada, be, and the same hereby is, withdrawn from the public domain: … And the above-named tract of land is hereby set apart as a reservation for the Western Shoshone Indians, subject to such modifications of boundary as a location of limits shall determine. R. B. HAYES.

Indian Agent John How, 1879: The Duck Valley Reserve, as set apart by President Hayes for the use of the Western Shoshones, has proved well suited for that purpose, both in regard to its distance from white settlements and the fertility of the soil. The Owyhee River, running through its center, gives ample water for irrigating purposes. The salmon ascending the river has aided us very much this season, and we hope in another year to utilize them as permanent food.[193]

1877: Reservation for Northwestern Shoshone at Carlin Farms

NEVADA. CARLIN FARMS RESERVATION.
EXECUTIVE MANSION, May 10, 1877.
It is hereby ordered that all that tract of country in the State of Nevada (known as the Carlin Farms) lying within the following boundaries, viz: … be, and the same hereby is, withdrawn from sale or settlement, and set apart as a reservation for the Northwestern Shoshone Indians. R. B. HAYES.

1879: Reservation for Northwestern Shoshone at Carlin Farms Canceled

EXECUTIVE MANSION, January 16, 1879.
It is hereby ordered that the order of May 10, 1877, setting apart as a reservation for the Northwestern Shoshone Indians of Nevada the following-described lands (known as the Carlin Farms), viz: … be, and the same is hereby, canceled and said lands are restored to their original status. R. B. HAYES.

1877: Whites Fomenting War at Duck Valley Indian Reservation

In a common trend, whites would circulate false rumors of war by Indians to foment war. War would result in a reduction of lands claimed by Indians and the input of federal dollars to bolster the non-Indian economy. In investigating a claim of war at Duck Valley Indian Reservation, the reports were found to be baseless. *"I believe that some of the white men were more anxious for an Indian war than the Indians themselves."* (Emphasis added).[194]

1878: Whites Trespassing at Pyramid Lake Paiutes' Reservation

On November 29, 1859, to preserve Indian rights to Pyramid Lake, located approximately 30 miles northeast of Reno, lands around the lake were withdrawn from the public domain by the U.S. General Land Office. On March 23, 1875, the Pyramid Lake Paiutes' Reservation was formally proclaimed by Executive Order of the President of the United States.

Nonetheless, given the valuable fisheries at Pyramid Lake Paiutes' Reservation and the slack enforcement of the law, whites were willing to run the slight risk of being caught trespassing. Agents consistently reported not having the numbers to adequately police Indian lands or courts willing to convict non-Indians. One readily available tactic was to 'skip town.'

> One great cause of discontent among these Indians is the *occupation of their fishing grounds on Pyramid Lake by white trespassers.* The *profits of this trade are large enough to induce these men to disregard the law* and its officers, and the want of definite monuments to define the boundaries seems to give them a technical defense before the courts. (Emphasis added).[195]

One result of the long-standing encroachment and harassment was that the Paiute were progressively restricted to the least productive parts of the original reservation. In a "Catch-22" situation, the Paiute were then accused of not making the best use of reservation lands, thus providing supposed justification for further attempts to reduce the size of the reserve.[196]

1879: Pyramid Lake Is within Valid Indian Reservation

After many years of controversy over fishing rights on Pyramid Lake, the Nevada State Journal (Reno) reported that on July 1, 1879, the [U.S.] Supreme Court "rendered a decision in the Pyramid Lake case...The decision...is to the effect that Pyramid Lake is within a valid Indian reservation..." This decision leaves the Indians in peaceful possession of the contested fishing lands.

1879: Lies about Pyramid Lake Paiutes' Improvement by Indian Agents

In Indian Agent Garvey's Annual Report, he noted a frequent occurrence by Indian agents—lying about the improvement of the conditions of the Indians under their jurisdiction. In this case, Agent Garvey disputed the past lies:

> Nevada Indian Agency, Pyramid Lake Paiutes' Reservation, August 16, 1879.
> I find that the Indians have been reported as steadily improving each year [for past decade when] these Indians have gradually been leaving the reservations for the past five years, caused by the failure of crops, for the want of irrigating ditches, encroachment of whites upon the fisheries, and an inadequate appropriation. W. M. Garvey, U.S. Indian Agent.[197]

1880: White Trespassers at Pyramid Lake Paiutes' Reservation Indicted

In a shameful manner, Indians would be falsely led to believe that something would be done about trespassers on their land. Federal cases in their favor were ignored by cunning, determined and patient whites who taunted the government to prosecute them. Just as President Jackson had allegedly said about the Supreme Court in 1830 when it ruled in favor of the Cherokee Nation: "John Marshall has made his decision; now let him enforce it!"

> A striking illustration of the inadequacy of the law is afforded in the case of the Pyramid Lake Reservation in Nevada. *At the February term of the United States district court for the district of Nevada, certain fishermen, trespassers, who had been previously removed from the reservation by the military, but who had returned thereto, were indicted, charged with having returned, in violation of section 2148, Revised Statutes. ... Upon appeal to the United States circuit court, the judgment of the court below was affirmed, thereby establishing: first, that the whole of Pyramid Lake is within an Indian reservation; and, second, that it is Indian country within the meaning of the intercourse laws, and that trespassers may rightfully be removed therefrom. ... Recent advices from the agent in charge state that the offenders*

and those whose interests prompt them to engage in this unlawful pursuit, emboldened by the delay in enforcing even the defective statutes which exist, conclude that they have nothing to fear, and are busily engaged in perfecting their plans, securing large quantities of minnows, purchasing boats, and getting in readiness for renewed operations on the lake. (Emphasis added).[198]

WHITE SETTLERS. At the time this reservation [Pyramid Lake] was set apart by Executive order there were a number of families settled in the valley, and they still remain for the purpose of holding their claims. *They occupy the best lands and control much of the water which is needed for the reservation*, and it was only by their sufferance that the Indians were able to plant a crop this fall. It will not be possible for the Indians to proceed with any extensive farming until these people are removed. There is danger of other troubles arising also, from their presence on the reservation, as there is *a constant conflict between them and the Indians, which becomes more bitter daily*, and, as the number of Indians is increased, it is liable to result in disastrous consequences. (Emphasis added).[199]

Some of their friends unite with them in an effort to have part of this fishery set aside from the reservation and thrown open to the public. This attempt by these violators of law to deprive these Indians of their most valuable franchise, I look upon as a piece of effrontery equal to that of a highwayman, who should ask the law-making power to so modify the laws that he could ply his vocation on certain designated highways. I must, therefore, enter my solemn protest against such a proposed dismemberment of any of the reservations under my charge.[200]

1881: President Hayes Pardons White Trespassers on Pyramid Lake Paiutes' and Walker River Indian Reservations

Relying on a legal technicality—the lack of an adequate boundary permitting a knowing trespass, President Rutherford B. Hayes set aside the conviction of trespassers at Pyramid Lake and Walker River Indian Reservations, undermining the ability to stop this poaching.

... in early January of 1879, the Pyramid Lake Paiute Reservation Indian agent called on the military to evict

~ 396 ~

six fishing companies, plus twenty independent-minded commercial fishermen, and confiscate 73,740 pounds of fish—with an estimated worth of more than $7,000—those criminals reportedly returned just as soon as the soldiers vacated. Nor did the 1879 arrest of nine fishermen for illegally sinking nets across the Truckee within (contested) reservation boundaries and for selling fish without a permit seem to mean much, insofar as those violators ultimately were granted a presidential pardon.[201]

Indian Agent McMaster attributed it to the frequent visits by whites:

> Pyramid Lake Paiutes' and Walker River Indian Reservations— Then, too, the lakes are visited by white persons, trespassers, which it is difficult to eradicate, as even after the conviction and sentence of the trespasser, a year ago, *sufficient influence was brought to bear on the President (Hayes) to induce him to pardon the trespassers.* (Emphasis added).[202]

> ... [the alleged trespasser had] *good reason to suppose he was without the limits of the reservation,* his case having been presented to the President for pardon and a pardon granted ... (Emphasis added).[203]

1873: Powell and Ingalls Report on Moapa Indian Reservation

Special Commissioners J. W. Powell and G. W. Ingalls reported on the condition of the Mo'apa Reservation in 1873 as follows:

> The Mo'apa Reservation [for the Moapa Band of Paiute Indians] though large in territory, is composed chiefly of arid, barren mountains and deserts of drifting sands. The only part of the valley fit for agricultural purposes is the few acres— not more than 6,000—which can be redeemed by the use of the waters of the Mo'-a-pa, and some grass-lands of no greater extent, for the *climate is so arid that agricultural operations cannot be carried on without artificial irrigation.* ... The reservation does not afford extensive facilities for cattle-raising, though a few cows can be kept with advantage. (Emphasis added).[204]

1874: President Hayes Sets Apart Moapa Reservation

> EXECUTIVE MANSION, February 12, 1874
>
> In lieu of an Executive Order dated the 12th of March last setting apart certain lands in Nevada as a reservation for the Indians of that locality, which order is hereby canceled, it is hereby ordered that there be withdrawn from sale or other disposition, and set apart for the use of the Pah-Ute and such other Indians as the department may see fit to locate thereon, the tract of country bounded and described as follows ...U.S. Grant[205]

1875: Moapa Reservation Reduced by Congressional Act

In 1875, the reservation was reduced to 1,000 acres. White settlers claiming land before the Reservation was set aside refused to sell their property and improvements to the U.S.

> DEPARTMENT OF THE INTERIOR, Washington, D. C., July 3, 1875.
>
> Sir: I return the report of William Vandever, United States Indian inspector, which accompanied your communication of the 28th ultimo, in which are defined the boundaries of the Pai-Ute Reservation in southeastern Nevada, embracing 1,000 acres, to which area said reservation was by act of March 8, 1875, declared to be reduced; the land to be selected by the Secretary of the Interior.
>
> The selection of the tract of country described in the report of Inspector Vandever is approved, and hereby set apart as a reservation for the Pai-Ute Indians.
> Very respectfully C. Delano, Secretary.

Senator William M. Stewart of Nevada led a legislative effort to reduce the Reservation to 1000 acres, through Congress without a hearing. By March of 1875, he had succeeded in passing a resolution reducing the entire reservation to 1000 acres, "in such manner as not to include the claim of any settler or miner." (18 Stat. 445). Secretary of Interior C. Delano confirmed the selection and reissued federal land for the reservation on July 3, 1875.

Despite formal designation of the Moapa Reservation, white settlers already established within the newly formed boundaries declined offered compensation and refused to move. As a result of this conflict, and of protests from mining interests, in 1875 the reservation was abruptly cut in size to 1,000 acres. (Emphasis added).[206]

1880: Appeals for Re-Expansion of Moapa Reservation

Indian agents made appeals for a re-expansion of the Moapa Reservation. One of these requests came from Nevada Indian Agent James Spencer. In 1880, Agent Spencer toured the reservations of the region and reported that conditions at Moapa were far worse than other reservations in his district:

> Moapa River *The reservation is entirely deserted by the Indians solely because it is unprotected from stock owned by herders [which] devour every green thing in their way... I am also informed that these Indians have reaped no benefit whatever from this reservation for several years ... This is a painful history for me to write, and reveals gross neglect or mismanagement of the affairs of the Moapa River Reservation.* (Emphasis added).[207]

> I ... recommended this enlarged reservation to be set aside by Executive order... No action, of which I am apprised, has yet been taken on my recommendation, and as a consequence the Indians are scattered over the surrounding country for 200 miles around, eking out a precarious existence by working, begging, root-digging, and insect-eating—a life not of their choice, but forced upon them for lack of a protected reservation equipped with a very few of the necessary appliances for commencing the work of tilling the soil.[208]

1881-1882: Pyramid Lake Paiutes' Reservation Fishery - Lifeline for Paiutes

In another testament relative to the importance of the Pyramid Lake Paiutes' Reservation fishery to the Paiute Indian Tribe, the new Indian Agent, Joseph M. McMaster noted in his annual report to the Secretary of Interior that "The most important means of livelihood to the Indians besides working for white people is their fisheries, the trout from Pyramid Lake and Walker Lake being accounted the very finest, and bring as high a price as any known to the writer." With respect to the numerous acts of trespassing on reservation lands, Mr. McMaster wrote: "And now if the department would order a survey of the reservation so that the lines could be positively defined, and authorize a sufficient force of Indian police, trespassers could be kept off or made to suffer, and the Indians get the benefit which is their due from the fisheries in these waters which have been reserved to them."[209]

In his 1882 annual report to the Secretary of Interior, Indian Agent Joseph M. McMaster noted that the "...[Pyramid Lake Paiute Indians] have an important fishery, which last season furnished over 70,000 pounds [of trout], for which the price was 8 cents per pound, or $5,600..."

1884: Trespassers Not Removed from Walker River Indian Reservation – One-Sided Justice

Whites encroaching on Indian lands on the Walker River Indian Reservation continued the argument there was no survey to prove up Indian title. It was the U.S.' responsibility to survey their lands and adequately mark the boundaries, which they negligently put-off. Due to the boundaries controversy the Indian Agent determined it was "inexpedient to undertake to remove any" of the trespassers.

> One thing that they (the Indians) do not just understand is why the trespassers are not removed from the reservation. The agent has informed them that the whole matter has been referred to Washington, and that soldiers have been promised to remove them. But the soldiers fail to come, and they think the law is all for the white man and none for the Indian.[210]

> At Walker River Reserve there has been considerable dissatisfaction among the Indians on account of trespassers on Walker Lake. ... Some of these farmers claim that they located their land prior to the time that the reservation was set aside for these Indians. Others claim they have purchased their lands from the State of Nevada under the school-land grant, while some of the fishermen insist that the reservation lines do not take in that portion of the river. Taking all these things into consideration, I have deemed it inexpedient to undertake to remove any of them. A survey ... of the outward boundaries of Pyramid Lake and Walker River Reservations should be made and properly marked with suitable monuments, substantially erected, defining the exact lines of said reserves.[211]

1885: Commissioner Recommends All Indians Be Removed to Two Indian Reservations

In 1885, in a continued effort to open even more Indian land to white settlers and ostensibly cut agency costs, Commissioner J.D.C. Atkins recommended there should only be two reservations, aside from the Indian Territory. Perfunctorily, the Department of the Interior advanced its reasons as bringing Indians under more rigid U.S. control, minimizing conflict between Indians and white settlers, and encouraging Indians to assimilate.

> Com. Report: [Recommended by Commissioner J.D.C. Atkins that all Indians] in Nevada, Upper California, Oregon, and Washington Territory, [be removed] to the Yakama Reservation, or some suitable one in that vicinity, selected for that purpose; while the southwestern Indians might be advantageously concentrated upon one or two existing reservations in that locality. Of course this policy could only be adopted by first obtaining the consent of the Indians already on the reservations upon which concentration is suggested, and the consent of those whom it is suggested to remove, all of which would be dependent upon action by Congress.[212]

1886: No Appropriations for Duck Valley Paiutes for Promised Equipment

In a continuing saga, Indians would settle on reservations based on promises made of supplying them with necessary farming equipment. They would accordingly relocate but the U.S. would fail to keep its end of the bargain. As late as 1886, this is reported by Indian Agent John B. Scott, Western Shoshone Agency:

> The destitute Piutes, who were induced to settle on this reservation (Duck Valley) under promises made them that they would this fall be furnished by the Government with wagons and farming implements, I regret to say have become greatly demoralized and discontented since learning that Congress had failed to make the appropriation necessary for that purpose.[213]

1887: Support Yourselves or Starve

With the Department of the Interior's lack of public support for continuing aid to Indians and the associated lack of Congressional appropriations, more and more Indians were being denied aid. In one case, John B. Scott, Indian Agent, reported his "regret to state there is very little agricultural or arable land, as well as an insufficiency of water for irrigating purposes" for the Paiutes, but then goes on to agree that the Indians should support themselves or starve.[214]

1888: Major Disputes over Pyramid Lake Paiutes' and Walker River Indian Reservations

Given the Pyramid Lake Paiutes' and Walker River Indian Reservations valuable fisheries, it is not surprising that encroachments would facilely be made by white settlers. Even with a resurvey made to determine the reservations boundaries, the agent in charge believed litigation would ensue as these whites were intransigent as to their occupancy and rights. The railroad depot town of Wadsworth had even been established and settled within the Pyramid Lake Paiutes' Reservation. This controversy would continue unresolved until 1897, with detrimental consequences following thereafter.

> Yet it is estimated that there is only about 5,000 acres of tillable land on both reserves, some 1,200 acres of which are occupied by whites ... Some of these people claim that they have a title from the State to the land they hold, while others claim their title by location prior to the Executive order setting apart this land from public domain for Indians. As a re-survey has been made within the year, no doubt, if it is approved, there will be some litigation involved before these people will consent to abandon their lands. ... The town of Wadsworth [situated within the exterior boundaries of the reservation] should be cut off from the reservation and the money derived therefrom applied for the benefits of the Indians in purchasing cattle, sheep, or otherwise.[216]

1891: Negotiations for Reduction of Pyramid Lake Paiutes' Reservation - Commission Appointed

Commissioner T.J. Morgan would report in 1891 that Congress' Indian appropriation act for the fiscal year ending June 30, 1892 (26 Stats., 1010) called for the appointment of a commission to negotiate with the Northern Paiutes for a reduction of their reservation at Pyramid Lake. Anytime a commission is appointed, the affected tribe(s) must be wary. Not only with the caution of a biased commission seeking reduction of the Pyramid Lake Paiutes' Reservation, Agent C.C. Warner would opine of the *advantages* to the Northern Paiutes. The revenues from the sale of the southern end of the Indian

Reservation would provide funds for a band of cattle. His recommendation would carry significant weight as the higher-up officials in the Department of the Interior supported the reduction and this Agent's input was from someone on the ground.

> White Settlers on the Reserve. This has become a hackneyed subject, but should be settled, which *can be done not only to the satisfaction of the Indians but to their very great advantage*. My plan would be to cut off a certain portion of the south end of the reserve, the extent to be determined on, where the thriving little town of Wadsworth is situated ... This sale would produce quite a fund which could be made of almost incalculable value to the Pah-Utes. With it I would recommend buying them a band of cattle ... (Emphasis added).[217]

However, once a plan is initiated for a reduction of an Indian reservation, other players introduce their desires. Suddenly added to the plan was cutting-off the northern end of the Pyramid Lake Paiutes' Reservation as well. Here, Agent Warner at least drew the line.

> I am reliably informed that there is a *movement on foot to have the north end of Pyramid Lake reserve cut off. Should this be done it would result in a very great wrong to the Indians,* and I am decidedly opposed to it. (Emphasis added).[218]

1892: Continued Negotiations for Reduction of Pyramid Lake Paiutes' Reservation, Termination of Walker River Indian Reservation and Removal of Walker River Indian Reservation Northern Paiutes to Pyramid Lake Paiutes' Reservation

As negotiations continued, an agreement was reached for the surrender by the Northern Paiutes of the southern end of the Pyramid Lake Reservation on October 17, 1891, including the town of Wadsworth. In spite of this initial plan being approved for payment of cattle to the value of $20,000, the people of Nevada added the surrender of the Walker River Indian Reservation into the parley, with the removal of the Walker River Indian Reservation Northern Paiutes to the Pyramid Lake Paiutes' Reservation.[219]

1895: Indians Opposed to Reduction of Pyramid Lake Paiutes' Reservation, Termination of Walker River Indian Reservation and Removal of Walker River Indian Reservation Northern Paiutes to Pyramid Lake Paiutes' Reservation

Given the disapproval of the proposed legislation by the Board of Indian Commissioners, headed by Albert Smiley, Commissioner Browning sought the input of Indian Agent I. J. Wootten to S. Bill 99.

Indian Agent Wootten replied:

> *The Indians of both of the reserves are unanimous in their opposition to the propositions contained in the bill,* and it would require the strongarm of the Government to force them to change their opinions. Moreover, even if the Indians were willing to give their voluntary approval to the provisions of the bill, I would deem it my bounden duty to enter a protest against its enactment, for the reason that it would be an *unfair, unjust, unwarranted, and uncalled-for piece of legislation, enacted solely in the interest of a few wealthy stockmen and mining men and the Carson and Colorado Railroad Company as against the best interests of the Pah-Ute Indians.* ... (Emphasis added).[222]

Commissioner Browning concluded that the proposed legislation did not contain a single meritorious feature and urged that it not pass.

> "Senator Stewart recently advised this office informally that he thought it best to abandon the proposed legislation."[223]

1896: Commissioner Recommends Reduction of Southern End of Pyramid Lake Paiutes' Reservation as Compromise

With five years having passed and the failure of 'Senate Bill 99,' the Pyramid Lake Reservation Indians approved the reduction of the southern end only. It is curious to know if the threatened reduction of a larger part of their reservation was merely a façade to get them to agree to the seven-mile reduction for $20,000 to be expended on cattle. Further, the purchase of cattle was fraught with frauds that could be perpetrated: age, weight of some but not all, place of weighing, quality, etc.[224]

In 1897, Congress approved the reduction of the southern end of the Pyramid Lake Paiutes' Reservation. In 1898, with the wheels of bureaucracy turning slowly, Congress' Indian appropriation act, approved July 1, 1898 (30 Stats., p. 594), contained the following clause relating to the Pyramid Lake Paiutes' Reservation, and the inhabitants of the town of Wadsworth located thereon:

> That the inhabitants of the town of Wadsworth, in the county of Washoe, State of Nevada, be, and they are hereby, *authorized to proceed and acquire title to the town site of ... Wadsworth ...* if there are any Indians residing in said town and in possession of lots of ground with improvements, they shall have the same rights of purchase under the town-site laws as white citizens... (Emphasis added).[225]

Pyramid Lake Paiutes' Defrauded for Payment of Reduction of Southern End of Reservation

So as not to have to pay for their land, the white settlers simply refused to take any legal action to secure title. In the meantime, the town of Wadsworth died as the new owner of the rail line, Southern Pacific, bypassed it for the nearby town of Sparks. Southern Pacific gave everyone clear deed to a 50' x 140' lot for the grand sum of $1 in the new town. "To make the deal more enticing, it offered to pick up and move—free of charge—every house in Wadsworth and reassemble it in this new town."[226]

The Northern Paiutes wouldn't receive the treasure trove for the seven-mile reduction from the sales to the citizens of Wadsworth, now long gone.

> I reiterate the statement contained in my last two reports that *I do not believe the citizens of the town will take any action toward acquiring title to the town site* under the provisions of the Indian appropriation act approved July 1, 1898. (Emphasis added).[227]

Unfounded Claims of Minerals within Pyramid Lake Paiutes' Reservation

As to claims of minerals within the Pyramid Lake Paiutes' Reservation, Fred B. Spriggs, Superintendent and Acting Indian Agent, "followed up some of the reports as to the presence of minerals within the limits of the reserve, but they have proved in every case to be without foundation."[228]

Fallon Paiute-Shoshone Indian Reservation (1894-1907)

The Fallon Paiute-Shoshone Indian Reservation was officially established in Churchill County, Nevada, when land allotments were granted from the public domain to certain Paiute and Shoshone Indians pursuant to the General Allotment Act, as amended. Originally, 50 allotments of 160 acres each (8,000 total acres) were granted to individual Indians.[220] In 1894, another 146 land allotments of 160 acres each (23,360 acres total) were granted to the Fallon Paiute-Shoshone Indian Reservation near the present-day city of Fallon in Churchill County, Nevada. Reservation acreage now totaled 31,360 acres. In 1906, an agreement was effected whereby the Fallon Paiute and Shoshone Indians of the Fallon Paiute-Shoshone Indian Reservation (initially established on February 8, 1887) would release their original 160-acre allotments of non-irrigable land and receive instead 10-acre allotments of irrigable land with paid up water rights. Of the original 196 allottees on the public domain, 189 consented to the exchange. Accordingly, this resulted in a reduction of the reservation acreage from 31,360 acres to 3,010 acres. In 1907, the U.S. Department of the Interior reserved an additional area of 4,640 acres for the reservation on behalf of the Fallon Paiute and Shoshone Indians who had relinquished their original allotments and such other Indians as might, on investigation, be found entitled to allotments thereon. (Later, in 1917, the USDI would add an additional 840 acres on the north boundary of the Fallon Paiute-Shoshone Indian Reservation, which then brought the reservation's total area up to 5,480 acres.)[221]

1889: Ghost Dance - "Father, I Come"

The Ghost Dance was the foundation of a spiritual movement that came about in the late 1880s when conditions were horrific on Indian reservations and American Indians needed something to give them hope. A Northern Paiute Indian named Wovoka claimed to have had a prophetic vision during the solar eclipse, on January 1, 1889, which entailed the resurrection of the Paiute dead and the removal of white settlers from their lands. To make the vision come true, he taught his people that they must live righteously and perform a circular dance called the Ghost Dance.

Mrs. Z.A. Parker, a teacher at Pine Ridge, observed the Ghost Dance on June 20, 1890, near White Clay Creek, Oglala Lakota County, South Dakota, and described it to James Mooney, an ethnographer for the Smithsonian Institution's Bureau of American Ethnology.

> ... Dancing in a circle, chanting, "Father, I come," they stopped ... set up the most fearful, heart-piercing wails I ever

heard-crying, moaning, groaning, and shrieking out their grief, and naming over their departed friends and relatives, at the same time taking up handfuls of dust at their feet, washing their hands in it, and throwing it over their heads. Finally, they raised their eyes to heaven, their hands clasped high above their heads, and stood straight and perfectly still, invoking the power of the Great Spirit to allow them to see and talk with their people who had died.

... [When they arose again,] the most intense excitement began. They would go as fast as they could, their hands moving from side to side, their bodies swaying, their arms, with hands gripped tightly in their neighbors', swinging back and forth with all their might. If one, more weak and frail, came near falling, he would be jerked up and into position until tired nature gave way. The ground had been worked and worn by many feet, until the fine, flour-like dust lay light and loose to the depth of two or three inches. The wind, which had increased, would sometimes take it up, enveloping the dancers and hiding them from view. In the ring were men, women, and children; the strong and the robust, the weak consumptive, and those near to death's door. They believed those who were sick would be cured by joining in the dance and losing consciousness. From the beginning they chanted, to a monotonous tune, the words:

> Father, I come;
> Mother, I come;
> Brother, I come;
> Father, give us back our arrows.

All of which they would repeat over and over again until first one and then another would break from the ring and stagger away and fall down.

When the dance spread to the Lakota, the BIA agents became alarmed. They claimed that the Lakota developed a militaristic approach to the dance and began making "ghost shirts" they thought would protect them from bullets. The BIA agent in charge of the Lakota sent the tribal police to arrest Sitting Bull, to force him to stop the dancing. Sitting Bull ended up being killed, along with a number of policemen.[229]

1902: Gold at Goldfield

In 1900, Nevada was entering its third decade of depression.

> The incomparable Comstock Lode, which had stimulated the migration of 60,000 people into Nevada Territory, spawned numerous smaller mining booms between 1805 and the 1870s, which died out by 1880. Since then, no new strikes of importance had been found, the state's population had fallen to 40,000, and the economy was suffering the effects of 20 years of decline. Some cynics even suggested that Nevada should revert to territorial status. *Such was the fate of a state whose entire economy was built around a mining frontier's boom and bust cycle.* (Emphasis added).[230]

> With gold discoveries at Tonapah (Goldfield), in December 1902, however, the cycle was reversed.

1904: Bullfrog Mining District, Rhyolite

Another gold rush was ignited with the discovery of gold in the Bullfrog District on August 9, 1904. High-grade surface ore assayed at $700 per ton.

> By 1906, 165 mining companies were reported working in the district, and all had hopes of developing another mother lode with just a few more feet of digging.[231]

> The Rhyolite Stock Exchange was incorporated and opened on March 25, 1907, to ease the effects of feverish stock trading on the overworked telegraph wires to Goldfield and San Francisco. In June, the Bullfrog-Goldfield Railroad came into town, opening rail connections with the north. In September, electric power was brought into Rhyolite over the poles of the Nevada-California Power Company. The power was hooked into the already-wired homes, stores, and offices of Rhyolite and into the machinery of the big Montgomery-Shoshone mill, which soon began operations.

> Several of these miscellaneous Bullfrog companies bought property in the district without ever planning to sink a pick in the ground, aiming to sell stock to gullible investors. Some of these included the Bullfrog Winner Mining Company,

the Bullfrog Western Mining Company, the United Bullfrog Mining Company, the Bullfrog Plutos Mining, and Milling Company, the Bullfrog Gold Note Mining Company, and the Bullfrog Jumper Company, and dozens of others.

In one fraudulent effort, J. P. Loftus and James R. Davis determined to mine the pockets of stockholders when it became evident that its Gold Bar Mine was low-grade.

> Like many mining promoters before and since Loftus' reply amply summed up the philosophy of the Bullfrog Gold Bar Mining Company. "I am not the guardian of the public. It is up to the public to decide these things for themselves." When further pressed by the reporter as to the lack of ethics displayed by the company, Loftus reiterated his feelings in the best tradition of the nineteenth-century robber barons — "The public be damned."[232]

The Bullfrog District produced $1,687,792 worth of ore between 1907 and 1910.

Nevada's Mining Magnates

John W. Mackay, James G. Fair, James C. Flood, William S. O'Brien formed the Bonanza Firm. They were known as the "Silver Kings" or the "Bonanza Kings." From the Big Bonanza on the Comstock Lode, they produced more than $180 million in ore in just over four years. The Silver Kings went on to dominate the Comstock, establishing the Pacific Mill and Mining Co. to monopolize the milling of ore. They financed operations through their Nevada Bank of San Francisco. They bought the Virginia and Gold Hill Water Co., which supplied the camps and mines with water from the Sierras; and formed the Pacific Wood, Lumber, and Fluming Co. to ensure supplies of timber for use in their mines. Their Pacific Lumber and Flume operation from the Lake Tahoe Basin of fifteen miles enabled trestled logs to be propelled by waters rushing faster than any train. "These acquisitions," one historian wrote, "gave the owners control of the whole mining process, excluding transportation via the Virginia & Truckee Railroad."[233] Bonanza dividends for the first three months of 1876 averaged $10 per share and then skidded to $2 per share by year's end. By the end of the decade, *dividends on the Comstock were down to 50 cents per share.*

Mid-1870s Millionaires' Club

In the mid-1870s, the Millionaires Club of the Washoe was formed by the 'elite gentlemen' of the Comstock in the hey-day of the mining activity, termed the "Silver Seventies." The Club's exclusive quarters housed one of the finest libraries east of San Francisco, an elegant billiard room, a parlor adorned with Italian marble and bronze statuettes, and a wine room that boasted an elaborately carved black walnut sideboard. The prominent members and guests included General Sheridan, President U.S. Grant, inventor Thomas Edison, General Sherman, mining tycoons James G. Fair, John Mackay, and many more of the Who's Who of Comstock and Pacific Coast history.

With the decline of mining came the demise of the Club. The *Territorial Enterprise newspaper, of September 9, 1897, said, "The Washoe Club is no more." "The closing of the Washoe Club marks an era in the history of Nevada, as did its opening."* (Emphasis added).[234]

Get in on "Ground Floor" to Make Money – 'Firstest Gets the Mostest'

One of the first rules of the mining game is to get in on the "ground floor" to make money. The process of becoming a ghost town after the ore is exhausted was organized as well.

> Investor confidence is weakened by the financial difficulties of a declining economy.
> Shady dealings come to the forefront.
> Stock prices plummet.
> Litigation ensues.
> The mills continue to mill, but only have low-grade ore.
> The mines close.
> The mills stop their machinery.
> Businesses began to decline; to cut their losses, they close up shop.
> Banks close their doors.
> Tax rolls reflect the death knell of owners. They leave town, letting their properties be confiscated by the county treasurer, rather than spending more money in paying property taxes to a losing cause.
> Newspapers close up the presses.
> The railroads discontinue service to the town.
> Electricity is cut off and the company salvages its poles and wire.
> The mines gas hoist and gallows frame are dismantled.
> The town is slowly dismantled to serve the needs of new boom camps, auctioning its property to satisfy the claims of its grumbling creditors.

~ 410 ~

There is no further word from the failed venture.
The crumbling remains of once imposing structures, dwindle among the scorpions and rattlesnakes, tumble weeds rolling through.

Nevada Indians never had a chance to take part in the mining truism: the *"firstest gets the mostest."*

Author Notes: Nevada

The Treaty of 1855 [NOT RATIFIED] (Contested by Shoshones Up to Present Day)

Eastern Shoshone Treaty, (18 Stat. 685), July 2, 1863

Northwestern Shoshone Treaty, (13 Stat. 663), July 30, 1863

Western Shoshone Treaty, Ruby Valley (Vigorously Contested by Shoshones Up to Present Day), 18 Stat. 689, October 1, 1863

Shoshonee-Goship Treaty, (13 Stat. 681), October 12, 1863

Mixed Bands Treaty, (5 Kapp. 693), October 14, 1863 (NOT PROCLAIMED)

Notes: Nevada

1. History of Humboldt County, Nevada. http://genealogytrails.com/nev/humboldt/history/histhum.html (accessed online January 17, 2023).
2. "Sagebrush and Salt Flats. Utah Crossroads of the West." National Trails System, National Park Service, 2010.
3. Twain, Mark. Roughing it. Vol. 1. Harper & Row, 1913.
4. Eugene S. Hunn, Knowledge Systems, in A COMPANION TO THE ANTHROPOLOGY OF AMERICAN INDIANS 148, 150 (Thomas Biolsi ed., 2004). 2006 DENVER UNIVERSITY LAW REVIEW SYMPOSIUM: BORROWING THE LAND: CULTURES OF OWNERSHIP IN THE WESTERN LANDSCAPE: ARTICLE: Listening to All the Voices, Old and New: The Evolution of Land Ownership in the Modern West, 83 Denv. U.L. Rev. 945, 958.
5. Stoffle, Richard W., and Henry F. Dobyns 1982 Navagantu: Nevada Indians Comment on the Intermountain Power Project, Nevada Section of Intermountain-Adelanto Bipole I Proposal. Manuscript on file at the Applied Urban Field School, University of Wisconsin Parkside, p. 12.

6. Ibid., p. 48.

7. Ibid., p. 32.

8. Washoe History. https://washoetribe.us/aboutpage/4-Page-washoe-history (accessed online January 21, 2023).

9. Nevers, Jo Ann. (1976). Wa she su: A Washo Tribal History. Inter-Tribal Council of Nevada. University of Utah Printing Service. Salt Lake City, Utah, p. 49.

10. Report of the Commissioner of Indian Affairs to the Secretary of the Interior, United States. Office of Indian Affairs. U.S. Government Printing Office, 1866, pp. 113, 115-116.

11. Ibid., p. 116.

12. Ibid., pp. 116, 118.

13. Report of the Commissioner of Indian Affairs to the Secretary of the Interior, United States. Office of Indian Affairs. U.S. Government Printing Office, 1901, p. 279.

14. Report of the Commissioner of Indian Affairs to the Secretary of the Interior, United States. Office of Indian Affairs. U.S. Government Printing Office, 1867, p. 171.

15. J. M. Lee, First Lieutenant, U.S. Army, Special Indian Agent for Nevada. Report of the Commissioner of Indian Affairs to the Secretary of the Interior, U.S. Office of Indian Affairs, Nevada Superintendency. U.S. Government Printing Office, 1870, p. 108.

16. Report of the Commissioner of Indian Affairs to the Secretary of the Interior, United States. Office of Indian Affairs, Nevada Superintendency. U.S. Government Printing Office, 1869, pp. 17-18.

17. H. Douglas, Major U.S. Army, Superintendent of Indian Affairs, To Hon. E. S. Parker, Commissioner of Indian Affairs. Report of the Commissioner of Indian Affairs to the Secretary of the Interior, United States. Office of Indian Affairs, Nevada Superintendency. U.S. Government Printing Office, 1870, pp. 97-98.

18. Report of the Commissioner of Indian Affairs to the Secretary of the Interior, United States. Office of Indian Affairs, Nevada Superintendency. U.S. Government Printing Office, 1870, p. 109.

19. Ibid., p. 112.

20. Powell and G. W. Ingalls, p. 23. Report of special commissioners J. W. Powell and G. W. Ingalls on the condition of the Ute Indians of Utah; the Pai-Utes of Utah, northern Arizona, southern Nevada, and southeastern California; the Go-si Utes of Utah and Nevada; the northwestern Shoshones of Idaho and Utah; and the western Shoshones of Nevada. United States. Bureau of Indian affairs. U.S. Government Printing Office, 1873, p. 23.

21. Levi A. Gheen, Farmer in charge of the Western Shoshone

Indians. Report of the Commissioner of Indian Affairs to the Secretary of the Interior, United States. Office of Indian Affairs, Nevada Superintendency. U.S. Government Printing Office, 1877, p. 153.

22. Report of the Commissioner of Indian Affairs to the Secretary of the Interior, United States. Office of Indian Affairs. U.S. Government Printing Office, 1885, p. 143.

23. Senate bill No. 99, Fifty-third Congress, first session, "To secure the relinquishment of the Indian title to a portion of the Pyramid Lake Paiutes' Reservation in Nevada, and to the entire Walker River Reservation in said State, and for other purposes." Pyramid Lake Reservation, S. Rep. No. 177, 53d Cong., 2nd Sess. (1894).

24. William Morris Stewart: A Featured Biography, United States Senate. .ps://www.senate.gov/senators/FeaturedBios/Featured_Bio_Stewart.htm (accessed online January 9, 2023).

25. Report of the Commissioner of Indian Affairs to the Secretary of the Interior, United States. Office of Indian Affairs. U.S. Government Printing Office, 1895, pp. 209-210.

26. Pyramid Lake Reservation, S. Rep. No. 177, 53d Cong., 2nd Sess. (1894).

27. Report of the Commissioner of Indian Affairs to the Secretary of the Interior, United States. Office of Indian Affairs. U.S. Government Printing Office, 1924, p. 18.

28. Report of the Commissioner of Indian Affairs to the Secretary of the Interior, United States. Office of Indian Affairs. U.S. Government Printing Office, 1864, p. 146.

29. The Indian Problem, Nelson A. Miles, North American Review 128, no. 268 (March 1879): 304–15.

30. Evans, Elwood. History of the Pacific Northwest: Oregon and Washington; Embracing an Account of the Original Discoveries on the Pacific Coast of North America, and a Description of the Conquest, Settlement and Subjugation of the... Original Territory of Oregon: Also Interesting Biographies of the Earliest Settlers and More Prominent Men and Women of the Pacific Northwest, Including a... Description of the Climate, Soil, Productions... of Oregon and Washington... Vol. 2. North Pacific History Company, 1889, p. 104.

31. Stoffle, Richard W., and Henry F. Dobyns 1982 Navagantu: Nevada Indians Comment on the Intermountain Power Project, Nevada Section of Intermountain-Adelanto Bipole I Proposal. Manuscript on file at the Applied Urban Field School, University of Wisconsin Parkside, p. 95.

32. Id.

33. Elliott, Russell R. 1987 History of Nevada. Second edition,

revised. Originally published in 1973, University of Nebraska, Lincoln. (hereinafter "History of Nevada").

34. Irving, Washington. The Adventures of Captain Bonneville, U.S.A., in the Rocky Mountains and the Far West. Edited by Edgeley W. Todd. University of Oklahoma Press, Norman. 1961, Appendix, p. 300.

35. NORTHERN PAIUTE AND WESTERN SHOSHONE LAND USE IN NORTHERN NEVADA: A CLASS I ETHNOGRAPHIC/ETHNOHISTORIC OVERVIEW. Submitted to BUREAU OF LAND MANAGEMENT, Ginny Bengston, p. 31.

36. History of Nevada, p. 145.

37. Bard, James C., Busby, Colin I. and Findlay, John M. 1981 A Cultural Resource Overview of the Carson and Humboldt Sinks, Nevada. Cultural Resources Series. No. 2, Bureau of Land Management, Reno, Nevada. Knack, Martha C., and Stewart, Omer C. 1999 As Long as the River Shall Run: An Ethnohistory of Pyramid Lake Paiutes' Reservation. Reprinted. University of Nevada Press, Reno. Originally published in 1984, University of California, Berkeley, p. 102.

38. California Historical Society, Quarterly, Vol. 1, Kit Carson in California, 1922 , p. 122.

39. Tustin, William Isaac (1880). Recollections of Early Days in California. Bancroft Library, p. 7.

40. https://www.oregonhistoryproject.org/narratives/nature-and-history-in-the-klamath-basin/inhabiting-the-land/fremont-and-kit-carson-at-upper-klamath-lake/#.Y8rrwOzMKw4 (accessed online January 20, 2023).

41. Frémont, John Charles. *Memoirs of My Life by John Charles Frémont, Explorer of the American West, Including Three Journeys of Western Exploration during the Years 1844, 1843-1844, 1845-1847* (1887), p. 496.

42. Frémont, John Charles, Mary Lee Spence, and Donald Dean Jackson. The expeditions of John Charles Frémont. Volume 2: The Bear Flag Revolt and the Court-Martial. Urbana, Il: University of Illinois Press, 1973, pp. 124-125.

43. Curran, Harold, Fearful Crossing – The Central Overland Trail Through Nevada, Great Basin Press, Reno, Nevada, 1982, p. 41.

44. Clark, Thomas D., ed. Gold Rush Diary: Being the Journal of Elisha Douglas Perkins on the Overland Trail in the Spring and Summer of 1849. University Press of Kentucky, 2014, p. 269.

45. Bryant, Edwin. What I Saw in California: Being a Journal of a Tour, by the Emigrant Route and South Pass of the Rocky Mountains, Across the Continent of North America, the Great Desert Basin, and Through California, in the Years 1846-1847. D. Appleton & Company, 1849, p. 268.

46. THE JOURNAL OF JAMES FRAZIER REED July 31-October

4, 1846, Utah Historical Quarterly, Vol. 19, WEST FROM FORT BRIDGER (January, April, July, October, 1951), University of Illinois Press , pp. 186-223 (40 pages).

47. Humboldt River Basin, Nevada, Water and Related Land Resources, Report Number Three, op. cit., page 2.

48. Moorman, Madison Berryman, and Louise Parks Banes. The Journal of Madison Berryman Moorman, 1850-1851. No. 23. California Historical Society, 1948.

49. "JOURNAL OF JOHN WOOD: As Kept By Him While Traveling From Cincinnati To The Gold Diggings In 1850." Nevins & Myers, Book And Job California, In The Spring And Summer Of Printers, Columbus, Ohio, 1871. https://homepages.rootsweb. com/~hoppes/booksdiaries.html (accessed online December 27, 2022).

50. James Reed, Pacific Rural Press, 1871.

51. The Journal of Heinrich Lienhard. Utah Historical Quarterly, Volume 90, Number 2, 2022. https://issuu.com/utah10/docs/ volume_19_1951/s/88944 (accessed online December 27, 2022).

52. https://ctic.oncell.com/en/outdoor-quotes-230451.html (accessed online January 17, 2023).

53. Id.

54. Thissell, G. W. Crossing the Plains in '49. G.W. Thissell, 1903, p. 129.

55. Comprehensive Management and Use Plan / Final Environmental Impact Statement for the Oregon, California, Mormon Pioneer, and Pony Express National Historic Trails, Department of the Interior, National Park Service, 1998, p. 278.

56. Ibid., p. 276.

57. Ibid., p. 278.

58. Ibid., p. 279.

59. Id.

60. Historic Nobles Trail Guide. http://npshistory.com/brochures/cali/ nobles-trail-guide-2017.pdf (accessed online December 27, 2022).

61. Around the world with General Grant: a narrative of the visit of General U.S. Grant, ex-President of the United States, to various countries in Europe, Asia, and Africa, in 1877, 1878, 1879 to which are added certain conversations with General Grant on questions connected with American politics and history, John Russell Young, 1879: 448.

62. Report of the Commissioner of Indian Affairs to the Secretary of the Interior, United States. Office of Indian Affairs. U.S. Government Printing Office, 1890, p. 64.

63. History of Nevada.

64. James B. Allen and Ted J. Warner, "The Goshute Indians in Pioneer Utah," Utah Historical Quarterly 39 (Spring 1971): 164.

65. History of Tooele County (Salt Lake City: Daughters of Utah Pioneers, 1961), 311–12, 325.

66. https://historytogo.utah.gov/uhg-history-american-indians-ch-4/ (accessed online December 28, 2022).

67. Record: Proceedings and Debates of the ... Congress, Volume 99, Part 4. United States. Congress. U.S. Government Printing Office, 1953, p. 1953.

68. George M. Stephenson, The Political History of the Public Lands from 1840 to 1862: From Pre-emption to Homestead (New York: Russell and Russell, 1967), 21.

69. St. Peter's Courier (Nicollet County, Minnesota Territory), April 26, 1855, as quoted in Stephenson, Political History, 21 n6.

70. History of Nevada, pp. 31-32.

71. History of Nevada, p. 146.

72. Id

73. Id.

74. Caning I. Malouf, "The Gosiute Indians," The Shoshone Indians (New York: Garland Press, 1974), p. 101.

75. Mary A. Helmich, THE STAGE COMPANY HIERARCHY, Interpretation and Education Division, California State Parks, 2008.

76. Mark Twain, Roughing It, Berkeley: University of California Press, 1995 reprint, pp. 35-37.

77. Report to the President by the Indian Peace Commission, 1868.

78. Geo. W. Manypenny, Commissioner to Secretary McClellan. Report of the Commissioner of Indian Affairs to the Secretary of the Interior, United States. Office of Indian Affairs. U.S. Government Printing Office, 1855, p. 23.

79. Report of the Commissioner of Indian Affairs to the Secretary of the Interior, United States. Office of Indian Affairs. U.S. Government Printing Office, 1855, p. 16.

80. Letter from Benjamin Alvord, Brigadier-General, U.S. Volunteers, Commanding District to Captain John Mullan, Second U.S. Army, Late in Charge of Walla Walla and Fort Benton Mil. Road Expedition, Washington City, DC. The War of the Rebellion: A Compilation of the Official Records of the Union and Confederate Armies, United States War Department, U.S. Government Printing Office, 1891. Series I, Chap. LXII, Operations on the Pacific Coast, CORRESPONDENCE, ETC. – UNION AND CONFEDERATE, p. 287.

81. https://www.nps.gov/places/virginia-city-historic-district.htm

(accessed online January 11, 2022).

82. Deur, Douglas and Confer, Deborah, "People of Snowy Mountain, People of the River: A Multi-Agency Ethnographic Overview and Compendium Relating to Tribes Associated with Clark County, Nevada." Pacific West Region: Social Science Series, National Park Service, Publication Number 2012-01, U.S. Department of the Interior, p. 96.

83. UNITED STATES DEPARTMENT OF THE INTERIOR NATIONAL PARK SERVICE THE NATIONAL SURVEY OF HISTORIC SITES AND BUILDINGS Theme XV, Westward Expansion and the Extension of the National Boundaries to the Pacific 1830-1898; THE MINING FRONTIER. Edited by William C. Everhart Region Four, San Francisco 1959, p. 40. http://npshistory.com/publications/nhl/theme-studies/mining-frontier.pdf (accessed online December 18, 2021).

84. Ibid., p. 31.

85. *Pyramid Lake Paiute Tribe of Indians v. Nevada, Dep't of Wildlife*, No. 11-16470.

86. Virginia City and the Comstock Lode. https://www.legendsofamerica. com/nv-virginiacity/ (accessed online January 17, 2023).

87. State of Nevada, Division of Water, Truckee River Chronology. http://cdn.ca9.uscourts.gov/datastore/library/2013/08/02/Pyramid_ TruckeeRiverChronology.pdf (accessed online December 23, 2021).

88. Ninth Judicial Circuit Historical Society, 184 WESTERN LEGAL HISTORY, VOL. 2, No. 2, Summer Fall 1989.

89. Comstock Lode – Creating Nevada History. https://www. legendsofamerica.com/nv-comstocklode/ (accessed online January 25, 2023).

90. Early Mining Discoveries in Nevada. https://www. legendsofamerica.com/nv-miningdiscoveries/ (accessed online January 25, 2023).

91. Id.

92. Report of the Commissioner of Indian Affairs to the Secretary of the Interior, United States. Office of Indian Affairs. U.S. Government Printing Office, 1876, p. 117.

93. Bowers, Michael W. The Sagebrush State, 4th Ed: Nevada's History, Government, and Politics, University of Nevada Press, 2013, Chapter One.

94. https://noehill.com/nv_washoe/nev0238.asp (accessed online January 29, 2023).

95. Dangberg, Conflict on the Carson, op. cit., pages 106-107.

96. Humboldt River Basin, Nevada, Water and Related Land Resources, Report Number Four, op. cit., p. 2.

97. Reports on the Statistics of Agriculture in the United States: Agriculture

by Irrigation in the Western Part of the United States, and Statistics of Fisheries in the United States at the Eleventh Census: 1890. U.S. Government Printing Office, 1895, p. 298.

98. History of Humboldt County, Nevada. http://genealogytrails.com/nev/humboldt/history/histhum.html (accessed online January 17, 2023).

99. J.A. Dun, Jas. A. Banks, Alen Peacock. A Compilation of the Official Records of the Union and Confederate Armies, series I, vol. L, part 2 (Washington, DC: Government Printing Office, 1880–1900), p. 1192.

100. Major C. McDermit, Second Cavalry California Volunteers. A Compilation of the Official Records of the Union and Confederate Armies, series I, vol. L, part 2 (Washington, DC: Government Printing Office, 1880–1900), p. 1192.

101. Proclamation—Rebellion in the Territory of Utah, American Presidency Project. https://www.presidency.ucsb.edu/documents/proclamation-rebellion-the-territory-utah (accessed online January 17, 2023).

102. Petersen, J. G. (2008). A route for the overland stage: James H. Simpson's 1859 trail across the Great Basin. Logan: Utah State University Press, p. 9.

103. Ibid., pp. 5-6.

104. Ibid., pp. 14-15.

105. Ibid., p. 20.

106. Ibid., p. 33.

107. Ibid., p. 161.

108. Ibid., p. 200.

109. Captain J.H. Simpson, Report of Explorations across the Great Basin of the Territory of Utah for a Direct Wagon-Route from Camp Floyd to Genoa, in Carson Valley in 1859 (Washington, DC: Government Printing Office, 1876).

110. National Historic Trails, National Park Service, Utah—Crossroads of the West. http://npshistory.com/publications/trails/ut.pdf (accessed online January 17, 2023).

111. Nevada Indian Battles. https://www.legendsofamerica.com/nevada-indian-battles/ (accessed online January 17, 2023).

112. https://nevadamagazine.com/issue/january-february-2014/1159/ (accessed online December 7, 2022).

113. Frank S. Popplewell. Pony Express – Fastest Mail Across the West. https://www.legendsofamerica.com/we-ponyexpress/ (accessed online January 17, 2023).

114. Twain, Mark. Roughing it. Vol. 1. Harper & Row, 1913.

115. Goodsprings, – Still Kicking the Desert Dust. https://www.legendsofamerica.com/nv-goodsprings/ (accessed online January 16, 2023).

116. John C. Burche, Local Agent, Humboldt County to James W. Nye, Governor and ex-officio Superintendent of Indian Affairs. Report of the Commissioner of Indian Affairs to the Secretary of the Interior, United States. Office of Indian Affairs, Nevada Superintendency. U.S. Government Printing Office, 1865, p. 148.

117. Annual Report of the Superintendent of Indian Affairs to the Secretary of Interior for the Year 1861, Report No. 40, James W. Nye, Governor, Acting Superintendent, Carson City, Nevada Territory, Government Printing Office, Washington, DC, July 19, 1861.

118. Report of the Commissioner of Indian Affairs to the Secretary of the Interior, United States. Office of Indian Affairs. U.S. Government Printing Office, 1861, p. 135.

119. *NW. Bands of Shoshone Indians v. United States*, 324 U.S. 335, 342 (1945).

120. Rusco, Elmer R. 1973 The Status of Indians in Nevada Law. In: Native American Politics: Power Relationships in the Western Great Basin Today, Ruth M. Houghton, ed., pp. 68-99. Reno: University of Nevada Bureau of Governmental Research, p. 79.

121. Report of the Commissioner of Indian Affairs to the Secretary of the Interior, United States. Office of Indian Affairs. U.S. Government Printing Office, 1863, p. 215.

122. Ibid., p. 222.

123. Allen and Warner, "Gosiute Indians," Hubert Howe Bancroft, History of Nevada, Colorado and Wyoming, 1540–1880 (San Francisco: A.L. Bancroft & Company, 1890), p. 219.

124. Amos Reed to William P. Dole, December 30, 1862, in "Letters Received by the Office of Indian Affairs, 1824–1881," National Archives, Microcopy M-243.

125. "A Needless War in Prospect," New York Times, May 26, 1862, p. 4.

126. P. Edw. Connor to Major Edward McGarry, September 29, 1862. The War of the Rebellion: A Compilation of the Official Records of the Union and Confederate Armies, series I, vol. L, part 2 (Washington, DC: Government Printing Office, 1880–1900), 144.

127. James Duane Doty, Commissioner of Indian Affairs. Report of the Commissioner of Indian Affairs to the Secretary of the Interior, United States. Office of Indian Affairs. U.S. Government Printing Office, 1865, p. 163.

128. Report of Colonel P. Edward Connor, March 29, 1863, The War of the Rebellion 1, 187.

129. Part 15 of Survey of Conditions of the Indians in the United States: Hearings Before a Subcommittee of the Committee on Indian

Affairs, United States Senate, Pursuant to S Res. 79, a Resolution Directing the Committee on Indian Affairs of the United States Senate to Make a General Survey of the Condition of the Indians of the United States, United States. Congress. Senate. Committee on Indian Affairs. U.S. Government Printing Office, 1929, p. 14955.

130. Report of the Commissioner of Indian Affairs to the Secretary of the Interior, United States. Office of Indian Affairs. U.S. Government Printing Office, 1865, p. 173.

131. Report of the Commissioner of Indian Affairs to the Secretary of the Interior, United States. Office of Indian Affairs, Nevada Superintendency, Western Shoshone Agency. U.S. Government Printing Office, 1878, p. 105.

132. Report of the Commissioner of Indian Affairs to the Secretary of the Interior, United States. Office of Indian Affairs. U.S. Government Printing Office, 1865, p. 176.

133. Printed in 39th Cong., 1st sess., House Executive Document 1 (Serial 1248), 326. Morgan, D. L., Saunders, R. L., & Smoak, G. E. (2007). Shoshonean peoples and the overland trails: Frontiers of the Utah Superintendency of Indian Affairs, 1849-1869. Logan: Utah State University Press, pp. 338-339.

134. Report of the Commissioner of Indian Affairs to the Secretary of the Interior, United States. Office of Indian Affairs. U.S. Government Printing Office, 1865, p. 158.

135. Pioche, Nevada – Wildest Town in the Silver State. https://www.legendsofamerica.com/pioche-nevada/ (accessed online January 25, 2023).

136. History of the Humboldt National Forest, Fred P. Frampton, Humboldt National Forest Cultural Resource Series #1, June 1992, Reformatted July 2008, Edited by Judith Frampton, p. 4. https://www.fs.usda.gov/Internet/FSE_DOCUMENTS/stelprdb5422498.pdf (accessed online January 17, 2023).

137. Jacob T. Lockhart, Indian Agent To W. Nye, Governor and Superintendent of Indian Affairs, Nevada Territory, 9/20/1864. Report of the Commissioner of Indian Affairs to the Secretary of the Interior, United States. Office of Indian Affairs, Nevada Superintendency. U.S. Government Printing Office, 1864, pp. 139-140.

138. Report of the Commissioner of Indian Affairs to the Secretary of the Interior (1864), United States. Office of Indian Affairs. U.S. Government Printing Office, 1865, pp. 144-145.

139. Ibid., p. 145.

140. Ibid., p. 16.

141. *Pyramid Lake Paiute Tribe of Indians v. Nevada, Dep't of Wildlife,* No. 11-16470.

142. History of Tahoe National Forest: 1840-1940, A Cultural Resources Overview History, CHAPTER V, Era of National Forest Management, 1906-1940. http://npshistory.com/publications/usfs/region/5/tahoe/history/chap5.htm (accessed online April 3, 2023).

143. Id.

144. Houghton, Samuel G., A Trace of Desert Waters: The Great Basin Story, University of Nevada Press, Reno, Nevada, 1994, p. 55.

145. Nevada State Journal, November 11, 1874, page 2.

146. McQuivey, Robert, "Habitat and Fisheries Historical Fact File," Habitat Bureau, Nevada Division of Wildlife (NDOW), Department of Conservation and Natural Resources, Reno, Nevada, 1996.

147. Humboldt River Basin, Nevada, Water and Related Land Resources, Report Number Eight, op. dt., p. 49.

148. Id.

149. "Going for Gold: How the Confederacy Hatched an Audacious Plan to Finance Their War." Daniel Seligman. https://www.historynet.com/confederate-plan-to-finance-war/ (accessed online January 19, 2023).

150. Id.

151. William P. Dole to O.H. Irish, March 28, 1865. Report of the Commissioner of Indian Affairs to the Secretary of the Interior, United States. Office of Indian Affairs. U.S. Government Printing Office, 1865, p. 149.

152. Idaho State Historical Society Reference Series, No. 238, Ruby and Silver City War Meetings. https://history.idaho.gov/wp-content/uploads/0238.pdf (accessed online January 17, 2023).

153. Representative Evans, speaking on S. 102, on May 18, 1830, 21st Cong., 1st sess., Register of Debates in Congress, p. 1049.

154. O. H. Irish to D. N. Cooley, Utah Superintendency, September 9, 1865. Report of the Commissioner of Indian Affairs to the Secretary of the Interior, United States. Office of Indian Affairs. U.S. Government Printing Office, 1865, pp. 146-147.

155. Report of the Commissioner of Indian Affairs to the Secretary of the Interior, United States. Office of Indian Affairs. U.S. Government Printing Office, 1866, p. 115.

156. H.G. Parker, Superintendent, Nevada to Commissioner Taylor. Report of the Commissioner of Indian Affairs to the Secretary of the Interior, United States. Office of Indian Affairs. U.S. Government Printing Office, 1868, p. 9.

157. Ibid., pp. 170, 171.

158. Report of the Commissioner of Indian Affairs to the Secretary of the Interior, United States. Office of Indian Affairs, Nevada Superintendency. U.S. Government Printing Office, 1872, p. 10.

159. Report of the Superintendent of Indian Schools. United States. Office of Indian Affairs, U.S. Government Printing Office, 1887, p. 38.

160. Report of the Commissioner of Indian Affairs to the Secretary of the Interior, United States. Office of Indian Affairs, Nevada Superintendency, Western Shoshone Agency. U.S. Government Printing Office, 1878, p. 104.

161. Franklin Campbell, Indian Agent to H. G. Parker, Superintendent of Indian Affairs for Nevada. Report of the Commissioner of Indian Affairs to the Secretary of the Interior, United States. Office of Indian Affairs. U.S. Government Printing Office, 1868, p. 170.

162. Report of the Commissioner of Indian Affairs to the Secretary of the Interior, United States. Office of Indian Affairs, Nevada Superintendency, Walker River Indian Reserve. U.S. Government Printing Office, 1868, p. 147.

163. American Indian Sovereignty: Now You See It, Now You Don't by Peter d'Errico, Legal Studies Department, University of Massachusetts/Amherst. https://people.umass.edu/derrico/nowyouseeit.html (accessed online January 21, 2023).

164. Report of the Commissioner of Indian Affairs to the Secretary of the Interior, United States. Office of Indian Affairs, Nevada Superintendency. U.S. Government Printing Office, 1868, p. 147.

165. Report of the Commissioner of Indian Affairs to the Secretary of the Interior, United States. Office of Indian Affairs. U.S. Government Printing Office, 1868, p. 6.

166. Humboldt River Basin, Nevada, Water and Related Land Resources, Report Number Three, op. cit., page 2.

167. Journal of California and Great Basin Anthropology Vol. 4, No. 2, pp. 203-221 (1982). Cultural Persistence in Nevada: Current Native American Issues Richard C. Hanes, p. 206.

168. Id.

169. Report of the Commissioner of Indian Affairs to the Secretary of the Interior, United States. Office of Indian Affairs, Nevada Superintendency. U.S. Government Printing Office, 1869, p. 18.

170. Agent H. G. Parker. Report of the Commissioner of Indian Affairs to the Secretary of the Interior, United States. Office of Indian Affairs, Nevada Superintendency. U.S. Government Printing Office, 1869, p. 203.

171. H. Douglas, Major U.S. Army, Superintendent of Indian Affairs. Report of the Commissioner of Indian Affairs to the Secretary of the Interior, United States. Office of Indian Affairs, Nevada Superintendency. U.S. Government Printing Office, 1870, p. 564.

172. Report of the Commissioner of Indian Affairs to the Secretary of the Interior, United States. Office of Indian Affairs, Nevada Superintendency. U.S. Government Printing Office, 1870, pp. 97-98.

173. Id.

174. J. M. Lee, First Lieutenant, U.S. Army, Special Indian Agent for Nevada. Report of the Commissioner of Indian Affairs to the Secretary of the Interior, United States. Office of Indian Affairs, Nevada Superintendency. U.S. Government Printing Office, 1870, p. 108.

175. H. Douglas, Major U.S. Army, Superintendent of Indian Affairs. Report of the Commissioner of Indian Affairs to the Secretary of the Interior, United States. Office of Indian Affairs, Nevada Superintendency. U.S. Government Printing Office, 1870, p. 106.

176. J. M. Lee, First Lieutenant U.S. Army, Special Indian Agent for Nevada. To: Major H. Douglas, U.S. Army, Superintendent of Indian Affairs, Carson City, Nevada. Report of the Commissioner of Indian Affairs to the Secretary of the Interior, United States. Office of Indian Affairs, Nevada Superintendency. U.S. Government Printing Office, 1870, p. 108.

177. George W. Dodge to F.A. Walker, February 2, 1872; George W. Dodge to F.A. Walker, August 31, 1872; Dennis Defa, The Goshute Indians of Utah, A History of Utah's American Indians 2000, Utah State History. https://issuu.com/utah10/docs/history_of_utah_s_american_indians/s/10988 (accessed online January 17, 2023).

178. https://district.mpcsd.org/Page/144 (accessed online January 14, 2023).

179. UNITED STATES DEPARTMENT OF THE INTERIOR NATIONAL PARK SERVICE THE NATIONAL SURVEY OF HISTORIC SITES AND BUILDINGS Theme XV, Westward Expansion and the Extension of the National Boundaries to the Pacific 1830-1898 THE MINING FRONTIER. Edited by William C. Everhart Region Four, San Francisco 1959, p. 33. http://npshistory.com/publications/nhl/theme-studies/mining-frontier.pdf (accessed online December 18, 2021).

180. Report of special commissioners J. W. Powell and G. W. Ingalls on the condition of the Ute Indians of Utah; the Pai-Utes of Utah, northern Arizona, southern Nevada, and southeastern California; the Go-si Utes of Utah and Nevada; the northwestern Shoshones of Idaho and Utah; and the western Shoshones of Nevada. United States.

Bureau of Indian Affairs. U.S. Government Printing Office, 1873, p. 20.

181. Ibid., p. 45.

182. Ibid., p. 23.

183. Ibid., p. 25.

184. DONALD WORSTER, A RIVER RUNNING WEST: THE LIFE OF JOHN WESLEY POWELL, p. 270 (2001) (quoting letter from John W. Powell to Senator Henry Teller (February, 1880) (File 3751) (Powell Papers, National Anthropological Archives). 2006 DENVER UNIVERSITY LAW REVIEW SYMPOSIUM: BORROWING THE LAND: CULTURES OF OWNERSHIP IN THE WESTERN LANDSCAPE: ARTICLE: Listening to All the Voices, Old and New: The Evolution of Land Ownership in the Modern West, 83 Denv. U.L. Rev. 945, 959.

185. DONALD WORSTER, A RIVER RUNNING WEST: THE LIFE OF JOHN WESLEY POWELL (2001), pp. 270-271.

186. The Letters of Mark Twain, Volume 2, 1867-1875. https://www. gutenberg.org/files/3194/3194-h/3194-h.htm (accessed online April 2, 2023).

187. UNITED STATES DEPARTMENT OF THE INTERIOR NATIONAL PARK SERVICE THE NATIONAL SURVEY OF HISTORIC SITES AND BUILDINGS Theme XV, Westward Expansion and the Extension of the National Boundaries to the Pacific 1830-1898 THE MINING FRONTIER. Edited by William C. Everhart Region Four, San Francisco 1959, p. 33. http://npshistory. com/publications/nhl/theme-studies/mining-frontier.pdf (accessed online December 18, 2021).

188. Id.

189. C. A. Bateman, Indian Agent, Nevada. Report of the Commissioner of Indian Affairs to the Secretary of the Interior, United States. Office of Indian Affairs. U.S. Government Printing Office, 1874, p. 279.

190. Executive Orders Relating to Indian Reservations, 1855-1922, Volumes 1-2, United States. President, 1912.

191. Report of the Commissioner of Indian Affairs to the Secretary of the Interior, United States. Office of Indian Affairs. U.S. Government Printing Office, 1874, p. 278.

192. Report of the Commissioner of Indian Affairs to the Secretary of the Interior, United States. Office of Indian Affairs. U.S. Government Printing Office, 1875, p. 343.

193. Report of the Commissioner of Indian Affairs to the Secretary of the Interior, United States. Office of Indian Affairs. U.S. Government Printing Office, 1876, pp. 115, 117.

194. Report of the Commissioner of Indian Affairs to the Secretary of

the Interior, United States. Office of Indian Affairs, U.S. Government
Printing Office, 1879, p. 111.

195. Levi A. Gheen, Farmer in charge of the Western Shoshone Indians.
Report of the Commissioner of Indian Affairs to the Secretary of the Interior,
United States. Office of Indian Affairs, Nevada Superintendency. U.S.
Government Printing Office, 1877, pp. 151, 152, 153.

196. A.J. Barnes. Report of the Commissioner of Indian Affairs to
the Secretary of the Interior, United States. Office of Indian Affairs,
Nevada Superintendency, Pyramid Lake Reserve. U.S. Government
Printing Office, 1878, p. 103.

197. Journal of California and Great Basin Anthropology Vol. 4,
No. 2, pp. 203-221 (1982). Cultural Persistence in Nevada: Current
Native American Issues, Richard C. Hanes, p. 208.

198. Report of the Commissioner of Indian Affairs to the Secretary
of the Interior, United States. Office of Indian Affairs, Nevada
Superintendency, Pyramid Lake Agency. U.S. Government Printing
Office, 1879, p. 109.

199. Report of the Commissioner of Indian Affairs to the Secretary of
the Interior, United States. Office of Indian Affairs. U.S. Government
Printing Office, 1880, p. xv.

200. Report of the Commissioner of Indian Affairs to the Secretary of
the Interior, United States. Office of Indian Affairs. U.S. Government
Printing Office, 1874, p. 55.

201. Report of the Commissioner of Indian Affairs to the Secretary of
the Interior, United States. Office of Indian Affairs. U.S. Government
Printing Office, 1880, p. 125.

202. Michael Hittman, Mabel Wright and the Prayer that Saved Cui-
ui Pah (Pyramid Lake), Nevada Historical Society Quarterly, Volume
56, Spring/Summer 2013, Numbers 1-2, p. 43.

203. Agent Joseph M. McMaster. Report of the Commissioner of
Indian Affairs to the Secretary of the Interior, United States. Office of
Indian Affairs. U.S. Government Printing Office, 1881, p. 132.

204. Congressional Record: Proceedings and Debates of the ...
Congress - Senate. U.S. Government Printing Office, 1884, p. 1147.

205. Powell & Ingalls, Report of special commissioners J. W.
Powell and G. W. Ingalls on the condition of the Ute Indians of
Utah; the Pai-Utes of Utah, northern Arizona, southern Nevada,
and southeastern California; the Go-si Utes of Utah and Nevada;
the northwestern Shoshones of Idaho and Utah; and the western
Shoshones of Nevada. United States. Bureau of Indian Affairs. U.S.
Government Printing Office, 1873, p. 14.

206. Executive Orders Relating to Indian Reservations, 1855-1922,

Volumes 1-2, United States. President, 1912.

207. Stoffle, Richard W. and Henry F. Dobyns. 1982 Navagantu: Nevada Indians Comment on the Intermountain Power Project, Nevada Section of Intermountain-Adelanto Bipole I Proposal. Manuscript on file at the Applied Urban Field School, University of Wisconsin Parkside, p. 136.

208. James E. Spencer. Report of the Commissioner of Indian Affairs to the Secretary of the Interior, United States. Office of Indian Affairs, Nevada Superintendency, Moapa River Reservation. U.S. Government Printing Office, 1880, pp. 125-126.

209. Ibid., p. 126.

210. Report of the Commissioner of Indian Affairs to the Secretary of Interior for the Year 1881, Joseph M. McMaster, Agent, Nevada Agency, Nevada, Pyramid Lake Reservation, U.S. Government Printing Office, Washington, DC, August 31, 1881.

211. Report of the Commissioner of Indian Affairs to the Secretary of the Interior, United States. Office of Indian Affairs. U.S. Government Printing Office, 1884, p. 171.

212. Report of the Commissioner of Indian Affairs to the Secretary of the Interior, United States. Office of Indian Affairs, Nevada Superintendency, Western Shoshone Agency. U.S. Government Printing Office, 1885, p. 147.

213. Report of the Commissioner of Indian Affairs to the Secretary of the Interior, United States. Office of Indian Affairs. U.S. Government Printing Office, 1885, p. XII.

214. John B. Scott, Indian Agent. Report of the Commissioner of Indian Affairs to the Secretary of the Interior, United States. Office of Indian Affairs. U.S. Government Printing Office, 1885, pp. 197-198.

215. Report of the Commissioner of Indian Affairs to the Secretary of the Interior, United States. Office of Indian Affairs. U.S. Government Printing Office, 1887, p. 166.

216. Annual Report of the Department of the Interior, Vol. II, Report of the Commissioner of Indian Affairs, Office of Indian Affairs, United States. U.S. Government Printing Office, 1916, p. 58.

217. Report of the Commissioner of Indian Affairs to the Secretary of the Interior, United States. Office of Indian Affairs. U.S. Government Printing Office, 1888, p. 179.

218. Indian Agent C.C. Warner. Report of the Commissioner of Indian Affairs to the Secretary of the Interior, United States. Office of Indian Affairs. U.S. Government Printing Office, 1891, p. 299.

219. Indian Agent C. C. Warner. Report of the Commissioner of Indian Affairs to the Secretary of the Interior, United States. Office of

Indian Affairs. U.S. Government Printing Office, 1891, p. 300.

220. Report of the Commissioner of Indian Affairs to the Secretary of the Interior, United States. Office of Indian Affairs. U.S. Government Printing Office, 1892, pp. 74-75.

221. FEDERALLY OWNED LAND IN NEVADA HELD IN TRUST FOR THE PAIUTE AND SHOSHONE TRIBES OF THE FALLON INDIAN RESERVATION GOVERNMENT BEFORE THE U.S. SENATE SELECT COMMITTEE ON INDIAN AFFAIRS S. 785 JULY 19, 1977, United States Government Printing Office, 1977.

222. Id.

223. Report of the Commissioner of Indian Affairs to the Secretary of the Interior, United States. Office of Indian Affairs. U.S. Government Printing Office, 1895, pp. 209-210.

224. July 9, 1892, Letter from Commissioner T.J. Morgan to Secretary Interior. Pyramid Lake Reservation, S. Rep. No. 177, 53d Cong., 2nd Sess. (1894).

225. Report of the Commissioner of Indian Affairs to the Secretary of the Interior, United States. Office of Indian Affairs. U.S. Government Printing Office, 1896, p. 207.

226. Report of the Commissioner of Indian Affairs to the Secretary of the Interior, United States. Office of Indian Affairs. U.S. Government Printing Office, 1898, p. 94.

227. https://www.up.com/goldenspike/sacramento-promontory.html (accessed online January 24, 2023).

228. Fred B. Spriggs, Superintendent. Report of the Commissioner of Indian Affairs to the Secretary of the Interior, United States. Office of Indian Affairs. U.S. Government Printing Office, 1904, p. 246.

229. Fred B. Spriggs, Superintendent and Acting Indian Agent. Report of the Commissioner of Indian Affairs to the Secretary of the Interior, United States. Office of Indian Affairs. U.S. Government Printing Office, 1901, p. 277.

230. The Ghost Dance – A Promise of Fulfillment. https://www.legendsofamerica.com/na-ghostdance/ (accessed online January 16, 2023).

231. Bull Frog Mining District, Nevada. https://www.legendsofamerica.com/nv-bullfrogdistrict/ (accessed online January 17, 2023).

232. Death Valley Historic Resource Study. https://www.nps.gov/parkhistory/online_books/deva/section4a5.htm (accessed online January 16, 2023).

233. Id.

234. "The Bank Crowd and Silver Kings Made a Fortune From the Comstock." Chuck Lyons. https://www.historynet.com/the-bank-crowd-and-

silver-kings-made-a-fortune-from-the-comstock/ (accessed online December 29, 2022).

235. The Washoe Club. https://www.thewashoeclubmuseum.com/history/ (accessed online January 17, 2023).

11: ARIZONA

Arizona, from its position and general geological features, so far as explorations have made them known, is believed to be stocked with mineral wealth beyond that of any other Territory of equal extent in the region under consideration. A recent letter, addressed to the Hon. John S. Watts, from this section, holds the following language: "*The country north of the Gila river is rich in gold, silver, and copper. In the new mines there is plenty of timber, water, and grass.*" (Emphasis added). *I think we will have one of the finest countries in the world if we can have some help to keep the Apaches and people from Sonora out of the country*. (Emphasis added).[1]

> The miners whom he met were almost all anxious to move east to the San Francisco and Salt rivers, where, they say, there is abundance of water at all seasons of the year, wide valleys of fertile land, good timber, and they believe gold, silver, and copper in much greater abundance than where they are at present. It was necessary, however, for them to wait until they could muster a much larger force to contend with the Coyotro Apaches, who are numerous and hostile. The mountains throughout this new mining district are everywhere intersected with quartz ledges, and it is believed that many of them are rich in gold and silver, but no assays had been made, and their value was unknown.[2]

1852: U.S.-Apache Treaty

The U.S.-Apache Nation Treaty (Treaty with the Apache, 1852) was signed in New Mexico Territory in July of 1852 by designated Apache and U.S. representatives. The agreement, occasionally referenced as "The Treaty of Santa Fe," was ratified by the U.S. Senate on March 23, 1853 (Kappler, 1904, pp. 598-600). The 1852 Treaty has not been altered or amended by subsequent ratified treaties or acts of Congress. Not all terms of the 1852 Treaty have been implemented, but no party has rescinded, modified, or disavowed the agreement.

Article 7 of the Treaty conveys to the U.S. the rights to use ANTT for "free and safe passage," a grant acknowledging and further enabling the surge of post-1848 east-west travel by non-Apaches through ANTT.

Article 9. Relying confidently upon the justice and the liberality of the aforesaid government, and anxious to remove every possible cause that might disturb their peace and quiet, it is agreed by the aforesaid Apache's that the government of the *United States shall at its earliest convenience designate, settle, and adjust their territorial boundaries*, and pass and execute in their territory such laws as may be deemed conducive to the prosperity and happiness of said Indians. (Emphasis added).

The 1852 Treaty includes 11 articles. The substance of each article is excerpted here:

"Said nation or tribe of Indians ... acknowledge and declare that they are lawfully and exclusively under the laws, jurisdiction, and government of the United States."

"hostilities between the contracting parties shall forever cease, and perpetual peace and amity shall forever exist between said Indians and the Government and people of the United States; the said nation or tribe of Indians, hereby binding themselves most solemnly never to associate with or give countenance or aid to any tribe or band of Indians, or other persons or powers, who may be at any time at war or enmity with the ... United States."

Apaches agree "to treat honestly and humanely all citizens of the United States [and] ... all persons and powers at peace with the said United States."

Apaches agree "to refer all cases of aggression against themselves or their property and territory, to the government of the United States."

Apaches agree "for all future time to desist and refrain from making any incursions within the Territory of Mexico of a hostile or predatory character ... [and to] refrain from taking and conveying into captivity any of the people or citizens of Mexico, or the animals or property of the people or government of Mexico ... [and to] surrender to their agent all captives now in their possession."

6. The parties agree that "persons subject to the laws of the United States [who should] murder, rob, or otherwise maltreat any Apache Indian ... shall be arrested and tried, and upon conviction, shall be subject to all the penalties provided by law for the protection of the persons and property of the people of the said States."

7. The parties agree that the "people of the United States of America shall have free and safe passage through the territory of aforesaid Indians."

8. The parties agree that "to preserve tranquility and to afford protection to all the people and interests of the contracting parties, the government of the United States will establish such military posts and agencies, and authorize such trading houses at such times and places as the said government may designate."

10. The government agrees to "grant to said Indians such donations, presents, and implements ... as said government may deem meet and proper."

11. The parties agree the "Treaty shall be binding [and] subject only to such modifications and amendments as may be adopted by the government of the United States ... [and] receive a liberal construction ... to the end that the said Apache Indians shall not be held responsible for the conduct of others, and that the government of the United States shall so legislate and act as to secure the permanent prosperity and happiness of said Indians."

The 1852 Treaty has no sunset clause and is not an agreement to end hostilities or cede contested lands.

1854: Mining Company

The first Anglo-American mining company to conduct business in Arizona, the Arizona Mining and Trading Company, was created in 1854 to mine the ores of Ajo. The first gold strike occurred in 1857 near the confluence of Sacramento Wash and the Colorado River. By 1864 almost one-fourth of the population of the Territory of Arizona was a prospector or a miner. Miners composed 44 percent of the first Territorial Legislature in the same year. The first Governor of the Territory, John N. Goodwin, and several members of his cabinet, were struck with gold fever and co-signed a number of mining claims. The American and Mexican Mining Exchange, established in 1880 at Tucson, provided a place for capitalists and engineers to view ore specimens, trade information and undoubtedly make deals.[3]

1861: Bascom Affair, Fort Bowie

Travel across southern Arizona is funneled by the formidable Chiricahua and Dos Cabezas mountains into a narrow, two-and-one-half mile corridor, known as Apache Pass. The Central Band of the Chiricahua Apaches settled in the region around Apache Pass. During the 1850s, after the Gadsden Purchase, Americans in increasing numbers used the Pass in their travels to California. In 1857, the Butterfield Overland Mail established a stone stage station in the Pass, taking advantage of the natural springs there. At first, the Chiricahuas, under the leadership of Cochise, left these travelers unmolested. However, two incidents provoked hostilities between Apaches and Americans and a military post became necessary, if the U.S. was to control this strategic location. The first incident was the tragic "Bascom Affair" of February 1861 in which American soldiers accused Cochise of stealing a young boy and some cattle.

Lieutenant Bascom set up a meeting with Cochise, leader of the accused Central Chiricahuas, and demanded the return of the boy and stock. Although Cochise returned the stock, he claimed to not have the boy, prompting Lieutenant Bascom to order his arrest. Cutting through the side of a tent, Cochise escaped, but a group of his band was captured. In response, Cochise captured civilian hostages from the Overland Line. After abortive negotiations, Lieutenant Bascom hung the Chiricahua captives, and Cochise did likewise with his civilian captives.

The second incident occurred a year later when General James Carleton, commander of the California Volunteers, ordered a detachment from Tucson to New Mexico through Apache Pass. A combined force of Apaches under Cochise and Mangas Coloradas prepared an ambush. The Union force, using artillery, managed to fight off the Apaches. The Chiricahua might have been successful had it not been for two Mountain Howitzer cannons. In reference to the Mountain Howitzers, an Apache warrior stated, "We would've won if you hadn't fired wagons at us." Bewildered by the destruction, the Chiricahua scattered and retreated.

Carleton, realizing the strategic importance of the Pass, ordered that a post be established there. Initially occupied by 100 men of the 5th California Volunteer Infantry, the post was named Fort Bowie after the 5th's regimental commander, Colonel George Washington Bowie.

1862: General James Carleton, Kill Apache Men

In 1862, General James Carleton, ordered Apache men to be killed wherever found.[4] General Carleton's May 1864 order, also reported in The Miner, required Apache "removal to a Reservation or by the utter extermination of their men, to insure a lasting peace and a security of life to all those who go to the country in search of precious metals."[5]

1863: Mangas Coloradas

Mangas Coloradas was a skilled war leader, chief and father-in-law to Cochise. He is considered by historians as one of the most important Indian leaders of the 19th century.

Long before the "White Eyes" came to the southwest, the Apaches had warred with Mexicans. So in 1846 when the U.S. went to war with Mexico, Mangas Coloradas saw them as heroes attacking their common enemy. He signed a peace treaty with the U.S., promising soldiers safe passage through Apache lands. That treaty was forgotten when gold and silver were later found. He long fought the "White Eyes" but came to understand he couldn't defeat them, so sought a peace treaty to save his people.

In January of 1863, under a flag of peace and with assurances of his safety, Mangas Coloradas went alone into Fort McLane in southwestern New Mexico to meet with General Joseph Rodman West. Instead of talking peace, General West ordered the chief's execution. Soldiers tortured and killed the chief– pretending he was trying to escape. They took his body outside the camp, dug a shallow grave and buried him. But the next day they returned, dug him up, cut off his head and boiled it in a big black kettle. The skull was sent to New York, where it was on display for a time. Native people believe it ended up in the Smithsonian Institution, but they have searched and found no record of it.[6]

The loss of Chief Mangas led Cochise to take up leadership of the Chiricahua. Capturing or defeating Cochise now became the key to U.S. victory.

1863–1874: Cochise Insurgency Tactics

Cochise ranged across a huge area--from Tucson, Arizona to Mesilla, New Mexico, and from Safford, Arizona to several hundred miles into Mexico. His Stronghold in the Dragoon Mountains was impregnable. Anyone approaching from far off could be seen from the tall rock spires. Many hiding spots allowed for easy ambush. It was never taken.

The U.S. military sought Cochise, but he proved far too elusive when chased, and far too effective a commander in battle. The Chiricahua people were more adapted to the land, better at hiding in it, and had better knowledge of it than the U.S. The military had many fights with Cochise and the Chiricahua Apache, but no single fight ended the war.[7]

1863: Territory of Arizona

The Arizona Territory was formed on February 24, 1863, from the New Mexico Territory. President Abraham Lincoln appointed John A. Gurley as Territorial Governor, but he died before taking office. He was replaced by John N. Goodwin.

Exterminating Apaches

In 1863, miners found gold and silver near present-day Prescott. Founded in April 1864, Prescott's importance for its mining led to the Army building and manning Fort Whipple to protect the fledgling settlement. Accusing the Apaches of raiding local ranches and committing depredations, groups of Prescott men formed into expeditions to retaliate against them. Irate citizens petitioned the first territorial governor John N. Goodwin, who wrote a letter to President Lincoln on February 20, 1864, requesting military escorts for the mail and exploring parties. Goodwin suggested utilizing native Arizonans as volunteers because of their knowledge of the terrain and Apache warfare.

With the ongoing Civil War, no immediate action was taken. When the miners asked General Carleton, commander of the Military Department of New Mexico, for troops, his reply was, "Until the Navajo War is off my hands, soldiers cannot be sent."

In the mean time, Governor Goodwin appointed King S. Woolsey, miner, rancher and Indian fighter, as Lieutenant Colonel to recruit and lead men against the Apaches. The editors of the Prescott Miner approved, reporting, *"He [Woolsey] is one of our most daring and skillful Indian fighters, and believes fully in the extermination policy."* (Emphasis added).[8] Three such expeditions in 1864, each led by King S. Woolsey, killed a total of 216 Western Apaches, including 131 women and children.[9] Likewise, in 1866, the ad hoc Volunteer Arizona Cavalry, mainly of Tucson, killed at least 60 Western Apaches. This pattern of violence continued unabated despite the Army's posting of two full regiments of infantry and nine cavalry companies to Arizona in 1868.

Mining Required Mercenary Protection

In 1871, Governor Spafford [sic], with 300 well-armed men and two months' provisions, entered the Pinal and Magallan Mountains ... determined to prospect fully the regions from which so many parties of whites have been driven back by Apaches.[10] General George Stoneman, the newly appointed Department Commander, ordered troops to "prosecute a relentless Winter campaign against the Pinal and Tonto branches" and "provide arms for civilians who desire to accompany them."[11]

Deathly Inflammatory Rhetoric

Mining proponents used propaganda to portray Apaches in the Pinal Mountains as subhuman impediments to civilization and profit. This inflammatory rhetoric ignited vigilante and military campaigns between 1859 and 1874 that killed over 380 Pinal Apaches—including many women and children— then confined survivors onto the San Carlos Reservation. Mining across Pinal Apache territory followed promptly, claiming additional Apache lands inside and outside reservation borders.[12] A Chart on **Annihilationist Government Policy and Miner Bombast Targeting Pinal Apaches is in the last chapter of this book.**[13]

An 1859 article in the New York Times used this rhetoric:

> *The Apache is as near the lobo, or wolf of the country, as any human being can be to a beast.* ... They neither cultivate nor hunt to any extent, but exist mainly ... by plunder. ... This is the greatest obstacle to the operations of the mining companies. ... [W]hipping these wild tribes ... into submission, and driving them into reservations ... with the penalty of death sternly enforced if they pass their limits, is the only prompt, economical, and humane process. ... My greatest hopes for

~ 435 ~

Arizona, however, rest on the army. ... Officers of various grades are becoming interested in mines throughout that region. *They ... have connections of influence and capital*. (Emphasis added).[14]

1865-1886: Apache Wars

The Apache Wars, though long, were not fought in the manner of most wars. There were very few open battles. Ambushes were common. They did not consider retreat shameful, but a useful tactic. They only engaged in open battle if they had greater numbers, the higher ground, or the element of surprise. Indian scouts were an essential component in tracking the Apaches. Governor Goodwin mustered in 103 Maricopa and Pima recruits to serve in the Arizona Volunteer Infantry as scouts in the Apache Wars.

More violence erupted as settlers pushed into Arizona and furthered displaced native peoples. To protect citizens from Indians, the U.S. intensified its military presence. Between 1865 and the late 1880s, military installations proliferated as the Army sought to contain and subjugate Indians. In the process, the Army built roads, a telegraph system, and a heliograph system, and also mapped the territory.

On March 2, 1865, *Arizona's Superintendent of Indian Affairs*, Charles D. Poston (1865), appealed to the U.S. House of Representatives for additional military support to protect the miners, not the Indians he represented:

> For three centuries they have stayed the progress of civilization.
> ... *Their subjugation would open to our hardy miners an unexplored gold field north of the Gila*. ... A sickly sympathy for a few beastly savages should not stand in the way of the development of our rich gold fields, or the protection of our enterprising frontiersmen. (Emphasis added).[15]

That same month, General John S. Mason assumed command of the District of Arizona. Mason was concerned with safeguarding the main supply routes across the territory, protecting miners and settlers, and establishing bases of operation for offensive sorties. Mason and his successors were faced with seemingly insurmountable problems as they attempted to manage their military domain. Supplies had to be shipped from San Francisco around the Baja Peninsula, then unloaded at Fort Yuma and dispersed to far-flung posts throughout the territory. Roads were poor, and rapid communication almost impossible. Supply trains were easy prey for Indian attacks. To avoid having to ferry supplies across the river from Fort Yuma, the Army in 1865 authorized the creation of the Yuma Supply Depot (later referred to as the Yuma Quartermaster Depot).

1866 Forward: Indian Scalp Bounties

On November 23, 1866, a town meeting in Prescott, AZ with "large attendance," appointed Thomas Hodges to organize a militia company, with pay and scalping bounties offered. A couple of years later, merchants from Prescott were reported to be travelling with mules decorated with scalps. In 1868, Tully & Ochoa Wagon Company reportedly paid its employees $150 per scalp, primarily targeting Apaches. The company, based in Tucson, Arizona, armed its wagon trains and was responsible for supplying army outposts in the region.

In 1882, according to a notice in the *Arizona Weekly Citizen*, the town of Tombstone "offers a reward of $200 for twenty-five Indian scalps and ten dollars for every additional one." There is no mention of who paid the bounty. A *New York Times* article in 1885, from Deming, New Mexico, reports on counties in Arizona that are "organizing in armed bodies for the purpose of going on a real old-fashioned Indian hunt, and they propose to bring back the scalps and obtain the reward. Word now comes from Tombstone, the county seat of Cochise County, that the reward … has been increased to $500 for a buck Indian's scalp."[16]

Another clip, published by the *Atchison Daily Champion* in Atchison, Kansas, October 9, 1885, tells of settlers in Arizona fanning out across the state to "hunt for redskins, with a view of obtaining their scalps." Scalps taken from the bodies of dead Indians were valued at $250, according to the report. The campaign was allegedly launched in an effort to end the Apache Wars.[17]

In early 1886, a horse breeder named H.G. Toussaint offered horses for the scalp of Geronimo and any other Apache. Geronimo, leader, warrior, and healer, fought against all who threatened the sovereignty and survival of his people. In May 1886, General Nelson Miles, hoping to attract both American and Mexican recruits on an expedition, offered $50 for the head of each Apache they killed and $2,000 for the head or capture of Apache leader Geronimo.[18]

1867-1870: Indian Attacks

From 1867 thru 1870, the Apache conducted fifty-four successful raids on civilian settlements, multiple cross border engagements in Mexico, and killed forty-four citizens.[19] See Chart in Notes hereto.

1862-1871: U.S. Military Campaigns

American campaigns killed over 380 Pinal Apaches, excluding the Camp Grant Massacre victims. The cost of the Apache pacification efforts was 5,000 American lives, thousands of dollars in property, and an estimated thirty eight million dollars between 1862 and 1871.[20]

1868: Department of the Interior - Indians

In 1868, Congress mandated the establishment of the Department of the Interior, Bureau of Indian Commissioners, to be the primary federal agency responsible for all Indian policies. For southwest pacification efforts, the War Department took a supporting role in execution of the policy. Political influences and the public's desire for limited military operations forced the military to operate within a confusing framework defined by divergent political agendas from the War Department and the Department of the Interior. Throughout the late 1860s, the War Department repeatedly requested that Indian affairs be placed under their control.

> The War Department struggled to understand its role in assisting the assimilation process. They attempted to understand the most effective way to accomplish the mission by questioning, "How did the policy apply to Indians such as the Apache in Arizona that had no reservation system established? How much force is sufficient to secure a reservation? When the civilian hierarchy asked for military intervention on the reservation who would be in command?"

> The Grant peace policy individually executed by the Department of Indian Commissioner agents, exacerbated hostilities and strained civilian and military relationships. The policy clouded the lines between civilian and military authorities, stymied effectiveness of military operations, hampered interagency coordination, emboldened hostile Apache forces, and placed the Army in a tenuous position to accomplish the strategic end state.[21]

President Grant initially planned for U.S. Army officers to have a more prominent role in implementing his Peace Policy, but in the Indian Appropriations Act of 1870, Congress included a provision making it illegal for military officers to accept civil appointments.

1871: Reservations Established

Vincent Colyer, a former colonel in the Union Army, representing President Ulysses S. Grant's administration, set aside a reservation for certain Mohave Apaches after inspecting their circumstances:

> "[H]aving personally inspected the country and condition of the Apache Indians on the Verde River ... and finding the Indians to be in considerable numbers, *destitute and in a starving condition, having no boundaries defining their homes, their country overrun by hunters who kill their game, and not infrequently kill the Indians*—gold prospectors and others ... I have concluded to declare [land described] to be an Indian reservation.(Emphasis added).[22]

In the fall of 1871, he created additional reservations. The citizens of Arizona were not enthused by his action. John Marion, editor of the *Arizona Miner*, wrote of Colyer that Arizonians should "dump the old devil into the shaft of some mine, and pile rocks upon him until he is dead. A rascal who comes here to thwart the efforts of military and citizens to conquer a peace from our savage foe, deserves to be stoned to death like the treacherous, black-hearted dog that he is.[23] It was clear that the population desired a more active solution than the Peace Policy envisioned.

1871: Camp Grant Massacre

On April 30, 1871, a group of seven Anglo-Americans, 48 Mexicans, and 92 Papagos killed an estimated 85 to 130 Aravaipa women and kidnapped 29 children sleeping near Camp Grant. The attackers claimed that the Indians were part of a band that had stolen some of their cattle and murdered an Anglo settler earlier that week. While papers in the East were outraged at the grisly murders, a local newspaper reflected the sentiment of the community:

> Sunday April 30, 1871 was a lucky day for the Americans, Mexicans and peaceable Indians of the territory, as on that day several citizens of southern Arizona and about a hundred Papago Indians surprized[sic] a rancheria of Apaches near Camp Grant on the San Pedro River and suceeded [sic] in killing 125 of the villanous [sic] wretches, who, while being fed from the public crib at Grant and treated by the military as though they were good Indians, had committed many murders and robberies for which they have been justly punished. Farewell, defunct Pinals, you have met a just fate...[24]

President Grant stated that the Camp Grant attack was "purely murder" and told Arizona Governor Anson P. K. Safford that if the people responsible were not brought to trial, he would declare martial law in Arizona. As a result of the President's threat, a trial was held.[25]

Skeleton Cave. In this fight, scores of Yavapai Indians were killed in their stronghold. The Cavalry troops, led by their Indian scouts, found their hideout-a cave in a canyon wall-on December 28, 1872. The soldiers rained bullets down upon the Yavapais by ricocheting them off the cave ceiling.

1871: General Crook, Apache Wars, Use of Indian Scouts

General Crook arrived in June 1871 and immediately issued orders to his subordinates to provide him first-hand accounts of: the current security situation by region, assessment of the terrain and impacts to cavalry operations, the status of military logistics, recent enemy actions and how they applied their tactics against Army formations, subordinates military views on the effectiveness of civilian led reservation system efforts, and the populace's perceptions of the Apache problem by sub-region.[26] "We have before us the tiger of the human species."[27]

Crook confirmed that Army forces in Arizona would rapidly have to adapt. His observations allowed him to understand how the enemy employed his tactics to prevent Army forces from gaining success. He assessed that the Apache excelled at controlling the terrain, employing deception, and expertly using ambushes to destroy superior forces. The Apache used terrain to their advantage and maintained a complex system of high mountain safe havens to conduct operations. Their tactics protected their logistical base and enabled mobility to strike at the time and place of their choosing. The Apache warrior acted as "his own general" when in contact but, could effortlessly combine action with adjacent elements to decisively halt Army forces in pursuit.

Crook applied his Civil War experiences fighting the confederate partisans to determine that, paramount to the Apaches' tactical success, was their ability to conduct a protracted running rear guard action. Their expert employment of the rear guard divided Army forces over time and terrain and allowed them to continually regroup while exploiting the Army's limited maneuver. General Sheridan skillfully described their advantage: "they attack and plunder, then scatter like quails over distance, then regroup at a previously planned point, making it exceedingly difficult for our troops to overtake and punish them."[28]

Based on analysis of terrain and mobility constraints, Crook assessed his forces lacked sufficient intelligence and reconnaissance resources to locate the enemy. Crook determined that Indian scouts were essential to his targeting effort to find and fix his adversary to gain the tactical advantage. They would give him a superior edge in locating the centers of the enemy and destroying them. Within a year after arriving, Crook had recruited Tonto, Cibecue, and White Mountain Apache, Walapai, Yavapai, Apache-Mohave, and Paiute warriors into his newly formed scout detachments.

> Crook reformed his cavalry to operate as small mobile strike forces capable of independent action. Crook's campaign framework focused on the use of Indian scouts to … "find, follow, and defeat" the enemy in their safe havens. … He adopted all weather campaigning to exploit the Apaches' winter encampments and destroy their logistic base and support zones. He summarized his campaign strategy in his 1870 guidance to his forces: "Indians should be induced to surrender in all cases where possible; where they prefer to fight they will get all the fighting they want, and in one good dose instead of a number of petty engagements, but in either case *they will be hunted down until the last one in hostility has been killed or captured.* Every effort should be made to avoid the killing of women and children." … *When prisoners can be induced to enlist as scouts, they should be so enlisted, because the wilder the Apache is, the more likely he is to know the wiles and stratagems of those still in the mountains, their hiding places and intentions.* No excuse is to be accepted for leaving the trail; if horses play out, the enemy must be followed on foot, and no sacrifice should be left untried to make the campaign, short, sharp, and decisive. (Emphasis added).[29] Crook theorized that the use of scouts against their own tribe would break the will of rogue Apaches quicker than any purely military application of force.[30]

They needed to raise the "surprise attack" in their arsenal, regardless of whether it meant killing women and children. The "cries of conscience" from the east had no play in this game. Indians fighting with less technology, armaments, and at times, numbers, knew survival is won and maintained at the point of the lance. This is why tribes had "warrior societies". This is why the Apache who faced war from the Mexicans, the Texans and other tribes had developed an elite society promulgated on the warrior and aggression.

Crook chose to ride a mule while in the Southwest. He felt it handled the heat and terrain better than a horse. He also developed the use of pack trains. Whether the task was battle or hard labor, Crook usually worked on the front lines with his men. Crook witnessed firsthand the ineffectiveness of the white man at tracking the Apache. He came up with perhaps the U.S.' most effective strategy in the Apache Wars--tracking Apache with defected Apache. He would later recall his time in the Apache Wars as one of the most difficult periods of his life.

Crook's General Order No. 10 (November 21, 1871) required all Apaches to remain within the boundaries of the recently established reservation or "be regarded as hostile."[31] In the Tonto Basin campaign authorized by that same order, Crook orchestrated a multipronged scouring of Tonto Apache homelands and northern reaches of Pinal Apache land. The campaign built on previous U.S. Army operations' effective tactics: relentless pursuits by cavalry units guided by Apache scouts, dawn ambushes, and destruction of homes, food stores, and agricultural fields.

Following General George Crook's successful 1872-1873 campaign against the Apache, the tribes were located on reservations after agreeing to the federal government's promise to provide provisions. Trouble began almost immediately after the Chiricahua were re-located to San Carlos in 1876, and thrown in with other Apache groups who regarded them as enemies. Also, leaders like Juh, Chatto, Chihuahua, and Victorio were unhappy with reservation life and continued escaping from the reservations, leading raids in Arizona and Mexico. This initiated the so-called "renegade" period in the Apache Wars where soldiers would go in pursuit of those who escaped from their reservations.

By early December 1872, he employed a force of over 1000 cavalrymen and hundreds of Apache scouts to encircle known hostiles, to force the bands through concentric mobile columns into the Tonto Mountain Basin where a decisive action could destroy their military ability to resist. His elements were destroying hostiles, forcing surrender, destroying winter stores, and controlling safe havens, which prevented the Apaches from collecting supplies for winter sustainment. ... To increase his effectiveness in pursuing hostiles he would employ his Apache scouts to "find, and fix the enemy". His operational objectives were to destroy their logistics, force engagements, and strike sanctuaries.[32] The resistance of the Tonto Apache was broken in an engagement at Turret Peak on March 27, 1873. It was the culmination of General Crook's campaign in the Tonto Basin.[33]

Chiricahua Apache Reservation Proposals

Finding or defeating the Chiricahua Apache, led by Cochise, had proven futile for the U.S. Army. The strategy shifted to relocating them to a reservation. Cochise was tired. He and his people had found life on the run and in hiding exhausting. However, the U.S. had what appeared to be an inexhaustible supply of soldiers and provisions.

Cochise bided his time and continued to avoid capture and defeat. He was asked repeatedly to meet and discuss relocating his people to a reservation. He would refuse because reservations at the time had poor conditions. The San Carlos Reservation, for instance, had bad water, rampant sickness, mandatory roll call, and forced menial labor which the people believed beneath them as warriors.

1872: Chiricahua Apache Reservation

In 1872, General O.O. Howard and Tom Jeffords, an Army scout, prospector, and employee of overland mail in Arizona, put their lives at risk by approaching Cochise's Stronghold with few troops. When confronted by the Chiricahua, Howard and Jeffords told them they were not there to fight but to talk.

Cochise made Howard and Jeffords wait several days before granting them entry into his camp. General Howard and Cochise entered into reservation talks. Both sides were very stubborn but after some time Cochise got the upper hand. Cochise procured a reservation for his people that spanned much of modern day Cochise County in southeast Arizona. Local newspapers slandered General Howard for giving up so much ground in the negotiations. Tom Jeffords was appointed as the Apache's agent.

The reservation brought about a peaceful period in the war which would last four years. Settlers did not approve of the reservation's loose authority over the Chiricahua. On the reservation, the Chiricahua were able to roam free and camp wherever they wanted. There was no roll call taken. They were even allowed to leave the reservation, and often raided in Mexico, which stirred tensions.

In Washington, DC, the Bureau of Indian Affairs and the Department of War fought over jurisdiction of the reservation. Given the peaceful period, however, General Crook headed north to fight with Lieutenant Colonel George Custer in the Dakotas.

1870s: Concentration of Apaches on San Carlos Reservation

In the 1870s, decision makers in Washington decided to consolidate the Chiricahuas with the Western Apaches at the San Carlos Agency in the new Arizona Territory. From Washington, it may have seemed that Apaches were all alike, but the Chiricahuas were not related to Western Apaches except in language and culture.

John P. Clum, despised Agent for the San Carlos Reservation pompously bragged:

> Since taking charge of the San Carlos agency in 1874 it
> has been my lot to consolidate five agencies into one, and
> to superintend the movement of about four thousand wild
> Indians to the San Carlos reservation; thus bringing together
> Indians, who, by their former locations, were separated by
> a distance of 600 miles; and also *opening to ranchmen and*
> *miners three Indian reservations, including important tracts*
> *of agricultural and mineral lands.* These movements have
> all been effected without the loss of a single life, and without
> destroying the property of citizens. ... *The Indians under*
> *my jurisdiction have been held in complete subjection,* and
> have remained quiet, industrious, and progressive. (Emphasis
> added).[34]

Western Apaches filled to capacity the San Carlos reservation, leaving very little area or resources for the Chiricahuas. Nevertheless, Cochise's band, now led by Geronimo because of Cochise's death, was moved to San Carlos in 1876. Victorio's Mimbres at Ojo Caliente were next. Forced to move to San Carlos in 1877, Victorio and his band of Mimbres soon departed the miserable conditions at San Carlos and took refuge in the Dragoon Mountains. Told once more that they could settle at Ojo Caliente, Victorio moved his band back to the old reservation. Inexplicably, in August 1879, the 9th Cavalry arrived at Ojo Caliente to guide Victorio's band back to San Carlos. Victorio had finally had enough; the 'Victorio War' had started.

1874: Death of Cochise

In 1874, Cochise died of what was likely stomach cancer. The whereabouts of his grave are still unknown, though it is thought to be somewhere in his Stronghold. Cochise was one of the Chiricahua's most effective leaders during the time of the Apache Wars. He was the only one able to bring prolonged peace and freedom to his people, even if it did not last long after his death. With Cochise's death, the Chiricahua were left without a strong central leader. The U.S. saw a chance to close the problematic Chiricahua Reservation. The final straw came when two Chiricahua warriors killed two white men for not selling them whiskey. The U.S. fired Agent Jeffords and abolished the reservation.

Pacification of Apaches Permits Mining

With the pacification of the Apaches in 1874, mining resumed in Arizona, with discoveries of silver, copper, and gold in Gila and Pinal counties. In 1878, Ed Schieffelin discovered the Tombstone mines in southeastern Arizona, and for several years Tombstone was noted as one of the wildest of the frontier mining towns, offering the talented Wyatt Earp an opportunity to make a lasting contribution. The Tombstone gold deposits were soon exhausted, but the district produced some $20,000,000 in silver within twenty years.[35]

1874: Indian Ring

The Indian Ring was comprised of crooked businessmen and Indian agents intermingling land speculation, mining, farming and ranching businesses. Contracts to supply military posts and Indian reservations were especially lucrative given the high prices set and the opportunities for fraud. Companies who had licenses to trade with Indians on the reservations would often cheat them and the government by supplying inferior goods, improperly weighing beef with rigged scales or weighing corn or seed that was soaked in water to provide less than the authorized daily rations, overcharging for freight, manipulating census numbers, signing incorrect vouchers, etc. The stolen surplus would then be sold on the open market.

In 1879 Inspector J. H. Hammond discovered that San Carlos Reservation Agent H. L. Hart and others were guilty of "gross frauds and dishonesty" concerning Indian cattle shipments. Agent Hart had a substantial interest in the Washington Mine, and he offered Inspector Hammond and Commissioner Hayt's son the option to buy the mine at a discount, in return for a promise not to prosecute. Commissioner Hayt's son closed the transaction, acting under the assumed name, "Edward Knapp."[36] Commissioner Hayt was forced to resign.

General Clinton B. Fisk, president of the Board of Indian Commissioners, reported to the Commission:

"Our Indian administration is made a stench in the nostrils of honest men by the shameful practices and personal conduct of our officials....San Carlos has suffered through the administration of a mining speculator, conducting his mining through means derived from the sale of agency supplies. Sugar, coffee, meat, blankets were taken by the wagon load from our warehouse to his mining camps. The purchase and sale of mines absorbed his thought. Finally, by the aid of one of our inspectors, he was enabled to sell his mines for a large sum and quietly leave the country, in genial social relations with the said inspector, who had been sent there to investigate abuses, and, as he said, to prosecute the agent."[37]

1882-1886: General Crook's Use of Apache Scouts in Second Apache Campaign

Incorporating many years of experience in conventional and irregular combat, Crook's second tour in the Arizona Territory differed from his first in that he relied more heavily on the use of Chiricahua Apache scouts to find and fight the hostile Chiricahuas. The General also employed seven secret observers to report any unrest or hostility among the reservation Indians.[38]

Once understanding the problem, Crook identified three major objectives according to noted historian Robert Utley: "To bring the reservation Indians under control, to give protection to the lives and property of citizens, and to subjugate the hostiles [led by Geronimo.]"[39] In order to surmount these challenges he had to divide the Indians into two groups: those living on the reservation in peace and accepting U.S. policy, and the hostiles that defied all manner of assimilation.

> Crook re-energized the cavalry and infantry to take on the mission of hunting down Geronimo's band as Sheridan had envisioned. He formed "an elite force of cavalry, mounted infantry, and Indian auxiliaries." After five months, the forces sent in pursuit of Geronimo were *virtually exhausted and no one "came in contact with or killed a hostile…"* (Emphasis added).[40]

1879-1886: Apache Wars

From 1879 through 1886, the U.S. Army fought almost continuously against Chiricahua bands under Victorio and then Geronimo. After fleeing the consolidated reservation system, Victorio established a stronghold in the northern mountains of Chihuahua, the Sierra Madres, and raided in New Mexico, Arizona, and Chihuahua. Despite employing several cavalry regiments, Victorio's band of less than 200 eluded capture by the U.S. Army and harassed civilian populations for over fourteen months.

In the summer of 1886, five thousand U.S. troops or some 20% of the U.S. Army were chasing less than two dozen warriors. Finally, crossing agreements were made between Mexico and the U.S., and Victorio was denied sanctuary. Mexico also organized forces to fight Victorio. In October 1880, Victorio was cornered by a combined U.S.-Mexico effort, and his band of Mimbres Chiricahuas was destroyed by Colonel Joaquin Terrazas' 400-man volunteer force, at Tres Castillas.

In 1885, the lack of social development for the Chiricahuas again created discontent on the San Carlos reservation. Geronimo and his Chiricahuas yet again departed the reservation for Mexico, committing depredations along the way. General Crook used the same techniques to end the final Apache insurgency.

Crook's humanitarian efforts in trying to assimilate the Apaches into society through his band of scouts, estranged him from his superiors, and ultimately led to his resignation of command of the Arizona Territory. All he had hoped to achieve for the Apaches was tragically wasted when the U.S. moved all Chiricahua Apaches, to include Apache scouts who faithfully served the U.S. Army, to Florida in order to refuse any possibility of support to those hostiles still resisting the Army. The Apaches were sent to a prison in Fort Marion, Florida. Learning of the fate of his family and band, Geronimo surrendered at Skeleton Canyon on September 3, 1886, and began the long trek into captivity in Florida. So ended the last Apache insurgency that had bested Spanish, Mexican, and American forces for over two centuries. The Chiricahua Apaches weren't allowed to return until 1913.

The Army became concerned in 1881 when a medicine man began spreading the new ghost dance ceremony to the White Mountain Apaches. After arresting the medicine man on August 30th, his followers attacked the soldiers in an attempt to free him. This is the only known fight where the Army's Apache scouts mutinied.

1871: Arizona Copper

What of the *development of the richest mineral* portion of the Territory that led to the *subjugation or extermination of the merciless Apaches?* Copper mining in the Morenci district of eastern Arizona began in 1871.

In 1874 the Commissioner of Indian Affairs persuaded President Ulysses S. Grant to restore the eastern portion of the Apache reservation in Arizona to the public domain by executive order. This portion of the reservation contained copper-bearing lands which non-Indians wished to mine. Both the Indian agent in Arizona and the Commissioner of Indian Affairs had financial holdings in the company which subsequently developed the copper mines.[41]

The Bisbee and Jerome districts were opened in 1877, and copper was mined at Globe the following year. By the 1880s two giants in the copper industry, the Calumet and Arizona Mining Company and the Phelps, Dodge Company, were leaders in production. The coming of the railroads opened a new era in the mining history of both Arizona and New Mexico...

Production data for the Magma Mine, the Superior District's largest and longest-lived, enumerate a small fraction of the billions in wealth extracted from Pinal Apache lands: "1,299,718 short tons of copper, 36,550 short tons of zinc, approximately 686,000 ounces of gold and 34.3 million ounces of silver."[42]

1885: Arizona Copper Mining Companies

Other large firms bought Arizona mines.

Pope, Cole and Company, one of the three largest U.S. refiners of copper, purchased the Old Dominion and Old Globe mines.
A group from Edinburgh, Scotland, composed of textile and insurance magnates, bought the Clifton copper mines and began constructing railroads, tramways, inclines, large smelting machinery, and other new apparatuses, thus making their Arizona Copper Company the most sophisticated operation in the Southwest.
The Calumet and Hecla Mining Company, the largest producer of copper in the U.S. during the late nineteenth century, formed the Cochise Copper Company and gained control of the Peabody Mine at Johnson.
Other Boston stockholders of the Calumet and Hecla also purchased and consolidated the old Santa Rita mines near Silver City, New Mexico, and formed the Santa Rita Copper and Iron Company. To cut costs they funded the construction of a railroad to Silver City and built the Southwest's first copper concentrator in 1882.

By 1883 six companies in Arizona each produced between 1 million and 7.5

million pounds of copper. Output expanded very rapidly. From a production record of only about 2 million pounds of copper in 1880, the copper mines of Arizona expanded in 1881 to 10 million pounds and doubled that figure the next year. Within a few years Arizona had become the second largest producer of copper in the U.S., after the mines at Lake Superior, Michigan.43

The Copper Queen, United Verde, Calumet and Arizona, Arizona Copper, Old Dominion (consolidated companies), Detroit Copper, Superior & Pittsburg, Miami Copper, Shattuck Arizona, Shannon Copper and Ray Consolidated, paid dividends of record in 1916, amounting to $225,000,000.[44]

1861–1868: Army's Constabulary Duties - Apache Wars

Western Army forces performed constabulary services conducting pacification, supporting the Bureau of Indian Commissioners with treaty enforcement, providing security for civilians and Apaches, and assisting the Department of the Interior with the implementation of a reservation system, and military governance.[45]

Second, the Army provided security from hostilities for the expanding western railroad and supporting infrastructure required for expansion. Hostilities economically affected U.S. mineral extraction and railroad expansion to the pacific coast.[46]

Southwestern territory politicians desired a purely lethal approach of extermination to mitigate threats to the civilian populace and increase economic development, while the "post-Civil War drawdown affected the military's ability to project enough force to achieve the prescribed military goals."[47] The situation in Arizona created a perpetual cycle of violence composed of raids, murder, and reprisals conducted by both civilian settlers and the Apache.

Railroads: Territories of New Mexico and Arizona

Emigration pouring in as a result of railroads "would soon solve the Indian problem by the extermination or complete subjugation of the hostile tribes." (Emphasis added).[48] Union Pacific Railroad's officials and employees favored war, since the government paid two cents a pound for freight and ten cents a mile for troops carried from Omaha to North Platte. In fact, two-thirds of the Union Pacific's business was with the War Department.[49]

1883: Indians Had "Little Use for Precious Metals"

Miners and their political pawns were unapologetic about killing Apaches, destroying their possessions, or taking their lands. In a further exposition of voracious frontier mentality, the Territorial Legislature (Legislature of the Territory of Arizona, 1885) petitioned the U.S. Congress for all lands remaining in Apache hands, asserting, that the Indians now occupying these vast reservations, comprising the richest mineral, agricultural and timber lands of the Territory, have made no use of said lands, but simply withhold the same from public use and occupation, and are a perpetual menace to the peaceful settler, retarding progress, paralyzing prosperity ...[50]

Indians had "little use for precious metals." (Emphasis added).[51]

1916: Arizona's Mineral Production

While it has been estimated that the dividends from gold, silver and lead produced in the early days of Arizona's history amounted to $100,000,000, it was not until the great copper properties of the State had begun to be developed that Arizona really became a world power in the wealth of its minerals, producing in one year, 1916, metals to the value of $203,000,000.[52]

Aftermath, Loss of ~5,900,000 Acres

A chart on Important Federal Government Acts Affecting Western Apache Lands[53] from Welch, J. R. (2017). Earth, Wind, and Fire: Pinal Apaches, Miners, and Genocide in Central Arizona, 1859-1874. SAGE Open, 7(4) is in the last Chapter.

Author Notes: Arizona

The advent of the Civil War, the formation of Arizona as its own territory in February 1863, and the discovery of gold and silver throughout the region, brought about the rapid militarization of the region, with *twenty-eight military outposts or forts being erected in Arizona during the decade*.

MILITARY POSTS, 1849-64, 1864–1897 [See cites for listing to demonstrate the extent of military assignments in the mid-1800s.][54 and 55]

A chart on **Thirty-Five Lethal Attacks on Apaches in and near Pinal Apache Territory, 1859–1874**[56] prepared by Berndt Kühn's, Chronicles of War: Apache & Yavapai Resistance in the Southwestern United States and Northern Mexico, 1821–1937, and included in Welch, J. R. (2017). Earth, Wind, and Fire: Pinal Apaches, Miners, and Genocide in Central Arizona, 1859-1874. SAGE Open, 7(4) is in the last Chapter.

A chart on **Lethal Attacks on Non-Apaches by Pinal Apaches or in Pinal Apache Territory, 1859-1874**[57] prepared by Berndt Kühn's, Chronicles of War: Apache & Yavapai Resistance and included in Welch, J. R. (2017). Earth, Wind, and Fire: Pinal Apaches, Miners, and Genocide in Central Arizona, 1859-1874. SAGE Open, 7(4) is in the last Chapter.

Notes: Arizona

1. Report of the Commissioner of Indian Affairs to the Secretary of the Interior United States. Office of Indian Affairs, U.S. Government Printing Office, 1864, p. 28.
2. General Land Office, Report of Commissioner Edmunds, October 22, 1863. https://www.nytimes.com/1863/12/10/archives/general-land-office-report-of-commissioner-edmunds-preemption-the.html (accessed online March 7, 2023).
3. ARIZONA MINING SCAMS AND UNASSAYABLE ORE PROJECTS OF THE LATE 20TH CENTURY. Open File Report 02-20 December 2002, W. Scott Donaldson.
4. General James H. Carleton, February 27, 1864. National Archives and Records Administration, Adjutant General File Number: 86 N 1864, National Archives Identifier: 300368, National Archives Series: Letters Received, 1805–1889. National Archives Record Group 94: Records of the Adjutant General's Office, 1762 – 1984, Microfilm publication: M619 Letters Received by the Office of the Adjutant General (Main Series), 1861-1870.
5. Welch, J. R. (2017). Earth, Wind, and Fire: Pinal Apaches, Miners, and Genocide in Central Arizona, 1859-1874. SAGE Open, 7(4).
6. https://truewestmagazine.com/article/mangas-coloradas-undue-fate/ (accessed online March 7, 2023).
7. https://www.nps.gov/chir/learn/historyculture/apache-wars-cochise.htm (accessed online March 7, 2023).
8. Indian Wars in Arizona Territory. https://dema.az.gov/sites/default/files/Publications/AR-IndianWars inArizonaTerritory-BORUNDA.pdf (accessed online September 5, 2022).
9. Siegrist, Jeremy T. *Apache Wars: A Constabulary Perspective*. ARMY

COMMAND AND GENERAL STAFF COLL FORT LEAVENWORTH KS SCHOOL OF ADVANCED MILITARY STUDIES, 2005, p. 53. Thrapp, Dan. The Conquest of Apacheria. Oklahoma City: University of Oklahoma Press, 1976, p. 32.

10. Welch, J. R. (2017). Earth, Wind, and Fire: Pinal Apaches, Miners, and Genocide in Central Arizona, 1859-1874. SAGE Open, 7(4).

11. Id.

12. Id.

13. Id.

14. Id.

15. Annual Report of the Secretary of the Interior, Office of Indian Affairs, United States. U.S. Government Printing Office, 1865, p. 155.

16. https://www.bountyfilm.org/lesson-four/bounties-in-pennsylvania (accessed online March 7, 2023).

17. Id.

18. Id.

19. PETITE GUERRE: BRIGADIER GEN. GEORGE CROOK, COMMANDER OF THE DEPARTMENT OF ARIZONA, APPLICATION OF SMALL WAR DOCTRINE AGAINST THE APACHE 1870-1873 MAJ Stephen P. Snyder United States Army, p. 26.

20. Ibid., p. 12.

21. Ibid., p. 18.

22. Annual Report of the Secretary of the Interior, Office of Indian Affairs, United States. U.S. Government Printing Office, 1886, p. 292.

23. Arizona Miner, May 20, 1871.

24. Arizona (Tucson) Citizen, 24 June 1871.

25. ETHNOGRAPHIC OVERVIEW AND ASSESSMENT OF CHIRICAHUA NATIONAL MONUMENT AND FORT BOWIE NATIONAL HISTORIC SITE, National Park Service Task Agreement J1233040013, Scott Rushforth, Ph.D. Department of Anthropology, New Mexico State University, Las Cruces, New Mexico 88003, July 2010, U.S. Department of the Interior, National Park Service, Intermountain Support Office, p. 137. General James H. Carleton, February 27, 1864. National Archives and Records Administration, Adjutant General File Number: 86 N 1864, National Archives Identifier: 300368, National Archives Series: Letters Received, 1805–1889. National Archives Record Group 94: Records of the Adjutant General's Office, 1762 – 1984, Microfilm publication: M619 Letters Received by the Office of the Adjutant General (Main Series), 1861-1870.

26. PETITE GUERRE: BRIGADIER GEN. GEORGE CROOK, COMMANDER OF THE DEPARTMENT OF ARIZONA, APPLICATION OF SMALL WAR DOCTRINE AGAINST THE APACHE 1870-1873 MAJ Stephen P. Snyder United States Army, p. 32.

27. https://www.nps.gov/chir/learn/historyculture/apache-wars-geronimo.htm (accessed online March 7, 2023).

28. PETITE GUERRE: BRIGADIER GEN. GEORGE CROOK, COMMANDER OF THE DEPARTMENT OF ARIZONA, APPLICATION OF SMALL WAR DOCTRINE AGAINST THE APACHE 1870-1873 MAJ Stephen P. Snyder United States Army, p. 34.

29. Robinson, Charles. General Crook and the Western Frontier. Norman: University of Oklahoma Press, 2001, p. 127.

30. Andrew Birtle, US Army Counterinsurgency and Contingency Operations Doctrine, 2nd ed. (Washington DC: Center of Military History, 1998), p. 69.

31. PETITE GUERRE: BRIGADIER GEN. GEORGE CROOK, COMMANDER OF THE DEPARTMENT OF ARIZONA, APPLICATION OF SMALL WAR DOCTRINE AGAINST THE APACHE 1870-1873 MAJ Stephen P. Snyder United States Army, p. 41.

32. Thrapp, Dan. The Conquest of Apacheria. Oklahoma City: University of Oklahoma Press, 1976, p.120. Robinson, Charles. General Crook and the Western Frontier. Norman: University of Oklahoma Press, 2001, p. 128.

33. PETITE GUERRE: BRIGADIER GEN. GEORGE CROOK, COMMANDER OF THE DEPARTMENT OF ARIZONA, APPLICATION OF SMALL WAR DOCTRINE AGAINST THE APACHE 1870-1873 MAJ Stephen P. Snyder United States Army, p. 43-44.

34. Report of the Commissioner of Indian Affairs to the Secretary of the Interior United States. Office of Indian Affairs, U.S. Government Printing Office, 1877, p. 34.

35. Geology, Mines and Minerals of Tombstone, Jan Rasmussen. https://janrasmussen.c om/pdfs/Tombstone%20abstract%202012.pdf (accessed online November 18, 2021).

36. Phillips, George H. "The Indian Ring in Dakota Territory, 1870-1890." South Dakota History 2.4 (1972): 350.

37. Annual Report of the Board of Indian Commissioners to the Secretary of the Interior ..., Volume II, U.S. Government Printing Office, 1880, pp. 54-55. New Mexico Historical Review, No. 1, January, 1958, pp. 88-90. Welch, J. R. (2017). Earth, Wind, and Fire: Pinal Apaches, Miners, and Genocide in Central Arizona, 1859-1874. SAGE Open, 7(4).

38. Crook, George. General George Crook: His Autobiography. University of Oklahoma Press, 1986, p. 245.

39. Utley, Robert. Frontiersman in Blue, the United States Army and the Indian 1848-1865. 2nd ed. Lincoln: University of Nebraska Press, 1981, p. 377.

40. Thomas W. Dunlay, Wolves for the Blue Soldiers: Indian Scouts and Auxiliaries with the United States Army, 1860-90 (Lincoln: University of

Nebraska Press, 1982), p. 181.

41. The 19th Century Indian Office, April 6, 2011. http://nativeameri-cannetroots.net/diary/912 (accessed online August 14, 2022).

42. Welch, J. R. (2017). Earth, Wind, and Fire: Pinal Apaches, Miners, and Genocide in Central Arizona, 1859-1874. SAGE Open, 7(4).

43. Spude, Robert L. "Mineral Frontier in Transition: Copper Mining in Arizona, 1880-1885." New Mexico Historical Review 51, 1 (2021).

44. Robinson, Will Henry. *The story of Arizona*. Berryhill Company, 1919, p. 263. https://books.google.com/books?id=I9Si1eQ1qQMC&q=ELEVEN+-COMPANIES#v=snippet&q=ELEVEN%20COMPANIES&f=false (accessed online October 4, 2022).

45. Andrew Birtle, US Army Counterinsurgency and Contingency Operations Doctrine, 2nd ed. (Washington DC: Center of Military History, 1998), p. 85.

46. Marszalek, John. Sherman a Soldiers Passion for Order. 2nd ed. New York: Free Press, 2007, p. 379.

47. PETITE GUERRE: BRIGADIER GEN. GEORGE CROOK, COMMANDER OF THE DEPARTMENT OF ARIZONA, APPLICATION OF SMALL WAR DOCTRINE AGAINST THE APACHE 1870-1873 MAJ Stephen P. Snyder United States Army. p. 3.

48. Statistics Of Mines And Mining In The States And Territories West Of The Rocky Mountains: Being The 6th Annual Report Of U.S. Commissioner Of Mining Statistics to Secretary of Treasury, 1871, p. 278.

49. Sen. Ex. Do. No , 13, 40th Cong., 1 sess. (Serial 1308), 1867, P. 60. Waltmann, Henry George, "The Interior Department, War Department and Indian Policy, 1865-1887" (1962). Dissertations, Theses, & Student Research, Department of History, p. 132.

50. Welch, J. R. (2017). Earth, Wind, and Fire: Pinal Apaches, Miners, and Genocide in Central Arizona, 1859-1874. SAGE Open, 7(4).

51. Arizona, Its Mineral Resources And Scenic Wonders 1940, Bureau of Mines, U.S. Department of the Interior, 1940. https://www.youtube.com/watch?v=2mMl4qmm1jA (accessed online August 17, 2022).

52. Old Time Arizona Copper Mines, Part I. http://nevada-outback-gems.com/Gold_rush_history/Arizona/Arizona18.htm (accessed online April 2, 2023).

53. Welch, J. R. (2017). Earth, Wind, and Fire: Pinal Apaches, Miners, and Genocide in Central Arizona, 1859-1874. SAGE Open, 7(4).

54. THE UNITED STATES MILITARY IN ARIZONA 1846-1945 A Component of the Arizona Historic Preservation Plan Prepared for: Arizona State Historic Preservation Office, Arizona State Parks Board. Prepared by: William S. Collins, Melanie Sturgeon, Robert Carriker Arizona State University. https://d2umhuunwbec1r.cloudfront.net/gal-

lery/0004/0051/37B1A5A99818499DB0DCA6E54DBE69E5/The%20United-%20States%20Military%20in%20Arizona%201846-1945.pdf (accessed online August 22, 2022).

55. Id.

56. Berndt Kühn's, Chronicles of War: Apache & Yavapai Resistance in the Southwestern United States and Northern Mexico, 1821-1937.

57. Id.

12: CALIFORNIA

1848: California Gold Discovered

Over 150,000 indigenous peoples lived in California prior to the Gold Rush with sustainable cultures and economies based primarily on hunting, gathering and fishing. To dispossess the indigenous peoples of their land, State militia companies, U.S. Army units, vigilante groups and individuals targeted the state's indigenous population. Acts of murder, enslavement, kidnapping, rape, child separation and displacement were widespread.[1]

On January 24, 1848, James W. Marshall discovered gold in the Sacramento Valley area describing it as follows: "I reached my hand down and picked it up; it made my heart thump, for I was certain it was gold." Marshall had discovered a mammoth lode of quartz more than 150 miles in length, lying along the western foothills of the Sierra Nevada. This discovery precipitated the California Gold Rush.[2]

In December 1848, aware of the discovery of gold, Congress excluded California's mineral lands from selection by the State and prohibited settlers' claims of preemption or settlement or location on them.

The population of California in 1848 was but a few thousand. The influx of white miners, settlers, farmers and ranchers reached its peak in 1849, resulting in the term "49'ers." By 1849, 84,000 gold miners had arrived at the California goldfields. By 1853 their numbers had grown to 250,000.

In 1850 the California legislature passed an Act for the Government and Protection of Indians that provided for the "apprenticing" or "indenturing" of Indian children to whites, and also punished "vagrant" Indians by "hiring" them out to the highest bidder at a public auction if the Indian could not provide sufficient bond or bail.

Peter Hardenman Burnett, the state's first governor, in his second state of the state legislative address in 1851 categorized indigenous Californians as lazy, thieves, and dangerous. Though he acknowledged that white settlers "appropriated whatever portion of it [land] we pleased to ourselves, without their consent and without compensation" and brought disease, he felt that it was the inevitable outcome of the meeting of two races.[3]

> That a war of extermination will continue to be waged between the races until the Indian race becomes extinct must be expected. While we cannot anticipate this result but with painful regret, the inevitable destiny of the race is beyond the power or wisdom of man to avert.[4]

Burnett didn't just refuse to avert such a conflict—he set aside state money to arm local militias against Indians. Up to 16,000 indigenous peoples died from the 1840s through the 1870s, in what California has officially recognized as "genocide.[5]

In a weak attempt to address the genocide occurring in California, in 1851, the U.S. Indian Agent for California, O.M. Wozencraft, advised Californians of the federal laws applicable to Indians which were being flaunted without consequence.

> TO THE PEOPLE LIVING & TRADING AMONG THE INDIANS IN THE STATE OF CALIFORNIA
> From information received, as well as from personal observation while traveling among the Indians, and in conformity with the requests made me by the inhabitants, more particularly the miners in sections of country occupied by Indians;
>
> It is deemed expedient to publish a communication, advisory of the proper policy to be pursued towards the Indians and the laws in relation thereto …
>
> *Since the discovery of gold in this region,* the section of country that was and is peculiarly the home of the Indians, has been found rich in the previous metal, and consequently filled with a population foreign to them; and this has been done in most instances without attempting to conciliate or appease them in their grief and anger at the loss of their homes. I am sorry to say that in many instances they have been treated in a manner, that were it recorded, would blot the darkest page of

history that has yet been penned …

Indians have been shot down without evidence of their having committed an offence, and without even any explanation to them of the nature of our laws …

This is not only inhuman and unlawful, but it is bad policy. …

In addition to the foregoing direct atrocious outrages so frequently perpetrated on the Indians by those claiming to be civilized men, there are those who indirectly cause as much … Selling those vile sanguinary beings intoxicating liquor, contrary to law … and likewise selling them arms and ammunition, thus inciting them to acts of violence and intoxication, and then placing in their hands those instruments with which they may and do seek vengeance, alike on the innocent and culpable. (Emphasis added).[6]

1852: California – Ratification of 18 Treaties Negotiated Withheld by Senate, Injunction of Secrecy; Indians Complied with Terms of Removal Only to Be Denied Land

In the Act of September 30, 1850, Congress made an appropriation of $20,000 "to enable the President to hold treaties with the various Indian tribes in the State of California."

Governor Burnett, in his second state of the state legislative address in 1851, had castigated the federal government for its neglect in making treaties with the Indians for their lands. Thereafter, the federal government appointed three commissioners, Oliver M. Wozencraft, Redick McKee and George W. Barbour, to negotiate treaties with California Indians. Between March 19, 1851, and January 7, 1852, 18 separate treaties had been negotiated with 139 tribes, setting aside 7,488,000 acres of land, or approximately one-third of California, for Indian use. The treaties met with vehement hostility in California.

On February 11, 1852, the California Assembly passed a resolution to "use all proper means to prevent Congress confirming the Indian reservations which have been made in the state." A similar resolution was passed by the California Senate which claimed that the *treaties "committed an error in assigning large portions of the richest mineral and agricultural lands to the Indians, who did not appreciate the land's value."* (Emphasis added).[7]
Among the many disparaging statements made about the Indian treaties were

the following:

> "To place upon our most fertile soil the most degraded race of aborigines upon the North American continent; to invest them with the rights of sovereignty, and to teach them that they are independent nations, is planting the seeds of future disaster and ruin.

> "As to the wild Indians now located within this State, your committee must protest against locating them within our limits. Occupying an important frontier position on the great Pacific...it is indispensable that this State should be wholly occupied by a homogeneous population, all contributing, by their character and occupation, to its strength and independence. To take any portion of the country west of the Sierra Nevada, for the home of the wild, and generally hostile Indians, would be manifestly unwise and impolitic."[8]

These Treaties were submitted to the Senate by President Fillmore on June 1, 1852, for action. The Senate went into secret session to discuss them. On July 2, 1852, the Senate by unanimous vote adopted a resolution refusing to consent to any of the treaties. The eighteen treaties were placed in secret files, where they remained for the next fifty-three years.

The tribes, believing that the treaties were valid, relinquished their historic territories and moved to the reserved acreage. However, once they reached their new locations, they were turned away. When the Northern California Indian Association [NCIA] sought government relief for destitute Indians in California not living on reservations, it had to build a case to justify their cause. The NCIA started its campaign methodically by doing research into the number, location, condition, and history of all the Northern California Indian bands. It sought government reports about the Indians from the Indian Bureau. They were told there were none and no mention was made of the eighteen unratified treaties.

Charles Edwin Kelsey, a lawyer, was one of several field workers for the NCIA in the early 1900s. He contacted Senator Thomas Bard of California who assigned his private secretary, R. Woodland Gates, to conduct research in Washington, DC on NCIA's behalf. Gates hit pay dirt in the archives of the Senate in September and reported to Kelsey about the unratified treaties. Gates wrote to Kelsey: *I am unable to find that the order of secrecy has been rescinded, and they are on file among the executive papers of the Senate.*

Under the circumstances it is impossible to obtain copies of these treaties. Later, on September 27, 1904, Gates wrote to Kelsey that he had finally found the *secret treaties* in the executive papers of the Senate. (Emphasis added). Location of the treaties made possible efforts to lift the secrecy and their publication. Kelsey reported: "The reservations proposed in the treaties are much more extensive than we knew and also the prices agreed to be paid by the Government." (Emphasis added).[9] This eventually led to aid for the tribes.

California: Gold Discovered on Indian Lands Forces Genocide of California Indians

In 1862, Commissioner of Indian Affairs William P. Dole summarized the impact of the Gold Rush on California's Indians:

> The emigration began, and every part of the State was overrun, as it were, in a day. All, or nearly so, of the fertile valleys were seized; the mountain gulches and ravines were filled with miners; and without the slightest recognition of the Indians' rights, they were dispossessed of their homes, their hunting grounds, their fisheries, and, to a great extent, of the productions of the earth. From a position of independence they were at once reduced to the most abject dependence. With no one of the many tribes of the State is there an existing treaty. Despoiled by irresistible force of the land of their fathers; with no country on earth to which they can migrate; in the midst of a people with whom they cannot assimilate, they have no recognized claims upon the government, and are almost compelled to become vagabonds-*to steal or to starve*.
>
> When the incalculable value of California, with its seven or eight hundred miles of sea-coast and its untold millions of wealth, is considered, how small, in comparison, is the value of such appropriations as would be sufficient to afford the Indians every aid and facility for the attainment of comfortable home; and the simple arts of civilization necessary to their subsistence! And when it is also considered that these people were in the almost undisputed possession of this beautiful domain, surely we, who have deprived them of their possessions, ought not to withhold the little which, by every consideration of humanity and justice, they may so imperatively and rightfully demand.[10]

In 1864, John C. Burche, Local Agent, Humboldt County, California, wrote the following to James W. Nye, Governor and ex-officio Superintendent of Indian Affairs, in an effort to prevent starvation of and disturbance by the Indians in the area.

> [T]he chances of subsistence of the Indians of this portion of the superintendency grow small by degrees … and where and how they are, in future, to subsist, in the absence of game, fish, pine-nuts, seeds, and roots, is altogether conjectural, unless their wants be supplied by the bounty of a protecting and beneficent government.[11]

In just 20 years, 80 percent of California's Indians were wiped out. And though some died because of the seizure of their land or diseases caught from new settlers, between 9,000 and 16,000 were murdered in cold blood—the victims of a policy of genocide sponsored by the state of California and gleefully assisted by its newest citizens.[12]

In 1944, the U.S. Court of Claims awarded $17 million to California Indians as a settlement for Congress's failure to ratify the 18 treaties. The Winnemem opposed the settlement as insufficient for the losses suffered and refused to accept payment.

Gold Production in California by 1852

A total of $2 billion worth of precious metal was extracted during the Gold Rush, which peaked in 1852. This was only a small part of "the incalculable value of California, with its seven or eight hundred miles of sea-coast and its untold millions of wealth."[13]

Notes: California

1. Revealing the history of genocide against California's Native Americans, Review of Benjamin Madley's Book, Jessica Wolf, August 15, 2017. https://newsroom.ucla.edu/stories/revealing-the-history-of-genocide-against-californias-native-americans (accessed online September 5, 2021).
2. UNITED STATES DEPARTMENT OF THE INTERIOR, NATIONAL PARK SERVICE, THE NATIONAL SURVEY OF HISTORIC SITES AND BUILDINGS, Theme XV, Westward Expansion and the Extension of the National Boundaries to the Pacific 1830-1898, THE MINING FRONTIER, 1959, p. 5. http://npshistory.com/publications/nhl/theme-studies/mining-frontier.pdf (accessed online November 18, 2021).

3. Governor Peter Burnett, State of State Address, January 6, 1851. https://governors.library.ca.gov/addresses/s_01-Burnett2.html (accessed online September 5, 2021).

4. Id.

5. https://www.nytimes.com/2019/06/19/us/newsom-native-american-apology.html (accessed online September 5, 2021).

6. O.M. Wozencraft [1851], "To the People Living and Trading Among the Indians in the State of California", Sen. Ex. Docs., 33 Cong., Spec. Sess., Doc. 4, pp. 115-117.

7. A History of American Indians in California:1849-1879. https://www.nps.gov/parkhistory/online_books/5views/5views1c.htm (accessed online September 5, 2021).

8. Journal of the Senate of the State of California, State Printing Office, 1852, Appendix, p. 598.

9. Larisa K. Miller, The Secret Treaties With California's Indians. https://www.archives.gov/files/publications/prologue/2013/fall-winter/treaties.pdf (accessed online March 30, 2023).

10. Abridgment ... Containing the Annual Message of the President of the United States to the Two Houses of Congress ... with Reports of Departments and Selections from Accompanying Papers, Volume 2, Report of the Secretary of Interior, 1862, pp. 78-79.

11. Report of the Commissioner of Indian Affairs to the Secretary of the Interior, United States. Office of Indian Affairs, U.S. Government Printing Office, 1864, p. 139.

12. California's Little Known Genocide, Erin Blakemore. https://www.history.com/news/californias-little-known-genocide (accessed online December 28, 2021).

13. Report of the Commissioner of Indian Affairs to the Secretary of the Interior, United States, U.S. Government Printing Office, 1863, p. 40.

13: DAKOTAS

Nakota, Dakota and Lakota were the names used by the Sioux in the Santee, Yankton, and Teton dialects respectively. These three divisions of the nation contained the following seven powerful sub-divisions:

Mdewakanton, Wahpeton, Wahpekute, Sisseton, Yankton, Yanktonai and Teton, each of which was again sub-divided into bands and sub-bands. These seven main sub-divisions are often called "the seven council fires". The Isanyati, Santee or eastern division, containing the first four groups, lived in Minnesota until 1862 and spoke one dialect. The Yankton and Yanktonia, the latter subdivided into Upper and Hunkpetine or Lower, held the middle territory between Lake Traverse and Missouri River in eastern Dakotas and together spoke one dialect.

The Teton (earlier Dwellers of the Prairie) were the Army's greatest antagonist. They comprised together more than half the nation, held the whole tribal territory west of the Missouri and spoke one dialect. The sub-divisions were Upper and Lower Brule (Burnt Thighs), Oglala (Scatter One's Own), San Arcs (Without Bows), Sihasapa (Blackfoot), Miniconjou (Those Who Plant by the Stream), Ooohenonpa (Two Kettles) and Hunkpapa (Those Who Camp at the Entrance).[1] Allied with the Teton Sioux were the Arapahoes and the Northern Cheyennes. Wasicu is the Dakota word for white man. The original meaning was "can't get rid of them."[2]

In early relations with the Indians, the U.S. determined it was cheaper to feed, bribe, and cajole, than to fight. The Treaty of Laramie of 1851, concluded with the Sioux and the other northern bands, was a manifestation of this policy. Major provisions of the agreement permitted the Government to establish roads, military and other posts, within their territory, granted annuities of trade goods and food to the Sioux for fifteen years, and designated specific tracts of land as hunting areas located north of the North Platte for individual tribes.

The Sioux territory recognized under the Fort Laramie Treaty of September 17, 1851, 11 Stat. 749, included all of the present State of South Dakota, and parts of what is now Nebraska, Wyoming, North Dakota, and Montana.

1855: Fort Pierre

Perhaps the most significant fur trade/military fort on the western American frontier, Fort Pierre Chouteau was the largest (almost 300' square) and best equipped trading post in the northern Great Plains. Built in 1832 by John Jacob Astor's (1763-1848) American Fur Company as part of its expansion into the Upper Missouri region, the trading activities at the site exemplified the commercial alliance between Indians and those engaged in the fur business.

The American military entered the northern Great Plains in the 1850s and the U.S. Army bought Fort Pierre Chouteau in 1855, making it the first military fort in the Upper Missouri River region. After purchasing the fort, the Army conducted nearly $20,000 worth of repairs to meet army standards.

Routes Connecting Forts Mapped

The importance of the forts and linkage between them is evidenced by U.S. Army Topographer, Lieutenant G.K. Warren's posting at Fort Pierre, under the command of General Wm. Harney, to *survey and map all possible supply routes that would connect the recently purchased Fort with other regional military forts, facilitating the delivery of provisions which would be shipped to Fort Pierre via steamboats on the Missouri River*.

1856: Fort Randall

Fort Randall was established on the right bank of the Missouri River in 1856, part of the system of forts to protect the Overland Trail. It housed four companies, and provided housing for twelve officers and their families in cottonwood log buildings. It served as an important outpost for operations against the Sioux in 1863-65 and was one of the chain of forts that surrounded the Sioux country from 1865 to 1876. It served until 1892, the longest continuously occupied military post on the upper river. The last company to leave the post on December 7th was composed entirely of Indians, commanded by two white officers.

P. Prescott, Superintendent for Farming for Sioux, reported in 1856 that the Sioux Agency was withholding annuities from the Sioux.

> The treaties say these funds shall be annually expended, whereas, large amounts have been kept back, and are now in arrears and that after repeated applications to have them expended. These arrears are not mere petty sums, surplusses or remnants of funds remaining unexpended, but large amounts, *thousand and tens of thousands, and in some cases the whole fund appropriated for a special purpose*. It cannot be wondered at that the Indians are dissatisfied and constantly complaining, making the want of faith on the part of the government officers their excuse for misconduct of every kind, and leading them to be at all times inattentive to the expressed wishes of the agent, superintendent and commissioner of Indian affairs. (Emphasis added).[3]

The only way for the Sioux to gain access to these unexpended funds returned to the U.S. Treasury would be to request and receive a new Congressional appropriation which was unlikely. *Commissioner Manypenny was unhappy with Prescott's Report and terminated him.*

Superintendent W.J. Cullen, Northern Superintendency, had another idea for reducing annuities. General Sherman had located fugitives from the Lac Traverse Band and Superintendent Cullen thought the following punishment would be warranted:

> It had been my intention to have had them whipped and their heads shaved, and thus disgrace them before all their people. But upon more mature reflection, I apprehended that men so degraded might be rendered desperate, become outlaws, and during the winter, commit murder or outrage upon some unprotected settler, to redeem themselves in the opinions of their people. I had withheld their share of the annuities, and *deducted from the annuity coming to their bands sufficient to cover the expense of my detention*. All the bands had been thoroughly humbled, great intercession was made in their

behalf; and their chiefs pledged themselves for their future good conduct, and for that of all their young men. (Emphasis added).

Superintendent Cullen was willing to charge all of the Yankton for the costs of apprehending and detaining the Lac Traverse fugitives, notwithstanding that he described the condition of the Yankton as follows:

They were literally half starved, their faces pinched with famine, and their bodies exhibiting extreme emaciation, with but shreds of blankets hanging about them.[5]

1858: "Treaty of Washington" or Treaty of Yankton Sioux

The Yankton Sioux signed a treaty with the U.S. in 1858, ceding more than 11 million acres of land known as the Yankton Delta … in exchange for a 430,000-acre reservation. They got an important concession in Article VIII: The said Yancton Indians shall be secured in the free and unrestricted use of the red pipe-stone quarry … and retain the same and keep it open and free to the Indians to visit and procure stone for pipes so long as they shall desire. [648 acres].

The U.S. later wanted the pipestone quarry and purchased it for $338,558. Today, the National Park Service oversees the property.

1860s: Suffering of Sioux - Starvation, Destitution, Exposure

The decade of the sixties was marked by the destitution, starvation and suffering of the Sioux due to lack of food and basic clothing. The lack of game for subsistence and land capable of sustainable agriculture left them in the position of stealing or starving. One agent couldn't take hearing of their misery so he ordered them not to return to their agency until he notified them.

The autumn of 1861 closed upon us rather unfavorably. The crops were light; especially was this the case with the Upper Sioux; they had little or nothing. As heretofore communicated to the Department, the cut-worm destroyed all the corn of the Sissitons, and greatly injured the crops of the Wahpetons, and Medewakaptons, and Wahpecutahs…

I advised them to go home, and admonished them not to come back again until I sent for them. I issued provisions, powder and shot, and tobacco to them, and they departed. How were over 4,000 annuity and over 1,000 Yanktonais Sioux, with nothing to eat, and entirely dependent on me for supplies, to be provided for? I supplied them as best I could; parsimoniously indeed, from necessity it was; still, I did all in my power. Our stock was nearly used up, and still, on the 1st day of August, no money had come. The Indians complained of starvation.[6]

At one hour a famishing, begging, and half naked crowd would surround my office on a freezing cold morning and implore me to go to their lodges and see their old people and children, who from starvation or want of clothing were unable to come out. To these I doled out provisions in quantities barely sufficient to keep them alive.

At another time, men wearing nothing but a stroud and robe or blanket, with a belt and knife in it, and carrying their tomahawks or other weapons, would come, and with loud, and, from starvation, hollow sounding voices, accompanied by exciting and threatening gestures, demand the cattle or other food. J. B. Hoffman, Indian Agent.[7]

The Indians who have been thus subsisted and belong to this agency are the Brule Sioux, numbering about 350 lodges; the Ogallalla Sioux, numbering about 350 lodges; the Northern Arapahoes, numbering about 150 lodges; and the Northern Cheyennes, numbering about 150 lodges, all averaging about six persons to the lodge. Many of these Indians are in a suffering condition, and must perish if not aided in some way. They have learned to depend upon the government for support and have made no provision for the approaching winter, and their suffering will be beyond endurance unless they are supplied by the government. M. T. Patrick.[8]

The greater portion of them, say four-fifths, live by pilfering grain, melons, and occasionally horses and cattle from the whites. There being no game for them to subsist on, starvation compels them to steal. R. N. Fenton, Captain U.S.A., Special Indian Agent.[9]

Sisseton and Wahpeton – Approaching Winter. A very few of them had some corn, but the majority were without food or clothing and were living on roots. I had known them for thirteen years, in peace and plenty, in famine and war, and never, at any time, was there so much suffering and utter destitution. I immediately called the chiefs and headmen together and told them I wanted the number of their people.[10]

1863: Yankton Sioux Must Be Whipped

Indian Agent Thomas J. Galbraith recommended whipping the Yankton Sioux to effect his espoused purpose of reducing the number to put up on a reservation since "many will be killed; more must perish from famine and exposure, and the more desperate will flee…"

> The remaining annuity Sioux, numbering some 4,800, are with the Yanctonais and other nomadic bands, numbering 3,000 or 4,000, doubtless banded together for hostile purposes, and must be caught before they are caged or cared for. Until these are severely chastised, nothing can be done with them. They will never deliver themselves up as prisoners … They can now be taken by force or fine strategy alone. The power of the government must be brought to bear upon them; they must be whipped, coerced into obedience. After this is accomplished, few will be left to put up on a reservation; many will be killed; more must perish from famine and exposure, and the more desperate will flee and seek refuge on the plains or in the mountains.[11]

Black Hills Should Be Exploited for Whites

In 1866, the Northwest Commission declared the Black Hills' considerable timber and coal could be readily exploited, advancing "the development of the northwest prairies." With no shame, they negotiated an annuity of 'three to six dollars' worth of clothing and food … enough to protect them from starvation…"[12]

On top of this, they disclosed the "more mortifying evidence of negligence by former agents, and most probably *stupendous frauds* and outrages in the administration of Indian affairs…" (Emphasis added).[13]

Commissioner Smith knew that the Black Hills were "best adapted to their [Sioux] immediate and paramount necessities. I doubt whether any land now remaining in the possession of the General Government offers equal advantages."[14] Yet, he took no action, as their trustee, to protect their property rights.

He reported in 1875 that since the Sioux were dependent on the U.S. for rations, and would starve if they were withheld, it provided a basis to negotiate with them for the Black Hills. Again, the U.S. would use the upper-hand it had in insuring the Sioux' starvation. They were doomed to lose the Black Hills from the get-go. *The unspoken threat of starvation would be weaponized to deliberately steal and undervalue the Black Hills, which the Sioux have not accepted to this day.*

> They are not now capable of self-support; they are absolute pensioners of the Government in the sum of a million and a quarter of dollars annually above all amounts specified in treaty-stipulations. *A failure to receive Government rations for a single season would reduce them to starvation.* They cannot, therefore, demand to be left alone, and the Government, granting the large help which the Sioux are obliged to ask, is entitled to ask something of them in return. On this basis of mutual benefit the purchase of the Black Hills should proceed. (Emphasis added).[15]

In a desultory repetition of what previously occurred, the claim of Manifest Destiny would rule. Miners had already staked out claims, expecting the Government to protect them or they would do it themselves.[16]

1866: U.S. Negligent and Fraudulent in Complying with Indian Treaties

In the 1866 Report of the Northwestern Treaty Commission to the Sioux of the Upper Missouri, the Commission confirmed the government's abject failure to honor its treaties with the Indians:

> In the preceding remarks we have said enough to show the very irregular and imperfect mode of our execution of treaties. Negligence and frauds have characterized this essential executive duty. Indians are like children, hopeful and anxious for the goods which the "Great Father" has promised as an annuity.[17]

From 1866 until the summer of 1868, Red Cloud's followers gave the occupants of Forts Phil Kearny, Reno, and C. F. Smith no respite from continuous observation, feints, and deadly attacks. The primary engagements of this period were: the massacre of Captain William J. Fetterman's column on December 21, 1866, at Fort Phil Kearny; the fight with Captain James W. Powell's woodcutters, on August 2, 1867, near Fort Phil Kearny (Wagon Box Fight); and the skirmish near Fort C. F. Smith on August 1, 1867 (Hayfield Fight).

The occupation of Forts Phil Kearny, Reno, and C. F. Smith was terminated in August 1868, by the Fort Laramie Treaty of 1868. Closing of the Forts resulted in the termination of travel over the Bozeman Trail to Montana.

1867: Department of the Interior and Dept. of Treasury Support Miners Who Want to Invade Black Hills

In 1867, Special Agent C.T. Campbell expressed his opinion of the obstacles Indians presented to the prosperity of the Dakota Territory:

> The Territory of Dakota today would be in a most prosperous condition, were it not for the hostile attitude of these Indians, or improving some of her best agricultural lands. Here, in this vicinity today, are 200 men ready to go to the Black Hills to locate and develop that country; said to be gold ... but they are suddenly met by thousands of hostile Indians, who say they shall not cross the Missouri. C. T. Campbell.[18]

> With the pacification of the Sioux Indians, and the establishment of emigrant roads, this district of Dakota would doubtless be the scene of great mining excitement, as the gold-field of the Black hills is accessible at a distance of 120 miles from the Missouri river.[19]

Fort Laramie Treaty of 1868 – Establishment of Great Sioux Reservation

The Fort Laramie Treaty of 1868 created the Great Sioux Reservation from a position of weakness during the U.S.' implementation of the concentration policy of Indians on small reservations. Prior to the negotiations of the treaty, Red Cloud had established the pre-condition that Forts Kearny, C.F. Smith and Reno be vacated before he would call off his war with the whites. The U.S. also granted an enormous tract of land for the creation of the Great Sioux Reservation.[20]

The 1868 Treaty set aside lands for the Lakota Sioux in two categories: (1)

the Great Sioux Reservation, made up of most of the western half of Dakota Territory, and (2) the so-called unceded lands north of the North Platte and east of the Bighorns—essentially the Powder River Basin of northeastern Wyoming and southern Montana. Tribes were allowed to hunt and live in these unceded lands, where buffalo were still plentiful. It also included the Black Hills region for their exclusive use.

The Treaty of 1868 pledged that the Great Sioux Reservation, including the Black Hills, would be "set apart for the absolute and undisturbed use and occupation" of the Sioux Nation, and that no treaty for the cession of any part of the reservation would be valid as against the Sioux unless executed and signed by at least three-fourths of the adult male Sioux population.

Most importantly, the treaty specified what Red Cloud sought: "no white person or persons shall be permitted to settle upon or occupy any portion" of the Powder River country "without the consent of the Indians first had and obtained, to pass through" the Powder River country.

The U.S. Army had given up their forts while the U.S. government had sworn to vacate Sioux land and had promised to feed the Sioux on the reservations. The U.S.' policies reinforced the concept that the 1868 Treaty was wholly in the Sioux's favor. With peace achieved, the Lakota and their allies were victorious. They gained legal control of the western Powder River country, took down the forts and permanently closed the Bozeman Trail. The Crow lost their hunting grounds in the Powder River region to their enemies. With the treaty, "... the [United States] government had in effect betrayed the Crows, who had willingly helped the army to hold the posts for two years." The victory of the Lakota and their allies, only endured for eight years until the Great Sioux War of 1876.

By 1868, the railroad terminal at Cheyenne, within the Rocky Mountain region, provided direct northward routes to Montana, west of the Big Horn Mountains, through safer territory. In brief, the wagon road through the western hunting grounds of the Teton Sioux was not worth a fight.[22]

It also provided for many things to be done for them among which was the furnishing of a certain quantity of subsistence for the period of four years. This treaty has been ratified, but no appropriation has been made to carry out its provisions, except so far as the funds appropriated in 1868, and placed at the disposal of General Sherman, were applied to that purpose.[23]

1868: Establishing Indian Agencies to Control Sioux – Barely Enough

Annuities Doled Out for Survival – Many Died

In 1868, between August 10 and November 23, General Harney spent $685,784.21 in feeding the Sioux and preparing agencies for them, this being $485,784.21 more than he had been allowed by General Sherman. During this time, he selected three different agencies for the Sioux and furnished them with proper buildings for the agents, employees and Indians.

The agencies were: Cheyenne River; Grand River established for Hunkpapa, Cut Heads, and as a temporary reservation for the Upper Yanktonia and Blackfeet; and Whetstone for Brules and Oglalas.[24]

Lakota Indian Agencies

The following agencies were created from the area formerly administered by the Upper Missouri Agency:

> 1846: Upper Platte Agency
> 1855: Blackfeet Agency
> 1859: Yankton Agency
> 1859: Ponca Agency
> 1864: Fort Berthold Agency
> 1869: Cheyenne River Agency
> 1869: Grand River Agency, Whetstone Agency, and Cheyenne River Agency
> 1871: Red Cloud Agency
> 1874: Crow Creek
> 1874: Standing Rock (formerly Grand River Agency 1869)
> 1874: Spotted Tail (Formerly Whetstone Agency succeeded the Upper Platte Agency in 1869)

1859: Yankton Agency

The Yankton Agency was established in 1859 and was located on the Missouri River near Greenwood in what is now South Dakota.

1869: Grand River Agency

The Grand River Agency was established in 1869, reporting to the Dakota Superintendency and associated with the Upper Platte Agency. After 1870, the Agent reported directly to the Office of Indian Affairs in Washington, DC. The Grand River Agency was primarily responsible for the Upper and Lower

Yanktonai, Hunkpapa, Cut Head (Pabaska), and Blackfeet Sioux. Other bands of the Sioux, including the Two Kettle (Oohenonpa), Sans Arcs, Oglala, and Brulé, also were associated with this agency. In July 1873, the agency was moved from the junction of the Grand and Missouri Rivers in South Dakota to its present location 50 miles up-stream on the Missouri River at Standing Rock, North Dakota. The name of the agency was officially changed to Standing Rock Agency in December 1874.

1869: Whetstone Agency (Name Changed to Spotted Tail Agency in 1874)

The Whetstone Agency succeeded the Upper Platte Agency in 1869, when it was moved from its Platte River location to the mouth of Whetstone Creek on the Missouri River in Dakota Territory. Whetstone Agency was primarily responsible for the band of Brulé Sioux under Spotted Tail, but it was also responsible for other bands of Brulé, Oglala, and Miniconjou Sioux who lived near the Agency. It was moved in 1871 and again in 1875, first to Big White Clay Creek and then to a site on the White River near the border between Dakota Territory and Nebraska. The name was changed in 1874 to the Spotted Tail Agency.

1869: Cheyenne River Agency

The Cheyenne River Agency was established in 1869, located just below the mouth of the Big Cheyenne River, on the west bank of the Missouri River about 6 miles from Fort Sully, South Dakota. It served the Minneconjou, SiHaSapa, Oohenumpa, and Itazipco bands of the Lakota or Great Sioux Nation. It was known as the Forest City Agency from 1892-1894.

1871: Red Cloud Agency (1877 Name Changed to Pine Ridge Agency)

The Red Cloud Agency was established in 1871 and was located on the North Platte River near Fort Laramie in Wyoming. In 1873, the agency was moved to the White River near Camp Robinson in northwestern Nebraska. In 1877, it was moved to the mouth of Medicine Creek on the Missouri River in present-day South Dakota. From that point on, it was known as the Pine Ridge Agency.

1874: Crow Creek Agency

The Crow Creek Agency at Fort Thompson, South Dakota was established in 1874 for the Santee, Sisseton, and Wahpeton Sioux Indians. From 1882 to 1896, Crow Creek and Lower Brulé Agencies were consolidated and called the Crow Creek and Lower Brulé Agency. In 1896, they were separated again and remained so until 1924, when Lower Brulé Agency became a subagency of Crow Creek.

1875: Lower Brule Agency

The Lower Brulé Agency was established in 1875 as the White River Agency and was renamed Lower Brulé in January 1876. It was first located on the western side of the Missouri River, 10 miles below Crow Creek in South Dakota. In the summer of 1876, it was moved to the mouth of American Crow Creek, 12 miles below the old site. In 1882, the Crow Creek Agency and the Lower Brulé Agency were consolidated. In 1896, they were again divided.

1869: General Sherman Publishes Letter in Press Advocating for Territorial or State Militias to Destroy Marauding Indians

> Letter in Cheyenne Star: As to the frontier settlements, I have again and again warned the governors and the people that until this Indian matter was finally concluded, their people should not spread out so much. Their isolated farms, with horses and cattle, are too tempting to hungry and savage bands of Indians. If, however, they will not be restrained by motives of prudence, the people should, as they used to do in Ohio, Kentucky, Iowa, and Missouri, make their settlements in groups, with block houses and a sod fort, so that when the savage comes, they may rally and defend themselves and their stock. It is a physical impossibility for the small army we all know [is the] kind Congress maintains, with yearly threats of further reductions, to guard the exposed settlements of Kansas, Nebraska, Dakota, Montana, Wyoming, Colorado, and New Mexico. *These states and territories must, by organizing their people into a sort of militia, be prepared to defend their exposed settlements, and to follow up and destroy the bands of marauding Indians and horse thieves, both red and white*, that now infest them, and carry on a profitable business. The army cannot do it, any more than we can catch all the pickpockets and thieves in our cities. Clamor on this subject against me, or General Augur, or General Sheridan, it is simply folly. We do our duty according to our means, and account to our superiors, and not to the people who neglect our advice and counsel. (Emphasis added).[25]

General Sherman summarized the dilemma of the frontier army as follows:

The army cannot resist the tide of emigration that is following toward these Indian lands, nor is it our province to determine the question of boundaries. When called on, we must, to the extent of our power, protect the settlers, and, on proper demand, we have to protect the Indian lands against the intrusion of the settlers. Thus we are placed between two fires, a most unpleasant dilemma, from which we cannot escape, and we must sustain the officers on the spot who fulfill their orders.[26]

July 1874: Custer's Black Hills Expedition

In July 1874, Lieutenant Colonel Custer led a *thousand-man expedition,* including 70 Indian scouts, four reporters and 110 wagons into the Black Hills. He was under orders to scout a suitable site for a military post, a mission personally approved by President Ulysses S. Grant, but *he also brought along two prospectors, outfitted at his expense*. William Illingworth took one of the most iconic photographs of the expedition.

Although largely unexplored by whites, the Black Hills were long rumored to be rich in gold, and *Custer's prospectors discovered what he reported as "paying quantities" of the precious metal*. A correspondent for the Chicago *Inter Ocean* who accompanied the expedition was less restrained in his dispatch: "From the grass roots down it was 'pay dirt.'" Taking him at his word, the nation's press whipped up a frenzy over a "new El Dorado" in the American West.[27]

> Commissioner Edward P. Smith reported on October 31, 1874, that *"The military reconnaissance of the Black Hills country was regarded by the Indians as a violation of their treaty*, and produced a turbulent feeling among them. Its objects, however, were peacefully accomplished. (Emphasis added).[28]

1875: Whites Taking Over Black Hills; Demand for President Grant to Annex Them

The U.S. was going into the second year of a crippling economic depression, and the nation desperately needed a financial lift. Within a year of Custer's discovery, more than a thousand miners had streamed into the Black Hills.

Soon Western newspapers and Western congressmen were demanding that President Grant annex the land.

There was one problem: The Black Hills belonged to the Lakota. Their treaty guaranteed their rights to the region. The Lakotas esteemed the Paha Sapa (literally, "hills that are black") for their material bounty. The Hills were their meat locker, a game reserve to be tapped in times of hunger.[29]

1875: USGS Newton Geological Expedition

To confirm Custer's Expedition Report, another Black Hills Expedition in 1875, was ordered by the Secretary of the Interior. It was led by Lieutenant Colonel Richard Irving Dodge and accompanied by Professor Walter P. Jenny, of the School of Mines, New York City. The 400 men included were experts in the fields of Geography, Geology, Paleontology, Microscopic Petrography, Botany and Astronomy and Barometric Hypsometry.[30]

Newton's Geological report concluded that the Black Hills were indeed gold bearing: [31]

> The report ... shows *a gold-field with an area of eight hundred square miles*, and around this gold region ... three thousand square miles of arable lands ... while the hill-sides and elevations contiguous thereto are equally adapted to purposes of grazing, *making the whole area of three thousand miles of timber, grazing, and arable land of great value for agricultural purposes*. (Emphasis added).[32]

As for the Reservation, excepting the Black Hills, Newton's data concluded:

> "it was a most inhabitable region, desolate and barren, and includes a large area of the well-known sterile and clayey tracts of "bad lands." Once abounding in buffaloes and smaller game, which afforded an abundant maintenance for the hunting Indians, it is now deserted... *The buffaloes have been destroyed ... and this large population of 50,000 Indians is held in a tract of country whose natural resources are utterly inadequate to maintain even a tithe of the number. ... The agricultural possibilities of the Sioux Reservation may practically be considered as nothing.* (Emphasis added).[33]

> Many parts of the reservation afford excellent grazing during the summer, though water is deficient, but the rigors of a

Dakota winter forbid any attempt at a systematic engagement in the grazing of stock, especially by the improvident Indians. *It may be said with truth that the Black Hills include all the desirable land in the reservation and all the useful timber, and by those who view the treatment and future of the Indians in this region in a purely humanitarian spirit the presence of gold in the Black Hills has been regarded as unfortunate* ... (Emphasis added).[34]

The Black Hills are pre-eminently a gold-producing region: the metamorphic rocks constituting the gold-field cover an area of nine hundred square miles, extending north and south through the central portions of the Hills for a distance of seventy miles, with a breadth of from five to twenty five miles. *"There's gold from the grass roots down, but there's more gold from the grass roots up."* (Emphasis added).[35]

While in the field, the various discoveries of the presence of gold ... were reported to the Commissioner of Indian Affairs. *From its immediate importance, this information was published by resolution of the Senate, April 18, 1876.*

April 1875: Military Command

As the tenuous situation between the U.S. and the Teton Sioux deteriorated, the quality of U.S. Army commanders in the northern Great Plains area became a subject of prime importance. The Department of the Platte was a region faced with an impending confrontation between the U.S. and powerful Sioux.

From April 27, 1875, to August 30, 1882, General Crook was assigned command of the Platte. His previous Indian combat experience included warfare with the Indians of northern California, Oregon, Washington and Arizona.

The Sioux presented a unique challenge. They were capable of united resistance and they were a warrior-oriented society. They inhabited a vast area, with extreme weather conditions. During winter the temperature dropped to minus thirty degrees Fahrenheit. Experienced in fighting small bands of Apaches, Crook was now to be pitted against an enemy who could—as a matter of official record—field one thousand warriors for a single occasion.

May 1875: Lakota Delegation to DC – President Grant - Cede Black Hills or Lose Rations

As the pressure rose on Grant to annex the Black Hills, his first resort was rough diplomacy. The Teton Sioux, were invited to the White House in 1875 and promptly met with President Grant. Grant attempted to convince the Teton Sioux to move to Indian Territory and relinquish their land rights to the Black Hills: "There is a territory south of where you now live, where the climate is very much better, and the grass is very much better, and the game is more abundant, including large game such as buffalo: where you can have good pasturage for animals; and where you can have teachers among you to teach you the arts of self-preservation and self support."[36]

The Lakota protested shortages of government rations, a corrupt Indian agent and the invasion of the miners onto their land. Grant seized the opportunity. First, he said, the government's treaty obligation to issue rations had run out and could be revoked; rations continued only because of Washington's kind feelings toward the Lakotas. Second, he, the Great Father, was powerless to prevent miners from overrunning the Black Hills (which was true enough, given limited Army resources). The Lakotas must either cede the Paha Sapa or lose their rations. (Emphasis added).

As the delegation to demand that the federal government adhere to the terms of the Treaty of Laramie went forward, miners continued to invade the northern Great Plains.

July-August 1875: Miners Settling in Black Hills Evicted by General Crook

The task of evicting the miners fell to General Crook, whose sympathies clearly rested with the miners. *General Crook evicted many of them that July, in accordance with standing policy, but before they pulled up stakes he suggested they record their claims in order to secure them for when the country opened up.*

Throughout these proceedings, General Crook thought the Lakotas had been remarkably forbearing. "How do the bands that sometimes roam off from the agencies on the Plains behave now?" a reporter asked him in early August. "Well," Crook said, "they are quiet." "Do you perceive any immediate danger of an Indian war?" the reporter persisted. "Not just now," Crook answered.[37]

September 17, 1875: Allison Commission to Buy Black Hills or Lease Mining Rights Fails

President Grant tried negotiations once more. Commissioner Smith estimated the reasonable value of the Black Hills to be:

The true equivalent to be offered the Sioux, as helpless wards of the Government, for the Black Hills will be found by estimating what eight hundred square miles of gold-fields are worth to us, and what three thousand square miles of timber, agricultural, and grazing lands are worth to them. (Emphasis added).[38]

The commission headed by Senator William B. Allison of Iowa and including Brigadier General Alfred H. Terry and others would offer to *buy the mining rights only* to the Black Hills, not a cession of the land.

Representatives of the Brules, Oglalas, Minneconjous, Hunkpapas, Blackfeet, Two Kettles, Sans Arcs, Lower Brule, Yankton, Santee, Northern Cheyenne, and Arapaho tribes attended. Crazy Horse refused to come. So did Sitting Bull. The Indians were divided into two parties: the larger was willing to sell the Black Hills if a satisfactory price could be obtained; the smaller party, composed of young warriors, resisted sale for any price. Intercession by Young Man Afraid of His Horses and his warriors prevented bloodshed.[39]

The essence of the Government's proposal: annual rental of mining rights for $400,000, or outright purchase for $6,000,000 to be paid in 15 annual installments; also, purchase of a right of way for the Bozeman Trail for $50,000 rental annually.[40] In their response to the proposal, the Sioux leaders, particularly Red Dog and Red Cloud, insisted that it must provide for the next seven generations of their people. At one time during negotiations, the Indians stated a price of $70,000,000.[41]

The Indians and the commission failed to reach an agreement for either the sale or the lease of mining rights. The Allison Commission Report stated the Lakotas could not be brought to terms "except by the mild exercise, at least, of force in the beginning."

Outright relinquishment of title was never seriously hoped for by the Allison Commission. The Treaty of Laramie of 1868 stated in Article 12 that any sale or cession of Indian land required the assent of three-fourths of the male Indians. This provision was considered an impossible obstacle to concluding an agreement for purchase.

October-November 1875: Presidential Scheming to Get Black Hills

On November 3, 1875, a mysterious meeting was convened at the White House. One news dispatch stated:

The president, Secretary [of War] Belknap, Generals Sheridan and Crook had a private interview yesterday regarding Indian matters in general and the Black Hills in particular. At the close, Secretary [of Interior] Chandler and General Cowen [Assistant Secretary of Interior] were sent for and the subject was discussed further. The result of this conference is that the government will preserve a neutral position towards the miners who are crowding into the Black Hills in great numbers. Four hundred men left Cheyenne a few days ago for the gold fields, and it may be said positively that they will not be molested by the troops. General Crook says that miners are crowding in from all directions, and that it is impossible to keep them out.[42]

Grant knew he could count on his Secretary of War, William Belknap. Also, he had personally appointed the Secretary of the Interior Zachariah Chandler, a former senator from Michigan and a hard-liner in Western affairs. The Assistant Interior Secretary, Benjamin R. Cowen, and the Commissioner of Indian Affairs, Edward P. Smith, would follow the direction of Secretary Chandler.

Opposition to Grant's plan might have come from General Sherman. He was one of the men who had signed the Fort Laramie Treaty on behalf of the U.S. He advocated using force against Indians when warranted, but he had once written Grant of his anger at "whites looking for gold [who] kill Indians just as they would kill bears and pay no regard for treaties." So, President Grant bypassed General Sherman and invited Lieutenant General Sheridan.

The conspirators believed that Sitting Bull and the non-treaty Lakotas had intimidated the reservation chiefs out of selling the mining rights to the Black Hills. Crush the non-treaty bands, they reasoned, and the reservation chiefs would yield. The Indian Bureau was to manufacture complaints against the Lakotas to justify military action; the Lakotas were to be given an *impossibly short deadline* to report to their reservation; and Lieutenant General Sheridan was to make ready for a winter campaign against the Lakota.

Lieutenant General Sheridan wrote in confidence to General Terry on November 9, 1875:

At a meeting which occurred in Washington on the 3d of November ... the President decided that while the orders

~ 482 ~

> *heretofore issued forbidding the occupation of the Black*
> *Hills country by miners should not be rescinded, still no*
> *fixed resistance by the military should be made to the miners*
> *going in. ... Will you therefore cause the troops in your*
> *Department to assume such attitude as will meet the views*
> *of the President in this respect.* (Emphasis added).[43]

Lieutenant General Sheridan sent a copy of the orders to General Sherman stating they "had best be kept confidential."[44]

General Crook shared the secret outcome of the meeting with his trusted aide-de-camp *Capt. John G. Bourke*. In Bourke's Herculean note-taking, in a 124-volume diary held at the West Point library, is this entry: "General Crook said that at the council General Grant had decided that the Northern Sioux [i.e, the Lakotas] should go upon their reservation or be whipped."[45]

November 3, 1875: President Grant Meets with Cabinet – White Miners May Enter Black Hills

On November 3, 1875, Grant convened his cabinet to announce that the Army would do nothing more to stop miners from entering the Black Hills.

November 9, 1875: Manufacture Complaints against Lakotas – Bureau Inspector Watkins' Report Completed Six Days after White House Secret Meeting

To manufacture complaints against the Lakotas, the Grant administration turned to an Indian Bureau Inspector, Erwin C. Watkins, who had just come back from a routine tour of the Montana and Dakota Indian agencies. Watkins' official duties were administrative, such as auditing Indian agents' accounts. His report singled the Lakota out as "wild and hostile bands of Sioux Indians" who "richly merit punishment for their incessant warfare, and their numerous murders of settlers and their families, or white men wherever found unarmed."

This report was dated November 9, 1875, or six days after the White House conference. Leaked to the press, it was to embody the Government's repressive measures against the Indians:

In my judgement, one thousand men, under the command of an experienced officer, sent into their country in the winter, when the Indians are nearly always in camp, and *at which season of the year they are almost helpless*, would be amply sufficient for their capture or punishment. ... The true policy, in my judgement, is to send troops against them in the winter, the sooner the better, and whip them into subjection. They richly merit the punishment for their incessant warfare on friendly tribes, their continuous thieving, and their numerous murders of white settlers and their families, or white men wherever found unarmed. (Emphasis added).

The United States troops are held in contempt, and surrounded by their native mountains, relying on their knowledge of the country and powerful endurance, they [the Sioux] laugh at the futile efforts that have thus far been made to subjugate them, and scorn the idea of white civilization. They are lofty and independent in their attitude and language toward the government officials, as well as the whites generally, and claim to be the sovereign rulers of the land. They say they own the wood, the water, the ground, the air, and that white men live in or pass through their country but by their sufferance.[46]

At General Crook's headquarters in Wyoming Territory, rations and ammunition were being stockpiled, pack trains prepared and troops marshaled in from outlying forts. The Chicago *Inter Ocean* correspondent who had stoked the gold frenzy, William E. Curtis, actually came close to exposing the plot. After sounding out his Army contacts, Curtis told his readers just five days after the White House meeting, "The roving tribes and those who are known as wild Indians will probably be given over entirely to the military until they are subdued." The precise identity of his source is unknown, but when Curtis took the matter up with the high command, a senior officer dismissed talk of war as "an idle fancy of a diseased brain." Curtis didn't press the matter, and an *Inter Ocean* correspondent in the field concluded that war was unlikely for the simple reason that Lakota Indian agents told him, truthfully, that the Indians had no wish to fight.

December 3, 1875: Impossible Deadline - Sioux Must Be on Reservation by January 31, 1876, or Be Attacked

Sitting Bull, and many other Lakota and Cheyenne chiefs and their followers, were living outside the reservation boundaries in the Unceded Territory, still preferring to live a nomadic lifestyle predicated on bison hunting.

On December 3, the Secretary of the Interior sent word to the Secretary of War that he had directed the Commissioner of Indian Affairs to notify the Indians that they must move to a reservation before January 21, 1876, or be deemed hostile and turned over the military force.[47]

December 6, 1875: Commissioner of Indian Affairs Sends Notice of Deadline to Agencies

This deadline notice was sent out to the Lakota Agencies on December 6, 1875.

President Grant's Indian Peace Policy Breached

The outcry for annexation brought President Grant to a crossroads. He had taken office in 1869 on a pledge to keep the West free of war. "Our dealings with the Indians properly lay us open to charges of cruelty and swindling," he had said, and he had staked his administration to a Peace Policy intended to assimilate Plains nations into white civilization.[48] Now, President Grant was forced to choose between the electorate and the Indians.

The Treaty between the Lakotas and the U.S. had been signed at Fort Laramie in 1868, the year before President Grant took office. "From this day forward," the document began, "all war between the parties to this agreement shall forever cease."[49] To entice Lakotas onto the reservation and into farming, the U.S. promised to give them a pound of meat and a pound of flour a day for four years. All Lakota land, however, was to be inviolate. President Grant would breach this Treaty.

December 7, 1875: President Grant's Message - Gold in Black Hills; Sioux Unwilling to Cede Them; End Rations

Succumbing to the demands of the voting electorate to open the Black Hills for mining, President Grant announced action would be taken to relieve the impasse, starting with denying food rations to the Sioux.

> The discovery of gold in the Black Hills, a portion of the Sioux Reservation, has had the effect to induce a large emigration of miners to that point. Thus far the effort to protect the treaty rights of the Indians to that section has been successful, but

the next year will certainly witness a large increase of such emigration. The negotiations for the relinquishment of the gold fields having failed, it will be necessary for Congress to adopt some measures to relieve the embarrassment growing out of the causes named. *The Secretary of the Interior suggests that the supplies now appropriated for the sustenance of that people, being no longer obligatory under the treaty of 1868, but simply a gratuity, may be issued or withheld at his discretion*. (Emphasis added).[50]

December 20, 1875: Deadline Notice Received by Cheyenne River Agency

The deadline Notice was received by the Cheyenne River Agency on December 20, 1875. Rounding up the Lakota was a near-impossible feat in the dead of winter, yet all who refused would be considered hostile and subject to attack. Many of the Lakotas were snowbound in villages scattered throughout the Unceded Territory. Their attitude hadn't changed; they had no problem with the wasichus so long as they stayed off Lakota land, which their chiefs had no intention of surrendering. Their response to Secretary Chandler's ultimatum was unthreatening and, from an Indian perspective, quite practical: They appreciated the invitation to talk but were settled in for the winter; when spring arrived and their ponies grew strong, they would attend a council to discuss their future.[51]

December 22, 1875: Deadline Notice Received by Standing Rock Agency, Agent Requests Extension of Time due to Weather Conditions

The Commissioner's deadline was received at Standing Rock on December 22, 1875. Agent Burke requested that the Indians be given an extension of time because of weather conditions.[52]

January 31, 1876: Deadline for Sioux to Be on Their Reservation

When January 31, 1876, arrived and only several bands of Indians had returned to the reservation, the mechanics for instituting war were set in motion.[53]

Prepare for Winter Military Campaign

The military strategic and tactical operations were directed toward an "end state" which included (1) breaking up the Great Sioux Nation; (2) destroying villages; (3) settling tribes on reservations; (4) subjugating the Northern Plains

Indians; (5) ceding the Black Hills to the U.S.; and (6) allocating Division of Missouri forces to provide wide area security.[54]

The military knew their supply lines would be stretched to the limit. Two new forts were built, along with two camps, to extend the operational reach of the military. They were to (1) provide a base for operations; (2) a refuge for settlers' and (3) to store the equipment and supplies for warfare against hostiles. Prior to any combat, the forts were stocked with (1) the military equipment necessary for Indian warfare (armaments, including howitzers and ammunition); (2) wagons, horses and mules to transport supplies needed for the soldiers in the field; and (3) the provisions to support the garrisoned soldiers. Food and supplies for soldiers in the field were cached at the camps to replenish the supply trains to support the soldiers in the vanguard.

January 21, 25, 1876: Department of the Interior to Provide Military Intelligence to War Department

The Department of the Interior was not a neutral party during the Sioux Wars; they were active participants providing military logistical support and intelligence. Commissioner Smith expressed his opinion on January 21, 1876, to Interior Secretary Chandler that:

> Certainly I can conceive of nothing more damaging to the authority of the Government, not yet fully recognized by other bands of Sioux, than a failure to execute threats of military operations so clearly made. … I directed, on the 19th instant, the agents at the Red Cloud, Spotted Tail, Standing Rock, and Cheyenne River agencies, who would in my view be most likely to obtain reliable and early news of Sitting Bull's intentions and movements, to keep me fully advised by letter and telegraph of his acceptance or rejection of the conditions imposed upon him, or of any other intelligence concerning him. On January 25, 1876, the Commissioner forwarded to the Secretary of War intelligence relative to the probable movements of Sitting Bull gathered by Agent Burke, Standing Rock Agency.[55]

February 1, 1876: Indians Turned Over to War Department

On February 1, the Secretary of the Interior notified the Secretary of War, "… Sitting Bull still refuses to comply with the directions of the Commissioner, the said Indians are hereby turned over to the War Department for such action on the part of the Army as you may deem proper under the circumstances."[56]

February 7, 1876: War Dept. Assumes Authority

On February 7, 1876, Generals Sheridan, Crook and Terry were notified to carry out the request of the Secretary of the Interior, but specific orders were not issued because of the uncertainty of the location of the Indians.[57] Simultaneous efforts were to be directed against Sitting Bull, Crazy Horse and Dull Knife.

> They [were] to find the enemy in his winter camps, kill or drive him from his lodges, destroy his ponies, food, and shelter, and hound him mercilessly across a frigid landscape until he gave up. If women and children fell victim to such methods, it was regrettable, but justified because it resolved the issue quickly and decisively, and thus more humanely.[58]

Base of Military Operations

Base of Operations: Fort Peck, Fort Fetterman and Fort Abraham Lincoln, along with four cantonments to support operations: Powder River Cantonment, Glendive Cantonment, Bighorn Cantonment and Tongue River Cantonment.

August 1876: Congress - Cede Black Hills or Lose Rations

Congress passed an act which provided:

> "...hereafter there shall be no appropriation made for the subsistence of the Sioux, unless they first relinquished their rights to the hunting grounds outside the [1868 treaty] reservation, ceded the Black Hills to the United States, and reached some accommodation with the Government that would be calculated to enable them to become self-supporting." (Emphasis added).[59]

February 1876: Preparations for U.S. Army's Big Horn Expedition

Preparations for the **Big Horn Expedition**, the official designation of the first campaign of the Sioux War of 1876, were undertaken immediately. The first action of importance was the destruction of Crazy Horse's village. Black Coal, an Arapahoe chief, told General Crook that he was encamped on the lower Powder River, about 150 miles from Fort Fetterman.[60]

March 1-26, 1876: U.S. Army's Campaign to Destroy Crazy Horse's Village

General Crook and the scouts formed the vanguard as the column departed from Fort Fetterman on March 1, 1876. They destroyed a village and captured a pony herd estimated at 400 to 700 head. It is uncertain if it was, in fact, Crazy Horse's village. *During withdrawal from the village, two soldiers—one still alive—were left on enemy ground.* With his men exhausted from marching seventy-three miles in extreme cold, Colonel Reynolds could not adequately guard the captured ponies. Only 100 head were left the next morning.

When General Crook arrived in camp on March 18, with nearly 100 ponies he had recovered, he *was upset to learn about the violation of the Army's cardinal rule—you do not leave a man behind.* Loss of the pony herd, as well, was considered inexcusable by the General.

As Crook's soldiers marched back to Fort Fetterman, the Sioux and Cheyennes kept the column under fire at night. Since the Indians wanted to regain the captured ponies, General Crook ordered them shot. Fort Fetterman was reached on March 26, and the Big Horn Expedition was dissolved on March 27.[61]

Failed Crazy Horse Village Attack Results in Court Martial of Colonel Reynolds and Others

Court-martial charges were preferred against Colonel Reynolds for leaving a wounded soldier behind who was captured by the Lakota.[62]

Troop morale would have been seriously compromised if he hadn't been charged. Reynolds could not overcome the stigma of substandard conduct and retired.[63]

The destruction of Crazy Horse's village yielded one important military lesson—winter campaigns could be conducted. Although Army combat forces would experience extreme discomfort, winter attacks were to be disastrous for the Indians.

Winter 1876: U.S. Army's Operations a Bust

The 1876 winter operations were a bust. General Terry was snowbound. General Crook mistakenly attacked a village of peaceable Cheyennes. Worse, the Army violated the code of not leaving a man behind.

April 1876: Black Hills Gold Rush

Miners continued invading the Black Hills. On April 9, 1876, brothers Fred and Moses Manuel, along with Hank Harney and Alex Engh, discovered a sizeable vein of gold-bearing ore near present-day Lead. This turned out to be the veritable mother lode deposit feeding the placer gold in the creeks. They staked a claim and named it the Homestake Mine, selling it to a group of out-of-state investors, George Hearst, in partnership with James Haggin and Lloyd Tevis (president of Wells Fargo, 1872-1892), the following year for $70,000. They had no way of knowing their discovery would end up being the most significant gold vein in American history, supplying 10 percent of the world's supply of gold over the next 125 years and yielding over 40 million ounces of gold.[64]

Spring 1876: U.S. Army's Yellowstone Military Expedition: Three Columns Led by General Crook, General Terry and Colonel John Gibbon

That spring, thousands of reservation Indians migrated to the Unceded Territory, both to hunt buffalo and to join the non-treaty Sioux warriors. The Army launched an offensive, the Yellowstone Military Expedition, under Generals Crook and Terry and Colonel John Gibbon. The plan was to trap the hostiles between the three forces.[65]

On June 14, one hundred seventy-five Crow scouts arrived. They were well mounted and armed, each warrior possessing an extra pony and a fifty caliber breech-loading rifle. A short time later, eighty-six Shoshones arrived. Crook's command was made up of a force of 1,325 men, comprised of 803 cavalry, 175 mounted infantry, 262 Indian scouts, twenty packers and sixty-five miners. The objective was a large Sioux village at the north end of the Rosebud Canyon.

June 17, 1876: Battle of Rosebud

The battle lasted six hours, when the Sioux suddenly retired. General Crook did not pursue. Neither the Indians nor the cavalry could claim overall victory in the fight on the Rosebud. This didn't stop General Crook from claiming victory in his report to General Sheridan dated September 25, 1876: "I invite attention to the fact that in this engagement my troops beat these Indians on a field of their own choosing, and drove them in utter rout from it, as far as the proper care of my wounded and prudence would justify."[66]

July 25, 1876: Little Big Horn Battle

Eight days later, some of General Terry's men—the 7th Cavalry, under Custer—set upon the Lakotas and their Cheyenne allies at the Little Bighorn (June 25–26, 1876). Custer was overwhelmingly defeated. Military witnesses estimated the Indians' strength from 5,000 to 6,000 warriors.

This was the third of four unsuccessful, disconnected engagements following General Crook's failures at the Powder River.

Summer 1876: General Crook's Operations

During the summer of 1876, the Indians evaded General Crook and Colonel Gibbon.

General Crook stated:

> I have never looked on any decisive battle with these Indians and in fact I have never expected any decisive battle at all. Indians do not fight such battles; they only fight boldly when they have the advantage or to cover the movement of their women and children... Indians have scarcely ever been severely punished unless by adapting their own mode of warfare, or tactics, and stealing on them.[67]

He focused his approach on relentless pursuit, denying the enemy resources and defeating them by starvation and exhaustion. Intelligence was provided by Department of the Interior agencies and Indian scouts.

August 1876: Lieutenant General Sheridan - Disarm and Dismount Lakota, Subjugate on Reservation

In August, Lieutenant General Sheridan issued a "dismount and disarm" order of agency Lakota. "A list of all Indians ... will be made and no Indian or their families now out or who may hereafter go out, will be permitted to return without unconditional personal surrender, as well as the surrender of all ponies, guns and property." He recognized that by taking the horses and weapons he was stripping away the key tools that allowed the Lakota and Cheyenne to hunt buffalo and raid their neighboring tribes or white settlers. The agency Lakota would no longer be able to roam and hunt freely in the summer, providing the fighting Sioux with food or military support.[68]

In Sheridan's mind, every Lakota disarmed and dismounted was separated from the hostiles and "a Sioux without a horse is not a Sioux." The disarmament represented the culminating act of the hard war mentality in Sheridan's mind against the Lakota. (Emphasis added).[69]

Failure of Summer 1876 Campaign

Historian Robert Utley summed up the failure of the Army's summer campaign very clearly:

> *Never before or after were the northern Plains tribes better prepared for war. They were numerous, united, confident, superbly led, emotionally charged to defend their homeland and freedom, and able, through design or good fortune, to catch their adversary in unfavorable tactical situations.* Even flawless generalship might not have prevailed over Sitting Bull's mighty coalition that summer [1876]. In large part the generals lost the war because the Indians won it. (Emphasis added).[70]

The summer campaign of 1786 confirmed that the Army could not decisively beat the Lakota and Cheyenne at the peak of their strength, while the Army was stretched beyond its limits of communication and logistical support. By any objective measure, the Lakota and Cheyenne in the spring and summer of 1876 decisively defeated, frustrated, and wore down the Army at the Powder River fight in March, the Battle of the Rosebud in mid-June, and the Battle of the Little Big Horn a week later.

The Army had to deal with poor communication due to long distances; confusion between the location of other companies; lack of linkage in the campaign; and insufficient supplies. Most importantly, the Army failed to anticipate the greater numbers and military prowess of the Lakota and their allies.

The failure of the 1876 summer campaign would require another large campaign the following summer.[72]

Great Sioux War: 1876-1877

A chart on BATTLES IN GREAT SIOUX WAR is in the last Chapter.

Fall 1876: Slim Buttes: Counterproductive: Lakotas Were Surrendering, Headed to Agencies

On the evening of September 8, 1876, Captain Mills' Third Cavalry troopers destroyed American Horse's village at Slim Buttes and killed American Horse. General Crook's report to Lieutenant General Sheridan acknowledged that the American Horse's people claimed that they were going back to the reservation.[73]

Appropriations Act of August 15, 1876, None for Sioux Until They Cede Black Hills

In the meantime, Congress was becoming increasingly dissatisfied with the failure of the Sioux to cede the Black Hills. The Sioux' entitlement to subsistence rations under the terms of the Fort Laramie Treaty had expired in 1872. Nonetheless, in each of the two following years, over $1 million was appropriated for feeding the Sioux. In August 1876, Congress enacted an appropriations bill providing that "hereafter there shall be no appropriation made for the subsistence" of the Sioux, unless they first relinquished their rights to the hunting grounds outside the reservation, ceded the Black Hills to the U.S., and reached some accommodation with the Government that would be calculated to enable them to become self-supporting. Toward this end, Congress requested the President to appoint another commission to negotiate with the Sioux for the cession of the Black Hills.

August 1876: Manypenny Commission Sent to Negotiate to Buy Black Hills

George W. Manypenny led the commission to try again to buy the Black Hills in August 1876. *The commissioners brought with them the text of a treaty that had been prepared in advance* under which the Lakota ceded the Black Hills and their rights to hunt in the Unceded Territory in exchange for subsistence rations. *It was signed by only 10% of the adult male Sioux population.* The deep political divisions continued for the next decade, and non-agency bands joined in the rise of the Ghost Dance movement in 1889–90.

November 25, 1876: U.S. Army's Dull Knife Battle in Wyoming

In November 1876, scouts informed Colonel Mackenzie that a large Cheyenne camp was situated along a canyon on the Red Fork of the Powder River. There were 200 lodges under Chiefs Dull Knife and Little Wolf, with 400 warriors. On November 25, 1876, a force 1,100 strong, including about 100 Pawnee scouts—attacked Dull Knife's village. It was destroyed and about 500 ponies were captured, leaving the surviving Cheyenne to face the winter without food and shelter. The battle ended Cheyenne resistance for all practical purposes.[74]

1877: Surrender of Northern Cheyenne and Sioux

Constant movement had ensured that the Sioux could not send out large hunting parties and the large Indian force could not logistically support itself. The Sioux and Cheyenne were reduced to choosing between starvation or fleeing to Canada. The Sioux War was concluded without a clear watershed moment or a decisive victory on the field of battle.

General Crook accepted the surrender of the Cheyennes on February 24, 1877, the Sans Arcs and Miniconjous on April 14, a second group of Cheyennes on May 1 and Crazy Horse and his Oglala on May 6.

As General Miles recorded, February 19, 1877, Little Chief stated the position of the remaining non-agency Lakota:

> "We are weak, compared with you and your forces; we are out of ammunition; we cannot make a rifle, a round of ammunition, or a knife; in fact we are at the mercy of those who are taking possession of our country; your terms are harsh and cruel, but we are going to accept them and place ourselves at your mercy."[75]

Congressional Inquiry

Then came the cover-up. A Congressional investigation was launched but the conspirators had prepared for congressional scrutiny. The new Secretary of War, J. Donald Cameron, took just three days to submit a lengthy explanation. Absent was Lieutenant General Sheridan's incriminating order to General Terry from November 9, 1875.

Military operations, Cameron assured Congress, targeted not the Lakota nation, only "certain hostile parts"—in other words, those who lived in the Unceded

Territory. Cameron attested: *"**The accidental discovery of gold on the western border of the Sioux reservation and the intrusion of our people thereon, have not caused this war***, and have only complicated it by the uncertainty of numbers to be encountered."* (Emphasis added).

Certainly many congressmen recognized Cameron's chicanery for what it was. But with the nation's press clamoring for retribution after the Little Bighorn, June 25–26, 1876, they dared not dispute the administration's line. Nearly everyone seemed content to blame them for the conflict. A singular dissenting voice was George W. Manypenny, a reform-minded former Indian Bureau commissioner. He surmised that "the Sioux War of 1876, the crime of the centennial year, [was] inaugurated" at the White House in November 1875. But he was dismissed as an Indian apologist, and no one took his allegations seriously. Nothing came of the investigation.[76]

Home for Arapaho

In the Fall of 1877, a Northern Arapaho delegation visited Washington, DC to request that the President not send them to the Indian Territory in Oklahoma. In 1878 they were settled on the Eastern Shoshone's Wind River Reservation. Their Southern Arapaho relatives were moved with the Southern Cheyenne to western Oklahoma.

1877: Forced Legislation Confiscates Black Hills

The Act of February 28, 1877 (1877 Act) abrogated the Fort Laramie Treaty of 1868, removing the Black Hills from the Sioux Nation.

Total Disrespect for Indian Commissioners

The following is a letter of General Crook to Mr. Tibbles, journalist, Indians' rights activist, and politician:

> … I will say without hesitation that our Indians have adhered more closely to the spirit of treaty stipulations than the white men or the white man's government has ever done. The leading chiefs thoroughly understand the changed condition of affairs-they see that they can no longer depend upon game for their support and are anxious to obtain cattle, seed, implements, and to have their children educated. They see the necessity of adopting the white man's ways and conforming to the established order of things. But I am very sorry to say they

have, to a very great degree, lost confidence in our people and their promises. Indians are very much like white men in being unable to live upon air. If you were to collate from treaties all the promises made to the red men, and contrast them with our performance, you would have to admit that there was a very serious margin of compacts broken and unfulfilled, upon which the Indians could ground their distrust and contempt. *We send them too many commissioners; there is no class of men for whom the Indian has less respect.* (Emphasis added).[77]

1889: Dawes Act

The Dawes Act had profound effects on the Lakota, beyond the loss of their land. First it removed control of the land from the tribe and placed it in the hands of the individual land owner, but more importantly, it separated the Lakota into six different reservations, making it far more difficult for the Lakota to organize and communicate as a single voice or unified force.

1889–1890: Ghost Dance Movement

In 1889, a Paiute medicine man's vision gave rise to a revivalist religious movement known as the Ghost Dance, which held out the promise of the disappearance of whites, the return of the buffalo, and the resumption of the traditional way of life. It attracted many fervent supporters. Although the movement did not call for violent action, some Indian agents and settlers feared that possibility, and the federal government responded by increasing the presence of the U.S. Army and ordering suppression of the Ghost Dance movement.

Pine Ridge Requests Troops

In October 1890, Daniel F. Royer arrived at Pine Ridge Agency, home of the Oglala Lakotas, to assume responsibility as agent. His selection as agent could not have been worse: he knew nothing about Indians and was irrationally fearful of them. His dispatches to Washington urged that troops be sent to protect citizens from war.

In Royer's paranoid mind the Ghost Dance was a war dance that threatened imminent bloodshed. His dispatches to Washington urged that troops be sent to protect citizens from war.

In mid-November 1890 President Benjamin Harrison responded to the fears of an Indian outbreak by ordering troops into the area. Regular troops were sent from Fort Robinson, Nebraska, and on November 18, 1890, the Second Nebraska Infantry left Fort Omaha in two special trains. On the train was also a cadre of newspaper reporters.

December 29, 1890: Massacre at Wounded Knee

The Interior Department was given the responsibility of preventing the Sioux from leaving their Reservations. Within a week, Army units began moving toward the Reservations. Major General Nelson A. Miles, Commander of the Military Division of the Missouri, assumed control of the troops converging on the Dakotas. Miles planned to anticipate the movement of the hostile Indians and arrest or overpower them in detail before they had time to concentrate in one large body. For this purpose, Miles had at his disposal almost half of the cavalry and infantry regiments in the Regular Army and two batteries of light artillery.

In the early morning hours of November 24, Captain Allyn Capron, Commanding Battery E, 1st Artillery, along with most of the 7th Cavalry regiment, entrained at Fort Riley for Pine Ridge. The battery, three officers and forty-seven enlisted men, arrived in South Dakota three days later. In addition to Capron, the battery's officers were Second Lieutenant John L. Hayden and Second Lieutenant Harry L. Hawthorne. Hawthorne was an officer of the 2nd Artillery regiment who had been attached to the battery for the move to Pine Ridge.

Shortly after arriving in South Dakota, the battery was issued six Hotchkiss 1.65 mountain guns and was ready to take the field by the third week in December. Lieutenant Hayden and a platoon (two guns) of Battery E joined Major Guy Henry's battalion of the 9th Cavalry on Christmas Eve. Henry was to patrol the White Clay River from his camp at Harney Springs. Hayden's detachment would remain with the 9th until the end of the campaign.

The 7th Cavalry intercepted the ailing Big Foot and his people and ordered them into confinement on Wounded Knee Creek. On the morning of December 29, Colonel James W. Forsyth convened a council with the Miniconjous. He had formed them in a semi-circle. Initially, B and K troop had been placed between the council and the cavalry camp. However, the two troops were shifted to prevent movement between the council and the village.[111]

Colonel Forsyth demanded that the Lakota surrender all their firearms and told them that they would be relocated to a new camp. While these discussions proceeded in the Lakota camp, a number of Indians began singing Ghost Dance songs, with some rising to throw handfuls of dirt in the air. The troops who surrounded them perceived the singing and dirt throwing as signals to attack, and at this tense moment the fuse was lit.

A single shot was sufficient to spark the following bloodshed. Battery E, 1st Artillery opened fire in support of the 7th Cavalry. The responsibility for many of the casualties on both sides, and for the obliteration of the village has been placed on the four mountain guns of Battery E. Capron opened fire with his two guns on a group of Indians fleeing southwest along the agency road. Hawthorne's guns engaged the warriors who had fled to the village and were firing at the 7th Cavalry from there. As Capron fired at any group of Indians firing at the Cavalry, Hawthorne shelled the ravine south of the Indian village. The warriors who had taken refuge in the ravine were pouring a chafing fire on the Cavalry. Corporal Paul H. Weinert, and one other artillery man, maneuvered the gun into the mouth of the ravine and opened fire.

The battery's guns were effective in neutralizing some of the pockets of resistance, but it did so at the high price of casualties among the women and children. At the ranges the guns were firing, it was impossible to distinguish Lakota men from women in those groups firing at the Cavalry. Even if the distinction could have been made, it would have been equally impossible to fire on the warriors without inadvertently hitting those around them.[112]

More than 200 Lakota were killed by the 457 U.S. soldiers. The Army conducted an investigation of the incident but never determined culpability.

1898–1904: Lakota Indian Reservations – Not Suitable for Farming, Not Enough Land for Ranching

Cheyenne River

First, the land of this reservation is not adapted to agriculture; second, the past season throughout this locality has been one of continuous drought, resulting in an almost entire failure of crops of all kinds.[113] This reservation is not adapted to farming.[114]

Devils Lake

Fort Totten and the Turtle Mountain, the former Sioux, the latter Chippewa—only about a third of the Reservation

~ 498 ~

is tillable. The condition of agriculture remains about the same as last year, notwithstanding the fact that $10,000 was appropriated by the last Congress for relief.

None of the machinery arrived in time for spring plowing and seeding and the stock estimated to run said machinery has not yet been furnished. The horses owned by the Indians are not, as a rule, large enough to run gang plows and the usual heavy farm machinery necessary for successful farming. We have planted an unusually large acreage of flax.[115]

Pine Ridge

As stated in previous reports, farming on this reservation is not practiced by these Indians, and is not practicable, except to a very limited extent where there are means of irrigating the land.[116]

These Indians, as a whole, can never, in my opinion, be entirely self-supporting. The only possible industry for them is stock raising, and this has a definite limit, as much of the land of the reservation produces grass so scantily that many acres are necessary to sustain one animal. Then, also, the bottomlands on which only in ordinary years hay can be cut, are limited in extent.[117] It is unfortunate that these Indians, once the owners of the fertile valley of the Platte and much other farming land, should have been relegated to a country like this, where farming is impossible even for white men.[118]

Rosebud

The land is all allotted as grazing land. The amount adapted to agriculture is very limited, and in consequence of the scarcity of water and timber in many portions of the reserve no use can be made of the land beyond grazing cattle during the summer and fall months in seasons when the rainfall is sufficient to fill the waterholes.[119]

Lower Brule Agency

Agriculture.-Results at this time show that nothing of any consequence has been accomplished in this direction during the year, as no seeds were furnished the Indians, though some have purchased a few garden seeds and planted them with little success on account of the drought. Many have planted corn in the face of repeated failures, only to be again disappointed at reaping time.

Stock raising.-As this country is mainly suited for stock raising, I have tried to instill into these people the importance of this industry, and quite a number of them have small bunches of cattle, of which they are very proud.[120]

Crow Creek

Climatic conditions—the season has not been a successful one. Neither Indians or whites have raised a good crop this year.[121]

Standing Rock

This proves how hard and risky farm operations are in this section of the country. They require an endless amount of work and care to produce any kind of fair results and then they often fail. If it is not drought, it is hail or insects or something else that destroys the hopes of the laborer.[122]

October 24, 1903: Battle of Lightning Creek

By the time this skirmish occurred, Indian battles had become a thing of the past and "civilization" had taken over Wyoming. However, on October 24, 1903, one more skirmish would occur. Also called Battle of Lightning Creek, the conflict occurred after Weston County Sheriff William Miller received word that several bands of Indians were roaming about the southern part of the county. The Indians, led by Chief Charley Smith had left the Pine Ridge Reservation in South Dakota to go hunting near Thunder Creek. Allegedly hunting illegally, the Indians had not only violated game laws but, were also said to have killed some stock on the range. Sheriff Miller and a posse caught up with a portion of the band on October 23rd and arrested 12 of them at the mouth of Lance Creek. The Indians were then disarmed and escorted back to Newcastle, Wyoming by Deputy Hilton, Ed Buchanan, and Arthur Edlund.

The remaining posse members, including Sheriff Miller, then went after the rest of the band, catching up with them on the Dry Fork of the Cheyenne River.

Finding a group of about 20 warriors and 30 women, he demanded that they surrender; however, Chief Charley Smith refused. Miller, in the meantime, realized he did not have enough men to make an arrest and withdrew. The next day after obtaining reinforcements, the posse caught up with the band near the confluence of Lightning Creek and Thunder Creek. Once again, Miller demanded that they surrender but they refused and one Indian opened fire on the posse. In the ensuing skirmish, Sheriff Miller suffered a fatal wound and bled to death, Deputy Louis Falkenberg was shot in the neck, five Indians were killed, and Chief Charley Smith was severely wounded. He died the next day.

The rest of the Indians fled and headed back to the reservation. Deputy Sheriff Lee Mather of Crook County and a posse set out to intercept the Indians in Edgemont, South Dakota. They were able to arrest nine braves and 12 women. The rest, it is believed, escaped to the reservation. On November 12, a preliminary hearing was held in which the Indians pled innocence, admitting they were part of the hunting party, but, denying having any part in the battle. They were all discharged for lack of evidence. Wyoming Governor Chatterton, upon hearing the news of the Indians' release, was outraged that the Indians, had gotten away with, not only the intentional murder of two fine lawmen but with killing game and the stock of area ranchers as well. However, there was nothing he could do about it.

Most Army officers resented the Interior Department's management of the reservations, and took it as a matter of gospel that the Indian agents were corrupt, and that flawed management caused most problems between Indians and whites.

Of the 60 million acres promised the Lakotas in 1868—including the Badlands—they've lost more than 55 million.

Summary of Military Operations

Base of Operations: Fort Peck, Fort Fetterman and Fort Abraham Lincoln, along with four cantonments to support operations: Powder River Cantonment, Glendive Cantonment, Bighorn Cantonment and Tongue River Cantonment.

The operational reach of the military forces was critical because Lieutenant General Sheridan knew there would be no decisive engagement with the Sioux. They used guerilla tactics. He focused his approach on denying the enemy resources and defeating them by starvation and exhaustion. Intelligence was provided by Department of the Interior agencies. Simultaneous efforts were directed against Sitting Bull, Crazy Horse and Dull Knife.

Tactics: converging columns were used in the 1876 Campaign but not in 1876-77. For the 1877 Campaign, the tactics focused on were relentless pursuit, destruction of personal possessions (including ponies), unconditional surrender, and the subsequent incarceration of prominent chiefs. Indian scouts were used; some were traditional enemies of the Lakota. Insurgents were to be isolated from the support of Indian non-combatants (disarm and dismount).

Obstacles included: severe weather (minus forty-degree Fahrenheit temperatures, waist deep snow); very long distances over the northern plains in converging, uncoordinated columns with insufficient supplies; lack of linkage in the campaign; poor communication due to distances; confusion between location of other companies; and failure to account for the greater numbers and military prowess of the Lakota and their allies. The U.S. Army could not maintain the pace of a coordinated offensive operation.

Cavalry columns, even with the use of mule trains for logistic support, could not keep up with the Sioux.

Notes: Dakotas

1. F. W. Dodge. Handbook of American Indians North of Mexico, American Bureau of Ethnology, Bulletin 30 (2 Vols., Washington, 1997), I, p. 376.
2. Robert H. Ruby, The Oglala Sioux, Warriors in Transition (New York: Vantage Press, Inc., 1955), p. 14.
3. Report of the Commissioner of Indian Affairs to the Secretary of the Interior, United States, U.S. Government Printing Office, 1857, p. 588.
4. Report of the Commissioner of Indian Affairs to the Secretary of the Interior, Northern Superintendency, Washington: Printer, George W. Bowman, 1860, p. 67.
5. Ibid., p. 65.
6. Report of the Commissioner of Indian Affairs to the Secretary of the Interior, Northern Superintendency, United States. Office of Indian Affairs, U.S. Government Printing Office, 1864, p. 273.
7. Report of the Commissioner of Indian Affairs to the Secretary of the Interior, Dakota Superintendency, United States. Office of Indian Affairs, U.S. Government Printing Office, 1865, p. 273.
8. Report of the Commissioner of Indian Affairs to the Secretary of the Interior, Northern Superintendency, United States. Office of Indi-

an Affairs, U.S. Government Printing Office, 1868, p. 250.

9. Report of the Commissioner of Indian Affairs to the Secretary of the Interior, United States. Office of Indian Affairs, U.S. Government Printing Office, 1870, p. 203.

10. Ibid., p. 320.

11. Report of the Commissioner of Indian Affairs, Northern Superintendency, Indian Agent Thomas J. Galbraith, Department of the Interior, United States. Office of Indian Affairs, U.S. Government Printing Office, 1864, p. 296.

12. Report of the Commissioner of Indian Affairs to the Secretary of the Interior, United States, U.S. Government Printing Office, 1866, p. 70.

13. Report of the Northwestern Treaty Commission to the Sioux of the Upper Missouri, August 25, 1866.

14. Condition of the Indian tribes: Report of the joint special committee, appointed under joint resolution of March 3, 1865. With an appendix. United States. Congress.

15. Report of the Commissioner of Indian Affairs to the Secretary of the Interior, Dakota Superintendency, U.S. Government Printing Office, 1875, p. 8.

16. UNITED STATES DEPARTMENT OF THE INTERIOR NATIONAL PARK SERVICE THE NATIONAL SURVEY OF HISTORIC SITES AND BUILDINGS Theme XV, Westward Expansion and the Extension of the National Boundaries to the Pacific 1830-1898 THE MINING FRONTIER. http://npshistory.com/publications/nhl/theme-studies/mining-frontier.pdf (accessed online August 1, 2022).

17. Report of the Commissioner of Indian Affairs to the Secretary of the Interior, Dakota Superintendency, U.S. Government Printing Office, 1866, p. 174.

18. Report of the Commissioner of Indian Affairs to the Secretary of the Interior, United States. Office of Indian Affairs, U.S. Government Printing Office, 1867, p. 240.

19. Browne, John Ross, and James Wickes Taylor. Special Commissioners, U.S. Dept. of Treasury, Reports upon the mineral resources of the United States. U.S. Government Printing Office, 1867, p. 5.

20. Wesley M. Pirkle, MAJ, MAJOR GENERAL GEORGE CROOK'S USE OF COUNTERINSURGENCY COMPOUND WARFARE DURING THE GREAT SIOUX WAR OF 1876-77, 2008, p. 35.

21. Ibid., p. 37.

22. Robert G. Athearn, William Tecumseh Sherman and the Settlements of the West (Norman: University of Oklahoma Press), 1956, p. 194.

23. S. Misc. Doc. No. 136, 41st Cong., 2nd Sess. (1870), p. 9. 4-29-1870. Letter of the Secretary of the Interior to the Chairman of the Committee on Indian Affairs of the Senate communicating a statement of the Commissioner of Indian Affairs [Ely S. Parker] in relation to all the Indian tribes within the bounds of the United States.

24. Clow, Richmond L. "General William Harney on the Northern Plains." South Dakota History 16 (1986): 229–48.

25. William T. Sherman "We Do Our Duty According to Our Means" Army and Navy Journal 6, no. 7 (September 26, 1868): p. 85.

26. Id.

27. https://www.pbs.org/wgbh/americanexperience/features/custer-timeline/ (accessed online January 3, 2022).

28. The Abridgment ... Containing the Annual Message of the President of the United States to the Two Houses of Congress ... with Reports of Departments and Selections from Accompanying Papers, United States, President, 1874, p. 641.

29. Library of Congress. Cozzens, Peter. "Ulysses S. Grant Launched an Illegal War Against the Plains Indians, Then Lied About it." Smithsonian Magazine, November 2016, https://www.smithsonian-mag.com/history/ulysses-grant-launched-illegal-war-plains-indians-180960787/?utm_medium=email&utm_source=govdelivery (accessed online September 11, 2022).

30. U. S. Department of the Interior, Geographical and Geological Survey of the Rocky Mountain Region; Report on the geology and resources of the Black Hills of Dakota: with atlas, Newton, Henry, 1845-1877, Jenney, Walter Proctor, 1849-1921, Washington: Govt. Print. Off., 1880, p. 1.

31. Id.

32. Ibid., p. 2.

33. Ibid., pp. 4-5.

34. Ibid., p. 5.

35. Ibid., p.225.

36. The Papers of Ulysses S. Grant, Vol. 26, 1875, xii. https://www.white-househistory.org/native-american-protests#footnote-23, (accessed online March 4, 2023).

37. Library of Congress. Cozzens, Peter. "Ulysses S. Grant Launched an Illegal War Against the Plains Indians, Then Lied About it." Smithsonian Magazine, November 2016. https://www.smithsonianmag.com/history/ulyss-

es-grant-launched-illegal-war-plains-indians-180960787/?utm_medium=e-mail&utm_source=govdelivery (accessed online September 11, 2022).

38. Report of the Commissioner of Indian Affairs to the Secretary of the Interior, Office of Indian Affairs, United States. U.S. Government Printing Office, 1875, pp. 7-9.

39. U.S., Congress, House, Report of the Secretary of the Interior. 44th Cong., 1st Sess., 1875, House Ex. Doc. 1, Part 5, pp. 688-689.

40. Ibid., pp. 692-93.

41. Ibid., p. 700.

42. Harry H. Anderson, "A Challenge to Brown's Sioux Indian Wars Thesis," Montana Magazine of Western History, XII, No. 1 (January, 1962), p. 46.

43. Library of Congress. Cozzens, Peter. "Ulysses S. Grant Launched an Illegal War Against the Plains Indians, Then Lied About it." Smithsonian Magazine, November 2016. https://www.smithsonian-mag.com/history/ulysses-grant-launched-illegal-war-plains-indians-180960787/?utm_medium=email&utm_source=govdelivery (accessed online September 11, 2022).

44. Id.

45. Id.

46. Letter of E. C. Watkins to Indian Commissioner E. C. Smith, November 9, 1876 U S , Congress, House, Military Expedition Against the Sioux Indians, 44 Cong. 1 sess. 1876, H. Ex. Doc. 184, pp. 8-9.

47. Letter from Secretary of the Interior Z. Chandler to Secretary of War Belknap, December 3, 1875, U.S., Congress, House, Military Expedition Against the Sioux Indians, 44 Cong. 1 sess. 1876, H. Ex. Doc. 184, p. 10.

48. Library of Congress. Cozzens, Peter. "Ulysses S. Grant Launched an Illegal War Against the Plains Indians, Then Lied About it." Smithsonian Magazine, November 2016. https://www.smithsonianmag.com/history/ulyss-es-grant-launched-illegal-war-plains-indians-180960787/?utm_medium=e-mail&utm_source=govdelivery (accessed online September 11, 2022).

49. Id.

50. Ulysses S. Grant, "Seventh Annual Message," December 7, 1875. Gerhard Peters and John T. Woolley, The American Presidency Project. http://www.presidency.ucsb.edu/ws/index.php?pid=29516#axzz2fUkFG2te (accessed online September 2, 2022).

51. Doane Robinson, History of the Sioux, op. cit., p. 422.

52. Letter of Indian Commissioner J. Q. Smith to Secretary of Interior Z. Chandler, 144 Cong. 1 sess. V. XIV, (ser 1691), H. EX. DOC. 184, p. 18.

53. U.S., Congress, House, Military Expedition Against the Sioux Indians, 44th Cong., 1st Sess., 1876, House Ex. Doc. 184, p. 10.

54. Blome, Matthew L. The Emergence of Operational Art in the Great Sioux War 1876-1877. ARMY COMMAND AND GENERAL STAFF COLLEGE FORT LEAVENWORTH KS SCHOOL OF ADVANCED MILITARY STUDIES, 2013.

55. 44 Cong. 1 sess. V. XIV, (ser 1691), H. EX. DOC. 184, pp. 13, 16.

56. Letters Received, Department of the Platte," Letter, Secretary of the Interior to the Secretary of War, 1 February 1876. 44 Cong, 1 sess, V. XIV, (ser 1691), H. Ex. Doc. 134. pp. 16-18.

57. U.S., Congress, House, Report of the Secretary War, 44th Cong., 2d Sess., 1876, House Ex. Doc. 1 , Part 2, p . 441.

58. Utley, Robert M. *Frontier Regulars: The U.S. Army and the Indian, 1866-1891*. Lincoln and London: University of Nebraska Press, 1973, p. 11.

59. Act of August 15, 1876, 19 Stat. 176, 192.

60. U.S., Congress, House, Report of Secretary of War, 44th Cong., 2d Sess., 1876, House Ex. Doc. 1, Part 2, p. 442.

61. J. W. Vaughn, The Reynolds Campaign on Powder River (Norman: University of Oklahoma Press, 1961), p. 214.

62. War Department, Record Group 94, Pile 6160 Adjutant General's Office. 1875, Powder River Expedition.

63. Id.

64. https://blackhillsvisitor.com/learn/history/the-black-hills-gold-rush/ (accessed online September 5, 2022).

65. Department of War, *Report of the Secretary of War, 1876* (Washington, DC: Government Printing Office, 1876), p. 441; from General Sherman's annual report. Sheridan, Phillip H. *Record of Engagements with Hostile Indians Within the Military Division of the Missouri*. Bellevue, NE: The Old Army Press, 1969, p. 50. U.S., Congress, House, Military Expedition Against the Sioux Indians, 44 Cong. 1.

66. U.S., Congress, House, Report of the Secretary War, 44th Cong., 2d Sess., 1876, House Ex. Doc. 1 , Part 2, p . 498.

67. Records of the War Department, Record Group 94, Document File 4163 (Sioux War) 1876, Item: 4718 AGO 1876.

68. Bailey, John W. Pacifying the Plains: General Alfred Terry and the Decline of the Sioux, 1866-1890. Westport and London: Greenwood Press, 1979, p. 167. Bourke, John G. *The Diaries of John Gregory Bourke, July 29, 1876: April 7, 1878*. Vol. 2. Edited by Charles M. Robinson. Denton, TX:

University of North Texas Press, 2005, p. 33.

69. Hutton, Paul A. *Phil Sheridan and His Army*. Norman: University of Oklahoma Press, 1985, pp. 182-3.

70. Utley, Robert M. *Frontier Regulars: The U.S. Army and the Indian, 1866-1891*. Lincoln and London: University of Nebraska Press, 1973, p. 262.

71. Blome, Matthew L. The Emergence of Operational Art in the Great Sioux War 1876-1877. ARMY COMMAND AND GENERAL STAFF COLLEGE FORT LEAVENWORTH KS SCHOOL OF ADVANCED MILITARY STUDIES, 2013, pp. 4-5.

72. Terry's Column in the Field, Camp on the Yellowstone, Mouth of Glendive Creek, Montana," *Chicago Tribune*, 6 September 1876. Cozzens, Peter, ed. *Eyewitnesses to the Indian Wars, 1865-1890*, Vol. 4. Mechanicsburg, PA: Stackpole Books, 2004, p. 407.

73. Bourke, John G. *The Diaries of John Gregory Bourke, July 29, 1876–April 7, 1878*. Vol. 2. Edited by Charles M. Robinson. Denton, TX: University of North Texas Press, 2005, p. 116. Greene, Jerome A., *Slim Buttes, 1876*. Norman and London: University of Oklahoma Press, 1982, p. 131.

74. Gerry Robinson, The Dull Knife Fight, 1876: Troops Attack a Cheyenne Village on the Red Fork of Powder River, 2014.

75. Nelson A. Miles, *Personal Recollections and Observations of General Nelson A. Miles*, (New York: De Capo Press, 1969 [1896]), p. 243.

76. Library of Congress. Cozzens, Peter. "Ulysses S. Grant Launched an Illegal War Against the Plains Indians, Then Lied About it." *Smithsonian Magazine*, November 2016. https://www.smithsonianmag.com/history/ulysses-grant-launched-illegal-war-plains-indians-180960787/?utm_medium=email&utm_source=govdelivery (accessed online September 11, 2022).

77. George Crook, The Council Fire 2, no. 12 (December 1879): 178-79.

78. Department of War, *Report of the Secretary of War, 1876* (Washington, DC: Government Printing Office, 1876), p. 441; from General Sherman's annual report. Sheridan, Phillip H. *Record of Engagements with Hostile Indians Within the Military Division of the Missouri*. Bellevue, NE: The Old Army Press, 1969, p. 50. U.S., Congress, House, Military Expedition Against the Sioux Indians, 44 Cong. 1 sess. 1876, H. Ex. Doc. 184, pp. 53-54.

79. Hutton, Paul A. *Phil Sheridan and His Army*. Norman: University of Oklahoma Press, 1985, p. 312.

80. U.S., Congress, House, Report of the Secretary War, 44th Cong., 2d Sess., 1876, House Ex. Doc. 1, Part 2, p. 460.

81. U.S., Congress, House, Report of the Secretary War, 44th Cong., 2d Sess., 1876, House Ex. Doc. 1 , Part 2, p. 498.

82. Graham, Colonel W. A. Abstract of the Official Record of Proceedings of the Reno Court of Inquiry. Harrisburg: The Stackpole Co., 1954.

83. Bourke, John G. *The Diaries of John Gregory Bourke, July 29, 1876– April 7, 1878*. Vol. 2. Edited by Charles M. Robinson. Denton, TX: University of North Texas Press, 2005, p. 116.

84. Charles F. Lummis, Genera Crook and the Apache Wars (Flagstaff, AZ, 1966), p. 17.

85. U.S., Congress, House, Report of the Secretary War, 44th Cong., 2d Sess., 1876, House Ex. Doc. 1 , Part 2, pp. 473-474, 506.

86. Records at the War Department Record Group 94, Document File 4164 (Sioux War) 1876, Item: 5184 AGO 1876.

87. Records of the War Department, Record Group 94, Document File 4163 (Sioux War) 1876, Item: 4718 AGO 1876.

88. Bailey, John W. Pacifying the Plains: General Alfred Terry and the Decline of the Sioux, 1866-1890. Westport and London: Greenwood Press, 1979, p. 167. Bourke, John G. The Diaries of John Gregory Bourke, July 29, 1876–April 7, 1878. Vol. 2. Edited by Charles M. Robinson. Denton, TX: University of North Texas Press, 2005, p. 33.

89. Hutton, Paul A. Phil Sheridan and His Army. Norman: University of Oklahoma Press, 1985, pp. 182-3.

90. Utley, Robert M. *Frontier Regulars: The U.S. Army and the Indian, 1866-1891*. Lincoln and London: University of Nebraska Press, 1973, p. 262.

91. Blome, Matthew L. The Emergence of Operational Art in the Great Sioux War 1876-1877. ARMY COMMAND AND GENERAL STAFF COLLEGE FORT LEAVENWORTH KS SCHOOL OF ADVANCED MILITARY STUDIES, 2013, pp. 4-5.

92. Paul L. Hedren, Great Sioux War Orders of Battle (Norman: Arthur H. Clark Company, 2011, pp. 40-48.

93. Blome, Matthew L. The Emergence of Operational Art in the Great Sioux War 1876-1877. ARMY COMMAND AND GENERAL STAFF COLLEGE FORT LEAVENWORTH KS SCHOOL OF ADVANCED MILITARY STUDIES, 2013, p. 30.

94. Bourke, John G. *The Diaries of John Gregory Bourke, July 29, 1876– April 7, 1878*. Vol. 2. Edited by Charles M. Robinson. Denton, TX: University of North Texas Press, 2005, p. 116.

95. Hutton, Paul A. *Phil Sheridan and His Army*. Norman: University of

Oklahoma Press, 1985, p. 222.

96. Charles M. Robinson III, Bad Hand: a Biography of General Ranald S. Mackenzie (Austin: State House Press, 2005), pp. 130-132.

97. "Terry's Column in the Field, Camp on the Yellowstone, Mouth of Glendive Creek, Montana," *Chicago Tribune,* 6 September 1876. Cozzens, Peter, ed. *Eyewitnesses to the Indian Wars, 1865-1890,* Vol. 4. Mechanicsburg, PA: Stackpole Books, 2004, p. 407.

98. Bourke, John G. *The Diaries of John Gregory Bourke, July 29, 1876– April 7, 1878.* Vol. 2. Edited by Charles M. Robinson. Denton, TX: University of North Texas Press, 2005, p. 116. Greene, Jerome A., *Slim Buttes, 1876.* Norman and London: University of Oklahoma Press, 1982, p. 131.

99. Crook, George W. General George Crook: His Autobiography. Edited by Martin F. Schmitt. Norman: University of Oklahoma Press, 1946, pp. 216-217.

100. Act of August 15, 1876, 19 Stat. 176, 192.

101. Gerry Robinson, The Dull Knife Fight, 1876: Troops Attack a Cheyenne Village on the Red Fork of Powder River, 2014.

102. Library of Congress. Cozzens, Peter. "Ulysses S. Grant Launched an Illegal War Against the Plains Indians, Then Lied About it." *Smithsonian Magazine,* November 2016. https://www.smithsonianmag.com/history/ulysses-grant-launched-illegal-war-plains-indians-180960787/?utm_medium=email&utm_source=govdelivery (accessed online September 11, 2022).

103. Blome, Matthew L. The Emergence of Operational Art in the Great Sioux War 1876-1877. ARMY COMMAND AND GENERAL STAFF COLLEGE FORT LEAVENWORTH KS SCHOOL OF ADVANCED MILITARY STUDIES, 2013, pp. 6-7.

104. Greene, *Yellowstone Command,* 1878. … Greene, Jerome A., *Yellowstone Command: Colonel Nelson A. Miles and the Great Sioux War, 1876-1877.* Lincoln and London: University of Nebraska Press, 1991, pp. 187-188.

105. Nelson A. Miles, *Personal Recollections and Observations of General Nelson A. Miles,* (New York: De Capo Press, 1969 [1896]), p. 243.

106. Nelson A. Miles The Future of the Indian Question, North American Review 152, no. 410 (January 1891): 1-10

107. 19 Stat. 254.

108. Hutton, Paul A. *Phil Sheridan and His Army.* Norman: University of Oklahoma Press, 1985, pp. 182-183.

109. George Crook, The Council Fire 2, no. 12 (December 1879): 178-79.

110. Report of the Commissioner of Indian Affairs to the Secretary of

the Interior, Reports of Agents in Dakota, U.S. Government Printing Office, 1888, p. 68.

111. Testimony of Major Samuel Whitside, Report of Investigation into the Battle at Wounded Knee Creek, South Dakota, Fought December 29th, 1890, February 4. 1891. As reprinted in U.S. Congress, Senate, Hearings before the Committee on the Judiciary on S. 1147 and S. 2900, 94th Cong., 2nd Sess., 1976.

112. Testimony of Major Samuel Whitside, Report of Investigation into the Battle at Wounded Knee Creek, South Dakota, Fought December 29th, 1890, February 4. 1891. As reprinted in U.S. Congress, Senate, Hearings before the Committee on the Judiciary on S. 1147 and S. 2900, 94th Cong., 2nd Sess., 1976. Larry D. Roberts, BATTERY E, 1ST ARTILLERY AT WOUNDED KNEE-DECEMBER, South Dakota State University.

113. Annual Report of the Department of Interior, Part 1, Report of the Commissioner of Indian Affairs to the Secretary of the Interior, Reports of Agencies in South Dakota, Report of Cheyenne River, Agency, ND, Office of Indian Affairs, United States. U.S. Government Printing Office, 1898, p. 267.

114. Annual Report of the Department of Interior, Part 1, Report of the Commissioner of Indian Affairs to the Secretary of the Interior, Reports of Agencies in South Dakota, Report of Agent for Cheyenne River Agency, Office of Indian Affairs, United States. U.S. Government Printing Office, 1899, p. 328.

115. Annual Report of the Department of Interior, Part 1, Report of the Commissioner of Indian Affairs to the Secretary of the Interior, Reports of Agencies in North Dakota, Report of Devils Lake Agency, Office of Indian Affairs, United States. U.S. Government Printing Office, 1899, p. 269.

116. Annual Report of the Department of Interior, Part 1, Report of the Commissioner of Indian Affairs to the Secretary of the Interior, Reports of Agencies in South Dakota, Report of Pine Ridge Agency, Office of Indian Affairs, United States. U.S. Government Printing Office, 1898, p. 276.

117. Annual Report of the Department of Interior, Part 1, Report of the Commissioner of Indian Affairs to the Secretary of the Interior, Reports of Agencies in South Dakota, Report of Pine Ridge Agency, Office of Indian Affairs, United States. U.S. Government Printing Office, 1899, p. 334.

118. Annual Report of the Department of Interior, Part 1, Report of

the Commissioner of Indian Affairs to the Secretary of the Interior, Reports of Agencies in South Dakota, Report of Pine Ridge Agency, Office of Indian Affairs, United States. U.S. Government Printing Office, 1899, p. 335.

119. Annual Report of the Department of Interior, Part 1, Report of the Commissioner of Indian Affairs to the Secretary of the Interior, Reports of Agencies in South Dakota, Report of Rosebud Agency, Office of Indian Affairs. United States. U.S. Government Printing Office, 1898, p. 220.

120. Annual Report of the Department of Interior, Part 1, Report of the Commissioner of Indian Affairs to the Secretary of the Interior, Reports of Agencies in South Dakota, Report of Agent for Lower Brule Agency, Office of Indian Affairs, United States. U.S. Government Printing Office, 1899, p. 333.

121. Annual Report of the Department of Interior, Part 1, Report of the Commissioner of Indian Affairs to the Secretary of the Interior, Reports of Agencies in South Dakota, Report of Agent for Crow Creek Agency, Office of Indian Affairs, United States. U.S. Government Printing Office, 1899, p. 330.

122. Annual Report of the Department of Interior, Part 1, Report of the Commissioner of Indian Affairs to the Secretary of the Interior, Reports Concerning Indians in North Dakota, Report of Superintendent of Agricultural School, Agricultural Boarding School, Standing Rock, Agency, ND, Office of Indian Affairs, United States. U.S. Government Printing Office, 1905, p. 280.

14: GEORGIA

The discovery of gold on Cherokee land and the removal of the Cherokees is discussed in depth in *The Earth Is Red: The Imperialism of the 'Doctrine of Discovery'*, **Chapters 25-29**, Roberta Carol Harvey, Sunstone Press (November 5, 2021).

Secretary of War Threatens Cherokees - They Will Be Left to Whims of Georgia

In 1824, Secretary of War John Calhoun threatened to leave the Cherokees "exposed to the discontent of Georgia and the pressure of her citizens" if they continued to refuse to exchange their land in Georgia for land west of the Mississippi. They responded: "Sir, to these remarks we beg leave to observe, and to remind you, that the Cherokees are not foreigners, but original inhabitants of America; and that they now inhabit and stand on the soil of their own territory; and that the limits of their territory are defined by the treaties which they have made with the Government of the United States."[1]

Arguments that that the Indians wanted to move were introduced:

> General Carroll, to the secretary of war, describing the difficulties he met with in inducing the Indians to emigrate, says, "The truth is, they rely with great confidence on a favorable report on the petition they have before Congress. If that is rejected, and the laws of the States are enforced, you will have no difficulty of procuring an exchange of lands with them."

General Coffee, upon the same subject says, "They express a confident hope that Congress will interpose its power, and prevent the States from extending their laws over them. Should they be disappointed in this, I hazard little in saying that the government will have little difficulty in removing them west, of the Mississippi."[2]

Reports from Indians that had moved west, however, were dismal and the Cherokees feared for their survival. General Clark, Superintendent of Indian Affairs, credits the southern Indians fear of moving with the dire stories of the Indians who had moved west. Senator Evans described it as follows:

> The condition of many tribes west of the Mississippi is the most pitiable that can be imagined. During several seasons in every year, they are distressed by famine, in which many die for want of food, and during which the living child is often buried with the dead mother, because no one can spare it as much food as would sustain it through its helpless infancy.[3]

Georgia Enacts Laws Abolishing Cherokee Indian Sovereignty, Self-Government and Right to Land

The State of Georgia enacted laws abolishing the Cherokee's right to sovereignty, self-government and land. President Jackson and Congress refused the direct request of the Cherokee Nation for federal intervention to uphold their Hopewell Treaty (1785) rights against Georgia's legislative encroachments.

Georgia's first act was passed the 12th of December 1829, and is entitled:

> An act to add the territory lying within the chartered limits of Georgia, and now in the occupancy of the Cherokee Indians, to the counties of Carroll, De Kalb, Gwinnett and Habersham, and to extend the laws of the State over the same, and to annul all laws made by the Cherokee Nation of Indians ... Resolved, *Indians are tenants at her will*, and that she may at any time she pleases, determine that tenancy, by taking possession of the premises. (Emphasis added).[4]

Gold Discovered on Cherokee Lands: 1829

When gold was discovered on Cherokee land in 1829, the State of Georgia passed another act, entitled An act to authorize the Governor to take possession of the gold, silver, and other mines lying and being in that section of the chartered limits of Georgia commonly called the Cherokee country, and those upon all other unappropriated lands of the State, and for punishing any person or persons who may hereafter be found trespassing upon the mines.[5]

Notes: Georgia

1. Bills and Resolutions, Senate, 21st Cong., 1st Sess., February 22, 1830.
2. Carroll Letter from General John Coffee to Secretary of War Eaton, October 14, 1829.
3. Evans *Speeches on the Passage of the Bill for the Removal of the Indians, Delivered in the Congress of the United States, April and May, 1830.* Perkins and Marvin, 1830: 172.
4. Foster, Arthur. *A Digest of the Laws of the State of Georgia: Containing All Statutes, and the Substance of All Resolutions of a General and Public Nature, and Now in Force, which Have Been Passed in Said State from the Year 1820 to the Year 1829 Inclusive: with Occasional Explanatory Notes and Connecting References, and a List of the Statutes Repealed Or Obsolete to which is Added an Appendix, Containing the Constitution of the State of Georgia, as Amended, Also References to Such Local Acts as Relate to Towns ....* Towar, J. & D.M. Hogan, 1831: 126-129.
5. Id.

15: IDAHO

History of Idaho Territory 1863-1890

In studying and writing about Idaho, it must be remembered that part of Idaho's history is included in the history of the Oregon Territory, the Washington Territory, and that parts of the Idaho Territory included what is today Montana and Wyoming. When Idaho became a state on July 3, 1890, the present boundaries became permanent.

For five years (from August 14, 1848, to March 2, 1853), Idaho was included in the Oregon Territory under the Oregon Organic Act of 1848. Then it was divided between the Washington Territory and the Oregon Territory until February 14, 1859. Oregon then became a state, and the entire Idaho area was attached to the Washington Territory. On March 4, 1863, President Abraham Lincoln approved Idaho becoming a Territory of the U.S. Exceeding Texas substantially in size, Idaho originally included all of present Montana, along with practically all of Wyoming as well. In 1864, Congress decided to set up a new Territory of Montana, taking the northeastern part of Idaho for the purpose. The remainder of original eastern Idaho was returned temporarily to the Dakota Territory when Montana was established, May 26, 1864. On July 25, 1868, President Andrew Johnson signed the Wyoming Organic Act creating the Wyoming Territory using lands from the Dakota, Idaho, and Utah Territories, and on April 17, 1869, the Territorial Government was organized. Idaho Indian history is thus a complicated amalgam of the histories of these various jurisdictions.

The Nez Perce War of 1877, the Bannock War of 1878, and the Second Bannock War of 1895 are discussed in Harvey, Roberta Carol. *The Iron Triangle: Business, Government, and Colonial Settlers' Dispossession of Indian Timberlands and Timber*, Sunstone Press, 2022.

1855: Nez Perce Treaty Establishing Reservation

In 1855, Territorial Governor Isaac I. Stevens met with representatives from the Umatilla, Yakama, Nez Perce, Cayuse, and Palouse to establish reservations for their protection from gold seekers.

> *Gold has been found in the country above yours [north of Nez Perce country]. Our people are very fond of it. When our people hear this they will come here by hundreds. Among them who come there will be some bad people.* Those bad people will steal your horses and cattle. There are but few of you. You cannot prevent it. When you are scattered over a great extent of country you cannot prevent it. *But if you are living on the Reservation we can protect you and your family. Why then would you refuse to receive our talk and refuse to allow us to protect you?* (Emphasis added).[1]

After more than a week of tense negotiations, the Nez Perce agreed to cede 7.5 million acres of tribal land while still retaining the right to hunt and fish in their "usual and accustomed places."[2]

Under Article 2, the Reservation for the exclusive use and benefit of the tribe was subject to the following proviso: "nor shall any white man, excepting those in the employment of the Indian Department, be permitted to reside upon the said reservation without permission of the tribe and the superintendent and agent."

1860: Idaho, Discovery of Gold, Nez Perce Reservation Overrun; Settlers' Lawlessness to Be Generously Rewarded at Substantial Cost to Nez Perce

In 1860, Elias D. Pierce found gold on a tributary of the Clearwater River near the present town of Orofino. News of this discovery spread through the Pacific Northwest like wildfire. At the time of the 1860 discovery Idaho was a part of Washington Territory. The miners in Idaho began to clamor for territorial status almost as quickly as they staked claims.

On July 2, 1860, Superintendent of Washington Indian Agency Geary reported to Acting Commissioner Charles E. Mix "that in consequence of the rumored discoveries of rich and extensive gold mines within the reservation of the Nez Perce, great excitement had been occasioned by the rush of a crowd of miners into the country of that tribe."[3]

Commissioner Mix strongly supported Superintendent Geary's decisions to protect the Reservation from invasion.

The action which you have taken in the premises toward the protection of the Reservation from lawless invasion is approved and you will further instruct the local agents to give public notice to all parties concerned that *the treaties with the Indians are paramount and the Government is determined to exercise its full authority to prevent intrusions upon the Reserves of the Indians*, under all circumstances, as no person except the proper officers of the Department have any right whatever under any pretense to go upon said Reservations. (Emphasis added).[4]

1860: Legislative Assembly of Washington Territory: MEMORIAL ASKING THE APPOINTMENT OF A COMMISSIONER TO TREAT WITH THE NEZ PERCE INDIANS FOR A CHANGE IN THEIR RESERVATION

On December 18, 1860, the Legislative Assembly of Washington Territory petitioned the President for the appointment of a commissioner to treat with the Nez Perce Indians to carve out the *"rich gold fields"* discovered on their land. They wanted to open the gold fields to enterprising miners.

To the President of the United States: Your memorialists, the Legislative Assembly of the Territory of Washington, would respectfully represent: that during the past year, *discoveries have indicated the existence of rich gold fields within the limits of the Nez Perce Reservation in this Territory*. This has caused great excitement among those Indians, as also among our white population, and it is feared that unless some action is taken by the general government, it may lead to serious difficulty between the whites and the Nez Perces who have been uniformly friendly to our citizens. It is believed that the lands upon which the gold is indicated may be peaceably procured of the Indians, should a commissioner be appointed to treat with them for a change in the boundaries of the Reservation.

We therefore request that such steps may be taken by such an appointment, to avoid difficulty with the Indians, and *open such portions of that country as may be found rich in gold, to the enterprise of our miners*. Passed December 18th, 1860. (Emphasis added).[5]

On February 14, 1861, Commissioner Greenwood endorsed appointing a commissioner to negotiate for the gold fields, which he represented as having "little or no value for Indian purposes:"

> *Recent discoveries of gold have been made on the Nez Perce Reservation* ... and a large emigration to that region of the country is anticipated ... in consequence of which serious apprehensions exist in regard to the ... invasion of the rights of the Nez Perce tribes guaranteed by the Treaty [of 1855]. It is recommended that further negotiations be entered into with the Nez Perce tribe, with a view to the purchase of that portion of their reservation containing the auriferous deposits, which is represented as rugged, barren, and mountainous, unfit for cultivation, and therefore of *little or no value for Indian purposes*. (Emphasis added).[6]

Whether the threat of hostilities was real or rumored, it resulted in prompt Congressional action. At stake were 960,000 acres of land for mining on the Reservation. Congress appropriated $50,000 for a commissioner.[7]

April 1861: Nez Perce Reservation Invaded by 10,000 Whites; Superintendent Geary Appeals for Military Aid

By the spring of 1861, the lawless invasion of Nez Perce lands had not been stemmed, but instead had worsened. Superintendent Geary, alerted Commissioner Dole, by letter dated April 23, 1861, of the Indians furor:

> *Great excitement prevailed among the Indians on finding that instead of the miners being expelled on the opening of spring, as they had been promised, their number on the Reservation was daily augmented*, and that thousands of white men were about to over run the country so recently

~ 520 ~

garanteed [sic] them as an asylum and permanent home by our government. (Emphasis added).[8]

The urgency of the settlers' invasion is seen in Superintendent Geary's communique to George Wright, Colonel, U.S. Army, on April 20, 1861, requesting a squadron of Dragoons and noting "[h]undreds of white men are already in [the Nez Perce's] country, and daily accessions will soon swell the number to thousands".[9]

August 1861: U.S. Army Alerted Its Command to Potential for Hostilities

The Army, having received notice of the potential for hostilities alerted its Command.

> "A large number of the Nez Perces are inclined to be hostile...
> It is feared by the agent, and in fact by all who are competent
> to judge, that there will be an outbreak [of hostilities] probably
> on Salmon River and the South Branch of Clearwater."[10]

November 1861: Commissioner Dole Alerts Secretary Smith to Invasion of Ten Thousand Whites on Nez Perce Land and Need for New Treaty

Without a dissipation of the whites' invasion onto the Nez Perce Reservation, Commissioner Dole reported to Secretary Caleb B. Smith, in his Annual Report on November 1861, that about *ten thousand whites had invaded the Nez Perce country in search of gold* and that a new treaty would have to be negotiated with the Nez Perce.

> The rush of white persons, probably to the number of ten
> thousand, into the country of the Nez Perces, in search of gold,
> of which it is reported that valuable discoveries have been
> made, will require on the part of our agents great vigilance
> and care in order that collisions of the two races may be
> prevented, and it will probably be necessary to negotiate an
> additional treaty with that tribe, in order to adapt the location
> of their reservation to the circumstances now surrounding
> them ...[11]

April 1861 Agreement: Unbelievable Encroachment - Nez Perce Give Right to Mine on Their Lands without Remuneration

Superintendent Washington Territory, C. H. Hale reported to Commissioner

Dole on October 19, 1862, of an April 10, 1861, Agreement negotiated by former Superintendent Geary and Agent Cain with "Lanyer, Head Chief Nez Perces nation, and forty-seven others," under which the Nez Perce granted to the whites a "right of way across the reserve to the gold fields," and "the privilege of working the mines," without any remuneration. They further agreed to a military force to locate on the Reservation. Without questioning the ability to negotiate such an arrangement, Superintendent Hale lauded the Nez Perce for this Agreement as follows:

> October 19, 1862: Whilst we were thus failing to execute our part of the contract, *gold is discovered within the bounds of their reservation*; application is made for privilege to mine on their land. *In their simplicity, and with full faith in the justice of the government, their consent is obtained* to make a steamboat landing and erect a warehouse at the mouth of the Clearwater; to a right of way across the reserve to the gold fields, and *to the privilege of working the mines*. This was done *without any remuneration* being asked on their part for the concessions thus made. It was, however, expressly provided that no settlements should be made by the whites, and that their root grounds and agricultural tracts should be preserved for the exclusive use and benefit of the Indians. To preserve the quiet of the country, and to protect their lands from trespass, it was furthermore agreed, on the part of the United States, that a sufficient military force should be placed on the reservation. (Emphasis added).

He then goes on to describe the outrageous behavior of the whites in response to this grant:

> October 19, 1862: No sooner were these privileges granted than the *landing and warehouse became a town, now known as Lewiston*; *their reservation was overrun*; their enclosed lands taken from them; stock turned into their grain fields and gardens; their fences taken and used by persons to enclose the lands to which they laid claim, or torn down, burned, or otherwise destroyed. (Emphasis added).[12]

The April 10, 1861, Agreement provided as follows:

> The 1861 Agreement made between Edward R. Geary, Superintendent of Indian affairs for Oregon and Washington,

~ 522 ~

and A.J. Cain, agent for the Nez Perces in behalf of the United States, and the chiefs and head men of the Nez Perces in behalf of the said nation, was made in accordance with the authority vested in them by the 2d article of the treaty between the United States and the Nez Perces of the 11th of June, 1855.

1. That portion of the Nez Perce reservation lying north of the Snake and Clearwater rivers, the south fork of Clearwater and the trail from said south fork by the Weipo root-ground, across the Bitter Root mountains, is hereby *opened to the whites in common with the Indians for mining purposes*, provided, however, that the root-grounds and agricultural tracts in said district shall, in no case, be taken or occupied by the whites, but shall remain for the exclusive use and benefit of the Indians.

2. No white person, other than those in the service of the United States, shall be permitted to reside upon or occupy any portion of the Nez Perces reservation south of the line above described, without the consent of the superintendent, agent, and tribe, except that the *right of way to the mining district* north of said described line may cross Snake river at any eligible point below the mouth of Clearwater.

3. *The entire portion of the Nez Perces reservation hereby opened to the whites for mining purposes*, shall in all respects be subject to the laws of the United States regulating trade and intercourse in the Indian country; and no person shall be permitted to trade therein without obtaining license and giving bonds as provided by law.

4. It is further agreed on the part of the United States that a *sufficient military force shall be placed on the reservation* to preserve the quiet of the country and protect the Indians in the rights secured to them by treaty and these articles of agreement. (Emphasis added).[13]

Superintendent of Indian Affairs for Oregon and Washington Geary and Agent Cain, *purported to have the authority* to enter into this "Agreement" under Article 2 of the 1855 Treaty. Article 2 allows them with the permission of the tribe to permit a "white man" to reside upon the Reservation. Reside is defined as to live in a particular place. The person would not have ownership of the property, just the right to live on the property as approved. They would not have the right to engage in practices that would reduce the value of the property, such as mining or cutting timber.

Under the interpretation of the occupancy rights of tribes, the Supreme Court had ruled in 1873 as follows: Indians, by virtue of a "right of occupancy," were entitled to no greater rights than those vested in a tenant for life. *United States v. Cook*, 19 Wall. 591 (1873). Under real property law, a life tenant who unilaterally developed minerals was deemed to have committed waste against the remainderman's inheritance. The 1873 *Cook* decision was reversed by the Supreme Court in 1938 in *United States v. Shoshone Indians*, 304 U.S. 111 (1938), holding that the minerals and every other element of value appurtenant to the land were beneficially owned by the tribes.

Geary and Cain did not have the authority to open the Nez Perce Reservation for *mining purposes.*

Spring 1862: Most Base Outrages by Whites on Indians; No Military Response

On March 20, 1862, the Indian Agent, Charles Hutchins informed Commissioner Dole of the severity of the continued "licentiousness" of the white settlers and the Indians complaints:

> It is not necessary that I should now enumerate instances of daily recurrences of overreaching, fraud, plundering, licentiousness, and rascality, that is incessantly practiced by unprincipled white men on the Nez Perce Indians. Sufficient to say that outrages the most base and glaringly mean are daily complained of to me, and I am without any force whatever for arrest or punishment, and without a dollar of public money to employ special police for prevention or redress of crime.[14]

The military refused to act. On June 30, 1862, Nez Perce Indian Agent Chas. Hutchins said in his Annual Report to the Commissioner:

> My repeated requisitions for troops, made on the military commanders of the adjoining post at Walla-Walla have not been supplied, and my representation of the necessity, of troops being permanently quartered here, made to the several alternate commanders of this district, at Vancouver, Washington Territory, during the past year, has likewise been of no avail.[15]

On June 30, 1862, the Indian Agent reported to the Commissioner:

[T]he funds appropriated for the maintenance of this agency, due on the expiring year, have been withheld, thus leaving this district without military force to compel obedience to the laws, and the agent with no means to employ special police to arrest and commit the most miscreant and infamous violators of the public peace.[16]

Brigadier-General, U.S. Volunteers, Benjamin Alvord explained that wherever these masses of gold miners and emigrants go, it has been my policy to encourage the formation of counties, and the putting in force of civil law and order as quickly as possible.[17]

Idaho Gold Rush: Nez Perce Reservation Completely Overrun by White Miners and Squatters

The Idaho Gold Rush resulted in the gross infringement of tribal land and property rights as described by Superintendent Hale:

June 20, 1862: At this time the Nez Perces are generally friendly (sic) disposed towards the whites, but the rush of citizens to the new gold fields within their country has repeatedly given occasion to sorely try their patience, and has also produced a complication that is thoroughly disastrous to elevating them to civilization. The entire eastern side of this reserve, from Salmon river on the south to the North fork of the Clearwater river, has been demonstrated to be an auriferous region. In some sections of that region *gold fields have proven richer than the known discoveries of any previous age*, and from the observation of many well informed persons who have had practical experience in the several mining localities. I deem it beyond question that the mines, for many years, will amply remunerate the gold-seekers. I think that at the present time the *number of white people that are dispersed through the several mining camps will closely approach the number of 15,000*, and the throng of new arrivals is steadily unabated. The travelled roads through the reservation to all of the mining localities pass by some one or more of the Indian villages, which brings the Indians in hourly contact with the whites. Such unrestrained intercourse is, of course, constantly abused by unprincipled white men, and drunkenness and licentiousness are alarmingly on the increase. There is no local force here of any avail to compel even the semblance of observance of the humane laws for the preservation and security of the Indian. (Emphasis added).[18]

~ 525 ~

No action whatsoever against the invaders, who by the tens of thousands squatted on tribal land in violation of the Nez Perce Treaty of 1855, was proposed or promulgated.

Superintendent Hale mentioned the 1851 Agreement but stated that it before it could go "practically into effect," with respect to its limitations, "the whole reservation was overrun in every direction to all the mines." With complete disregard for the public notice by the Superintendent that the law forbade the location of a town within the Reservation, Lewiston was established with a population at the time of 1,200 persons.

> June 20, 1862: *Your predecessor, Mr. Geary, and Agent Cain, in April, 1861, after the existence of the gold mines about "Oro Fino" was made known, made an agreement with the Nez Perces, permitting our citizens to mine in that section,* and opened a route of travel for them on the north side of the Clearwater river. *Before that agreement could go practically into effect,* richer gold fields were found to the south of that limit, and headlong thitherward rushed the miners and soon discovered the chief "El Dorado," the Salmon river mines. These united discoveries establishing the mines to course on the whole western foothills of the Bitter Root mountains, no regard was paid to the restriction against travelling on the south side of the Clearwater river; so *the whole reservation was overrun in every possible direction to all the mines.* During last season but little injury was really suffered by the Indians in consequence, for a general regard was entertained to respect their rights, which feeling was in no little assisted by the presence of Captain A. J. Smith, with a detachment of United States dragoons, who remained here till the mining season was nearly closed and the miners and travellers commenced to seek their own winter quarters. In the month of October, of last year, a town site was laid off on the reservation on Snake river, at the confluence of the Clearwater, which is now known as "Lewiston;" and despite my calling public attention to the laws forbidding it, a small but active town has rapidly sprung up, numbering, perhaps, two hundred tenements of various descriptions, with a population approximating 1,200 white persons. (Emphasis added).[19]

Military Command Garrisoned at Lewiston

While a military presence was established at Lewiston, Brig General Alvord wrote to Governor Pickering, on July 28, 1862, that hopefully the multitude of whites in the region would keep the Indians at bay. The Department of the Interior, the Territorial Governor and the Volunteer Militia all supported extinguishing the Nez Perce's Indian title. All they awaited was the imprimatur of Congress.

William Wallace wielded substantial legislative influence. In time, he had served as governor and Congressional delegate from both Washington Territory and Idaho Territory. He successfully lobbied for Idaho's territorial status. In 1863, President Lincoln appointed him the Territorial Governor of Idaho.

> *Brig General Alvord to Governor Pickering, July 28, 1862.* The command of Major Rinearson, which has gone to the vicinity of Lewiston, will have an important and delicate duty to perform in the preservation of peace by protecting the Nez Percé Indians from outrages by the whites. Those Indians are of superior character; have always been warmly our friends, but they are now rudely dispossessed of their lands on the reservation secured to them by a sacred treaty; their women treated with outrage by the miners; liquor is sold to them by lawless whites, and great danger apprehended of collision. I learn that Senator Nesmith has pushed through the Senate a measure appropriating $50,000 to enable the Indian Department to take steps to extinguish the Indian title. I hope and trust Colonel Wallace will get it through the House. From this statement you will see that I have taken such measures as lay in my power to preserve the peace. The multitude of whites pervading that region may possibly hold the Indians in check. Benj. Alvord, Brigadier-General, U.S. Volunteers Commanding District.[20]

New Treaty Will Take More than Clothing

1862 The need to negotiate a new treaty was clear to the U.S. *Queries were sent to the Superintendent and to the volunteer militia.* Superintendent Hale reported to Commissioner Dole that *"ten millions of gold will be taken from the mines within the bounds of this reserve"* and the "prospects are that [in] another year this amount will be doubled." Already, thirty thousand persons—miners, traders, and others were directly or directly connected with mining. The writing was on the wall—a new Treaty with the Nez Perce would be the result. The "steal treaty" in 1863, which reduced the size of the tribe's Reservation by 90 percent to make way for the miners, was preordained.

Superintendent Hale pronounced outright that offering them clothing would be "rejected with disdain." The U.S. could afford otherwise given the immense wealth to be gained.

Superintendent Hale to Commissioner Dole, October 19, 1862:

> The Nez Perces, as a body, know the value of money, understand its uses, and can manage their own business affairs with as much shrewdness as the majority of white men, and I am well satisfied that any proposition to pay them, even partially, in clothing will be rejected with disdain. They will require money, or its equivalent in stock, or valuable permanent improvements upon the lands to which they may be removed. This the United States can well afford to do, when it is considered that *about ten millions of gold will be taken from the mines within the bounds of this reserve* before the winter compels the miners to suspend their operations. The prospects are that [in] *another year this amount will be doubled*, especially if the mining population continues to increase. It is estimated that not less than thirty thousand persons-miners, traders, and others have been employed the past season, in one way or other, either directly or directly connected with mining operations. (Emphasis added).[21]

No New Reservation Location Available

Gold was present on and around the Reservation in every direction. There was no new location for a Reservation; yet a new treaty was mandated to avoid an *"Indian war of gigantic proportions."*

Superintendent Hale to Commissioner Dole, October 19, 1862:

> *The question of a new location is also attended with much difficulty, as to where they can be placed with any prospect of not being again disturbed by gold-seekers, or speedily overwhelmed by the surging waves of civilization.* North, east, and south of the present reservation is gold found, and further examinations may develop it to the west; where, then,

~ 528 ~

can we place them so as not to render it necessary, in a year or two at most, to remove them again. The question in reference, not only to these Indians, but the Flatheads and confederate tribes, the Spokanes and others, forces itself upon us, and we had as well meet it at once. They are residing in a gold-bearing country, and before another year rolls around provision will have to be made for treating with these, or ere *we are aware an Indian war of gigantic proportions will be on our ha*nds. (Emphasis added).[22]

Volunteer Militia's Opinion: If Nez Perce Reservation Opened, Millions Will Be Added Annually to Moneyed Wealth of U.S.

Surprisingly, Superintendent Hale sought the opinion of Captain Hays, Volunteer Militia. Perhaps, he wanted to know in advance the opinion of the military should he need their aid. Superintendent Hale was getting his ducks in a row.

Captain Hays to Superintendent Hale, October 30, 1862:

> In your letter of several days ago, you ask me for information on various subjects connected with the Nez Perce reservation.
>
> First. You desire to know whether, in my opinion, a treaty can be made with the Nez Perce tribe for their reserve. My impression is that a treaty may be made with them for their reservation. In conversation with some of the leading men of the tribe, I learned substantially from them this: That they had heard that money had been appropriated to have a talk with them to see if they would sell out; that they were disposed to accommodate and let us have the country on some terms, but said they were at a loss to know where they could go; they preferred to remain where they were if they could be permitted to do so in peace and safety, but they had their fears that the vast numbers of white men who were coming to their country would overrun them and seize not only their gold lands, but would also take from them their agricultural and grazing lands. They seem to have lost confidence in our government as a treaty-making power. They say we talk much and promise much, but that we are very slow in making good our promises. *They complain and say we have not complied with existing treaty stipulations; that we ought to pay up*

what we now owe them before we ask them to treat again.
I have said that I believed a treaty could be made with them
for their reservation. *If the Indian department have (sic) the
means to make good all former treaty obligations to date,
and present them something tangible, in the shape of money
or stock, I believe they can be treated with for their country
on terms advantageous to both themselves and the United
States.*

The Nez Perce Indians are far above other tribes on this coast
for intelligence and virtue. They know the value of money,
property, and merchandise. They know just what blankets and
other articles of clothing costs them when paid in annuities.
They know equally well that if the amount of annuity was paid
them in money that with it they could buy better and cheaper
goods from any merchant or trading post in the country.

Secondly. You ask me the *probable amount of gold taken
from the Nez Perce gold fields this season.* This is a question
very difficult to answer. *The Portland dailies make the sum
between six and seven millions. These papers, I think, have
rather underrated than overrated the amount. I should think
between seven and ten millions would be a fair estimate.*

Third. You want to know my opinion relative to the next
year's yield. My impression is that it will be greater than that
of the present year. The country is better known; roads have
been made, claims found and opened; miners will get to work
earlier in the season, and they will understand the mining arts
better than heretofore.

Fourth. You inquire as to the amount of the agricultural land
on the Nez Perce reserve. [If opened] the yield would be ample
to sustain a mining population of twenty thousand souls. ...
Open the Nez Perce country to cultivation, and supplies are
raised in the vicinity of the mines, transportation measurably
dispensed with, and millions will be added annually to the
moneyed wealth of the country. (Emphasis added).[23]

Unauthorized Occupation of Gold Mines

Rather than stop the newcomers from trespassing on reservation land, the U.S. government instead initiated another treaty council at the Lapwai Agency, Wash. Terr. In a talk with the Nez Perce on October 24, 1862, General Alvord stated the common refrain: *"It is very sad to find that the discovery of gold and the consequent rush of miners to this country should have brought such a mass of the very worst white men in contact with you …"*

> I have come to see you in order to *assure you that the Government desires to do all in its power to protect you*. … the best the Government can do for you is to provide, as it has, for the making of a new treaty, so as to *compensate you as far as possible for the unauthorized occupation of the gold mines by our people*. (Emphasis added).[24]

Major General Howard, No Spirit Will Hinder Me

During the treaty negotiations in 1863 with Major General O. O. Howard, *Nez Perce Chief Toohoolhoolzote became enraged and asked: "What person pretends to divide the land, and put me on it."*[25] *General Howard replied: "I am that man. … I stand here for the President, and there is no spirit good or bad that will hinder me."* (Emphasis added).[26]

1863: Nez Perce "Thief Treaty"

Under the new treaty, the Nez Perce would cede ninety percent of the lands reserved in 1855, including all of the known mining lands. In consideration for this cession, the U.S. would pay $1,626,222.00, among other consideration. (Treaty between the United States of America and the Nez Perce Tribe of Indians, U.S.-Nez Perce Indians, June 9, 1863, 14 Stat. 647 (1863 Treaty)). Fifty-one headmen affixed their marks to the new treaty. The bands that lived outside of the proposed reservation boundaries walked out of the proceedings and refused to endorse this land grab.[27]

The 1863 Treaty became known amongst the Nez Perce as the 'Thief Treaty' or 'Steal Treaty' and created the conditions that would eventually lead to the armed clash between the Nez Perce and the U.S. Army, now known as the Nez Perce Flight of 1877.[28] The U.S. Senate ratified the document in 1867.

1863: General Land Office Recommends Appropriation for Surveys

With the Idaho Territory established and the Thief Treaty signed, the General Land Office recommended a "liberal appropriation for surveys" given the "rich mineral deposits known to exist over a considerable portion of Idaho."[29]

1864: "Inquietude and Discontent" of Nez Perce

Idaho's Governor Caleb Lyon reported to Secretary of Interior Harlan on Sep. 20, 1865, that the violation of the Nez Perce's "sacred rights," as their Reservation was overrun by miners, resulted in their "discontent." Given the complete disregard for their legal rights—with no preventive government action other than to take their lands under a new treaty—would make anyone more than "discontent." This common trajectory of the theft of Indian lands would occur over and over among tribes across the country.

> Nez Perce: But with the discovery of gold, their reservation was overrun by the enterprising miners, treaty stipulations were disregarded and trampled under foot, towns were established thereon, and all the means that cupidity could invent or disloyalty achieve were resorted to shake their confidence in the government. They were disturbed in the peaceable possession of what they regarded as their vested rights, sacredly secured by treaty. They were informed that the government was destroyed, and that whatever treaties were made would never be carried out. All resistance on their part proved unavailing, and inquietude and discontent predominated among them.[30]

1865: Kootenai and Coeur d'Alene Indians Retarding Development of Minerals and Agricultural Land

Given the federal government's need for money, Indians were seen as an obstacle whenever their interests collided with the U.S.' support for mining.

Commissioner Cooley *authorized Governor Lyon to "conclude a treaty, if possible, with the Kootenai's and Coeur d'Alene Indians in the extreme northern part of Idaho" to open large tracts of mining and agricultural land" to the public.* (Emphasis added).[31]

1866: Governor Ballard: Idaho's Precious Metals, Profitable Investments for Capitalists

Notwithstanding the maltreatment of the Nez Perce, Governor Lyon's successor did not seem concerned about the extinguishment of Indian title. Almost in a promotion of the state - a solicitation for new settlers, Governor Ballard accented the valuable minerals located throughout the state, available for the taking by capitalistic investors.

> The immense wealth of the Pacific coast has had the effect to people our shores with a vast population in advance of the extinguishment of what is called "the Indian title." Idaho is not an exception to other States and Territories west of the Rocky mountains, and all the unhappy consequences resulting from a promiscuous intermingling of whites with the Indians have been painfully experienced in our Territory. The mountains of *Idaho, abounding as they do in many rich deposits of precious metals, some of them, perhaps, the richest known to the world*, will still continue to invite an increasing population to our Territory. These deposits of mineral wealth not being confined to any particular locality, but abounding in both northern and southern Idaho, some of them almost fabulous in richness, will continue to present in the future, as now, the most profitable fields of labor for the active and industrious miner and tradesman, and as profitable investments for the capitalist as can be found in any other part of our Union. David W. Ballard, Governor and Superintendent of Indian Affairs, Idaho Territory. (Emphasis added).[32]

1866: Concentration of Indians on Single Reservation

Without consulting the tribes in Washington, Idaho and Montana, Idaho's Governor Ballard was instructed to determine the feasibility of locating these tribes on the Flathead Reservation in Montana.

> In accordance with instructions received at this office from the department, dated June 13, 1866, I opened a correspondence with Superintendent Waterman, of Washington Territory, and the governor of Montana, touching the practicability of collecting the tribes in the northeast of Washington Territory and northern Idaho on the Flathead reservation in Montana.[33]

Fortunately, Montana's Acting Governor Meagher wrote directly to the Commissioner advising against such a plan.

Bounty for Scalps

Adding fuel to the fire, inflammatory reports from the media didn't help. Idaho's Owyhee Avalanche reported a meeting of citizens who chose twenty-five men to go Indian hunting and offered bounties of $100 for an Indian man's scalp, $50 for a woman's scalp, and $25 for the scalps of children under ten years of age, provided that "each scalp shall have the curl of the head."[34]

1867: Decaying Carcasses

On July 29, 1867, an editor for the *Idaho Statesman* was of the opinion: ... that the military should continue killing Indians 'until the last Indian in the Territories was either on his reservation or enriched the sagebrush with his decaying carcass.' ... 'The idea that the Indians have any right to the soil is ridiculous. ... They have no more rights to the soil of the Territories of the United States than wolves or coyotes...'[35]

Repeatedly, Indians were referred to as animals to eliminate any residue of immorality in murdering them.

1868: Governor Duplicitous in Pushing for Cession of Mineral and Agricultural Lands of Shoshone and Bannock Indians

Governor Ballard "proposed" moving the Shoshone and Bannock Indian to Fort Hall Reservation. In fact, previously to Governor Ballard meeting with them, the President had already decided this removal should occur. It wasn't a proposal; it was a fait acompli. They had no option but to accept it. The only delay was securing the approval of the Eastern Shoshone as part of the proposed Fort Hall Reservation overlapped on the Eastern Shoshone's Wind River Reservation. Governor Ballard anticipated no problem with the Eastern Shoshones.[36]

In his meeting with the Shoshone and Bannock Indians, Governor Ballard declared that no power on earth could restrain the whites' unlawful intrusion on their lands for the minerals and fertile lands. He focused on the lie that he wanted them to be "comfortable and happy' with the underlying threat of their disappearance from the earth with the increasing penetration of whites into their country.

August 21, 1867: I desire peace and good will between the white and red men. I desire to see all the Bannocks comfortable and happy, and so situated that they may become a prosperous people, skilled in the arts of civilization. To this end the *President of the United States proposes to place you upon a reservation*, and afford you the facilities for farming, thereby enabling you to make your livelihood by tilling the soil, raising and herding stock, &c., instead of depending upon roots and the uncertainties of the chase. The white people are numerous in the United States; *the mountains of your country are filled with minerals; the white people seek them; your valleys and plains are productive, they want to cultivate them; they are spreading all over this vast country, even as you see the grasshoppers and crickets around you; no power on earth can restrain them*. Common contact between the white and the red man has always resulted badly to the latter; it always will; and while the white people increase in numbers, the Indians gradually disappear from the earth. (Emphasis added).[37]

Chief Tygee said:

I thought when the white people came to Soda Springs and built houses and put soldiers in them, it was to protect my people, but now they are all gone, and I do not know where to go nor what to do. *The white people have come into my country, and have not asked my consent. Why is this*? And why have no persons talked to me before? I have never known what the white people wanted me to do. (Emphasis added).[38]

Governor Ballard used the Civil War as the excuse. Governor Ballard continued about how he had selected Fort Hall for them.

August 21, 1867: As the whites approach your hunting-grounds, the game recedes; as they cultivate the fields, wild roots, upon which you depend for subsistence, disappear. In view of these facts, and that the Bannocks have been a good and loyal people, the *President of the United States directed me to select a suitable place for a reservation on which all your people can live happily, and in time become independent. I therefore, last summer, selected a tract of country at Fort Hall*, which I understand unofficially has been set apart for that purpose. It is a good place for you, with fish in the streams, game in the hills, an abundance of timber, and good water-power for mills to saw your lumber, grind your grain, &c., &c. (Emphasis added).[39]

After which the following articles were read, explained to them, and signed by the Indians:

LONG-TOM CREEK, IDAHO TERRITORY, August 26, 1867.

I, Tygee, head chief of all the Bannock Indians, in council with Governor D. W. Ballard, ex officio superintendent Indian affairs, do hereby agree that I, my under chiefs, headmen, and all Indians of my tribe, will remove to the reservation at Fort Hall, known as Bannock and Shoshone reservation, at any time designated by the said D. W. Ballard between now and the 1st day of June, 1868: that we will submit to the usual rules and regulations of reservations: Provided, that the said reservation belong forever to the Bannocks and such other Indians as may be placed thereon; and Provided, that the government of the United States furnish the necessary facilities for learning and prosecuting farming, with an agent, teachers, mechanics, books, implements of husbandry, and such other appliances and conveniences as are usual on reservations.

And I further agree to relinquish all right and title on the part of the Bannock Indians to all the country we have claimed, which is understood to embrace all between the 42° and 45°parallel of latitude and the 113th meridian and the summit of the Rocky mountains.[40]

1887: Dawes Act

In 1887, Congress passed the General Allotment Act, commonly referred to as the Dawes Act. General Allotment Act, ch. 119, 24 Stat. 388 (1887). The Dawes Act authorized the Secretary to allot reservation lands to individual Indians and to negotiate with tribes for the sale of unallotted portions of their reservation lands. The Secretary could then make surplus lands available for non-Indian settlement.

1893: Nez Perce Agreement

An agreement between the United States and the Nez Perce Tribe of Indians was concluded on May 1, 1893, and ratified by Congress on August 15, 1894 (1893 Agreement). *The lands ceded in the agreement totaled 549,559 acres.*[41] *The Secretary allotted reservation lands to individual Indians on the Nez Perce Reservation from 1892 to 1899.*

President Cleveland proclaimed the unallotted and unreserved lands acquired from the Nez Perce open to settlement on November 18, 1895. Within the first 13 days after opening to entry, 507 homestead filings were made on the ceded lands. Prior to the 1893 agreement ceding unallotted reservation lands, the Nez Perce Reservation consisted of 762,236 acres. (Emphasis added).[42]

Values of Minerals in Idaho

Gold

Total reported gold production for the period of *1860-70* was 2,728,300 ounces with an estimated *value of $50,000,000*. This production far exceeds that of any subsequent 10-year period and is almost one-third of Idaho's total gold recovery to date. (Emphasis added).[43]

Silver

Silver was discovered in Idaho almost as early as gold. After the discovery of rich silver lodes near Silver City, Owyhee County, in 1863, this district was second only to the Comstock lode of Nevada in silver output. However, the bonanza days were short-lived. In the 1870s activity dropped.[44]

Production revived in the early 1880 with the discovery of the lead-silver ores in Blaine County, and by 1882 the value of Idaho silver exceeded the value of the gold produced. Shoshone County became a major producer of silver around 1885. Most of the bonanza silver lodes worked in the 1880s had been exhausted of high-grade ore.[45]

Notes: Idaho

1. Record of Official Proceedings of the 1855 Treaty Negotiations at the Council in Walla Walla Valley, Which Culminated in the Stevens Treaty of 1855, p. 68.

2. Treaty between the United States of America and the Nez Perce Indians, June 11, 1855, 12 Stat. 957 (1855 Treaty), ratified by the U.S. Senate on March 8, 1859 and proclaimed by the President on April 29, 1859.

3. https://archives.yvl.org/bitstream/handle/20.500.11867/6818/TRA-042-03-003.pdf?sequence=1&isAllowed=y (accessed online July 12, 2022).

4. Letter from Charles E. Mix, Acting Commissioner of Indian Affairs, Department of the Interior, to Edward R. Geary, Superintendent of Indian Affairs, Portland, Oregon (July 2, 1860) (on file with the U.S. National Archives). https://archives.yvl.org/bitstream/handle/20.500.11867/6818/TRA-042-03-003.pdf?sequence=1&isAllowed=y (accessed online July 12, 2022).

5. Lyman Shaffer, Speaker House of Representatives Memorial from Lyman Shaffer, Speaker of the House of Representatives, to James Buchanan, President of the U.S. (December 18, 1860); Laws of Washington, Washington (State) Legislative Assembly, G.B. Goudy, public printer, 1861, pp. 136-137.

6. Letter from the Secretary of the Treasury, Transmitting Estimates of Additional Appropriations ... United States. Dept. of the Treasury, 1861, p. 36.

7. Ibid., pp. 37-38.

8. https://www.doi.gov/sites/doi.gov/files/uploads/m-37033.pdf at p.6, fn 44 (accessed online March 24, 2023).

9. The War of the Rebellion: A Compilation of the Official Records of the Union and Confederate Armies, United States War Department, U.S. Government Printing Office, 1891. Series I, Chap. LXII, Operations on the Pacific Coast, CORRESPONDENCE, ETC. – UNION AND CONFEDERATE, p. 467.

10. Letter from Enoch Steen, Major, U.S. Army, to A.C. Wildrick, Lieutenant, U.S. Army (August 19, 1861). The War of the Rebellion: A Compilation of the Official Records of the Union and Confederate Armies, United States War Department, U.S. Government Printing Office, 1891. Series I, Chap. LXII, CORRESPONDENCE, ETC. – UNION AND CONFEDERATE, p. 575.

11. Report of the Commissioner of Indian Affairs to the Secretary of the Interior, United States. Office of Indian Affairs. U.S. Government Printing Office, William P. Dole to Secretary Caleb B. Smith, 1861, p. 26.

12. Report of the Commissioner of Indian Affairs to the Secretary of the Interior, United States. Office of Indian Affairs. U.S. Government Printing Office, 1863, p. 395.

13. Ibid., pp. 430-431.

14. Letter from Charles Hutchins, Indian Agent, Washington Territory, to W.P. Dole, Commissioner of Indian Affairs, Washington DC (March 20, 1862) (on file with the U.S. National Archives).

15. Report of the Commissioner of Indian Affairs to the Secretary of the Interior, United States. Office of Indian Affairs, Washington Superintendency. U.S. Government Printing Office, 1863, p. 422.

16. Ibid., p. 423.

17. Letter from Benjamin Alvord, Brigadier-General, U.S. Volunteers, to W.P. Dole, Commissioner of Indian Affairs, Washington DC (September 8, 1863) (on file with the U.S. National Archives).

18. Report of the Commissioner of Indian Affairs to the Secretary of the Interior, United States. Office of Indian Affairs, Washington Superintendency. U.S. Government Printing Office, 1863, p. 422.

19. Ibid., p. 423.

20. The War of the Rebellion: A Compilation of the Official Records of the Union and Confederate Armies, United States War Department, U.S. Government Printing Office, 1891. Series I, Chap. LXII, Operations on the Pacific Coast, CORRESPONDENCE, ETC. – UNION AND CONFEDERATE, p. 43.

21. Report of the Commissioner of Indian Affairs to the Secretary of the Interior, United States. Office of Indian Affairs. U.S. Government Printing Office, 1863, p. 397.

22. Id.

23. Ibid., pp. 431-432.

24. The War of the Rebellion: A Compilation of the Official Records of the Union and Confederate Armies, United States War Department, U.S. Government Printing Office, 1891. Series I, Part II, Chap. L, Operations on the Pacific Coast, CORRESPONDENCE, ETC. – UNION AND CONFEDERATE, pp. 192-193.

25. Mark H. Brown, Flight of the Nez Perce (New York: Capricorn Books, 1971; reprint, Lincoln, Nebraska: University of Nebraska Press, 1982), p. 82.

26. L. V. McWhorter, Hear me my Chiefs: Nez Perce History and Legend (Caldwell, Idaho: The Caxton Printers, Ltd., 1952), p. 166.

27. Treaty between the United States of America and the Nez Perce Tribe of Indians, June 9, 1863 (1863 Treaty) (14 Stat. 647).

28. The Treaty Period, National Park Service. https://www.nps.gov/nepe/learn/historyculture/the-treaty-era.htm#:~:text=After%20more%20than%20a%20week,the%20US%20Senate%20in%201859 (accessed online December 28, 2021).

29. General Land Office, October 22, 1863, p. 57.

30. Report of the Commissioner of Indian Affairs to the Secretary of the Interior, United States. Office of Indian Affairs. U.S. Government Printing Office, 1865, p. 232.

31. Report of the Commissioner of Indian Affairs to the Secretary of the Interior, United States. Office of Indian Affairs. U.S. Government Printing Office, 1866, p. 191.

32. Ibid., p. 192.

33. IDAHO STATE HISTORICAL SOCIETY REFERENCE SERIES RUBY

AND SILVER CITY WAR MEETINGS, FEBRUARY 14-15, 1866, Number 238. https://history.idaho.gov/wp-content/uploads/0238.pdf (accessed online March 21, 2023).

34. Madsen, Brigham D. The Northern Shoshoni. Caxton Press, 1980, p. 51.

35. Report of the Commissioner of Indian Affairs to the Secretary of the Interior, United States. Office of Indian Affairs. U.S. Government Printing Office, 1868, p. 14.

36. Ibid., p. 197.

37. Ibid., p. 198.

38. Ibid., p. 197.

39. Ibid., p. 198.

40. https://www.lib.uidaho.edu/mcbeth/governmentdoc/1893www.htm (accessed online March 23, 2023).

41. https://www.presidency.ucsb.edu/documents/proclamation-381-opening-nez-perce-indian-lands-settlement-idaho (accessed online December 29, 2021).

42. Charles R. Hubbard, SURVEY OF THE MINERAL RESOURCES OF IDAHO (With Map), Pamphlet No. 105, August 1955, p. 18.

43. Ibid., p. 37.

44. Id.

45. Id.

16: WYOMING

The Indians in Wyoming fought hard for their lands. The number of battles which many are not aware of, or overlook, is astonishing. It involved tribes fighting singly and tribes allying together to fight against the U.S. invasion of their lands. They could not match (1) the technological superiority of the military's armaments, (2) the U.S. Army's manned forts crisscrossing their lands with the avowed purpose of providing protection to white settlers traveling westward on the Oregon-California Trails, (3) the surging emigration with wagon and supply trains of more than 100 wagons, and (4) the fortresses provided by the transcontinental railroads bisecting Indian lands. More deadly was (1) the threat of outright extermination by the highest levels of Army officers and volunteer militias (goon squads), (2) a Congress that played with appropriations to punish Indians who refused to give sway to their despotic power, (3) presidential abdication in enforcing treaties, and (4) barricaded judicial portals.

The repeated refrain, that Indians considered precious metals valueless or useless justifying the expropriation and exploitation of the highly valuable gold, silver, copper, lead, zinc and iron ore on Indian lands, was simply a lie. The federal government as its trustee knew the value of these metals yet failed to protect its guardians' right to these extremely valuable non-renewable resources. At times, it actively assisted in the expropriation and exploitation through rapacious federal policies.

These stolen Indian resources still have value today, something the federal government refused to consider in valuing the loss to the Indian nations as their minerals were depleted, wasted, stolen, exchanged on the black market, and underreported to the taxing and regulatory authorities. Fortunes were made as Indians starved, froze to death, had limbs amputated due to frostbite, suffered from syphilis and other white diseases, and died on the battlefield fighting for their peoples and lands. They were reduced to paupers and vagabonds by the U.S.' overarching strategy of settler colonialism.

Indians in Powder River Basin

"This story of Powder River is—in reality—the story of grass. The search for it. The fight for it. The slow disappearance of it."[1]

The Powder River country encompasses the numerous rivers (the Bighorn, Rosebud, Tongue and Powder) that flow northeastward from the Bighorn Mountains to the Yellowstone. In the 18th century, the Powder River Basin was home to the Crow Indians, and towards the turn of the 19th century, Oglala and Brulé Lakota tribes arrived from Minnesota. The Minniconjou, Hunkpapa and Sans Arc Lakota followed them in the 1820s, around the time bison were driven to extinction east of the Mississippi River. For many years, this country was largely unvisited by white people, other than fur trappers.

The Fort Laramie Treaty of 1851 acknowledged the Crow Nation's land west of the Powder River and the Lakota Nation's land to its east.

Manifest Destiny

The westward migration of white settlers imperiled the lives of American Indians through sanctioned extermination, strategic U.S. military warfare, the theft of their economic resources, removal and the reservation system. In 1857, Congress approved the construction of a number of wagon roads across the territories to expedite emigrant travel and speed mail delivery to the West Coast. Frederick West Lander, a transatlantic explorer, engineered the Pacific Land Route, and served as the chief engineer for the Fort Kearny, South Pass, and Honey Lake Wagon Roads. As an aide-de-camp to General McClellan in the Union Army, and as a Brigadier General, he was sent on a secret mission to Texas to dissuade Sam Houston from leaving the Union. So, Lander possessed not only civil engineering experience, but military competence, as well.[2]

The Oregon Trail, the California Trail and the Mormon Pioneer Trails became the route for the invasion of white settlers, the Pony Express, and the federal overland mail. These trails crossed through Indian lands across the west. Wagon trains of 100 or more Conestogas beat the Earth into submission, eliminating its agricultural or grazing capacity. Professional and sport hunters decimated the game subsistence of the Indians, bringing to extinction the massive buffalo herds stewarded in the past by tribes. Manned forts were constructed to protect white settlers. Massive herds of cattle endured the long runs from Texas to feed on the lush Wyoming grasses.

These corridors, which included many cutoffs and variations, were designed to cut down traveling time in the rush for California gold and Oregon's settlement. The associated north-south routes such as the Bozeman and Bridger Trails, opened up the interior of Wyoming to eventual exploitation and settlement, leading to the discovery of gold at South Pass.

The Manifest Destiny pushing white settlers to the ocean, helped spawn important Euro-American mining, agricultural, ranching and financial ventures. Western businessmen funded by European and eastern capital became millionaires supplying these industries. The financial bounty of Indian nations from their valuable natural resources was siphoned off as a reward for theft. Land speculators fed off the hunger of the white settlers who could never dream of land ownership on their Continent. The wealthy preyed on the poor for cheap labor to fund their enterprises.

Given the initial small numbers of Wyoming white settlers, Indians were unprepared for the prolific invasion that would follow. The sparse groups of white settlers trespassing on tribal lands didn't initially raise the fears of Indian nations. Many of the tribes maneuvered around them, to avoid clashes.

With the California Gold Rush, the waves of emigrants trespassing across Indian lands marked the real beginning of ill feeling and open hostility. The transients disturbed game herd movements and utilization of the plentiful grasses upon which they depended. Livestock overgrazed the range as they were transported for food supplies during the cross-country cavalcade and as feedstock for new ranches at their destination. All available wood within the trail corridor was cut and used, without permission or compensation. Exacting tributes to cross tribal lands was a common practice that was highly resented or refused by the emigrants.

The increasing spiral of violence between emigrants and Indians ultimately pitted the tribes against the U.S. executive, congressional and judicial branches. The overland migrations initiated a series of wars that lasted for decades and robbed Indians of their political and economic independence.[3]

Indian Battles in Wyoming

Lest the reader question this recitement of battles and wars, it is imperative for indigenous readers to be cognizant of the sacrifice Indians endured for their lands and peoples. Having visited Wyoming several times, I was completely unaware of the numerous battle sites. Today, I hope to make a journey to these sites to honor the Indians who risked and lost their lives and land and resources.

When I was a child, Daddy told me the Earth was red from the Blood of our People who fought for their land. I told my children the same story so they can tell their children the same story and it will never be forgotten.

A chart on Indian Battles in Wyoming is in the last Chapter.

1863: Bozeman Trail

In 1863, John Bozeman established the Bozeman Trail up the east side of the Bighorns as a route for white settlers and prospectors from the North Platte River emigrant trails to newly discovered gold fields in Montana and then on to connect with the Oregon Trail. It appropriated many of the accustomed north-south trails which the Indians had used since prehistoric times. The first three major river crossings on the Bozeman Trail were the Powder River Crossing, the Crazy Woman Crossing and the Clear Creek Crossing (present-day Buffalo, Wyoming). At each water ford, emigrants would often camp at least one night to rest and water their stock. This behavioral routine translated into an awareness of repeat areas for Indians to plan their attacks. It gave an advantage to Indians who were familiar with the Bozeman Trail, its path, times between arranged stops by wagon trains, and strategic areas such as amenable terrain for attack, grass stock feed and water sources.

Between 1864 and 1868, the high risk of Lakota and allied attacks resulted in fewer than a thousand people using the Bozeman Trail.

Frontier Forts

Demonstrating the strategic role Army frontier forts played in warfare and settlement of the west, they were strategically located to protect white settlers. Soldiers built and used military roads to stockpile supplies at the forts as military supply depots and to enable military-escorted wagon trains to rest, regroup and resupply.

The high cost of military campaigns and the need for new roads with safe travel impressed upon the United States Government the need for new negotiations with the Northern Plains Indians. These negotiations began at Fort Laramie in June, 1866. While the intent of the Treaty of 1866 was to allow the construction of forts and roads in exchange for bi-annual annuities, government officials failed to recognize the complexity of tribal politics. Some Indian leaders did sign the treaty and government officials assumed they had a treaty with all members of the tribes. When Carrington's command arrived under orders to establish three forts on the Bozeman Trail, Red Cloud and other Indian leaders walked out of the talks declaring that war would occur if the trail was used and the forts constructed.[4]

Cantonment Reno

On August 11, 1865, General Patrick Edward Connor's troops reached the Powder River Crossing, where they began building Cantonment Reno, a temporary post. At about the same time, another group of soldiers under Colonel James Sawyer were ordered to build a military road for freighting supplies along the Bozeman Trail. The post garrison consisted of detachments of the 4th, 9th, and 23rd Infantry, commanded by Captain Edwin Polluck.

Fort Kearny

The information is this section is derived from Records Relating to Investigations of the Fort Philip Kearny (or Fetterman) Massacre. Testimony of Colonel Henry B. Carrington, Page 1, M740 roll 1 of 1, National Archives & Records Administration. Senate documents, Volume 1; Volume 390, Indian Operations on the Plains. 1888, pp. 25-55.

In July 1866, a military force under Colonel Henry B. Carrington established Fort Kearny, with 700 soldiers and 300 civilians, to further secure the route of the Bozeman Trail. This angered Red Cloud, leader of the Oglala Lakota.

While Fort Kearny was under construction, Carrington suffered about 50 Indian attacks, losing more than 20 soldiers and civilians. In November, a cavalry company of 63 soldiers would be assigned, as well.

On July 16, Carrington met with a contingent of Cheyenne Chiefs who relayed their ultimatum that no settlement be allowed further west and no new forts were to be constructed: the principal chiefs were "'Black Horse", "Pretty Bear", "Dull Knife", "Red Arm", "Little Moon", Man that stands alone on the ground", "Wolf that lies down", "Rabbit that jumps", "Bob Tail", and "Dead White Leg, the brave soldier." These chiefs claimed to represent one hundred and seventy-six lodges of Cheyenne Indians.

They expressed their opposition to the U.S. taking their hunting grounds and making a road through them, without their consent. From 1866-1868, Red Cloud, accompanied by Crazy Horse and other warriors, repeatedly attacked wagon trains escorted by U.S. military troops in the Powder River Basin. Knowing of the military superiority of the U.S. forces, they still attacked military troops and garrisons, notably Fort Phil Kearny.

Colonel Carrington described Fort Kearny in his July 30, 1866, report to Major Litchfield: Fort Philip Kearny is, in all directions familiarly related to the Indians.

1st. It occupies the very heart of their hunting grounds. In my ride of the 14th I saw Bear, buffalo, elk, deer, antelope, rabbits and sage hens.

2nd. It is the natural middle and semi-neutral ground of Crows, Snakes, Cheyennes, Sioux and Arapahoes. Not that all claim equal right to, or, in fact equally visit this tract, but it is to all a favorite field.

3rd. It is a natural source of recuperation and supply to moving, hunting, and roving bands of all tribes, and their lodge trails cross in great numbers from north to South between Piney junction, near the post, and the mountains that lie behind.

The mountains five miles distant are precipitous, but the gorges are full of pine, hemlock, balsam, fir, and spruce. This ridge is about eight hundred feet above the Piney bottoms, but behind, and stretching to the foot of the next, or "snow capped range", is a sweep of prairie, as rich in game as it is in grass and flowers. Here Indians hunt unmolested by travel, and from this great basin, or plateau, then move unexpectedly, north, south, east or west. Their fires are visible, and I doubt not I shall find there much stolen stock.

1866: Colonel Carrington – Whip Indians

The information is this section is derived from Records Relating to Investigations of the Fort Philip Kearny (or Fetterman) Massacre. Testimony of Colonel Henry B. Carrington, Page 1, M740 roll 1 of 1, National Archives & Records Administration. Senate documents, Volume 1; Volume 390, Indian Operations on the Plains. 1888, pp. 25-55.

Each of his reports documents the numerous Indian attacks.

> The [Peace Treaty] Commissioners did all they could, but, as when I left I wrote you so, since, my impressions derived from closest scrutiny of the Indians I saw, are confirmed that *I shall have to whip the Indians*, and they have given me every provocation. (Emphasis added).

> A large force of miners from Virginia City have recently located in the mountains, furnishing no mean auxiliaries in fighting Indians. It is near the western limit of the best hunting grounds. It assures Indians that this movement is not temporary, but a substantial fixed occupation.

Carrington's September 17th, 1866, report to Major Litchfield included the following:

> The following facts are important by way of review.
> 1st. The Indians are well armed, with revolvers as well as rifles.
> 2nd. Red Cloud is known to command the parties now immediately engaged. White flags were used as signals between the different bands, thus covering a line of at least seven miles.
> 3rd. There are men with them who dress and appear to be white men, and swear and talk in good English.
> 4th. They are determined to burn the country, cut off supplies, and hamper every movement.
>
> I believe the force I have is well disposed and effective for its strength, and I did not permit presence of the Indians to stop the hay wagons from going back to the hay field.

Carrington's September 26, 1866, reported to Major Litchfield the mineral, agricultural and other resources of the new route to Montana. As to minerals, "Coal abounds in exhaustless supply."

In regard to agriculture: "The valleys of Piney, Clear, Goose and Peno Creek, also of Tongue and the Big Horn rivers, with their numerous tributaries, afford fine grass, with wheat and oats. Their soil is a rich loam, and susceptible of full culture with rich returns. ... Irrigation of this grass region is most ample."

Concerning timber: "The following timber, additional to exhaustless supplies of evergreen varieties, is found upon various creeks and Mountain slopes, viz.:—ash, box-elder, willow and cottonwood in all its forms. ... The boards from [the pine timber] take the plane, and polish equal to No. 1 merchantable seasoned pine timber."

His summary [in part] was as follows:

This country is susceptible of the highest development. There is no land on the Platte that will rival the average bottoms of Creeks referred to. The inducements to substantial emigration and permanent homes for people who do not hunt gold as the final desideratum, are unquestionably great. Neither do I think the Indian troubles will be permanent or general. Losing no opportunities to ascertain facts respecting their animus towards the whites and their relation to each other, I can see no indications of harmony in action, combined operations.

They have a common antipathy to the loss of this splendid hunting sphere, this centre of natural advantage, where all game is found and whence they can at all times replenish their supplies when elsewhere unsuccessful. But the occupation by the troops has so far advanced this fall, the defences are so stable, and the purpose of the Government is so decided that they must yield. ....

Colonel Carrington reported the lack of discipline on the part of non-commissioned officers and soldiers.

[T]roops were in the habit of dashing helter skelter over the stockade whenever an Indian appeared, without regard to orders, and generally before the Commanding Officer knew there were Indians about, or had issued any orders. Frequently bodies of twenty or thirty mounted men would dash out without orders, on receipt of reports that Indians were driving off herds.

The caliber of soldier which effected discipline was impacted by low morale related to pay problems, a lack of civilian education, poor military training, lack of arms and munitions, and the hardships associated with soldiering. Cultural stereotypes and misunderstandings about Indian culture led to miscalculations and underestimations of their abilities; all of which translated to operational and tactical blunders for the Army.[5]

Capt. Fetterman Disobeys Orders Resulting in Destruction of His Command

The information is this section is derived from Records Relating to Investigations of the Fort Philip Kearny (or Fetterman) Massacre, National Archives & Records Administration.

With the Civil War over, the U.S. Army was able to shift trained veterans to active duty on the western front. Capt. William J. Fetterman and Lieutenant Horatio S. Bingham were Civil War veterans but had no experience fighting Indians. Fetterman criticized Carrington's defensive posture and was contemptuous of their Indian foes. He allegedly boasted, "Give me 80 men and I can ride through the whole Sioux nation." Many other officers shared Fetterman's feelings about pursuing an aggressive offense.

On January 14, 1867, Brevet Major General Commanding P. St. George Cooke summarized his understanding of the battle to his superior officer, Brevet Major General W. A. Nichols:

> [M]y judgment of the probabilities is, that on the 21st December hostile Indians, in number between 1,500 and 3,000, formed an ambush within five or six miles of Fort Phil Kearny; that they sent a party to decoy the garrison; that all the available horses (which I believe were kept saddled) were mounted, and that hastily and irregularly they sallied out to engage or pursue; that the Indians skillfully managed to lead the pursuit of the whole into ground selected as forbidding escape; and that there, by so greatly superior numbers, the troops were surrounded and massacred, no quarter asked or given.

A telegram from Colonel Carrington to Brevet Major General General Sherman on January 1, 1867, states that Fetterman disobeyed specific orders from Colonel Carrington:

> *They were sent to relieve, and pushed over Lodge Trail ridge in order of pursuit, after orders three times given not to cross that ridge.* ... Fetterman and Brown — evidently shot each other. (Emphasis added).

C. M. Hines, A.A. Surgeon, confirmed that Fetterman disobeyed orders, was decoyed by the Indians, resulting in the destruction of Fetterman's command.

Captain and Brevet Lieutenant Colonel Fetterman, Captain Brown and Lieutenant Grummond were ordered out by the colonel to protect our wood train, which had been attacked. Captain Fetterman commanded the infantry, Lieutenant Grummond the cavalry, (twenty-seven men,) and Captain Brown some mounted teamsters and citizens, the whole amounting to eighty-one men, about fifty of whom were armed with the Spencer carbine and pistols, one or two with Henry rifles, and the balance with the Springfield musket. No men were better armed. Instead of obeying orders, these officers (than whom there were none better or braver in the service) allowed themselves to be decoyed from the position ordered to be taken, and the whole command were butchered, (eighty-one officers and men.) I was ordered by Colonel Carrington, with one man, to go out to the wood train, (five miles off,) and if I found them safe to join the other command.

General Wessel's January 21, 1867, Report on the Fort Phil Kearny Massacre to the Adjutant General:

On the 21st December last the usual wagon train with an armed escort, left the post about 8 o'clock [sic] a. m. for the purpose of procuring timber for the saw mills. Not long after their departure, perhaps an hour, firing was heard in the direction they had taken, and the alarm was given that the train was attacked by the enemy. Capt. and Brevet Lieutenant Colonel W. J. Fetterman 18th Infantry with a detachment of forty nine (49) men Infantry soldiers, made up by details from the different Companies was directed to proceed at once to the assistance of the train, and *conduct it in safety to the post but not to pursue the enemy.* Lieutenant Grummond 18th Infantry was then ordered to report to Lieutenant Colonel Fetterman with twenty seven men of the 2nd Cavalry and to reiterate to him the orders previously given, this detachment left the post within fifteen minutes after the Infantry, and soon joined it. (Emphasis added).

The attack on the wagon train appears to have been only a feint, as it returned safely to the post. *Why Colonel Fetterman should have failed to join it, can only be conjectured, he may have seen from the Valley that it was not seriously threatened, and in his zeal for soldierly distinction, have determined to*

~ 550 ~

attack the enemy the latter showing only small parties, and leading him to the position selected by themselves. (Emphasis added).

Testimony of Assitant Surgeon Horton:

Question: Please state with what weapons those persons were killed, and the appearance of their bodies, whether they were mutilated and if so how mutilated. Answer: Lieutenant Bingham was killed with arrows and a pistol ball in the head, Sgt. Bowers was killed with a tomahawk driven into his brain, and they were otherwise mutilated.

From the appearance of all the persons in Colonel Fetterman's party I believe the majority of them were killed by clubs with which the Indians crushed their skulls and brains, after having fallen wounded. A few were disemboweled with knives which I believe was done after they were wounded. The brains of some of them were found lying beside their bodies, some of them were killed by arrows after they had fallen and were stripped, as their bodies contained a great number of arrows. One body had as high as sixty five arrows in it, which seemed to have been unmolested by removing clothing. Every man was stripped of all his clothing, with but few exceptions, [as?] when bloody stockings remained on their feet. Colonel Fetterman's body showed his thorax to have been cut crosswise with a knife, deep into the viscera; his throat and entire neck were cut to the cervical spine all around. I believe that mutilation caused his death.

Capt. Brown's body showed gashes inside of both thighs, to the bone, from his body to his knees, both ears had been cut off and his body otherwise horribly mutilated and a hole made in his left temple [caused?] by a small pistol ball; the latter most probably caused his death. Lieutenant Grummond's body showed his head to have been crushed by a club; and his legs were slightly scorched by fire.

One body was found with a large stake driven into it, as high as the chest. One body was found with one arm cut off at the shoulder joint. One found with both hands and both feet cut off, one with the entire head crushed away, except the lower jaw. All the bodies were more or less mutilated, and presented in nearly every instance a horrible sight, never to be forgotten by those who saw them.

Question: Was there any evidence presented by these bodies of death from torture. Answer: No. In place of torture, by far the majority of men, in my opinion, were fallen upon by the Indians and butchered after they were wounded.

The display of mutilated corpses were messages for the U.S. government and for the emigrating population. The Indians were willing to fight to defend their control in the territories they claimed, demonstrating to the public the force they would employ to protect their lives and land. Under this logic, the scenes of mutilation are telling: exposure of the private parts, the skulls are shattered, faces mutilated, penises cut off and the bodies burnt.

The Indians were using their own version of "shock and awe," broadcasting a willingness to fight to the end. Killing so graphically was to sap public confidence in the government, hoping the U.S., its trustee, the guarantor of the treaties entered into, the promisor, would act to protect their land and their traditional lifestyles.

As the invasion of white settlers increased, the violence grew bolder and more grotesque. The hyperviolence, the grotesque acts and the decapitations were meant to be destabilizing—acts of psychological warfare against a government and public willing to exterminate them for their land and resources.

Testimony of J.B. Weston, Lawyer

Question: In your opinion what was the cause, that led to the Indian War now existing in the Powder River country.
Answer: Very many causes led to this result. Some of the more immediate causes are as follow.

1st On account of attempting to take possession of a country by an inadequate military force, without having obtained consent of the Indians who occupied it.

2nd The Indians in this country are very numerous, very wild, well armed, mounted and appointed; and their constant and repeated successes, against the weak and poorly appointed Government force in the country, has tended to strengthen, encourage and embolden them; has enabled their Chiefs to unite and consolidate the various tribes to the present very formidable force, embracing, as I believe more than six thousand warriors.

Also the Indians naturally resist the opening up of a great National highway to Virginia City, through a fine country abounding in game, upon which they rely for their subsistence.

3rd *The Indians have been cut off and driven back from every quarter, and this Powder River country alone remains to them intact. It is the last and perhaps the finest Indian country extant. The Indians are well aware that the country besides posessing [sic] almost unlimited resources, such as they require for their sustenance and support, is also a country rich in agricultural and mineral resources.* They know that while coal and iron are abundant, that the more precious minerals exist in paying quantities, in some parts of the country; and they have always been jealous of the Whites getting a foothold in the country on that account. They are no fools. They see the results in other mining territories; and know perfectly well that a knowledge of these mineral resources would only result in an absorption of the country by the Whites.

Lastly: Stupid and criminal management of our Indian Affairs by the U.S. Government. The Government, as represented by the Officials of the Indian Bureau, has never seemed to have any clear understanding of the Indian problem. Instead of preparing the way for the inevitable advance of civilization over this country, they have, *as far as my observation has gone, been absorbed in some scheme of personal [s]peculation.* And when this management has resulted in bringing on an Indian war, the War Department has failed to appreciate its extent and magnitude; has sent a military force to this country so small, inadequate, and insufficient in numbers, arms and supplies, that instead of conquering a peace, it has aggravated and augmented the troubles. (Emphasis added).[6]

Indians refer to it as "The Battle of the Hundred Slain." Americans refer to it as the Fetterman Massacre.

After the defeat, civilians John "Portugee" Phillips and Daniel Dixon were hired to carry a message to the telegraph station at Horseshoe Bend requesting reenforcements. Phillips made a 236-mile ride through a snowstorm. This need to engage a civilian graphically demonstrates the unpreparedness of the military.

President Andrew Johnson ordered an investigation, which would result in the withdrawal of U.S. troops from the Powder River country, in accordance with treaties then in existence.

The 1868 Fort Laramie treaty granted the whole northeast corner of what is now Wyoming to the Indians, who burned to the ground the hated forts the U.S. Army had built along the Bozeman Trail as the troops marched away. Red Cloud's War of 1866–68 clearly established the dominance of the Oglala Sioux over U.S. forces in northern Wyoming and southern Montana east of the Bighorn Mountains.

Battle at Crazy Woman Creek

On July 20, 1866, Sioux and Cheyenne warriors attacked a military-escorted wagon train at Crazy Woman Creek. Lieutenants Napoleon H. Daniels and George M. Templeton and twenty-nine soldiers had been appointed as the protection detail. A second wagon train of 34 wagons and 47 soldiers under Captain Thomas B. Burrowes from Fort Reno rescued the military commands which incurred fatalities. This was not the last ambush on Crazy Woman. The high hills surrounding the crossing offered excellent opportunities for observation or attack, which became common occurrences during the next two years.

Battle of Clear Creek

On July 24, 1866, at the Battle of Clear Creek (Buffalo, Wyoming), the Indians would face more than 60 soldiers from Fort Kearny, armed with a twelve pound and mountain howitzers, along with white settlers from four wagon trains, consisting of about 200 wagons, stretching six miles across the plains. Demonstrating the strategic role Army forts played in warfare, the two wagon trains from the battle at Crazy Woman Creek had regrouped at Fort Reno and were headed to Fort Kearny. They caught up with two large civilian wagon trains, led by Hugh Kirkendall and William Dillon.
Joining forces, they were still not able to maintain one solidified group. Indians

attacked whites from each split group, mortally wounding train leader Dillon in the attack on his train.

Wyoming Territory

Wyoming was recognized as a Territory in the spring of 1869. On April 3, 1869, President Ulysses S. Grant appointed John A. Campbell as the Governor of the Wyoming Territory and, as such, the ex oficio Superintendent of Indian Affairs and trustee for Indians in the Territory.

From the gilded safety of his office, Governor Campbell wrote in 1869:

> *This reservation (Shoshone) includes a large extent of country, bordering in the southwestern part on the Sweetwater gold-mining region. The river valleys included in it contain the only arable land within one hundred miles of the gold mines, and the miners are very anxious to obtain possession of these valleys, in order to raise vegetables and other produce for their subsistence.* (Emphasis added).[7]

The decision of the white settlers to supplant the Indians was evidenced by their organization of counties with appointed officials. There were originally five counties in the Wyoming Territory: Laramie and Carter, established in 1867; Carbon and Albany established in 1868; and Uinta, an annexed portion of Utah and Idaho, extending from Montana (including Yellowstone Park) to the Wyoming–Utah boundary. More would be added such that by the time Wyoming was admitted to statehood in 1890, there were 10 counties.

Discovery of Gold at South Pass

Placer gold panning started in the South Pass area of Wyoming as early as 1842. After the Civil War ended, gold fever resulted in accelerated emigration. The Carizzo (renamed Carissa) lode was discovered in June 1867. In April and May 1868, Indians raided the South Pass area, confiscating an estimated 100 horses and mules, taking stock, supplies and mercantile goods, and killing four men.[8]

By 1870 South Pass City boasted a population estimated at between 2,000 and 4,000 and in 1870 as much as *$5,000,000 in gold* may have been taken from this district. During the peak summers of 1870 and 1871 as many as 12,000 souls lived in the Sweetwater Mining District. In 1873 most of the mines played out. (Emphasis added).[9]

The white settlers drive to supplant the Indians was also evidenced by the organization of mining districts and towns, such as Sweetwater, with the towns of Atlantic City and Miners Delight. The rich Carissa mine, discovered in June 1867, was attacked by Sioux Indians who killed three miners and drove the rest away but the continuing raids did not stop the invasion of whites. By 1868, there were seventeen saloons, brothel and gambling houses, and the accompanying lawlessness in the new South Pass City. There were 1,517 people in the Sweetwater Mining District by 1869. As mentioned, transportation routes were built from the Union Pacific mainline to serve the mines and *aided in opening up the region.*

Mining districts enacted laws concerning the location and representation of quartz leads or lodes of gold or silver bearing rock such as the Lincoln Mining District on November 11, 1865:

> Sec. 1. Any person locating quartz lodes or leads of gold bearing rock shall not be entitled to more than 200 feet in one claim by location, and no person shall hold more than one claim on the same lead by excavation... All persons shall define the limits of their claims by a stake at each end of the claim not less than three (3) inches in diameter nor less than two (2) feet in height, with the name of person or persons and date of location thereon written.
>
> Sec. 2. All persons shall have their claims recorded in the district recording office within ten (10) days from the time of their location... claims [shall be improved], by work in or for the benefit of the claim to the amount of fifty ($50) dollars.[10]

Along with the immigration came military camps and manned forts. Camp Stambaugh, built in 1870, was an army post constructed near Atlantic City to offer protection to the white miners and other white settlers from hostile Indians. Occupied until 1877, the Camp was not involved in hostilities; instead, it became an important supply station for the local area.[11] In the alternative, local governments armed their populace, sometimes paid for with federal dollars, and established volunteer, untrained squads to unilaterally determine how to protect themselves. *Territorial governors with the dual role of superintending the territory and acting as trustee for its Indian inhabitants issued "kill Indians on-site orders" to its armed squads, with the reward of booty for destroying villages and monies for Indian scalps.*
The County Commissioner reported Indian raiding in the Sweetwater District to the Governor, the trustee for the Indians. The Governor immediately demanded troops for the protection of the white settlers. His clout resulted in

two companies being despatched to the Valley and the establishment of Camp Augur in June 1869.

On July 28, another Indian raid near Atlantic City resulted in *Governor Campbell ordering the military commander to arm and provide ammunition to the area to be distributed among the citizens*. (Emphasis added). With the closest military base at Fort Bridger, over 150 miles away, the white settlers turned to self-help.

However, by 1875, the Sweetwater District had become idle with most of the miners moving on to other strikes in a combination of factors, including poor management and fraud. Also, recovering ores became more complex as greater depths were reached, therefore requiring more expensive milling processes. The mines were far from rail transportation with limited water and timber for milling and mine construction.

Cattle Business

With the opening of the Powder River country and the removal of the Indians after 1876, the cattle industry soon filled the void and occupied the vast grasslands north of the North Platte River and Oregon Trail. The industry also spread westward into the Sweetwater country along the Oregon Trail and in western Wyoming, wherever the range was suitable for cattle.

Cattle drovers ran livestock on the hoof over the Texas Trail, with over 100,000 head of cattle coming from Oregon to Wyoming by 1879. The Union Pacific opened up trade to distant markets. Cowboys poured into the Powder River country to work at the 20-some established cattle companies worth a cumulative $12 million. In 1885, the Powder River Cattle Company owned more than 50,000 cows.

However, federal land policy was not practicable in a semi-arid region where, according to John Wesley Powell, at least 2,560 acres or 40 acres per cow were needed for a successful cattle operation. By 1880, a Wyoming rancher could use all the existing land laws to obtain a maximum of 1,120 acres, and still fall far short of what he needed to conduct a successful cattle operation. As a result, ranchers resorted to fraudulent and illegal measures such as 'dummy' filings, controlling water sources, and fencing the public domain.[12]

As available range became overstocked, flooding of the market brought about a decline in prices. European and eastern investment which had fueled emerging business during the era of the cattle barons in the late 1870s and early 1880s dried up.

Farming

Settlement in terms of the small farming homesteads envisioned by the federal government was hindered in Wyoming Territory for a number of reasons. First, the cattle interests were the first to take advantage of Wyoming's grasslands, and they required large amounts of land which they controlled by any means, fair or foul. Secondly, fertile lands in Oregon and California as well as the eastern fringes of the Great Plains were still available into the 1880s. Therefore, until these lands were saturated, the homesteader had little incentive to venture forth onto the Great Plains to brave the harsh semi-arid climate, the cattle rancher, or the Indians.

Most successful farming efforts occurred along the North Platte River, along the eastern portion of the Oregon Trail corridor, where rich bottomland existed and irrigation of crops was possible.[13]

Wyoming Superintendency, Fort Bridger Treaty, 1868

The gold rush at South Pass with the concomitant raids hastened plans for Indian removal. The Bridger-Teton Treaty with the federal government in 1868 established the Wind River Reservation, comprising 4,200 square miles, for the Eastern Shoshone tribe, numbering about 2,000, *which acted as a buffer between the mines and the more hostile Sioux Nation to the east*.

In violation of the Treaty, the incursions of the miners continued as more gold veins were discovered and exploited. The federal government took no action to enforce the Treaty. Annuities guaranteed under the Treaty were constantly short or delivered late or missed.

The 1868 treaty set aside lands for the Lakota Sioux in two categories—the Great Sioux Reservation, made up of most of the western half of Dakota Territory, and the Powder River Basin of northeastern Wyoming and southern Montana. Tribes were allowed to hunt and live in these unceded lands, where buffalo were still plentiful.

1872: Reduce Wind River Indian Reservation ("WRIR")

By 1872, miners were trespassing on the mineral area and agitating for a reduction of the WRIR Reservation. The Commissioner again capitulated to their demands, relying on the trite excuses that the Indians didn't need the land and it was "rendered undesirable" due to the discovery of gold and silver.

The [Wind River] reservation containing an area far beyond what is required by the Indians entitled thereto, who number less than 4,000, and discoveries of gold and silver being credibly reported in the southern portions of the same, and miners entering and preparing to enter thereon in considerable numbers, it was deemed expedient that negotiations be entered into with these Indians for the relinquishment of the portion of their reservation thus rendered undesirable for Indian occupation. (Emphasis added).[14]

Relinquish Part of WRIR with Mineral Discoveries, 1874 Lander Purchase

In 1872, Congress authorized the President to negotiate with the Eastern Shoshone Indians for the relinquishment of *all of that part of their reservation embracing the mineral discoveries,* in exchange for lands to the north. 17 Stat. 214 (1872). The best gold mines in the district had been found to be located within the reservation. On September 26, 1872, Felix Brunot, commissioner for the United States, entered into an agreement with the Shoshone Indians for lands within the southern portion of the Reservation where whites were actively mining. Rather than an exchange for additional lands to the north, the Shoshone Tribe agreed to relinquish approximately 700,000 acres for a fixed sum payment of $25,000 to be paid over five years for the purchase of cattle and a $500 annual payment to the Chief for five years.[15] On December 15, 1874, Congress ratified the agreement, also known as the "Lander Purchase." 18 Stat. 291 (1874). The purpose of the 1874 Lander Purchase Act, as expressly set forth in the statute, was to sell lands south of the 43rd parallel for $25,000 in order "to change the southern limit of said reservation."[16]

Allegedly, it was not the intention to include any of these settlements in the reservation. The mistake arose from the inaccuracy of a map in their possession ... (Emphasis added).[17]

> The portion of the reservation ceded is supposed to include the mines and all the gold-bearing district. It also includes the valleys of the two Popoagies ... to contain from twenty-five to thirty sections of tillable land for agricultural purposes ... The Popoagie Valleys, like Wind River, are of a low altitude, sheltered from the west by the Wind River Mountains, and almost free from winter snows. This makes them of great value to the mining district, which is from 8,000 to 10,000 feet above sea level, and is rendered almost uninhabitable by

~ 559 ~

the deep snows in winter. The mining camps have no other source of agricultural supplies nearer than one hundred miles. The area of land ceded is almost 700,000 acres.[18]

Commissioner Brunot obtained an agreement from the Shoshones ceding 700,642 acres of the reservation for a total consideration of $27,500. At that time the Indians had no conception of the value of money or the value of the property they were surrendering to the Government and they accepted, without question, Brunot's first offer of the amount stated. With reference to the consideration to be paid for this cession, Brunot reported to the Commissioner of Indian Affairs that "Acting upon my experience of the general habit of Indians, the Shoshones were offered a sum as the basis of further negotiation, and which I supposed would have to be increased to meet the demand of the Indians. When the terms first offered were promptly accepted, I did not feel at liberty to make an addition it seems eminently proper to solicit from Congress." (Emphasis added).[19]

No further amount was ever paid for this cession.

In 1872 gold miners who were operating illegally on the southern part of Wind River demanded the land be opened, prompting Commissioner of Indian Affairs Francis A. Walker to announce:

"It is the policy of the government to segregate such [mineral] lands from Indian reservations as far as may be consistent with the faith of the United States and throw them open to entry and settlement in order that the Indians may not be annoyed and distressed by the cupidity of the miners and settlers who in large numbers, in spite of the efforts of the government to the contrary, flock to such regions of the country on the first report of the gold discovery."[20]

Further Reduction of WRIR with Agricultural Land, Coal and Minerals

Again in 1874, a further reduction of the WRIR was sought for its *agricultural lands and the coal and other minerals it contained. If the Shoshones were unwilling to agree to a cession, legislation would be imposed on them. The justification by the Commissioner of Indian Affairs - it was of "so little real value to the Indians" and it was a great wrong to the white settlers "that its domain should not be settled."*

Besides, this unceded territory embraces the most productive part of Wyoming Territory, in an agricultural view and on account of the coal and other minerals it contains. It is a great wrong to the citizens of this Territory that its domain should not be settled. (Emphasis added).[21]

U.S. Army's Sioux Nation Mission

As tensions rose, the U.S. government officials decided the Indians needed to stay on the reservation lands and in December 1875 declared that all Indians not on those lands by January 31, 1876, would be deemed hostile and subject to attack. In 1876, the U.S. assigned the Army the mission of forcing the Sioux Indians onto their reservations permanently. Armies marched from every direction of the compass to confront them in the Powder River Country. The standard strategy for defeating hostile Indian tribes was based upon exhaustion as the Army simply sought to wear the enemy down by eroding the hostile tribe's will or means to resist.

Retrospective View of Military Policy by General John Pope

In considering military policy in hindsight, General John Pope thought it would have been better to pursue open conquest. Indians did not stand a chance against the odious apparatus of a superior armed force. Yet they chose to fight to the death in many instances, knowing their defeat was inescapable, because they had no choice other than surrendering their heritage and legacy from time immemorial of their predecessors.

> It is hard to believe that open conquest would not have resulted in the extinction of Indians. It is equally incredulous that the victorious white men would have acted honorably to the vanquished Indians. *Over and over again what we have heard repeatedly from the federal government was that if Indian lands were valuable, they were doomed to be stolen due to the cupidity of the white man. When Indians have not been exterminated, they have been forcibly removed to concentration camps, lacking in area and resources that would permit a sustainable livelihood. "It would have been a conflict between men only, and unattended by the massacre of the innocent and helpless, nor would it have led to such rapid and violent extinction of the Indian race."* (Emphasis added).[22]

Notes: Wyoming

1. Struthers Burt, Powder River: Let 'er Buck. 1938. "The search for it. The fight for it. The slow disappearance of it."

2. Comprehensive Management and Use Plan / Final Environmental Impact Statement for the Oregon, California, Mormon Pioneer, and Pony Express National Historic Trails, pp. 45, 47. http://npshistory.com/publications/oreg/cmup.pdf (accessed online August 17, 2022).

3. Ibid., p. 29.

4. Historical Markers and Monuments in the Fort Kearny area. Courtesy of Wyoming Division of State Parks, Historic Sites & Trails. https://www.fortphilkearny.com/historical-markers (accessed online August 17, 2022).

5. Records Relating to Investigations of the Fort Philip Kearny (or Fetterman) Massacre. Testimony of Colonel Henry B. Carrington, Page 1, M740 roll 1 of 1, National Archives & Records Administration. Senate documents, Volume 1; Volume 390, Indian Operations on the Plains. 1888, pp. 25-55.

6. Records Relating to Investigations of the Fort Philip Kearny (or Fetterman) Massacre, National Archives & Records Administration.

7. Report of the Commissioner of Indian Affairs to the Secretary of the Interior, United States. Office of Indian Affairs, Wyoming Superintendency. U.S. Government Printing Office, 1870, p. 271.

8. http://sites.rootsweb.com/~wytttp/history/countant/chapter43.htm (accessed online August 18, 2022).

9. Wild and Scenic River Study June 1979. Prepared by Department of the Interior, National Park Service, Denver Service Center, pp. 11-33.

10. History of Wyoming, Volume I, Charles Griffin Coutant, 1899.

11. Proposed Resource Management Plan and Final Environmental Impact Statement for the Lander Field Office Planning Area. United States, Bureau of Land Management, Wyoming State Office, 2013, p. 436.

12. Oregon/Mormon Pioneer National Historic Trails Management Plan. United States. Bureau of Land Management, 1986, p. 50.

13. History of Wyoming, Volume I, Charles Griffin Coutant, 1899.

14. Report of the Commissioner of Indian Affairs to the Secretary of the Interior, United States. Office of Indian Affairs. U.S. Government Printing Office, 1872, pp. 89-90.

15. Ibid., p. 512.

16. Ibid., p. 292.

17. Ibid., p. 478.

18. Ibid., p. 511.

19. Ibid., p. 511.

20. Ambler, Marjane, Breaking the Iron Bonds: Indian Control of Energy Development, University Press of Kansas, 1990, p. 33. Indian History in Wyoming, Needs and Opportunities for Study, Colin G. Calloway. https://archive.org/stream/annalsofwyom63141991wyom/annalsofwyom63141991wyom_djvu.txt (accessed online December 23, 2022).

21.Report of the Commissioner of Indian Affairs to the Secretary of the Interior, United States. Office of Indian Affairs. U.S. Government Printing Office, 1874, Appendix A, Report of Chris C. Cox, Special Indian Commissioner, pp. 89-90.

22. Address by General Pope before the Social Science Association, at Cincinnati, Ohio, May 24, 1878. Delivered by Request of the Association (Cincinnati: n.p., 1878). Excerpt From: Editor, Cozzens, Peter. "Eyewitnesses to the Indian Wars: 1865-1890: Vol. 5, The Army and the Indian." Apple Books.

17: MICHIGAN

The Iron Triangle, **Chapter 6, The Carving Up of Michigan,** centers on the massive cession of lands, removal, concentration and consolidation of tribes on small tracts of non-arable land, establishment of reservations, and allotment of tribal land such that Indian Nations once self-sufficient became destitute paupers. It is only through the courage of the Indians that lived through the era of 1850-1900 that there are currently twelve (12) federally recognized Indian Nations in Michigan able to exercise their sovereignty and self-determination to thrive.

Indigenous Discoveries of Copper in Keweenaw Peninsula

The Keweenaw Peninsula, approximately 50 miles long and 15 miles wide, lies at the northernmost tip of Michigan as it juts out into Lake Superior. The copper range forms a narrow spine running down the peninsula, with copper occurring in a pure metallic state, unalloyed with other elements.[1]

Prehistoric copper mining in the Lake Superior region is clearly evident. From Isle Royale and the surrounding area, it was used in jewelry and ornamentation, and for tools such as arrow and spear points.[2] Lake Superior copper has also been found at prehistoric sites around the eastern U.S., demonstrating its value for trading, and the existence of extensive trading networks across the continent.

The Minong Mining District is known for more than 1,000 pits dug by indigenous people and evidences their extraction and processing of the copper. The prominent site featured native copper close to the surface. Its raw, concentrated form permitted the creation of usable material, without any heating or other processing.[3]

Later, European mines included open pits and underground shafts, and left much of the surface evidence undisturbed.[4]

1805: Michigan Territory, Extinguish Indian Title in State

As early as 1805, Michigan Territory's inhabitants petitioned President Jefferson to extinguish Indian title in the territory. The petition was submitted by the Officers of Militia at Detroit representing the non-Indian inhabitants. This was a consistent trend across the continent. Indians would be characterized as an obstacle to emigration, economic development and progress. It was a predictor of the opening of Indian lands for white settlement, with or without purchase. Many times, the invasion of white settlers, the establishment of communities, and the reduction of game which eliminated the Indians subsistence base, was enough to drive Indians away from their homeland.

> It is also desired that after our claims are settled the Indian title in this Territory may be extinguished and the sales of the United States lands commence, to open the door to emigration, for without it we must remain of little worth to the United States.[5]

1820: Mineral Survey

Under the U.S. flag, Henry R. Schoolcraft surveyed the area in 1820 and recommended that the federal government mine the deposits. The discovery of minerals is another unquestionable precursor to the invasion of Indian lands. It started early and is reported by the Commissioner of Indian Affairs as a constant:

> Wherever an Indian reservation has on it good land, or timber, or minerals, the cupidity of the white man is excited, and a constant struggle is inaugurated to dispossess the Indian, in which the avarice and determination of the white man usually prevails.[6]

1840: Report on Keweenaw's Copper Deposits

In 1840, Douglass Houghton, Michigan's State Geologist, reported on the geology of the Upper Peninsula describing the Keweenaw's copper deposits. The upshot of the publication was a land rush to acquire copper-rich real estate by miners, entrepreneurs and investors.[7]

Copper Mining

Copper was classified in the Lake Superior country in three grades according to its state of occurrence in the rock: "mass," "barrel-work," and "stamp." Masses were large sheets of pure copper occurring in the vein, and weighing from a few hundred pounds to many tons. Smaller masses were taken from the mine intact; larger chunks were divided by means of chiseling.

Barrel-work consisted of smaller pieces of copper in bundles and string-like form, bound together with veinstone-the worthless rocky material in the ore bearing vein. With these, as much of the adhering rock as possible was picked free with a hammer, and the copper was barreled up in casks holding from 500 to 800 pounds.

Stamp copper consisted of pebble-sized or smaller pieces of metallic copper bound in rock which had to be pulverized by stamping. In this process, the ore was first roasted to make the veinstone friable, so it would yield to the blows of the stamps. The stamp mills consisted of a series of heavy metal shoes operating from a cam shaft driven by water or steam power. The shoes would crush the ore, and the metal would be separated from the copper through a series of washings.

F.C.L. Koch, German Mining Engineer, 1850

The Isle Royale copper lode is about two and one half feet thick, but the copper has penetrated into the foot and hanging wall beyond and outside of it. At many points the copper occurs in thin plates, which now and then thickens to larger pieces, up to several pounds in weight.

Most of the copper shipped from Isle Royale-the ore was taken down the lake to Sault Ste. Marie, and thence across to the lower lakes to be smelted-was mass or barrel work. Only two stamp mills operated on the island during this first frontier.

The underground workings consisted of vertical shafts about six feet by eight feet sunk to a suitable depth-generally about sixty feet- where stoping would begin, that is, excavation of the ore made accessible by the shaft.

The mining boom came to an end as rapidly as it had started. By the end of 1847 about half the companies that had been in operation the earlier part of the year were closed. By 1850 only two companies were in operation, and in 1855 the last of these companies closed up.

Saginaw Mining Company

The Saginaw Mining Company, apparently backed by Marquette capital, sent out a small work force in 1877 to mine an old location formerly prospected by the Ohio and Isle Royale Company. They sank two shafts with a winze connecting them and took out a limited amount of copper. But operations ceased after 1879. This company went through a series of early changes, beginning as the Isle Royale Union Company in 1844, reorganizing as the Siskowit Mining Association in 1847, and becoming the Siskowit Mining Company in 1849.

Ohio and Isle Royale Company

The short-lived Ohio and Isle Royale Company, like the Siskowit, was given permission by the Secretary of War to locate claims on Isle Royale locations between Rock Harbor and Chippewa Harbor. A townsite named Ransom, after the Agent, Leander Ransom, was established.

Pittsburg & Isle Royale Mining Company

This company, incorporated in Pittsburg about 1846, began its mining activities in 1847 in the Todd Harbor area.

1842: Ojibwe Treaty of La Pointe

It is not surprising that a cession of lands would be sought from the Chippewa Indians of the Mississippi and Lake Superior.

> As reported by Michigan Superintendent Robert Stuart, by the Treaty with the Chippewa Indians of the Mississippi and Lake Superior, dated on the 4th October, 1842, a "valuable mineral region" and the southern shore of Lake Superior is secured to the U.S. *There were copper ores of the "purest quality;" silver ores and fisheries on Lake Superior and its island which would result in a "considerable source of revenue" to the colonial settlers.* (Emphasis added).[8]

In 1843, the U.S. opened a mineral land office in Copper Harbor to record non-Indian property acquisitions, protecting their title.

1843: Department of the Interior's Continued Celebration of U.S. Stripping of Tribes Agriculturally Valuable Land and Mineral Resources

In 1843, Commissioner Crawford bore witness to the stripping of Indian land that was agriculturally valuable and also, valuable for its mineral resources.

> The treaty with the Chippewa Indians of the Mississippi and Lake Superior, dated on the 4th October, 1842, was ratified on the 10th February last. It secures to the United States a large body of land, said to *be agriculturally desirable, but especially valuable for its mineral resources* while the right to the exclusive possession of the southern shore of Lake Superior is commercially important, and will become more and more so as the settlements extend and the mineral resources of its vicinity are developed. (Emphasis added).[9]

1844: Continued Removal, Re-Locating Tribes Delayed; Chippewas of Mississippi and Lake Superior

In 1844, the Chippewas of Lake Superior challenged the inclusion of Isle Royale in their past Treaty. In order to avoid a possible war, the U.S. gave the Chippewas $400 worth of gunpowder and $100 worth of fresh beef.

> Whereas a difference of opinion has heretofore existed between the United States and a portion of the Chippewa Indians of the Mississippi and Lake Superior; in relation to the cession of Isle Royale, by the treaty concluded with them on the 4th day of October, 1842, at Lapointe; in the Territory of Wisconsin, be it therefore known, that the said Indians hereby declare themselves satisfied with the explanations now made by the commissioner of the United States, of the said Isle Royale having been included in the cession of that treaty, and by these presents they ratify and confirm the said cession. In consideration of which, and the regard which the President of the United States bears to his red children of the Chippewa nation, four hundred dollars worth of gunpowder and one hundred dollars worth of fresh beef shall be delivered to the said Indians, on their signing this compact.[10]

Repeating this refrain, Alex Ramsey, Governor of Michigan Territory, reported to Commissioner Lea the valuable mineral district present, but emphasized the fact that the Chippewa Treaty of 1842, required the Chippewas to *move from the ceded territory when the President of the United States so ordered*.

> The most important treaties to which the Chippewas have at any time been parties, are the treaties of 1837 and of 1842. In these, *they ceded to this government all their possessions in Michigan and Wisconsin, comprising the rich mineral district...* For these cessions, the United States agreed to pay them in money, goods, &c., the sum of $1,865,000... (Emphasis added).[11]

1846: President Polk, Removal of Chippewa Indians from Mineral Lands on Lake Superior

In a move typical of Indian lands abounding in agricultural lands and minerals, the Chippewa Indians' removal from the mineral lands on Lake Superior would be ordered by President Polk. Michigan Territory Governor Ramsey's plea to open these lands had not gone unheeded. Territorial governors coveted the grant of statehood which rose them in political standing to governor of a state, putting them in an enviable position for a U.S. Senate seat. Statehood required a population of 60,000.

> Removal of the Chippewa Indians from the mineral lands on Lake Superior. James K. Polk. June 24, 1846.

> The Lake Superior country is capable of sustaining a dense population. ... It abounds in fine streams and water privileges, and the character of the timber is that of the western part of the State of New York, with the exception of hickory and chestnut. The soil is excellent for the growing of wheat, and Indian corn comes to maturity, and it is a remarkably fine grazing country. Farmers would find a ready sale for all the produce they could raise, and at high prices; and they could raise it with as much ease as in western New York. The fisheries bid fair to become, at some future time, a matter of very great commercial importance.
> Lead and bismuth have been found ... and also *many valuable veins of copper ore; and there can be little doubt, from the character of the discoveries already made, that large portions of that country are quite valuable for their mineral*

~ 570 ~

properties. Upon the banks of the St. Croix, Black, and Chippewa rivers, and between the Mississippi and Kickapoo rivers, quite rich veins of copper ore have been discovered and opened during the last year. (Emphasis added).[12]

1846: Commandeering Valuable Chippewa Land and Resources

In 1846, Commissioner Medill announced a plan to commandeer the remaining land of the Chippewas of the Mississippi and Lake Superior of agricultural and mineral value.

> The Chippewas of the Mississippi and Lake Superior still own a considerable extent of country east of that river and in the vicinity of that lake. A portion is said to be so well adapted to agricultural purposes, and *a part so rich in minerals and ores, that it will probably at an early day attract a considerable white population.*
>
> While they remain in their present situation, but little if anything can be done to give them the benefit of the benevolent policy of the government for the improvement of the Indian race. ... Such a change can be brought about only by concentrating them within fixed and reasonable limits, where they are given to understand that they are to reside permanently, and where they will reap the benefit of any arrangements they may make for their subsistence and comfort. The purchase of the lands of the Chippewas east, and their removal to those owned by them west of the Upper Mississippi, which are believed to be ample for their accommodation, and suited to their condition and wants, would be the first and necessary step towards bringing about those desirable results among these people. (Emphasis added).[13]

Wealth Derived from Ancillary Businesses

The Michigan Copper Rush enabled enterprising entrepreneurs to sell goods, to speculate in real estate and open banks. The rapid growth and consequent demand led to individuals amassing fortunes. During the rush, logging, farming, developing waterways and transport enabled the Great Lakes region to grow.

~ 571 ~

1875: Copper Extracted

During the second half of the 1800s, the region including Isle Royale and Michigan's Keweenaw Peninsula produced more than half of the world's copper. The largest and most productive 19th-century mine on Isle Royale, the Minong Mining Company, extracted more than half a million pounds of copper in the nine years between 1874 and 1883. (Emphasis added).[14]

In fact, in 1875, the Minong Mining Company triumphantly announced - "In the opening of our principal mines we have followed in the path of our ancient predecessors, but with much better means of penetrating the earth to great depths."[15]

With these actions by (1) the President; (2) the Department of the Interior, the Indians' trustee; (3) mining and other businesses; and (4) white settlers, the Indians of Michigan were stripped of their valuable mineral lands.

Notes: Michigan

1. Options For National Park Service Involvement In The Management Of Historic Copper Mining Resources On Michigan's Keweenaw Peninsula, National Park Service, 1988, p. 7. http://npshistory.com/publications/kewe/copper-mining-mgt.pdf (accessed online November 18, 2021).
2. Copper mines many millennia old on Isle Royale designated as National Historic Landmarks. February 5, 2021. https://queticosuperior.org/blog/copper-mines-many-millennia-old-on-isle-royale-designated-as-national-historic-landmark/ (accessed online November 18, 2021).
3. Id.
4. Id.
5. "To Thomas Jefferson from Elijah Brush, 11 December 1805," Founders Online, National Archives. https://founders.archives.gov/documents/Jefferson/99-01-02-2799 (accessed online November 18, 2020).
6. Report of the Commissioner of Indian Affairs to the Secretary of the Interior, United States. Office of Indian Affairs. U.S. Government Printing Office, 1876, pp. VI-VIII.
7. Options For National Park Service Involvement In The Management Of Historic Copper Mining Resources On Michigan's Keweenaw Peninsula, National Park Service, March 1988. http://npshistory.com/publications/kewe/copper-mining-mgt.pdf (accessed online November 18, 2021).
8. United States Congressional Serial Set, Volume 413, U.S.

Government Printing Office, 1842-1843, p. 409. http://images.library.
wisc.edu/WI/EFacs/transactions/WT199101/reference/wi.wt199101.
i0022.pdf (accessed online November 18, 2021).

9. Report of the Commissioner of Indian Affairs to the Secretary of
the Interior, United States. Office of Indian Affairs. C. Alexander,
Printer, 1844, p. 5.

10. United States Congressional Serial Set, Volume 463, U.S.
Government Printing Office, 1844, p. 319.

11. Report of the Commissioner of Indian Affairs to the Secretary
of the Interior, United States. Office of Indian Affairs. Robert
Armstrong, Printer, 1852, p. 39.

12. Message from the President of the United States, communicating,
in compliance with a resolution of the Senate, information in relation
to the removal of the Chippewa Indians from the mineral lands of
Lake Superior. S. Doc. No. 403, 29th Cong., 1st Sess. (1846).

13. Copper mines many millennia old on Isle Royale designated as National
Historic Landmarks. February 5, 2021. https://queticosuperior.org/blog/
copper-mines-many-millennia-old-on-isle-royale-designated-as-national-
historic-landmark/ (accessed online November 18, 2021).

14. Id.

18: MINNESOTA

The Iron Triangle, **Chapter 7: Minnesota: Fraudulent Legislation Enabling Acquisition of Indian Land,** details the Department of the Interior's solution to the (1) colonial settlers' illegal encroachment on Indian lands; (2) the even more unlawful extermination of the Indians themselves; and (3) the President's refusal to engage the U.S. military to remove squatters and to punish the murder of any Indians. Instead, Indians were removed from their valuable agricultural and mineral lands, purportedly out of harm's way. Repeatedly, throughout the fulfillment of the U.S.' Manifest Destiny to build a continental empire, Indians would be forced off of their prime land and be relocated on 'government assigned lands.' If they did not willingly move, they would be placed under military control and the U.S. Army would forcibly evict them. The lands assigned lacked the resources necessary for them to thrive.

> In 1865, on the floor of the House, Minnesota's eloquent congressman, Ignatius Donnelly stated: "We... are a superior race sharing its noblest privileges with the humblest of mankind and lifting up to the condition of freedom and happiness those who from the dawn of time have been either barbarians or slaves ..."[1]

1866: Gold Mining NE Minn (Bois Forte Impacted)

Minnesota's first governor, Henry Sibley, latched on to gold mining as a get-rich-quick scheme. It began when the Minnesota State Geologist misidentified iron pyrite as gold in the northern part of the state. This mistake was a catastrophe for the Bois Forte Band whose reservation was located in the purported mining area. Gold mining companies quickly organized and incorporated in Minnesota. These speculative mining companies attracted capital from throughout the U.S. "One of the most secure, both financially and politically, was the Minnesota Gold Mining Company, headed by Henry Sibley, which rapidly sold $5,000,000 in shares."[2] An *armed* contingent of miners moved to Lake Vermillion in December of 1865. ... On April 7, 1866, the Bois Forte Band was forced to cede lands for Minnesota's fake 'Gold Rush.'[3]

Value of an Indian Scalp

Minnesota Paid Its Pioneers a Bounty for Every Redskin Killed

It is not generally known ... that the state treasury once paid out cash as bounties for Sioux Indian scalps ... State Treasurer Koerner yesterday, in looking over the 1863 report of State Treasurer Charles Schaff, discovered the following item among the disbursements of that year: J.C. Davis, Sioux scalp ... $25. This Item occurs in the list of disbursements, amounting in all to $7,870.06, under the head "Suppressing Indian War." The $25 paid to J.C. Davis for the Indian scalp in question, therefore, had its niche in the cause of suppressing, or spreading, the Sioux outbreak.[4]

Minnesota's "Knights of the Forest"

Minnesota had a violent organization similar to the Ku Klux Klan. The Knights of the Forest members took a solemn oath to do everything in their power to remove "all tribes of Indians from the State of Minnesota." They promised to be bound "together as brothers in common" so they could go forth "stronger and braver in the determination to banish forever from our beautiful State every Indian who now desecrates our soil." A candidate for membership in the Knights of the Forest took the following oath (quoted in part):

I __ do most solemnly promise, without any mental reservation whatever, to use every exertion and influence in my power to cause the removal of all tribes of Indians from the State of Minnesota.[5]

New initiates were welcomed because they had "chosen the only path which will give security and safety to the future and prevent the blow of the glittering knife and merciless tomahawk." An article in a local newspaper reported the following:

One noteworthy act of the Mankato Lodge, however, merits particular attention. This was the employment of a certain

~ 576 ~

number of men whose duty was to lie in ambush on the outskirts of the Winnebago Reservation, and shoot any Indian who might be observed outside the lines. It is not the province of this sketch to relate how many, if any, Indians were thus disposed of. It is sufficient to say that the designated parties went out on their scouting excursions, and in due time returned and reported. For obvious reasons their reports were not made a matter of record.[6]

The state of terror imposed on Winnebagoes to relinquish their lands is confirmed by the Department of the Interior:

The hostile feelings of the white people are so intense that I am necessitated to use extra efforts to keep the Indians upon their own lands, for the reason that *I have been notified by the whites that the Indians will be massacred if they go out of their own country;* and it is but a few days since *a Winnebago was killed* while crossing the Mississippi river for no other reason than that he was an Indian, and such is the state of public opinion that the murderer goes unpunished. (Emphasis added).[7]

Reign of Terror for Bowels of Earth

Minnesota's brutal terror tactics in persecuting Indians played a major role in the implementation of the "Final Solution" - the treaties with the Dahcotas evidence this abusive reign of unrestricted power:

The region of country acquired lies in the great heart of the North American continent, is larger than the island of Cuba, and computed to contain over thirty-five millions of acres. It is so diversified in natural advantages, that its productive powers may be considered almost inexhaustible. Probably no tract upon the surface of the globe is equally well watered. ... A large part is rich, arable land; portions are of unsurpassed fertility, and eminently adapted to the production in incalculable quantities of the cereal grains. The boundless plains present inexhaustible fields of pasturage, and the river bottoms are richer than the banks of the Nile. *In the bowels of the earth there is every indication of extensive mineral fields, which only await the energies of an American population to reveal hidden treasures of uncounted wealth.* (Emphasis added).[8]

Notes: Minnesota

1. Congressional Globe, 38th Congress., 2 sess., appendix,
61. Waltmann, Henry George, "The Interior Department, War
Department and Indian Policy, 1865-1887" (1962). Dissertations,
Theses, & Student Research, Department of History, p. 4.
2. Why Treaties Matter. 1866 Treaty with the Chippewa - Bois Forte Band,
Signed April 7, 1866 in Washington, D. C. https://treatiesmatter.org/treaties/
land/1866-ojibwe (accessed online August 14, 2022).
3. https://healingmnstories.wordpress.com/2020/04/07/this-day-in-history-
april-7-1866-bois-forte-band-forced-into-treaty-to-open-land-for-minnesotas-
gold-rush/ (accessed online August 14, 2022).
4. Minneapolis Times, Reprinted in Los Angeles Herald,
Volume 27, Number 24, 24 October 1897. https://cdnc.ucr.
edu/?a=d&d=LAH18971024.2.212&e=-------en--20--1--txt-txIN
(accessed online December 3, 2022).
5. Initiation, Grand Lodge of the Knights of the Forest. Old Main
Cornerstone. Collection. MSU Archives Collection 200. Mankato
State University Library, Mankato, Minn., 1869-1969.
6. Mankato Review, April 27, 1886; Mankato Daily Review, April
18, 1916. Coats, Catherine M., "Extermination or Removal": The
Knights of the Forest and Ethnic Cleansing in Early Minnesota"
(2017). Culminating Projects in History, p. 62. https://repository.
stcloudstate.edu/hist_etds/11 (accessed online April 21, 2022).
7. Report of the Commissioner of Indian Affairs to the Secretary of
the Interior, United States. Office of Indian Affairs. U.S. Government
Printing Office, 1863, p. 92.
8. Report of the Commissioner of Indian Affairs to the Secretary
of the Interior, United States. Office of Indian Affairs, Minnesota
Superintendency. U.S. Government Printing Office, 1851, p. 156.

19: WISCONSIN

The Iron Triangle, **Chapter 8: Wisconsin's Forced Indian Removal**, focuses on how the history of the Great Lakes Indians is intertwined since the Wisconsin Territory established in 1836 included all of the present-day states of Wisconsin, Minnesota, Iowa and parts of North and South Dakota. Many of the early Indian treaties crossed the boundaries of the current states.

Approximately 4,000 square miles of hilly, unglaciated terrain spanning Illinois, Iowa and Wisconsin made up the historic lead and zinc mining district of the Upper Mississippi River Valley. The Sioux, Sauk and Fox, Ojibwe (or Chippewa), Pottawatomie, Illini, Menominee, and Ho-chunk (or Winnebago) occupied the Upper Mississippi long before the arrival of European white settlers.

Numerous treaties were entered into with the various tribes in Wisconsin ceding large tracts of Indian lands to the U.S. The Ho-Chunk and the Pottawatomi were left without land at all, other than what they purchased. Others were left with a vastly diminished base and were confined to reservations. In a tragedy of vast dimension, the federal and state governments knowingly and deliberately dispossessed the Indians of "fertile tracts" and "mineral wealth" and "pineries," leaving them in a "destitute and starving condition."

Mining in Northern Wisconsin

Indians mined copper on the shores of Lake Superior in prehistoric times. Between 4,000 and 1,200 B.C., copper jewelry and implements from Wisconsin and Upper Michigan were part of a trade network that stretched from the Rocky Mountains to the Gulf Coast.[1]

In 1739 a French officer attempted the first systematic mining of copper in northern Wisconsin. After French officials left about 1760, subsequent English-speaking travelers such as Jonathan Carver and Henry Schoolcraft commented on the abundant mineral wealth of the region.[2]

Nevertheless, for several more decades northern Wisconsin remained largely untouched by white settlement, with only a few fur trading posts and lumber camps.

1827: Upper Mississippi Valley: Illinois, Wisconsin and Iowa

In his 1827 Report, Secretary of War Barbour confirmed the importance of purchasing the land encompassing the Upper Mississippi Valley Lead-Zinc area which included northwest Illinois, southwest Wisconsin, and northeast Iowa. The expected annual supply of lead was equal to 10,000,000 pounds. One critical use at the time was for the manufacturing of bullets.

> To obviate any ground of complaint, and to meet the wishes of our Western citizens, it is proposed to procure, by purchase, an enlargement of our boundaries in that quarter, so as to embrace the whole of the highly valuable lead mines, said to abound in that region, and for which an appropriation will be hereafter asked.[3]

1829: Lead Mining in Southwestern Wisconsin

Many of the first miners came to Wisconsin from Missouri, which had experienced a lead boom a few years earlier. They brought with them their expertise in mining lead. Communities sprang up quickly around the mines, as other industries and businesses were founded to serve the residents that mining attracted. *More than 4,000 miners worked in southwestern Wisconsin, producing 13 million pounds of lead a year.*[4] The cession of Chippewa lead lands in 1832 coincided with this strong demand.[5]

1832: City of Galena

Colonel Whittlesey described the lead deposits in Galena in 1832: "the supply appears to be inexhaustible," and he found conditions as follows:

> Arriving at Galena, we found the place crowded with people. The mineral riches of the Dubuque country were well known... Thousands of adventurers lined the eastern shore of the Mississippi, ready to seize upon the possession and pre-emption rights in the new territory the moment they became

perfect. *In this case as in many others, guards of soldiers were necessary to keep the whites from taking unlawful occupancy of Indian lands*. (Emphasis added).[6]

Eliminating Indians' Land Base

Mining and logging created an insatiable demand for land for white settlement. The Legislature of Wisconsin sent a Memorial to the President and Senate in 1838 supporting ratification of the Treaties entered into which would open the mineral and timber lands of the Winnebago, Sioux, and Chippewa Indians for white settlement:

> The land thus purchased of the Winnebagoes, from its geographical position, from the nature and quality of the soil, and *from the mineral wealth* which it is believed to contain, may be considered as a *most valuable acquisition* to the Territory of the United States: - And the country purchased of the Sioux and Chippewas, *embracing, as it does, all, or nearly all, the pineries on the head waters of the Mississippi*, is of great importance in affording supplies of pine lumber to the inhabitants residing on the borders of that river. (Emphasis added).[7]

> A very large number of people have, upon the faith of the treaties made, taken up their residence on the land purchased: they are engaged in cutting and rafting the pine lumber, and in the construction of mills; and difficulties of a very serious character between the white and red men upon our borders must immediately ensue, upon the rejection of the treaties by your honorable body. The combined forces of the Winnebagoes, Sioux, and Chippewas, assisted as they naturally would be by the Sacs and Foxes, would form a powerful alliance, and it would cost the General Government much blood and treasure to protect her citizens from the aggressions of an enemy so strong and so evil minded.[8]

1842: Confirmation by Army of Vast Quantity of Mineral Land

In a report to his superior officer, in 1842, Capt. William H. Bell, of the Ordnance Department of the Army, stated: "The amount of mineral land in Wisconsin is more than four times as great as is to be found in Iowa and Illinois combined."[9] This did not bode well for the Indians of Wisconsin. Northern settlement was shaped largely by and for the benefit of people outside Wisconsin, especially investors from Eastern cities who hoped to make a quick fortune through mining.

As it was more profitable to ship the ore east for refining, a canal at Sault Ste. Marie was needed to connect Lake Superior to the other lakes. It was opened in 1855 and led to markets in Chicago, Cleveland, or Pittsburgh where the ore was turned into iron and steel, developing a multi-state interdependence.[10]

Copper Mining in Northern Wisconsin

Writing in 1855, James Gregory declared, "Iron ore of unlimited extent and of great purity may be found at Lake Superior, in the Baraboo district, and at the Iron Ridge in Dodge and Washington counties." The investment opportunities for eastern capital were short-lived. The financial panic of 1857, the Civil War and the high grading of the ore left northern Wisconsin abandoned. (Emphasis added).[11]

1865: Post Civil War

After the Civil War, the discovery and mapping of high-grade Bessemer ore in the Gogebic Range of northern Wisconsin and Michigan in 1872 renewed interest in the region. Fortunes were made -- and lost -- overnight in northern Wisconsin during the 1880s. The investment that peaked in 1886 and 1887 was soon followed by a crash that eliminated most of the smaller companies.[12]

Resolution of Legislature of Wisconsin for Removing Wisconsin Indians

The decline in mining did not end the State's interest in ridding itself of its Indian population. As with many other states, Wisconsin's state legislature would endorse the removal of all Indians from the State to Indian Territory or any other western location.[13]

Notes: Wisconsin

1. Mining in Northern Wisconsin, Wisconsin Historical Society. https://www.wisconsinhistory.org/turningpoints/tp-029/ (accessed online October 24, 2022).
2. Id.
3. Documents from the War Department accompanying the

President's Message to Congress, Part II, 1827. http://images.library. wisc.edu/History/EFacs/CommRep/AnnRep2639/reference/history. annrep2639.i0003.pdf (accessed online November 18, 2021).

4. Economy and Environment, Wisconsin Historical Society. https:// wisconsinhistory.org/Records/Article/CS16466 (accessed online October 24, 2022).

5. Lead Mining in Southwestern Wisconsin, Wisconsin Historical Society. https://www.wisconsinhistory.org/turningpoints/tp-026/ (accessed online October 24, 2022).

6. Wisconsin: Its Story and Biography, 1848-1913, Volume 1; Ellis Baker Usher; Publ. 1914.

7. Journal of the Council, Volume 1, Part 2, Wisconsin. Legislative Assembly. Council, 1838, p. 248.

8. Ibid., p. 14.

9. History of Wisconsin. Wisconsin: Its Story and Biography, 1848-1913, Volume 1; Ellis Baker Usher; Publ. 1914. http:// genealogytrails.com/wis/history_wisconsinstory.html (accessed online October 24, 2022).

10. Mining in Northern Wisconsin, Wisconsin Historical Society. https:// www.wisconsinhistory.org/turningpoints/tp-029/ (accessed online October 24, 2022).

11. Current, Richard Nelson. The History of Wisconsin. State Historical Society of Wisconsin, 1976.

12. Mining in Northern Wisconsin, Wisconsin Historical Society. https:// www.wisconsinhistory.org/turningpoints/tp-029/ (accessed online October 24, 2022). The History of Wisconsin, vol. 3 and 4 (Madison: State Historical Society of Wisconsin); Kasparek, Jon, Bobbie Malone and Erica Schock. Wisconsin History Highlights: Delving into the Past (Madison: Wisconsin Historical Society Press, 2004); Wagner, Herbert "Wisconsin's Ancient Copper Miners," Wisconsin Outdoor Journal. http://www.atthecreation.com/ wis.anc/%20cu.mines.html) (accessed online September 5, 2022).

13. H.R. Misc. Doc. No. 155, 43d Cong., 1st Sess. (1874).

20: MONTANA

***The Iron Triangle*, Chapter 9: Montana: Big Business' Corrupt Political Clout**

The web of interlocking mining, lumber and railway companies' tremendous political and economic power in the U.S.' westward expansion is discussed in *The Iron Triangle*, **Chapter 9: Montana: Big Business' Corrupt Political Clout**, specifically, "the continuous failure of the U.S. to protect the sovereignty, lives, land and property of Indians." Congress and the executive branch repeatedly sacrificed its wards to the dominating control of colonial settlers and businesses, actively aligning against Indians. Their deceptive justifications, that removing Indians from their land was for their benefit or ceding valuable lands was in their interest, went unchecked.

1862: Gold Discovered

The discovery of gold in Montana in 1862 brought in the first rush of miners. The mining industry demanded support in the form of towns, railroads, logging, ranching, and farming.

Montana had three major strikes that produced large amounts of gold. In July 1862, Grasshopper Creek was discovered with the production of $5,000,000 in gold dust in its first year. Alder Creek's discovery led to $30,000,000 in production from 1863-1866 with $10,000,000 taken out in the first year. The Last Chance Gulch discovery produced $19,000,000 in gold.[1]

More gold was available but it would require the costly digging of shafts and tunnels into the hillsides. Quartz mining used large, expensive equipment in order to retrieve the buried gold. Large corporations, such as the Anaconda

Company owned by Marcus Daly, were the only ones with the resources to purchase the equipment needed to successfully mine ore from these deep veins. With new equipment to retrieve the ore came the ability to mine many different precious and base metals including gold, silver, copper, zinc, aluminum, iron, lead, tungsten, uranium, platinum, manganese, and cobalt.

Historians continued to state the usual refrain: The nomadic tribes didn't consider gold useful or valuable.[2]

Railroads

Railroads allowed the expansion of mining operations with the ability to transport ore and the heavy equipment for successful development. It also permitted the transport of settlers to the west, with the population needed for territorial and statehood status. The impact on Indian reservation lands is described in the Boom and Bust: The Industries That Settled Montana. Railroads Exhibit:

> As the planning began on massive railroad lines across the southern and northern parts of the territory, railroad companies realized that they would need control of more Indian lands. They pressured the government to negotiate reductions of Indian reservation land through new agreements. Through these corrupt dealings, in 1882, the Crow would lose 1.5 million acres to the Northern Pacific Railroad, while in 1887, northern tribes would sell 17 million acres of land—including the sacred Sweetgrass Hills region—to the Great Northern Railway for 1.5 million dollars that was never paid in full.[3]

1862 Homestead Act; 1877 Desert Land Act

The Homestead Act of 1862 alone wasn't sufficient for attracting farmers and cattle men. The 160 acres granted to U.S. citizens didn't provide enough of a land base for dry farming, given Montana's climatic conditions; nor did it provide an adequate base for cattle ranching. Congress passed several supplementary laws including the 1877 Desert Land Act, which allowed homesteaders to claim 640 acres of land if they irrigated within three years. By 1882, 370 desert claim filings were made in the Montana Territory covering 122,000 acres. Many cattle companies hired entrymen to file for desert land claims who had no intention to settle on the land. The false entrymen would then assign their acreage to these companies.[4]

As more and more gold miners and prospectors poured into Montana, more and more food was needed to feed them. These new hunters quickly depleted Montana's wild game populations and then turned to ranchers for their meat supply. With a new market for their cattle, ranchers liked Montana for its abundant open land for grazing as well as its high quality grass. The hardy Montana grasses dried standing up and strong winter winds blew snow away so the grass did not flatten, making it edible all winter. As hunters seeking furs decimated the bison herds, open-range ranching grew.

Indian Hostilities

As immigration to Montana increased in the 1860s, so did the hostility of the Indians, who specifically directed attacks on forts and steamboats along the Missouri River.[5]

1864: Montana Territory Created

On May 26, 1864, Congress created the Montana Territory. President Lincoln appointed Sidney Edgerton as the first Territorial Governor and ex-officio Superintendent of Indian Affairs. With regard to his Indian policy, Edgerton stated:

> "I trust that the Government will, at an early day, take steps for the extinguishment of the Indian title in this territory, in order that our lands may be brought into market."[6]

His statement evidences the conflict of interest he would have as Territorial Governor and ex officio Superintendent of Indian Affairs. His lack of attention to his duties as Superintendent of Indian Affairs was blatant, as reported by the Commissioners of Indian Affairs in 1865 and 1866 in their Annual Reports to the Secretary. Commissioner Dole singled out individuals by name, and he included Edgerton in his remarks describing Montana's conditions:

> No annual report from this superintendent has been received. The governor, and ex-officio superintendent, Ho. Sidney Edgerton, has been absent from the Territory a considerable portion of the time, and the general interests of the service have been in the hands of General Meagher, secretary and acting governor, who, at last accounts was about to leave the capital of the Territory to visit the Flathead agency.[7]

Edgerton simply neglected his role as ex-officio Superintendent of Indian

Affairs. He complained to Secretary of State Seward that:

> "...the duties devolved upon me by virtue of my office,
> as Superintendent of Indian Affairs, were not defined by
> any instructions from the Department, and the subordinate
> agencies were securing supplies from other channels than
> through me. The Indians within my Superintendency, with
> an unimportant exception, held the title to the mineral and
> agricultural portions of the Territory, which were settled;
> some of them were intensely hostile, and not a soldier was in
> the Territory, nor had any force been ordered there, so far as
> I could learn, to protect the rapidly increasing and important
> interest there existing."[8]

1864: Commissioner of Indian Affairs' Indian Policy

The 1864 Commissioner of Indian Affairs Report addressed all of the issues affecting Montana: the discovery of gold, the influx of miners and settlers and the impact of railroads on trade. It also raised the question of what Indian policy should be pursued:

> Important changes have taken place in this country during the
> last two years. *Extensive gold fields have been discovered,
> and millions of gold dust secured*; emigration has wended its
> way here by thousands, and at this present time a population
> of not less than thirty thousand are within the limits of this
> Territory. The trade of the country is extensive and rapidly
> increasing; over one thousand tons of freight has passed
> through this place the present season, and this is but a very
> small portion of what has been received in the Territory.
> (Emphasis added).[9]

> Hundreds of men are now in the mountains prospecting for
> the "precious metals" and new placers and leads are being
> discovered weekly; the pick and shovel are in constant and
> daily use; the valleys and streams are being occupied for
> agricultural purposes, and everything indicates activity, thrift,
> and prosperity. The future of the Territory is indeed hopeful.
> With these facts before us, the question naturally arises, what

policy shall be pursued towards the Indians. This subject demands the most serious attention of the department, and I hope will receive that consideration the coming year which its importance demands. Gad. E. Upson, Indian Agent.[10]

Upson's question of what Indian policy the Department of the Interior would follow was answered by diminishing Indian lands, the establishment of reservations, the reduction of Congressional appropriations, and the use of starvation as a tactic of war.

1865: Indian Policy: Protect White Settlers and White Miners Over Indian Interests

The Indian policy response would once more be to protect the settlers and miners' interests, given the complete lack of civilization attributed to the Indians. The mineral wealth and concomitant business growth surpassed any concern of the trust relation of the U.S. to the Indians.

BLACKFEET AGENCY, October 2, 1865.

The moral condition of the Indians in this country is truly lamentable. Not one spark of civilization appears to have dawned upon their ignorant minds, and their capacity for improvement, if they ever had any, seems to have risen and set in total darkness. They appear not to have been benefited one iota from their intercourse with the whites, but rather to have imitated their vices, instead of their virtues. War with each other, and disease, are fast taking them away to their "spirit home," and unless a change for the better appears soon to improve their moral condition, but a few years will elapse before all but a remnant of what they once were will have passed to their last "hunting lands," to return no more forever.

The rapid increase of population in this Territory, the new and rich placer and lode discoveries, the extensive and fast increasing business, the immense mineral wealth, and the rapid development of the country, demand the fostering and protecting arm of the government. … If this trade and this Territory receive from the general government the protection and encouragement their importance and geographical position demand, then but a few years will elapse before

another rich and powerful State, rivaling in mineral wealth
California itself, will be ushered into the great American
Union, adding another brilliant star to the constellation,
unsurpassed by any now set in that great temple of liberty.
(Emphasis added).[11]

Copper Kings

Butte's copper deposits became world famous as did the Copper Kings,
Marcus Daly and William Clark. These two men owned the largest copper
mining interests in Montana and waged war for control of the resources and
politics of the state. The massive copper deposits on "The Richest Hill on
Earth," supported the Anaconda smelter. Daly's railroad company, the "Butte,
Anaconda and Pacific Railway," hauled ore to the smelter.[12]

> The Anaconda Copper Company, called "the company" by
> the employees, was a huge political power. The company
> owned the mines, smelters, and many of the state newspapers,
> and bribed politicians. Men under the control of the company
> were said to wear the "copper collar."[13]

Daly organized affiliated corporations with numerous shareholders: Bitter
Root Development Company, Anaconda Mining Company, Anaconda Copper
Company, Anaconda Copper Mining Company and Mining Improvement
Company. In addition to mining copper and silver, these companies owned
timber lands, timber cutting privileges and rights, timber, logs, mills, water
rights, and water ditches, flumes, pipe lines, and rights of way.

U.S.' Failure to Fulfill Treaty Obligations Causes Indian Depredations

In reporting on Montana's Indians, the U.S.' failure to fulfill treaty obligations
was highlighted as the cause for Indian depredations

> Blackfeet, Bloods, and Piegans ... have been committing
> depredations during the past year, and may, at the present
> time, be considered as being in a state of semi-hostility to the
> government... owing in a great measure, to [the] failure on
> the part of the government to carry out the stipulations of [yet
> unratified] treaties.

> The Mountain Crows, under a treaty made with them in
> 1868 ... were, among other things, to be furnished with

subsistence for four years. No appropriation has been made by Congress to carry out this stipulation, and ... they are uneasy and dissatisfied, and may, at any time, break out into open hostilities. They number about two thousand souls, and live principally, by hunting.

The Flatheads, Kootenays, and Upper Pend d' Oreilles, numbering about fifteen hundred, are on a reservation in ... accordance with a treaty made with them in 1855. ... no fear need be entertained of their committing depredations upon the whites, unless it may be to steal when hungry and to prevent starvation. Many of these Indians are engaged in agriculture, but the limited assistance rendered them by the government prevents their accomplishing much in that pursuit. They have a small annuity, 84,000, which is expended for their benefit.[14]

1868: Bitter Root Valley - White Intruders on Flathead Tribal Lands

In 1868, the Flathead Tribe refused to move away from the Bitter Root Valley, demanded by the U.S. due to the invasion of hundreds of white families since the discovery of gold in the vicinity. The Montana Indian Agent reported it would become "the centre of an enterprising, industrious, and intelligent population."[15] Indian Commissioner N. G. Taylor ordered extinguishing the Indian title to lands in Montana and locating them upon suitable reservations.[16]

In 1871, the Secretary of Treasury, reported a minimum of $12,000,000 in bullion production from the Montana Territory. Again, the Indians didn't stand a chance of holding onto their lands.

Although the governor of the Territory, in a recent letter (February 17, 1871,) has given the bullion product as $12,000,000 ... The exact sum is more difficult to ascertain. The very high rate charged ... for the transportation of bullion, and the fact that most of the product is gold dust, lead to a heavy undervaluation of bullion by shippers (from 25 to 30 per cent,) and an extraordinary amount of transportation in private hands. The latter item is estimated by the express agents at half the product of the Territory ... What the experiences of the future may demonstrate no one can tell - "the miners light but seldom going beyond the end of his pick."[17]

Montana's Indian Wars (1865-1887)

Even though Montana's Indian Tribes were outnumbered by and lacked the armaments of the U.S. military forces, they fought against the invasion of their lands. The Indian Wars (1865-1887) discussed in *The Iron Triangle*, can be condensed into three groups: (1) the Blackfeet Wars of northwestern Montana; (2) the Nez Perce's 1,170-mile march from eastern Oregon to Canada; and (3) the U.S. Dakota War of 1862, the battles of which were led by Chiefs Sitting Bull, Crazy Horse, Dull Knife, and Two Moons against U.S. military officers George Custer, Nelson Miles, George Crook and Alfred Terry.

A chart on Indian Battles in Montana is in the last Chapter.

1869: Use of "Hard" Military Tactics

Lieutenant General Sheridan used the "hard" tactics of the Civil War against Indians:

> In taking the offensive, I have to select that season when I can catch the fiends; and if a village is attacked, and women and children killed, the responsibility is not with the soldier, but with the people whose crimes necessitate the attack. During the [Civil] war, did any one hesitate to attack a village or town occupied by the enemy because women or children were within its limits? Did we cease to throw shells into Vicksburg or Atlanta because women or children were there?[18]

1870: Piegan Massacre (aka Baker Massacre)

With more forays into Indian country in Montana by the military and white settlers, the Indians engaged in retaliatory strikes.

August 18, 1869: Department of the Interior Superintendent General Sully Reports Blackfeet in State of War

On August 18, 1869, Superintendent General Alfred Sully reported:

> "I fear we will have to consider the Blackfeet in a state of war. In addition to the late attack by these Indians on a train near Fort Benton; a large number of horses have been stolen within fifty miles of here and early this morning a ranch twenty-five miles from here was attacked and two men shot. The miners are very much exasperated."[19]

will end Indian troubles in Montana, and will do away with the necessity of sending additional troops there in the spring as contemplated. (Emphasis added).[26]

February 1, 1870: General Sully Reports Massacre of Women and Children

On February 1, 1870, General Sully reported to Colonel de Trobriand that it had been reported to him that there were only twenty or thirty warriors, the rest were women and children.[27]

February 10, 1870: Montana Resolutions Praise Military Victory

The attack was celebrated as a great military victory by the Army and by residents of Bozeman and Helena. The Bozeman Pick and Plow newspaper reported on February 10, 1870, on a mass meeting, which passed several resolutions: "That our thanks are due, and are hereby gratefully tendered, to Colonel Baker and his men, for their toilsome march in an inclement season to chastise our savage robber foes, and for the deserved though terrible punishment inflicted upon them.... That the Indian of poetry and romance is not the Indian of fact: The former is said to be noble, magnanimous, faithful and brave; the latter we know to be possessed of every attribute of beastly depravity and ferocity."[28]

Lieutenant William Pease, the Blackfeet Agent, reported more specifically that of 33 Indian men killed, only 15 were of fighting age, and the dead included 18 old men, 90 women and 55 children and babies. He accounted for only fifty-one Blackfeet survivors: eighteen women, nineteen small children and infants. Weakened by small pox, they were undefended, as the able-bodied men had gone out to hunt buffalo.[29]

February 23, March 9, 10, 1870: New York Times Reports Massacre

Secretary of the Board of Indian Commissioners Vincent Colyer sent Chairman Felix Brunot a summary of the destruction of Heavy Runner's village based on Pease's report, which the New York Times published. The letter was read in

Congress, and news of the atrocity spread across the nation.[30]

March 12, 1870: General Sherman Requests Detailed Report of Indians Killed

On March 12, 1870, with the massacre reported in The New York Times, General Sherman wrote to General Sheridan requesting a more complete report from Colonel Baker:

> I think Colonel Baker should have reported more exactly the number, sex, and kind of Indians killed; and in view of the severe strictures in Congress on this act as one of horrible cruelty to women and children, I wish you would require, by telegraph, Colonel Baker to report specifically on this point.[31]

March 18, 1870: Lieutenant General Sheridan Justifies Killings

On March 18, 1870, a clearly exasperated Sheridan wrote the following unsubstantiated justifications for the killings to General Sherman:

> Since 1862, at least eight hundred men, women, and children have been murdered within the limits of my present command, in most fiendish manner, the men usually scalped and mutilated, their--- cut oft and placed in their mouths; women ravished sometimes fifty and sixty times in succession, then killed and scalped, sticks stuck up their persons before and after death. I have myself conversed with one woman who, while some months gone in pregnancy, was ravished over thirty times successively by different Indians, becoming insensible two or three times during this fearful ordeal; and each time on recovering consciousness, mutely appealing for mercy, if not for herself, for her unborn child. Also another woman ravished with more fearful brutality, over forty times, and the last Indian sticking the point of his saber up the person of the woman. I could give the names of these women were it not for delicacy.[32]

March 24, 1870: Military Investigation – No Guilt

Sherman responded to the claims of a massacre by issuing a press release denying military guilt. Neither Baker nor his men faced a court martial or any other disciplinary actions.

"I prefer to believe," Sherman wrote, "that the majority of those killed at Mountain Chief's camp were warriors; that the firing ceased the moment resistance was at an end; that quarter was given to all that asked for it; and that a hundred women and children were allowed to go free ... rather than the absurd report that there were only thirteen warriors killed, and that the balance were women and children, more or less afflicted with small pox."[33]

Afterward, a brief storm of outraged protest occurred in Congress and the eastern press. However, Sherman deflected a public inquiry by silencing the protests of Superintendent General Alfred Sully, and Lieutenant Pease, the Indian Agent who had reported the damning body count.

March 27, 1870: Colonel Baker Files Second Report; Reports Vast Majority Killed Were Male Warriors

THE WESTERN UNION TELEGRAPH COMPANY, Chicago, Illinois, March 27, 1870. To General W. T. Sherman: I have the honor to transmit the following dispatch, just received from Colonel Baker: Fort Ellis, M. T., March 23, 1870. In answer to your telegram received on the 22d instant, I report that after having made every effort to get the judgment of the officers of the command, I am satisfied that the following numbers approximate as nearly to the exact truth as any estimate can possibly be made; that the number killed was one hundred and seventy-three. Of those there were one hundred and twenty able men, fifty-three women and children; that of captives, (afterward released,) there were of women and children one hundred and forty. I believe that every effort was made by officers and men to save the non-combatants, and that such women and children as were killed were killed accidentally. The reports published in the Eastern papers, purporting to come from General Alfred Sully, are, wholly and maliciously false ...[34]

The Helena Daily Herald wrote in support of Baker: "General Sheridan ordered men to hunt them down, just as we hunt down wolves. When caught in camp they were slaughtered, very much as we slaughter other wild beasts, when we get the chance."[35]

Indians to Stay Under Control of Department of the Interior

In 1870, the Department of the Interior controlled the Office of Indian Affairs, to the dissatisfaction of General Sherman, who sought its return to the War Department so that the army would have complete control over Indian affairs on and off the reservations. But after the massacre, President Grant's administration put reservations under the Interior Department. It is **alleged** that Congress' move was partly its way of "reclaiming the lucrative patronage powers lost to it."[36]

Itomot' ahpi Pikun'i: "Killed Off the Piegans"

In Montana, Piikuni descendants of Heavy Runner's band know the site on Big Bend on the Marias River where their families and friends perished as Itomot' ahpi Pikun'i: "Killed Off the Piegans."[37]

1870-1890: Montana's Unswaying Industrial Boom

Montana's non-Indian population grew from 20,595 people in 1870 to nearly 143,000 people by 1890. The boom and bust nature of Montana industries kept people on the move.

Starvation of Montana's Reservation Indians

General John Pope's admission of the starvation of reservation Indians severely impacted Montana Indians.[38] The Blackfeet Indians endured starvation in the Winters of 1881-1882 and 1883-1884. Men women and children died.[39] Speaking of the Blackfeet, Blood, and Piegan Indians in a report dated July 26, 1883, an Indian inspector documented this starvation: "There can be no doubt but many of the young children died from lack of food during last winter and spring." In reference to the same Indians, a Special Agent reported on August 21, 1883, the extensive numbers in need of food: "Last week 3,200 persons presented themselves as actually in need of subsistence ... I am fearful that unless additional supplies are furnished depredations must be expected to prevent starvation, and early action is necessary ..."[40]

Again, as to the Blackfeet:

> *Their supplies had been limited and many of them were gradually dying of starvation.* I visited a large number of their tents and cabins. All bore marks of suffering from lack of food, but *the little children seemed to have suffered most; they were so emaciated that it did not seem possible for them to live long, and many of them have since passed away.* To feed these Indians, I was reduced to such a strait that *I was compelled to issue over 2,000 pounds of bacon which had been condemned.* Indians stripped the bark from saplings to eat. The buffalo, on which these people formerly subsisted, is now extinct.[41]

In regard to the Crow Indians, the Indian Agent stated, without irrigation, no farming is possible:

> I had to feed a certain number of people for a period of fifty-two weeks and was allowed enough supplies to feed them but sixteen or seventeen weeks. ... *It is not pleasant to be importuned, day after day, by hordes of half-fed women and children for something more to eat, and not have it in your power to alleviate their suffering.* (Emphasis added).[42]

1884: Fort Belknap Reservation - Gold Discovered While Whites Illegally Prospecting

In 1884, Pike Landusky and Pete Zortman discovered gold while illegally prospecting on the Fort Belknap Reservation. To facilitate the mining of the gold, the federal government appointed a three-man commission, headed by George Bird Grinnell, which was tasked with negotiating with the Assiniboine and Gros Ventre for a tract of land overlying the gold deposits. *In 1895, the tribes, under duress, sold the land to the U.S. government for a paltry $360,000.* (Emphasis added).[43]

Notes: Montana

1. Boom and Bust: The Industries That Settled Montana, Mining: There's Gold in Them There Hills!, Introduction. https://dp.la/exhibitions/industries-settled-montana/mining (accessed online January 2, 2022).
2. The Bozeman Trail: A Rush to Montana's Gold Wyoming, PBS. https://

www.youtube.com/watch?v=_7YhMJutbQc (accessed online August 17, 2022).

3. Boom and Bust: The Industries That Settled Montana. Railroads. https://dp.la/exhibitions/industries-settled-montana/early-settlement/railroads (accessed online January 2, 2022).

4. Boom and Bust: The Industries That Settled Montana, Early Settlement, Homestead Acts. https://dp.la/exhibitions/industries-settled-montana/early-settlement/homestead-act (accessed online January 2, 2022).

5. Adams, Tammie, editor. 2021.The Road to Garnet's Gold: A brief history of Montana's Gold Rush featuring one of the last ghost towns. Bureau of Land Management, National Operations Center, Denver, Colorado. https://www.blm.gov/learn/blm-library/agency-publications/cultural-resource-series (accessed online January 2, 2022).

6. House Journal of the First Session of the Legislative Assembly of the Territory of Montana, 1864, p. 21. https://ia800300.us.archive.org/4/items/housejournaloffi1864mont/housejournaloffi1864mont.pdf (accessed online January 2, 2022); Governor Edgerton's First Message, Contributions to the Historical Society of Montana, Vol. III, 1900, p. 344.

7. Report of the Commissioner of Indian Affairs to the Secretary of the Interior, United States. Office of Indian Affairs, 1866, p. 40.

8. Secretary of the Interior Jason Harlan to Commissioner of Indian Affairs D.N. Cooley, April 4, 1866, Letters Received, Office of Indian Affairs, Montana Superintendency, Roll 488, Microcopy 234, RG 75, NA.

9. Report of the Commissioner of Indian Affairs to the Secretary of the Interior, United States. Office of Indian Affairs, Montana Superintendency. U.S. Government Printing Office, 1864, p. 295.

10. Ibid., p. 298.

11. Report of the Commissioner of Indian Affairs to the Secretary of the Interior, United States. Office of Indian Affairs. U.S. Government Printing Office, 1865. Appendix, p. 515.

12. Boom and Bust: The Industries That Settled Montana, The Treasure State. https://dp.la/exhibitions/industries-settled-montana/mining/treasure-state (accessed online January 2, 2022).

13. Boom and Bust: The Industries That Settled Montana. European Immigrants. https://dp.la/exhibitions/industries-settled-montana/industry-displaced-people/european-immigrants (accessed online April 13, 2022).

14. S. Misc. Doc. No. 136, 41st Cong., 2nd Sess. (1870), p. 10-12. 4-29-1870. Letter of the Secretary of the Interior to the Chairman of the Committee on Indian Affairs of the Senate communicating a statement of the Commissioner of Indian Affairs [Ely S. Parker] in relation to all the Indian tribes within the bounds of the United States.

15. Report of the Commissioner of Indian Affairs to the Secretary of the

Interior, United States. Office of Indian Affairs, Montana Superintendency.
U.S. Government Printing Office, 1868, p. 673.

16. Ibid., p. 223.

17. Statistics Of Mines And Mining In The States And Territories
West Of The Rocky Mountains: Being The 6th Annual Report Of U.S.
Commissioner Of Mining Statistics to Secretary of Treasury, 1871,
pp. 204, 220.

18. H.R. Exec. Doc. No. 269, 41st Congress, 2nd Sess. (1870), pp. 8-11.

19. Piegan Indians. Letter from the Secretary of War in answer to a resolution
of the House, of March 3, 1870, in relation to the late expedition against the
Piegan Indians, in the Territory of Montana. H.R. Exec. Doc. No. 269, 41st
Congress, 2nd Sess. (1870), p. 4.

20. Ibid., p. 57.

21. Ibid., p. 7.

22. Ibid., p. 8.

23. Henderson, Rodger C. "The Piikuni and the US Army's Piegan
Expedition." Montana; The Magazine of Western History 68.1
(2018): 48-96, pp. 49, 55.

24. Ibid., p. 56.

25. Ibid., p. 49.

26. Piegan Indians. Letter from the Secretary of War in answer to
a resolution of the House, of March 3, 1870, in relation to the late
expedition against the Piegan Indians, in the Territory of Montana.
H.R. Exec. Doc. No. 269, 41st Congress, 2nd Sess. (1870), p. 8.

27. Ibid., p.11.

28. Blackfeet remember Montana's greatest Indian massacre, Gail
Schontzler, January 25, 2012, Updated March 30, 2017, Bozeman
Daily Chronicle. https://www.bozemandailychronicle.com/news/
sunday/blackfeet-remember-montana-s-greatest-indian-massacre/
article_daca1094-4484-11e1-918e-001871e3ce6c.html (accessed
online March 29, 2023).

29. Henderson, Rodger C. "The Piikuni and the US Army's Piegan
Expedition." Montana; The Magazine of Western History 68.1 (2018): 48-96.
p. 60.

30. Henderson, Rodger C. "The Piikuni and the US Army's Piegan Expedition." Montana; The Magazine of Western History 68.1 (2018): 48-96. p. 62.

31. Piegan Indians. Letter from the Secretary of War in answer to a
resolution of the House, of March 3, 1870, in relation to the late expedition against the Piegan Indians, in the Territory of Montana. H.R.
Exec. Doc. No. 269, 41st Congress, 2nd Sess. (1870), p. 70.

32. Piegan Indians. Letter from the Secretary of War in answer to a
resolution of the House, of March 3, 1870, in relation to the late ex-

pedition against the Piegan Indians, in the Territory of Montana. H.R. Exec. Doc. No. 269, 41st Congress, 2nd Sess. (1870), p. 9.

33. Piegan Indians. Letter from the Secretary of War in answer to a resolution of the House, of March 3, 1870, in relation to the late expedition against the Piegan Indians, in the Territory of Montana. H.R. Exec. Doc. No. 269, 41st Congress, 2nd Sess. (1870), p.72.

34. Ibid., p. 73.

35.Blackfeet remember Montana's greatest Indian massacre, Gail Schontzler, January 25, 2012, Updated March 30, 2017, Bozeman Daily Chronicle. https://www.bozemandailychronicle.com/news/sunday/blackfeet-remember-montana-s-greatest-indian-massacre/article_daca1094-4484-11e1-918e-001871e3ce6c.html (accessed online March 29, 2023).

36. U.S. Cavalry Massacre of Piegan Blackfeet Indians on the Marias River in Montana. https://legallegacy.wordpress.com/2020/01/23/january-23-1870-u-s-cavalry-massacre-of-piegan-blackfeet-indians-on-the-marias-river-in-montana (accessed online March 29, 2023).

37. Henderson, Rodger C. "The Piikuni and the US Army's Piegan Expedition." Montana; The Magazine of Western History 68.1 (2018): 48-96. p. 49.

38. Address by General Pope before the Social Science Association, at Cincinnati, Ohio, May 24, 1878. Delivered by Request of the Association (Cincinnati: n.p., 1878).

39. Report of the Commissioner of Indian Affairs to the Secretary of the Interior, United States. Office of Indian Affairs. U.S. Government Printing Office, 1881, p. XV.

40. Report of the Commissioner of Indian Affairs to the Secretary of the Interior, United States. Office of Indian Affairs. U.S. Government Printing Office, 1883, p. LX.

41. Report of the Commissioner of Indian Affairs to the Secretary of the Interior, Vol. 2, United States. Office of Indian Affairs. U.S. Government Printing Office, 1884, p. 151.

42. Ibid., p. 115.

43. https://opi.mt.gov/Portals/182/Page%20Files/Indian%20Education/Indian%20Education%20101/Montana%20Indians%20Their%20History%20and%20Location.pdf (accessed online January 2, 2022).

21: WASHINGTON

***The Iron Triangle*, Chapter 11: Washington: Governor Stevens' Private Wars of Extermination**

What is so tragic about the history of Washington Indians is the skirmish after skirmish, battle after battle, war after war engaged in between the mobster Volunteers, the U.S. Army and Indian Nation after Indian Nation, when Governor Stevens, the Indians' trustee, could have engaged in legitimate diplomacy and avoided war. *The Iron Triangle, Chapter 11: Washington: Governor Stevens' Private Wars of Extermination* documents the numerous wars fought as Indians sought to hold onto their lands.

1848: Oregon Territory; 1853 - Washington Territory

The creation of the Washington Territory in 1853 triggered the treaty process.[1] General Pope's disclosure of the U.S.'s artifice in treaty making applied to many of the tribes, reducing their land-holdings, with Indians working as menial laborers in the white-owned hop fields.

> This **process [treaty-making] was repeated** at short intervals, the Indians becoming less numerous and more debased by every treaty, **until finally they were left with a small fragment of the possessions** they once occupied, and being no longer able to subsist themselves and **emasculated of their manhood, they became paupers and vagabonds** dependent upon the government for support. ...[2]

Federal Policy: Dispossess Indians of Land; Destroy Tribal Relations

The same federal policies would play out in Washington: removal, cession, concentration on reservations, allotment, sale of surplus lands, sale of allotments and sale of decedent estates. Under the paternalistic and deceitful guidance of Territorial Governor Stevens, tribes would be pressured to sign treaties. Knowing it to be false, Stevens, the Indians' trustee, would promise protection from the "bad white men" and punishment for their offenses. These hollow promises echoed in the Official Proceedings at the Walla Walla Valley Council:

> Governor Stevens said, " ... the Great Father has been for many years caring for his red children across the mountains; there (points at) many treaties have been made. Many councils have been held; the red man could be protected. The Great Father therefore desires to make arrangements so you can be protected from these bad white men, and so they can be punished for their misdeeds; and the Great Father expects you will treat his white children as he will make a law they shall treat you."[3]

On June 9, 1855, the Yakama, Umatilla, Cayuse, and Walla Walla tribes signed treaties which ceded more than six million acres in exchange for $200,000. Walla Walla Chief Peopeomoxmox carved out a separate reservation for the Walla Walla, Cayuse, and Umatilla. The Nez Perce were to be consolidated with these tribes but refused. Instead, they were permitted to remain in their territory, on the condition that they relinquish nearly 13 million acres to the U.S. government.

Governor Stevens' Breach of Promise

At the time the treaties were signed, Governor Stevens assured the Indians that white miners and settlers would not be allowed to trespass on tribal lands before the U.S. Senate ratified their treaties, which stipulated the tribes had two years to relocate to their new reservations. Governor Stevens didn't hesitate in breaching his promise. On June 23, 1855, The Oregon Weekly Times, proclaimed the opening of the ceded treaty lands for settlement:

> "By an express provision of the treaty, the country embraced in these cessions and not included in the reservation is open to settlement, excepting that the Indians are secured in possession of their buildings and implements till removal to the reservation."

The three treaties signed by Washington tribes, resulting in the Yakama, Nez Perce, and Umatilla reservations, were not ratified by Congress until 1859.

General John Pope's Admission that Congress Lacked Ability to Prevent White Intrusion on Indian Reservation Lands

General Pope's speech in 1878 fully confirmed that Congress agreed to many treaty terms that it was incapable of fulfilling just to get a treaty signed by a tribe; that a governor would do the same is not surprising.

> *The first demand by the Indians, as the principal condition of the treaty, is that the white man shall not intrude upon his reserved lands, nor destroy his game, nor interfere with his people.* This condition is the first and most important to the Indian. … *What means has the government to enforce compliance? … Look at the great numbers of adventurous people pressing forward, urged by curiosity, speculation, love of excitement, thirst for gold, or craving for land. … Who is to keep them from crossing imaginary lines of Indian country?* (Emphasis added).[4]

Even though many tribes knew they didn't stand a chance against the U.S. military and state militias, they still were willing to die because war was there only recourse against a federal government that didn't keep its word.

Law of Nations regarding Treaties

The acknowledgement of the sovereign status of Indian Nations is confirmed by the understanding under the Law of Nations regarding the status of the parties to treaties. Vattel states that treaties are made "between sovereigns who acknowledge no superior on earth."

§219. Treaties are sacred between nations.

> … Between bodies politic,—between sovereigns who acknowledge no superior on earth,—treaties are the only means of adjusting their various pretensions,—of establishing fixed rules of conduct,—of ascertaining what they are entitled to expect, and what they have to depend on.[5]

§221. He who violates his treaties, violates the law of nations.

> He who violates his treaties, violates at the same time the law of nations; for he disregards the faith of treaties,—that faith which the law of nations declares sacred; and, so far as

depends on him, he renders it vain and ineffectual. Doubly guilty, he does an injury to his ally, he does an injury to all nations, and inflicts a wound on the great society of mankind.[6]

Regardless of the alleged sanctity of treaties, those entered into with Indian Nations were treated as only so many words. Long before Commissioner Smith confirmed this in his 1876 Report to the Secretary, it had become part of the lexicon of the federal government.

> "There is a very general and growing opinion that observance of the strict letter of treaties with Indians is in many cases at variance both with their own best interests and with sound public policy. Public necessity must ultimately become supreme law…"[7]

1853–1854: Railroad Routes Predominate over Indian Rights

In 1853, the U.S. War Department dispatched five separate survey parties to map out the most economical and practical railroad routes. General Pope's speech in 1878 set out the real reason that the U.S. War Department and Governor Stevens wanted railroads to the Pacific Coast:

> **Every proposition to build railroads … and for the establishment of a territorial government, has but one object … the dispossession of the Indian and the occupation of his lands by white men. …"** (Emphasis added).[8]

Governor Stevens was determined to impose treaties on the Indian Nations of what is now Washington, Idaho, and Montana - to move Indians out of the way of the railroads and the white settlers that the railroads would bring in. This resolve surpassed any trust obligation to the Indians. If gold entered the picture, Stevens steadfastness was unstoppable. Railroads served not only for transport, but most importantly, as fortresses against Indian attacks across Indian lands.

Gold Discovery in Colville Leads to Yakima War

Capt. George McClelland, in exploring for a possible railroad route, discovered gold in 1853 in the Yakima River Valley. The record shows that as early as January 1855, Governor Stevens was notified of the discovery of *gold* on the Columbia and Pend d'Oreille Rivers.

The following account in the Weekly Oregonian of July 21, 1855, gives a public account:

Latest from the Colville Mines.

Gold!! *Gold*!! Since our last we have received additional confirmation of former reports from these newly discovered *gold* mines. So far as examinations have been made, these mines are the richest yet discovered on the Pacific coast. Their extent is unknown to any degree of certainty ...[9]

Local newspapers would report the entry of hundreds of miners into the area during the following summer. The familiar pattern of trespass on Indian lands, theft of horses and property and mistreatment, with no accountability, ensued. The U.S. failed to initiate any punitive or protective action on behalf of the Yakamas. When prospectors mobbed the area, Yakama warriors retaliated by killing miners in random incidents, Andrew J. Bolon, the Indian sub-agent, was sent to investigate. When he, too, was killed, troops were sent into the Yakama Valley, starting the Yakama War in October 1855.

General Pope's speech in 1878 confirmed the unremitted outrages Indians experienced at the hands of miners.

> *The Indian country is penetrated everywhere by the seekers for gold or for land; highways are made through it without his consent, and the game driven off or destroyed. No one will say, even if he can, what outrages are committed upon the Indian by irresponsible crowds of white men...* It is only what the Indian does to the white man which reaches the public. (Emphasis added).[10]

U.S. Army and Governor Stevens Condone Gold Mining on Indian Lands in Colville District

Trespassing on and gold mining on Colville Indian lands was expressly permitted in an Order by General Wool, Commander of the Department of the Pacific:

> No emigrants or other whites, except the Hudson Bay Company, or persons having ceded rights from the *Indians*, will be permitted to settle or remain in the Indian country, or on lands not ceded by treaty, confirmed by the Senate and approved by the President of the United States.

These orders are not however to apply to the Miners engaged in collecting gold at the Colville mines. (Emphasis added).[11]

Governor Stevens transmitted a copy of the above order to Secretary of the Interior McClelland on August 20, 1856. The Governor complained, not about allowing settlement at the Colville mines, but that settlement was not allowed on all lands, whether or not Indian title had been extinguished. Developing Colville gold would eclipse the protection of Indian rights.

1857: Gold Discovered East of Cascade Mountains

The Department of the Interior was aware of the "constant difficulties" due to the discovery of gold east of the Cascade Mountains. To contain the numerous and warlike tribes under the Oregon and Washington Superintendency, more Indian agents were requested.

> The region of country east of the Cascade mountains is daily becoming of more importance to the whites, by reason of the *discovery of gold* in its northern limits, and its being traversed by the great thoroughfares leading to the States. Our people are being continually brought in contact with its Indian occupants, which compose several numerous and warlike tribes. In order to maintain friendly relations with them, and prevent constant difficulties, it requires the presence of several reliable agents. (Emphasis added).[12]

The land laws which permitted the occupation and settlement of both Washington and Oregon Territories, regardless of the rights of the Indians, led to Indian lands being overrun by white settlers, who intended permanent ownership. If the Indian rights were not protected and supplies provided, the Department of the Interior forecast the *extermination [of the Indians] at the hands of the whites:*

> The present condition of things cannot last long, and some permanent policy must be speedily adopted by the government for the protection of the whites and subsistence of the Indians. As the lands of the latter are entirely occupied by the whites, their means of obtaining a living are greatly curtailed. *The wants of those "untutored wards of the government" should be supplied, and their rights protected, unless the government has determined that they should be doomed to extermination at the hands of the whites*. (Emphasis added).[13]

J. W. Nesmith, Superintendent of Indian Affairs, Oregon and Washington Territories asked for the authority to negotiate treaties.[14]

Puget Sound, M. T. Simmons – 1859: Gold

The discovery of gold continued to boom across the Washington Territory. Even with the Department of the Interior's knowledge, they took no preventive action. It was merely announced as a fait accompli, as also was the case with the Puget Sound.

> During last summer and autumn, this country was overrun with adventurers seeking for gold.[15]

1862: Washington Territory, Volunteer Militia Used to Protect White Settlers from Snake Indians

While Indian rights were ignored, William Pickering, Governor of Washington Territory would seek the protection of white settlers by volunteer militias. These militias were known for their extermination of Indians in their path, killing them at will.

By letter dated August 2, 1862, *William Pickering, Governor of Washington Territory, requested Lieutenant Colonel George S. Evans, Second Cavalry, California Volunteers, to provide military protection to all the vast mass of defenseless men, women, and children now on their overland routes to this Territory and Oregon, and thereby save them all from the savage and butchering attacks of the merciless and brutal Snake Indians and other murdering, thieving, and unfriendly tribes.* (Emphasis added).[16]

The reality was that the Snake Indians had been decimated by "war, starvation and pestilence." The Salem Oregon newspaper, The Guard, reported the following on the Snake Indians:

> [T]he tribe has diminished fearfully since 1861. In that year it was estimated by competent judges at 10,000 souls. Now, there are not more than 1,500 or at most 2,000 alive. War, starvation and pestilence have nearly annihilated them. They succumb to inevitable necessity and yield scornfully and proudly that which they cannot longer retain. Their race is run! Once powerful, self-reliant and brave, they owned, occupied and controlled the territory from the Sweetwater on the East, to the Cascade mountains of the West; from the Gila of the

South, to the Fraser river of British Columbia. These were
nomadic monarchs, whose title though often viewed with
jealous eye, was never contested. They reigned supreme.[17]

The same was true of the Chehalis, Cowlitz, and Chenooks Tribes.

These Indians present a melancholy picture of the wasting
influences of contact with the whites. ... *They were the
original possessors of the largest and one of the richest
tracts of agricultural lands lying west of the Cascades, over
the most valuable portion of which the public surveys have
been extended, and the principal settlements made, while as
yet the Indian title is unextinguished.* (Emphasis added).[18]

1862: Preeminence of Gold

On December 31, 1862, Governor Pickering used his influence to seek
Congress' aid in purchasing Indian lands along the Oregon Trail and enlisting
the U.S. Army's protection to protect emigrants seeking to capitalize on the
millions of dollars worth of gold:

*Taking into consideration the fact that full ten millions of
gold has been gathered from the tributaries of the Columbia
River during the past season; with upwards of twenty
millions of dollars worth being the result of the labors of
miners during the next year; and the certain prospects of
thirty millions the 2nd year and forty millions the third
year and fifty millions carried away every year from then
on, these gold fields will operate as a magnet of attraction
to encourage and entice many thousands of new emigrants
every year, from all parts of the Northern, and Middle States,
who will not only need, but will surely merit this protection
of their lives and property at the hands of the United States
Congress.* (Emphasis added).[19]

1896: Fraudulent Mineral Entries on Colville Reservation

The federal government would delay for a decade before seeking to protect
Indian lands from white settlers who filed fraudulent entries under the Mining
Act of 1872 for alleged mineral discoveries on land *valuable for agricultural
or town-site purposes*, located within the Colville Reservation, in anticipation
of the surplus Reservation lands being restored to the public domain.

On March 20, 1896, Acting Indian Agent Bubb reported many complaints from Indians that placer claims were being located on their farms, following Congressional legislation which authorized mineral locations and entries on the Colville reserve.

Placer claims were staked off on lands which were inclosed with fence and cultivated by Indians. In the language of one of these would-be settlers, this was done with the "intention of proving up and then laying-off a townsite." He frankly stated that "there is not enough gold to pay to work, and in many places hardly enough to swear by," and that although the lands he desired were inside of an Indian's inclosure he wished to make himself secure in his location for a business place as quickly as possible, in order "to get the start of all other placers." (Emphasis added).[20]

On July 7, 1896, Special Agent T. D. Rockwell, of the General Land Office, reported to the Commissioner of the Land Office that none of the lands on the northern portion of the reservation contain minerals in such quantities that they can be profitably mined, and that none of them can be classed as mineral lands. On August 5, 1896, the United States land office at Spokane, Wash , was instructed *not to accept any mineral entries on any agricultural or grazing land on the Colville reservation and to "exercise the greatest care to protect Indian occupants of lands in that reservation."* (Emphasis added).[21]

In 1905, this was again brought to the attention of the Secretary of the Interior.

1905 The rich soil of the valleys of the Colville Reservation along the rivers has tempted the cupidity of numerous persons who have made thousands of entries of quartz and placer mining claims on splendid fruit, wheat, and timber lands. In this process many Indians have been cheated, frightened, cajoled, or bought out of their rightful possessions, and it has been claimed by some eminently respectable people that such entries are justifiable on the ground that there is no other way in which the lands can be obtained within a reasonable time. (Emphasis added).[22]

In 1907, eleven years after the fraudulent entries, the Department of the

Interior requested the DOJ to institute suits against white settlers for mineral entries made on non-mineral lands within the Colville Reservation for the purpose of *securing title to lands valuable for agricultural or town-site purposes.* **It is uncertain how successful these suits were.**[23]

Notes: Washington

1. https://www.nps.gov/nepe/learn/historyculture/the-treaty-era.htm (accessed online January 18, 2022).
2. Address by General Pope before the Social Science Association, at Cincinnati, Ohio, May 24, 1878. Delivered by Request of the Association (Cincinnati: n.p., 1878). Excerpts From: Editor, Cozzens, Peter. "Eyewitnesses to the Indian Wars: 1865-1890: Vol. 5, The Army and the Indian." Apple Books.
3. Record of the official proceedings at the Council in the Walla Walla Valley, held jointly by Isaac I. Stevens Governor & Supt. W. T. and Joel Palmer Supt. Indian Affairs O.T. on the part of the United States with the Tribes of Indians named in the Treaties made at that Council June 9th and 11th 1855, National Archives of the United States of America, Washington, D. C.
4. Address by General Pope before the Social Science Association, at Cincinnati, Ohio, May 24, 1878. Delivered by Request of the Association (Cincinnati: n.p., 1878). Excerpts From: Editor, Cozzens, Peter. "Eyewitnesses to the Indian Wars: 1865-1890: Vol. 5, The Army and the Indian." Apple Books.
5. de Vattel, Emerich, *The Law of Nations or the Principles of Natural Law*, 1797, trans. Charles G. Fenwick (New York: Oceana Publications for the Carnegie Institute, 1964), § 219.
6. Ibid., §221.
7. Report of the Commissioner of Indian Affairs to the Secretary of the Interior, United States. Office of Indian Affairs. U.S. Government Printing Office, 1876, pp. VI-VIII.
8. Address by General Pope before the Social Science Association, at Cincinnati, Ohio, May 24, 1878. Delivered by Request of the Association (Cincinnati: n.p., 1878). Excerpts From: Editor, Cozzens, Peter. "Eyewitnesses to the Indian Wars: 1865-1890: Vol. 5, The Army and the Indian." Apple Books.
9. Oregon Historical Quarterly, Volume 18, 1917.
10. Address by General Pope before the Social Science Association, at Cincinnati, Ohio, May 24, 1878. Delivered by Request of the Association (Cincinnati: n.p., 1878). Excerpts From: Editor, Cozzens, Peter.

"Eyewitnesses to the Indian Wars: 1865-1890: Vol. 5, The Army and the Indian." Apple Books.

11. Trimble, William Joseph. The mining advance into the inland empire: a comparative study of the beginnings of the mining industry in Idaho and Montana, eastern Washington and Oregon, and the southern interior of British Columbia; and of institutions and laws based upon that industry. Vol. 3. No. 2. University of Wisconsin, 1914, p. 22. 34th Cong. 3rd Session, Vol.1, pt. 2, p. 169.

12. Report of the Commissioner of Indian Affairs to the Secretary of the Interior, United States. Office of Indian Affairs, Oregon and Washington Superintendency. U.S. Government Printing Office, 1857, pp. 319-320.

13. Ibid., pp. 218, 317.

14. Ibid., pp. 323-324.

15. Report of the Commissioner of Indian Affairs to the Secretary of the Interior, United States. Office of Indian Affairs, Oregon and Washington Superintendency. U.S. Government Printing Office, 1859, p. 393.

16. Civil War, 29 Series I Volume L-II Serial 106 - Pacific Part II, p. 29. http://ww12.civilwar.com/official-record/951-pacific-part-ii/252077-29-series-i-volume-l-ii-serial-106-pacific-part-ii.html (accessed online December 21, 2022).

17. *The Guard (Eugene, OR) – December 12, 1868.*

18. Report of the Commissioner of Indian Affairs to the Secretary of the Interior, United States. Office of Indian Affairs, Washington Superintendency. U.S. Government Printing Office, 1862, p. 392.

19. WASHINGTON NATIONAL GUARD PAMPHLET THE OFFICIAL HISTORY OF THE WASHINGTON NATIONAL GUARD VOLUME 3 WASHINGTON TERRITORIAL MILITIA IN THE CIVIL WAR HEADQUARTERS MILITARY DEPARTMENT STATE OF WASHINGTON OFFICE OF THE ADJUTANT GENERAL CAMP MURRAY, TACOMA 33, WASHINGTON, p. 37.

20. Report of the Commissioner of Indian Affairs to the Secretary of the Interior, United States. Office of Indian Affairs. U.S. Government Printing Office, 1896, p. 83.

21. Id.

22. Annual Reports of the Secretary of the Interior, Report of the Commissioner of Indian Affairs, Reports Concerning Indians in Washington, Report of Agent for Colville Agency, Office of Indian Affairs. U.S. Department of the Interior, United States. U.S. Government Printing Office, 1906, p. 371.

23. Annual Reports of the Secretary of the Interior, Report of the Commissioner of Indian Affairs, U.S. Department of the Interior, United States. U.S. Government Printing Office, 1907, p. 128.

22: OREGON

The Iron Triangle, **Chapter 10: Oregon: Governor Curry's Private Wars of Extermination**

The study of timber theft in Oregon in *The Iron Triangle*, **Chapter 10: Oregon: Governor Curry's Private Wars of Extermination**, discussed the settlement of non-Indians in Oregon and the resulting wars. By early 1856, it was obvious to the U.S. military that the warfare occurring in Oregon was due to the desire of white settlers to rid Oregon of Indians, and not the actual threat imposed by the Indians. As a result, lives were needlessly lost, Indians were deliberately exposed to cruel and barbarous suffering - exposure, starvation and death - while federal dollars were being expended on a private war.

> The United States government had made no serious preparations for dealing with the indigenous peoples of the West during the early stages of the migration. ***The mood of the country at the time was expressed by the policy of Manifest Destiny - the Indians had no right to these lands and stood in the way of the expansion of the American empire.*** (Emphasis added).[1]

Indian Wars

The Cayuse (1847–1855), Rogue River (1853–1856), Yakama (1855–1858) and Snake (1864–1868) Indian Wars would result in treaties of duress signed between the U.S. and the tribes. The Modoc (1872–1873), Nez Perce (1877) and Bannock (1878) Wars would result in Indians being imprisoned, with others scattered among different reservations, and still others escaping to Canada.

1848: Cayuse Indians Fight Invasion of Their Lands, Resulting in Forfeiture

In a July 6, 1848, Proclamation, the Superintendent of Indian Affairs, Oregon declared Cayuse Indian lands forfeited as a result of their fight against the invasion of their lands. The Proclamation read in part:

> In consideration of the barbarities and insufferable conduct of the Cayuse indians [sic] tribe as portrayed in the massacre of American families at Waiilatpu, and the subsequent cause of the hostilities against Americans generally, and with a view to inflict upon them a just and proper punishment, as well as to secure and protect our fellow citizens immigrating from the United States to this territory against a course of reckless aggression so long and so uniformly practiced upon them by the said Cayuse indians [sic] I, H.A.G. Lee, Superintendent of Indian Affairs [Oregon Provisional Government] hereby *declare the territory of said Cayuse indians [sic] forfeited by them, and justly subject to be held by American residents in Oregon*. (Emphasis added).[2]

1850: Gold Discovered

Gold was first discovered in southern Oregon in 1850 by prospectors from the state of Illinois. These early Oregon miners had chartered a boat to the mouth of the Klamath River, hiked over the mountains, and discovered gold.

1850: Donation Land Claim Act

To encourage settlement, Congress passed the Donation Land Claim Act of 1850 permitting *qualifying adult U.S. citizens 320 federal acres at no charge,* subject to the claimant residing on the property on or before December 1, 1850, and occupying it for four consecutive years, which could be counted retroactively. (Emphasis added).[3] The donated land in Oregon, in part, which was inhabited by Indians is described as follows by the Department of the Interior's Agent:

> Though this region, for its timber and agricultural productions, may justly be regarded as valuable, yet when its mineral wealth is taken into consideration ... The beach, through the whole extent of the district, is a deposit of the precious metals, and is already dotted with towns and villages of miners; and it has

been recently discovered that its mountains abound in placers equal in richness to those of California ... and thousands are now rushing to offer their devotions at this nearer shrine of mammon. J. L. Parrish, Indian Agent, Port Orford District.

The act known as the Oregon land bill, making donations to settlers, positively and without reference to the previous extinction of the Indian title, precluded us from getting reservations, except of ground entirely clear, or with a saving of claims heretofore made ...[4]

1851: Oregon Legislature, Extinguish Indian Title

Almost immediately, the Legislature of Oregon petitioned for the extinguishment of Indian title to the soil:

The first, and one of the most momentous interests of this Territory to which we wish to invite your attention, is the extinguishment of the Indian title to the soil, and their early removal from those portions of the Territory needed for settlement, and their location in some district of country where their wretched and unhappy condition may be ameliorated [5]

The Governor and Superintendent of Indian Affairs, Samuel Thurston, worked in concert to secure Congressional authority and funding to commence negotiations for the cession of Indian lands. This occurred without contest.[6]

Indian Agents were ordered and empowered to negotiate treaties which would dispossess Indians of their homelands. One example of this authority is set forth in the Special Instructions to Special Agent E. P. Drew from Superintendent Palmer, dated September 30, 1854:

The policy of the government in regard to the Indians in Oregon is to extinguish their title to the country and colonize them on suitable reserves.[7]

The Department of the Interior's broad brushed mandate to extinguish the Indian title was acted upon quickly.

1851: Rich Gulch Discovery

In 1851, two men, James Poole and James Clugage, were traveling through the area on their way south from the Willamette Valley to sell supplies to miners in California. They stopped to camp for the night along Jackson Creek, a tributary of the Rogue River, and, while watering their horses, noticed something shiny in the creek. The men had accidentally stumbled upon what would be one of the largest gold strikes in Oregon. Poole and Clugage immediately filed a claim on the land and named it "Rich Gulch."

> It is estimated that over the years more than 80,000 pounds of gold have been taken out of the streams and streambanks of the Rogue Valley.[8]

Under the Treaty of September 10, 1853, with the Rogue River Indians, they would be forced to cede a vast amount of their land for a mere Forty Thousand Dollars in Sixteen Equal Annual Installments - $2.50 Per Annum Per Person.

> The country which they ceded embraces nearly the whole of the valuable portion of the Rogue River valley, embracing a country *unsurpassed in the fertility of its soil and value of its gold mines*; and the compensation which those nine hundred and nine people now living receive for this valuable cession is forty thousand dollars, in sixteen equal annual instalments of two thousand five hundred dollars each, a fraction over two dollars and fifty cents per annum to the person, which is the entire means provided for their clothing and sustenance. (Emphasis added).[9]

> The discovery of gold in the Rogue river country has attracted, with many well disposed persons, some of the most unprincipled and ungovernable white men of all countries; to keep in check these men troops are indispensable.[10]

> From the frequent recurrence of similar atrocities against the Indians in southern and southwestern Oregon, the conviction is forced upon me that a premeditated and combined effort on the part of reckless and evil-disposed whites roaming through that country has been, and continues to be made, to plunge the government into another Indian war, and to carry out their favorite scheme of annihilating those Indians.[11]

> Port Orford District: Though this region, for its timber and

~ 618 ~

agricultural productions, may justly be regarded as valuable, yet when its mineral wealth is taken into consideration, its value in all other respects sinks into insignificance.[12]

Many, and perhaps most persons then in this valley, had been attracted hither in advance of the settlement to any considerable extent of the country by the rich gold discoveries made in the valley, actuated by the same laudable motive of gain as miners generally, without the intention of remaining in the country, and alike without a wish to sow the seeds of future discord between the natives and our own people, to the injury of those of their friends who might wish to reside permanently in the valley. Their minds were upon but the one object; they did not care about or think of Indians.[13]

Whites could move Indians off their land in Oregon and California, whenever and wherever they wanted. Indians in Oregon and California had no rights to land, whatsoever. It created the legitimized free-for-all stage for the execution of 'might makes right.'

1852: Attitude of White Settlers in Willamette Valley

The Oregon Statesman ranted at length about the reckless disregard of the Indian commissioners for the welfare of the white settlers in the Willamette Valley:

They made reservations of large tracts of country in the heart of our valley--in the very neighborhood of white settlements, and sometimes including and surrounding the claims of white settlers [....] those who had settled in the vicinity of the reservations, were compelled either to abandon their property or consent to live upon it with but the filthy Indians for neighbors and companions, and all white persons were forbidden to settle on them.[14]

1854: White Miners at Rogue River

Anson Dart: I am sorry to record here that serious difficulties have from time to time occurred in that portion of southern Oregon known as the Rogue's River country, between the miners engaged in digging gold and the Indians.[15]

1854: Inexhaustible Mineral and Agricultural Wealth on Indian Lands

The Indian Agent J. L. Parrish, for the Port Orford District, corroborated the immense value of the Indian lands, on the southern coast alone, to Joel Palmer, Superintendent, on July 10, 1854:

> What the value of this region may be to the government, or what it may yield to the world's wealth when tenanted and cultivated by enlightened industry, are questions which it may not be proper for me to introduce into this report. Its value to government may be inferred from what I have heretofore said of the *inexhaustible mineral wealth* of its mountain lands, and the adaptation of its plains and valleys to the agricultural pursuits of the white man. (Emphasis added).[16]

1855-1856: Rogue River War Culminates in "Oregon's Trail of Tears"

On October 15, 1855, Governor Curry enlisted two battalions of mounted volunteers from southern and middle Oregon, for the purpose of suppressing Indian hostilities.

E. M. Barnum, Adjutant General of Oregon, filed a damning report, on October 20, 1855, condemning the "war of extermination" waged by the Governor's volunteers:

> ... armed parties have taken the field in southern Oregon, with the *avowed purpose of waging a war of extermination against the Indians* in that section of the Territory, and have *slaughtered, without respect to age or sex, a friendly band of Indians upon their reservation*, in spite of the authority of the Indian agent and the commanding officers of the United States troops stationed there, and contrary to the peace of the Territory. (Emphasis added).[17]

After their defeat in June 1856, the Rogue River Indians were removed forcibly to the Grande Ronde Reservation. Their removal is known as "Oregon's Trail of Tears."

The Grande Ronde Reservation would include the Umpqua-Cow Creek Band, the Rogue River Indians, the Chasta, the Umpqua and Kalapuya, and the Molalla. A. G. Henry M.D., the Resident Physician at the Grand Ronde

Agency would report on January 2, 1857, of the Indians sick and dying:

> I found that very little preparation had been made for ... the large number of naked, diseased Indians. I found them sick & dying. *We find them most generally destitute of every [omission] necessary, often suffering extremely for want of sufficient covering, and in such cases we could not refrain from loaning them a blanket... [A] large number who apply for medicine are suffering mainly from mental depression.* (Emphasis added).[18]

1856: President Pierce: Remove Indian Obstacle

The brutal treatment of Indians by whites resulted in war across Oregon. Fully aware of the bloody war going on under his watch, President Pierce gave carte blanche authority to the state and federal governments to chastise the Indians, by whatever means necessary. As the highest government official to protect Indians, he chose to focus, instead, on the agricultural and mining riches on Indian lands. They were being dedicated wholesale to the white settlers, by the President.

> Extensive combinations among the hostile Indians of the Territories of Washington and Oregon at one time threatened the devastation of the newly formed settlements of that remote portion of the country. From recent information we are permitted to hope that the *energetic and successful operations conducted there will prevent such combinations in future and secure to those Territories an opportunity to make steady progress in the development of their agricultural and mineral resources.* (Emphasis added).[19]

1857: Oregon Indians Destitute

Oregon Indians had no alternatives to the plans presented in the treaties planned by the Interior Department. For a while, a number of the southern Oregon tribes resisted, but the white settlers had more men and firepower. Robert B. Metcalfe, Indian Agent, confirmed this when he wrote on July 1, 1857, to Superintendent J.W. Nesmith:

> They are all wretchedly poor, and destitute of all the necessaries and comforts of life, except what is supplied them by the government. At present they regard the white

man as their natural enemy, and recognize no other principle of government than that of force, the weaker yielding to the stronger in all instances; and as they regard the whites as superior in number and in the use of fire-arms, they have determined to submit to such regulations as we may think best for their future government and advancement in civilization.[20]

General Pope: Indians Emasculated, Reduced to Paupers & Vagabonds

The Oregon Indians, as did the rest of the Indians across the country, became destitute as part of the plan of the U.S. General Pope describes this accurately:

But a little while and the resistless movement of the white race began again to be felt upon the lands not ceded by the Indians. Of course, the Indian, after more or less resistance, again sold, mainly because he had not power to keep, and the same results followed. This process was repeated at short intervals, the Indians becoming less numerous and more debased by every treaty, *until finally they were left with a small fragment of the possessions they once occupied, and being no longer able to subsist themselves and emasculated of their manhood, they became paupers and vagabonds dependent upon the government for support.* (Emphasis added).[21]

1861: Gold Discovered in Northeastern Oregon

In the fall of 1861 gold was discovered in northeastern Oregon near what is now Baker in Baker County. According to Browne and Taylor, the output in 1865 may have been as high as $20 million.[24] Due to the great influx of miners, the cream of the placers was skimmed off within a few years, and production declined to less than a million dollars annually during 1882-1888. Lode mining developed rapidly in the 1890s.

1864–1868: Snake War - Indians Hunted like Wolves

The Snake Indians was the white settlers' term for Northern Paiute, Bannock and Western Shoshone bands who lived along the Snake River. Fighting took place in the states of Oregon, Nevada, California, and Idaho. The hostilities of the Snake Indians would result in General Alvord declaring a military response of "a good whipping."[22]

Subsequently, Indian Agent L. Applegate informed Superintendent Huntington of the Snake Indians' destitute condition, on August 28, 1868, and their removal to the Klamath Reservation.

> ... Wal-pah-pe Snake Indians ... have all come onto the reservation. ... *They have been reduced to great extremity, having been hunted like wolves until they have eaten their last horses. Not having had any ammunition for many months, they have been able to get but little game, and their fear of the troops has kept them confined to mountain fastnesses where it is impossible to dig roots or gather wocus. They say they have long had a desire to get onto the reservation, but fear of the troops prevented them. Beside their want of provisions they are almost entirely naked, and if possible should be supplied with some blankets and clothing before winter.* (Emphasis added).[23]

1866: Umatilla Indians Threatened with Violent Removal by White Settlers

Superintendent Huntington reported to Commissioner Cooley on October 26, 1866, the attempts by whites to take over the Umatilla Reservation due to its fertile land, timber, water resources and location. They were willing to encroach on the Umatilla's land, to locate on it, and to incite war.

> The superior quality of the land, and its location on a great thoroughfare convenient to the gold mines of Powder River, Boise Basin, Owyhee and other points, of course make it attractive to whites. *There are constant attempts to encroach upon it, constant attempts under various pretexts to locate upon it, and occasional attempts to exasperate the Indians into the commission of some overt act which will justify-- or at least palliate--retaliation and thus give an excuse for plunging the country into another Indian war, the end of which, they well know, would be the expulsion of the Indians from the coveted tract. This cupidity is the cause of constant trouble to the agent and apprehension to the Indians.* (Emphasis added).[24]

Umatilla Indian Reservation, Oregon, Indian Agent Wm. H. Barnhart reported threats of violent removal of the Umatillas by local citizens and the state legislature also requested that Congress remove them.

The reservation is completely surrounded by white settlements ... So anxious are the white people in the vicinity to possess this land, that *threats to remove the Indians by violence are not unfrequently heard*. ... At the last session of the legislature of Oregon, a memorial to Congress was passed asking the removal of these Indians ... (Emphasis added).[25]

Congress enacted legislation in the late 1800s, which continued reducing the size of the Umatilla Reservation. The legislation created land allotments for the individual tribal members at that time, then proclaimed the remaining acres as surplus and opened it up for settlement by non-Indians.[26]

1871: U.S. Secretary of Treasury Documented Gold Yield in NE Oregon

The U.S. Secretary of the Treasury documented the gold yield in 1871 justifying the need for a railroad which would result in the settlement of millions of acres.

Mining Statistics: We trust our Senators and Representatives may induce Congress to pass a bill for a railroad to connect [Baker and Union Counties to Central Pacific Railroad], and would, by giving means of transportation for our products, lead to the settlement of millions of acres of land valuable for farming and grazing purposes. ... *The gold yield should not be one million, but from three to five million dollars yearly from these two counties*, and from agricultural and grazing products a like sum. (Emphasis added).[27]

As the placer mines decline, persons forsake them for the more permanent pursuits of farming and stock-breeding, and in the end the country will undoubtedly be the gainer.[28]

White Settlers Demand Removal of Modoc Indians

The Oregon Trail cut right through the traditional lands of the Modoc Indians along what is now the California-Oregon border.[29] White settlers demanded that the Modocs be removed from their lands along Lost River to the Klamath Reservation which was done. The Klamath Indians were their hereditary enemy so consolidating the Modocs on the Klamath Reservation was a disaster.

As documented by a January 27, 1872, Letter from Superintendent Meachem to Commissioner Walker, the Department of the Interior failed to protect the Modocs who were forced onto the Reservation:

> *They were ill treated and abused by the Klamath Indians, and the sub-agent failing to protect them, they vacated. Peace has been disturbed and danger seems imminent,* and on a strong petition of the white settlers of the Modoc country I have made a requisition on the commander of the Dept. of the Columbia for assistance ...(Emphasis added).[30]

They returned to Lost River. General E.R.S. Canby in a letter to his superior, the Adjutant General, dated February 21, 1872, informed him that the Department of the Interior had given permission to the Modocs to remain at Lost River, pending a determination of a new location for them, other than the Klamath Reservation.[31]

1873: Peace Commission Doomed to Fail

A Peace Commission was appointed to mediate a peace. It was doomed from the start. In a February 10, 1873, Letter from Oregon Governor L. F. Grover to the commissioners, he vehemently refused to consider a Modoc reservation on the Lost River, claiming it was Oregon's land.[32]

Even though the commissioners were repeatedly warned that the Modocs planned an ambush, they proceeded with their plan to meet with them.[33] Capt. Jack's military control as leader of the Modocs would have been lost if he didn't carry through with his warning that he did not wish to meet with the Peace Commission. General Canby was fatally shot and *others were wounded.*

1873: Modocs to Be Punished

President Grant sanctioned the most severe punishment of the Modocs. The U.S. Army combined its forces against the *60 Modoc warriors. The total number of officers and soldiers was approximately 375.* (Emphasis added).[34] After the Modoc defeat, six of them were hung. *"The warriors' heads were cut off and shipped in alcohol to the Army Medical Museum for "scientific investigation."* (Emphasis added).[35] Twelve days after the hanging, 163 Modocs were taken in cattle cars, as prisoners of war, to the Quapaw Agency in Oklahoma.[36] Over one-half of the prisoners died.

1877: Nez Perce 'Thief' War

In the Treaty of 1855, the Nez Perce ceded 5.5 million acres of their 8-million-acre Reservation, reserving the right to off-reservation hunting, fishing, and gathering. The Senate ratified the Treaty, creating the Nez Perce Reservation. This Treaty was negotiated at the same time the Cayuse War was winding down and the Rogue River Wars were ongoing. Unfortunately, the government's promise to them of a permanent home didn't last long. Gold was discovered.

> Recent discoveries of gold have been made on the Nez Perce Reservation ... and a large emigration to that region of the country is anticipated ... in consequence of which serious apprehensions exist in regard to the ... invasion of the rights of the Nez Perce tribes guaranteed by the Treaty [of 1855]. It is recommended that further negotiations be entered into with the Nez Perce tribe, with a view to the purchase of that portion of their reservation containing the *auriferous deposits*, which is represented as rugged, barren, and mountainous, unfit for cultivation, and therefore *of little or no value for Indian purposes.* (Emphasis added).[37]

This amounted to 960,000 acres of land and an appropriation of $50,000 was made.

> In a talk with the Nez Perce on October 24, 1862, General Alvord stated the common refrain: "It is very sad to find that the discovery of gold and the consequent rush of miners to this country should have brought such a mass of the very worst white men in contact with you ..." I have come to see you in order to assure you that the Government desires to do all in its power to protect you. ... the best the Government can do for you is to provide, as it has, for the making of a new treaty, so as to compensate you as far as possible for the unauthorized occupation of the gold mines by our people. (Emphasis added).[38] In treaty negotiations in 1863 with Major General O. O. Howard, the Nez Perce were pressured into ceding 1,750,000 acres.[39]

> *After [General] Howard spoke, Nez Perce Chief Toohoolhoolzote became enraged and asked "What person pretends to divide the land, and put me on it?" General Howard had lost his patience, and replied to Toohoolhoolzote,*

"I am that man. … I stand here for the President, and there is no spirit good or bad that will hinder me." (Emphasis added).[40]

On May 16, 1877, the fragile peace broke. *For four months, ten different Army units fought against Chief Joseph's impressive band of around eight hundred Nez Perce Indians. During those four months, some of the toughest battles were fought by the troops under the command of Brigadier General Oliver Otis Howard.* (Emphasis added).[41]

With elements of the 7th and 2nd Cavalries, the 5th Mounted Infantry, and 30 to 40 Cheyenne and non-Indian scouts, Colonel Miles' command totaled 400 men. In the Bear Paw Mountains, the depleted band of 418 Nez Perce, three quarters of them women and children, surrendered after a final five-day battle that took the lives of Looking Glass and twenty-four others.

During the war, the Army failed to decisively defeat the Indians in any of the thirteen battles and engagements fought over a four-month period, along a 1,350-mile trek, prior to the Bear Paw Battle that resulted in the Nez Perce finally surrendering due to exhaustion. (Emphasis added).[42]

Chief Joseph and the remaining survivors were force marched and imprisoned at Fort Leavenworth and in the Indian Territory for *eight years*. When released, some went to Lapwai, but Chief Joseph and 150 others were sent to the Colville Reservation in Washington, not to Nez Perce, and certainly not to their home in the Wallowa Valley.

1878: Bannock War

General George Crook warned of the possibility of a Bannock war due to the starvation they were facing:

> "It cannot be expected that they will stay on reservations where there is no possible way to get food, and see their wives and children starve and die around them. We have taken their lands, deprived them of every means of living."

> With the Bannocks and Shoshones our Indian policy has resolved itself into a question of war-path or starvation, and being merely human, many of them will always choose the former alternative, where death shall at least be glorious.[43]

The war that resulted ended in internment for some at the Yakama Indian Reservation in southeastern Washington Territory. Others were scattered among different reservations.

1878: President Hayes: Lack of Food

In his 1878 State of the Union address, President Hayes pointed to the leading cause of the Bannock War: Congress' abject failure to appropriate monies enough even for their bare subsistence.[44]

President Hayes acknowledged the moral duty of the U.S. to the Indians. Unfortunately, he was in the minority. Those that followed would violate his trust.

> It may be impossible to raise them fully up to the level of the white population of the United States; but *we should not forget that they are the aborigines of the country, and called the soil their own on which our people have grown rich, powerful, and happy.* We owe it to them as a moral duty to help them in attaining at least that degree of civilization which they may be able to reach. It is not only our duty, it is also our interest to do so. (Emphasis added).[45]

1895: Second Bannock War

In 1895, several Bannock were arrested for elk hunting off-reservation at Jackson Hole which was allowed under their Treaty. They paid the fine and there was no conflict. The news media though reported, "Settlers Massacred: At Least Sixteen Families Butchered in Jackson Hole by the Red Devils." Troops responded unnecessarily. Wyoming's U.S. Attorney wrote, "The whole affair was, I believe, a premeditated and prearranged plan to kill some Indians ... and ultimately have the Indians shut out from Jackson's Hole."[46]

Litigation would follow regarding off-reservation hunting rights, continuing into the twenty-first century.

Stolen Opportunities

Given the Indians' sustained warfare and loss, miners staked claims, mined the gold and left the land depleted.

Notes: Oregon

1. Oregon/Mormon Pioneer National Historic Trails Management Plan United States. Bureau of Land Management, Publisher: The Bureau, 1986, p. 49.
2. O'Callaghan, Jerry A. The Disposition of the Public Domain in Oregon. U.S. Government Printing Office, 1960, p. 24.
3. Donation Land Claim Act of 1850, ch. 76, 9 Stat. 496 (1850).
4. Report of the Commissioner of Indian Affairs to the Secretary of the Interior, United States. Office of Indian Affairs, Printed for the Office of the Commissioner of Indian Affairs, 1850, pp. 207-208.
5. Memorial of the Legislature of Oregon, praying for the extinguishment of the Indian title and the removal of the Indians from certain portions of that territory; payment of the debt growing out of the recent Indian War, and the debt occasioned by the maintenance of the provisional government; establishment of military posts for the protection of emigrants; donations of land to citizens and emigrants … S. Misc. Doc. No. 5, 31st Cong., 2nd Sess. (1851).
6. Act of June 5, 1850, ch. 16, 9 Stat. 437.
7. Microcopy of Records of the Oregon Superintendency of Indian Affairs, Reel 11, Instructions and Reports 1854-1855, pages 179-181. A copy can be found on NARA Series M234, Letters Received by the Office of Indian Affairs, Reel 608 Oregon Superintendency 1853-1855, frames 713-715.
8. An introduction to the History of the Rogue Valley With a focus on the Ashland area North Mountain Park Nature Center A division of the Ashland Parks and Recreation Department Version 4: December 2012. https://www.ashland.or.us/Files/HistoryBackgroundBook-Web1-3-13.pdf (accessed online October 9, 2022).
9. Report of the Commissioner of Indian Affairs to the Secretary of the Interior, United States. Office of Indian Affairs, Oregon and Washington Superintendency. U.S. Government Printing Office, 1857, p. 321.
10. Report of the Commissioner of Indian Affairs to the Secretary of the Interior, United States. Office of Indian Affairs. Gideon & Co. Printers, 1851, p. 211.
11. Ibid., p. 267.
12. Ibid., p. 289.
13. Oregon Statesman, November 16, 1852: 4.

14. Report of the Secretary of the Interior, United States. Office of Indian Affairs. Robert Armstrong Printer, 1852, p. 447.

15. Report of the Commissioner of Indian Affairs to the Secretary of the Interior, United States. Office of Indian Affairs. A.O.P. Nicholson, Printer, 1855, p. 291.

16. War Department, 1855, p. 87. NARA Series M234, Letters Received by the Office of Indian Affairs, Reel 610 Oregon Superintendency 1857, frames 267-288.

17. http://www.let.rug.nl/usa/presidents/franklin-pierce/state-of-the-union-1856.php (accessed online April 27, 2022).

18. Report of the Commissioner of Indian Affairs to the Secretary of the Interior, United States. Office of Indian Affairs. U.S. Government Printing Office, 1857, p. 357.

19. "The Indian Question" John Pope. Address by General Pope before the Social Science Association, at Cincinnati, Ohio, May 24, 1878. Delivered by Request of the Association (Cincinnati: n.p., 1878).

20. Browne, John Ross, and James Wickes Taylor. Reports upon the mineral resources of the United States. U.S. Government Printing Office, 1867, p. 9.

21. THE OFFICIAL HISTORY OF THE WASHINGTON NATIONAL GUARD VOLUME 3 WASHINGTON TERRITORIAL MILITIA IN THE CIVIL WAR HEADQUARTERS MILITARY DEPARTMENT STATE OF WASHINGTON OFFICE OF THE ADJUTANT GENERAL CAMP MURRAY, TACOMA 33, WASHINGTON, p. 34. https://mil.wa.gov/asset/5ba41fe280330 (accessed online May 8, 2022).

22. NARA Series M2, Microcopy of Records of the Oregon Superintendency of Indian Affairs 1848-1873, Reel 25; Letters Received, 1868-1870, No. 111.

23. NARA Series M2, Microcopy of Records of the Oregon Superintendency of Indian Affairs 1848-1873, Reel 10; Letter Books I:10, pages 51-63.

24. Report of the Commissioner of Indian Affairs to the Secretary of the Interior, United States. Office of Indian Affairs. U.S. Government Printing Office, 1868, p. 83.

25. https://ctuir.org/about/brief-history-of-ctuir/ (accessed online April 27, 2022).

26. Statistics Of Mines And Mining In The States And Territories West Of The Rocky Mountains: Being The 6th Annual Report Of U.S. Commissioner Of Mining Statistics to Secretary of Treasury, 1871, p. 186.

27. Ibid., p. 193.

28. https://modocnation.com/history/ (accessed online December 21, 2022).

29. NARA Series M2, Microcopy of Records of the Oregon Superintendency of Indian Affairs 1848-1873, Reel 10; Letter Books I:10, page 657. Original on NARA Series M234 Letters Received by the Office of Indian Affairs 1824-81, Reel 617 Oregon Superintendency, 1872, frames 435-437. A copy is on NARA Series M234 Letters Received by the Office of Indian Affairs 1824-81, Reel 617 Oregon Superintendency, 1872, frames 709-710.

30. NARA Series M2, Microcopy of Records of the Oregon Superintendency of Indian Affairs 1848-1873, Reel 27; Unregistered Letters Received, 1870-73. A copy of the February 7 letter and many of the attachments are on NARA Series M234 Letters Received by the Office of Indian Affairs 1824-81, Reel 617 Oregon Superintendency, 1872, frames 688-741.

31. NARA Series M234 Letters Received by the Office of Indian Affairs 1824-81, Reel 617 Oregon Superintendency, 1872, frames 1105-1108.

32. Report of the Commissioner of Indian Affairs to the Secretary of the Interior, United States. Office of Indian Affairs. U.S. Government Printing Office, 1874, p. 77.

33. Thompson, Erwin N. Modoc War; Its Military History & Topography, Argus Books, 1971.

34. Fort Klamath, Post Medical History, p. 142, Record for October 1873.

35. Letter from Brigadier General Howard to 1st Lieutenant M. C. Wilkinson, dated November 3, 1873. NARA Series M234 Letters Received by the Office of Indian Affairs 1824-81, Reel 618 Oregon Superintendency, 1873, frames 1246-1251.

36. Letter from the Secretary of the Treasury, Transmitting Estimates of Additional Appropriations ... United States. Dept. of the Treasury. 1861, pp. 36-37.

37. Letter from Benjamin Alvord, Brigadier-General, U.S. Volunteers, to W.P. Dole, Commissioner of Indian Affairs, Washington DC (September 8, 1863) (on file with the U.S. National Archives).

38. Major General O. O. Howard, Famous Indian Chiefs I Have Known (New York: Century Co., 1908), 192-194.

39. Williams, Mathyn D. Indian Wars: Failings of the United States Army to Achieve Decisive Victory During the Nez Perce War of 1877. ARMY COMMAND AND GENERAL STAFF COLL FORT LEAVENWORTH KS, 2005, p. 94; L. V. McWhorter, Hear me my

Chiefs: Nez Perce History and Legend (Caldwell, Idaho: The Caxton Printers, Ltd., 1952), 166.

40. Ibid., p. 94.

41. Ibid., p. 90.

42. Ibid., p. 8.

43. George Crook, in J.F. Santee, "Egan of the Piutes," Washington Historical Quarterly 26, 1 (January, 1935), 18-19. Report of the Secretary of War, Executive Documents, Vol. II, 90.

44. https://www.infoplease.com/primary-sources/government/presidential-speeches/state-union-address-rutherford-b-hayes-december-2-1878 (accessed online May 8, 2022).

45. http://www.let.rug.nl/usa/presidents/rutherford-birchard-hayes/state-of-the-union-1878.php (accessed online April 28, 2022).

46. July 27, 1895, Cheyenne Daily Sun Leader.

23: NEW MEXICO

1850: New Mexico Established as Territory

James S. Calhoun was appointed to head the Santa Fe Indian Agency on April 7, 1849. When New Mexico became a Territory in 1850, he became territorial governor, an office which carried with it the Superintendency of Indian Affairs. As a Georgian politician, military officer, and bureaucrat in the U.S., he was part of the era of Indian removal.

It is not surprising that Governor Calhoun's advocacy for Indians would be in direct conflict with his role as the Indians' trustee. In his opinion, "The Comanches and Apaches, with all the adjacent fragments of other tribes must be penned up." As to the mineral resources in the State, he declared the Indians incapable of developing their resources with the implication that they should be opened to the "energy and enterprise" of white miners.

> The mineral resources of New Mexico are believed to be equal to those of any country; and yet the most daring and enterprising dare not venture so far abroad as to ascertain, with any degree of certainty, the mineral wealth of the territory. *It would be a blindness to well-established historical facts to suppose the native population of this territory, in its present demoralized and subdued condition, could develop its resources*; and unless American energy and enterprise are properly protected here, as elsewhere, it must ever remain a heavy charge upon the treasury of the United States. J.S. Calhoun, Indian Agent.[1]

To protect the people of the Rio Grande Valley from the alleged threat of the Mescalero and other Apache groups, Calhoun issued a Proclamation on March

18, 1851, authorizing the formation of voluntary militia to protect the white settlers' families by pursuing and attacking "hostile" Indians.

> To the People of Said Territory The present condition of the Territory of New Mexico, surrounded as it is by hostile tribes of Indians, whose almost daily incursions and depredations are the source of the greatest evils which afflict the country, has induced me to issue by virtue of my powers, as Commander-in-Chief of the Militia of the Territory, this proclamation.

> I recommend to all able-bodied male citizens of the Territory, capable of bearing arms, the formation of Volunteer Corps to protect their families, property and homes ... they are then authorized to pursue and attack any hostile tribe of Indians which may have entered the settlements for the purpose of plunder and depredation. 18th day of March, A. D. 1851. James S. Calhoun, Governor.[2]

1852: Territory Governor Calhoun Fears Indian Hostilities

Nearing death and fearing that Indians would take advantage of the political void left at the end of his tenure as governor, Governor Calhoun sought military assistance. As was the case in other territories, the fabrication of Indian hostilities was a ruse to foment war for personal gain. In an April 22, 1852, letter from Colonel E. V. Sumner to Major Gen. R. Jones, Adjutant General, Colonel Sumner confirmed this.

> I saw no appearance of disaffection as I passed through the country, and I think if there is anything in these rumors, it is confined to the lower classes, *instigated, perhaps, by a few desperate, unprincipled, gamblers and speculators, who have everything to gain and nothing to lose by fomenting commotions*. (Emphasis added).

In fact, the anarchy was due to the white settlers and their fear of a Mexican revolution.

> On my arrival in this town I was surprised to find it in a state of anarchy. All prisoners had been released for want of means

to subsist them and all law seemed to be set at naught. At the same time there was a constant dread of revolution, which kept up a feverish excitement, that was likely, every moment, to lead to some collision with the Mexicans. ...[3]

1862: Military's Objective - Subjugation of Mescalero Apaches

By 1862, the military's objective was the complete subjugation of the Mescalero Apache. General James Carleton ordered Colonel Kit Carson, on October 12, 1862, "to kill them wherever you can find them..."

> "*All Indian men of that tribe are to be killed whenever and wherever you can find them.* The women and children will not be harmed, but you will take them prisoners... If the Indians send in a flag and desire to treat for peace, say to the bearer that when the people of New Mexico were attacked by the Texans, the Mescaleros broke their treaty of peace, and murdered innocent people, and ran off their stock; that now our hands are untied, and you have been sent to punish them for their treachery and their crimes; that *you have no power to make peace*; *that you are there to kill them wherever you can find them;* that if they beg for peace, their chiefs and twenty of their principal men must come to Santa Fe to have a talk here; but tell them fairly and frankly that you will keep after their people and slay them until you receive orders to desist from these headquarters; that this making of treaties for them to break whenever they have an interest in breaking them will not be done any more; that that time has passed by; that *we have no faith in their promises*; that we believe if we kill some of their men in fair, open war, they will be apt to remember that it will be better for them to remain at peace than to be at war. I trust that this severity, in the long run, will be the most humane course that could be pursued toward these Indians." (Emphasis added).[4]

1863: Mescalero Apaches Imprisoned at Fort Sumner

By February 1863, General Carleton considered that the Mescalero were completely subdued. Over 350 Mescaleros were *imprisoned* at Fort Sumner or on the way there. About a hundred were known to have fled to Mexico.[5] The Mescalero Apache resented the Navajo and, in 1865, fled from Fort Sumner back to their homelands in the mountains of Sierra Blanca.

1863: Geological Surveys

With the Mescaleros interned at Fort Sumner, the Territory of New Mexico engaged its Surveyor General, John Anderson Clark, in 1863, to ascertain the locality, and extent of the various silver, gold, and copper mines then extant. This intelligence was to be communicated to Congress.[6]

In 1867, John Ross Browne and James Wickes Taylor were instructed to perform a mineral survey of the "vast resources of our new States and Territories" which would "add to the wealth of the whole country." The survey, ordered by Congress, including New Mexico, overseen by the U.S. Department of the Treasury, was to include the following:

> The geological formation of the great mineral belts and the general characteristics of the placer diggings and quartz ledges ...

> The different systems of mining in operation since 1848, showing the machinery used, the various processes of reducing the ores, the percentage of waste, and the net profits.

> The population engaged in mining, exclusively and in part; the capital and labor employed; the value of improvements; the number of mills and steam-engines in operation; the yield of the mines worked; the average of dividends and average of losses, in all the operations of mining.

> The proportion of agricultural and mineral land in each district; the quantity of wood land; facilities for obtaining fuel; number and extent of streams and water privileges.

> Salt beds, deposits of soda and borax, and all other valuable mineral deposits.

> The altitude, character of the climate, mode and cost of living; cost of all kinds of material; cost of labor, &c.

> The population of the various mining towns; the number of banks and banking institutions in them; the modes of assaying, molting, and refining bullion; the charges upon the same for transportation and insurance.

> Facilities in the way of communication; postal and telegraphic lines;

stage routes in operation; cost of travel; probable benefits likely to result from the construction of the Pacific railroad and its proposed branches.

The necessity for assay offices and public depositories; what financial facilities may tend to develop the country and enhance its products.

Copies of all local mining laws and customs now regulating the holding and working of claims.

The number of ledges opened and the number claimed, the character of the soil and its adaptation to the support of a large population.

The importance of the Report was evidenced by the ten thousand copies ordered for the Senate and the House of Representatives upon its completion. It recommended a permanent system of collecting mineral statistics, lacking in the U.S. The importance of the information for the "national welfare" was highlighted by the fact that gold and silver production from the Pacific Coast alone for the then present year exceeded the amount of gold and silver in the national treasury and in all the banks in all the States.[7]

Browne and Taylor, declared the following as to New Mexico:

The indispensable conditions to the development of the mines of New Mexico are, *first, Indian pacification*; second, railway communication with New Orleans, Vicksburg, Memphis, and St. Louis; third, a geological reconnaissance. (Emphasis added).[8]

Even though Browne and Taylor's conditions were not then met, gold placers in Dry Gulch, northeast of Nogal Peak, were located in 1865, and lode deposits were found at the site of the American Lode mine in 1868. *Mining did not begin, however, until this region was deliberately withdrawn from the Mescalero Indian Reservation in 1882*. (Emphasis added).[9]

1866: Volunteer Campaigns against Indians

Indian populations were declining up to 50%. According to the 1866 Commissioner's Report:

This decrease is accounted for, in a great measure, by the

incessant warfare carried on against the Indians. A practice, sanctioned by territorial law, has obtained, by which the whites are encouraged to make volunteer expeditions or campaigns against the Indians. Theoretically, those participating in these raids are rewarded with the plunder obtained, but should report at the territorial offices all the captives; while practically, in most cases; the captives are either sold, at an average of $75 to $400, or held in possession in practical slavery. This state of things of course keeps up a state of hostility among the Indians. The intervention of Congress is asked to put a stop to this practice.[10]

1866: Concentrating Indians on Reservations

If these volunteer militias weren't enough, the political forces were in play *within* the Office of Indian Affairs to dispossess the Mescalero Apaches of their mineral wealth. In concentrating Indians on reservations in New Mexico for agricultural purposes, the Office of Indian Affairs was adamant that military forces be posted nearby. Significantly, the reservations were not to be located in areas abounding in mineral wealth.

> A military force should be posted at or near each reservation. ...
> *The reservations should not be selected near the mountains, which abound in mineral wealth and will attract the whites*.
> J.K. Graves, Special Agent Relative to Indian Affairs in New Mexico. (Emphasis added).[11]

1871: Scalping Apaches

Also in 1871, soldiers from Fort Bayard, New Mexico killed and scalped Apaches. That same year, U.S. soldiers led by Captain Kelly were "cleaning out that nest of Indians" and returning to town with, and publicly displaying (and even gifting) several scalps. A scalp bounty offered by the Mexican state of Chihuahua was advertised in an Arizona newspaper in 1880. Another article mentions that several residents of Silver City killed and scalped four men and that one scalp was displayed on the wall of the Exchange Hotel there. A scalp bounty funded by citizens of Silver City, New Mexico, promised a reward of $100 in 1881. A group of miners and cattlemen in Sierra County, New Mexico, offered a bounty of $50 for scalps in 1885.[12]

Indian Battles in New Mexico

A number of battles occurred in New Mexico as Indians sought to protect their lands from invasion. In September 1867, a Mescalero Apache raid resulted in the capture of 150 head of stock near Mora. Soldiers from the Third Cavalry, under the command of Capt. Francis H. Wilson, immediately rode out of Fort Union in pursuit. On October 18, they caught up with the raiders in western Texas. After a three-hour battle in Dog Canyon, the Third Cavalry destroyed a winter camp of 400 Mescaleros and drove the warriors into the mountains.[13]

In another instance, on December 31-January 1, 1875, Mescaleros were attacked by a party of white settlers resulting in the murder of three Indians, the loss of their property, and, subsequently, the abandonment of their reservation. The attack occurred within the hearing and reach of the military stationed at Fort Stanton, who rendered no relief, with the excuse that they thought the Indians were fighting amongst themselves. The Mescaleros retaliated and a further attack on the part of *citizens and outlaws* ensued. The Mescaleros fled to the mountains. Here they were attacked by the military who confiscated and destroyed their clothing, and fifty-five horses which were captured and sold. Three mules remained in the possession of the quartermaster. The Indians thereafter were induced to return to the reservation.

Hon. John McNulta, a late member of the Indian Committee of the House of Representatives, was appointed on March 11, 1875, by the Secretary of the Interior, to investigate the attack by the American citizens. The Indians were exonerated of any fault. As usual, no action was taken against the unknown white perpetrators. It would just be another report gathering dust on the shelves of the Department of the Interior.

While investigating the unwarranted Fort Stanton attack, McNulta uncovered extensive fraud in the Mescalero Agency. Suppliers expected the Agent to let them make money by under-delivering on contracts and boosting the average weight of cattle. In testimony, one supplier is alleged to have told the Agent "the Department at Washington expects us to make money and it is expected that the agent will aid us and we all make money including the agent." Agent Crothers was threatened with removal and appointment of a man "who would work-in harmony with the Indian Department and the contractors."[14]

> In a joint affidavit Roman, Caballero, Jose de la Paz, Antonio, Quintana, Jose Dios, Francisco, Juan del Navajo, and Cochito swore that an agency contractor, A.W. Sharpe, had planned to kill Crothers, and had also tried to induce the Mescaleros to

murder their agent. Moreover, Sharpe had urged the Indians to steal stock from ranchers in the vicinity. Sharpe told them he would take the horses to another section of the Territory, sell them, and give the Mescaleros their cut. The Apaches believed Crothers to be a good man and were satisfied with him as their agent. In his report McNulta entirely exonerated Crothers of any mismanagement or fraud. [15]

1877: Carve Up Mescalero Reservation to Exclude Discoveries of Silver

As part of the common pattern of defining reservation boundaries to exclude bountiful agricultural and grazing lands, McNulta recommended that the boundaries of the reserve be changed:

> The existing boundaries did a great injustice to the Indians and would impair their confidence in the government. *The lines as projected in the executive order of February 2, 1874, had left most of the White Mountains off the reservation, which was a violation of the word given the Mescaleros. The tablelands to the west of the reservation, which embraced good grazing lands, were also excluded, along with a large portion of excellent agricultural lands along the upper Ruidoso River. The Indian Bureau replied there was no need for haste.* (Emphasis added).[16]

Exclude Discoveries of Silver

A decade after J.K. Graves, Special Agent Relative to Indian Affairs in New Mexico, reported that reservations should be located away from mineral discoveries, silver was discovered on the western edge of the Mescalero Reservation. Given this oversight, a powerful array of political and business forces would align to carve this section out of the Reservation.

> On September 27, 1877, Henry M. Atkinson, Surveyor General of New Mexico, sent a petition to the Indian Bureau. Dated July 27, it requested that several townships on the western edge of the reservation be "restored to market." The seven signers of the petition, David M. Easton, James West, C. P. Frederick, Andrew Wilson, John Walters, Benito Montoya, and Wesley Fields had settled on parts of this land before it was embraced by the extension of the reservation westward. But in 1877 the government decided to take no action.[17]

Agent Russell, on August 11, 1879, had stated that the reserve was "well suited to wild, roving Indians," but useless for agricultural purposes. Less than 600 acres of reservation land were suitable for cultivation, and if all the Mescaleros were to farm at the same time there would scarcely be enough land. "Is not this statement of facts the strongest possible argument in favor of their removal to the Indian Territory?" he asked.[23]

On November 1, 1880, the Commissioner of Indian Affairs also recommended removal of the Mescaleros. He wanted the Indians placed on the Ojo Caliente Reservation west of the Rio Grande. If placed there it would be difficult for them to raid into Mexico and Texas without passing one of the several military posts in southwestern New Mexico. He recommended that a council be held to see if the Mescaleros would be willing to go to the Ojo Caliente Reserve.[24]

On September 1, 1881, the Commissioner outlined yet another plan for Mescalero removal. *Noting that citizens in New Mexico and Texas were clamoring for their removal and that Lincoln County was still "under the control of cutthroats and thieves," he suggested the Mescaleros be sent to the Jicarilla Reservation in northern New Mexico.* Moreover, three companies of Cavalry and one of Infantry were stationed at Fort Stanton. If the Mescaleros were removed, the government could abandon the post, resulting in a cost savings for the War Department. (Emphasis added).[25] As the Commissioner predicted, the idea of removal was dropped.

The Department of the Interior never considered the alternative of using the military to disperse the desperadoes. It was used as a ruse to gain control of valuable Indian mineral, agricultural and grazing lands.

1880: Mescaleros Accused of Supporting Victorio's Outbreak

During the early months of 1880, Agent Russell had to contend with Mescaleros leaving their Reservation to join with Victorio's band of warriors at Warm Springs. Victorio was the chief of the Chihenne band of the Chiricahua Apache. By April 1, an estimated 250 Mescaleros had left. Army officers were convinced that a majority of the Mescaleros were actively supporting and aiding Victorio. To reduce the threat, Major General John Pope employed the tactic being used against other Apaches: disarming and dismounting every Apache on the reservation and treating all Apaches off the reservation as hostile. Secretary Schurz concurred.

The military under General Philip Sheridan used the disarming and dismounting program. He recognized that by taking the horses and weapons he was stripping away the key tools that allowed hunting and raiding neighboring tribes or white settlers.

> With great secrecy, Negro troops of the Tenth Cavalry began marching from Texas to rendezvous at the agency. Colonel Edward Hatch, commanding the District of New Mexico, informed Russell that troops would arrive at the agency on April 12, but he did not mention the Indians would be disarmed and dismounted. Russell was to gather the Mescaleros and their stock at the agency on that day. All Apaches not at the agency would be considered hostile.[26]

Nautzilla, the chief of the Mescaleros, was led by false statements to bring in his people. They were confined at Fort Stanton in a corral, where the manure was 5 to 8 inches deep. Many became sick. Others escaped and fled to the mountains. Colonel Hatch claimed that this justified his indiscriminate slaughter of 14 Indians.[27]

General Pope considered that the sole cause of this outbreak was the determination of the Office of Indian Affairs to remove the Mescaleros from Warm Springs to San Carlos. He stated:

> *"Both Victorio and his band are resolved to die rather than go to the San Carlos Agency, and there is no doubt, it will be necessary to kill or capture the whole tribe before present military operations can be closed successfully.* The capture is not very probable, but *the killing (cruel as it will be) can, I suppose, be done in time*. I am trying to separate the Mescaleros from Victorio, and yet hope to do so, but there is not the slightest prospect that Victorio or his band will ever surrender under any circumstances." (Emphasis added).[28]

1880: Gold Discovered on Mescalero Reservation

If Victorio's hostilities weren't enough for Agent Russell to contend with, on July 14, 1880, S. W. Dorsey, the secretary of the Republican National

Committee, engaged in cattle raising and mining, informed Commissioner Smith that *gold had been discovered on the Mescalero Reservation, and he asked that a strip twelve miles wide, running north-south, be detached and restored to the public domain.* (Emphasis added).[29]

Though Agent Russell tried to remove the trespassers on the Mescalero Reservation with military assistance, they would "step quietly across the line, and wait until they [soldiers] leave, and then come back again." *Russell posted a notice that after August 28 anyone on the reservation would be treated as a trespasser.* Samuel A. Russell to Commissioner Trowbridge, August 31, 1880. *But no miners left.* (Emphasis added).[30]

Instead, the politically-connected Dorsey was supported in his request by the military.

> *Colonel Purington noted that gold, silver, copper, and cinnabar deposits indeed existed on the western slope of the White Mountains. The Mescalero Reservation was much too large as it existed, Purington declared, and a twelve mile section on the western boundary could easily be restored to the public domain.*

Further adding to the political clout of businessmen, on September 27, 1880, Henry M. Atkinson, *Surveyor General of New Mexico, again sent a petition to the Indian Bureau that several townships on the western edge of the reservation be "restored to market."* (Emphasis added).[31]

On December 14, 1880, Indian Agent Russell caved in to this proposal. It was *"impossible to keep miners away from where there is mineral."* (Emphasis added).[32]

Going a step further, on December 15, 1880, Surveyor General Atkinson pressured President Hayes by presenting a petition, signed by some 160 persons, demanding the abolishment of the Mescalero Reservation. If abolishment was impracticable, the petitioners asked for the restoration of the western edge of the reservation to the public domain.

The indefatigable march was on to dispossess the Mescalero Indians of the minerals on their Reservation.

1881: Nogal Mining District Petitions Military Support in Reducing Size of Mescalero Reservation

Yet again on February 1, 1881, the miners in the Nogal Mining District would petition the military for support in reducing the size of the reservation. They were afraid that Colonel George P. Buell, Fifteenth Infantry, commanding Fort Stanton, would receive orders to force the white miners off the reserve, and asked that he use his influence to get a reduction of the reservation. The petition was signed by some 114 persons … J. Sligh et al. to G. P. Buell, February 1, 1881. Buell favored the request, as did his powerful and influential superiors Brevet Major General John Pope and Lieutenant General Philip H. Sheridan.

On March 9, 1881, Agent Russell wrote to Commissioner Trowbridge that more miners were flocking to the Reservation. There was a "prevailing opinion throughout this country" that the Reservation would soon be thrown open to miners and settlers." Russell to Trowbridge, March 9, 1881.[33]

On May 28, 1881, Indian Agent *Russell reported the miners had commenced building a town on the reservation.* He feared to take any action "without special and specific instruction, lest I get myself into trouble." … Again, the Indian Bureau delayed action. (Emphasis added).[34]

On July 13, 1881, William H. H. Llewellyn, who had replaced Indian Agent Russell, reported that forty log houses, a blacksmith shop, and a supply store had been built in Nogal Cañon.[35]

On Sep. 1, 1881, Agent Llewellyn described the Reservation as follows:

> *The entire north half of the reservation, including Nogal and White Mountain Peaks, is alleged to be rich in gold and silver mines, while on the west line of the reservation, near the Mexican village of Tularosa good copper mines are said to exist.* (Emphasis added).[36]

1882: President Arthur's Executive Order to Redefine Mescalero Reservation Boundaries

Finally on May 19, 1882, President Arthur by executive order redefined the reservation boundaries to give the miners the land they demanded.[37]

Early in the present year a considerable change was made in the boundaries of the Mescalero Apache Reservation in New Mexico, by which a goodly portion thereof was restored to the public domain from the north and west, while a tract containing an area equal to about five townships was added thereto on the east. This change was made to *satisfy the wishes of the white population of the "Nogal Mining District,"* so called, and by so doing to allay the ill feeling against the Indians which it was not difficult to see was fast taking the place of previously acknowledged friendship for them. *It appears that upon the discovery of gold in the Nogal Mountains a large body of miners and prospectors were attracted there, and that in due time what is now known as the "Nogal Mining District" was organized. New veins were discovered, and many locations were made upon lands afterwards discovered to be within the reservation.* As was natural, when a knowledge of these facts reached the Indians a spirit of dissatisfaction was manifested, and *the miners, fearing that they might lose the results of their enterprise and labor, appealed to the government through the military. Upon a proper presentation of the facts by their agent, the Indians appeared to appreciate the situation, and finally became convinced that it would be to their interest to yield to the fair demands of the miners.* Accordingly they decided to interpose no objection to such reduction of the reservation on the north and west as in the judgment of the department might seem expedient, with the understanding, however, that a strip of country should be added to the reservation on the east, which would afford them additional grazing ground. The existence of certain claims within the reservation alleged to have been acquired prior to its establishment, and upon which the claimants resided has been a fruitful source of trouble. This was an additional reason for desiring a reduction of the reservation. By the reduction all but two have been placed outside the limits of the reservation, thereby disposing of a much-vexed question. (Emphasis added).[38]

This reconstruction met the approval of the Indians, and has afforded relief to the miners on the excluded parts of the reservation, and the addition of the strip on the east was not met with any opposition from the citizens of the country, it not embracing any mineral lands and there being no settlers thereon.[39]

1883: Lincoln County Exhibit

In an 1883 mineral survey, the following was reported regarding Lincoln County:

The White Mountains have been little explored but the specimens give evidence of great wealth in that part. *They are from claims that are on the ground recently thrown open by the changing of the lines of the Mescalero Reservation.* (Emphasis added).

Red Chief, eight foot vein; gangue spar; averages 50 ounces silver.

Flower Pot, four foot vein; copper glance; assays $37.00 silver, 20 per cent. copper.

Copperhead, 10 foot shaft only; a new discovery; three foot vein, grey copper; quartz and carbonate of copper; $17.00 silver, 27 per cent. copper.

Blue Stone, is an azurite; $150 to $200 ounces silver, three foot vein.

Minnie Lee, two feet wide; $59.00 silver and 50 per cent. lead.

Center Crickett, quartzite; $230 to $600 gold; width five and a half feet, depth of shaft 65 feet.

Santa Ana, six foot vein of quartz; $300 in silver; 12 foot shaft.

Neptune, decomposed quartz, vein six feet wide on surface; 10 pounds of the ore assayed $200 to the ton.

Mazeppa, lead carbonate; width of vein five feet; pay streak 14 inches; 169 ounces of silver.

Accident, four feet pay; ore carbonate and galena; 111 ounces silver.

Oreland, 100 feet deep; four and a half feet wide galena, quartzite; 64 ounces silver, 10 to 20 ounces gold.

Christmas, has two crevices eight feet apart, one three feet wide, 100 to 2,500 ounces silver; other crevice four feet wide, 50 to 500 ounces silver; lead carbonate and galena.

High Line Chief, gold quartz; $38 to $130.

White Oaks district was represented by some of the finest specimens of free gold there were in the exposition, taken from the Little Mac, Homestrike, Old Abe, Henry Clay, and others.

The gangue is a quartz trachyte carrying the gold in wires and also in flour form. The veins are from four feet up in width and a mill is all that is needed to take out enormous values at once. Recent discoveries of excellent bituminous and semi-bituminous coal from White Oaks, were displayed. The veins from which they were taken being five feet in thickness. Iron from 40 foot vein within five miles of the coal beds was also shown.[40]

The Texas Pacific railroad and the Atchison, Topeka and Santa Fe railroad were reaching out their line of road to avail itself of the rich coal deposits. In addition to the coal the mountains are heavily timbered with pine, spruce, pinon and cedar, and an abundance of lumber for building and other purposes can be readily obtained.[41]

1900: Proposal to Open Mescalero Reservation for White Settlement

In 1897, Agent Captain V.E. Stottler recommended allotment whereby boundaries of each family's possession would be set so as to give them assurance of permanency. Based on his recommendation, in 1900, the House of Representatives instructed the Department of Interior to allot the reservation upon receipt of a favorable inspector's report. **Superintendent and Special Disbursing Agent Walter Luttrell argued successfully for the Mescaleros against opening the Reservation.**

If the reserve should be thrown open it should be immediately embodied in a forest reservation, and the forest perpetually protected. The ruin of the forest not only means ruin to the agricultural land now occupied and cultivated by the Indians, but to thousands of acres occupied and cultivated by white settlers outside of the reservation. ... The water supply and the farming lands of the Indians and the Mescalero boarding school will be ruined. ... *The Mescalero Indians are bitterly opposed to the opening of the reserve.* They do not ask of the Government one cent of money for their support, but do ask the Government to protect their water supply, and to secure to them a permanency to their peaceable occupations. They do not want to have the same trouble over their water supply as other Indians in New Mexico and Arizona are having. (Emphasis added).[42]

Notes: New Mexico

A chart on Indian Battles in New Mexico is in the last Chapter.

1. Report of the Commissioner of Indian Affairs to the Secretary of the Interior, United States. Office of Indian Affairs, J.S. Calhoun, Indian Agent, 1850, p. 109.
2. THE OFFICIAL CORRESPONDENCE OF JAMES S. CALHOUN WHILE INDIAN AGENT AT SANTA FE AND SUPERINTENDENT OF INDIAN AFFAIRS IN NEW MEXICO COLLECTED MAINLY FROM THE FILES OF THE INDIAN OFFICE AND EDITED, UNDER ITS DIRECTION, BY ANNIE HELOISE ABEL, WASHINGTON, GOVERNMENT PRINTING OFFICE, 1915, pp. 300-301.
3. Twitchell, Ralph Emerson. The Leading Facts of New Mexican History. Vol. 4. Torch Press, 1917, p. 219.
4. Opler, Morris Edward and Catherin H. Opler. "Mescalero Apache History in the Southwest." New Mexico Historical Review 25, p. 13 (1950). https://digitalrepository.unm.edu/nmhr/vol25/iss1/2 (accessed online December 7, 2022).
5. Opler, Morris Edward and Catherin H. Opler. "Mescalero Apache History in the Southwest." New Mexico Historical Review 25, 21-22 (1950). https://digitalrepository.unm.edu/nmhr/vol25/iss1/2 (accessed online December 7, 2022); Twitchell, Ralph Emerson. The Leading Facts of New Mexican History. Vol. 4. Torch Press, 1917, p. 484.
6. Annual Report of the Secretary of the Interior, United States. Office of Indian Affairs. U.S. Government Printing Office, 1863, p. 26.
7. Browne, John Ross, and James Wickes Taylor. *Reports upon the mineral resources of the United States*. U.S. Government Printing Office, 1867, pp. 4-5.
8. Ibid., pp. 4-5, 10.
9. Lincoln County New Mexico Gold Production, A. H. Koschmann and M. H. Bergendahl, United States Geological Survey, 1968. https://westernmininghistory.com/library/170/page1/ (accessed online December 28, 2021).
10. Report of the Commissioner of Indian Affairs to the Secretary of the Interior, United States. Office of Indian Affairs. U.S. Government Printing Office, 1866, pp. 135-136.
11. Ibid., p. 136.
12. https://www.bountyfilm.org/lesson-four/bounties-in-pennsylvania (accessed online March 7, 2023).
13. https://www.nps.gov/parkhistory/online_books/foun/adhi/adhi2.htm

(accessed online December 7, 2022).

14. Affidavit of W. D. Crothers, July 21, 1875. Mehren, Lawrence Lindsay. "A history of the Mescalero Apache Reservation, 1869-1881." 1969, p. 101.

15. Affidavit of Head Chief Roman, et al., July 16, 1875. Mehren, Lawrence Lindsay. "A history of the Mescalero Apache Reservation, 1869-1881." 1969, pp. 102-103.

16. McNulta to Smith, June 30, 1875, LRNMS, Roll 564; Mehren, Lawrence Lindsay. "A history of the Mescalero Apache Reservation, 1869-1881." 1969, pp. 104-105.

17. Mehren, Lawrence Lindsay. "A history of the Mescalero Apache Reservation, 1869-1881." 1969, pp. 223-224. Purington to Acting Assistant Adjutant General, District of New Mexico, July 19, 1877, Special Case 108, BIA; H. M. Atkinson to Hayt, September 28, 1877.

18. Mehren, Lawrence Lindsay. "A history of the Mescalero Apache Reservation, 1869-1881." 1969, p. 150.

19. Ibid., p. 150.

20. Ibid., p. 161.

21. Ibid., p. 185.

22. Ibid., p. 224.

23. Report of the Commissioner of Indian Affairs to the Secretary of the Interior, United States. Office of Indian Affairs. U.S. Government Printing Office, 1879, pp. 113-114.

24. Report of the Commissioner of Indian Affairs to the Secretary of the Interior, United States. Office of Indian Affairs. U.S. Government Printing Office, 1880, pp. 44-45.

25. Report of the Commissioner of Indian Affairs to the Secretary of the Interior, United States. Office of Indian Affairs. U.S. Government Printing Office, 1881, pp. 5-7.

26. Report of the Commissioner of Indian Affairs to the Secretary of the Interior, United States, Office of Indian Affairs. U.S. Government Printing Office, 1880, pp. 129-130; Report of the Secretary of War, 1880, U.S. Government Printing Office, 1881, p. 154.

27. Report of the Commissioner of Indian Affairs to the Secretary of the Interior, United States. Office of Indian Affairs. U.S. Government Printing Office, 1880, p. 130.

28. Worcester, Donald Emmet. *The Apaches: Eagles of the Southwest.* Vol. 149. University of Oklahoma Press, 1979; Opler, Morris Edward and Catherin H. Opler. "Mescalero Apache History in the Southwest." New Mexico Historical Review 25, 29 (1950). https://digitalrepository.unm.edu/nmhr/vol25/iss1/2 (accessed online December 7, 2022); Dunn, Jacob Piatt. Massacres of the Mountains: A History of the Indian Wars of the Far West.

Stackpole Books, 2002, p. 742.

29. Mehren, Lawrence Lindsay. "A history of the Mescalero Apache Reservation, 1869–1881." 1969, p. 223.

30. Ibid., pp. 225-226.

31. Ibid., pp. 223-224.

32. Samuel A. Russell to Commissioner Trowbridge, December 14, 1880. Mehren, Lawrence Lindsay. "A history of the Mescalero Apache Reservation, 1869–1881." 1969, p. 226.

33. Mehren, Lawrence Lindsay. "A history of the Mescalero Apache Reservation, 1869–1881." 1969, p. 227.

34. Russell to Hiram Price, May 28, 1881.

35. Mehren, Lawrence Lindsay. "A history of the Mescalero Apache Reservation, 1869–1881." 1969, p. 227.

36. Report of the Commissioner of Indian Affairs to the Secretary of the Interior, United States. Office of Indian Affairs. U.S. Government Printing Office, 1881, p. 135.

37. Mehren, Lawrence Lindsay. "A history of the Mescalero Apache Reservation, 1869–1881." 1969, FN 44, p. 227.

38. Report of the Commissioner of Indian Affairs to the Secretary of the Interior, United States. Office of Indian Affairs. U.S. Government Printing Office, 1882, p. lxvii.

39. Ibid., p. 123.

40. Ritch, William Gillet. Illustrated New Mexico. New Mexican Print & Publishing Company, 1883, pp. 135-136.

41. Ibid., p. 85.

42. Report of the Commissioner of Indian Affairs to the Secretary of the Interior, United States. Office of Indian Affairs. U.S. Government Printing Office, 1900, p. 288.

24: UTAH

Utah's Metals

Utah has a rich history in mining metals that has been integral to the development of the state since the 1860s. From these holdings came mining millionaires such as David Keith, Thomas Kearns, John Judge, and Susanna Emery Holmes (known as the Silver Queen).

The development of mining in the West drew Thomas Kearns in 1883 to Park City, Utah, where he worked, prospected, and developed with others the Silver King mine that made him a millionaire. He worked to secure regimental post status for Fort Douglas and for opening the Uintah Indian Reservation to settlement. Kearns and David Keith owned the Salt Lake Tribune and the evening Salt Lake Telegram.

The total historical value of metal mining in the state is valued at over $215 billion, placing Utah as the third largest metal-producing state in the U.S. The Bingham Canyon district alone has produced approximately 80 percent of Utah's total historical metal production value.

Copper is the most valuable mined commodity in the state, making Utah the second-highest copper-producing state, behind Arizona, in the U.S. More than 50 percent of copper supply is used for infrastructure applications such as electrical wiring, plumbing, electronic equipment, and more.

Through 1960 Utah produced about 17,765,000 ounces of gold and ranked sixth among the States in total gold production. However, the Bingham open-pit mine has continued to produce significant gold as a byproduct of copper production, and Utah has likely moved up at least a few spots on this list.[1]

1858: Gold Discovery

It wasn't until 1858 that a gold discovery was reported. Westbound travelers on their way to California found gold in Tooele County. Indians initially drove away prospectors, discouraging any mining in the area. Prospectors were persistent, however, and in 1869, the Clifton (Gold Hill) district was organized. Small amounts of gold, silver, and lead were produced over the next few years. Mining activity and production increased in 1892, when a mill was constructed to treat the ores.

The discovery and development of mineral deposits was delayed due to the opposition of the Mormons, who intended to make agriculture the basis of their development and therefore discouraged the search for minerals.

> They feared "that the excitement and unsettling influence of mining would turn away their people from the more monotonous and peaceful occupations of agriculture and thereby interfere with their great work of reclaiming the desert, and fearing, also, that the restless and sometimes rather lawless class of people who are attracted by mining excitement might prove a disturbing element in the population and tend to subvert their almost autocratic authority."[2]

Indian Tribes in Utah

Utes

Ute Indians (who call themselves Nuciu, "The People") are Southern Numic speakers of the Numic (Shoshonean) language family. At the time of Euro-American contact, twelve informally affiliated Ute bands inhabited most of Utah and western Colorado. They included the Cumumba (probably a Shoshone band), the Tumpanuwac, Uinta-at, San Pitch, Pahvant, and Shebaretch in Utah, and the Yamparka, Parianuc, Taviwac, Wiminuc, Kapota, and Muwac in Colorado.

Utes acquired horses from the Spanish by 1680. Horses facilitated Ute raiding and trading, making them respected warriors and important middlemen in the southwestern slave and horse trade. While involved in this trade with Hispanic settlers, Utes remained independent from colonial control.

Beginning in 1847, Utes experienced the full impact of Euro-American contact with the arrival of Mormon settlers. The initial Mormon settlement in the Salt Lake Valley occurred in a joint occupancy zone between Utes and Shoshones.

Paiutes

The establishment of the first Southern Paiute Agency at Saint Thomas in 1869 and also the Moapa Indian Reservation in 1873 resulted from tensions between the Nevada Paiutes and miners when mineral discoveries were made in Meadow Valley and Pahranagat Valley in the late 1860s and early 1870s. The Southern Paiutes would be removed to a reservation in accordance with current government policy. In 1865, a few Utah Paiutes had signed a treaty relinquishing southern Utah in return for their removal to the Ute reservation in the Uinta Basin. This treaty was never ratified, but, nevertheless, it became the basis of government policy.

John Wesley Powell and George W. Ingalls were sent to the area to determine the conditions of the Paiutes. In 1873, they recommended that all of the Southern Paiutes be removed to Moapa. With lack of supervision and aid, the Moapa reservation sank into corruption and neglect.

In 1891, the U.S. provided a reservation for the Southern Paiutes in an area cut through by the Santa Clara River. This location had historically supported one of the largest segments of the Paiute population.

In the early part of the twentieth century a partial attempt was made by the government to regain control over Indian affairs at Moapa. Land was acquired at Las Vegas for an Indian colony, and the Moapa Agency was temporarily moved there in 1912. Other Paiute reservations were established: the Kaibab Reservation in northern Arizona in 1907, the Koosharem Reservation in central Utah in 1928, and the Indian Peaks Reservation in western Utah in 1915.

Gosiutes

Two reservations were eventually established for the Gosiutes on their own lands: in 1912 eighty acres were reserved for their use in Skull Valley with an additional 17,920 acres added in 1919, and in 1914 the Deep Creek Reservation in western Tooele County and eastern Nevada was founded with 34,560 acres.[3]

Conflicts

All Utah tribes have experienced difficulty. For the Shoshone, it was the Bear River Massacre of 1863. For the Utah Utes, it was forced removal in 1865 from their beloved Utah Valley into the arid Uinta Basin. For the Goshutes, it was broken promises and removal from traditional sacred lands. For the Navajo and Paiute, it was countless skirmishes with Mormon settlers in southern Utah.

Indian Wars

1849: Battle Creek Massacre

On March 5, 1849, Mormon settlers ambushed Timpanogos who were outnumbered and outgunned. They had no defense against the Mormon militia that crept in and surrounded their camp before dawn. Mormon settlement of the Utah Valley came upon the heels of the attack at Battle Creek.

1853: The Walker War [Mormons and Utes]

By the time the Mormons arrived in Utah, there were different tribes living in Utah territory: the Shoshone in Northern Utah, the Goshute in Eastern Utah, the Cumumba Utes, in what is now Ogden, the Timpanogos Shoshones in the Provo area (Central Utah), the Sanpit Utes in Central Utah, the Pahvant Utes in Southern Utah, the Uinta Utes in the Uintas, the Seberecheth Utes in the Moab area, the Weeminuche Utes in Southwestern Utah and the Paiutes in southeastern Utah. The end of the Mexican War enlarged the U.S. territory to include Ute lands. Mormon settlers' occupation of lands that the Utes used for hunting and gathering, along with Mormon attempts to suppress the New Mexican trade, disrupted the Ute economy and society.

On July 17, 1853, several Utes were trading at James Ivie's home near Springville when Ivie intervened in a dispute between a Ute man and his wife over her failure to strike a good bargain. In the ensuing melee, Ivie killed one of the Ute men, a relative of Walkara's named Shower-O-Cats.

Under orders from Colonel George A. Smith, Capt. Stephen C. Perry of the Springville Militia, garrisoned just south of Provo, led a unit the next day into Walkara's camp to try to placate the outraged Utes. The Springville Militia (aka Mormon Iron County or Nauvoo Legion) was the 10th Regiment of the Utah Territorial Militia. Unable to appease the infuriated Utes, they beat a hasty retreat. Walkara bargained with the settlers, demanding the usual Numic retribution--the death of one Euro-American. The settlers refused to pay that price, and two of Walkara's associate chiefs, Arapeen and Wanship, opposed compromise.

After leaving Walkara's camp, Arapeen killed a guard named Alexander Keel. Recognizing that Keel's death would bring the wrath of the Mormon settlers on his followers, Walkara led his people on a flight up Payson Canyon. On the way, they fired on settlers' cabins and stole about twenty head of cattle and six horses. Hearing of Keel's death and Walkara's flight, Colonel Peter

W. Conover of the Nauvoo Legion led a punitive expedition of more than 150 men in pursuit.

Dreading a return to the bloodshed of 1849 and 1850, *General Wells ordered Conover to disband his troops and to act entirely on the defensive.* Before he received the orders, however, Conover had sent out a patrol to attack a Ute camp east of Pleasant Creek. The militiamen killed six Indians in a skirmish. After receiving General Wells's orders, Conover prepared to return to Utah Valley, but in the meantime, General Wells and Brigham Young issued further orders that anticipated even more thorough disengagement.

Ordering George A. Smith to assume command of all units south of Salt Lake County, they instructed the settlers to abandon small outlying settlements and to gather in larger communities within secure forts. Also, they ordered the settlers to immediately send all stock not needed for teams and milk to Salt Lake City for safekeeping. *Later, Smith relieved Conover of command and arrested him for his failure to implement the ordered defensive and conciliatory policy.*

Smith encountered considerable hostility in effecting his policy of defense and conciliation. Walkara made Smith's job more difficult since his soldiers attacked the settlers at Allred Settlement, driving off virtually all the community's livestock. Smith also encountered an open rebellion within the Mormon community and had to accept the resignation of the Cedar City Militia commander, Major Mathew Caruthers, before the community agreed to send their stock to Salt Lake.

Attacks continued into August 1853 as Utes tried to take a Salt Lake-bound herd of surplus cattle near Clover Creek in the Rush Valley. The war spread into northern Utah as Utes attacked four men hauling lumber near Park City, killing two and wounding one other. Walkara left for northern Arizona for the winter, but Wyonah, brother to Shower-O Cats, and other sympathetic Utes continued fighting. During the fall, Utes killed and mutilated settlers, most of whom were working in isolated parties outside the towns in defiance or disregard of the orders to remain in large groups.

Instead of following a conciliatory policy as Young had directed, Mormon settlers responded in brutal kind. A militia unit in Utah County assaulted a Ute camp near Goshen, killing four or five people. At Nephi, on October 2, 1853, after eight or nine Utes came to the fort seeking protection, a group of townspeople slaughtered them and then reported the murders as deaths that occurred during a skirmish.

Following the violence of late 1853 and early 1854, a number of Ute leaders offered terms for peace. Walkara, who had since returned from Navajo country, petitioned the settlers and Brigham Young for peace as well. Walkara asked for food, guns, and ammunition, offering to sell portions of central Utah lands in return for annuities to be paid in cattle and horses over a twenty-year period.

Young also favored the renewal of normal relations and an end to war and murder but solved none of the underlying issues. In fact, bloody skirmishes continued through the Black Hawk War of the 1860s.

1853: Gunnison Massacre

Eager to determine the most feasible and politically acceptable route from the Mississippi Valley to the Pacific Coast, Congress had authorized four surveys of possible transcontinental corridors. Unaware that the Walker War had broken out between the Ute Indians of central Utah and the Mormons, Capt. John W. Gunnison of the Corps of Topographical Engineers, the leader of the 38th Parallel Railroad Survey, and seven men set out on October 21, 1853, from their camp at Cedar Springs, just west of Fillmore, Utah, to explore the Sevier Lake country. On October 26, 1853, they were killed. Anti-Mormons attributed the death to Mormons acting under Brigham Young's instructions.

1856: Tintic War [Mormons and Utes]

In February 1856, the Tintic War, a series of skirmishes inflamed the people in the Tintic and Cedar Valleys, largely because Indians, who were starving in the drought, began taking cattle from the settlers. The war resulted in a number of clashes and deaths.

1857–1858: Mormon War

The Mormon War was an armed confrontation between Mormon settlers in the Utah Territory and the armed forces of the U.S. The confrontation lasted from May 1857 to July 1858. There were some casualties, most of which were non-Mormon civilians. The war had no notable military battles.

In 1857–1858, President James Buchanan sent U.S. forces to the Utah Territory in what became known as the Utah Expedition. Rather than engaging the Army directly, the Mormon strategy was one of hindering and weakening them. Daniel H. Wells, Lieutenant-General of the Nauvoo Legion, instructed Major Joseph Taylor:

On ascertaining the locality or route of the troops, proceed at once to annoy them in every possible way. Use every exertion to stampede their animals and set fire to their trains. Burn the whole country before them and on their flanks. Keep them from sleeping by night surprises; blockade the road by felling trees or destroying the river fords where you can. Watch for opportunities to set fire to the grass on their windward so as, if possible, to envelop their trains. Leave no grass before them that can be burned. Keep your men concealed as much as possible, and guard against surprise.[4]

The confrontation between the Mormon militia and the U.S. Army involved some destruction of property and a few brief skirmishes in what is today southwestern Wyoming, but no battles occurred between the contending military forces.

On September 11, 1857, at least **120** California-bound settlers from Arkansas, Missouri and other states, including unarmed men, women, and children, were killed in remote southwestern Utah by a group of local Mormon militia. They first claimed that the migrants were killed by Indians but it was proven otherwise.

Indeed, the report of Mr. I. Forney, the Superintendent of Indians in Utah, of September 29, 1859, fixes the stigma of this horrible outrage on the Mormons. Commissioner Greenwood, in his report of November 26, 1859, to Secretary of the Interior, says in relation to this matter:

> The reports of the condition of the Indians in Utah present a melancholy picture. The whites are in possession of most of the little comparatively good country there is, and the game has become so scarce as no longer to afford the Indians an adequate subsistence. ... Many of the numerous depredations upon the immigrants have doubtless been committed by them in consequence of their destitute and desperate condition. They have, at times, been compelled either to steal or starve; but there is reason to apprehend that in their forays *they have often been only the tools of lawless whites residing in the Territory*. In some of the worst outrages of this kind,

involving the lives as well as the property of our emigrants, the latter are known to have participated. That this was the case in the atrocious and dreadful massacre at "Mountain Meadow' in September, 1857, the facts stated in the report of the superintendent, in regard to that occurrence, leave no room for doubt. (Emphasis added).[5]

This event was later called the Mountain Meadows Massacre.

The Aiken massacre took place the following month. In October 1857, Mormons arrested six Californians traveling through Utah and charged them with being spies for the U.S. Army. They were released but were later murdered and robbed of their stock and money.

President Buchanan issued a lengthy Proclamation—Rebellion in Territory of Utah, on April 6, 1858, with a history of events in the hostilities and notice that the force of the U.S. would be brought to bear if the Mormons did not cease their disobedience.

> Whereas the Territory of Utah was settled by certain emigrants from the States and from foreign countries who have for several years past manifested a spirit of insubordination to the Constitution and laws of the United States. ... The officers of the Federal Government have been driven from the Territory for no offense but an effort to do their sworn duty; others have been prevented from going there by threats of assassination... Indeed, such is believed to be the condition to which a strange system of terrorism has brought the inhabitants of that region that no one among them could ... even propose to obey its laws, without exposing his life and property to peril. ...
>
> After carefully considering this state of affairs and maturely weighing the obligation I was under to see the laws faithfully executed ... I accordingly ordered a detachment of the Army to march for the city of Salt Lake ... While the troops of the United States were on their march a train of baggage wagons, which happened to be unprotected, was attacked and destroyed

by a portion of the Mormon forces and the provisions and stores with which the train was laden were wantonly burnt. ... Their determination to oppose the authority of the Government by military force has not only been expressed in words, but manifested in overt acts of the most unequivocal character.

Fellow-citizens of Utah, this is rebellion against the Government to which you owe allegiance; it is levying war against the United States, and involves you in the guilt of treason. ...

Do not deceive yourselves nor try to mislead others by propagating the idea that this is a crusade against your religion. ...

But being anxious to save the effusion of blood ... I offer now a free and full pardon to all who will submit themselves to the just authority of the Federal Government. ...

Now, therefore, I, James Buchanan, President of the United States ... declar[e] that the military forces now in Utah and hereafter to be sent there will not be withdrawn until the inhabitants of that Territory shall manifest a proper sense of the duty which they owe to this Government. April 6, 1858.[7]

Brigham Young accepted Buchanan's terms and pardon, although he denied Utah had ever rebelled against the U.S. Utah was under nominal military occupation. Historian Leonard J. Arrington noted that "the cream of the United States Army" reviled the Mormon settlers. Fortunately, the near isolation of Camp Floyd kept interaction to a minimum, as troops stayed on or near their base.

1860: SW States' Residents Petition for Extinguishing Indian Title

In 1860, President Buchanan transmitted eight memorials to Congress from residents of New Mexico, Utah, Kansas, and Nebraska "for the early extinguishment of the Indian title, a consequent survey and sale of the public land, and the establishment of an assay office in the immediate and daily reach of the citizens of that region," along with granting territorial status.[8]

1860: Indians Surrounded by Mormons (Indian Agent)

> Thus it will be seen that they are entirely surrounded by a large Mormon population extending over three counties, having no sympathy or interest in them, which deprives them of all chances of killing game, even for their partial subsistence, and leaves them destitute of any other source from whence to look for the commonest necessaries of life than the government; and here I would state that in consequence of the great damage to their crops by grasshoppers and crickets in 1859, the sufferings of these poor Indians during the past winter were horrible, many of them dying from starvation and exposure. It was a common circumstance to find them frozen to death. I made frequent requisitions ·upon and earnest appeals to the superintendent. He steadily refused to relieve their sufferings, notwithstanding he had in his possession at the time some $5,000 or $6,000 worth of Indian goods. I was compelled to witness the sufferings and death of these poor creatures, without money, provisions, or clothing wherewith to relieve them. On several occasions I parted with my own blankets to bury them in. A. Humphreys, Indian Agent, Utah Territory.[9]

1860: President Sets Aside Uinta Valley Reservation

By 1860, Ute Indian agents suggested removing these Indians to the Uintah Basin.

In 1861, President Abraham Lincoln set aside the two-million-acre Uinta Valley Reservation for the tribes of the Utah Territory. Executive Order 38-1 of the United States, President Abraham Lincoln, October 3, 1861. A September 25, 1861, editorial in the Deseret News described the Uinta Basin as "*one vast contiguity of waste,*" fit only for "nomadic purposes, hunting grounds for Indians and to hold the world together." (Emphasis added).

Congress confirmed establishing the Uinta Valley Reservation on May 5, 1864 (13 Stat. 63); section 2 of this act provides as follows:

> And be it further enacted, That the *superintendent of Indian affairs for the territory of Utah be, and he is hereby, authorized and required to collect and settle all or so many*

of the Indians of said territory as may be found practicable in the Uintah valley, in said territory, which is hereby set apart for the permanent settlement and exclusive occupation of such of the different tribes of Indians of said territory as may be induced to inhabit the same. (Emphasis added).

Thereafter, the Mormons petitioned for the Utah Indians removal to the new Reservation. Sometime thereafter the Uinta Valley Reservation was referred to as the Uintah Reservation.

1863: Bear River Massacre

On January 29, 1863, Colonel Patrick Edward Connor and about 200 California Volunteers attacked a Northwestern Shoshoni winter village located a short distance north of the present Utah-Idaho boundary line. This band of 450 Shoshoni under war chief Bear Hunter had opposed the expropriation of all the land and water in the mountain valley. The young men of the tribe had struck back at the white settlers prompting Utah territorial officials to call on Connor's troops to punish the Northwestern Shoshoni Band.

> *Before [Colonel Connor] led his men from Camp Douglas at Salt Lake City north to Bear River, he had announced that he intended to take no prisoners.* As the troopers approached the Indian camp in the early morning darkness at 6:00 a.m., they found the Shoshoni warriors entrenched behind the ten-foot eastern embankment of Beaver Creek. By 8:00 a.m., the Indian men were out of ammunition, and the last two hours of the battle became a massacre as the soldiers used their revolvers to shoot down all the Indians they could find. *Approximately 250 Shoshoni were slain, including 90 women and children. After the slaughter ended, some of the undisciplined soldiers went through the Indian village raping women and using axes to bash in the heads of women and children who were already dying of wounds. Chief Bear Hunter was killed along with sub-chief, Lehi. The troops burned the seventy-five Indian lodges, recovered 1,000 bushels of wheat and flour, and appropriated 175 Shoshoni horses. While the troops cared for their wounded and took their dead back to Camp Douglas for burial, the Indians' bodies were left on the field for the wolves and crows.* Although the Mormon settlers in Cache Valley expressed their gratitude for "the movement of Colonel Connor as an intervention of the Almighty" in their

behalf, the Bear River Massacre has been overlooked in the history of the American West chiefly because it occurred during the Civil War when a more important struggle was taking place in the East. (Emphasis added).[10]

1864: Gold Discovery in Bingham Canyon

Placer gold was discovered in Bingham Canyon in 1864. *Connor, stationed with his regiment at Camp Douglas, east of Salt Lake City, formally organized the first mining district, West Mountain (currently Bingham) in 1863, after the discovery of lead-silver ore in Bingham Canyon in the Oquirrh Mountains of Salt Lake County.*

Thomas C. W. Sale, an Indian subagent sent to investigate reported problems with the Southern Paiutes, pursued his personal agenda of prospecting, allowing his soldiers to do the same.[11] Without railroad transport, commercial mining of these resources did not commence until 1869.

Captain N. Baldwin, Company A, Second Cavalry, was ordered by Connor on May 11, 1864, to Uinta Valley to "afford ample protection to prospectors and miners … [and] cause the valley and vicinity to be thoroughly prospected by your men..." On May 13, 1864, he dispatched Captain David J. Berry to the Meadow Valley Mining District in southwestern Utah to "afford protection to miners from Mormons and Indians [and to] explore and prospect the country over which you travel, and if successful in finding placer diggings, you will at once report the fact to these headquarters."[12]

Connor reported to his commanding officer that he was spending "every energy and means" he possessed, "both personal and official, towards the discovery and development of the mining resources of the Territory, using without stint the soldiers of my command, whenever and wherever it could be done without detriment to the public service."[13]

In a July 4, 1866, letter to Grenville Dodge, Chief Engineer for the Union Pacific Railroad, Connor confirmed an agreement between the two regarding minerals. Connor was to engage two prospecting parties to locate any valuable silver, gold, coal, or iron mines and then bill Dodge, by voucher, for the expenses.[14]

Indian Battles in Utah

A chart on Indian Battles in Utah is in the last Chapter.

Mining as Vital Industry

With the completion of the Transcontinental Railroad on May 10, 1869, mining emerged as a vital industry. The scarcity of water and placer gold that could be panned limited activity. Silver ores kept the district alive until around 1880. About 1883, gold-bearing ores were found, but the gold could not be separated from the rock. With the newly developed cyanide leaching process, production renewed in 1880. From 1890 to 1900, almost 2 million tons of gold ore were treated, producing over 380,000 ounces of gold worth about $8 million.

1865: Congress Authorizes President to Enter into Treaties with Indians in Utah Territory to Extinguish Indian Title to Lands Suitable for Agricultural and Mineral Purposes

In February 1865, Congress passed a law authorizing the President to enter into treaties with Indians in the Utah Territory that would extinguish Indian title. An Act, To Extinguish the Indian Title to Lands in the Territory of Utah Suitable for Agricultural and Mineral Purposes. The Act also provided for the establishment of reservations as far as practicable from areas of white settlement.[15]

1865-1867: Black Hawk War - Mormons and Utes (April 9, 1865)

On April 9, 1865, the long simmering conflict between the Ute and Mormons erupted into the Black Hawk Indian War. Black Hawk united factions of the Ute, Paiute, and Navajo tribes into a loose confederacy which stole cattle and killed settlers from 1865 to 1867 The Mormons formed local militia to defend against the raids. They built scores of forts and deserted dozens of settlements while hundreds of Mormon militiamen pursued the Indians. Their distrust of the federal government resulted in the prolonged war as federal troops did not intervene until 1872 when 200 federal troops were finally ordered to step in.[16]

1865: Silver Discovered in SW Utah, May 4, 1865

> *Report of Thomas C. W. Sale, Special Indian Agent, May 4, 1865: Important silver mines having recently been discovered in the southeastern part of Nevada or southwestern Utah ... it is probable that it will be the means of introducing a large emigration into a portion of the country that has been heretofore wholly occupied by the Indians.* (Emphasis added).[17]

1865: Spanish Fork Treaty between U.S. and Ute Tribes in Utah, June 8, 1865 (Unratified)

Under the Spanish Fork Treaty, signed on June 8, 1865, Indians relinquished the "right of possession to all of the lands within Utah Territory occupied by them. ... With the exception of the Uintah valley, which [was] to be reserved for their exclusive use." The treaty required Indians to give up their Spanish Fork, San Pete, and Corn Creek reservations. It also gave the president of the United States authority to place other bands of "friendly Indians" on the Uintah reservation without prior Indian approval, and the Indian signatories agreed to move to the reservation "within one year after ratification of the treaty."[18]

Indians were to receive annual payments of $25,000 for ten years, followed by $20,000 per year for the next twenty years, and finally $15,000 for an additional thirty years. Congress did not ratify the treaty, though, and it is of no legal effect.

1865: Weber (Cumumbah) Treaty between U.S. and Weber Ute Indians, October 1865 (Unratified)

On October 30, 1865, the Weber (Cumumbah) Utes signed a treaty incorporating the terms of the Spanish Fork Treaty. From 1865-1866 most of the Utes were removed to the Uintah Reservation. In March 1866 President Johnson submitted the Spanish Fork Treaty to Congress for ratification. Three years later, on March 11, 1869, Congress rejected the Spanish Fork Treaty and it is of no legal effect.

1866: Circleville Massacre [Mormons and Koosharem Band of Paiute Indian Tribe of Utah]

In 1866, the Parowan Militia Officer decided to round up all Indians, including the Paiutes, who at the time remained peaceful, and demand they appear in Fort Sanford to be questioned. The Militia distrusted the Paiutes because they felt the Paiutes and Utes were in alliance with each other, but historically this was never proven.

The local settlers and the Mormon Leaders of Circleville took it upon themselves to decide the fate of roughly 30 Paiute men, women and children.

~ 666 ~

They tricked the Paiutes into coming to Circleville by imploring them, that Bishop Allred had a letter to read to them from Brigham Young. The Indians were asked to surrender their guns and were then placed under guard. *All of the Indians were killed*. Panicked by the bloody incident, the soldiers felt it necessary, as one resident put it, to *"dispose of the squaws and papooses" to prevent them from telling of the massacre and inciting further violence."* (Emphasis added). No one was prosecuted for the murders.[19]

1867: Most of Uintah Utes Removed to Uintah Valley Reservation

By 1867, most of the Uintah Utes were removed to the Uintah Valley Reservation.

1870: Vernon H. Vaughan, Eighth Governor of Utah Territory, 1870–1871

In 1870, President Grant named Vernon H. Vaughan as the Eighth Governor of the Utah Territory. The only event of consequence during his administration was the Wooden Gun Rebellion—an illegal drill in November 1870 by members of the Mormon Nauvoo Legion. The incident resulted in the arrest and trial of those involved, but all were released. Vaughan was not reappointed.

1871: George Lemuel Woods, Ninth Governor of Utah Territory, 1871–1875

In 1871, President Grant named George Lemuel Woods as the Ninth Governor of the Utah Territory, He saw the Mormon Nauvoo Legion as a threat to federal authority. He urged the establishment of free public schools, comprehensive mining legislation, the abolition of polygamy, further railroad development and federal funds to improve irrigation. He was not reappointed and returned to practicing law.

1875: George W. Emery, Eleventh Governor of Utah Territory, 1875–1880; Advocated for Abolishing Tribal Relations

In 1875, President Grant named George Emery as the Eleventh Governor of the Utah Territory. Emery was in favor of abolishing tribal relations and reported his opinion in 1878:

> *The sooner the tribal relations can be done away with, and the Indian understands that he is individually responsible to the laws for his acts, and that he is to be protected in all his*

rights in the same manner as white men, the better it will be for the Indian and the country. (Emphasis added).[20]

1879: Uintah Utes at Peace

Notwithstanding the Meeker Incident, the Uintah Utes, although neighbors, remained at home in peace, and under the control of their agent.[21]

1880: Eli Houston Murray, Twelfth Governor of Utah Territory, 1880–1886

In 1880, President Hayes named Eli Houston Murray, the Twelfth Governor of Utah Territory. Murray's attacks on the Mormons influenced national policy. Importantly, he reported that mining entries had increased by 4%. Also, railroad connections had increased the connection of mining districts to markets.[22]

1881: White River & Uncompahgre Utes Removed from Colorado

The White River Utes were removed from Colorado by the U.S. to the Uinta Valley Reservation, Utah, 20 years after the Uinta Valley Reservation was established. The Uncompahgre Utes, led by Chief Ouray, managed to obtain their own reservation in 1882 - the 1,912,320 acre Ouray Reservation, situated on the Tavaputs Plateau, immediately south of the Uinta Valley Reservation.[23]

In 1881, the Indian Agent expressed his concern with the location of the White River Utes and their bad influence on the Uintah Utes:

> The [White River Utes] have been the larger number; they are indolent and know nothing of farming or caring for themselves by civilized pursuits, and what is worse, many of them have no desire to learn, and are free to express their intention of avoiding anything of the kind. They laugh at the Uintahs for farming, and say they ought to fight and then Washington would furnish them plenty to eat. ... It is true that the White River are under treaty stipulations and therefore well provided for, and it is also true that the Uintahs are not, and therefore are unfortunate. J. J. Critchlow, Indian Agent.[24]

1886: Fort Duchesne

Secretary Lamar's report that the Utes would not send their children to school or adapt to "civilized pursuits," led the Secretary of War to establish Fort

Duchesne in September 1886. The Utes were angered at the arrival of troops but decided that resistance was useless. In 1886, with the new fort in existence, the Uintah Agency and the Ouray Agency were combined and the agent moved to Fort Duchesne.[25]

1886: Uncompahgre Band of Utah Indians Reservation Barren; Vile and Hateful Report on Utes by Agents

The Indians belonging to the Ouray Agency are the Tabequache or Uncompahgre band of Utes, about 1,087 in number. Those belonging to the Uintah Agency are the Uintah and White River bands of Utes (about 481 of the former and 575 of the latter), 1,056 in all.

> The Ouray (Uncompahgre) Reservation is a desert. Of the 1,933,440 acres embraced therein not one can be relied on to produce a crop without irrigation, and not more than 3 per cent. (sic) of the whole is susceptible of being made productive by process of irrigation.... In my judgment an abundant supply of water can be carried within convenient reach of all this land at a cost of $3,000 or less.

> There are no Indians within the range of my knowledge lower down in the scale of civilization than the Utes. ... The most advanced members of the tribe barely know enough of the arts of industry to drive a team, or plant, cultivate, and harvest a crop in the crudest possible way. Blankets, leggings, moccasins, gee-strings, paint and feathers constitute the fashionable or prevailing Ute costume, and the brush wickiup or the cloth and skin tepee is the almost universal Ute habitation. ...

> [T]hey are impatient of the restraints of government, distrustful of whites, opposed to any sort of improvement, and by nature nomadic and savage in their habits and instincts. Eugene E. White, Special Agent at Large in Charge of Uintah and Ouray Agency.

> These Indians are what is known as "blanket" Indians; as a rule are lazy, shiftless, vicious, and densely ignorant; content to live the barbarous life of their ancestors; perpetually loafing around, when not on their wandering hunting trips, ever waiting for something to turn up; without energy, ambition, or any thought of their future. They have no respect for the white

man or his ways, and but little for the Government ...

Polygamy and gambling are their prevailing vices ... This vice has not been broken or checked, simply because the means or power is not at hand to do so. Thus it is that while various misdemeanors and three murders occurred during the year, it was found impossible to bring the offenders to justice.

There is here no police force or court of Indian offenses ... The Indian is the master of the situation, and he knows it. He won't work, because he isn't forced to it and it is beneath his dignity. Besides, that far away, mystical, beneficent "Washington" kindly furnishes him with food, clothing, and pocket money (which is quite natural and just, and will always continue, he thinks). Then why should he work? He don't [sic]. He placidly sits on the banks of the White and Green Rivers, kicks his feet in the muddy waters, longing and dreaming, perhaps, for the coming of the Indian millennium—the downfall of the whites, his country regained, the delights of the chase and trail, as in days of yore. Wm. A. McKewen, Clerk in Charge Ouray Agency.[26]

1887: Illegal Grazing on Uintah Indian Reservation

Illegal grazing on the Uintah Indian Reservation was a problem for many years. By 1887 prospectors and stockmen had moved onto reservation land. Preston Nutter was one of Utah's greatest cattle barons. In 1893, Nutter was able to secure a five-year lease of range land (665,000 acres) on the western portion of the reservation, and his business began to grow.

1888: Southern Utes Agree to Move to Utah, But Congress Fails to Ratify Agreement

Colorado continued to advocate for removal to Utah of the one remaining Indian tribe in Colorado, the Southern Utes. In 1888, the Southern Utes agreed to move to Utah, but Congress failed to ratify the agreement. Utah was vehemently opposed to this move.

1888: Congress Reduces Uintah Reservation for Mining of Gilsonite by Whites

In 1885, asphalt, known as gilsonite, was discovered on [the Uintah]

Reservation, was being worked by the white miners who were trespassing on the Reservation, and the substance shipped to Eastern markets. No effort had been made to stop them. In *1888*, Congress removed approximately 7,000 acres from the eastern portion of the Uintah Reservation, freeing the gilsonite deposits for legal mining claims.

> In response to Ute complaints about white trespassing in the eastern end of the Uintah Valley Reservation, Agent Byrnes recommended that the "Gilsonite Strip" be removed from the reservation; after all, the lands "are not, nor have they been, used or occupied by the Indians, for the reason that they are not fit for agricultural or grazing purposes." Letter of Agent Byrnes to J. Atkins of February 18, 1888. Speaking of the Gilsonite Strip, Captain J. Randlett of Fort Duchesne observed:
>
> > [D]etachment by sale will occasion no inconvenience to the tribes. If the Gilsonite enterprise proves a success, the Indians will see how profits are made from industry and will also to some extent find at the mines a market for their own products... It will be very agreeable to the isolated garrison to have a settlement near it. Letter of Capt. Randlett to Agent Byrnes of February 18, 1888.
>
> Congress soon joined in the view that the best interests of everyone would be served by excising the Gilsonite Strip from the Uintah Reservation. See H.Rep.No.791, 50th Cong., 1st Sess. (1888) LD 15; S. Rep. No.1198, 50th Cong., 1st Sess. (1888) LD 17; 19 Cong. Rec. 1927-1929, 3776, 3821 (1888), LD 16. By the Act of May 24, 1888, ch. 310, 25 Stat. 157, I Kapp. 271 (2d ed. 1904) Congress mandated that the 7,040-acre triangular Gilsonite Strip be "declared to be public lands of the United States and restored to the public domain." Id. § 1. The Act directed the Secretary of the Interior to procure the approval of a three-fourths majority of the adult male Indians on the reservation and upon such ratification, to sell the lands at not less than $1.25 an acre. Id. §§ 2, 3. After "much proselyting" the ratification by the Indians was secured on October 8, 1888, and on October 22, the Secretary of the Interior restored the land to the public domain and ordered

surveys to be conducted. See Letter of Acting Comm. of Ind. Aff. to Secretary of the Interior of September 9, 1899; Report of Uintah and Ouray Agency in Rept. of the Comm. of Ind. Aff., 1890, at 280.[27]

1889: Unlawful Gilsonite Mining by Whites Continues after Establishment of Uintah Reservation in 1881

In 1889, trespassers were required to move off the Uintah Reservation established in 1881.

> The parties in interest claimed that the lands upon which the [gilsonite] mineral was found were off the reservation. I investigated the matter [in 1889] and found ... that the lands on which they were mining were a part of the reservation. I then ordered all work on such lands stopped and compelled the parties to leave the reservation. Mr. J. T. McConnell with the agency police force removed therefrom all trespassers, destroying 10 houses, erected and in course of erection, and Mr. McConnell also collected $511 from cattle men trespassing in that vicinity. Since that time I have kept the reservation clear of all intruders.[28]

1889: Arthur Lloyd Thomas, Fourteenth Governor of Utah Territory, 1889–1893; Requests Early Allotment of Uintah Reservation Lands

Thomas was appointed as Governor in 1889 by President Harrison. He reported that the Uintah Reservation lands are

> "some of *the most fertile and well-watered lands within the Commonwealth*. As the acreage per capita for the Indians is so unnecessarily large as to be entirely beyond reason, I have to recommend that *early provision be made for the allotment in severalty* of suitable quantities of such land to the Indians, and that the remainder of the lands be then thrown *open to the public for settlement*. I ought also to say that any further removal of the Indians [Southern Utes] from Colorado or elsewhere to this Territory, would be such a grave injustice and impediment to the progress of the Territory that it ought not to be considered, much less permitted. (Emphasis added).[29]

1890: Utah Opposed to Southern Utes Removal from Colorado to Utah

Governor Thomas' reports continued to oppose the removal of the Southern Utes from Colorado to Utah.

The people of Utah are almost unanimously opposed to the bringing of these Indians to the Territory. (Emphasis added).[30]

In regard to Southern Utes, the presence of these Indians would be a menace and a hindrance to the settlement of the country. (Emphasis added).[31]

The people of the Territory through their legislative assembly have protested against the unloading of the Indians upon them. After a full investigation of the matter by the Senate Committee on Indian Affairs it was decided not to recommend the passage of the bill authorizing the removal. In justice to the Territory the matter should no longer be agitated.[32]

1891: Members of Former Pi Ute, Shoshone, Pah Vants, Piedes and Ute Tribes Need Aid

Governor Thomas also reported on the Indians in Utah without a reservation as needing aid.

In other counties small bands of Indians may be found who like most of the Indians not on the reservations, have abandoned their tribal relations. They are objects of pity, and their numbers are being rapidly reduced by disease. The Government ought to provide for them in some way.[33]

> *About fifteen hundred Indians, remnants of former Pi Ute, Shoshone, Pah Vants, Piedes and Ute tribes*, are to be found scattered throughout the Territory, mostly in the southern and eastern counties. About six hundred of these obtain a livelihood by farming, raising live stock, etc., and are gradually becoming accustomed to peaceful pursuits. The remainder are engaged in fishing, hunting, begging and, too often, stealing. *As a rule their condition is a pitiable one, but they must be seen before their condition can be appreciated. They long ago renounced their tribal relation and now roam at will. They are degraded and very ignorant.* (Emphasis added).[34]
>
> *I again recommend that the Government provide in some way for their care and support.* Several petitions have been presented to me signed by citizens residing in Grand and San Juan counties, asking me to lay before the Department of the

~ 673 ~

Interior the fact that straggling bands of Ute Indians from the Uintah Reservation in Utah and the Pine Ridge Reservation in Colorado, and the Navajo Reservation in New Mexico, are committing serious depredations upon the property of residents in the counties named; that they are stealing horses, killing cattle, stealing produce from the farms and killing game for the hide alone. (Emphasis added).[35]

I have nothing new to add to my former statements respecting the 1,500 or more Indians who have renounced their tribal relations and are scattered throughout the Territory. At the last session of Congress an appropriation of $10,000 was made for the relief of the Shebit Indians. Similar action should be taken for the relief of the Indians in Tooele County, who are anxious to own their land, and those in Garfield, San Juan, Sevier, Kane, and Iron counties.[36]

1893: Value of Gold & Silver Extracted $16,276,818

Caleb Walton West was selected by Grover Cleveland as Governor in 1886. *In his 1893 Report to the Sec. of Interior, Governor West reported the metal values from Utah at $16,276,818*. (Emphasis added).[37] West served as Territorial Governor twice, between 1886 and 1888 and between 1893 and 1896.

1894: Utah's Legislative Push for Opening Both Uintah and Ouray Reservations

Utah's territorial delegate to Congress, Joseph L. Rawlins, sponsored a bill in 1894 to *open both the Uintah and Ouray Reservations in eastern Utah to white settlement*. Under provisions of his bill, certain land within the reservation would be given in severalty (individual ownership) to the resident Utes, and the rest of the land would then be sold in lots not exceeding 160 acres to whoever submitted the highest sealed bid.

In his proposal for severalty of Ute lands, Rawlins was marching in cadence with the reform movement of the times. Feeling that the reservation policy had been a failure, certain social thinkers, particularly in the East, began working for an Indian policy that de-emphasized tribal life-styles in favor of individualism, education, vocational training, and property ownership.[38]

Utah's Governor West continued his advocacy for opening the Reservations:

The Congressional legislation authorizing the allotment to the Indians, in severalty, of certain of the lands embraced within the Uintah and Uncompaghre reservations and the opening for settlement and sale of the remaining lands, as recommended by me in my last report, will prove of untold advantage and wealth to the new State. *It will open for settlement millions of acres of the most fertile and perfectly watered lands, and will furnish homes for thousands* of our young people who need no longer emigrate to the valleys of adjoining States for suitable locations. The undeveloped mineral resources will undoubtedly attract much attention, and, together with the magnificent opportunities afforded the home seeker of the already overcrowded East, will be the means of causing a material increase in our population and taxable wealth. (Emphasis added).[39]

Under the State government we confidently anticipate an influx of population sufficient to strengthen our cities, cultivate our valleys, and *as soon as the Indian reservations are thrown open for settlement, to completely transform them into productive gardens and fields, thrifty villages and towns.* (Emphasis added).[40]

The General Government, holding a paternal relation toward the people in its Territories, is looked to by them for fostering aid in the work of developing the Territory in many ways, and especially in matters beyond private control, as in the matter of undeveloped mineral deposits within the limits of our Indian reservations. Much land within these reservations is useless for either cultivation or grazing, while some of it is of immeasurable value for mining. When such circumstances are combined, the effect of the reservation is clearly that of restriction of the best interests of the Territory and its people, and without any advantage to anyone else. *The early adoption of an Indian policy which will abolish the tribal organization of the Indians, and give them in severalty whatever land they can use, will be worth millions of dollars to the people of the Territory.* (Emphasis added).[41]

1898: Allotments Made on Ouray (Uncompahgre) Reservation

The Act of Jun 7, 1897, first opened the Uncompahgre Reservation for location and entry to non-tribal settlement on April 1, 1898. The Utes were not ready for the allotments when the bill was passed and avoided partitioning of reservation lands for several years. Congress finally took notice of this situation, and on May 27, 1902, another Act of Congress authorized an allotment of 80 acres of irrigable, agricultural land for each head of a family, and forty acres of such land to each other member of the Ute tribe then residing at the reservation. By Acts of Congress on June 19, 1902, March 3, 1903, and March 3, 1905, about 250,000 acres of non-irrigable land were set aside as a grazing reserve, to be kept intact as tribal land. By June, 1905, the allotment of land to individual Indians was completed, and unallotted land was opened to sale to whites by lottery.

1904: Congress Approved Allotments for Uintah and White River Utes of Uintah Reservation

In 1904, Congress approved 80-acre individual allotments for the Uintah and White River Utes of the Uintah Reservation.

In 1905, the federal government opened the Uintah Valley Reservation to non-tribal settlement. Land ownership within the boundaries of the Reservation is complicated due to both the checkerboard surface land ownership and differing subsurface ownership.

1905: Uintah Forest Reserve Established

By act of March 3, 1905 (33 Stat. 1070) it is provided:

> That before the opening of the Uintah Indian Reservation the President is hereby authorized to set apart and reserve as an addition to the Uintah Forest Reserve, subject to the laws, rules, and regulations governing forest reserves, and subject to the mineral rights granted by the Act of Congress of May twenty-seventh nineteen hundred and two, such portion of the lands within the Uintah Indian Reservation as he considers necessary ...

Acting on the authority granted in the provision just quoted President Roosevelt by proclamation made June 14, 1905 (34 Stat. 3116), withdrew over 1,004,285 acres for the Uintah National Forest and opened the Uintah Reservation for sale of surplus land after the allotments were made.[42]

Some 1,600 Indian allotments were made, and 5,772 homesteading permits were issued in the lottery that followed. In 1909, 56,000 acres were withdrawn from the Reservation for the Strawberry Valley Reclamation project.

1906: White River Utes Head to Pine Ridge

In 1906, approximately 400 members of the White River Band of Utes left the Uintah Reservation in Utah and made their way across northern Wyoming on their way to the Pine Ridge Reservation, where they hoped to find refuge. Their trek was peaceful, but for alleged theft from local ranches. However, the press became overly excited, including the New York Times, which reported on October 31, 1906, that the Utes were prepared to fight to the death. When they were intercepted by the Army, 40 Indians elected to return to Utah and the remainder were escorted to Fort Meade, South Dakota, and were later placed on the Cheyenne River Reservation. Two years later, they also elected to return to Utah.

1934: Ute Indian Tribe of the Uintah and Ouray Reservation

In 1934, the three Bands organized pursuant to the provisions of the Indian Reorganization Act of June 18, 1934 (48 Stat. 984, as amended), and formed the Ute Indian Tribe of the Uintah and Ouray Reservation.

Bingham Canyon Silver and Gold

In 1863, the West Mountain Mining District, the first in the Territory, was organized. It included the whole of the Oquirrh range. Mining of ores at Bingham, Stockton, Ophir, and Mercur would follow. The ore grade was low, only 39 pounds of copper per ton of ore, due to its minute dissemination.[43] V. C. Heikes of the U.S. Geological Survey considered the operation at Mercur "a pioneer" in the development of the cyanide-electric process, "which transformed the operations of the Mercur camp from a forlorn hope to an important commercial enterprise."

1902: MacNeill-Penrose Group ($250,000 Cash Investment)

In 1902, with the Colorado Cripple Creek gold rush slowing down, three miners, Charles MacNeill, Charles Tutt and Spencer Penrose, hired Daniel Jackling, a well-known mineralogist who had been working on the possibility of processing porphyry copper in Bingham Canyon, Utah. Jackling believed that if bulk-mined, this low-grade copper could be profitable. Penrose used Cripple Creek profits to bankroll Jackling.

On June 4, 1903, the Utah Copper Company was born and duly incorporated under the laws of Colorado with a nominal capital of $500,000 in one-dollar shares. MacNeill and Penrose took 250,000 shares, and their friends paid $250,000 in cash for the others. That same month Jackling was given the go-ahead to build a 300-ton experimental concentrator, and a lease was firmed up for the surface rights on 20 acres in lower Bingham Canyon, along with the rights to dump tailings. Utah Copper paid $250 a month for the surface rights, which it would terminate upon abandoning the mill. Rather than follow high-grade veins, they moved and milled vast tonnages of low-grade rock.[44]

Jackling's theory that the porphyry copper deposits could be profitably mined proved to be correct - $250,000 was all the cash that was put up at the start in order to launch the Utah Copper enterprise.[45]

Copper Enterprise's Financial Backing

With financial backing from Swiss born Philadelphia smelting entrepreneur Meyer Guggenheim, Utah Copper applied industrial technology such as steam shovels, railroad cars, and dump cars to scrape off the overburden and remove and transport the ore to a concentrator. After concentrating the ore, they shipped it to a smelter at Midvale, and after 1906 to the ASARCO smelter at Garfield, which the company later purchased. George Hearst, James Ben Ali Haggin and William Rockefeller also invested in the Company.[46]

Smelters - Bingham Consolidated Mining and Smelting Company, United States Mining Company ("ASARCO"), Utah Consolidated

The rapid change from gold to copper and the resulting success prompted the formation of numerous companies and exchange of shares of existing companies. Among them were the Bingham Consolidated Mining and Smelting Company and the United States Mining Company (later to become the United States Smelting, Refining and Mining Company). Those two concerns, plus Utah Consolidated and the American Smelting and Refining Company (ASARCO), built large smelters. ASARCO came on the industrial scene in early 1899, soon becoming the dominant nonferrous smelting firm in Utah. In early1904 there were three large copper smelters at the south end of the Salt Lake Valley in Murray and Midvale, and ASARCO had a large lead smelter in Murray.[47]

Railroad Lines

In 1905, the Denver & Rio Grande Western railroad extended its line from Bingham to the mill-site at Garfield. The Bingham & Garfield Railway, controlled by the Utah Copper Company, was completed and the first ore shipped over this line on September 14, 1911.

Notes: Utah

1. Koschmann, A. H., and M. H. Bergendahl. "Principal Gold-Producing Districts." United States Geological Survey Professional Paper 610, U.S. Government Printing Office, 1968. Statistics Of Mines And Mining In The States And Territories West Of The Rocky Mountains: Being The 6th Annual Report Of U.S. Commissioner Of Mining Statistics to Secretary of Treasury, 1871, p. 281.
2. Rickard, Thomas Arthur. The Utah Copper Enterprise. Abbott Press, 1919, p. 14.
3. Utah's First People: The Utes, Paiutes, and Goshutes, April 21, 2016, Peoples of Utah, Floyd A. O'Neil. https://historytogo.utah.gov/first-peoples/ (accessed online October 11, 2022).
4. Bancroft, Hubert Howe, Bates, Alfred (1889), "Chapter XIX: The Utah War", History of Utah, 1540–1886, The Works of Hubert Howe Bancroft, vol. XXVI, San Francisco: History Company.
5. Report of the Commissioner of Indian Affairs to the Secretary of the Interior, United States. Office of Indian Affairs. U.S. Government Printing Office, 1859, p. 21.
6. Proclamation by the Governor, September 15, 1857, Brigham Young. http://law2.umkc.edu/faculty/projects/ftrials/mountainmeadows/martiallaw.html (accessed online January 24, 2023). Hafen, Leroy R., Hafen, Ann W., eds. (2006). Mormon Resistance: A Documentary Account of the Utah Expedition, 1857–1858. Lincoln, NE: University of Nebraska Press.
7. James Buchanan, Proclamation—Rebellion in the Territory of Utah. https://www.presidency.ucsb.edu/node/202635 (accessed online October 11, 2022).
8. https://www.presidency.ucsb.edu/documents/special-message-2969 (accessed online October 4, 2022).
9. Report of the Commissioner of Indian Affairs to the Secretary of the Interior, United States. U.S. Office of Indian Affairs. Washington, DC: George W. Bowman, Printer, 1860, p. 394.
10. Brigham D. Madsen, The Shoshoni Frontier and the Bear River Massacre (1985).

11. Silver Reef and Southwestern Utah's Shifting Frontier, W. Paul Reeve, p. 254.

12. Whitley, C. (2006). From the ground up: The history of mining in Utah. Logan, UT: Utah State University Press, p. 60.

13. Tullidge, Edward William. History of Salt Lake City, Star Printing Company, 1886, p. 698.

14. Whitley, C. (2006). From the ground up: The history of mining in Utah. Logan, UT: Utah State University Press, p. 65; Grenville M. Dodge, "Personal Biography of Major General Grenville Mellon Dodge, 1831 to 1870," 2:569–70.

15. 13 Stat. 432 (1865).

16. Peterson, John Alton, "Utah's Black Hawk War," University of Utah Press, 1999.

17. Report of the Commissioner of Indian Affairs to the Secretary of the Interior, United States. Office of Indian Affairs, Utah Superintendency. U.S. Government Printing Office, 1865, p. 156.

18. O. H. Irish to Wm. P. Dole, "Utah Superintendency," June 29, 1865, in Report of the Commissioner of Indian Affairs. 1865, 150.

19. Albert Winkler, "The Circleville Massacre: A Brutal Incident in Utah's Black Hawk War," Utah Historical Quarterly 55 (1987); Carlton Culmsee, Utah's Black Hawk War (Logan: Utah State University Press, 1973), 90-91.

20. Governor of Utah Notes 1878, Geo. W. Emery, Governor of Utah Territory. Hon. Carl Schurz, Secretary of the Interior. H.R. Exec. Doc. No. 1, 45th Cong., 3rd Sess. (1878), p. 1117.

21. H.R. Exec. Doc. No.1, 46th Cong., 2nd Sess. (1879), p. 457.

22. Governor of Utah Notes H.R. Exec. Doc. No. 1, 46th Cong., 3rd Sess. (1880).

23. Letter from the Secretary of the Interior, transmitting, in response to Senate resolutions of January 27, 1881, copy of report of Ute Commission, and copies of all correspondence between this department and the Ute Commission, and also the Governor of Colorado S. Exec. Doc. No. 31, 46th Cong., 3rd Sess. (1881).

24. Report of the Commissioner of Indian Affairs to the Secretary of the Interior, United States. Office of Indian Affairs. U.S. Government Printing Office, 1881, p. 157.

25. Thomas G. Alexander and Leonard S. Arrington, "The Utah Military Frontier, 1872-1912: Forts Cameron, Thornburgh, and Duchesne," Utah Historical Quarterly 32 (Fall 1964); June Lyman and Norma Denver, compilers, Ute People: An Historical Study (1970); Couben and Geneva Wright, "Indian White Relations in the Uintah Basin," Utah Humanities Review 2 (October 1948).

26. Report of the Commissioner of Indian Affairs to the Secretary of the

Interior, United States. Office of Indian Affairs. U.S. Government Printing Office, 1886, p. 226.

27. *Ute Indian Tribe v. State of Utah*, 521 F. Supp. 1072, 1098-1099 (D. Utah 1981).

28. Report of the Commissioner of Indian Affairs to the Secretary of the Interior, United States. Office of Indian Affairs. U.S. Government Printing Office, 1889, p. 280.

29. Governor of Utah Notes, 1889. H.R. Exec. Doc. No. 1, 51st Cong., 1st Sess. (1889).

30. Governor of Utah Notes, 1890. Report of the Governor of Utah, 1890, p. 488.

31. Governor of Utah Notes, 1891. Arthur L. Thomas, Governor. Hon. John W. Noble, Secretary of the Interior, H.R. Exec. Doc. No. 1, 52nd Cong., 1st Sess. (1891), p. 645.

32. Ibid., p. 368.

33. Ibid., p. 487.

34. Ibid., p. 644.

35. Ibid., p. 645.

36. Ibid., p. 367.

37. Governor of Utah Notes, 1893. H.R. Exec. Doc. 1, 53rd Cong., 2nd Sess. (1893), p. 397.

38. Stanford J. Layton, History Blazer, July 1995.

39. Governor of Utah Notes, 1893. H.R. Exec. Doc. 1, 53d Cong., 2nd Sess. (1893), p. 464.

40. Ibid., p. 473.

41. Ibid., p. 375.

42. https://www.presidency.ucsb.edu/documents/proclamation-581-opening-uinta-indian-reservation-lands-utah (accessed online October 9, 2022).

43. Thomas G. Alexander Progression to Maturity, 1847–1945. University Press.

44. Whitley, C. From the ground up: The history of mining in Utah. Logan, UT: Utah State University Press, 2006, p. 228.

45. Ibid., p. 226.

46. Id.

47. Ibid., p. 225.

25: MAYHEM

The U.S.' primary function is to protect its territorial integrity and sovereignty over its claimed lands, resources, and population, which includes Indian lands which they hold in trust.

Doctrine of Settler Colonialism

General Pope best expressed the Doctrine of Settler Colonialism in 1878:

> It is absolutely imperative that Indian Nations realize the U.S. premeditated and calculated determination of *"the dispossession of the savage and the occupation of the lands by civilized man"* and that *"it is certain that the larger part of the country claimed by him will, in some manner, pass into the possession of the white race."*(Emphasis added).[1]

Fraudulent Doctrine of Discovery

In 1991, University of Oklahoma Law Professor Lindsay G. Robertson found *fifty years* of corporate records of the United Land Company documenting the collusive effort to confirm title to the purchased Indian lands through the *Johnson v. M'Intosh* case. These records are now in the University of Oklahoma's Law Digital Collection.[2]

Even though the United Land Company was unsuccessful in its legislative petitions, it thought it could win a case that the purchases from Indians were valid before the U.S. Supreme Court - if it controlled the case. The Company planned and funded the entire court proceeding for the prosecution and the defense.[3] The parties entered into an agreed Statement of Facts and Decision.

Fifty years after the alleged dispute arose, it reached the U.S. Supreme Court. The case would set precedent on the validity of title as between private purchases of Indian land and purchases from the federal government after extinguishing Indian title. There was an *enormous interest* in this case given the many land speculators who held titles from varying parties. The Chief Justice of the U.S. Supreme Court, John Marshall, had 240 square miles of family-owned land purchased under state law, not directly from Indians, at stake. Even though the case afforded Marshall the opportunity to bolster the legitimacy of his family's land claims, resulting in an undeniable conflict of interest in the outcome of the case, Chief Justice Marshall failed to recuse himself from hearing the case. He had recused himself in similar previous cases in which he had an interest. Justice James Wilson also had a vested interest in the case and similarly failed to recuse himself. As President of the United Company in 1780, he was the largest single investor with an interest totaling over 1,000,000 acres.

Without citing any statutes or legal cases or other authority for his decision, Chief Justice Marshall's decision held that, under the European 'doctrine of discovery,' the land discovered in the 'New World' belonged to the 'discovering' sovereign, so long as there were no Christian sovereign or Christian inhabitants. The thirteen colonies, having defeated Great Britain in the American Revolution, succeeded to its title which was based on the 'doctrine of discovery.'

The 'doctrine of discovery' promulgated for the U.S. by Chief Justice Marshall was as follows:

> They (Indians) were admitted to be the rightful occupants of the soil, with a legal as well as just claim to retain possession of it, and to use it according to their own discretion; but their rights to complete sovereignty as independent nations were necessarily diminished, and their power to dispose of the soil at their own will to whomsoever they pleased was denied by the original fundamental principle that *discovery gave exclusive title to those who made it*. (Emphasis added).[4]

Under this infamous doctrine, the U.S. was the only party with the rightful authority to convey Indian land. The wait of fifty years had been well worth it to those who had purchased their land from the federal government.[5]

Grants of Right of Way for Railroads and Locations for Settlements

Up to 1853 there had been no treaties made with the tribes of the southwest, but in that year Thomas Fitzpatrick, Indian Agent of the Upper Platte and Arkansas

Agency, was *sent as the sole commissioner to make a treaty* of friendship with these Indians. Under instructions dated May 5, 1853, his first meeting was with the Comanche, Kiowa and Apache. A treaty was concluded with them at Fort Atkinson and his lengthy report was included in the Commissioner Report to Secretary McClelland.

Agent Fitzpatrick's Report was endorsed by Commissioner George Manypenny and commended for the consideration of all concerned with the welfare of these Indians.

> The report of this officer, herewith transmitted, evidences the satisfactory manner in which he has discharged the important duties confided to him in this connection, and as containing highly valuable information touching our relations with the prairie and mountain tribes, and grave suggestions relative to our future policy in reference to them, *commends itself to the attention and consideration of all who may take an interest in the future of this unfortunate class of our Indian population*. (Emphasis added).[6]

Agent Fitzpatrick's interpretation of Article 3 of the Treaty is a clear example of what Peter d'Errico denominates as a **"semantic world created by one group to rule another."** *The explanation of the import of* **Article 3 of the Treaty** *in Fitzpatrick's Report demonstrates the extremely broad interpretation given the Treaty.*

Article 3 is as follows :

> "Article 3. The aforesaid Indian tribes do also hereby fully acknowledge the right of the United States to lay off and mark out roads and highways, to make reservations of land necessary thereto - to locate depots - and to establish military and other posts within the territory inhabited by the said tribes; and also to prescribe and enforce, in such manner as the President or Congress of the United States shall from time to time direct, rules and regulations to protect the rights of persons and property among the said Indian tribes." [10 Stat. 1013]

Agent Fitzpatrick was extremely proud of what he achieved in negotiating Article 3:

"The mere acknowledgment of a right of way through their country was readily conceded, because it had been long enjoyed; but upon the subjects of military posts, and reservations of land, and hostilities against the Republic of Mexico, they were found to be far more tenacious…

[I]n view of the fact that at no distant day the whole country over which those Indians now roam must be peopled by another and more enterprising race… [and that] a great central route to the Pacific by railway has become deeply impressed upon the public mind; and while many courses are contemplated two of them at least are designed to pass through this section of the country. [T]he acknowledgment contained in [Article 3] may be found of inestimable value. *It will afford all the concession necessary for locations, pre-emptions, reservations, and settlements, and avoid, besides, the enhanced costs of secondary treaties with those tribes.* (Emphasis added).[7]

In James Malin's analysis of this Treaty he concludes:

The underlying motives in making the Fort Atkinson treaty in this particular form are certainly sufficiently clear and impressive. Its provisions were designed to admit of the interpretation that they might be considered as *grants of right of way for railroads and locations for settlements*. The Laramie treaty contained practically the same provisions for the grant of right of way for roads and locations for military and other posts. It is evident that they also would be open to the same kind of an interpretation. Thus by these two great Indian treaties the two most practicable railroad routes to the Pacific were opened through the country of the prairie and mountain tribes. (Emphasis added).[8]

Railroads Recruited Emigrants

Railroads were expensive to build and operate. They needed passengers, freight and income, and their publicity staffs recruited emigrants to settle in cities and on farms — and, of course, rely on the railroads for goods and services.[9]

Military Posts Built Along Transcontinental Routes

~ 686 ~

Given the importance of westward expansion to the U.S. economy, military posts were built along the transcontinental routes. The passage of the Homestead Act opened the west to settlers of more modest means. What started as a trickle became a steady flow of migration that would last until the end of the century. Nearly 400,000 settlers had made the trek westward by the height of the movement in 1870.

> Development of a basic defense system in the trans-Mississippi West had followed the course of empire; territorial acquisition and exploration succeeded by emigration and settlement brought the whites increasingly into collision with the Indians and progressively raised the need for military posts along the transcontinental trails and in settled areas.[10]

Requiem for Buffalo

> The decimation of the buffalo is not a tale of glory, but of immense sorrow. European settlers in the Great Plains are estimated to have reduced the American bison population from 30 million to just 325 by the 1880s. It was a means for destroying the subsistence base of the Indians, a source of income and most horribly, of fun, for those participating and those watching.

John Putnam's article on *A Trip on the Union Pacific* confirms the tragedy. The sacredness of the buffalo was lost on the plains.

> Then Buffalo-singly-in couples-in groups-in countless herds. ... There we come on a herd. The cars stop. Now the fun begins. Every body runs out and commences shooting-Nothing hurt. ... With the same result this performance is repeated again and again- the stopping of the train- the brave charge- the ignominious return.

> We failed to bag a buffalo. I did not shoot having ill defined ideas as to hunting rifles, which end you put the load in and which end you get it out at. (I never hunted any game with guns except men, you know.) But I rushed out with the rest - yelled promiscuously "Buffalo"- "Stop the train"- "let me out"- "there they are" - "Whoop-pey" - "Give 'em thunder" - "no go" - "Come back" - "drive on"- So you see I helped a good deal.[11]

The Department of the Interior witnessed the near extinction event as helpful in the assimilation of Indians to an agricultural lifestyle, yet recognized the difficulties in generating hostility among the Indians. Secretary of Interior Columbus Delano stated in 1873:

> While I would not seriously regret the total disappearance of the buffalo from our western prairies, in its effect on the Indians, regarding it as a means of hastening their sense of dependence upon the products of the soil and their own labors, yet these encroachments by the whites upon the reservations set apart for the exclusive occupancy of the Indian is one prolific source of trouble in the management of the reservation Indians ...[12]

Reservation Policy

The 1851 Indian Appropriations Act allotted funds to move western tribes onto reservations. The Bureau of Indian Affairs defines a reservation as "an area of land reserved for a tribe or tribes under treaty or other agreement with the United States, executive order, or federal statute or administrative action as permanent tribal homelands, and *where the federal government holds title to the land in trust on behalf of the tribe*." (Emphasis added).[13]

Commissioner N.G. Taylor expressed the government's position on the need to dispossess Indians of the abundant and valuable natural resources on their aboriginal homelands. In 1868 he stated as follows:

> "The steady approach of emigration ... imperiously demand that the policy of concentrating them upon reservations should, whenever practicable, be adopted. ... The Indians are in possession of vast tracts of country, abounding in precious metals, or rich in sources of agricultural wealth. These invite the enterprise of the adventurous pioneer, who, in seeking a home and fortune, is constantly pressing upon the abode of the red man."[14]

Commissioner Morgan in 1890 in hindsight reflected on the infinite horror of the reservation system:

> The entire system of dealing with them is vicious, involving, as it does, the installing of agents, with semi-despotic power

over ignorant, superstitious, and helpless subjects; the keeping of thousands of them on reservations practically as prisoners, isolated from civilized life and dominated by fear and force; the issue of rations and annuities, which inevitably tends to breed pauperism; the disbursement of millions of dollars worth of supplies by contract, which invites fraud; the maintenance of a system of licensed trade, which stimulates cupidity and extortion, etc.[15]

U.S. Mission to Destroy Tribal Governments, Decimate Sovereignty and Obliterate Indian Individual Identity

Citizenship was a cruel irony for Indians. Described as a badge of honor, it was instead, a weapon of destruction, of the ultimate control of Indians. It was a token reflecting the collapse of tribal existence, much less sovereignty. How cruel to Indians, to extend quasi-citizenship, necessary to allow the federal government to continue its role as guardians and Indians as wards, maintaining an imperial control over everything Indian. The silent deletion of the statutory grant of "full" citizenship to Indians in the proposed Indian Citizenship Act is shrouded in silence and secrecy. What is the substance of Indian citizenship? It didn't include suffrage and it eliminated the right of individual Indians to sue the federal government, forever indemnifying the U.S. for the documented and substantiated atrocities against Indian peoples.

As the 1870s progressed, federal officials further recommended that the entirety of the indigenous population be "brought within the protection and restraint of ordinary law" and that civilized Indians be permitted to adopt American citizenship. In his 1874 report, Indian Affairs Commissioner Smith argued that such measures would benefit the Native population, *reflect the fact that their tribal government structures had collapsed*, and put an end to the "fiction of sovereignty" by which the tribes were described as independent nations. Commissioner. J.Q. Smith. (Emphasis added).[16]

"[T]he domination of the chiefs should be broken up." (Emphasis added).[17] "It has become the settled policy of the Government to break up reservations, *destroy tribal relations*, settle Indians upon their own homesteads, incorporate them into the national life, and deal with them not as nations or tribes or bands, but as individual citizens. The American Indian is to become the Indian American." (Emphasis added).[18]

Savage Aristocracy

> It has seemed to me ... that the system of large reservations as has hitherto prevailed, is not only no longer desirable either in the interest of the Indians or of the whites, but will, in the course of time become utterly untenable. As our white settlements in the West multiply, as the development of the country advances, *available lands become more and more scarce and valuable*, and so it is not unnatural that the withholding of large tracts from settlement and development so as to maintain a savage aristocracy in the enjoyment of their chivalrous pastimes, should be looked upon by many as a system incompatible with the progress of civilization and injurious to the material interests of the country. As an inevitable consequence, we have witnessed many encroachments, lawless and wrongful in character, upon Indian lands and rights, and constant efforts to drive the red men from the reservation belonging to them. ... as long as the Indians hold very large tracts of land, in great part useless to themselves and useless to other people, their tenure will, under existing circumstances become practically more and more precarious. It is most desirable for the interests of the Indians themselves, therefore, that we should substitute for the system of large reservations another system that will protect the rights and interests of the Indians without standing in the way of the progress and development of the country. *The ultimate end of this new system, in my opinion, must necessarily be that the Indians be gradually assimilated to and merged in the body of citizens.* In the direction of this end, some things are necessary, which have been done as far as the Executive could do them under the laws of the country as they stand: First, to set the Indians to work; second, to educate them; and, third, to individualize the Indians by settling them in severalty, with the expectation of giving them fee-simple title by patent to their allotments, the same title by which white citizens hold their lands under the protection of law. (Emphasis added).[19]

Policy Conflict between War Department and Interior Department

Congress created the Joint Committee Appointed to take into Consideration the Expediency of Transferring the Indian Bureau to the War Department (hereafter referred to as the Joint Committee) in 1878. The Doolittle Committee of 1865, the Peace Commission of 1867 and the Banning Committee of 1876 all had expressed their opinion on the transfer issue. Even though the Committees had partisan views and differences, it brought into the public forum the intense and hostile division between the two entities.

The Banning Committee's report concluded by stating:

> In view of all the evidence adduced, we are of the opinion that the ***conduct of Indian affairs*** under civil administration, after a practical working of twenty-seven years, has proved ***fraudulent, expensive, and unsatisfactory*** to the Indians, provoking them to hostilities that have cost the Government many millions, besides the lives of thousands of citizens and destruction of their property, whereas the affairs of this branch of the public service, while under the control of the War Department, were honestly, economically, and firmly administered and executed." (Emphasis added).[20]

General Sherman voiced his concern on defining the Army's role in relation to government civil servants when he stated:

> I dont [sic] care about interesting myself too far in the fate of the poor devils of importance of Indians who are doomed from the causes inherent in their nature or from the natural & persistent hostility of the white race. All I aim to accomplish is to so clearly define the duties of the Civil & Military agents of Govt so that we wont [sic] be quarrelling all the time as to whose business it is to look after them.[21]

With the focus on agency dominance and budgets, the divided responsibility over the Indians was not based on concern for them but was marked by a conflict of authority at every echelon. This resulted in territorial governors favoring military control of the BIA. Arizona Territory Governor John P. Hoyt argued that under the current system, if an Indian rebellion were to break out, the Department of the Interior would then be required to notify the War Department. The lag in communication concerned Hoyt because he recognized the tension between the two departments that might effect response time to such an event.[22]

Failure to Fulfill Trust Relationship

Maura Grogan in her article, "Native American Lands and Natural Resource Development," Revenue Watch Institute, identifies three components of the federal trust responsibility: "the protection of Indian trust lands and Indian rights to use those lands; the protection of tribal sovereignty and rights of self-governance; and the provision of basic social, medical and educational service for tribal members."[23]

The information in this Chapter will demonstrate how the federal government has completely failed in these responsibilities.

The extract below is from the Report of a commission of citizens appointed by the President under the act of Congress of April 10, 1869, to cooperate with the administration in the management of Indian affairs. The commissioners included: Felix R. Brunot, Chairman, Robert Campbell, H. S. Lane, W. E. Dodge, Nathan Bishop, John V. Farwell, Vincent Colyer, George H. Stuart and Edward S. Tobey.

> While it cannot be denied that the government of the United States, in the general terms and temper of its legislation, has evinced a desire to deal generously with the Indians, *it must be admitted that the actual treatment they have received has been unjust and iniquitous beyond the power of words to express*. Taught by the government that they had rights entitled to respect; when those rights have been assailed by the rapacity of the white man, *the arm which should have been raised to protect them has been ever ready to sustain the aggressor*. The history of the government connections with the Indians is a shameful record of broken treaties and unfulfilled promises. The history of the border white man's connection with the Indians is a sickening record of murder, outrage, robbery, and wrongs committed by the former as the rule, and occasional savage outbreaks and unspeakably barbarous deeds of retaliation by the latter as the exception.
>
> In addition to the class of robbers and outlaws who find impunity in their nefarious pursuits upon the frontiers, there is a large class of professedly reputable men who use every means in their power to bring on Indian wars, for the sake of the profit to be realized from the presence of troops and the expenditure of government funds in their midst. They proclaim

death to the Indians at all times, in words and publications, making no distinction between the innocent and the guilty. They incite the lowest class of men to the perpetration of the darkest deeds against their victims, and, as judges and jurymen, shield them from the justice due to their crimes. Every crime committed by a white man against an Indian is concealed or palliated ... (Emphasis added).[24]

Concealing Peace Treaty Commissions' Purpose

On June 5, 1850, An Act Authorizing the Negotiation of Treaties with the Indian Tribes in the Territory of Oregon, for the Extinguishment of their Claims to Lands Lying West of the Cascade Mountains was passed into law. The act established a commission to negotiate treaties with western Oregon Indians for the *purpose of extinguishing all Indian claims to lands west of the Cascade Mountains and removing over two thousand members of thirty tribes to a reservation east of the mountains*. (Emphasis added).[25]

Samuel Thurston, territorial delegate to Congress in 1849–1851, lobbied for the removal of the western Oregon Indians to east of the Cascade Mountains to further enable settlement in the Willamette Valley.[26]

In a letter to the Secretary of War on June 17, 1867, General Sherman made it clear that "if fifty Indians are allowed to remain between the Arkansas and Platte we will have to guard every stage station, every train, and all railroad working parties. In other words, fifty hostile Indians will checkmate three thousand soldiers." Making sure the Secretary of War understood him, he proclaimed that "*it makes little difference whether they be coaxed out by Indian commissioners or killed,*" but the government needed to get the Indians out as soon as possible. (Emphasis added).[27]

Most likely, Indians were not aware of the long term policies of the various Treaty and Peace Commissions to extinguish Indian title and take their lands en masse with the ultimate goal of their assimilation into the American melting pot.

U.S.' Willingness to Break Indian Treaties

There is no question that the U.S. was willing to break the Indian treaties it entered into and that the judiciary backed them up. Plenary authority over the tribal relations of the Indians has been exercised by Congress and is considered a political matter, not subject to judiciary review. As evidenced in *Lone Wolf v. Hitchcock*, 187 U.S. 553, 565-66 (1903), the legislative power may pass laws in conflict with treaties made with the Indians, to the point of completely abrogating them.

General Pope knew of the fate of Indian tribes entering into solemn treaties with the government:

> I have, for instance, known of more than one case in which a treaty with the Indians contained a solemn provision that their country should not be intruded on by the whites—a treaty duly ratified by the Senate ... *The very fact that this provision of all treaties with Indians is constantly and systematically violated, and that the Indian wars and outrages have occurred with increasing frequency on that very account, created the necessity of almost continuous treaty-making, even with the same tribe, until there remained of the tribe no one to treat with, and this I believe to be the natural end of all Indians who engage in this sort of diplomacy.* (Emphasis added).[28]

In 1876, Commissioner Smith recognized the practicality of breaching Indian treaties:

> There is a very general and growing opinion that observance of the strict letter of treaties with Indians is in many cases at variance both with their own best interests and with sound public policy. Public necessity must ultimately become supreme law...[29]

Brigadier General Nelson A. Miles clearly addressed this topic recognizing that the U.S. had transgressed the Indian treaties it entered in to from the Atlantic to the Pacific and much of the intergenerational wealth in the U.S. was derived as a result.

> *Our relations with the Indians have been governed chiefly by treaties and trade, or war and subjugation. By the first we have invariably overreached the natives, and we find the record of broken promises all the way from the Atlantic to the Pacific, while many of the fortunes of New York, Chicago, St. Louis, and San Francisco can be traced directly to Indian tradership.* (Emphasis added).

In our treaty relations, most extravagant and sacred promises have been given by the highest authorities, and yet these have frequently been disregarded.[30]

Failure to Protect Indian Land

The U.S.' failure to protect Indian land is wrapped up in its aim of pauperizing Indians as documented by General Pope and Secretary Delano.

"Every year's advance of our frontier takes in a territory as large as some of the kingdoms of Europe. We are richer by hundreds of millions; the Indian is poorer by a large part of the little that he has. This growth is bringing imperial greatness to the nation; *to the Indian it brings wretchedness, destitution, beggary*..." (Emphasis added).[31]

"Thus, by the process of two treaties, between the civilized and the savage, the strong and the weak, the *Arapahoes and Cheyennes* were stripped of their magnificent possessions, larger than the States of Pennsylvania, New York, and New Jersey, and *left without a foot of land they could call their home*." (Emphasis added).[32]

The famed Comstock lode lay right on Northern Paiute land.

The discovery was unusual not only for the large presence of silver as well as gold, but also for the spectacular amount of wealth it generated. Almost seven million tons of ore were extracted and milled between 1860 and 1880, with the mines producing what today would equal approximately $700 million in profits.[33]

Executive Order Reservations

As with treaty or statutory reservations, under Executive Order reservations Indians have the exclusive right to possession, with title to the lands in the U.S. Congress has plenary authority to control use, grant adverse interests or extinguish the Indian title. The one difference is that so long as Congress has not recognized compensable interests in the Indians, executive order reservations *may be terminated by Congress or the Executive without payment of compensation.* (Emphasis added).[34]

The creation of new executive order reservations was prohibited by the Act of June 30, 1919, ch. 4, § 27, 41 Stat. 34 (codified at 43 U.S.C. § 150) and changes in the boundaries of existing reservations by executive order were prohibited by the Act of March 3, 1927, ch. 299, § 4, 44 Stat. 1347 (codified at 25 U.S.C. § 398d).

Encroachments on Indian Lands by White Settlers

Economic pressures from private settlers and companies in search of valuable resources continued to infringe on the rights of tribes to reside without interference on their reservations.

> There is scarcely one of the ninety-two reservations at present established on which white men have not effected a lodgement: many swarm with squatters, who hold their place by intimidating the rightful owners; while in more than one case the Indians have been wholly dispossessed, and are wanderers upon the face of the earth. So far have these forms of usurpation been carried at times in Kansas, that *an Indian reservation there might be defined as that portion of the soil of the State on which the Indians have no rights whatsoever*. (Emphasis added).[35]

Government's Segregation of Minerals from Indian Lands

In 1860, the year before the American Civil War started, the U.S. Government debt was $64.8 million. Once the war began, debt grew quickly. The financial cost of the war was significant, totaling an estimated $5.2 billion. Individual Confederate States owed $67 million. The Confederated States of America owed about $1.4 billion. Following the Civil War, the South was bankrupt. It's industry and farms were unserviceable and their credit was depleted. The federal government needed the value of the vast mineral production from the west to pay off this debt.

In a Bureau of Mines documentary about Arizona, including gold, mineral, copper, and silver mining, agriculture, and features such places as Montezuma Castle and Oregon Pipe Cactus National Monuments, Petrified Forest, Painted Desert, Mission of St. Xavier Del Bac, Hope Creek Canyon, Dragoon Mountains, and Sunset Crater, the Bureau of Mines made the common refrain *Indians had "little use for precious metals."* (Emphasis added).[36]

Deliberate Undervaluation of Indian Mineral Lands by U.S.

Superintendent Nesmith described the sharp techniques negotiators used to get bargain prices on Indian land in Oregon. His Report that the Indians didn't receive "fair compensation" was included in the Congressional debate in 1928 on this topic.

> My own observation in relation to the treaties which have been made in Oregon leads me to the conclusion that in most instances the Indians have not received a fair compensation for the rights which they have relinquished to the government.
>
> It is too often the case in such negotiations that the agents of the government are over anxious to drive a close bargain … The Indians … begin to conclude that they have been defrauded, finally resort to arms … and the government expends millions in the prosecution of a war.
>
> A notable instance of this kind is exhibited in the treaty of September 10, 1853, with the Rogue River Indians. … The country which they ceded embraces nearly the whole of the valuable portion of the Rogue River valley, embracing a country unsurpassed in the fertility of its soil and value of its gold mines; and the compensation which those nine hundred and nine people now living receive … [amounts to] *two dollars and fifty cents per annum to the person*, which is the entire means provided for their clothing and sustenance. (Emphasis added).[37]

Felix Brunot admitted his willingness to cheat Indians by offering low prices for their land. At the same time, respected and renowned, he was appointed in 1868 as the Chairman of the Board of Indian Commissioners to investigate Indian grievances. He negotiated the Brunot Agreement with the Utes by which they surrendered their valuable mineral land in the San Juan Mountains. He also negotiated the 1868 cession agreement with the Shoshones which diminished the original reservation by nearly one third and opened the ceded southern portion to white settlement.

Mining Dependent on Timber, Agricultural Land and Water

Shafts in mines depended on timber for support. Philip Deidesheimer invented square-set timbering, a framing system that used interlocking rectangular timber sets to support unstable rocks. An enormous amount of timber was used so that it was said "a forest of underground timbers of enormous dimensions" lay under Virginia City, Nevada.

The first gold deposits were found primarily along streams, and early miners usually established claims along the stream banks, where they could pan for gold directly. Hydraulic mining utilized water pushed through hoses under great pressure to wash entire hillsides directly into wooden sluices. The use of water was so basic to the production of gold that enterprising miners discovered that they could make more money providing water to the mines than they could from mining the gold itself.[38]

In addition, food was necessary for the mining communities and agriculture needed water.

Theft of Indian Mineral Resources

The effect of the theft of Indian mineral resources is still with Indians today. The Department of the Interior could have held the minerals in trust for the Indians until they could be developed for their benefit. It faced a huge conflict of interest: the revenue was needed to pay off the national debt from the Civil War and to aid in the reconstruction of the south. It was needed to fund the industrial engine that would make the U.S. a dominant world power. Indians were a mere obstacle to subdue through all the brutality imaginable. Combat would be conducted by a technologically superior Army, by vigilante forces armed by the government, by miners and colonial settlers. Indian country was invaded and Indians incarcerated on reservations.

In 1885, Commissioner Atkins stated the following in his Report to Secretary Lamar:

> Mines, real or prospective, have tempted thousands of men into localities heretofore occupied only by Indians. Without regard to the rights of the Indians, they are constantly trespassing, harassing the Indians, provoking quarrels, thieving, and making the life of the agent one of constant anxiety and vigilance.[39]

Theft of Indian Timber

In 1880, Commissioner Marble pronounced the absolute need for legislation prohibiting the theft of Indian timber. In 1882 and 1884, Commissioner Price *reiterated* the continuing occurrence of the wanton theft of Indian timber. In 1885, Commissioner Atkins alerted the Secretary of the Interior to the "incessant spoliation of timber on Indian lands" due to Congress' repeated failure to act on preventive legislation. In 1888, Congress finally amended section 5388 to cover timber trespass "upon any Indian reservation, or lands belonging to or occupied by any tribe of Indians under authority of the United States,"[40] but did not include allotted land.

Theft of Indian Water Resources

Due to state allocation of water to private users, and in most cases over-allocation, Indian tribes were often left without water. They came late to the game of quantifying their right to water such that they *must* litigate in state court or negotiate settlements with private users and states to determine their water rights. Executive Orders, federal statutes and treaties reserving land for Indian reservations typically did not address water needs of these reservations.

The courts have held that Indians have the following types of water rights:

> **Reserved**: water allocated to fulfill the purpose of the Indian reservation established by the federal government. Winters v. United States, 207 U.S. 564 (1908).
> **Allotted**: when the Indian reservation was allotted, each allotment possesses the right to a portion of tribal waters needed for agriculture. U.S. v. Powers, 305 U.S. 529 (1939).
> **Aboriginal**: in some cases, water used by Indians pre-dating European colonization. United States v. Adair, 723 F.2d 1394 (9th Cir. 1983).

In *Winters v. United States*, non-Indians had built large and substantial dams and reservoirs and, by means of canals and ditches and waterways, diverted waters of the Milk River from its channel, above the points of diversion by the U.S. and the Indians on the Fort Belknap Reservation in Montana, which deprived the U.S. and the Indians of the use of water. The U.S. Supreme Court explained that lands provided under the Fort Belknap agreement for the purpose of developing an agrarian society "were arid and, without irrigation, were practically valueless." Water was thus necessary for agriculture. The Supreme Court held that the federal government reserved water rights for the Fort Belknap Reservation and for a use which would be necessarily continued through the years. The amount must satisfy the present and future needs of the reservation. The water rights vest on the date that Congress reserves the land and are not lost if a tribe does not maintain continuous use.

> As for the holding in the *Winters* decision, Utah's Senator George Sutherland spoke for many others when he dismissed it as "one of those unfortunate statements that sometimes courts, and the highest court, lapse into." Sutherland was a renowned legal scholar and politician, having served in the Utah State Senate, U.S. Congress, and U.S. Senate.[41]

Congress passed the McCarran Amendment in 1952, 43 U.S.C. § 666 (1952), under which state courts could hear disputes involving Indian reserved water rights. All water rights adjudication cases must originate in state court, including those of Indian Nations.

The McCarran Amendment general stream adjudications have proved to be extremely costly and protracted. Since all water users on a given stream system must be joined as parties, hundreds or even thousands of parties are commonly involved. Each party is adverse to every other party. The rights of each party must be proven: the priority date, quantity of use, place of use and purpose of use must be established for each water user. Trials take many years, and millions of dollars in costs, fees for expert witnesses and attorney's fees. As a result, very few of these cases involving tribal reserved water rights have been litigated to final judgment. In one example, in a general stream adjudication of the Big Horn River system initiated by the state of Wyoming in 1977, the State reportedly spent $14 million in attorney's fees during a twelve-year period in the 1970s and 1980s.[42]

Given the prospect of having state courts adjudicate Indian reserved water rights, tribes prefer negotiated settlements. Since 1978, 36 Indian water rights settlements have been federally approved with 40 individual Indian tribes.

The primary challenge in pursuing settlement agreements is the availability of federal funds to implement ongoing and future agreements. Indian water rights settlements often involve construction of major new water infrastructure to allow tribal communities access to water. Many times the funding for these delivery systems is not allocated and tribes suffer in the drought-stricken west. Farming ventures are shut-in, people laid off, and healthy food replaced by canned and processed commodities.

Mining Magnates

Colorado's mining and business magnates gained wealth as the result of the ethnic cleanings of Colorado by removing the Cheyenne, Arapahos and the Utes. It was a pattern repeated across Indian country.

> Official statistics show that Colorado produced from 1859 to December 31, 1904 at the current market prices for the metals: Gold $355,014,347; silver $386,457,857; lead $121,118,146; copper $17,835,820; zinc (a recent product); $10,740,207; total, $891,259,375.

> The total Colorado production of the precious and allied metals from 1859 to 1870, inclusive, was: Gold $27,213,081; silver $330,000; copper $40,000; total, $27,583,081.[43]

Strategic Military Policy

A military command structure was put in place, with designated zones of operations, the establishment of forts to assure the control of territory and the ability to procure, transport and distribute armaments and supplies. The most elite U.S. generals were given carte blanche to eliminate Indian resistance in the west.

> The annexation of Texas in 1845, the settlement of the Oregon boundary dispute in 1846, and the successful conclusion of the Mexican War with the cession to the United States in 1848 of vast areas of land all drew the outlines of the primary duties facing the Army in the West in the middle of the nineteenth century: **the facilitation of westward expansion and the pacification or defeat of the Indian tribes that actively fought or resisted this expansion.** (Emphasis added).[44]

Cost-Benefit Analysis of Total Destruction of Indians

In an Extract from the 1865 Commissioner of Indian Affairs Report to the Secretary of the Interior, we find the following cost-benefit analysis of the total destruction of the Indians:

> The *policy of the total destruction of the Indians has been advocated by gentlemen of high position, intelligence, and personal character*; but no enlightened nation can adopt

or sanction it without a forfeiture of its self-respect and the respect of the civilized nations of the earth.

Financial considerations forbid the inauguration of such a policy. The attempted destruction of three hundred thousand of these people, accustomed to a nomadic life, subsisting upon the spontaneous productions of the earth, and familiar with the fastnesses of the mountains and the swamps of the plains, *would involve an appalling sacrifice of the lives of our soldiers and frontier settlers, and the expenditure of untold treasure*. It is estimated that the maintenance of each regiment of troops engaged against the Indians of the plains costs the government two million dollars per annum. All the military operations of last summer have not occasioned the immediate destruction of more than a few hundred Indian warriors. Such a policy is manifestly as impracticable as it is in violation of every dictate of humanity and Christian duty. (Emphasis added).[45]

Shock and Awe Tactics

Joseph Lane, the Late Superintendent and Isaac I. Stevens, Delegate to the U.S. House of Representatives from Washington Territory, proposed to the House of Representatives and Chas. E. Mix, Acting Com. Ind. Aff., on February 17, 1858, that a group of Indian leaders from Oregon and Washington be taken on a tour of the principal cities to realize that there was no way they could fight the array of forces possessed by the U.S. or the policies imposed by them.[46]

Railroads: Weapon against Indians

Railroads served not only for transport, but most importantly, as fortresses against Indian attacks across Indian lands. They also aided in emigrant transport and development of towns and cities. Bisecting Indian country they reduced the possibility of tribes integrating their forces. Such alliances would have augmented war fighting capacity and supplies against a common shared enemy.

The railroads now under construction, or projected with a reasonable assurance of early completion, will *multiply fourfold the striking force of the Army* in that section; the little rifts of *mining settlement, now found all through the mountains of the southern Territories will have become self-protecting communities...* (Emphasis added).[47]

Military Massacres

Colonel John M. Chivington, First Colorado Cavalry, Citizen Militia, reported on November 29, 1864, that his command killed between *400 and 500 Indians* at Sand Creek. (Emphasis added).[48] Many times this number is lessened, but it was the number he used in his two official military reports of record.

Two hundred fifty Shoshoni were slaughtered by Colonel Patrick Edward Connor and about 200 California volunteer thugs at the Bear River Massacre.[49] Others included the Piegans at the Baker Massacre in Montana (1870) Arapahoes and Cheyennes at the Washita River, Indian Territory (1868); the Apaches at Camp Grant, Arizona (1871); the Modocs in Oregon Territory (1873); and the Lakotas at Wounded Knee, Dakota Territory (1890).

Consequences of Indian War

Bribery through annuities and treaties without substance were cheaper than outright warfare with the Indians. From the time of President Jefferson, the plan was to drub them or bribe them.

From Thomas Jefferson to James Monroe, April 17, 1791:

> I hope we shall *drub the Indians well this summer and then change our plan from war to bribery*. We must do as the Spaniards and English do, keep them in peace by liberal and constant presents. They find it the cheapest plan, and so shall we. The expence of this summers expedition would have served for presents for half a century. ...Every rag of an Indian depredation will otherwise serve as a ground to raise troops... (Emphasis added).[50]

Generals Sherman, Harney, Augur and Terry knew the cost of war:

> *Fifteen or twenty Indians had been killed at an expense of more than a million dollars apiece, while hundreds of our*

soldiers had lost their lives, many of our border settlers had been butchered, and their property destroyed. This was the experience of the United States in a contest with an Indian tribe numbering perhaps four thousand men, women, and children, and able to bring into the field not one-fifth as many warriors as the Sioux bands of today. (Emphasis added).[51]

The elite generals, most of them graduates of the U.S. Military Academy, that fought in the Civil War, assumed duty in the west to fight the Indians. Trained in war and combat, they would use their forces as needed to "drub" the Indians. The guerilla warriors would be worn down by constant pursuit, by using Indian scouts and warriors to destroy the enemy forces, by attacking villages by surprise and wasting them, by forcibly disarming and dismounting the Indians, and imprisoning them on reservations so they couldn't offer sustenance to their warriors.

Six years into the Navajo-American War of 1860-1868, Navajo War Leader Manuelito surrendered with 23 warriors:

> *They were all in rags, their bodies emaciated. They still wore leather bands on their wrists for protection from the slaps of the bowstrings but they had no bows or arrows. One of Manuelito's arms hung useless at his side from a wound. Now there were no more war chiefs.* (Emphasis added).[52]

As Manuelito said:

> We fought for that country because we did not want to lose it. We lost nearly everything. The American nation is too powerful for us to fight. When we had to fight for a few days we felt fresh, but in a short time we were worn out and the soldiers starved us out.[53]

He was incarcerated at Fort Sumner.

Military Used to Enforce Reservation, Assimilation Policies

President Hayes' national objectives were to promote economic development and settlement in the West. To accomplish these objectives, three goals were incorporated into Indian policy and adopted by the military: first, the removal of Indians from the major east-west immigration trails where they were an obstacle to emigration and the development of the transcontinental railroad routes; second, the increase of the reservation system to reduce contact and conflict between the races; and third, the use of the reservation system to assimilate the Indians into mainstream American culture.

The military would be used to accomplish these objectives. Importantly, they would be used to force Indians to stay on their reservations. Akin to an *occupation* of the reservations, the nearby forts and the deterrence of insurgency were key to ensuring the success of the President's objectives. The military assumed leading responsibility for security, forcible settlement and regulating the Indians, along with intelligence collection and analysis.

> Those tribes that refused federal "protection" on reservations or rejected the government's assimilation programs were subjected to military action, an approach Harper's Monthly referred to in 1870, as "the iron fingers in a velvet glove."[54]

> Commissioner Smith further asserted that *Indians* throughout the country needed to understand that when outside of their reservation lines they are *subject to severe treatment by the military*. (Emphasis added).[55]

Private Vigilante Wars Paid for by U.S.

In a deplorable Report from General Wool to Lieutenant Colonel L. Thomas, Assistant Adjutant General, U.S. Army, Benicia Headquarters, Department of the Pacific, dated January 19, 1856, he cited the frightening motives of the white settlers engaging in "private wars:"

> *As long as individual war is permitted and paid for by the United States, and which is expected by all the citizens of Oregon, we shall have no peace,* and the war may be prolonged indefinitely, especially as it is generally asserted that the present war is a God-send to the people. (Emphasis added).[56]

> "*[T]here is a large class of professedly reputable men who use every means in their power to bring on Indian wars, for the sake of the profit to be realized from the presence of troops and the expenditure of government funds in their midst.* They proclaim death to the Indians at all times, in words and publications, making no distinction between the

innocent and the guilty. They incite the lowest class of men to the perpetration of the darkest deeds against their victims, and, as judges and jurymen, shield them from the justice due to their crimes." (Emphasis added).[57]

The cry of wolf by the governor and people of Kansas over Indian troubles was evidenced by General William T. Sherman, who had been touring Kansas and Colorado in the fall of 1866. General Sherman encountered no Indian troubles other than rumors. In referring to the latter he said, *"These are all mysterious, and only accountable on the supposition that our people out West are resolved on trouble for the sake of the profit resulting from the military occupation."* (Emphasis added).[58]

Extermination of Indians by Pioneer Vigilantes

California Governor Gavin Newsom in 2019 acknowledged that "California must reckon with our dark history … California Native American peoples suffered violence, discrimination and exploitation sanctioned by state government throughout its history. … It's called a genocide. That's what it was. A genocide."[59]

Up to 16,000 indigenous peoples died from the 1840s through the 1870s, in what California has officially recognized as "genocide." California Governor Burnett didn't just refuse to avert such a conflict—he set aside state money to arm local militias against Indians.

This goal of absolute extermination was recognized within the Department of the Interior as well:

> **"All this high-sounding talk about the hardy pioneer coming and mingling among them "with the Bible in one hand" and a patent to their land in the other, the latter backed by force, means in effect the absolute dispersion and ultimate extermination of the Indian. Pioneers and frontier settlers are not missionaries, and they are not fond of close contact with the Indian race." (Emphasis added).[60]**

Mayhem to Instill Fear among Indians

The volunteer goons fighting against the Walla-Walla Indians Oregon engaged in the following atrocity:

Chief "Pu-pu-mux-mux met them under a flag of truce, and declared "He was for peace ... He, however, was taken prisoner, and afterwards barbarously murdered, scalped, his ears and hands cut off, and these preserved and sent to the friends of the volunteers in Oregon, all [of] which was reported by volunteers." (Emphasis added).[61] Preserved in a jar, the ears were on exhibition for several years.

A December 20, 1933, letter written by F. B. Warfield, grandson of Samuel Newton Warfield, gives a graphic account of the incidents attending the passing of Pio-Pio-Mox-Mox. This account agrees in the main with other versions of the affair, and perhaps supplies additional items.

The relevant part of the letter reads substantially as follows:

> Vernonia, Oregon, December 20, 1933. ... Grandfather took the chief's scalp, which was a beauty-hair about 18 inches long, all braided in with beads, eagle feathers, etc. This scalp was buried in Linn County, near Shedd, Oregon ... After keeping the scalp for several years, my step-grandmother persuaded Grandfather to bury it.... F. B. Warfield. This letter is in the possession of Miss Edna Headrick of the Library Department, Oregon Normal School, Monmouth.[62]

These parties' desocndants should be contacted for information and a Native American Graves Protection and Repatriation Act claim should be pursued, if possible. The manner of treatment of this Chief's body, killed under a flag of truce, is despicable.

Reducing Reservation Size to Acquire More Indian Land

General Pope elucidated the procedure used by the U.S. to expropriate Indian lands through treaty-making. An example of this in regard to the Eastern Shoshone's Wind River Reservation is described below. They were not alone—three concession treaties were made with the Utes each time a mineral discovery was made on their lands.

> *"The first treaty made with an Indian tribe only alienated a small portion of his lands, but as the emigrants pressed forward, increasing daily both their numbers and the routes*

by which they entered the Indian country, it soon became
necessary to make another treaty, and then another, until
in time, and a very short time, as it appears, one tribe of
Indians after another was dispossessed of its lands ..."
(Emphasis added).[63]

1872: Reduce Wind River Indian Reservation to Get Mineral Lands

By 1872, miners were trespassing on the Wind River Indian Reservation's ("WRIR") mineral area, agitating for a reduction of the WRIR Reservation. The Commissioner again capitulated to their demands, relying on the trite excuses that the Indians didn't need the land and it was "rendered undesirable" due to the discovery of gold and silver.[109] *The area of land ceded was almost 700,000 acres.* (Emphasis added).[64]

1874: Further Reduction of WRIR to Get Agricultural Land, Coal and Minerals

Again in 1874, a further reduction of the WRIR was sought for its *agricultural lands and the coal and other minerals it contained. If the Shoshones were unwilling to agree to a cession, legislation would be imposed on them. The justification by the Commissioner of Indian Affairs - it was of "so little real value to the Indians" and it was a great wrong to the settlers "that its domain should not be settled."* (Emphasis added).[65]

Consolidation of Different Indian Tribes to Free Up Lands for White Settlers

To free up Indian land for "white settlement and cultivation," the Department of the Interior recommended and engaged in tribal consolidations. The effort to consolidate the Modoc Indians at Lost River on the Klamath Reservation led to the Modoc War. The sentence for the six Modoc leaders, including Captain Jack, read "to be hanged by the neck until they be dead." President Grant approved the findings on August 22. General Court Martial Orders No. 32, War Dept. On October 3, 1873, Captain Jack, Schonchin John, Black Jim, and Boston Charley were hanged. "The warriors' heads were cut off and shipped in alcohol to the Army Medical Museum for "scientific investigation.""
(Emphasis added).[66]

Loss of Tribal Lands due to Allotment

As early as 1838, the federal government advocated for allotment. *"Unless some system is marked out by which there shall be a separate allotment of land to each individual* whom the scheme shall entitle to it, you will look in vain for any general *casting off of savagism.* Common property and civilization cannot co-exist." (Emphasis added).[67] The severalty policy reduced Indian-owned lands from 155 million acres in 1881 to 77 million in 1900 and just 48 million acres in 1934.[68]

In *Hodel v. Irving*, 481 U.S. 704, 707 (1987), the U.S. Supreme Court declared the allotment policy "disastrous." Within a few decades, the Indian land base had been reduced by two-thirds and reservations were transformed into ungovernable checkerboards of Indian and non-Indian land.

Commissioner Morgan said in 1892:

> If the policy of allotting lands is conceded to be wise, then it should be applied at an early day to all alike wherever the circumstances will warrant. If we have settled upon the breaking up of the tribal relations, the extinguishment of the Indian titles to surplus lands, and the restoration of the unneeded surplus to the public domain, let it be done thoroughly. If reservations have proven to be inadequate for the purposes for which they were designed, have shown themselves a hindrance to the progress of the Indian as well as an obstruction in the pathway of civilization, let the reservations, as speedily as wisdom dictates, be utterly destroyed and entirely swept away.[69]

Opening Surplus Reservation Lands after Allotment to White Settlers

The allotment policy was vigorously endorsed within the Indian Service. "The common field is the seat of barbarianism," proclaimed an Indian agent; "the separate farm is the door to civilization." Commissioner of Indian Affairs Oberly explained in 1880, "the Indian must be imbued with the exalting egotism of American civilization so that he will say "I" instead of "We" and "This is mine" instead of "This is ours.""[70]

Truth about Quality of Indian Lands

Commissioner Cato Sells issued this strong rebuke of the allotment policy in 1915. It is still apt today.

> *I know of many allotments depending entirely upon which an Indian family would starve to death* and where no white family could be induced to attempt to make a living, and yet under these circumstances an unsuccessful Indian farm is apt to be declared a failure. There are thousands of acres of land on Indian reservations where *100 hundred acres would not feed a rabbit*. I suggest that hereafter we photograph the "painted desert" more frequently and less often the small alfalfa patch on a great reservation. We should at least tell the whole truth. It is prejudicial to the Indian to emphasize the small part of their possessions that are productive and withhold from the public the very large unproductive portion. In this wise it becomes wrongfully understood that they have vast and valuable possessions unused by them which should be otherwise utilized. (Emphasis added).[71]

Unfair Advantage due to Indians Unfamiliarity with English Language

Stuart Banner's book, *How the Indians Lost Their Land: Law and Power on the Frontier*, describes the many disadvantages Indians faced in land transactions due to their unfamiliarity with the English language and the methods used by whites to cheat the Indians.[72]

Commissioner Sells graphically described the greed and the unparalleled ruthlessness of the white man:

> While corruption and inefficiency may find its way into the rank and file of Government employees, the greatest danger to the Indian lies in the greed of the white man for his land and money. Where a tribe has these the grafter is sure to be in evidence. He comes from every breed known to mankind, and in the past has despoiled the Indian with a ruthlessness unparalleled.[73]

Land Descriptions

> Devious purchasers could also slip misdescriptions of the land past Indian sellers, Colden explained, by drafting deeds

to express boundaries not in terms of natural landmarks but "by points or Degrees of the Compass & by English Measures which are absolutely unknown to the Indians."[74]

Deeds for Land Transactions

The deeds for land transactions were written in English which allowed white purchasers to commit fraud in buying Indian land from Indian sellers.

Fraud could take many shapes. In several cases English purchasers told the Indians they wished to buy parcels of a given size but then, without alerting the Indians, inserted in the deeds descriptions of parcels much larger. As one duped seller complained, "when a Small parcel of Land is bought of us a Large Quantity is taken instead."[75]

Type of Document Proffered

The effect of the allotment on the Whites near White Earth was immediate. Mushroom banks sprang up in the surrounding small towns. The Indians in their affidavits (of which Linnen and myself took 505) testified that lawyers, banks, county officials, and business men of prominence in Detroit, Ogema, Mahnomen, and other towns, joined in the scramble to secure their pine lands and farm tracts… in the majority of cases, *as the Indian could neither write nor read, he did not know whether he was signing receipts, mortgages, deeds or releases*. (Emphasis added).[76]

Traders' Bills

There was absolutely no accounting for verification or auditing of the claims asserted by traders for debts due, with accumulated usurious interest. Indians lacked the capacity to assure debts were properly charged.

Sharp Business Practices

In leaving Indians to the sharp business practices of whites to learn by the harsh experience of financial loss, one hard blow could wipe out a whole Indian family's future economic well-being for generations to come.

"[A]s soon as an Indian of either mixed or full blood becomes capable of taking care of himself, we should set him upon his feet and sever the ties which bind him either to his tribe, in the communal sense, or to the Government. This principle is imperative as to both land and money. ... *[A]fter we have taken our hands off he may fall a victim to sharp practices; but the man never lived-red, white, or any other color-who did not learn a more valuable lesson from one hard blow than from twenty warnings*." (Emphasis added).[77]

Inadequate Appropriations

The inadequate appropriations by Congress for food, clothing and other needs of Indians resulted in some of the bleak stories of man's inhumanity. Indian men, women and children, unable to meet their most basic needs, died from starvation and exposure.

In 1862, only 247 blankets were furnished the tribe, or one blanket to six Indians, and 4,393 yards of calico, which was less than two yards to each Indian. Giving a blanket to one Indian works no satisfaction to the other five, who receive none, and two yards of calico to each Indian affords but little help and no advancement; yet this was all that could be distributed owing to the meagre appropriations allowed.[78]

The appropriations by the Government for their education and support are year by year growing less and less. *Our Congress seems to pass these bills for the assistance of the Indians grudgingly, as if it was a disagreeable duty, and they would do just as little of it as possible, or as is compatible with any sort of compromise with conscience.* (Emphasis added). A. J. Barnes, Indian Agent.[79]

Our wise Congress has appropriated lands, money, and legislation upon railroads, rivers, and harbors, public buildings, and monuments to the dead ... while within our own borders men, women, and children have been in a state of starvation, in actual want of sufficient to sustain life, and all this in the interest of economy. I believe the nation paid, and dearly, too, for the great *crime of slavery* and I believe that a just God will exact the tribute for our treatment of the Indian race.[80]

Tens of Thousands of Appropriation Dollars Withheld from Sioux

Sioux Agency, Withholding Appropriations, P. Prescott, Superintendent for Farming for Sioux

The treaties say these funds shall be annually expended, whereas, large amounts have been kept back, and are now in arrears and that after repeated applications to have them expended. These arrears are not mere petty sums, surplusses or remnants of funds remaining unexpended, but *large amounts, thousand and tens of thousands*, and in some cases the whole fund appropriated for a special purpose. It cannot be wondered at that the Indians are dissatisfied and constantly complaining, making the want of faith on the part of the government officers their excuse for misconduct of every kind, and leading them to be at all times inattentive to the expressed wishes of the agent, superintendent and commissioner of Indian affairs. There are always about the Indians people disposed to give them ill advice. (Emphasis added).[81]

Withholding Annuities

Through withholding food and clothing, the U.S. utilized a strong lever. A starving, freezing people were much more likely to surrender or sell their lands or submit to government orders. A letter to Thomas Jefferson from Meriwether Lewis, December 15, 1808, details the withholding of goods as intimidation to require land cessions:

> ... they were reduced in the course of a few months to a state of perfect submission without bloodshed; this has in my opinion very fairly proven the superiority which the policy of withholding merchandize from the Indians has over the chastizement of the sword, when their local situations are such as will enable us to practice it. In this state of humiliation General Clark found them in September (sic) last when he established the post near the Fire Prarie (sic); he very properly seized this favourable moment, to enter into a treaty with them ... It extinguishes their title to a country nearly equal in extent to the state of Virginia and much more fertile.[82]

Use of Annuities as Economic Sanctions

Annuities in monies and goods that were a federal obligation were used as economic sanctions to get Indians to cede lands and to move out of the State of Wisconsin. Governor Ramsey and John Watrous, an Indian Agent at La Pointe, conspired to lure the Ojibwe's to Minnesota and then extend the time for payment, making it impossible for them to return home in the dead of winter. They were forced to travel three to five hundred canoe and portage miles to Sandy Lake in Minnesota to receive their annuities. While waiting to receive their annuities at Sandy Lake, Agent Watrous wrote to Governor Ramsey that as many as 150 Ojibwe had died. With the waterways frozen over, the Ojibwe abandoned their canoes and returned home to Wisconsin on foot in what is referred to as the Wisconsin Death March. Chief Buffalo told Commissioner Luke Lea that another 230 died during the long, cold march home.[83]

Distribution of annuity goods was at times based on behavior creating internal dissension within tribes.

> *The policy of rewarding the progressive by a generous issue of the articles furnished by the Government and imposing privation upon others who obstinately persist in refusing to adopt civilized habits has been productive of good results.* It has brought forcibly to them an object lesson and the realization of the fact that, while the Government is disposed to be kind and generous to them if they will accept the instruction and advice imparted through its representatives, it will not support them in idleness. (Emphasis added). Mescalero Apache Indians.[84]

Annuities Late

For Indian agents, distribution of annuity goods was also a major task, and when goods failed to arrive at the promised time or at all, they had to face disgruntled Indians and defend the government in its failure.

> None of their annuity goods (and but part of their supplies) have reached this agency during the year. Goods purchased in August of last year have been lying in the railroad depot, 175 miles away, since November last, a period of over nine months. Flour purchased the first of June is still at Rawlins. No clothing, blanket, tent, implement, or utensil of any kind

has been issued at this agency for nearly two years; no flour, except once, 15 pounds to a family, since May.[85]

Annuity Goods Useless

Indian Agent Paige questioned the uselessness of the goods being sent to the Pacific Coast Indians and even more importantly, whether the New York contractors sent whatever they had just to make money at the expense of the Indians:

> "[T]he annuities they received, consisting, in part, of shoes, coats, pitchforks, sickles, scythes without snaiths, frying pans, and other loose odd ends of New York stores, are bartered off to white men on every opportunity. The articles that would be acceptable to them are such as are useful to the inhabitants of any fishing village; but I doubt the practicability or economy of sending goods from the Atlantic States for the Indians of this coast. ... *The high prices and inferior quality of the goods would seem to indicate that the main object of the persons engaged in furnishing them was simply to make as much money as possible, without regard to law or justice.* The invoice price of some of the articles is greater than the retail prices of the same things here. Such as they are, the packages are short. (Emphasis added). Agent G. A. Paige.[86]

Annuity Goods Damaged

With the federal government entering into contracts with New York business men, transport of goods to Indians covered long distances, at a time when transport was limited to shipping and wagon trains. Many times, the goods delivered were damaged or destroyed. Substitute goods were unlikely to be sent to replace the useless ones.

> The goods purchased for the Creeks and Seminoles in 1854, and which were so seriously damaged in transportation that their acceptance was formally declined by them, still remain here in storage, as I have received no instructions as to their disposition. The purchase of agricultural implements, &c., made last year on account of the Creeks, reached here a few days ago, but had been so badly handled in transportation that several of the original packages were broken and destroyed, their contents imperfectly and carelessly repacked, and a part

of some of the articles called for by the invoices lost in toto. Southern Superintendency, Fort Smith, Arkansas, C. W. Dean, Superintendent.[87]

Fraud within Department of the Interior

Repeatedly, fraud within the Department of the Interior was reported without accountability:

"It is a well-known fact that for years, Indian agents and Indian traders, as a class, have made immense fortunes in their positions. Even honest men have not failed to yield to the temptations set before them, and to forget their principles in the thirst for gain. The reason is obvious—the opportunity to make fortunes is great, the chances of detection in case of a breach of trust, very small. We cannot expect man to be any more scrupulous or conscientious on the distant frontier, surrounded by savages, than he is in Wall Street, surrounded by bulls and bears."[88]

Similar fraud existed under the War Department's control, also. In 1842, for example, an investigation revealed "an almost total want of method and punctuality" in business affairs. Millions had been spent without proper accounting, to the "great loss" and "heavy responsibility" of the government. Likewise, appropriations had been wasted or expended so as to "degrade" and "demoralize" the Indians.[89]

There is no doubt that fraud in the performance of contracts, and dishonest practices in the delivery and distribution of supplies and annuity goods, have frequently been the cause of just discontent among the Indians, sometimes resulting in trouble and disaster. I do not deem the present machinery of the Indian service sufficient for the prevention or discovery of abuse and fraudulent practices. The Inspectors and Superintendents who are charged, among other things, with such duty, have in but rare instances been successful in ferreting out the wily expedients resorted to by dishonest contractors or agents. The records of the Indian Office bear out this assertion.[90]

With the Indian agent ... He issues when he pleases, how he

pleases, and in what quantity he pleases. A wandering tribe reaches his agency, and he reports he has issued to it ten thousand pounds of flour and a thousand blankets. He may not have issued a hundred pounds of flour nor ten blankets. No receipts are required as vouchers by the accounting officers. I know such a statement will be received with incredulity by all businessmen and an indignant denial by the Indian Department, and therefore must explain that I mean no receipts that are worth the paper they are written on. Of course, what is called a receipt is, I presume, sent; but, when it is remembered that an Indian has about as much idea of the weight of a pound or the length of a yard as he has of the horizontal parallax of the fixed stars, and that in addition to this he knows neither how to read nor to write and is just as apt to put "his mark" to a receipt for ten thousand pounds of bacon as to one for ten. John Gibbon, Fort Shaw, M.T., December 1, 1875.[91]

Incompetent Accounting

The following changes were made in procurement in 1878 by the Department of the Interior, recognizing the flawed accounting of the past. Whether these changes were monitored or not is questionable, given the repeatedly reported lack of personnel.

All expenditures are made by payment through the Treasury Department for goods purchased under contracts made by the Commissioner of Indian Affairs.

Formerly agents were the sole judges of the necessities for making purchases. Now they must submit their proposals and estimates and give satisfactory reasons.

Formerly there was nothing to prevent contractors putting in straw bids, or withdrawing after a contract had been awarded to them, in order that a bidder at a higher price (often times the same party under another name) might receive the award.

Formerly contracts were so drawn that those to whom beef and flour contracts were awarded could and did habitually take advantage of the necessities of the Indians to accept grades inferior to those called for by the contracts.

Formerly agents hired as many employes as they saw fit and

paid them such salaries as they chose. Now all employes must be approved by the Secretary of the Interior, and legal limits are fixed to the amounts which may be expended for agency employes.

Formerly agents' accounts ran on for years without settlement. Now, their accounts are settled quarterly.

Formerly funds were remitted quarterly to agents, even though their accounts might not have been sent in for two or three years. Now remittances to agents are not made and the salaries of their employee, cannot be paid until their accounts for the preceding quarter have been received in the Indian Office.

Formerly the unexpended balances of funds which remained in the hands of agents at the end of a fiscal year were carried over by them to succeeding years until their retirement from the service. Now balances are covered into the Treasury at the end of each fiscal year.

Formerly agents expended government property in such manner as they thought best. Now sufficient reasons must be given for the disposal of any government property, and authority must be obtained from the Secretary of the Interior before any expenditure can be made.

Formerly supplies issued to Indians by Indian agents were receipted for by the chiefs. Now each head of a family and each individual Indian who is of age must receipt for himself.

Formerly when annuity moneys were paid to Indian tribes in fulfillment of treaty stipulations a large percentage of the whole sum was divided (or supposed to be) among a few prominent chiefs. Now each individual Indian, including chiefs, receives his per capita share.

Formerly flour was accepted at an Indian agency without any inspection. Now it is inspected before shipment and again upon its arrival at the agency.

Formerly when beef cattle were delivered at agencies two or

three head were selected for their weights and an estimate was made for the weight of the whole herd. Now the agent must render a certified weigher's return for all animals received.

Formerly Indian traders were permitted to charge whatever prices they might elect to put upon their goods. Now their prices are controlled by the Indian Office.

Formerly a trader might charge an Indian two or three times the price charged a white man for the same kinds of goods. Now traders are forbidden to make any distinction in prices, under pain of the forfeiture of their licenses.

Formerly contracts were made with Indians collecting claims against the government, by which attorneys took from one-half to two-thirds of the sums which were collected. Now all contracts made with Indians must be approved by the Commissioner of Indian Affairs.[92]

Incompetent Legal Representation

In 1911, the Commissioner of Indian Affairs had reported that more than 1,700 Indians, forming almost 34 per cent of the White Earth allottees lost 142,000 acres, *valued at over $2,000,000, and for timber valued at $1,755,000*, due to fraud. More than 2,000 suits were filed by the federal government involving over 2,300 allotments and 142,000 acres of land, asserting that allotments had been wrongfully obtained from both full-bloods and minors. The timber company's attorney, Ransom Powell, won on three points: (1) delay - ten years passed since the DOJ started the litigation making prosecution impossible due to lack of witnesses, etc.; (2) litigating to determine full-blood Indians reducing the pool to Indians who could bring suit to *102 full-blood White Earth Chippewas;* (3) successfully litigating that individual Indians had to bring their fraud cases in state court, without DOJ support - Indians lacked the money to pay for prosecuting a case. *Powell ensured that most of his clients' purchases were protected for a comparatively small cost. Nichols-Chisholm paid out only $48,497 and its sister firm, Park Rapids Lumber, only $23,015.*

Skull Studies

In 1914 with timber-company funds, Powell hired two social science physical anthropologists for the identification of full-bloods and mixed-bloods Chippewas, since the mixed-bloods had the right to sell their land and would drop out of the case. Dr. Albert E. Jenks, a professor at the University of Minnesota, and Dr. Ales Hrdlicka conducted studies using their theoretical studies.

In 1915 and 1916, they examined 696 allottees who claimed to be full bloods, comparing their physical attributes to the Pima Indians of the southwestern U.S., whom the anthropologists considered the most racially "pure" American Indians. They carefully measured and calibrated hair, eyes, nails, gums, head shapes, and teeth of White Earth Ojibwe and compared this data to measurements of the Pima.[94]

Their studies narrowed the pool of full-bloods. *Of the 5,173 White Earth allottees, only 408 were considered to be full bloods - and 306 of them died before the roll was finalized in 1920.* Based on the government studies, in 1920, there were only *102 full-blood White Earth Chippewas*. [The results of this study still stand today.]

Government's Cases Weakened by Powell's Advocacy

Due to Powell's *first defense*—the mere passage of time, he had won. The DOJ determined that it would be difficult to successfully prevail at trial given the *decade* that had passed since starting the litigation. They agreed on a settlement basis:

> Land would be restored to full bloods; the cases involving mixed bloods who were competent to sell would be dismissed; and others who were defrauded, such as minors, would receive the difference between their original payments and the fair value of the property at time of sale, plus six percent interest to the time of settlement [not their land]. Significantly, no remedy was established for mixed bloods who had been defrauded.[95]

Fraudulent Land Transactions

As evidenced below and in the history on this subject, fraudulent land transactions with Indians were common, frequent and not limited to any tribe.

Commissioner Burke Confirms U.S. Fraudulent Land Transactions with Indians across U.S.

Applications for patents in fee have too often been adroitly supported by influences which sought to hasten the taxable status of the property or to accomplish a purchase at much less than its fair value, or from some other motive foreign to the Indian's ability to protect his property rights. Notwithstanding the sincere efforts of officials and competency commissions to reach a safe conclusion as to the ability of an Indian to manage prudently his business and landed interests, experience shows that *more than two-thirds of the Indians who have received patents in fee have been unable or unwilling to cope with the business acumen coupled* with the selfishness and greed of the more competent whites, and in many instances have lost every acre they had. (Emphasis added).[96]

Puyallup Indians, near Tacoma, Washington

The Puyallup tribe lives near *Tacoma* and are now, by act of Congress, citizens. The giving of unrestricted freedom to these Indians, ignorant and incapable as they are, and *owning as they do the most valuable agricultural lands in the State of Washington, has made them the mark for every unprincipled schemer and blackleg in Tacoma* and vicinity and will soon result in their destruction. They are continually being robbed, and several even now, who a very short time ago were owners of very valuable property, are entirely destitute. Some have received a fair price for their property and have squandered it, while others have received practically nothing for theirs. (Emphasis added).[97]

Citizen Potawatomi, the Absentee Shawnee, and the Mexican Kickapoo Indians, Oklahoma

Various acts of Congress have been past (sic) permitting these Indians to sell their allotments and, in my opinion, all have been detrimental to them… At the time most of the Indians of this agency sold their own allotments the surrounding country had not as yet been settled up and the Indians could not realize the great importance of their holding the lands set aside to them by the Government. *They did not know what the absolute title to a tract of land meant*-that to dispose of such title and spend the proceeds of the sale, left them to live upon the section lines without a home or the means with which to buy one. Those who were unfortunate enough to sell all of their land are now, generally speaking, in this condition. They not only have no financial means with which to get a home, but they are also unable to compete with their white neighbors in the securing of such means, and therefore *they seem to be left by the wayside in this seeming uncontrollable strife of the "survival of the fittest."* (Emphasis added).[98]

Since the purchase of these lands the title thereto has past thru several hands, and mortgages have been recorded against nearly every tract. Why were these rapid transfers made? Plainly to *get the title into the hands of so-called "innocent purchasers,"* with the hope of heading off any possible efforts in behalf of the Indians by the Department of Justice or by Congress. A "guilty conscience" seems to be clearly defined in a person taking such steps in regard to the title of land he may have purchased from an ignorant Indian. (Emphasis added).[99]

Forced Assimilation

Pratt the Baptist

In a speech in 1892, The Advantages of Mingling Indians with Whites, Captain Pratt said: "A great general has said that the only good Indian is a dead one, and that high sanction of his destruction has been an enormous factor in promoting Indian massacres. In a sense, I agree with the sentiment, but only in this: that all the Indian there is in the race should be dead. Kill the Indian in him, and save the man." Also, "In Indian civilization I am a Baptist," Pratt wrote, "because I believe in immersing the Indians in our civilization and when we get them under holding them there until they are thoroughly soaked."[100]

1870: Washington Territory's Superintendent Advocated Taking Children Away from Their Parents by Cajolery, by Threats, by Bribery, by Fraud, by Persuasion or by Force

In Washington Territory, Sam'l Ross, Brevet Colonel, U.S. Army, Superintendent of Indian Affairs, advocated taking children away from their parents, by compulsion or by compensation, to be placed in industrial schools for their civilization. He believed parents would part with their children *"for a small compensation in blankets and presents."*

If it is really the intention of the governing powers to civilize the Indians-to transfer the bold spirit of the daring savage warrior to the level such an intellect should occupy in civilized life, and save the red man, who has become a part of our national history, from extinction, then it becomes necessary to adopt a new mode for his civilization. The way to accomplish this is plain, and I think there is but one way, and that is as follows: All Indian children between the ages of five and twelve should be taken from their parents, either by compulsion or compensation, and removed from the influences of all Indian tribes, and placed in industrial schools. At first this might appear to be a cruel measure; but it is really an act of humanity. *I am satisfied that many of the Indians would really part with their children for a small compensation in blankets and presents.* (Emphasis added).[101]

In his 1901 Annual Report, Commissioner W. A. Jones spitefully states as follows: "There are in operation at the present time 113 boarding schools, with an average attendance of something over 16,000 pupils, ranging from 5 to 21 years old. These pupils are gathered from the cabin, the wickiup, and the tepee. *Partly by cajolery and partly by threats; partly by bribery and partly by fraud; partly by persuasion and partly by force,* they are induced to leave their homes and their kindred to enter these schools and take upon themselves the outward semblance of civilized life." (Emphasis added).[102]

Indenturing of Indians

In 1860, the California legislature amended an Act for the Government and Protection of Indians that provided for the "apprenticing" or "indenturing" of Indian children to whites… "male Indian children under fourteen years could be indentured until they were twenty-five, and females under fourteen until they were twenty-one years old. If they were over fourteen but under twenty, males were indentured until they were thirty, and females until they were twenty-five years."[103]

Starvation of Indians

General Pope best described the starvation as "spectacles of suffering, which human nature could not contemplate without horror." Indian families still suffer today from being unable to put food on the table.

There can be no doubt but many of the young children died from lack of food during last winter and spring. Never before have I been called upon to listen in an Indian council to such tales of suffering. Three or four years ago this reservation abounded in game and these Indians were, practically, independent of the Government; now, nowhere else have I ever seen a country so destitute of it as this, and there is, practically, nothing for the people to live upon but what is furnished by the Government. I cannot believe that Congress was fully aware of the change in the surroundings of these Indians when the *annual appropriation was diminished*. ... I am fearful that unless additional supplies are furnished depredations must be expected to prevent starvation, and early action is necessary, as the severe winter here renders transportation of supplies at that time impossible in this country. (Emphasis added).[104]

Superintendent Rector reported on September 2, 1862, that Indians had died from starvation and exposure:

> ... the *suffering among the Indians [Siletz] has been severe*. I have good authority, together with the statements of the Indians, for saying that *quite a number of them died from cold and hunger*. ... The Indians generally are dissatisfied. They complain to me very bitterly in regard to their treatment; the bad faith of the government towards them; that their treaty was not ratified &c., &c. *To compel even Indians to remain on a reservation without food and clothes, or even the means of obtaining them, is unjust and inhuman*. (Emphasis added).[105]

Diseases

The extensive illnesses and diseases suffered by Indians have resulted in severe intergenerational health complications, infant and youth mortality, suicides and deaths.

Syphilis

Commissioner Dole reported on syphilis:

> If you wish to exterminate the race, pursue them with the ball and blade; if you please, massacre them wholesale, as

~ 724 ~

we sometimes have done; or, to make it cheap, call them to a peaceful feast, and feed them on beef salted with wolf bane; but, for humanity's sake save them from the lingering syphilitic poisons, so sure to be contracted about military posts.[106]

Alcoholism

Another usual tactic was to get Indians inebriated, complained of by Indian leaders as early as 1753. In an October 3, 1753, meeting at Carlisle between colonial Commissioners and Ohio Indians, Scarrooyady, substantiated this practice:

> Traders come, They bring thirty or forty kegs and put them down before us, and make us drink, and get all the Skins that should go to pay the debts we have contracted for goods bought of the Fair Traders; and by this means, we not only ruin ourselves but them too.

The Commissioners, replying to Scarrooyady, including Benjamin Franklin, confirmed this practice:

> THUS, may it please the Governor, we have given a full and just Account of all our Proceedings ... we cannot close our Report, without taking Notice, That the *Quantities of strong Liquors sold to these Indians in the Places of their Residence, and during their Hunting Season, from all Parts of the Counties over Sasquehannah, have encreased of late to an inconceivable Degree, so as to keep these poor Indians continually under the Force of Liquor*, that they are hereby become dissolute, enfeebled and indolent when sober, and untractable and mischevious in their Liquor, always quarreling, and often murdering one another. RICHARD PETERS, ISAAC NORRIS, BENJ. FRANKLIN. (Emphasis added).[107]

Criminal Rules to End Indian Cultural Practices

Secretary of the Interior Teller recommended the drafting of civil and criminal rules for use on Indian reservations to end the Indians' "savage and barbarous practices," which were "a great hindrance to [their] civilization."[108] This was done.

Stereotypes Justifying Mistreatment and Extermination of Indians

Commissioner John N. Oberly, in his Annual Report to the Secretary of the Interior in 1888, inscribed the stereotypical view of Indians that dominated federal and state policymaking in the nineteenth century:

> The Indian has indeed begun to change with the changing times. He is commencing to appreciate the fact that he must become civilized-must, as he expresses it, "learn the white man's way" - or perish from the face of the earth. He can not sweep back with a broom the flowing tide. The forests into which he ran whooping from the door of "William and Mary" [Indian School in Virginia] have been felled. The game on which he lived has disappeared. The war-path has been obliterated. He is hemmed in on all sides by white population. The railroad refuses to be excluded from his reservation-that hot-bed of barbarism, in which many noxious social and political weeds grow rankly. The Christian missionary is persistently entreating him to abandon paganism. Gradually the paternal hand of the Government is being withdrawn from his support. His environments no longer compel him, or afford to him opportunities, to display the nobler traits of his character. On the war-path and in the chase he was heroic: all activity; patient of hunger; patient of fatigue; coolheaded-a creature of exalted fortitude. "But, says a writer, sketching his character, "when the chase was over, when the war was done, and the peace-pipes smoked out, he abandoned himself to debauchery and idleness. To sleep all day in a wig-wam of painted skins, filthy and blackened with smoke, adorned with scalps, and hung with tomahawks and arrows, to dance in the shine of the new moon to music made from the skin of snakes, to tell stories of witches and evil spirits, to gamble, to sing, to jest, to boast of his achievements in war, and to sit with a solemn gravity at the councils of his chiefs constituted his most serious employment. His squaw was his slave. With no more affection than a coyote feels for its mate, he brought her to his wigwam that she might gratify the basest of his passions and minister to his wants. It was Starlight or Cooing Dove that brought the wood for his fire and the water for his drink, that plowed the field and sowed the maize."[109]

These stereotypes became embedded in the consciousness of whites and are still expressed today.

Ridiculing Indians: Ration Day

> On Mondays we issue rations. At the beef corral a large concourse of Indians assembles for beef, and at the commissary for flour. When the cattle are issued they have an exciting time; the frightened and desperate animals rush madly around pursued by from one to a dozen savages, yelling, whooping, and firing their guns, reminding one of the early days when buffalo-hunting was their chief sport. When the beef is killed the voracious bucks and their families eat the raw entrails with great satisfaction. The squaws take charge of the carcass, dry the meat, and the "buck" takes the hide to the traders.[110]

U.S. Aim to Weaken Indians, Then Expropriate Their Lands

William Clark in 1826, dismally described the impact of the government on *"weakening"* Indians so their lands could be expropriated:

> ... *"Their power has been broken, their warlike spirit subdued, and themselves sunk into objects of pity and commiseration,"* he wrote to his superiors in Washington. *"While strong and hostile, it has been our obvious policy to weaken them; now that they are weak and harmless, and most of their lands fallen into our hands, justice and humanity require us to cherish and befriend them.* (Emphasis added).[111]

U.S. Impotent to Protect Indians

Throughout all of this, Commissioner E. A. Hayt in 1879 announced the impotency of his agency to protect Indians:

> The experience of the Indian Department for the past fifty years goes to show that the *government is impotent to protect the Indians on their reservations, especially when held in common, from the encroachments of its own people, whenever a discovery has been made rendering the possession of their lands desirable by the whites*. The evidently growing feeling in the country against continued appropriations for the care and support of the Indians indicates the necessity for a radical change of policy in affairs connected with their lands. (Emphasis added).[112]

~ 727 ~

Federal Indian Law

As Philip Frickey notes, the "practical effect" of federal Indian law "has been to legitimate the colonization of this continent--the displacement of its native peoples--by the descendants of Europeans."[113]

Citizenship

The U.S. unilaterally declared Indians to be U.S. citizens by a series of legislative enactments. It was simply another exercise of the U.S.' claimed prerogative to define Indians as citizens, though not "*full*" citizens. The imposition of American citizenship is still contested by some.[114]

On January 29, 1924, the bill (H. R. 6355) that was to become the Indian Citizenship Act was introduced in the House by Homer P. Snyder of New York and referred to the Committee on Indian Affairs. The *proposed bill stated*: That the Secretary of the Interior is hereby authorized, in his discretion, under regulations to be prescribed by him, to issue a certificate of citizenship to any noncitizen Indian born within the territorial limits of the United States who may make application therefor, and upon the issuance of such certificate to any Indian, he or she shall become a *full citizen* of the United States: Provided, that the issuance of a certificate of citizenship shall not in any manner impair or otherwise affect the right of any Indian to tribal or other property. (Emphasis added).[115]

The Senate removed the word "full." There isn't any legislative history to explain this modification other than the amendment being offered and agreed to on March 18, 1924.

> The committee amendment was read as follows:
>
> Page 1, line 8, strike out the words "become a full" and insert in lieu thereof "be a."
> The amendment was agreed to.
> The bill as amended was ordered to be engrossed and read a third time, was read the third time, and passed.[116]

It is unclear from the legislative history what the difference is between a "full citizen" and "a citizen."

The bill was further modified significantly in the Senate. *The original language had called for the Secretary of Interior to be authorized to grant citizenship to those Indians who applied, but this was removed by the Senate and the blanket grant to all Indians* not previously made U.S. citizens was included. It was then approved by both houses and signed by President Calvin Coolidge on June 2, 1924. So, without consultation with Indians, the U.S. simply imposed citizenship onto them.

> "BE IT ENACTED by the Senate and house of Representatives of the United States of America in Congress assembled, That all non citizen Indians born within the territorial limits of the United States be, and they are hereby, declared to be citizens of the United States: Provided That the granting of such citizenship shall not in any manner impair or otherwise affect the right of any Indian to tribal or other property. (Approved June 2, 1924)[117]

Bureau of Indian Affairs Citizenship Ceremony: Stripping Indian of His/Her Indian Identity, The Last Arrow

The following Bureau of Indian Affairs Citizenship Ceremony exemplifies the meaning of U.S. Citizenship—it was meant to strip the Indian of his/her Indian identity. This 'last arrow' ceremony is grotesque and obscene.

The Indian person becoming a citizen was asked to wear traditional regalia. A tipi was set up. For men, *after shooting his last arrow* he entered the tipi and changed into white man's clothing. He also was given a white man's name.

This photo was taken on the Standing Rock reservation during a citizenship ceremony. *One man poses with a drawn bow and arrow, others hold their "last arrows."* The plow and the flag are displayed as symbols of U.S. citizenship. Major McLaughlin stands at the table. Two women and one man to the right of the table appear to be wearing the citizenship badge.

Introduction for Ceremony:

> The President of the United States has sent me to speak a solemn and serious word to you, a word that means more to some of you than any other that you have ever heard. He has been told that there are some among you who should no longer be controlled by the Bureau of Indian Affairs, but should be given their patents in fee and thus become free American citizens. It is his decision that this shall be done, and that those so honored by the people of the United States shall have the meaning of this new and great privilege pointed out by symbol and by word, so that no man or woman shall not know its meaning.

> **For Men:**
> (Read Name.)

> _____ (white name). What was your Indian name? (Gives name.)

> _____ (Indian name). I hand you a bow and an arrow. Take this bow and shoot the arrow. (He shoots.)

> _____ (Indian name). You have shot your last arrow. That means that you are no longer to live the life of an Indian. You are from this day forward to live the life of the white man. But you may keep that arrow, it will be to you a symbol of your noble race and of the pride you feel that you come from the first of all Americans.

> _____ (white name). Take in your hand this plow. (He takes the handles of the plow.) This act means that you have chosen to live the life of the white man—and the white man lives by work. From the earth we all must get our living and the earth will not yield unless man pours upon it the

~ 730 ~

sweat of his brow. Only by work do we gain a right to the land and to the enjoyment of life.

_____ (white name). I give you a purse. This purse will always say to you that the money you gain from your labor must be wisely kept. The wise man saves his money so that when the sun does not smile and the grass does not grow, he will not starve.

I give into your hands the flag of your county. This is the only flag you have ever had or ever will have. It is the flag of freedom; the flag of free men, the flag of a hundred million free men and women of whom you are now one. That flag has a request to make of you, _____ (white name), that you take it into your hands and repeat these words:

"For as much as the President has said that I am worthy to be a citizen of the United States, I now promise to this flag that I will give my hands, my head, and my heart to the doing of all that will make me a true American citizen."

And now beneath this flag I place upon your breast the emblem of your citizenship. Wear this badge of honor always; and may the eagle that is on it never see you do aught of which the flag will not be proud.

(The audience rises and shouts: "_____ (white name) is an American citizen.")

For Women:

_____ (white name). Take in your hand this work bag and purse. (She takes the work bag and purse.) This means that you have chosen the life of the white woman—and the white woman loves her home. The family and the home are the foundation of our civilization. Upon the character and industry of the mother and homemaker largely depends the future of our Nation. The purse will always say to you that the money you gain from your labor must be wisely kept. The wise woman saves her money, so that when the sun does not smile and the grass does not grow, she and her children will not starve.

I give into your hands the flag of your country. This is the only flag you have ever had or ever will have. It is the flag of freedom, the flag of free men, a hundred million free men and women of whom you are now one. That flag has a request to make of you, _____ (white name), that you take it into your hands and repeat these words:

"For as much as the President has said that I am worthy to be a citizen of the United States, I now promise to this flag that I will give my hands, my head, and my heart to the doing of all that will make me a true American citizen."

And now beneath this flag I place upon your breast the emblem of your citizenship. Wear this badge of honor always, and may the eagle that is on it never see you do aught of which the flag will not be proud.

(The audience rises and shouts: "_____(white name) is an American citizen.")[118]

Chief Old Dog, 1851–1928

A revered chief, Old Dog, photographed in 1909 by Edward Curtis, was born in 'the old world' and died, in 1926, in an era of modernization that his own parent's could not have imagined. He never spoke a word of English, and when citizenship was offered him in 1922, he declined, saying that he had never needed the white man's blessing to make him a free man.

"I do not want the white man's offer of citizenship. I have lived a long life, and I have seen many of the Great White Fathers' promises vanish on the winds. I do not need the white man's government to tell me that I am free."[119]

Indian Claims Commission

The Indian Claims Commission was established to provide a forum for the adjudication of all claims by Indian tribes against the United States that existed on the date of the act, August 13, 1946.[120] Tribes with pending claims were given 5 years in which to file them, and the Commission was given until April 10, 1957, to complete its work. In March 1976, Congress extended the life of the Commission, but provided for its termination effective September 30,

1978. Congress also provided for the transfer of any unresolved ICCA claims to the United States Court of Federal Claims. However, not until October 2006 was the last case filed under the ICCA.

The most fundamental problem with the act, from the tribes' point of view, was that it provided for payment in money and not land. The Indian Claims Commission arbitrarily assigned a monetary value to those lands, paid it into a trust fund of their own making, and declared the matter closed.

> We have had enough experience with the Indian Claims Commission Act to know that it has not benefited most tribes. Approximately $800 million was awarded through the Indian Claims Commission. If you divide the number of acres of land that those particular cases involved, the United States government ended up paying Indian people fifty cents an acre for the United States of America. The title was quieted, but in many cases it is still unsettled. Roger Buffalohead, Ponca, project director, MIGIZI Communications.[121]

Notes: Mayhem

1. General John Pope, Social Science Association speech, May 24, 1878, on 'The Indian Question.'
2. Robertson, Lindsay G. *Conquest by law: How the discovery of America dispossessed indigenous peoples of their lands*. Oxford University Press, 2005.
3. Letter from Brinton to Ingersoll, 02/26/1822. Illinois Wabash Land Company. https://digital.libraries.ou.edu/IWLC/paper.asp?pID=52&doc_type=Corr (accessed online November 14, 2020).
4. *Johnson v. M'Intosh*, 21 U.S. 543, 574 (1823).
5. See Harvey, Roberta Carol. The Earth Is Red: The Imperialism of the Doctrine of Discovery, Sunstone Press, 2021.
6. Report of the Commissioner of Indian Affairs to the Secretary of the Interior, United States. Office of Indian Affairs. U.S. Government Printing Office, 1853, p. 12.
7. Sen. doc. No. 1. pt. 1. ls. 330. p. 363. Pub. doc. No. 690.
8. Malin, James C. *Indian Policy and Westward Expansion*, BULLETIN OF THE UNIVERSITY OF KANSAS HUMANISTIC STUDIES, Vol. II, November 1, 1921, No. 3, University of Kansas.
9. https://www.nwcouncil.org/reports/columbia-river-history/railroads/ (accessed online April 8, 2022).

10. https://www.history.army.mil/books/AMH-V1/ch14.htm (accessed online April 8, 2022).

11. Putnam, A TRIP ON THE UNION PACIFIC IN 1868, August 1944, Kansas Historical Society (Vol. 13. No. 3), pp. 198-199. https://www.kshs.org/p/a-trip-to-the-end-of-the-union-pacific-in-1868/12969 (accessed online March 24, 2023).

12. House Documents, Volume 1; Volume 4; Volume 270. USA Congress House of Representatives, U.S. Government Printing Office, 1874, p. VI.

13. https://www.bia.gov/faqs/what-federal-indian-reservation (accessed online September 1, 2022).

14. Report of the Commissioner of Indian Affairs to the Secretary of the Interior, United States. Office of Indian Affairs. U.S. Government Printing Office, 1868, Extract, p. I.

15. Report of the Commissioner of Indian Affairs to the Secretary of the Interior, United States. Office of Indian Affairs. U.S. Government Printing Office, 1890, p. V.

16. Report of the Commissioner of Indian Affairs to the Secretary of the Interior, United States. Office of Indian Affairs. U.S. Government Printing Office, 1874, p. 15.

17. Report of the Commissioner of Indian Affairs to the Secretary of the Interior, United States. Office of Indian Affairs, Report of the Sioux Commission. U.S. Government Printing Office, 1878, pp. 655-656.

18. Report of the Commissioner of Indian Affairs to the Secretary of the Interior, United States. Office of Indian Affairs. U.S. Government Printing Office, 1890, p. VI.

19. Report of the Commissioner of Indian Affairs to the Secretary of the Interior, United States. Office of Indian Affairs. U.S. Government Printing Office, 1872, pp. 9-10.

20. H.R. Report No. 354, 44th Cong., 1st Sess. (1876), 6.

21. Marszalek, John F. Sherman: A Soldier's Passion for Order, SIU Press, 2007, p. 390.

22. S. Misc. Doc. No. 53, 45th Cong., 3rd Sess. (1879), Testimony, 214. Cited in White, Eric M., "Interior vs. war: The development of the Bureau of Indian Affairs and The Transfer Debates, 1849–1880." (2012). Masters Theses. 366, p. 79. https://commons.lib.jmu.edu/master201019/366 (accessed online March 24, 2023).

23. Maura Grogan, "Native American Lands and Natural Resource Development," Revenue Watch Institute, NY, NY, 2011, pp. 3, 6, 10, 11.

24. Annual Report of the Board of Indian Commissioners (Washington, 1869), pp. 5-11.

25. https://www.oregonencyclopedia.org/articles/willamette_valley_treaty_commission/#.Y6ca6exKiw4 (accessed online October 5, 2022).

26. https://www.oregonencyclopedia.org/articles/willamette_valley_treaty_commission/#.Yz41mOxKiw4 (accessed online October 5, 2022).

27. Letter to the Secretary of the Interior, communicating. In compliance with a resolution of the Senate of the 8th Instant, information touching the origin and progress of Indian hostilities on the frontier, 40th Cong., 1st sess., S. Ex. Doc. 13, 1867, serial 1279, p. 121.

28. General John Pope, Social Science Association speech, May 24, 1878, on 'The Indian Question.'

29. Report of the Commissioner of Indian Affairs to the Secretary of the Interior, United States. Office of Indian Affairs. U.S. Government Printing Office, 1876, pp. VI-VIII.

30. The Indian Problem, Nelson A. Miles, North American Review 128, no. 268 (March 1879): 304–15.

31. Annual Report of the Superintendent of Indian Schools, United States. Office of Indian Affairs. U.S. Government Printing Office, 1887, p. 38.

32. Report of the Commissioner of Indian Affairs to the Secretary of the Interior, United States. Office of Indian Affairs. U.S. Government Printing Office, 1870, p. 57.

33. https://www.nps.gov/places/virginia-city-historic-district.htm (accessed online January 11, 2022).

34. *S. Pac. Transp. Co.*, 543 F.2d 676, 687 (1976).

35. "The Indian Question, Francis A. Walker" (2017). US and Indian Relations, p. 60.

36. Arizona, Its Mineral Resources and Scenic Wonders 1940, Bureau of Mines, U.S. Department of the Interior, 1940. National Archives Identifier: 12496. https://www.youtube.com/watch?v=2mMl4qmm1jA (accessed online August 17, 2022).

37. Report of the Commissioner of Indian Affairs to the Secretary of the Interior, United States. Office of Indian Affairs. William A. Harris, Printer, 1858, p. 321.

38. Apple, Daina Dravnieks, Evolution of U.S. Water Policy: Emphasis on the West, women in Natural Resources, Vol. 24 No. 3, 2003-04.

39. https://www.webpages.uidaho.edu/winr/applewater.htm (accessed online December 25, 2022).

40. Report of the Commissioner of Indian Affairs to the Secretary of the Interior, United States. Office of Indian Affairs. U.S. Government Printing Office, 1885, p. XXIII. Report of the Commissioner of Indian Affairs to the Secretary of the Interior, United States. Office of Indian Affairs. U.S. Government Printing Office, 1880, pp. XX, XXIX. Report of the Commissioner of Indian Affairs to the Secretary of the Interior, United States. Office of Indian Affairs. U.S. Government Printing Office, 1882, p. 14. Report of the Commissioner of Indian Affairs to the Secretary of the Interior,

United States. Office of Indian Affairs. U.S. Government Printing Office, 1884, p. XVI. Report of the Commissioner of Indian Affairs to the Secretary of the Interior, United States. Office of Indian Affairs. U.S. Government Printing Office, 1885, pp. XXXII-XXXIII. Report of the Commissioner of Indian Affairs to the Secretary of the Interior, United States. Office of Indian Affairs. U.S. Government Printing Office, 1890, p. XXXIV.

41. Hoxie, Frederick E. A final promise: The campaign to assimilate the Indians, 1880-1920. U of Nebraska Press, 2001, p. 184.

42. Wyoming's Water Dilemma, Denver Post, July 9, 1989.

43. Mining and Engineering World, Volume 22, 1905, pp. 604-605.

44. Stewart, R. "Winning the West the Army in the Indian Wars, 1865-1890." American Military History (2001). p. 301.

45. Report of the Commissioner of Indian Affairs to the Secretary of the Interior, United States. Office of Indian Affairs. U.S. Government Printing Office, 1865, p. viii.

46. House Documents, U.S. House of Representatives, Volume 112, U.S. Government Printing Office, 1858, p. 83.

47. Report of the Commissioner of Indian Affairs to the Secretary of the Interior, United States. Office of Indian Affairs. U.S. Government Printing Office, 1872, p. 397.

48. The War of the Rebellion: A Compilation of the Official Records of the Union and Confederate Armies, United States War Department, U.S. Government Printing Office, 1891. Series I, Vol. XLI, Part I, LOUISIANA AND THE TRANS-MISSISSIPPI, Chapter LIIIO, p. 948.

49. Brigham D. Madsen, Utah History Encyclopedia, 1994.

50. "From Thomas Jefferson to James Monroe, 17 April 1791," *Founders Online*, National Archives, https://founders.archives.gov/documents/Jefferson/01-20-02-0051. [Original source: *The Papers of Thomas Jefferson*, vol. 20, *1 April–4 August 1791*, ed. Julian P. Boyd. Princeton: Princeton University Press, 1982, pp. 234–236.] (accessed online November 13, 2020).

51. Report of the Commissioner of Indian Affairs to the Secretary of the Interior, United States. Office of Indian Affairs. U.S. Government Printing Office, 1868, Accompanying Papers, p. 42.

52. Brown, Dee. Bury My Heart at Wounded Knee: An Indian History of the American West. Macmillan, 2007.

53. Brown, Dee. *Bury My Heart at Wounded Knee: An Indian History of the American West*. Macmillan, 2007.

54. George Ward Nichols, "The Indian: What we should do with Him," Harper's Monthly 40 (April 1870): 732.

55. Report of the Commissioner of Indian Affairs to the Secretary of the Interior, United States. Office of Indian Affairs. U.S. Government Printing Office, 1875, p. 323.

56. Senate Documents, Otherwise Publ. as Public Documents and Executive Documents: 14th Congress, 1st Session-48th Congress, 2nd Session and Special Session, Volume 10, 1856, p. 50.

57. Report of the Commissioner of Indian Affairs to the Secretary of the Interior, United States. Office of Indian Affairs. U.S. Government Printing Office, 1870, p. 47

58. Letter to John Sherman, October 20, 1866. The Sherman Letters (Correspondence between General W. T. Sherman and Senator John Sherman, 1837-1891). Edited by Raphael Sherman Thorndike. New York, Charles Scribner's Sons, 1894), p. 277.

59. https://www.indianz.com/News/2019/06/19/california-governor-apologizes-for-genoc.asp (accessed online November 13, 2022).

60. Report of the Commissioner of Indian Affairs to the Secretary of the Interior, United States. Office of Indian Affairs. U.S. Government Printing Office, 1886, p. 118.

61. The Congressional Globe, Volume 37, Blair & Rives, March 31,1856, p. 782.

62. THE SLAYING OF PIO-PIO-MOX-MOX, Victor, Frances Fuller: The Early Indian Ways of Oregon, 445. University of Washington.

63. General John Pope, Social Science Association speech, May 24, 1878, on 'The Indian Question.'

64. Report of the Commissioner of Indian Affairs to the Secretary of the Interior, United States. Office of Indian Affairs. U.S. Government Printing Office, 1872, pp. 89-90.

65. Report of the Commissioner of Indian Affairs to the Secretary of the Interior, United States. Office of Indian Affairs. U.S. Government Printing Office, 1874, Appendix A, Report of Chris C. Cox, Special Indian Commissioner, pp. 89-90.

66. Thompson, Erwin N. Modoc War; Its Military History & Topography. Argus Books, 1971, p. 110.

67. Report of the Commissioner of Indian Affairs to the Secretary of the Interior, United States. Office of Indian Affairs. Blair & Rives, Printers. 1838, p. 17.

68. https://www.digitalhistory.uh.edu/disp_textbook.cfm?smtID=3&psid=4029 (accessed online September 1, 2022).

69. Report of the Commissioner of Indian Affairs, Department of the Interior, Vol. 1, United States. Office of Indian Affairs, U.S. Government Printing Office, 1891, p. 8.

70. H.R. Rep. No. 1401, 46th Cong., 2nd Sess. (1880), p. 2.

71. Annual Report of the Department of the Interior, Vol. II, Report of the Commissioner of Indian Affairs, Office of Indian Affairs, United States. U.S. Government Printing Office, 1916, p. 58.

72. Banner, Stuart. *How the Indians lost their land: Law and power on the frontier*. Harvard University Press, 2005:64.

73. United States. Office of Indian Affairs. *Annual Report of the Secretary of the Interior, Vol. II, Report of the Commissioner of Indian Affairs*. US Government Printing Office, 1917, p. 71.

74. Banner, Stuart. How the Indians lost their land: Law and power on the frontier. Harvard University Press, 2005:64.

75. Id.

76. William W. Folwell, History of Minnesota, rev. ed. (St. Paul: Minnesota Historical Society, 1969), 4: 278-279.

77. Report of the Commissioner of Indian Affairs to the Secretary of the Interior, United States. Office of Indian Affairs. U.S. Government Printing Office, 1900, p. 6.

78. Report of the Commissioner of Indian Affairs to the Secretary of the Interior, United States. Office of Indian Affairs. U.S. Government Printing Office, 1877, p. 10.

79. Report of the Commissioner of Indian Affairs to the Secretary of the Interior, United States. Office of Indian Affairs. U.S. Government Printing Office, 1877, p. 151.

80. Report of the Commissioner of Indian Affairs to the Secretary of the Interior, United States. Office of Indian Affairs. U.S. Government Printing Office, 1884, p. 115.

81. Report of the Commissioner of Indian Affairs to the Secretary of the Interior, United States. Office of Indian Affairs. U.S. Government Printing Office, 1857, p. 588.

82. "To Thomas Jefferson from Meriwether Lewis, 15 December 1808," Founders Online, National Archives, https://founders.archives.gov/documents/Jefferson/99-01-02-9323 (accessed online November 5, 2020).

83. Buffalo et al., to Lea, November 6, 1851. Fish in the Lakes, Wild Rice, and Game in Abundance: Testimony on Behalf of Mille Lacs Ojibwe Hunting and Fishing Rights, Editor James M. McClurken, MSU Press, 2000, p. 39.

84. Annual Report of the Secretary of the Interior, Part 1, United States, Report of the Commissioner of Indian Affairs, Office of Indian Affairs, Reports Concerning Indians in New Mexico. U.S. Government Printing Office, 1905, p. 251.

85. Report of the Commissioner of Indian Affairs to the Secretary of the Interior, United States. Office of Indian Affairs, Reports of Agents in Colorado. U.S. Government Printing Office, 1877, p. 46.

86. Report of the Commissioner of Indian Affairs to the Secretary of the Interior, United States. Office of Indian Affairs, Washington Superintendency. U.S. Government Printing Office, 1863, p. 410.

87. Report of the Commissioner of Indian Affairs to the Secretary of the

Interior, United States. Office of Indian Affairs. U.S. Government Printing Office, 1857, p. 683.

88. The Indian Department John Gibbon, Army and Navy Journal 13, no. 21 (January 1, 1876): 388.

89. HR No. 93, 45th Cong., 3 sess. (Serial 1866), 1879, p. 7. Waltmann, Henry George, "The Interior Department, War Department and Indian Policy, 1865-1887" 1962). Dissertations, Theses, & Student Research, Department of History, p. 16.

90. Report of the Secretary of the Interior on the Operations of the Department, U.S. Government Printing Office, 1877, p. XIII.

91. John Gibbon, Fort Shaw, M.T., December 1, 1875. John Gibbon, The Indian Department, Army and Navy Journal 13, no. 21 (January 1, 1876): 388.

92. Report of the Commissioner of Indian Affairs to the Secretary of the Interior, United States. Office of Indian Affairs, Methods of Conducting Business in Indian Office, U.S. Government Printing Office, 1878, pp. LXV-LXVI.

93. Peterson, Ken. "Ransom Powell and the Tragedy of White Earth." Minnesota History 63.3 (2012): 91.

94. Id.

95. Id.

96. Annual Reports of the Department of Interior, Part 1, Report of the Commissioner of Indian Affairs to the Secretary of the Interior, United States Office of Indian Affairs, As to Indian Competency. U.S. Government Printing Office, 1921, p. 25.

97. Report of the Commissioner of Indian Affairs to the Secretary of the Interior, United States. Office of Indian Affairs. U.S. Government Printing Office, 1905, p. 353.

98. Report of the Commissioner of Indian Affairs to the Secretary of the Interior, United States. Office of Indian Affairs. U.S. Government Printing Office, 1906, p. 325

99. Report of the Commissioner of Indian Affairs to the Secretary of the Interior, United States. Office of Indian Affairs. U.S. Government Printing Office, 1906, p. 326.

100. https://upstanderproject.org/firstlight/pratt (accessed online March 29, 2023).

101. Report of the Commissioner of Indian Affairs to the Secretary of the Interior, United States. Office of Indian Affairs. U.S. Government Printing Office, 1870, p. 137.

102. Report of the Commissioner of Indian Affairs to the Secretary of the Interior, United States. Office of Indian Affairs. U.S. Government Printing Office, 1902, p. 2.

103. Johnston-Dodds, Kimberly. Early Laws and Policies Related to California Indians. 2002. California State Library.

104. Annual Report of the Secretary of the Interior, Vol. II, United States. Report of Commissioner of Indian Affairs to the Secretary of the Interior, United States. Office of Indian Affairs. Deplorable Conditions of Indians in Montana. U.S. Government Printing Office, 1883, p. 48.

105. Report of the Commissioner of Indian Affairs to the Secretary of the Interior, United States. Office of Indian Affairs. U.S. Government Printing Office, 1863, p. 255.

106. Report of the Commissioner of Indian Affairs to the Secretary of the Interior, United States. Office of Indian Affairs. U.S. Government Printing Office, 1868, p. 11.

107. Treaty of Carlisle, 1 November 1753," *Founders Online*, National Archives, https://founders.archives.gov/documents/Franklin/01-05-02-0026. [Original source: *The Papers of Benjamin Franklin*, vol. 5, *July 1, 1753, through March 31, 1755*, ed. Leonard W. Labaree. New Haven: Yale University Press, 1962, pp. 84–107.] (accessed online November 6, 2020).

108. The Bureau of Indian Affairs promulgated "Rules Governing the Court of Indian Offenses" on April 10, 1883, which criminalized traditional Indian dances, traditional marriage and divorce, community and social gatherings, traditional probate, traditional burials and mourning practices, and religious practices of medicine men, etc.

109. Report of the Commissioner of Indian Affairs to the Secretary of the Interior, United States. Office of Indian Affairs, Reports of Agents in Indian Territory. U.S. Government Printing Office, 1888, p. lxxxviii.

110. Report of the Commissioner of Indian Affairs to the Secretary of the Interior, United States. Office of Indian Affairs, Reports of Agents in Indian Territory. U.S. Government Printing Office, 1885, p. 179.

111. Civilization of the Indians," March 23, 1824, ASP: Indian Affairs, 2: 458.

112. Department of the Interior Bill to Allot Indian Land, H.R. Rep. No. 165, 45th Cong., 3rd Sess. (1879), p. 2.

113. Philip P. Frickey, Adjudication and Its Discontents: Coherence and Conciliation in Federal Indian Law, 110 Harv. L. Rev. 1754 (1997).

114. Robert B. Porter, The Demise of the Ongwehoweh and the Rise of the Native Americans: Redressing the Genocidal Act of Forcing American Citizenship upon Indigenous Peoples, 15 Harv. Blackletter L.J. 107, 108 (1999).

115. Proposed bill U.S., Congress, 68th Cong., 1st sess., 1924, Congressional Record, XV, p. 347.

116. Cong. Rec., March 18, 1824, p. 4446.

117. Citizenship Act (43 Stat. 253).

118. https://www.ndstudies.gov/curriculum/high-school/standing-rock-oyate/ documents-standing-rock (accessed online April 9, 2023).
119. MHA Website.
120. Act of August 13, 1946, 60 Stat. 1049.
121. Philip, Kenneth. Indian Self Rule: First-Hand Accounts of Indian-White Relations from Roosevelt to Reagan. First edition ed. Utah State University Press, 1995. Chapter 4, The Indian Claims Commission, Charles F. Wilkinson, W. Roger Buffalohead, E. Richard Hart, Edward C. Johnson.

26: VATICAN REPUDIATES 'DOCTRINE OF DISCOVERY;' IT MUST RESCIND ALL UNDERLYING BULLS

The Vatican issued the following statement on March 30, 2023, *repudiating* the 'doctrine of discovery':

> The legal concept of "discovery" was debated by colonial powers from the sixteenth century onward and found particular expression in the nineteenth century jurisprudence of courts in several countries, according to which the discovery of lands by settlers granted an exclusive right to extinguish, either by purchase or conquest, the title to or possession of those lands by indigenous peoples. Certain scholars have argued that the basis of the aforementioned "doctrine" is to be found in several papal documents, such as the Bulls *Dum Diversas* (1452), *Romanus Pontifex* (1455) and *Inter Caetera* (1493).

The statement went on to say:

> The "doctrine of discovery" is not part of the teaching of the Catholic Church. Historical research clearly demonstrates that the papal documents in question, written in a specific historical period and linked to political questions, have never been considered expressions of the Catholic faith. At the same time, the Church acknowledges that these papal bulls did not adequately reflect the equal dignity and rights of indigenous peoples. The Church is also aware that the contents of these documents were manipulated for political purposes by competing colonial powers in order to justify immoral acts against indigenous peoples that were carried out, at times, without opposition from ecclesiastical authorities. It is only just to recognize these errors, acknowledge the terrible

effects of the assimilation policies and the pain experienced by indigenous peoples, and ask for pardon. …The Catholic Church therefore repudiates those concepts that fail to recognize the inherent human rights of indigenous peoples, including what has become known as the legal and political "doctrine of discovery".[1]

The National Congress of American Indians issued the following statement on March 30, 2023, in part:

"It is no secret that many governments—including the United States—have relied on this doctrine to justify the mistreatment of Indigenous peoples and the taking of our lands. It is our sincere hope that today's announcement is more than mere words, but rather is the beginning of a full acknowledgement of the history of oppression and a full accounting of the legacies of colonialism — not just by the Roman Catholic Church, but by all the world governments that have used racism, prejudice and religious authority to not only justify past inequalities, but to allow, fuel, and perpetuate the institutionalization of those inequalities that continue to this very day.[2]

Rescind All Underlying Bulls

It is not enough for the Vatican to repudiate the Doctrine of Discovery; it must rescind all of the underlying Bulls - *Dum Diversas* (1452), *Romanus Pontifex* (1455) and *Inter Caetera* (1493) and all other related Bulls. The action taken in *Non indecens videtur* below serves as precedent: "by virtue of Apostolic authority, we revoke, invalidate, and annul the previous letter(s) and whatever is contained in it (or them)." The word "repudiates" is ambiguous and does not have a set meaning. It is imperative that the Church act with order and clarity.

An English translation of certain of the Bulls is reproduced below, as published in *European Treaties bearing on the History of the United States and its Dependencies to 1648*, Frances Gardiner Davenport, editor, Carnegie Institution of Washington, 1917, Washington, DC ("Davenport").

Catholic Church Must Accept Full Accountability for Abuses

The Catholic Church, through the Pope, must accept full accountability for the abuses by competing colonial powers *"to justify immoral acts against Indigenous peoples that were carried out, at times, without opposition from*

~ 744 ~

ecclesial authorities." It was not only without opposition; it was under the AUTHORITY of the Catholic Church. The Church may not use this statement to distance itself from acknowledging its actual culpability in the abuses that occurred.

Canon Law

Canon law was developed and decrees published which were binding on the entire Church membership. A papal bull, a document sealed with the insignia of the pope, from the Latin word bulla, was not only a binding, enforceable document, it addressed doctrine universal to the Church. In 494, Pope Gelasius I impressed on Emperor Anastasius, the primacy of papal power: *"[a]lthough you take precedence over all mankind in dignity... Nevertheless, you piously bow the neck to those who have charge of divine affairs ..."*[3]

Catholic Church's Infallibility

What made this system ironclad was the Church's infallibility proclaimed in 1090 by Pope Gregory VII in Dictatus Papae, The Dictates of the Pope: *"That the Roman church has never erred; nor will it err to all eternity, the Scripture bearing witness."*[4]

Dum Diversas (June 18, 1452)

Pope Nicholas V issued the papal bull *Dum Diversas* on 18 June, 1452. It authorized Alfonso V of Portugal to reduce any *"Saracens (Muslims) and pagans and any other unbelievers"* to perpetual slavery. This facilitated the Portuguese slave trade from West Africa.

> *"We weighing all and singular the premises with due meditation, and noting that since we had formerly by other letters of ours granted among other things free and ample faculty to the aforesaid King Alfonso—to invade, search out, capture, vanquish, and subdue all Saracens and pagans whatsoever, and other enemies of Christ wheresoever placed, and the kingdoms, dukedoms, principalities, dominions, possessions, and all movable and immovable goods whatsoever held and*

possessed by them and to reduce their persons to perpetual slavery, and to apply and appropriate to himself and his successors the kingdoms, dukedoms, counties, principalities, dominions, possessions, and goods, and to convert them to his and their use and profit—by having secured the said faculty, the said King Alfonso, or, by his authority, the aforesaid infante, justly and lawfully has acquired and possessed, and doth possess, these islands, lands, harbors, and seas, and they do of right belong and pertain to the said King Alfonso and his successors".[5]

Romanus Pontifex (January 5, 1455)

The kingdoms of Portugal and Castile had been jockeying for position and possession of colonial territories along the African coast for more than a century prior to Columbus' "discovery" of lands in the western seas. On the theory that the Pope was an arbitrator between nations, each kingdom had sought and obtained Papal bulls at various times to bolster its claims, on the grounds that its activities served to spread Christianity.

The bull *Romanus Pontifex* is an important example of the Papacy's claim to spiritual lordship of the whole world and of its role in regulating relations among Christian princes and between Christians and "unbelievers" ("heathens" and "infidels"). This bull became the basis for Portugal's later claim to lands in the "new world," a claim which was countered by Castile and the bull *Inter caetera* in 1493.

The Roman pontiff, successor of the key-bearer of the heavenly kingdom and vicar of Jesus Christ, contemplating with a father's mind all the several climes of the world and the characteristics of all the nations dwelling in them and seeking and desiring the salvation of all, wholesomely ordains and disposes upon careful deliberation those things which he sees will be agreeable to the Divine Majesty and by which he may bring the sheep entrusted to him by God into the single divine fold, and may acquire for them the reward of eternal felicity, and obtain pardon for their souls. This we believe will more certainly come to pass, through the aid of the Lord, if we bestow suitable favors and special graces on those Catholic

kings and princes, who, like athletes and intrepid champions
of the Christian faith, as we know by the evidence of facts,
not only restrain the savage excesses of the Saracens and of
other infidels, enemies of the Christian name, but also for
the defense and increase of the faith vanquish them and their
kingdoms and habitations, though situated in the remotest
parts unknown to us, and subject them to their own temporal
dominion, sparing no labor and expense, in order that those
kings and princes, relieved of all obstacles, may be the more
animated to the prosecution of so salutary and laudable a
work.[6]

Bull *Inter caetera* (May 3, 1493)

By the **Bull *Inter caetera*** of May 3, 1453, clarified thereafter to Spain's advantage, the Pope granted to Ferdinand II and Isabella and their descendants all lands lying west of a line joining the North and the South Poles, 100 leagues west of the Azores, so long as they had not already been seized by any other Christian Prince. Lands east of the line were awarded to Portugal.[7]

Bull *Inter caetera* (May 4, 1493)

The language in the Bull *Inter caetera* made it clear that the Pope regarded his grant as giving the Spanish monarchs full power of sovereignty and dominion over the territories 'discovered,' with the primary objective of spreading Christianity. The indigenous inhabitants' sovereignty and dominion were completely ignored. The Church further ceded all of its authority in the 'New World' to the Spanish Crown in three famous bulls. The first bull, *Inter caetera*, in 1493 delegated the exclusive privilege of Christianizing and civilizing the natives to the Spanish monarchs.

Alexander, bishop, servant of the servants of God, to the
illustrious sovereigns, our very dear son in Christ, Ferdinand,
king, and our very dear daughter in Christ, Isabella, queen of
Castile, Leon, Aragon, Sicily, and Granada ...

And, in order that you may enter upon so great an undertaking
with greater readiness and heartiness endowed with the benefit
*of our apostolic favor, **we, of our own accord, not at your***
***instance nor the request of anyone else in your regard,** but*
of our own sole largess and certain knowledge and out of the

fullness of our apostolic power, by the authority of Almighty God conferred upon us in blessed Peter and of the vicarship of Jesus Christ, which we hold on earth, do by tenor of these presents, should any of said islands have been found by your envoys and captains, give, grant, and assign to you and your heirs and successors, kings of Castile and Leon, forever, together with all their dominions, cities, camps, places, and villages, and all rights, jurisdictions, and appurtenances, all islands and mainlands found and to be found, discovered and to be discovered towards the west and south, by drawing and establishing a line from the Arctic pole, namely the north, to the Antarctic pole, namely the south, no matter whether the said mainlands and islands are found and to be found in the direction of India or towards any other quarter, the said line to be distant one hundred leagues towards the west and south from any of the islands commonly known as the Azores and Cape Verde (Emphasis added).[8]

Spain and Portugal's dispute over which lands were actually conveyed to it was resolved in the Treaty of Torsedillas, ratified by the Pope June 7, 1494.[9]

Dudum siquidem (September 26, 1493)

Dudum siquidem (Latin for "A short while ago") is a papal bull issued by Pope Alexander VI Borgia on September 26, 1493, addressed to the Catholic Monarchs Isabella I of Castile and Ferdinand II of Aragon which supplemented the bull *Inter caetera* and purported to grant to them *"all islands and mainlands whatsoever, found and to be found, discovered and to be discovered, that are or may be or may seem to be in the route of navigation or travel towards the west or south, whether they be in western parts, or in the regions of the south and east and of India."*[10]

Eximae Devotionis (1501)

A second bull in 1501, *Eximae Devotionis*, extended to the Spanish monarchs all rights of royal patronage, including the selection of all persons for ecclesiastical offices and the right to collect and use for itself all ecclesiastical tithes throughout its dominions.[11]

Universalis Ecclesiae (1508)

Still another bull, *Universalis Ecclesiae*, issued in 1508 by Pope Julius II, declared the King of Spain to be the head of the Church in Spain and its empire.[12]

Intra arcana - 1529: Papal Permission to Use Force for Catholic Conversion

Intra arcana, a papal bull issued in 1529 by Pope Clement VII to Charles V, authorized the use of force and arms, if necessary, to convert Indians to Catholicism:

> *We trust that ... you will compel and with all zeal cause the barbarian nations to come to the knowledge of God ... not only by edicts and admonitions, but also by force and arms, if needful ...*[13]

Sublimus Dei: Prohibiting Enslavement and Forced Conversion of Indians (May 29, 1537)

Sublimus Dei (On Prohibiting the Enslavement and Forced Evangelization of Indians) was promulgated, decreeing that Amerindians were not to be deprived of their liberty or the possession of their property:

> "*The said Indians and all other people who may later be discovered by Christians, are by no means to be deprived of their liberty or the possession of their property, even though they be outside the faith of Jesus Christ ...*"[14]

Non indecens videtur (June 19, 1538): Pope Paul III Retracts Penalties for Violating Sublimus Dei in Papal Letter

Under pressure though from Emperor Charles V, Pope Paul III succumbed to the Emperor's diatribe that the punishment of excommunication or interdict for violating Sublimus Dei, contained in a contemporaneous Apostolic Brief (Pastorale official), was injurious to the imperial right of colonization and harmful to the peace of the Indies. *The Pope retracted the ecclesiastical censures in another papal letter, Non Indecens Videtur, dated June 19, 1538.*

In *Non indecens videtur*, Pope Paul III wrote,

> *It does not seem to us improper if the Roman Pontiff...revoke, correct, or change those [dispositions] ... **from whom they were extorted by stealth at a time when he was engaged in other matters** and that it caused disruption to the peaceful*

> *state of the islands of the Indies ... Accordingly, by virtue*
> *of Apostolic authority, we revoke, invalidate, and annul the*
> *previous letter(s) and whatever is contained in it (or them).*
> (Emphasis added).[15]

Thus, the sanctions for excommunication for violating Sublimus Dei were removed, leaving it without any penalties or enforceability.

King Philip II Decree (1589)

In an 1859 decree ('cedula') King Philip II sent to his viceroy in Spanish America, he forthrightly proclaimed:

> *... the right of the ecclesiastical patronage belongs to us*
> *throughout the realm of the Indias-both because of having*
> *discovered and acquired that new world, and erected there*
> *and endowed the churches and monasteries at our own cost*
> *... and because it was conceded to us by bulls of the most holy*
> *pontiffs, conceded of their own accord.[16]*

Atrocities that Resulted from 'Doctrine of Discovery'

In Roberta Carol Harvey's following books the atrocities that resulted from the 'doctrine of discovery' are plainly laid out: *The Earth Is Red: The Imperialism of the Doctrine of Discovery; The Iron Triangle: Business, Government, and Colonial Settlers' Dispossession of Indian Timberlands and Timber* and *All That Glitters Is Ours: The Theft of Indian Mineral Resources.*

Indian lives, land, timber, mineral, agricultural, water and identity were stolen by the government in concert with big business and settlers. The U.S. government's agenda was and still is the theft of all Indian lands and is well-stated by General Pope in his Address before the Social Science Association in 1878:

> **We bought his lands by driblets, knowing very well that every**
> **purchase demanded another purchase in geometrical ratio,**
> **and that with every sale the means of livelihood upon which**
> **the Indian race had depended for ages, and which was the**
> **only mode they knew, were restricted more and more, and**
> **that in time every tribe of Indians must, in the nature of the**
> **case, be left destitute, except insofar as the government chose**
> **to feed and clothe them. The Indian did not know this in the**

beginning, nor indeed until want was upon him. We knew that he must relinquish in time all of his country. He did not know it, nor in the least comprehended the merciless and resistless progress of white populations. In short, we began the system, knowing perfectly what would be the results; the Indian began and for a long time continued it in ignorance of these ends." (Emphasis added).[17]

This is the horror brought on by the Catholic Church and its propagation of the Doctrine of Discovery and it is this the Catholic Church must be accountable for before all is lost by indigenous peoples worldwide.

Notes: Vatican Repudiates 'Doctrine of Discovery;' It Must Rescind All Underlying Bulls

1. Joint Statement of the Dicasteries for Culture and Education and for Promoting Integral Human Development on the "Doctrine of Discovery", 30.03.2023. https://press.vatican.va/content/salastampa/en/bollettino/pubblico/2023/03/30/230330b.html (accessed online April 3, 2023).

2. https://www.ncai.org/news/articles/2023/03/30/ncai-statement-onvatican-s-repudiation-of-doctrine-of-discovery (accessed online April 3, 2023).

3. Gelasius I on Spiritual and Temporal Power, Robinson, James Harvey. *Readings in European history.* Wildside Press LLC, 2008: 72-73.

4. Gregory VII, Dictatus Papae, Translated in Ernest F. Henderson, *Select Historical Documents of the Middle Ages*, (London: George Bell and Sons, 1910): 366-367.

5. https://doctrineofdiscovery.org/dum-diversas/ (accessed online April 3, 2023).

6. *European Treaties bearing on the History of the United States and its Dependencies to 1648*, Frances Gardiner Davenport, editor, Carnegie Institution of Washington, 1917, Washington, DC ("Davenport"), pp. 20-21.

7. [Inter Caetera, 1493. https://www.papalencyclicals.net/Alex06/alex06inter.htm] (accessed online November 17, 2020).

8. [Inter Caetera, 1493. https://www.papalencyclicals.net/Alex06/alex06inter.htm] (accessed online November 17, 2020).

9. https://avalon.law.yale.edu/15th_century/mod001.asp (accessed online April 3, 2023).

10. Davenport, p. 82.

11. Editorial: Church and State in Latin America, J. E. W., JR., Journal of Church and State, Volume 8, Issue 2, Spring 1966, pp. 173, 174.

12. Editorial: Church and State in Latin America, J. E. W., JR., Journal of Church and State, Volume 8, Issue 2, Spring 1966, pp. 173, 174.

13. https//suburbanbanshee.wordpress.com/2015/09/28/intra-arcana-the-good-bits/ (accessed online November 5, 2020).

14. https://www.papalencyclicals.net/paul03/p3subli.htm (accessed online November 5, 2020).

15. Parish, Helen Rand, Harold E. Weidman, and Bartolomé de las Casas. *Las Casas en México: historia y obra desconocidas*. Fondo de cultura económica, 1992: 303 –305, 310-312.

16. Ibid., p. 175. http://www.philippinehistory.net/1589philipII.htm (accessed online November 5, 2020).

17. Address by General John Pope before the Social Science Association, at Cincinnati, Ohio, May 24, 1878. Delivered by Request of the Association (Cincinnati: n.p., 1878).

Brief Statement regarding Catholic Church's Canon Law

Papal Influence

To understand the impact of the Papal Bulls *Dum Diversas* in 1452, *Romanus Pontifex* in 1455 and *Inter Caetera* in 1493, it is important to understand the authority of the Church. In brief, from the early part of the fourteenth century, it was generally accepted that the entire globe was the property of God and, as such, distributable by the Pope as His delegate on earth. The Church claimed authority from God through Jesus Christ who designated His apostle Peter as "the rock upon which my church will be built."[1] Peter was regarded as the first Pope, the head of the Church, and all others as his successors were endowed with the same divine authority.

Primacy of Papal Power

As between secular and spiritual authority, the Church reigned supreme. In 494, Pope Gelasius I impressed on Emperor Anastasius, the primacy of papal power: "[a]lthough you take precedence over all mankind in dignity... Nevertheless, you piously bow the neck to those who have charge of divine affairs ..."[2]

~ 752 ~

The Bull *Unam sanctam*, promulgated by Pope Boniface in 1302, reasserted the Church's primacy as follows: "We are informed by the texts of the gospels that in this Church and in its power are two swords; namely, the spiritual and the temporal. ... However, one sword ought to be subordinated to the other and temporal authority, subjected to spiritual power."[3]

Church's Infallibility

What made this system ironclad was the Church's infallibility proclaimed in 1090 by Pope Gregory VII in *Dictatus Papae*, The Dictates of the Pope: "That the Roman church has never erred; nor will it err to all eternity, the Scripture bearing witness."[4] According to Church dogma, in certain circumstances, the pope alone can speak with an infallibility by virtue of a gift (charism) allegedly bestowed by Christ and passed down through apostolic succession.[5]

For a statement of the pope to be considered infallible, it must meet three conditions:

> (1) The Pope must be speaking *ex cathedra* (lit., "from the chair" of Peter), or in the capacity as chief shepherd and teacher of the universal church.
> (2) The Pope must explicitly declare ("by a definitive act") that this doctrine is a truth of faith and so define it.
> (3) This doctrine must pertain to either "faith" or "morals".[6]

ex cathedra Authority of Pope

Ex cathedra is a Latin phrase which means "from the chair." It refers to **binding and infallible** papal teachings which are promulgated by the pope when he officially speaks by virtue of his supreme Apostolic authority on a matter of faith or morals and addresses it to the entire world.[7] Its present meaning was formally determined by the Vatican Council, Sess. IV, Const. de Ecclesiâ Christi, c. iv. (Emphasis added).

Dum Diversas (1452) Invoked Under *ex cathedra* Authority of Pope

Dum Diversas (English: Until different) is a papal bull issued on June 18, 1452, by Pope Nicholas V. It authorized Afonso V of Portugal to conquer Saracens and pagans, confiscate their property and consign them to "perpetual servitude". It is a **binding and infallible** promulgation by the pope as (1) it is made by virtue of his supreme "Apostolic authority;" (2) expressed a definitive act of subjugation by which they could 'missionize' the pagans and bring them to Christ; and (3) concerned faith—subjugating unbelievers and enemies of Christ.

> We grant you by these present documents, *with our Apostolic Authority*, full and free permission to invade, search out, capture, and subjugate the Saracens and pagans and any other unbelievers and enemies of Christ wherever they may be, as well as their kingdoms, duchies, counties, principalities, and other property [...] and to reduce their persons into perpetual servitude.[8]

Romanus Pontifex (1455) Invoked Under *ex cathedra* Authority of Pope

Romanus Pontifex (from Latin: "The Roman Pontiff") are papal bulls issued in 1436 by Pope Eugenius IV and in 1455 by Pope Nicholas V praising Catholic King Afonso V of Portugal for his battles against the Muslims and instructing him to capture and subdue all Saracens, Turks, and other non-Christians to reduce their persons to perpetual slavery. The Crown of Portugal was entitled to dominion over all lands south of Cape Bojador in Africa. The bulls forbade other Christian kings from infringing the King of Portugal's practice of trade, including the slave trade, and colonization in these regions. Again, these papal bulls would be considered *ex cathedra*, binding and infallible: (1) The Pope is designated as the *successor of the key-bearer of the heavenly kingdom and vicar of Jesus Christ*; (2) it expressed a definitive act—many Guineamen and other negroes, taken by force, and some by barter of unprohibited articles, or by other lawful contract of purchase, have been sent to the said kingdoms. A large number of these have been converted to the Catholic faith, and it is hoped, by the help of divine mercy, that if such progress be continued with them, either those peoples will be converted to the faith or at least the souls of many of them will be gained for Christ;" and (3) *pertained to faith* - "the reward of eternal felicity, and "pardon for their souls." Any violator would *incur the wrath of Almighty God and of the blessed apostles Peter and Paul.*[9]

Inter Caetera (1493) Invoked Under *ex cathedra* Authority of Pope

The Papal Bull, *Inter Caetera*, issued by Pope Alexander VI in 1493, granted certain designated lands to the Catholic monarchs of Spain. It was considered binding on the Church because it (1) invoked "the *fullness of our apostolic power;*" (2) expressed a definitive act—"extending and spreading [Catholicism] everywhere, securing the salvation of souls and subduing the barbarous nations and bringing them back to the faith itself;" and (3) addressed faith by imposing the sanction of "the wrath of Almighty God and of the blessed apostles Peter and Paul" if violated. As such, the bull would be considered *ex cathedra* and vested with the infallibility of the pope.[10]

Other Bulls Pertaining to Spanish Monarchy

In 1501, Pope Alexander VI issued *Eximae Devotionis*, which extended to the Spanish monarchs all rights of royal patronage, including the selection of all persons for ecclesiastical offices and the right to collect and use for itself all ecclesiastical tithes throughout its dominions.[11] Still another bull, *Universalis Ecclesiae*, issued in 1508 by Pope Julius II, declared the King of Spain to be the head of the Church in Spain and its empire.[12]

Treaty of Tordesillas, June 7, 1494

After continuing military conflict between Spain and Portugal over control of 'discovered' land and peoples, Don Ferdinand and Dona Isabella, King and Queen of Castile, and Dom John, King of Portugal, agreed to re-establish the line of partition of the globe set forth in the Bulls promulgated by Pope Alexander VI. The new line of demarcation was confirmed under The Treaty of Tordesillas on June 7, 1494, ratified thereafter by Spain on July 2, 1494, and by Portugal on September 5, 1494.[13] *Since it didn't have the approval of the Pope, King Emmanuel of Portugal sought Pope Julius II's approval and confirmation,* given the quarrels between the Christian princes of Europe.

Pope Julius II's Bull: *Ea quae pro bono pacis* (For the Promotion of Peace)

On January 24, 1506, Pope Julius II issued the Bull Ea quae pro bono pacis (For the promotion of peace) "to approve and confirm" the Treaty of Torsedillas, such that it would possess "perpetual authority" and "remain forever firm and unshaken."[14]

Sublimis Deus

The Joint Statement cited a subsequent Papal Bull, *Sublimis Deus* (On Prohibiting the Enslavement and Forced Evangelization of Indians), issued in 1537 by Pope Paul III, decreeing that Amerindians were not to be deprived of their liberty or the possession of their property: "The said Indians and all other people who may later be discovered by Christians, are by no means to be deprived of their liberty or the possession of their property, even though they be outside the faith of Jesus Christ ..."[15] *However,* the Joint Statement did not mention the subsequent edict of the Pope in *Non indecens videtur (1538).*

Pope Paul III Retracts Penalties for Violating *Sublimus Dei* in Papal Letter Using Words "Revoke, Invalidate and Annul:" *Non indecens videtur* (1538)

Under pressure from Emperor Charles V, Pope Paul III retracted the penalties of excommunication or interdict for violating *Sublimus Dei as injurious to the imperial right of colonization* and harmful to the peace of the Indies. In a papal letter, *Non indecens videtur*, dated June 19, 1538, Pope Paul III wrote:

> It does not seem to us improper if the Roman Pontiff...revoke, correct, or change those [dispositions] ... *from whom they were extorted by stealth at a time when he was engaged in other matters* and that it caused disruption to the peaceful state of the islands of the Indies ... Accordingly, by virtue of Apostolic authority, we revoke, invalidate, and annul the previous letter(s) and whatever is contained in it (or them).[16]

So much for papal infallibility, if the request comes from the Emperor and injures the imperial right of colonization.

King Confirms Concession of the "Indias" by the Papal Bulls

In a decree ('*cedula*') King Philip II sent to his viceroy in Spanish America in 1589, he forthrightly proclaimed: "... the right of the ecclesiastical patronage belongs to us throughout the realm of the Indias-both because of having discovered and acquired that new world, and erected there and endowed the churches and monasteries at our own cost ... and because it was *conceded to us by bulls of the most holy pontiffs*, conceded of their own accord."[17] (Emphasis added).

France's Reliance on Pope Clement VII's Reinterpretation of the Bull *Inter Caetera*

Official French exploration of the 'New World' lagged some thirty years behind Spain, beginning in the reign of Francis I. France claimed all of Canada and Louisiana based on its 'discovery,' when Indians occupied almost the entire area. As a Catholic ruler, Francis I was restricted by the Papal Bull *Inter Caetera*. *In 1533, King Francis I met with Pope Clement VII to 'reinterpret' the Bull, thus protecting France's 'discovery.'* By 1540 though, Francis I openly challenged not just the scope of *Inter Caetera* but its legitimacy, asserting that popes had no power to distribute lands among kings and asking "to see Adam's will to learn how he had partitioned the world."

England Was Catholic Nation When Letters Patent Issued to Cabot in 1496

England was a Catholic nation under the rule of Henry VII (1485-1509), during much of Henry VIII's (1509-1547) reign and for the period 1685-1688 under James II. *While still under the authority of the Roman Catholic Church*, though without regard to the Papal Bull *Inter Caetera*, *King Henry VII, in 1496, granted Letters Patent to John Cabot and his sons to discover countries then unknown to Christian people, and to take possession of them in the name of the king of England*. Subsequent grants to others were made thereafter. The Letters Patent used wording similar to *Inter Caetera* and *Romanus Pontifex*.

> [T]o find, discover and investigate whatsoever islands, countries, regions or provinces of **heathens and infidels**, in whatsoever part of the world placed, which before this time were **unknown to all Christians** ... they may be able to **conquer, occupy and possess**, as our vassals and governors lieutenants and deputies therein, **acquiring for us the dominion, title and jurisdiction** of the same towns, castles, cities, islands and mainlands so discovered...[18]

In Johnson v. M'Intosh, Chief Justice Marshall relied on the Letters Patent as the basis of England's 'discovery' claim - its sovereignty over the lands so discovered.19

Church as Economic Juggernaut

Emperors and empresses, monarchs, landowners and high officials sought papal favor, endowing the Church with treasure and land, and it became hugely wealthy. In addition, the Church collected a tithe of 10% of its members income, either in cash or goods. The Church was an economic juggernaut and acted as a financier and lending agent as well. E. de Vattel, a prominent eighteenth-century scholar of international law, notes the immense sums raised through tithes and indulgences:

> § 155.10 ... Over every affair of life they extended their authority, under pretence that was conscience. They obliged new-married husbands to purchase permission to lie with their wives the first three first nights after marriage.

§ 156. Money drawn to Rome. This burlesque invention leads us to remark another abuse ... the immense sums which bulls, dispensations, &c., annually drew to Rome, from all the countries in communion with her. How much might be said on the scandalous trade of indulgences![20]

Papal Permission to Use Force for Catholic Conversion

Intra arcana, a papal bull issued in 1529 by Pope Clement VII to Charles V, authorized the use of force and arms, if necessary, to convert Indians to Catholicism:

> We trust that ... you will compel and with all zeal cause the barbarian nations to come to the knowledge of God ... not only by edicts and admonitions, but also by force and arms, if needful ...[21]

Dominican Friars Silenced for Disclosing Atrocities Committed by Conquistadors

Antonio de Montesinos, and other Dominican friars, denounced the "cruel and horrible servitude" to which Amerindians were being reduced:[22]

> Tell me by what right of justice do you hold these Indians in such a cruel and horrible servitude? On what authority have you waged such detestable wars against these people who dwelt quietly and peacefully on their own lands? Wars in which you have destroyed such an infinite number of them by homicides and slaughters never heard of before. Why do you keep them so oppressed and exhausted, without giving them enough to eat or curing them of the sicknesses they incur from the excessive labor you give them, and they die, or rather you kill them, in order to extract and acquire gold every day.

The friars were silenced by the King and their superiors in Rome.

Catholic Church's Code of Canon Law No. 10

Book I of the Catholic Church's Code of Canon Law contains general norms that govern the nature and application of ecclesiastical laws and processes.

Canon 10 states: "*Only those laws must be considered invalidating or disqualifying which expressly establish that an act is null or that a person is unqualified.*" (Emphasis added).[23]

Annul All Underlying Bulls

It is not enough under the Church's Canon Law for the Dicasteries to "repudiate" the 'concept' of the 'doctrine of discovery.' The Church must "annul" all of the underlying Bulls - *Dum Diversas, Romanus Pontifex, Inter Caetera, Ea quae pro bono pacis* and all other related Bulls. The action taken in *Non indecens videtur* serves as precedent: "*by virtue of Apostolic authority, we revoke, invalidate, and annul the previous letter(s) and whatever is contained in it (or them).*"[24] (Emphasis added). The word "repudiates" is ambiguous and does not have a set meaning. It is imperative that the Church act with order and clarity.

Confusion over Joint Statement

Robert J. Miller, an expert on this subject, noted the confusion regarding the Joint Statement: The Vatican News posted an article with a title that the "'Doctrine of Discovery' was never Catholic." Plus, the Canadian Bishops Conference on March 30 rejected the idea that the papal bulls were ever the basis of the international law of colonialism."[25] It is certain that many questions still remain to be answered.

Notes: Brief Statement regarding Catholic Church's Canon Law

1. Matthew 16:18-19.
2. Gelasius I on Spiritual and Temporal Power, Robinson, James Harvey. *Readings in European history*. Wildside Press LLC, 2008: 72-73.

3. English translation of 'Unam' is taken from a doctoral dissertation written in the Dept. of Philosophy at the Catholic University of America and published by CUA Press in 1927.

4. Gregory VII, *Dictatus Papae*, Translated in Ernest F. Henderson, *Select Historical Documents of the Middle Ages*, (London: George Bell and Sons, 1910): 366-367.

5. *Lumen Gentium*, 25. https://www.ewtn.com/catholicism/library/dogmatic-constitution-on-the-church-1513 (accessed online April 15, 2023).
6. https://www.newadvent.org/cathen/05677a.htm (accessed online April 15,

2023).

7. https://www.newadvent.org/cathen/05677a.htm (accessed online April 15, 2023).

8. https://en.wikipedia.org/wiki/Dum_Diversas (accessed online November 17, 2020).

9. https://www.papalencyclicals.net/nichol05/romanus-pontifex.htm (accessed online November 17, 2020).

10. *Inter Caetera*, 1493, https://www.papalencyclicals.net/Alex06/alex06inter.htm (accessed online November 17, 2020).

11. https://clc-library-org-docs.angelfire.com/Eximiae.html (accessed online November 17, 2020).

12. Editorial: Church and State in Latin America, J. E. W., JR., Journal of Church and State, Volume 8, Issue 2, Spring 1966, pp. 173, 174.

13. https://avalon.law.yale.edu/15th_century/mod001.asp (accessed online November 17, 2020).

14. https://clc-library-org-docs.angelfire.com/ea.html (accessed online April 15, 2023).

15. https://www.papalencyclicals.net/paul03/p3subli.htm (accessed online November 5, 2020).

16. Parish, Helen Rand, Harold E. Weidman, and Bartolomé de las Casas. *Las Casas en México: historia y obra desconocidas*. Fondo de cultura económica, 1992: 303–305, 310-312.

17. Editorial: Church and State in Latin America, J. E. W., JR., Journal of Church and State, Volume 8, Issue 2, Spring 1966, p. 175.

18. Skelton, Raleigh Ashlin. *The Cabot voyages and Bristol discovery under Henry VII*. Routledge, 2017: Document 18.

19. *Johnson v. M'Intosh*, 21 U.S. 543, 576-577 (1823).

20. de Vattel, Emerich. *The Law of Nations or the Principles of Natural Law Applied to the Conduct and to the Affairs of Nations and of Sovereigns*. Carnegie Institution of Washington, 1916. Book I, Chap. XII, Of Piety and Religion §155.10, §156.

21. Translation from: https//suburbanbanshee.wordpress.com/2015/09/28/intra-arcana-the-good-bits/ (accessed online November 5, 2020).

22. Hanke, Lewis. *The Spanish struggle for justice in the conquest of America*. Southern Methodist University Press, 1949: 17.

23. Code of Canon Law. https://www.vatican.va/archive/cod-iuris-canonici/eng/documents/cic_lib1-cann7-22_en.html#:~:text=10%20Only%20those%20laws%20must,that%20a%20person%20is%20effected (accessed online April 15, 2023).

24. Parish, Helen Rand, Harold E. Weidman, and Bartolomé de las Casas. *Las Casas en México: historia y obra desconocidas*. Fondo de cultura económica, 1992: 303 –305, 310-312.

25. "ASU Law professor talks about the history of 'Doctrine of Discovery' and what the Vatican's repudiation of it really means," April 14, 2023, Robert J. Miller. https://news.asu.edu/20230414-discoveries-repudiation-without-reparations (accessed online April 15, 2023).

27: CHARTS

ARIZONA

Arizona's Indian Battles[58]	
1856	First Battle of Fort Defiance
1857	Battle of Pima Butte
1860	Second Battle of Fort Defiance
1860–1868	Navajo War
1862	Apache Pass/Fort Bowie
1862	First Battle of Dragoon Springs
1862	Big Dry Wash
1864	Canyon de Chelly
1865	Battle of Fort Buchanan
1865–1868	Hualapai War
1871	Camp Grant Massacre
1871–1875	Yavapai War
1872	Salt River Canyon Skeleton Cave Battle
1873 and 1885–1886	Apache War Campaign
1873	Turret Peak
1881	Cibecue Creek
1886	Geronimo meets with U.S. Gen. Crook near Tombstone, Arizona

Indian Battles in Arizona

Arizona Annihilationist Government Policy and Miner Bombast Targeting Pinal Apaches[13]

Date and Source	Statement(s) (Emphasis added).
October 26, 1864 ("Apache rangers" 1864, p. 1, col. 2)	"a bill ... adopted by the Legislature, authorizing the raising of not more than six companies of rangers to fight Apaches. ... [I]f we do not conquer the savages they will ... drive us from the country. ... *Extermination is our only hope, and the sooner it is accomplished the better.* ... Let the necessary work go on."
October 31, 1865 (Farish, 1916, Vol. 4, p. 126)	General John S. Mason, issues General Order No. 11: *"All Apache Indians in this Territory are hostile and all men old enough to bear arms who are encountered will be slain.* ... All rancherias, provisions and whatever of value belonging to the Indians ... will be destroyed."
September 22, 1868 (Major General H. W. Halleck, 1869, p. 49)	"The Apaches ... are the natural and hereditary enemies of the whites. ... They have successfully expelled from that Territory the Aztecs, the Spaniards and the Mexicans; and they will yield to our people only when compelled to do so by the rifle. ... Murder and robbery constitute almost the sole occupation of the Apaches ... plundering and destroying unprotected agricultural and mining settlements. ... They will observe no treaties, agreements, or truces. *With them there is no alternative but active and vigorous war, till they are completely destroyed.*"
September 27, 1869 (General Ord, 1870, pp. 121-122)	"On taking command of the department I was satisfied that the few settlers and scattered miners of Arizona were the sheep upon which these wolves habitually preyed. ... *I encouraged the troops to capture and root out the Apache by every means, and to hunt them as they would wild animals* ... over two hundred have been killed, generally by parties who have trailed them for days and weeks. ... lying in wait for them by day and following them by night. Many villages have been burned, large quantities of arms and supplies of ammunition, clothing and provisions have been destroyed. ... Some of the bands, having the fear of extermination before them, have sued for peace."
January 23, 1871 ("The Pacific Coast," 1871, p. 1) (Emphasis added).	*"Governor Safford ... recommends a war of extermination against Apache Indians, and favors the employment of volunteers composed of settlers ... as more effective and cheaper than regular troops."*
August 26, 1871 ("Indian War in Arizona," 1871, p. 1)	"Crook is bent on exerting the fullest strength of his command to punish hostile Indians. ... The Territory will be scoured as it never has been, and the Apaches warred upon in a manner that will strike them with awe, and we believe produce an early peace."
September 26, 1871 ("The Indians: The Campaign," 1871, p. 1)	"Governor Sofford [sic] and a company of 200 miners and Indian hunters had found rich gold placers in the Pinal country, and were still scouting after gold and Apaches."
March 30, 1872 ("Arizona," 1872, p. 1)	"not only mining, but all classes of industry are seriously hindered by the atrocities of the murderous Apaches. ... Peaceable miners in the pursuit of their vocation are shot down, pick and shovel in hand. ... *The inhabitants saw a glimmer of hope in the arrival of General Crook, whose policy is to exterminate the Indians entirely as the most efficient means of making peace with them.*"

Annihilationist Government Policy
and Miner Bombast Targeting Pinal Apaches

Aftermath, Loss of ~5,900,000 Acres

Important Federal Government Acts Affecting Western Apache Lands,[53]

Action and Date	Affected land (Mostly Severed Acres)
Executive order to establish White Mountain Reservation, November 9, 1871	Original White Mountain Indian Reservation: Add ~4,000,000 acres
Executive order to increase size of White Mountain Reservation and create "San Carlos division," December 14, 1872	Add ~1,250,000 acres
Assumption of U.S. jurisdiction over Western Apaches and their territory, per Finding of Fact No. 11 (21 Ind. Cl. Comm. 189, 218), May 1, 1873	Western Apache Aboriginal Territory: ~9,400,000 acres
Executive order to open White Mountain Reservation land in Gila River Valley to non-Indian use, August 5, 1873	Subtract ~1,300,000 acres
Executive order to open Reservation land east of 109° 30' west longitude (east-most 26 miles, approximately) for non-Indian use, July 21, 1874	Subtract ~950,000 acres
Executive order to open Reservation land east of Globe to non-Indian use, April 27, 1876	Subtract ~100,000 acres
Executive order to open Reservation land along western boundary for non-Indian use, March 31, 1877	Subtract ~55,000 acres
Congressional act to open Reservation land south of Salt River and north of Chromo Butte to non-Indian use, February 20, 1893	Subtract ~115,000 acres
Agreement to exclude from Reservation the "Mineral Strip" south of Gila River, February 25, 1896 (ratified by Congressional act June 10, 1896, 29 Stat. 358)	Subtract ~230,000 acres
Congressional act to partition White Mountain Reservation into Fort Apache and San Carlos reservations, June 7, 1897 (30 Stat. 64, 86)	San Carlos acres; Fort Apache Reservation ~1,700,000 acres Indian Reservation since 1990, ~1,800,000
Congressional act to open a "small tract" to mining and give proceeds to tribe, March 2, 1901 (31 Stat. 952)	Subtract ~231 acres (location indeterminate)
Executive order to open San Carlos Reservation land in southwest corner to non-Indian use, December 22, 1902	Subtract ~39,000 acres
San Carlos Mineral Strip Act to return land to Reservation for benefit of the San Carlos Apache Tribe, 1990 (104 Stat. 1047)	Add 10,650 acres (104 Stat. 1047)
Approximate difference between Western Apache Aboriginal title lands (~9,400,000 acres) and remaining Reservation land (~3,500,000 acres) =	(~5,930,000 acres)

Aftermath, Loss of ~5,900,000 Acres

Date	Personnel, location, description & casualties	Kühn Page
November 19, 1859	8th Infantry command kills 3 Apaches and captures 15 cattle in attack on Pinal Apaches near San Pedro River	71
December 25, 1859	U.S. Army command kills 6 Apaches in skirmish, Pinal Mountains (Capt. Elliott wounded)	72
May 7, 1863	Command of California Volunteers and civilians kills about 50 Apaches (1 soldier killed) and captures 16 Apache children in attack on camp in Aravaipa Canyon	99
November 5, 1863	Command of California Volunteers kills 1 Apache in ambush of 7 Apaches at Gila River near Pinal Mountains	103
June 8, 1864	Command of 58 California Volunteers kills 8 Apaches, captures 9 Apache women and children, in attack in Aravaipa Canyon	108
July 31, 1864	Command of California and New Mexico Volunteers kills 2 Apaches (1 woman, 1 boy) shooting at 2 Apache prisoners attempting to escape, near Pinal Creek	110
August 1, 1864	Command of California and New Mexico Volunteers kills 1 Apache woman and captures 1 Apache woman in attack on Apaches east of Pinal Creek	110
August 3, 1864	Command of California and New Mexico Volunteers executes 2 Apache prisoners (men) at Pinal Creek	110
August 5, 1864	Command of California and New Mexico Volunteers kills 5 Apaches in ambush on 15 Pinal Apaches at Pinal Creek	110
March 31, 1866	Command of 1st Infantry and 200 Pimas kills 25 Pinal Apaches and captures 16 in attack on camp about 25 miles north of the Gila River	122
April 21, 1868	8th Cavalry command kills 2 Apaches near Camp Grant	138
May 1, 1868	8th Cavalry command kills 6 and mortally wounds 2 Apaches in an attack on a small camp at the Gila River, near Camp Grant	138
April 29, 1869	Command of 1st Cavalry and 14th Infantry kills 25 Pinal Apaches and captures 8 in attack on camp in Santa Teresa Mountains	150
May 24, 1869	Command of 1st Cavalry and 32nd Infantry kills 4 Pinal Apaches and captures 2 in attack on 42 dwellings near Mineral Creek	152
June 3, 1869	Command of 1st Cavalry kills 2 Pinal Apaches in attack on camp near Mineral Creek	152
June 4, 1869	Command of 8th Cavalry, 1st Cavalry, and 14th Infantry kills 20 Pinal Apaches and captures 4 children in attack near Pinto Creek	152
August 11, 1869	Command of 1st Cavalry under Major John Green kills 3 Apaches and captures 2 children in attack on camp near Aravaipa Creek	155
December 16, 1869	Command of 8th Cavalry and 1st Cavalry kills some Apaches and captures Apache women and children at Pinto Creek	161
January 7, 1870	Command of 1st Cavalry kills 3 Apaches after pursuit to the Gila River near Camp Grant	162
April 30, 1870	Command of 1st and 3rd Cavalry and 21st Infantry kills 11 Apaches in attack on camp in Pinal Mountains	165
June 5, 1870	Command of 1st and 3rd Cavalry kills at least 30 Apaches (9 men and 21 women and children) in attack in Apache Mountains	167
October 29, 1870	Command of 1st Cavalry kills 4 Apache men in Pinal Mountains	170
January 1, 1871	Command of 1st and 3rd Cavalry kills 9 Apaches and destroys a camp, Pinal Mountains, near the Gila River	171
February 1871	Cavalry command kills 1 Apache in attack on a Pinal Apache camp, Pinal Mountains	173
April 11 & 12, 1871	Command of 3rd Cavalry kills 29 Apaches in two attacks on camps, Apache Mountains	175
March 8, 1874	Command of 5th Cavalry kills 13 Apache men and captures 34 women and children at Eskiminzin's camp, Pinal Mountains	198
March 25-26, 1874	Command of 5th Cavalry kills 12 Western Apaches in attack on camp, Superstition Mountains	198
April 2, 1874	Command of 5th Cavalry kills 47 Apaches and captures 50 women and children in attack on camp, Pinal Mountains	198
April 3-14, 1874	Command of 5th Cavalry kills 14 Apache men and captures 30 women and children in attacks on camps, Pinal, Mescal, and Santa Teresa Mountains	198
April 28, 1874	Command of 5th Cavalry kills 23 Western Apaches in attack on a camp in Aravaipa Mountains	199
April 28-30, 1874	Two 5th Cavalry attacks kill 3 Apaches and capture 11	199
May 23, 1874	Apache scouts kill 4 Pinal Apaches, Santa Catalina Mountains	200
June 6, 1874	Command of 5th Cavalry kills 4 Aravaipa Apaches, Santa Teresa Mountains	200
ca. June 7, 1874	Apache scouts kill 1 Pinal Apache	200
July 1874	Apache scouts kill 7 Pinal Apaches	201

Thirty-Five Lethal Attacks on Apaches in and near Pinal Apache Territory, 1859–1874

Lethal Attacks on Non-Apaches by Pinal Apaches or in Pinal Apache Territory, 1859–1874[57]		
Date	Personnel, location, description & casualties	Kühn page
August 3, 1860	Pinal Apache attack on engineering party in San Pedro River Valley mortally wounds 1 civilian	77
April 25, 1861	Attacks by Pinal Apaches in Santa Rita Mountains kill 3 civilians	83
January 8, 1865	Pinal Apache attack west of Fort Grant kills 1 civilian	120
March 22, 1866	Ambush of 7 soldiers by at least 75 Apaches west of Cottonwood Springs, kills 4 soldiers, mortally wounds 1 soldier	121
May 20, 1867	Attack by Pinal Apaches at Cañada del Oro kills 1 Mexican and 2 'tame' Apaches	129
June 4, 1867	Attacks by Apaches on ranches near Camp Grant kill 1 Mexican and 1 civilian and wound 2 Mexicans and 1 Indian	130
March 25, 1868	14th Infantry command led by Captain Guido Ilges attack on 50 Apaches near Cottonwood Springs results in death of 1 soldier	137
July 9, 1868	Fight near Camp Grant kills 1 Mexican	140
July 15, 1868	Apache attack near Camp Grant kills 1 Mexican	140
February 26, 1869	Attack by 50 Western Apaches, probably Pinals, on 2 wagons near Camp Grant kills 2 civilians and wounds 1 soldier	148
March 21, 1869	Attack by 30 Apaches on 2 wagons 10 miles from Camp Grant kills 1 civilian and wounds 2 infantrymen	149
May 11, 1869	Attack by ~200 Apaches on wagons at Cañada del Oro claims 3 Mexican lives	151
October 5, 1869	Ambush of mail coach by Pinal and Chokenen Apaches at Dragoon Pass kills 4 soldiers and 2 civilians	157
November 25, 1869	Apaches mortally wound 1 civilian 6 miles from Florence	160
November 30, 1869	Apaches kill 1 prospector 9 miles from Florence	160
February 1, 1870	Attack by ~50 Pinal Apaches on wagon train north of Tucson kills 1 soldier and 2 civilians	163
April 13, 1870	Apache ambush kills 1 civilian near San Pedro settlements	165
May 28, 1870	Attack by Pinal, Aravaipa, and Cibecue Apaches on wagon train south of Camp Grant kills 1 civilian and 2 Mexicans	166
January 31, 1871	Apache attack on wagon near Florence kills 1 Pima	172
February 14, 1871	Pinal Apache attack 12 miles west of Camp Pinal kills 1 Mexican	173
March 9, 1871	Pinal Apache attack on a wagon between Camp Grant and Camp Pinal kills 1 soldier and 1 Mexican	174
March 14, 1871	Apache attack on herd at Camp Pinal kills 2 civilians	174
May 28, 1871	Attack by Eskiminzin on ranch near Camp Grant kills 1 civilian	177
July 13, 1871	Attack led by Eskiminzin on wagon train east of Cienega Station kills 1 soldier; soldiers kill 13 Apaches	178
August 4, 1872	1 Mexican killed in vigilante attack on Apaches	186
November 22, 1872	Apache attack on Ward's camp near Camp Grant kills 1 Mexican	188
May 27, 1873	Apache attack on ration day at San Carlos kills 1 soldier	193
September 12, 1873	Apache attack on 4 prospectors on Pinal Creek kills 1 civilian	195
January 31, 1874	Apache attack led by Chunz and Cocinay on wagons at San Carlos Agency kills 1 civilian and mortally wounds 1 civilian	197
February 3, 1874	Apache attack on ranch near Camp Grant kills 6 Mexicans	197
February 8, 1874	Apache attack on wagon southeast of Florence kills 1 civilian	197
March 1874	Attack by Eskiminzin on wagon train near Florence kills 1 civilian	198
March 9, 1874	Pinal Apache attack northwest of Tucson kills 1 Mexican	198

Lethal Attacks on Non-Apaches by Pinal Apaches
or in Pinal Apache Territory, 1859–1874

COLORADO

COUNTY	COUNTY SEAT	TRIBES
A		1840 ALLIANCE ARAP/CHEY/COMANCHES/ KIOWAS (1864 ALLIANCE ARAP CHEY LAKOTA & PLAINS IND.)
ADAMS	AURORA, ARVADA, COMMERCE CITY	ARAPAHO & CHEYENNE
ALAMOSA	SAN LUIS, SAND DUNES	CAPOTE & MOUACHE UTES
ARAPAHOE	LITTLETON AURORA ENGLEWOOD	ARAP/CHEY (1867 MEDICINE LODGE TREATY - OK IND. TERR. RES.)
ARCHULETA	PAGOSA SPRINGS	UTES
B		
BACA	SPRINGFIELD, COMANCHE NATIONAL GRASSLANDS	COMANCHES
BENT	LAS ANIMAS	CHEYENNE, COMANCHES, KIOWAS
BOULDER	BOULDER	ARAP/CHEY
BROOMFIELD	BROOMFIELD	ARAP/CHEY
C		
CHAFFEE	SALIDA	
CHEYENNE	CHEYENNE WELLS	ARAP/CHEY
CLEAR CREEK	IDAHO SPRINGS, LOVELAND, GEORGETOWN	ARAP/CHEY (UTES)
CONEJOS	ANTONITO	UTES - CAPOTES
COSTILLA	SAN LUIS	UTES - FT. GARLAND
CROWLEY	ORDWAY	ARAP/CHEY (KIOWAS, JICARILLA APACHES, COMANCHES)
CUSTER	WESTCLIFFE - SOUTH CENTRAL CO	UTES
D		
DELTA	DELTA	PARIANUCHE UTES TABEGUACHE UTES
DENVER	DENVER	ARAP/CHEY
DOLORES	DOVE CREEK	WEEMINUCHE UTES
DOUGLAS	CASTLEROCK, LONE TREE PARKER	ARAP/CHEY (UTES)
E		
EAGLE	EAGLE, VAIL, WHITE RIVER NATL FOREST	PARIANUCHE, YAMPA UTES
EL PASO	PIKES PEAK	TABEGUACHE UTES
ELBERT	ELIZABETH	ARAP/CHEY (COMANCHE, KIOWA, UTES)
F		
FREMONT	ROYAL GORGE, CANON CITY	MUACHE UTES (CHEYENNE, ARAP, KIOWA, COMANCHES)
G		
GARFIELD	GLENWOOD SPRINGS	PARIANUCHE UTES
GILPIN	CENTRAL CITY	UINTAH & YAMPA UTES (ARAP)
GRAND	GRANBY (WINTER PARK)	UINTAH UTES (MIDDLE PARK INDIAN AGENCY) ARAP
GUNNISON	CRESTED BUTTE	PARIANUCHE UTES, TABEGUACHE UTES

Colorado Counties

U.S. Colorado Indian Treaties			
Year	Treaty	Purpose	Outcome
1849	Abiquiu	Pacify the Territory of NM and San Luis Valley acquired as result of Mexican-American War (1846-48).	Capote and Muache Ute bands agree to U.S. jurisdiction over them, safe passage for settlers, presence of military forts and trading posts.
1851	Fort Laramie	Ensure protected right-of-way for emigrants crossing Indian lands.	White travelers permitted free and unmolested travel across Great Plains and Army could build and man forts.
1861	Fort Wise	Allow for continued settlement and mining for gold in Colorado without fear of Indian violence.	Cheyenne and Arapaho cordoned onto small triangular reservation, cede lands granted them under 1851 Fort Laramie Treaty; 1/13 of their original land base retained.
1863	Conejos	Avoid hostilities that resulted when white immigrants occupied Ute lands during Colorado Gold Rush and after passage of the Homestead Act in 1862.	Relinquished claims to all land in Colorado Rocky Mountains east of Continental Divide (Front Range of the Rockies), along with Middle Park basin in Rockies in north-central Colorado.
1865	Little Arkansas Treaty	Remove Cheyenne and Arapaho Tribes from Colorado to Indian Territory in Oklahoma.	Cheyenne and Arapaho chiefs sign treaty creating a reservation in western Indian Territory.
1867	Medicine Lodge	Establish security for person and property along the lines of railroad.	Utes cede Central Rockies; Reservation for Utes on Colorado's Western Slope; reservation for Uintah Utes in Utah.
1868	Ute	Open Central Rocky Mountains for mining.	
1874	Brunot Agreement	Permit mining in San Juan Mountains (silver and gold).	Utes reduce reservation through cession of San Juan Mountains.
1880	Legislation, Forced Treaty	Punish Utes for Meeker "Massacre, dispossess them of their reservation, and remove them from Colorado.	Forced removal to Utah of White River and Uncompahgre Utes; small reservation for Southern Utes in SE Colorado.

U.S. Colorado Indian Treaties

BATTLES IN GREAT SIOUX WAR [LIST NOT MEANT TO BE INCLUSIVE]		
Battle of Powder River	March 17, 1876	Montana
Battle of Prairie Dog Creek	June 9, 1876	Wyoming
Battle at Warbonnet Creek	July 17, 1876	Nebraska
Battle of Rosebud Creek	June 17, 1876	Montana
Battle of the Little Bighorn	June 25, 1876	Montana
Battle of Slim Buttes	September 9, 1876	South Dakota
Battle of Glendive Creek	October 10, 1876	Montana
Battle of Cedar Creek	October 21, 1876	Montana
Dull Knife Fight	November 25, 1876	Wyoming
Battle of Wolf Mountain	January 8, 1877	Montana
Battle of Little Muddy Creek	May 7, 1877	Montana

Great Sioux War

MONTANA INDIAN BATTLES [Not Inclusive of All Battles]		
September 1, 1865	Battle of Alkali Creek, Powder River War	Sioux
September 8, 1865	Battle of Dry Creek, Powder River War	Sioux, Cheyenne, Arapaho
August 1, 1867	Hayfield Fight, Red Cloud's War	Cheyenne and Sioux
April 7, 1869	Battle of Sixteen Mile Creek	Blackfoot
January 23, 1870	Marias Massacre	Blackfoot
August 11, 1873	Battle of Bighorn River	Sioux
March 17, 1876	Battle of Powder River, Great Sioux War of 1876	Cheyenne and Sioux
June 17, 1876	Battle of the Rosebud, Great Sioux War of 1876	Cheyenne and Sioux
June 25–26, 1876	Battle of the Little Bighorn, Great Sioux War of 1876	Sioux, Cheyenne, Arapaho
October 21, 1876	Battle of the Cedar Creek, Great Sioux War of 1876	Sioux, Shoshone, Crow
January 8, 1877	Battle of Wolf Mountain, Great Sioux War of 1876	Cheyenne and Sioux
May 7, 1877	Battle of Little Muddy Creek, Great Sioux War of 1876	Cheyenne and Sioux
July 17, 1879	Battle of Milk River	Sioux
February 7, 1880	Battle of Pumpkin Creek	Sioux
January 2, 1881	Battle of Poplar River	Sioux
November 5, 1887	Battle of Crow Agency	Crow

Indian Battles in Montana

NEVADA

NEVADA'S INCOHERENT INDIAN POLICY

Territory or State	Year	Officials	Office	Jurisdiction
Utah Territory	1850	Brigham Young, Territorial Governor and ex oficio Superintendant of Indian Affairs (1850–1860).	Utah Superintendency of Indian Affairs, Agencies in Salt Lake City, Provo, Uintah Valley, Fort Bridger and Carson Valley.	Utah Territory
California	1852, Abolished 1873.		Superintendency of Indian Affairs.	
California	1859		California created Colorado District.	Tribes between Mojave and Colorado Rivers.
Utah Territory	1858	Agent: Frederick Dodge 1858.	Carson Valley, 1858.	Walker River Indian Reservation set aside (1859). Pyramid Lake Paiutes' Reservation set aside (1859).
Nevada Territory	1861	Agents: Jacob T. Lockhart 1861, Franklin Campbell 1865, Lieutenant Jesse M. Lee 1869, George Balcom 1870, Calvin A. Bateman 1871, A. J. Barnes 1875, William M. Garvey 1879, and James E. Spencer 1879.	Carson Valley Agency became Nevada Superintendency in 1861; abolished in 1921; re-established in 1952 - Paiute, Shoshone, Washoe Tribes.	**Paiutes**: Fort McDermitt Reservation (1936); Summit Lake Reservation (1913); Yerington Colony (1916 and 1936). **Shoshone**: Fallon Colony and Reservation (1907); Fort McDermitt Reservation (1936); Yomba Reservation (1934). **Washoe**: Carson Colony (1917), Dresslerville Colony (1917), Reno Sparks Colony (1917), Stewart Colony.
State of Nevada	1869	Agents: Captain Reuben N. Fenton 1869, Henry G. Stewart 1870, Charles F. Powell 1871, George W. Ingalls 1873, and A. J. Barnes 1874.	SE Nevada or Pi-Ute Agency.	Southern Nevada and adjacent parts of Arizona and Utah Tribe also in California: Moved from Hiko to St. Thomas, to Pioche.
	1870		Larger State Superintendencies discontinued.	
State of Nevada	1870–1883		Shoshone and Bannock Agency from its establishment in 1870 until 1883, when it became Shoshone Agency; 1937, name was changed to Wind River Agency.	
Utah Territory (State in 1896)	1870		Saint George Agency	Portions of Utah. **Today**: *Kaibab Band of Paiute Indians of the Kaibab Indian Reservation, Arizona,* Fredonia, Arizona. *Las Vegas Tribe of Paiute Indians of the Las Vegas Indian Colony, Nevada,* Las Vegas NV. *Moapa Band of Paiute Indians of the Moapa River Indian Reservation,* Moapa, NV. *Paiute Indian Tribe of Utah,* Cedar City, Utah. *San Juan Southern Paiute Tribe of Arizona,* Tuba City, Arizona
Nevada	1875		Moapa River Reservation and Agency	

Nevada's Incoherent Indian Policy

MONTANA INDIAN BATTLES [Not Inclusive of All Battles]		
September 1, 1865	Battle of Alkali Creek, Powder River War	Sioux
September 8, 1865	Battle of Dry Creek, Powder River War	Sioux, Cheyenne, Arapaho
August 1, 1867	Hayfield Fight, Red Cloud's War	Cheyenne and Sioux
April 7, 1869	Battle of Sixteen Mile Creek	Blackfoot
January 23, 1870	Marias Massacre	Blackfoot
August 11, 1873	Battle of Bighorn River	Sioux
March 17, 1876	Battle of Powder River, Great Sioux War of 1876	Cheyenne and Sioux
June 17, 1876	Battle of the Rosebud, Great Sioux War of 1876	Cheyenne and Sioux
June 25-26, 1876	Battle of the Little Bighorn, Great Sioux War of 1876	Sioux, Cheyenne, Arapaho
October 21, 1876	Battle of the Cedar Creek, Great Sioux War of 1876	Sioux, Shoshone, Crow
January 8, 1877	Battle of Wolf Mountain, Great Sioux War of 1876	Cheyenne and Sioux
May 7, 1877	Battle of Little Muddy Creek, Great Sioux War of 1876	Cheyenne and Sioux
July 17, 1879	Battle of Milk River	Sioux
Febuary 7, 1880	Battle of Pumpkin Creek	Sioux
January 2, 1881	Battle of Poplar River	Sioux
November 5, 1887	Battle of Crow Agency	Crow

Indian Battles in New Mexico

UTAH INDIAN BATTLES/MASSACRES (Not intended to be inclusive of all battles).		
1853	Walker War	Mormons and Utes
January 29, 1853	Bear River Massacre	Shoshoni
October 26, 1853	Gunnison Massacre	Pahvant
April 9, 1865–1872	Black Hawk War (Peace Treaty 1868)	Mormons and Utes
April 1866	Circleville Massacre	Paiutes

Indian Battles in Utah

WYOMING

INDIAN BATTLES IN WYOMING 1853–1865 (This list is not meant to be inclusive.)			
Date	**Location**	**Event**	
June 15, 1853	Fort Laramie Skirmish		Chiefs proclaimed soldiers "the first to make the ground bloody."
August 19, 1854	Grattan Fight	Lieutenant Grattan sought to arrest Sioux Indian for killing a cow. All troops killed.	
November 13, 1854	Horse Creek Skirmish	Mail stage attacked.	
September 3, 1855	Battle of Ash Creek	General William S. Harney sent to Fort Kearny, Nebraska 2nd U.S. Dragoons. Assignment: Exact retribution on Sioux.	Several Brule Sioux warriors killed.
February 20, 1863	Pass Creek Skirmish	Stage station attacked.	One soldier killed, 6 wounded. 20 Indians killed, more wounded and more possibly dead.
July 7, 1863	Battle of Grand Pass		
July 7, 1864	Townsend Wagon Train attacked.	Traveling on Bozeman Trail through Indian country.	
July 12, 1864	Kelly Wagon Train		Four white settlers killed. Two women and two children captured – Mary Hurley killed.
May 20, 1865	Deer Creek Station	In two battles, 5 Indians killed, 9 wounded. One soldier killed.	Two companies of **Kansas Cavalry** garrisoned at Station. August 1866 – Indians burned Deer Creek Station.
June 3, 1865	Battle of Dry Creek, Wyoming	Two soldiers killed.	Lieutenant Colonel Preston B. Plumb, in command of 11th **Kansas Cavalry**, 10 men from **Ohio Cavalry**.
June 8, 1865	Sage Creek Station	4 men of **Ohio Cavalry** killed.	
July 26, 1865	Battle of Platte Bridge Station	Number of Indians and soldiers killed.	Commanded by Major Martin Anderson of 11th **Kansas Cavalry**.
July 26, 1865	Battle of Red Buttes, Wyoming (aka Battle of Custard's Wagon Train)		Wagon train guarded by Sergeant Amos J. Custard and 25 **Kansas Cavalry** soldiers.
August–September, 1865	Powder River Expedition	Colonel James H. Kidd to build Fort Connor, aka, Fort Reno – 200 men of 6th **Michigan Volunteer Cavalry**.	Brigadier General Patrick E. Connor led campaign carried out by U.S. Volunteer soldiers (675 troops), 7th **Iowa** and 11th **Ohio Cavalries** and 95 **Pawnee scouts**, Captain Albert Brown of 2nd **California Cavalry** (116 volunteers and 84 **Omaha scouts**). Expedition failed to defeat Indians in any decisive battle.
August 13, 1865	Crazy Woman's Fork		
August 13–15, 1865	Battle of Bone Pile Creek	Expedition to locate shorter route to Montana; escorted by Captain George Williford, 143 men of Volunteer **Dakota Cavalry**.	2 soldiers killed, 2 Indians killed.
August 16, 1865	Powder River	Captain Frank North, volunteers, and **Pawnee** scouts.	Killed 27 Indians, including Yellow Woman.

Indian Battles in Wyoming

Printed in the USA
CPSIA information can be obtained
at www.ICGtesting.com
LVHW031932111123
763680LV00010B/690

9 781632 936295